SALAMANDER

THE STORY OF THE
MORMON
FORGERY
MURDERS

SECOND EDITION

SALAMANDER

THE STORY OF THE
MORMON
FORGERY
MURDERS
WITH A NEW AFTERWORD

Linda Sillitoe and Allen Roberts

forensic analysis by
George J. Throckmorton

Signature Books
Salt Lake City
1989

FOR THE SURVIVORS,
ESPECIALLY THE FAMILIES OF

Steven F. Christensen,

Kathleen W. Sheets, and

Mark W. Hofmann

Copyright © 1989, Signature Books, Inc. All rights reserved.
Signature Books is a recognized trademark of Signature Books, Inc.
First edition 1988.
Printed in the United States of America.
94 93 92 91 90   6 5 4 3 2

Book and cover design by Traci O'Very Covey

Library of Congress Cataloging-in-Publication Data

Sillitoe, Linda, 1948–
    Salamander.

    Includes bibliographical references
    1. Hofmann, Mark.   2. Church of Jesus Christ of
Latter-Day Saints--History.   3. Criminals--Utah--Salt
Lake City--Biography.   4. Murder--Utah--Salt Lake City--
Case studies.   6. Mormon Church--Case studies--History.
I. Roberts, Allen D., 1947-   . II. Title.
[HV6248.H467S55 1989]   364.1'523'0979225   89-70093
ISBN 0-941214-87-7

TABLE OF CONTENTS

PREFACE

By February 1986, when Mark W. Hofmann was charged with two bombing murders, document forgery, and fraud, the research for this book was well underway. While we initially reserved judgment on Hofmann's guilt or innocence, four months of investigating the story convinced us that the secrets, targets, and motives in this mystery lay in a Mormon subculture—an unstructured, diverse community of about 3,000 academics, historians, writers, artists, researchers, and readers. It was a community both of us knew well.

Fortunately, for this project, the vast majority of that community is highly literate. Because of their educational background, religious instruction, and interest in the flow of information, many kept journals, daily appointment books, and even recorded their conversations and participation in events surrounding contemporary Mormon history, document discoveries, and church politics. The information made available to us included excerpts from the diary and "daytimer" entries of high church officials, rare book and document dealers, financial victims, historians, and Mormon critics. Letters and journal entries written by the murder victims and the perpetrator also proved helpful, as they became available through family members or investigators. We also depended upon written accounts of complicated document or business transactions provided to us by those involved.

Within the voluminous evidence collected by investigators, we found much that proved invaluable, particularly when the case did not go to trial. Our own research uncovered several interesting pieces of evidence, including a plan for another murder.

The bombings were investigated by the Salt Lake City Police Department, the Salt Lake County Attorney's Office, the Federal Bureau of Investigation, The Federal Bureau of Alcohol, Tobacco, and Firearms, the United States Attorney General's Office and its grand jury, and LDS Church Security. Following a preliminary hearing, thirty felony counts against Mark Hofmann were bound over for trial in Third District Court. Since the investigative reports and evidence gravitated to the Salt Lake Police Department and the county attorney's office, we spent many hours interviewing and reinterviewing key investigators and prosecutors, comparing theories, and tracing the investigation itself. Our presence during the lengthy preliminary hearing provided us not only with the drama—and tedium—of the courtroom, but with the best accounts of forty-one witnesses. Some testimony required follow-up interviews, as well; nevertheless, the extensive public record established in court offered a reliable framework for making sense of an immense amount of information.

Only through portraying a few key investigators were we able to avoid the use of composite characters to represent the scores of officers involved. Similarly, we are forced to minimize or omit mention of many people whose individual experiences are part of the larger story—witnesses, reporters, collectors and dealers, investors, and family members and friends of the murder victims. Even then, dozens of names and details were removed from the text by our editors. This was done neither because the individuals or their accounts were unimportant, nor to protect sources, but to simplify for the reader a story that involved hundreds of people in complex situations. In only two instances did we agree to use pseudonyms—"Kate Reid" and "Gene Taylor"—due to issues of privacy and because their real names were unessential to either the story or the public record.

Throughout this process, information was both a goal and a distraction. A continually updated chronology of dates, times, and events eventually covered thirty years and represented, in itself, 145 pages. Keeping this timeline brought together seemingly unrelated incidents in new ways and became the backbone of the book.

The story was fleshed out by hundreds of additional interviews ranging from brief telephone calls to all-day sessions. Information we found vital during our first year coalesced during the second year, providing a steady base for more central and focussed interviews and investigation. We learned very early the necessity of segregating information that originated with Mark Hofmann. Although his interviews with the prosecutors became available about twenty months into our research, we did not rely on them for our basic storyline, but rather upon verifiable and independent accounts. Hofmann's early interviews, writings, and depositions are represented here but are clearly identified.

In order to recount a coherent story, we have woven into narrative form the information and insight from all these sources. Naturally, we do not claim that the conversations, which occurred over a period of years, are reported verbatim. Rather, we have relied on our sources' memories and, where possible, on other documentation. Regarding contested or especially significant incidents, we have compared accounts, paying attention to specificity, detail, bias, consistency with the whole, and point of view. Despite those precautions, we recognize that individual viewpoint and memory are such that these renderings cannot possibly seem entirely accurate to all involved. However, we have made a sincere attempt to tell the story as accurately, fairly, and sensitively as our own limitations permit. The synthesis of information this book represents is ours alone, and we accept responsibility for inadvertent errors.

Readers unfamiliar with Mormon terms need only understand the basic organizational structure of the Church of Jesus Christ of Latter-day Saints, which forms a pyramid with a wide base and a narrow top. At the pinnacle is the church president/prophet and his two counselors. These three men form the First Presidency of the church and, along with the Council of Twelve Apostles, are sustained by Mormons as "prophets, seers, and revelators," who devote their lives to the church. Other "general authorities," the First Quorum of Seventy and Presiding Bishopric, form the tier below and fill full-time ecclesiastical callings. These leaders are assisted by the descending ranks of male priesthood holders; virtually every active Mormon adult holds at least one lay church position, supervised by the priesthood. Presiding over the bottom of the pyramid are bishops, the equivalent of ministers, priests, or rabbis, except that Mormon bishops hold a lay calling that rotates about every five years. Each bishop leads a ward (parish or congregation), and six or so wards are grouped into a stake (or diocese), led by a stake president.

Throughout our research and writing, we have been encouraged by various groups and individuals who have been eager to have this story told. Specifically, we would first like to thank our colleagues who initially worked with each of us on this story: Fred C. Esplin and Paul Swenson at *Utah Holiday* magazine; and the "bombings team" at the *Deseret News*, including Jerry Spangler, Kathy Fahy, Max Knudsen, Marianne Funk, Brett Del Porto, Carrie Moore, and Bob Bernick, Jr., as well as assistance later from Robert D. Mullins, Jan Thompson, Audrey Clark, and Brent Israelson. Other reporters and journalists have offered encouragement and shared information and deserve our thanks, as well.

We are grateful to George D. Smith, our publisher, whose optimism, faith, and unflagging support made this project possible; to Peter Wiley for the benefit of his experience and perception, as well as his insightful suggestions, draft by draft; also to Gary J. Bergera, who skillfully and diplomatically performed the painstaking task of synthesizing comments and styles. We appreciate the expertise of Connie Disney, production manager; Susan Staker, our copy editor; Mark W. Beck, who provided the maps; and Traci O'Very Covey, who designed the book and cover. In addition, we sincerely appreciate the responsive readings contributed by George J. Throckmorton, Lavina Fielding Anderson, Ron Priddis, Richard Van Wagoner, Deborah Hirth, Paul Ginsburg, and Richard Ouellette, and the consistent encouragement of John R. Sillito, DeAnn Evans, Levi and Althea Peterson, Bruce and Donna Jorgensen, Dennis and

Valerie Clark, Wallace Cooper II, Dawn Roberts, Randall Mackey, Linda Thatcher, and Jack and Linda Newell.

During the two years we worked on the book, we depended on a talented and versatile part-time staff. Kathy Buhler Ballard transcribed the bulk of our interview notes and kept us organized. Lin Ostler was chief researcher and archivist and contributed significantly to the historical material in the technical analysis. Additional typing was done by Dan Maryon, Pat Fought, Janean Buhler Ayers, Annie Brewer, and Melissa Sillitoe; they, too, are appreciated. Frank McEntire, Steven L. Mayfield, and Paul Bennion offered media clippings or videos that were useful, as well.

We regard all of our interviews as gifts that we can only repay through whatever benefit there is in bringing them together in this book. Most of all, then, we are indebted to those whose story this is, some of whom would prefer not to be thanked by name, but who include: Douglas Alder, Tom Alexander, John Alleman, Gary Anderson, Richard Anderson, George Aposhian, Leonard Arrington, Edward Ashment, Brent and Charlene Ashworth, Danel Bachman, Grant Ballam, Don Bell, Jim Bell, Curt Bench, Grant Bierer, David Biggs, David John Buerger, Robert and Phyllis Buhler, Jerry Cahill, Harry Campbell, Ted Cannon, Paul Cheesman, Fred Collier, Everett Cooley, Peter Crawley, Betty Lynn Davis, Louise Degn, Gerry D'Elia, Scott Dunn, George Easter, Tom Eatchel, Andrew Ehat, Ronald Esplin, Bill Evans, Mildred Evans, Kenneth Farnsworth, Scott Faulring, Robert Fillerup, Peggy Fletcher, Shannon Flynn, William J. Flynn, Richard Forbes, David L. Freed, Michael George, Joan Gorton, Paul Grant, Rick Grunder, Van Hale, Jay Haymond, Blaine Harris, Dave Harrison, Harold Hill, Gordon B. Hinckley, Ron Hofmann, Richard Howard, Robert Howell, Lyn Jacobs, Rhett James, Dean Jessee, Franklin Johnson, Jeffery O. Johnson, Heidi Sheets Jones, Joseph Judd, Dale Kaufmann, Edward Kimball, Faye Kotter, C. Dean Larsen, Terri Christensen, Gordon P. Liddle, Wade Lillywhite, Matt Limburgh, Wes Losser, Richard Lindsay, Randall Mackey, H. Michael Marquardt, Brian McGavin, Sterling McMurrin, Brent Metcalfe, Jill Metcalfe, George Mitton, Tom Moore, Jack and Linda Newell, Hugh Nibley, Dallin H. Oaks, David Olds, Emma

Olsen, Blake Ostler, Richard Ostling, Lynn Packer, Grant Palmer, Steve Palmer, Hugh W. Pinnock, D. Michael Quinn, Tim Rathbone, Bradley Rich, Randy Rigby, Kenneth Rigtrup, Joe and Katie Sheets Robertson, Larry Rock, Glenn Rowe, Alvin Rust, Jeff Salt, Darlene Sanchez, Hal Schindler, Donald Schmidt, John Schumann, J. Gary Sheets, Jan Shipps, Steven Shields, Bernard Silver, A. J. Simmonds, John Simmons, Alan L. Smith, David E. Sorenson, Jeff Sorenson, Susan Southworth, Robert L. Stott, Lorie Winder-Stromberg, Don A. Tanner, Jerald and Sandra Tanner, Linda Thatcher, Greg Thompson, Scott G. Thompson, George J. Throckmorton, Paul and Margaret Toscano, Dawn Tracy, Richard Turley, Bradley C. Volmar, Dorothy Walker, Ronald Walker, Wesley Walters, Cecelia Warner, David E. and Dixie West, Walt West, David Whittaker, E. L. Willoughby, Randy Wilson, Michael Woolley, Ruth Woolley, Ronald Yengich, David Yocom, and Buddy Youngreen.

We are also grateful to representatives and staff of the Church of Jesus Christ of Latter-day Saints, particularly in the departments of genealogy and history; the Reorganized Church of Jesus Christ of Latter Day Saints; the University of Utah Marriott Library; the Salt Lake City Police Department; the Salt Lake County Attorney's Office; the Bath, England, public library; Olympus High School; Bountiful High School; the Utah State Historical Society; KSL-Television; the Fifth Circuit and Third District courts; the Daughters of the Utah Pioneer Museum; the Utah Lighthouse Ministry; the Brigham Young University Archives; the Utah State University Special Collections; *Utah Holiday* magazine; the Sunstone Foundation and *Sunstone* magazine; and *Dialogue: A Journal of Mormon Thought*; with special thanks to the *Deseret News* library, which provided many of the photographs.

Finally, we thank our families for their generous accommodation to this two-year murder mystery. Their interest, encouragement, practical and moral support, cooperation, and, ultimately, endurance were essential and much appreciated.

"I take Joseph aside and he says it is true . . . the next morning the spirit transfigured himself from a white salamander in the bottom of the hole & struck me 3 times & held the treasure and would not let me have it . . . the spirit says I tricked you again . . ."

--Letter dated October 23, 1830, from Martin Harris to W. W. Phelps

SECTION ONE

1

PIPE BOMBS IN
THE CITY OF THE SAINTS

Between the dark land and sky, the Great Salt Lake held the morning light. Steering his jeep through rush-hour traffic south toward Salt Lake City, Steven F. Christensen looked like any other commuter. A thatch of brown hair was brushed back above intent blue eyes. The extra weight he carried on a sturdy frame and his businesslike demeanor made him seem older than his thirty-one years.

Christensen had more than financial consulting on his mind this morning, Tuesday, October 15, 1985. After weeks of delay, the day promised the long-awaited closure of a transaction involving a cache of controversial documents he knew was destined for the secret vaults of the Mormon church. As a bishop in the Church of Jesus Christ of Latter-day Saints, Christensen was committed to defending his religion. But as an inquiring student of Mormon history, he was also devoted to intellectual honesty. Thus torn between the competing demands of faith and reason, Christensen had become something of a double agent in a drama as convoluted as the suspense novels he devoured for recreation.

Only the year before, Christensen had indulged his passion for history by purchasing for $40,000 the "salamander letter," an 1830 document signed by a close friend of church founder Joseph Smith. Smith claimed that an angel revealed the location of buried gold plates, which Smith translated into The Book of Mormon. But this early letter recounted how a white salamander, guarding the plates, transformed itself into

3

an "old spirit," struck Smith three times, and forbade him to take the ancient treasure. Christensen had the letter authenticated and then donated it to the church. Church leaders released the text of the letter, but rumors surfaced that they were hiding other potentially embarrassing documents.

According to Mark Hofmann, the same dealer who had sold Christensen the salamander letter, the collection Christensen would be helping to authenticate this morning could be devastating to the six-million-member church. The papers of renegade Mormon apostle William McLellin, Hofmann explained, contained diaries, affidavits, and other artifacts that had been lost for nearly a century. Collectively, they painted a portrait of early Mormonism far different from traditional Mormon history. With luck, today's transaction would not attract media attention, thereby engendering yet another crisis in the church over Mormon origins.

All summer, as the McLellin deal twisted through one complication after another, Christensen had tried to expedite its acquisition. He appreciated the practical value of assisting top church leaders whose power extended from their status as men of God to corporate boardrooms throughout the Salt Lake Valley. But, just as important, he was also eager to examine the papers personally as they changed hands.

Despite Christensen's busy schedule, the church leaders overseeing the deal had made the collection his priority. His wife, Terri, pregnant with their fourth child, was tired of the frequent calls that pulled her husband away from home and family. Last weekend, they'd even had to cancel a family vacation to Wyoming after the transaction stalled again.

First on Christensen's agenda this morning was a meeting with business partner Randy Rigby. (On his way into the city, Christensen had stopped for doughnuts and soft drinks, their usual snack-food breakfast.) Until that August, Christensen had been a vice-president of CFS Financial Corp., founded by his boss and mentor, J. Gary Sheets. But as the real estate investment company floundered deeply into debt, Christensen and Sheets had parted ways. Since then, Christensen and Rigby had opened a new office in the Judge Building down the street. Christensen understood Sheets's inability to admit defeat. Many

Salt Lake City businessmen ran on Sheets's heady optimism that "the righteous shall prosper."

The morning was postcard blue and gold by 8:00 a.m. as Christensen passed the copper-domed Capitol. To the south, the twenty-six story Church Office Building, tallest of the city's high-rises, overshadowed the nearby granite Salt Lake Temple and the turtle-backed Mormon Tabernacle. The church-owned Hotel Utah, and the Lion and Beehive houses built over a century before for Brigham Young's wives, flanked the classical-columned Church Administration Building where Christensen met with Mormon officials to discuss the deal. Descending into the valley, Christensen could see the business area stretching from the city center, then the older residential districts, and finally the suburbs. In the distance, a soft rim of pollution clung to the base of the Wasatch Mountains fortressing the valley.

In pioneer times, Brigham Young had laid out the city on a grid numbered according to distance and direction from the temple site. Turning east at 300 South and Main Street, Christensen parked in front of the Judge Building, an old brick and stone edifice, its name incised in Roman letters above the northern entry. He picked up his sack of doughnuts, Tab, and ginger ale, stepped out of the jeep, and walked toward his office.

Earlier that morning, about 6:45, before Christensen awoke, Bruce Passey walked into the Judge Building where he and his father were jewelers on the third floor. With his father not far behind him, Passey paused in the lobby. As he waited, he saw a young man wearing a green letterman's jacket, minus the letter, enter the building. Passey idly read the writing on the package the man carried: "To Steve Christensen."

Passey recognized the name. Several times people had stopped by their store to ask directions to Christensen's office. The Passeys eventually learned that Christensen had rented an office two months earlier on the sixth floor, but they had never met him.

In a moment, Hal Passey entered the lobby and joined his son and the young man by the elevators. The freight elevator arrived first and they all stepped on. Hal Passey pushed three.

"I'll take five," the young man said. The Passeys knew that this was not Christensen's floor but said nothing. When the elevator stopped at the third floor, the jewelers got off.

A few minutes later, Janet McDermott, a sales representative, boarded the elevator. She was generally the first at work on the sixth floor; but as she walked to her office, 610, she noticed a man in a jacket walking away from her. She did not recognize him; and at such an early hour, the presence of a stranger was disturbing. However, she was soon distracted by a cardboard box propped against door 609, Steve Christensen's office. Night-maintenance personnel usually placed deliveries inside the offices.

Strangely, there were no postal or other markings. The package was about a foot square and six inches deep. Letters, printed in black felt-tipped pen, spelled, "To Steve Christensen." Suddenly, she realized that the man she had seen walking toward the end of the blind hallway had turned and passed behind her. At the end of the hall, he glanced over his shoulder at her. Then he opened the door to the stairs and was gone.

Shortly after Christensen had rented the neighboring office, he and McDermott had agreed to accept one another's packages, since both were frequently out and had only part-time secretaries. Christensen's mail always read, "Steven Christensen" or "Steven F." This one looked personal. Perhaps it was a box of cookies from a member of Christensen's ward. She decided to leave it.

Peering apprehensively at the door to the stairs, she stepped into her office and deadbolted the door.

An hour later, she left to feed her car's parking meter. Her uneasiness was gone. When she came back, she did not bother to relock her door. Christensen's package was still by his door.

A few minutes after 8:00, she came out again on her way to an appointment. This time she decided to collect the package for safekeeping. Just then she remembered to call-forward her telephone, something she usually forgot. She walked back into her office and dialed hurriedly.

As the heavy door hissed shut behind her, a violent blast jolted her, then arrows of flying glass sprayed from the shattering picture on the wall across the room. Shrapnel ripped through the wooden door and cut her leg. Panicked, she ran to the far side of her desk. As she crouched, she heard an operator's voice from the dangling receiver. Terrified, she assumed that the gunman in the hall would also hear the voice and know someone was in the office. Then she heard another sound, one that chilled her — high-pitched human cries.

Later she could not remember if she had smelled smoke or heard an alarm, but she immediately became convinced there was a fire. Fearing that she would be trapped at the end of the hall, she snatched her suit jacket, purse, and briefcase, and, trembling, stepped into the hall.

There was no gunman, only Steven Christensen, barely recognizable, lying on the floor. His entire chest was oozing scarlet. Blood pooled around his eyes and ran in stripes down his face. The pitiful sounds were deeper now. McDermott stared for what seemed a long time. As she became aware of people gathering at the end of the hall, she screamed for an ambulance. Another woman ran up and knelt by Christensen, trying to find a pulse. Nothing. Shaking, McDermott walked slowly toward the elevator where frightened people began to gather.

Randy Rigby pulled into the CFS company garage down the street a little past 8:00 a.m. to pick up some papers for his meeting with Christensen. He tried phoning Christensen but only got the answering machine. Steve must be running late, too, he figured. By the time he'd walked down the block, Steve should be arriving.

As Rigby hurried west toward Main Street, he noticed a fire truck blocking the intersection. A crowd was gathering, and now he could see emergency vehicles. He heard people talking about an explosion.

Christensen's jeep was parked on Main Street. *I wonder if Steve knows what's going on?* Rigby thought. He darted in the back door and, avoiding the elevators in case of fire, ran up the five flights of stairs. Midway to the sixth floor, he was joined by the building's manager. They emerged into the hallway of the sixth floor together.

Staring the length of the hall, Rigby could see only that the door on his and Christensen's office was down. Fragments of Tab soft drink cans—Christensen's favorite—were scattered through the hall with other debris. Rigby imagined, odd as it seemed, that their small office refrigerator had somehow blown up.

Beside him, the manager whistled. "What the hell do you guys do up here?"

Rigby rushed toward a police officer and began explaining that this was his office, that he was concerned about his partner. The officer assured him everything was under control. In a moment, Rigby was evacuated with everyone else while trained dogs searched for bombs.

Rigby gave the officers his name, then gathered what information he could from those who had been inside the building at the time of the explosion. He soon learned the bare facts—a bomb of some sort had gone off and Christensen had been badly hurt, maybe killed.

Rigby felt the impact of the news in the center of his chest, squeezing the breath out of him. This has something to do with that screwy document deal Steve's been working on night and day, he thought. He went with a friend to a nearby office and both began making calls. His friend called CFS president Gary Sheets. Rigby urgently dialed the Christensens' home number, but there was no answer. "Terri knows," he muttered, assuming she had fled to safety. He looked up the number for Mr. Mac retail clothing store in the ZCMI Mall a few blocks north. He got the owner, Mac Christensen, Steve's father, on the phone.

"Mac, this is Randy Rigby. I have some very bad news for you. A bomb went off in our office this morning and I think Steve's seriously injured or maybe even dead." Rigby felt brutal but did not know how else to put it.

Stunned, Mac Christensen thanked him for calling and asked him to call back if he learned anything more.

It took a minute to get the next number Rigby needed—that of Elder Hugh Pinnock in the Mormon Church Administration Building. He dialed it quickly, hoping his warning would be in time.

"Hello, you don't know me, but my name is Randy Rigby. Steve Christensen and I are partners in a business we're starting up. Steve told me he was involved in a document deal with you and Elder Dallin Oaks and President Hinckley."

Pinnock made no comment. Oaks, fifty-three, had recently been appointed to the Quorum of the Twelve Apostles where he was a tier above Pinnock, fifty-one and a member of the First Quorum of the Seventy. As second counselor in the church's First Presidency, Gordon B. Hinckley held still higher rank. With church president Spencer W. Kimball, whom faithful Mormons revered as a living prophet, now old and ailing, Hinckley, seventy-five, was *de facto* president in directing church affairs worldwide.

"Because of that deal," Rigby continued, "I thought I'd better tell you there was a bomb in Steve's and my office this morning. As far as I can tell, Steve's badly injured. He might even be dead."

A pause. "Well, Randy, do you know any more?"

"No, that's all I know right now."

"I appreciate your call. I'm sure that this has to do with CFS Financial Corp., not the document transaction you mentioned. If you find out any more, will you please let me know?"

"Yes, I will." Rigby hung up, recalling that Pinnock and Gary Sheets, the head of CFS, were longtime friends. Pinnock had no doubt already heard of the company's mounting financial problems — word was spreading. Next Rigby called his wife, Sandra, and told her about the bomb. She asked about Terri Christensen.

"I called her first. She didn't answer, so I think she knows."

"She was in the shower, Randy. She just called me because some reporter called and wanted to know which office you and Steve rent."

Rigby was floored. "How much did she find out?"

"Just that there was an explosion. What are we going to do, Randy? She doesn't know anything."

"Sandra, go across the field and tell her. It's better for her to have someone who loves her there than for me to telephone."

By the time the Rigbys hung up, several friends had arrived at the Christensen home north of Salt Lake in Centerville, alerted by bits of bad news. But no one was certain what had happened.

A petite, brown-eyed woman, her long blond hair still damp from the shower, Terri Christensen hunted frantically for a copy of her husband's new letterhead. She called his office number but reached the answering machine. She then tried Sandra Rigby and learned that the bomb had been in or near their husbands' office. "It can't be Steve," Sandra wept.

The person who had been hurt or killed must have been a janitor or someone else, Terri told herself. She called her mother-in-law and asked if she had heard anything. "Mac's coming home," her mother-in-law said, then added that someone was badly hurt.

At that, Terri decided that if a bomb had exploded in or near Steve's office, she did not want to be at home alone. "I'm not going to learn anything out here," she told friends. A friend volunteered to drive her to her in-laws, and she accepted. The ride seemed maddeningly slow. When at last she looked into Mac and Joan Christensen's devastated faces, she did not need to ask anything. She sat down quietly on a couch.

In shock, Terri was also five months pregnant and had miscarried the year before. Her obstetrician prescribed Valium, and all day she lay on the couch, benumbed. When she found a coherent thought, it was, "There's no way I can have this baby by myself."

Friends collected her three sons from school and preschool. One asked, "What are you thinking, Terri?"

"I don't dare to think," she answered, but then the realization of her loss broke through her haze and she wept hysterically.

Randy Rigby was at the police station giving a statement when his description of Christensen's involvement in the document deal reminded him of his promise to Hugh Pinnock. He asked for a phone. When Pinnock's secretary transferred him to Apostle Oaks's office, Rigby was not surprised. He introduced himself to Pinnock again and said, "I just wanted to tell you that the victim was Steve Christensen and he is dead."

"I very much appreciate your call, Mr. Rigby. I want to confirm to you that this tragedy involves CFS," Pinnock said. Amazed, Rigby said good-bye. Elder Pinnock seems pretty definite about that, he thought.

As emergency vehicles were converging on the Judge Building, suburbs like Holladay, southeast of the city, remained quiet. Kathleen Sheets, a gregarious, graying woman of fifty, stepped into the sunshine at about 8:30 a.m. for her regular morning walk with friends through the hilly neighborhood.

Sheets's home was a haven, largely of her own creation. Inside, her collection of signs included one that informed husband Gary, an early riser, "The Early Bird Fixes His Own Breakfast." Gary usually went to work by 6:30, but this morning he had waited to take their youngest, Jimmy, to volleyball practice at Churchill Junior High.

Kathy usually stayed up for hours after Gary went to bed, and last night she had tended their three grandchildren. Their oldest daughter, Heidi, and her husband, Roger Jones, were fixing up the home they had purchased nearby. Heidi had come for her two children about 11:45 p.m. Kathy and Gary's second daughter, Katie, whose husband, Joe Robertson, like Roger, was connected to Gary's company, had brought their newborn over last night, too.

This morning everything seemed late and disorganized. Jimmy's carpool had stopped though he had already left. Gretchen, Kathy's youngest daughter, had hurried off to her University of Utah classes. On her own way out, Sheets passed another of her signs, "When you reach the end of your rope, tie a knot and hang on."

"Hanging on," Kathy knew, was what she and her family had been doing lately. For months she had grown increasingly concerned about her husband's impending business failure, though she tried to talk optimistically to others. She worried what people would think and felt heartsick for Gary's investors. Her daughters' families would suffer, too, and most likely she and Gary would lose everything—though Gary had said maybe they would not lose their home. Still, she realized, there were no guarantees.

Sheets hurried around the U-shaped wooden walkway to the garage and found that the family dog had scattered the trash. Since she was driving to her friend Faye Kotter's house rather than walking, as she usually did, she hastily stuck a bag of trash into her red Audi and backed out of the garage, leaves crunching under the tires. At the top of the driveway, she exchanged the trash bag for the morning newspaper.

Sheets and Kotter had missed their walk the day before but had still talked. She'd had such a good time last week in New York with Gary, she had told Kotter. Business for Gary, Christmas shopping for her. But even there reality had eventually caught up with them. Gary had said he might be charged with fraud, though he swore no one could ever prove it. The family had a high profile in the neighborhood, and failure would be conspicuous. Gary was bishop of their local Mormon ward. Kathy had a gift with people and compensated for her husband's occasional social gaffes. When he had been called as bishop, she had begun her comments to the congregation by asking, "Does this mean I have to call him 'the bishop' instead of 'the nerd'?" The story quickly became part of Gary's repertoire of anecdotes.

When Sheets pulled up at the Kotter home, she appeared subdued. "Let's walk somewhere different," she suggested. They drove a little distance in a silence so companionable that neither thought to turn on the radio.

By that time, Gary Sheets was reading the *Salt Lake Tribune* in his CFS office. A big, energetic man with white hair and dark eyes, Sheets had gone to the YMCA for his morning swim, steam, and shave. With his company in trouble, Sheets had been paying attention to managerial details, trying to sell the company's assets, save a few jobs, and arrange some provision for his own future once his personal indebtedness was resolved. Surely, he reassured himself, he was salesman enough to do that. He recalled how Steve Christensen, before he left the company, liked to say, "When you're up to your waist in alligators, try working while they're asleep."

When a telephone call alerted Sheets to the explosion in the Judge Building, he tried first to call his wife, then ran into the hall where he saw his son-in-law, Joe Robertson. Sheets told him the news, then headed for the Judge Building. He stood with others outside the building until it seemed definite that Steve Christensen had been killed by a bomb.

For years, Sheets had thought of Christensen almost as a

son. Instinctively, he headed for Mr. Mac in the ZCMI Mall. He hugged the distraught father and again called home. There was no answer, so he called his daughter Heidi Jones. "Try to get your mother. I know she'll be terribly upset."

Jones said she had a morning full of errands but would go by her parents' house afterward; meanwhile, she would keep calling. Hanging up. Sheets thought of Terri Christensen. She was too young to be a widow. Impulsively, he decided to drive to the Christensens' Centerville home to do his best to comfort Terri. He could try Kathy again from there.

As Sheets left Mr. Mac on the mall's second floor, Curt Bench was on his way up. Manager of the successful Fine and Rare Books department at Mormon-owned Deseret Book, Bench was alarmed by reports of a bomb at the Judge Building where his friend and good customer Steve Christensen had an office. Christensen's ties to the notorious salamander letter nagged at Bench. Some Mormons had been deeply troubled by the letter, Bench knew, and Mormonism had its share of fanatics. He hurried up the stairs, entered the mall, and walked around the corner to Mr. Mac. He caught a painful glimpse of Mac Christensen in tears, talking with police.

Sickened, Bench went back to the store. Unbelievably, he concluded, Steve must be dead. Murdered. Despite a wash of helplessness, Bench telephoned another friend, the one who had sold Christensen the salamander letter—Mark Hofmann. As usual, he could not reach Hofmann but left a message on his answering machine.

Soon the telephone rang. "Curt, this is Mark." Bench told him about Christensen's death and heard Hofmann draw in his breath. The two exchanged feelings of shock and disbelief, then wondered—could the reason be the salamander letter?

"Be careful, Mark."

"I'll call Dori and tell her to get herself and the kids out of the house."

"Good idea. And Mark, keep in touch."

Transplanted New Yorker and arson prosecutor Gerry D'Elia (De-LEE-a) heard the garbled radio report of a bombing as he drove to work at the Salt Lake County Attorney's Office (CAO).

He decided to get over there as soon as he finished in court. Explosives fell under arson prosecution and he did not want to hear evidence from police three weeks later. A homicide case could take years to come before a jury, but D'Elia knew that someday his closing arguments would begin with his own memory of the crime scene.

By 9:15 D'Elia finished his court business and jaywalked across 400 South Street to the CAO. As he told the justice administrator where he was headed, David Biggs, an attorney the CAO had recently recruited from the Legal Defenders office, overheard and offered to go. The pair left, Biggs, blond and impeccable trailing the broad-shouldered and shorter D'Elia, who even in a sportcoat and slacks seemed slightly scruffy. When they reached the Judge Building, they worked their way inside, past the police blockade, as D'Elia hailed officers and introduced Biggs as a new prosecutor.

On the sixth floor they saw a scene television stations would afterwards play repeatedly: officers from the Salt Lake City Police Department (SLCPD) and the Federal Bureau of Alcohol, Tobacco, and Firearms (ATF) on their hands and knees taping and numbering hundreds of bits of evidence.

"Hi, Kenny, what have we got here?" Detectives Ken Farnsworth, tall and outgoing, and Jim Bell, shorter and deadpan, were both utterly serious as they organized the crime scene. With a thumb, Farnsworth gestured toward a cardboard fragment protruding from the ceiling. The detectives were looking at the first death by bombing anyone could remember in Salt Lake, and they were determined not to make any mistakes. D'Elia chatted with the ATF people, too. He had worked with them before on arson cases and had attended the ATF training school.

D'Elia called this part of his job "making friends." In New York, he knew, a prosecutor could run the whole crime scene, but here police were fiercely autonomous until they brought their evidence to the county attorney's office for screening. He pointed out the officers of the separate agencies to Biggs. "Now, look, David," he cautioned, "don't assert yourself. They all want the scene. This will migrate to us in time. We're not investigators."

D'Elia moved toward the victim. For several minutes he stood over the body, memorizing what he saw. He could not even determine an age for this businessman, whose face was obscured by black powder burns, soot, and blood. The bomb had opened him like a can opener, D'Elia thought, staring at the deep chest wound. His right foot had been nearly severed.

Nails lay everywhere. D'Elia looked at one closely and whistled. Whoever had built this bomb had not only wanted to kill, but to disfigure, to obliterate. D'Elia contemplated that rage.

The officers told him what had been gleaned from interviews with people in the building. The victim was Steven Christensen, son of Mac Christensen of Mr. Mac clothing stores. That summer Steven had left CFS, the big investment company a block east on State Street. Word was that CFS was in trouble. Christensen had been a vice president under Gary Sheets. They were looking for Sheets now. Also, someone had seen an unusual package outside Christensen's door that morning.

One more possibility: Christensen had bought that controversial early Mormon document, the salamander letter. D'Elia nodded. He knew little about the Mormon church. He wore his hair longer than the Mormon attorneys in the office and, unlike his Mormon colleagues, enlivened his everyday speech with street terms. Still, he remembered hearing a joke or two about the salamander letter. Maybe not everybody laughed at jokes like those, but could a 150-year-old letter get someone killed?

Roger and Heidi Sheets Jones listened to the radio to catch what they could about Steve Christensen's death. Suddenly Heidi felt threatened and mortal. "You know," she said, turning to her husband, "these things are hitting a little close to home."

About 9:30 a.m., Kathy Sheets started up the wooden walkway of her home. She had dropped off Faye Kotter, then gone to the bank before coming home. As she drove down the driveway, she saw a square brown box. She parked the car in the garage and walked over to the package. There were no postal marks, but it was addressed to "Mr. Gary Sheets" in black felt-tipped pen. She picked it up and took a few steps to the walkway.

There, investigators would later surmise, Sheets shifted her burdens—the package, the newspaper, her purse—and the motion-sensitive pipe bomb inside the package exploded. Metal, newspaper bits, cardboard, and leaves shot in all directions. As Sheets's body took the impact, the corner of the garage fractured and fell. One steel fragment soared across the creek between the garage and the house and pierced a pane in the far door, lodging in the wall by the mud room.

The neighbors in the home nearest the Sheets house heard the blast and looked out their window to see a flurry of leaves. They assumed a tree had gone down. Another neighbor, down the street, concluded the same. She stopped and listened before driving away for an appointment but heard nothing more.

More than an hour later, a friend pulled in the driveway and saw Kathy's red Audi in the garage. At first, she thought a dummy lay on the walkway—Kathy was such a practical joker. This close to Halloween, she was likely to set a scarecrow on the bench near the house. However, a long second look told her she was staring at Kathy Sheets's body.

A police officer, stationed with a walkie talkie down the hall from the homicide on the sixth floor, grabbed Gerry D'Elia's shoulder. "We've got another one."

"Another what?"

"Another bomb."

"Where?"

"Out in the county. The county's handling it."

"Oh, Christ! Is it a homicide?"

"Yes."

"Male or female?"

"Female. On Nan . . . Nanny-ola Drive."

"Where the hell's that?"

"I'll get the coordinates."

D'Elia caught Farnsworth. "We've got another one, Ken. Look, I've seen the scene here. You've got it under control. If you need me, I'll be with the county."

"Right."

"C'mon, Biggs," D'Elia called. "You want to see one in the county?"

The two prosecutors circled through the Holladay streets southeast of the city for ten or fifteen minutes before they rounded a corner to Naniloa and saw the fire trucks, news cameras, and county sheriff's deputies.

D'Elia had worked in the CAO's southeast satellite office before coming downtown. "Hey, D'Elia, how's it going?" he heard repeatedly, as he made his way down Naniloa Drive. Again D'Elia shook hands, introduced Biggs, and waved at the ATF officers, trying to forge a few links between them and the deputies. This time, he thought, everyone has to pull together.

By now his head was clear with an adrenaline-laced calm. This was big. Two bombings, not simultaneous, nothing under control. This has got me worried, D'Elia thought, striding down a steep driveway toward a triple garage. Two homicides and no real suspects.

D'Elia did not see the victim until he turned toward the wooden walkway that crossed a stream. The body lay in the corner of the walkway with pieces of the splintered garage overhang on top of her. Unlike Christensen, her face was visible, surrounded by wavy, gray hair. She had only a few nicks and powder burns around the shocked, half-open eyes, the startled mouth. No pain, D'Elia thought; she went just like that.

"It's Kathy Sheets," someone said, "married to Gary Sheets."

D'Elia absorbed that fact, still looking at the victim. Her left arm had been severed, her left breast removed, her internal organs exposed both above and below the lacerated skin of her waist. He wondered how long she had lain there.

He followed the walkway to the house and observed the shrapnel in the wall. Slowly, he paced through the rooms. He read the tennis dates on Kathy Sheets's calendar, saw that she had just returned from a trip to New York, and paused. There was a lot of talk among officers about assassins and hit men. This New York trip made him wonder—CFS trouble and New York. The victims were Gary Sheets's former business partner and Gary Sheets's wife. What was going on?

So Kathy Sheets was a grandmother, judging from the photographs and drawings on the wall, D'Elia mused as he joined the officers gathering evidence outside. It was a beautiful day for a bombing, they agreed; this time of year there could be snow, making their job more difficult. The sheriff's communication van had been set up, so D'Elia called the office. He began comparing the murder scenes, compiling information from investigators at both locations.

Now they knew that both bombs had been motion-sensitive, though they were not sure of the detonator. And both probably contained smokeless gunpowder. Just that much indicated that the bomber was fairly knowledgeable and skilled. Both bombs had used battery packs with C-cell batteries and were contained in closed boxes. Yet they had been carried, D'Elia reasoned, and placed as bait. So where was the off switch?

"No switch," D'Elia mumbled. "*No* switch. Somebody's got a lot of gazoombies."

The investigators also knew from a brown paper scrap recovered on the walkway that Gary Sheets's name had been on the second package in the same type of printing as on the Christensen package. So, Sheets was a target. Yet he had to be a suspect, at least in the general sense. "Get on CFS," D'Elia told the investigators. "If Gary Sheets had nothing to do with this, we'll have to disprove him as a possible suspect."

Gary Sheets had returned to CFS when he found that Terri Christensen was not home. He had barely reached his office when a phone call told him there had been a bombing on Naniloa Drive. He hung up and quickly called home. No answer. He called the neighbors. No answer. He called the sheriff's office. Yes, he was told, there was an explosion and we have a female fatality.

Kathy or Gretchen? Sheets wondered, racing to his car. A friend, Dean Larsen, pulled up and told Sheets to get in. "It's Kathy," he said, throwing an arm around Sheets's shoulders. When the car stopped on Naniloa Drive, Sheets got out, grabbed Katie with one arm and Joe with the other. He hugged them close as they wept and news cameras hummed. Then they got in the car and went to the police substation, where they found Roger and Heidi Jones. There, the police told Sheets he had been the bomber's target. He agreed that he must be a marked man; no one could have intended to kill Kathy.

Deputies and police officers began searching the homes

and cars of CFS officers looking for other suspicious packages. The valley's nightmare had begun.

By noon, Judge Building jewelers Bruce and Hal Passey had helped a detective prepare a composite sketch of the man they had seen in the elevator. The drawing depicted such an ordinary face that police decided releasing it would serve no purpose. Dozens of officers began interviewing people in the Judge Building and CFS employees.

The morning's *Salt Lake Tribune* and early editions of the afternoon's *Deseret News* carried no news of the bombings. However, the later city edition of the church-owned *News* came off the press with several front-page stories, gingerly treating Christensen's connection with the salamander letter. "In pursuing his interest in Mormon historical documents, Christensen puchased what has become known as the salamander letter in January 1984; it created a ripple among church historians when its contents were made public.

"However, Christensen considered the letter a tool that would help researchers working on a book about the history of the Book of Mormon rather than something that might cast doubt on the credibility of church founder Joseph Smith."

The information about Kathy Sheets, whose body was discovered just before the newspaper's deadline, was scant, but she, too, was praised by neighbors and friends.

Hugh Pinnock, alerted quickly about the first bombing, left his office after hearing about the second. He had known Gary and Kathy Sheets for years and more recently became acquainted with Christensen. In one unforgettable morning, he had lost two friends.

Nearly a decade earlier, Pinnock had been ordained a full-time high-ranking "general authority," as members of the Mormon hierarchy are called. The general authorities, numbering seventy-five men, lead the church they believe Jesus Christ restored to the earth through Joseph Smith in 1830. The programs they administer—from the priesthood for men to the Relief Society for women to Primary for children—are intended to meet members' spiritual, religious, and social needs, and to prepare the faithful for the Millennium and "eternal progression" toward godhood.

Pinnock, like many general authorities, had been a businessman before joining the hierarchy, and his financial acumen had benefitted the church. The church's true power, however, stemmed not only from the influence of general authorities sitting on many major local corporate boards but also the deference of bishops and stake presidents who virtually comprised Utah's legislature, business community, and political party structure. Even among non-Mormons operating in Mormon arenas, consideration for the church's wishes tended to be automatic.

Pinnock and Sheets had both belonged to the same fraternity at the University of Utah, and later Sheets had worked for Pinnock selling insurance. Since Pinnock had befriended Christensen before the McLellin deal came along, he had a lot on his mind as he drove to Holladay where the Sheets were planning a funeral.

When Pinnock arrived, he did his best to console Gary and his children and readily accepted an invitation to speak at Kathy's funeral. Arrangements were being made quickly because Sheets was being taken into protective custody, his children scattering to the homes of friends or relatives.

Between conversations with the family, Pinnock was on the phone, relaying expressions of sympathy from church leaders whose names were as familiar as the men themselves were personally unknown. Once, however, fifteen-year-old Jimmy Sheets heard Pinnock try to reach a man he had never heard of—someone named Mark Hofmann.

Heidi Jones went outside to escape the talk. Watching the breeze stir the leaves, she tried to comprehend what was happening. My mother's dead, she told herself. They're trying to kill my father. But we're just an ordinary family!

While Pinnock was meeting with the Sheets and trying to telephone Mark Hofmann, Hofmann was trying to reach him, too. He called ahead on his mobile phone to the Church Administration Building before pulling into the underground parking plaza at about 2:15 p.m. Instead, he met Apostle Dallin Oaks. Before his appointment to the Twelve, Oaks had been a Utah

Supreme Court justice, president of church-owned Brigham Young University in Provo, a professor of law at the University of Chicago, and executive director of the American Bar Association.

When Hofmann entered his office, Oaks met a nondescript young man in his early thirties, of average height and weight, with medium brown hair and glasses. The firm set of his lower lip seemed to compensate for a receding chin.

Pinnock was out of the office, but Oaks explained that he was fully informed about the McLellin transaction. This brought the conversation to Christensen, and the two exchanged expressions of shock. Hofmann's voice was soft and rapid, his words crisp.

"Sit down," Oaks urged. "How can I help you?"

"I think the police might want to question me," he explained. He said he didn't know how best to respond, implying that Oaks might make some suggestions.

"Why would the police want to question you?" Oaks had talked with Pinnock earlier and had just read in the *Deseret News* that the bombings seemed tied to CFS. He had never heard of Gary Sheets until Pinnock had rushed away upon word of the second victim. The second bombing seemed to define the motive for the first. "Their business activities with CFS don't have anything to do with you, do they?"

"No, not at all."

A pause. "Well, do you have any reason to suppose that the bombings had anything to do with your connections with Christensen?"

No.

"Do you know anyone in your document business who would enforce his contracts with bombs?"

No.

"Well, then, what do you have to worry about? The police probably won't question you, and if they do, just tell them the truth."

Then Hofmann made it clear that Oaks was missing the point, for Hofmann could not discuss Christensen with the police without getting into the confidential McLellin deal.

"From all I know," Oaks said firmly, "your activities with

21

the McLellin collection represent an ordinary commercial transaction, even though it has been treated confidentially. If it turns
out to be relevant to a murder investigation, or if the police
question you about it, you'd better answer truthfully."

But if Hofmann intended to delay, Oaks was ready. "Are
you prepared to close on the deal despite Christensen's death?"
he pressed.

"Well, I'd planned to go to New York."

"Can't you stay in town long enough to get this matter
resolved?"

Hofmann agreed, and Oaks turned to specifics. "You'd
better contact the attorney who's representing your buyer. He'll
be wondering what's going to happen."

Christensen had agreed to verify the value and authenticity of the collection. Now they decided that Donald Schmidt,
recently retired from a long stint as Church Archivist, could
replace Christensen. Hofmann knew Schmidt well from frequent trades and sales.

As Hofmann prepared to leave, Oaks rose and thanked
him for his efforts in discovering church documents and for
seeing to it that the McLellin collection reached friendly hands.
A handshake, and Hofmann was out the door.

In the parking lot, Hofmann stopped to chat with Pinnock,
who had just arrived. Afterward, Pinnock called his friend David
E. Sorenson, an LDS mission president in Nova Scotia and the
buyer who had agreed to purchase the McLellin collection and
donate it to the church. The deal is still on, Pinnock assured
him. Sorenson then telephoned his attorney, David E. West,
and asked him to contact Christensen's replacement, an archivist named Don Schmidt.

With one bombing in Salt Lake City and another in the
county, traditionally rival law enforcement departments formed
a task force. Prosecutor David Biggs wrote up the first investigative subpoena, seizing file cabinets and other materials in
Christensen's office.

"You think the bombings have to do with the Mormon
documents?" the judge asked D'Elia as he signed the subpoena.

"If I did, I wouldn't be going after CFS."

That afternoon, local television stations carried Police Chief E. L. (Bud) Willoughby live, outlining the investigation. Soon both national and local stories were identifying CFS's financial problems as the probable motive for murder, perhaps accomplished by hired assassins. The *Deseret News* even quoted an unnamed source that CFS had lost some $400 million — a figure television reporters were repeating. Gary Sheets, watching television with a county deputy in a downtown hotel room, saw his dream company sink into the quicksand of public panic.

Reports on Christensen's connection to the salamander letter followed, and the coverage ended with sympathetic profiles of the murder victims by neighbors and friends.

The 10:00 p.m. news was not yet over when David West, the attorney representing McLellin purchaser David Sorenson, called Donald Schmidt in Provo. West introduced himself, then asked if Schmidt could come to Salt Lake in the morning to verify the value of a collection about to be sold.

"What will I be looking at?" Schmidt asked.

"It's called the McLellin collection."

"Who's selling it?"

"Mark Hofmann."

Schmidt agreed to meet West at 10:00 the next morning in West's Main Street office and hung up. The usually taciturn Schmidt was more than a little curious. Hofmann had dropped by his Provo home last June to talk about the McLellin collection. He had described the contents, then said it was for sale in Texas and that he was going to pick it up. What did Schmidt think he should do with it? Hofmann had asked. Would the church buy it? Or should he contact private collectors?

Schmidt had said he thought the church would be interested but had not pressed the issue. Hofmann had brought so many items to Schmidt at LDS archives; a few documents had been truly remarkable. Still, Schmidt did not feel it fair to pressure Hofmann to give or sell every document he found to the church, even though he personally believed they belonged there, not with private collectors. Besides, Schmidt knew that the Mormon document market was not so different from a poker game — showing a strong interest might raise the asking price.

Now Schmidt stood by the telephone a moment, puzzling.

So Hofmann had the McLellin collection and was selling it, evidently not to the church—or not directly. Strange. In August, he had asked Hofmann about the collection. Hofmann had replied in just four words: "It has been sold." But how many times could a major collection like that hit the Mormon market without someone like Don Schmidt hearing about it?

Mormon researcher Brent Metcalfe was so alarmed by the bombings that he took his wife and daughter to his parents' condominium complex to spend the night. Metcalfe, in his late-twenties, had worked for Christensen at CFS; to Metcalfe's delight, Christensen had asked him to research the salamander letter. He had become the letter's most ardent defender against the surprisingly few critics who attacked its authenticity or disliked its content. He believed the letter was incredibly significant, a document that ultimately would force the Mormon church to admit that its traditional history was not so simple as its missionaries made it sound. A former Mormon missionary himself, Metcalfe's primary ties to the church now consisted of an abiding interest in Mormon history and his devout extended family.

Metcalfe had been bitterly disappointed when he had lost his job with Christensen earlier that year. Now he worked for Mark Hofmann, who knew more about collecting documents than anyone. In fact, Metcalfe had been on the telephone with Hofmann only minutes before he had heard on television that a bomb had exploded in the Judge Building, followed by the report of Christensen's death. Kathy Sheets's death had come as a second shock, leaving Metcalfe too uneasy to stay at home.

Before driving his family to safety, he talked again with Hofmann on the phone. Hofmann's family, too, had stayed away all day, eaten dinner with Hofmann's parents in Sandy, and arranged to spend the night. Yet Hofmann sounded more relaxed than Metcalfe felt and mentioned the news coverage. "Isn't it great how all of this is going toward CFS?" he offered.

Metcalfe assumed Hofmann was relieved that the murders did not seem related to the salamander letter, but the CFS angle did not bring much comfort. "Mark, it isn't necessarily that way. Don't you know that Gary Sheets was involved in paying for the research on the salamander letter? I was on the CFS payroll."

Hofmann didn't say much. Metcalfe had gone through all that before, blaming "Bishop Sheets" for his dismissal. But tonight Metcalfe had other things on his mind. He brought up Terri Christensen, whom he had met and admired. "Who could ever do this to Terri and those little kids, let alone to Steve?" The question was rhetorical, and in a minute they hung up.

Metcalfe had missed a television interview with Bruce Passey, who described the man he had seen in the Judge Building carrying a package with Christensen's name on it. On her way to bed, Metcalfe's mother mentioned the description: a white male, about five foot eight to ten inches, medium brown hair, possibly with a moustache, wearing a green letterman's jacket without the letter.

Metcalfe froze. "Jill," he whispered after his mother went down the hall, "that's like Mark's jacket. That description kind of sounds like him." They looked at each other and shook their heads in disbelief.

Ernest Salt, one of Hofmann's neighbors, also heard the description that night. Hanging inside the living room closet was a green letterman's jacket his son Jeff had worn. Jeff had run with Hofmann on the Olympus High School track team and later roomed with him in college. He had seen his son and Mark together in those jackets hundreds of times. There must be a thousand jackets like that around, he assured himself. What nagged him, however, was Passey's description of the man's attitude, his nod and calm smile as he stood in the elevator, the box bearing Christensen's name under his arm.

Now that, he thought, sounds like Mark Hofmann.

A few blocks east and south in Millcreek, Curt Bench heard the description and turned to his wife, Pat. "You know who they're describing, don't you? Mark Hofmann."

"Oh, come on."

Bench padded to the telephone in his stocking feet and called Shannon Flynn, who worked document deals for Hofmann.

"Shannon, did you hear that description on television?"

"Yeah, I know what you're saying. But it can't be."

Agreeing, Bench hung up. If Mark were a murderer, Bench told himself, at least he would be intelligent enough not to wear that stupid jacket to deliver a bomb.

2

THE THIRD BOMB VICTIM

Wednesday, October 16, 1985, began early for law enforcement officers. Before dawn, county, city, and federal investigators began checking hundreds of leads surrounding Tuesday's bombings. Gerry D'Elia and David Biggs issued search warrants and subpoenas one after another. The bombings case represented a major break in both men's careers. Biggs had worked on capital punishment cases before as a prosecutor in California, and in Utah he had served as co-counsel defending a child-murderer. D'Elia, backed by a physics degree, had tried arson and explosives cases. But neither had prosecuted a capital case in Utah, and this one promised to scream in the headlines for a long time.

Tuesday's plague of bomb threats carried over to Wednesday morning—all false alarms. Law officers were a little edgy. Later there was one near-miss when Utah's governor stepped out of his car for a meeting at the Hotel Utah. A security guard noticed a man running toward the governor, carrying a package and yelling. The guard shouted, drew his gun, took aim, but then lowered his weapon as the pedestrian swung unaware onto a bus about to leave without him.

Wednesday morning, Gary Sheets handed investigators a list of disappointed investors. "Here are your suspects," he said. But Sheets was not about to hide in a hotel room. Accompanied by a bodyguard, he called on newspaper editors, then visited television stations, intent on correcting media stories from the day before.

27

Meanwhile, Jerry Taylor, western regional officer for the Federal Bureau of Alcohol, Tobacco, and Firearms (ATF), had arrived from San Francisco and accompanied officers to the Judge Building. During his briefing, any suggestion of Mafia hit men left Taylor unimpressed. The Mafia did not take chances on who would get hurt, as this bomber apparently had. A professional hit man made sure the intended target died.

At the Judge Building, Taylor picked up a few missed wires. Then, assessing the damage to the floor, hallway, door, and ceiling, he calculated the exact location of the explosion. The blast was centered, he concluded, above the floor inside the doorway of office 609 where even the concrete floor under the carpet was fractured. He picked up a few more fragments and blunt nails, then returned to police headquarters to continue his analysis.

In addition to the physical evidence gathered at the crime scenes, investigators also began pursuing CFS's complex finances. Their interviews, scores of them, introduced the detectives to a labyrinth of multi-level financing beyond their expertise.

Unknown to most investigators, the community of Mormon scholars—a diverse group of professional and amateur historians connected by an information network so effective it seemed telepathic—was growing uneasy. Although police said that Christensen's involvement with the salamander letter was a less likely motive for murder than CFS's troubled finances, others connected to the controversial letter were concerned.

That loosely knit group had long subsisted on quiet controversy. A Camelot for historians, as one of them christened it, had reigned during the 1970s. In April 1972, for the first time ever, a professional historian, Leonard J. Arrington, had been sustained in General Conference by a show of hands as Church Historian. Under Arrington, the LDS history division blossomed and access to the church's archives increased. Independent Mormon journals—such as *Dialogue: A Journal of Mormon Thought*, *Sunstone*, and *BYU Studies*—carried what was being called the "new Mormon history" to interested readers. The diverse ranks of Mormon intellectuals flourished in the booming Mormon History Association and the new Sunstone Theological Symposium. Official church periodicals, too, reflected a growing historical emphasis.

But as Mormon history became grounded in time and place, some ranking church officials feared that more objective or critical accounts might shake the faith of the weak, and tremors began running through Camelot. A sixteen-volume history of the church was scrapped even before the first volume appeared, and in 1982 a general authority replaced Arrington as Church Historian. Never officially "released" from his position by church members, Arrington and his remaining associates were relocated to Brigham Young University in Provo. When Arrington's portrait was removed from the gallery of Church Historians, Camelot fell.

The powerful and controversial "Joseph Smith story" that began a church and was the focus of many new Mormon historians, had been dictated by Smith in 1838 and canonized in 1880. As a boy of fourteen, Smith said, he was moved by Protestant revivals near his rural New York home in the early 1820s. Following an admonition to pray, which he read in the New Testament, he went into the woods near his home and beseeched God for guidance.

"I had scarcely done so, when immediately I was seized upon by some power which entirely overcame me, and had such an astonishing influence over me as to bind my tongue so that I could not speak. Thick darkness gathered around me, and it seemed to me for a time as if I were doomed to sudden destruction. . . . just at this moment of great alarm, I saw a pillar of light exactly over my head, above the brightness of the sun, which descended gradually until it fell upon me. It no sooner appeared than I found myself delivered from the enemy which held me bound. When the light rested upon me I saw two personages, whose brightness and glory defy all description, standing above me in the air. One of them spake unto me, calling me by name and said, pointing to the other — 'This is My Beloved Son. Hear Him!' "

Smith recounted how his first vision, as it became known, was followed several years later by a visitation from an angel named Moroni. "He said there was a book deposited, written upon gold plates, giving an account of the former inhabitants of this continent, and the source from whence they sprang. He also said that the fulness of the everlasting Gospel was contained in it, as delivered by the Savior to the ancient inhabitants." Ultimately, Smith published the Book of Mormon, which he said he translated from the gold plates "by the power of God," as a companion to the Bible. On April 6, 1830, with six members, the church was organized.

For the next fourteen years, his flock moved westward from state to state, always at odds with its neighbors. Smith reached the apex of his influence when his 10,000 followers built the city of Nauvoo, Illinois, on the Mississippi River, where he was mayor, general of a large, private militia, and candidate for president of the United States. Intent on restoring "all things" lost from biblical epochs, Smith was also a polygamist. Although plural marriage was practiced secretly by select church leaders, rumors of its existence mixed with other troubles. Finally, in June 1844, after being charged with treason for having ordered the destruction of an anti-Mormon newspaper, he and his older brother, Hyrum, and other Mormon leaders, turned themselves over to authorities. On June 27, both Joseph and Hyrum Smith were shot and killed when a mob stormed the Carthage, Illinois, jail.

When the embattled saints regrouped, the majority followed Smith's senior apostle and leader of the Quorum of the Twelve, Brigham Young, to the Great Basin. A minority, including Smith's wife, Emma, and her children, stayed in the midwest, disavowing polygamy and helping to establish the Reorganized Church of Jesus Christ of Latter Day Saints.

While the strong-willed, sometimes fiery Joseph Smith occasionally demanded the obedience of disciples, soft-spoken twentieth-century LDS authorities simply expected it. Yet when Elder Hugh Pinnock arrived at his office on Wednesday morning, October 16, he was less than delighted to learn that Mark Hofmann's wife, Doralee, had called at 7:30 to say that her husband was busy and could not close the McLellin deal until 2:00 that afternoon.

There was not much Pinnock could do about this additional delay. Two o'clock was better than nothing. Once again, calls circled the McLellin deal, from Pinnock in the Church Administration Building to Mormon mission president David Sorenson in Nova Scotia to lawyer David West on Main Street in Salt Lake to former church archivist Donald Schmidt in Provo—except that Schmidt was already on his way to Salt Lake. Another complication, West thought. Already he was holding a check made out to two men, one of whom was dead. And he had heard that there had been an additional bomb scare in the Judge Building that morning. Neither thought was reassuring.

West had represented Sorenson many times over the years, but neither had dealt with Mormon documents before. This transaction was a personal favor to Pinnock and the church and a potential tax write-off for Sorenson, so West had agreed to help. Still, he thought the whole arrangement unusual, to say the least.

Don Schmidt arrived at West's office a little late, about 10:30. He knew Hofmann too well to expect that the meeting would begin on time. After introductions, West told Schmidt two things. That Hofmann would not show until afternoon did not surprise Schmidt. However, that the McLellin deal was to have closed on the very day Christensen had been killed was unnerving. West assured Schmidt that the bombings had nothing to do with the McLellin collection, and the two men agreed to meet again in the afternoon.

At 2:00 they met and waited for Hofmann. As they chatted, West found Schmidt reassuring. Schmidt had known Hofmann for years and had heard about the McLellin collection. After waiting for Hofmann nearly half an hour, West, who had not dealt directly with church officials downtown, decided to call Sorenson again in Nova Scotia. Sorenson insisted that the deal was still on. But no sooner had West hung up than he and Schmidt heard sirens—lots of them, like the day before.

West suddenly felt sick. "I just know that's Hofmann," he muttered, reaching for the radio.

As Schmidt and West had waited for Hofmann, a young flower shop owner, Brad Christensen (no relation to Steven), had left Crossroads Mall two blocks north of West's office and walked uphill to his car on 200 North Street, where he could park for free. The street was lined with old apartment buildings, and ahead and across Main Street on the northeast corner of 200 North rose the red turret of the McCune Mansion. The Deseret Gym, owned by the church, was across the street to the southwest.

As he approached the gym, Christensen noticed a man a few years older than he coming out of the gym and walking toward a blue Toyota MR2 sports car. Christensen, who drove a truck, had noticed this particular sports car parked there before. He assumed the car's owner must be a gym regular. He watched the man unlock the door and bend inside, his arms and shoulders moving as if he were rearranging something on the front seat. Then Christensen traversed Second North, waited for traffic, and crossed Main.

Behind him, he heard a loud explosion. He whirled and saw debris cartwheel through a haze of smoke. The young man was sprawled on the street near the sports car. For a second or two no one along the street moved.

Christensen did not see a nearby meter officer telephone a police dispatch operator—it was 2:41 p.m. He raced across the street toward the victim, who lay flat on his back, his legs spread, knees in the air. One knee had a gaping hole in it, and a fingertip had been blown off his right hand, exposing bone. Christensen looked inside the car. He saw that the front portion of the driver's seat had been blown out. On the passenger's side, he saw part of a cardboard box. Small flames licked toward the rear of the car, burning brown wrapping paper.

Now others were coming to help—attorneys who had offices in the McCune Mansion and patrons of the gym. Christensen helped carry the victim across the street, away from the burning car. Someone brought towels from the gym, and they applied them to the victim's chest, head, and knee wounds, now bleeding profusely. They looked for signs of breath.

Christensen, a returned Mormon missionary, noticed that the man wore temple garments—symbolic white clothing worn next to the skin by devout Mormons as a reminder of religious vows. Immediately Christensen performed a healing ordinance

to try to save the victim's life. He removed a vial of conse-
crated olive oil from his pocket. A man near him noticed the
oil and offered to help. He poured a drop of oil on the young
man's brown hair and invoked the power and authority of his
priesthood. Then he and Christensen placed their hands over
the oil, as Christensen commanded the victim to live until medical help arrived.

Within a few minutes of the blast, Brent Ashworth, vice-
president and corporate attorney for Nature Sunshine Products,
received four phone calls at his Spanish Fork, Utah, office, a
few miles from his Provo home. Each was from a different
Salt Lake City friend, warning: "Look out, Brent. You could
be next."

Ashworth, thirty-six, collected Mormon and American
manuscripts with a passion and considered himself one of Mark
Hofmann's best customers. A Mormon bishop and father of
seven children, he typified the ideal Mormon with his business
suits, closely trimmed hair, glasses, and well-ordered life. His
regret at never having filled an LDS mission had lessened lately,
for with the encouragement of several general authorites, he
now served a self-styled mission buying and speaking about
historical documents to thousands of Mormons.

Ashworth usually went to Salt Lake on Wednesdays, frequently meeting Hofmann at "their spot" by the elevators in
Crossroads Mall downtown. But since he had already been in
Salt Lake this Monday and Tuesday, he remained at his Spanish Fork office on Wednesday.

Alarmed by the spate of telephone calls, Ashworth called
his father in Provo and asked him to check on his family. In
panic, he recalled the bomb at the Sheetses' house and anxiously called the Provo police. By the time he reached home,
officers were searching his house, using mirrors to check under
vehicles. The Ashworths gathered their children and left. Soon
others in the LDS historical community would do the same.

With the third bomb, the entire murder scenario changed.
If Mark Hofmann had been hurt, then the Salt Lake bombings
had everything to do with the salamander letter, for the letter

linked the bomb targets, Steven Christensen, Gary Sheets, and Mark Hofmann. And who else?

Security officers swarmed the archives of BYU's library in Provo as police searched the homes of faculty members Ronald Walker and Dean Jessee, both of whom had researched the salamander letter. Phone lines buzzed as colleagues traded information and warnings. A few hours later, a bomb threat caused the evacuation of Temple Square, the usually tranquil heart of Salt Lake City.

Salt Lake City police officer James Bryant waited at LDS Hospital for the third bombing victim to arrive. When the ambulance screamed to a halt, medical personnel raced out to receive Mark Hofmann. Bryant met them about halfway down the hall as they entered with the victim on a stretcher.

Within a few minutes, the victim's father arrived. William Hofmann was a printing sales representative and Mormon "temple worker," who, with his wife, Lucille, assisted church members in performing temple rites for the dead. Bill Hofmann had been on his way to the Salt Lake Temple when he had heard a blast a block to the north. Inside the temple he had learned that his son had been the victim of a third bomb.

Bryant stayed close to the stretcher. The police dispatcher had notified Bryant that the victim might somehow be involved with setting the bombs. He listened in on the conversation between the shaken father and his injured son.

"What happened, Mark?"

Hofmann said he had left the Church Office Building and walked to his car, which was locked. He had opened the door and an object had started to fall out. He had reached for it and did not remember anything else.

Bryant stepped forward and asked a few questions. "Did anyone know you were parking there?"

Hofmann told him that a brown pickup had followed him earlier, and he had noted the license number in an address book in his car. The truck was a light tan, full-size pickup with a damaged right front fender.

"Who was driving it?"

"A white male about thirty-five years old."

"Did this truck follow you to Deseret Gym where you parked?"

"No, I don't think so."

Then Hofmann asked Bryant to relay a message to two friends, Brent Ashworth, and Hofmann's sometimes-partner Lyn Jacobs. "Tell them to get out of town."

When Hofmann was wheeled to x-ray, Bryant followed. Bill Hofmann called an attorney friend and got the name of Ron Yengich, a defense attorney best known for appealing the case of convicted Utah heiress/murderess Frances Schreuder.

At the county attorney's office, Gerry D'Elia had been in his office screening routine cases for prosecution when his secretary burst in excitedly. Until now, despite a rash of bomb scares, the day had been relatively quiet.

"There's another one!" she exclaimed.

"Another threat?"

"No, this time someone's been injured."

"Where?" D'Elia grabbed his coat.

She told him a radio report said 200 North Main.

D'Elia yelled for Biggs and tore out the door. He was supposed to be in charge of the damn investigation, and not one agency had let him know about this bombing.

"They're all out pissing on fenceposts," he told Biggs, "marking their territory."

In Biggs's car, the two drove a few blocks west and north.

"Biggs, one thing I can tell you," D'Elia said. "Bombers usually blow themselves up. Just hope that's what this is. Otherwise, I don't know where we'll go with it. You're a religious person, Biggs. Why don't you pray that this is the bomber?"

By the time D'Elia and Biggs arrived, the victim had been taken to the hospital. D'Elia looked at the victim's blue sports car. The fire was out, but the car was still hot. Fire fighters and reporters mixed with spectators.

Mike Carter, police reporter for the *Salt Lake Tribune*, approached D'Elia. Carter's usual cockiness was gone, D'Elia noticed.

"The victim this time," Carter said, "is Mark Hofmann — he went to Olympus High School. I used to run against him in track. The Olympus colors are green and gray like that letterman's jacket in the description from the Judge Building. You know what else? Mark is the guy who sold the salamander letter to Steve Christensen."

D'Elia listened carefully, then went to talk with Ken Farnsworth. Suddenly, a tall, muscular young man was brought over to them by a uniformed officer.

"I'm Brent Metcalfe," he said.

"We've been looking for you," Farnsworth told him. He knew that Metcalfe had been mentioned in more than one interview as a person who might have a grudge against Christensen, Sheets, or the Mormon church. He had been fired by LDS church security because of his interest in controversial Mormon subjects, and he had been dismissed by Christensen when the salamander letter project was disbanded at Sheets's urging.

"Is that Mark Hofmann's car?" Metcalfe asked.

"Yes, it is."

"Is he dead?"

"No, he's at the hospital. I think he's going to be okay."

"I used to work for Steve Christensen." Metcalfe was shaking. "Now I work for Mark Hofmann. Do you know what's going on?"

D'Elia gave Metcalfe a hard look. Here's a guy who's scared down to his toenails, he thought. Whatever Metcalfe knew, he was not a bomber. He sent Metcalfe to police headquarters for an interview.

The fire hoses had washed bomb and car parts down the gutter, so the entire block had to be secured and searched. Meanwhile, identification officers scanned the crowd with video cameras since arsonists and bombers often stick around to watch the show. ATF expert Jerry Taylor sent officers to both the rooftops and sewers to collect the scattered evidence. As he had done at the Judge Building, Taylor began his calculations from the physical evidence of exactly how and where the blast occurred.

The explosion of a third bomb easily tripled the panic of the previous day. The victim, soon identified by radio as Mark Hofmann, was unknown to most people, including those associated with CFS. But his name was well known to Mormon scholars, historians, collectors, and dealers in old books and rare papers.

The smoke from the car bombing could be seen by employees working on the upper floors of the Church Office Building. Hofmann's name, some of them knew, was irrevocably linked with church history and documents and, lately, with controversy. In Utah, church involvement in any event was as presumable as fresh drinking water from the canyons. If Hofmann had been bombed, some murmured, somehow the church must be involved.

Rumors raced through the Church Office Building, particularly the history and genealogy departments. Hofmann was dead, one rumor reported. Hofmann has a green letterman's jacket; even he could be a suspect. Hofmann was not dead. Yes, he was. Church security said so. What did church security know? Were they a part of the investigation?

Across the plaza in the Church Administration Building, Apostle Dallin Oaks heard of the bombing with consternation. Oaks on Tuesday had told Hofmann to close the McLellin transaction Wednesday. Hofmann had missed the morning appointment and, obviously, the postponed meeting at 2:00 p.m. Now he had been bombed. Oaks picked up the telephone and called the FBI.

Coin dealer Alvin Rust, in his shop near the Judge Building, had had enough. First Steven Christensen on the sixth floor, then that poor woman in Holladay, and now Mark Hofmann, whom Rust treated as a son. Maybe Mark owed him money now, a lot of money. He had borrowed $150,000 from Rust for the McLellin collection last April and so far had repaid only $17,000. But Mark always came through eventually.

Recently Rust had grown tired of waiting for repayment, let alone a profit, so last June when Hofmann had told him that President Gordon B. Hinckley had the McLellin collection, Rust had tried to call Hinckley. Hinckley's secretary told him to put his information in a letter. Rust did and sent the letter.

When Hofmann learned of the end-run, he had been

annoyed. "I talked with President Hinckley," he told Rust later. "Everything's taken care of, but I don't think you'll hear from him." And Rust had not. You had to hand it to Mark; not many people could walk in and see Hinckley.

But this was too much. Maybe the McLellin deal was confidential and church leaders were busy men. Still, Rust had been a bishop in the church; he had done a lot for the church. He picked up the telephone and called President Hinckley's office. He ended up with church security and they would not put him through.

"I need to talk with President Hinckley," Rust insisted, not about to be put off again. "You wouldn't know anything about the McLellin papers."

"Mr. Rust," said the voice on the other end, "we know all about the McLellin papers."

"You do?"

"Yes. Did *you* know that Mark Hofmann was supposed to get them from you and deliver them today?"

"That's news to me. I've never seen the McLellin papers."

"Mr. Rust," the guard said, "we have reason to believe that your life is in extreme danger and you'd better take precautions."

Rust called his wife and told her to leave the house and go to the neighbors. When he hung up, the phone rang. Suddenly certain church leaders wanted to meet with him. Rust went directly to see Dallin Oaks and two church security representatives to tell them what he knew about the McLellin collection.

A few blocks away, with the burned sports car cooling, Jerry Taylor, other ATF agents, and police officers were checking the car for more bombs. They popped the trunk and sped out of range. Ken Farnsworth raised his head and was astonished to see spectators saunter over to the trunk and peer inside.

He and the other investigators pushed the onlookers back and inspected the trunk. Old papers and postcards were everywhere. So were negatives, cans of diet supplement, a papyrus piece encased in plastic, rubber gloves, and a felt-tipped pen. The agents suspected anyone with a bomb in his or her car, and the odd contents of the trunk piqued their interest. Farnsworth fixed his eyes on a pipe elbow. The bombs would use straight pipe—but what if someone was trying to purchase pipe the day after a double bombing? Wouldn't buying an elbow look less suspicious? Farnsworth had no experience with bombing homicides, but he trusted Taylor as the best man in his field. When Jerry got a free minute, Farnsworth decided, he would see what he had to say about bomb victim number three.

Farnsworth's partner, Detective Jim Bell, had hurried to LDS Hospital to interview Hofmann. He arrived about 3:45 but had to wait a few minutes to be taken down to x-ray. There, he passed Officer Bryant. "Did you get the victim's clothes as evidence?" Bell asked.

"We got them," Bryant said. Bell nodded and entered the anteroom. He talked with a doctor, who showed him an x-ray posted on a lighted panel. A steel fragment extended from the victim's knee.

"Can I talk to the victim?" Bell asked.

The doctor agreed. Bell went into the adjoining room, where two nurses were working on the victim's head wound.

Mark Hofmann looked up at him.

"Can we talk for a few minutes?" Bell asked.

"Yes, but you'll have to speak loudly," Hofmann said, his voice a little above a whisper. Bell realized that his hearing had been damaged.

"Can you understand what I'm saying?"

"Yes."

"Can you tell me where you were going when you were injured?"

Hofmann replied that he had been on his way to sell some documents to an attorney in town.

Bell asked him to relate his day's activities.

Hofmann said he had gotten up at about 7:00 a.m. and gone to McDonald's for breakfast. After that, he had been driving around.

"Driving around where?"

Hofmann was indefinite. Finally he said he had been driving around Emigration Canyon.

"What were you doing up there?"

"Nothing. Just thinking."

Next Bell asked Hofmann what had happened when he got to his car. The victim said that when he opened the car door, a package had fallen onto the floor of the car.

Bell asked if he could describe the package. No, Hofmann said, he couldn't.

How about size? Color?

No, he didn't remember.

Bell wanted to press further but was sent from the room while more x-rays were taken. When he returned, Bell brought up Emigration Canyon again. During what time period had Hofmann been driving around there?

Just part of the day, Hofmann said, softly. After medical personnel wheeled Hofmann into the CAT scan room, Bell waited outside for half an hour, completed his notes on the conversation with Hofmann, then left.

Bell had plenty to do back at the office but instead drove to the crime scene to talk with Ken Farnsworth and Jerry Taylor. Taylor told him that the third bomb was similar in structure and components to the first two, but only the first bomb had contained the ferocious spray of concrete nails. Bell listened, then related Hofmann's account of how the explosion occurred.

"That did not happen," Taylor said succinctly, adding, "he's your bomber." Taylor explained to Bell the way the bomb had exploded, at the height of the console between the bucket seats, with one end pointing back over the victim's shoulder, the other toward the floor. Bell listened in a growing fury—at himself. The victim's evasive answers, which he had thought might be due to injury and shock, hit him like thunder.

D'Elia went back to the office to prepare search warrants for Hofmann's car and house. He sent one back to the car with Bell. Within ten minutes, Bell and Farnsworth had Hofmann's address book. They found no license plate number for a truck.

The Salt Lake County Sheriff's Department, working the Sheets murder, was not excluded from Wednesday's excitement. Around 4:00 p.m. the department got a report of an explosion in Holladay, near the home of Elder Hugh Pinnock. More than a dozen sheriffs' cars rushed to the scene. So did reporters. Officers canvassed the area in a door-to-door search, but no explanation was found for the loud noise that reportedly had caused dogs to bark, windows to rattle, and people to rush from their houses. Rumors about a fourth bomb wove into the growing mystery, which would be solved repeatedly on radio talk shows and in private conversations for months to come.

Detective Don Bell (no relation to Jim Bell), at the site of the car bomb, noticed that a car with California plates had left the scene soon after the explosion. He made a note to check the license plate against CFS investors. Yesterday his interviews had switched from the salamander letter to CFS. A switch back might be imminent, but Bell had not made it yet.

Then Bell and another detective were summoned at about 5:30 p.m. to First Interstate Bank to meet the head of bank security. Ushered in, they rode an out-of-the-way elevator to the thirteenth floor and were led down a thickly carpeted, walnut-lined hallway to a plush conference room. Inside, they were introduced to several banking officials and their attorneys, who were engaged in a hot debate about whether or not they should give the detectives the information that prompted their call. After checking law books, they decided to proceed, and everybody sat down. Harvey Tanner, head loan officer, acted as spokesman.

Tanner told the detectives, who by then were as baffled as interested, that on June 28, 1985, he had received a telephone call from an important man in the LDS church. He said he was sending over Steven Christensen and his friend Mark Hofmann to get a loan for $185,000, which, Tanner said, the church was authorizing.

Only the detectives' pens edged the silence. "Is that all it takes?" Bell asked, trying to lighten the meeting's tension.

"Well," Tanner said, "this had been done in the past and we knew everything was okay."

Silence fell and heads turned toward a small man wearing bifocals in the back of the room. Bell had noticed him before, since he was the only man who had not been introduced. Mr. Bifocals, Bell dubbed him mentally. The man said nothing, and the heads turned toward Tanner again.

Tanner described how Hofmann had filled out the loan application while Christensen observed.

A little odd, Bell thought. "Were you concerned about that?"

"No, because I'd had a call from this man at the LDS church."

"What's his name?"

"I can't tell you right now." He handed Bell a folder. "Here's the file." It contained an application form without much writing. No collateral was listed.

Bell handed the folder to his partner and looked at Tanner. "This is all you require for a $185,000 loan?"

Heads turned toward the man in back again, and this time he spoke. "No, it is not proper and that's not all it takes to get $185,000."

In a moment Tanner continued. "A couple of weeks later I saw Mark come into the bank and do some business. He didn't make any payment on the loan although he deposited $26,000."

"What happened next?"

"The loan came due and there was no payment. Then we received a check in the mail, which arrived on September 3, for the principal and the interest. We sent it to Rocky Mountain State Bank and it was returned for insufficient funds. At that point, I was very concerned. I called the man at the church and Mark Hofmann and Steve Christensen.

"On September 16," Tanner continued, "Mark Hofmann came back in the bank to discuss the bounced check. He said he needed a little more time. A little later, I saw him in the bank with two men. I confronted him about payment, and he denied ever having sent a bad check. He was very uptight, close to angry. I got the feeling he didn't want those guys to know about the problem. I made more calls to the man at the church and Steve Christensen."

Bell looked Tanner squarely in the eye and pressed, "I need to know who the person is at the LDS church. This is a murder case and we need the facts."

Another debate raged among bank officers and attorneys as to whether that information could be supplied. Finally, the man in back spoke again. "Stop it. Tell him the man's name."

In the silence, Harvey Tanner said, "Hugh Pinnock."

"Oh," Bell said. He had never heard of him.

Tanner said when he had called Pinnock he had been reassured that Hofmann was good for the money, the church was behind it, not to worry. "You see," Tanner added, "we had done business with Pinnock before, obtaining money for the church without the church being involved."

"Okay," Bell said, writing it down carefully. If such things were done, he mused, they certainly were not publicized. He decided Mr. Bifocals was from out of town and did not approve of local customs. Suddenly he felt very sorry for Tanner.

"On October 4 we got a payment for $20,000 by way of a check made out to a Shannon Flynn but endorsed to Mark Hofmann and then to First Interstate." At that point, Tanner had made more phone calls. "Around the same time, Steve Christensen and Mark Hofmann told me about a document Mark was selling in the east called the 'Oath of a Freeman.' They gave me the names Raymond Wapner and Justin Schiller and said I could call them to be sure of payment. I called, and they agreed they would be paying Hofmann $150,000 for the document and that the money would be coming to him. Of course," he added, "Hofmann would still be about $15,000 short."

Bell wondered if they would let him off on the interest. Tanner continued: "Mark Hofmann was going to go to New York and get the money, then pay off the loan on October 15. Actually, it was due on October 14, but that was Columbus Day, a bank holiday, so the money would be wired on the 15th."

"What was Christensen's part in this?"

"Steve was there, but he never participated in the conversations. He was more like a witness. My impression was that Steve was working for the LDS church. After they told me about the Oath, I felt better."

Tanner said he later found out that Christensen had rented two safe deposit boxes on October 7 at First Interstate Bank and would place the McLellin collection there as collateral for the loan.

"When Steve was killed I called Hugh. He told me not to worry, that the deal had been rescheduled for today and the money was coming. So then I felt okay until Mark was bombed."

When Tanner heard about the third bomb victim, he flew

for the telephone but found that Pinnock would not return or accept his calls, nor would any other church leader. He wondered if he had been stuck with a paper for $185,000. At that point, the bank officers decided to convene, and someone eventually called the police.

Bell and his partner arranged protection for Tanner, in case he was a bomb target, and then returned to the station. Bell went to see police chief Bud Willoughby, who was supervising the high-profile case. "Chief," he said, "I've got your motive. I don't know what it is, but I've got it."

The Salt Lake police station was crowded that night with witnesses and other informants. Curt Bench was one of them. Bench had been driving back to Deseret Book after completing a deal, which Hofmann had initiated, when he had heard on the radio that a third bomb had exploded in downtown Salt Lake and that the victim was thought to be Mark Hofmann. Bench nearly drove off the road: Steve killed yesterday, Mark bombed today. He hit his fist against the steering wheel, shouting, "Why didn't he listen to me!"

When Bench reached South Temple Street he was too upset to park his car. He pulled into the Hotel Utah garage across from Deseret Book. "This is an emergency," he told the attendant. "Would you please just park this for me?"

Bench ran inside the store and began calling people and talking to employees. Within minutes he confirmed that Hofmann had been the victim of the third bomb and he learned something new and even more terrible—that Hofmann might be a suspect. Word was trickling back from comments overheard at the scene.

Bench looked at his assistant, Wade Lillywhite. "We'd better tell the police what we know," Lillywhite suggested.

Bench nodded. They dealt with Hofmann frequently, and Bench had talked several times with Steve Christensen lately. At the police department, Bench and Lillywhite joined the general pandemonium. Brent Metcalfe was in tears, a reporter wanted to interview Bench on camera (which he declined), while officers brought in Hofmann's bloody clothes. Bench grimly waited his turn, then told the police what he knew about

Christensen, Hofmann, and various documents, including the McLellin deal.

Shannon Flynn, who, like Lyn Jacobs, had worked document transactions for Hofmann, finished talking with the police about the same time Bench did and offered to drive him back to his car. The two walked out, talking. "They're thinking that Mark's a suspect," Bench said. It suddenly hit him that he had told Hofmann about Christensen's death the day before.

"No, no, no, that's impossible," Flynn insisted. "There's no way Mark would hurt Steve. Steve was making things come together for Mark."

"Well, that's what they think. It's obvious."

"I'm going to have to talk to some people," Flynn said. Bench looked at Flynn curiously, but Flynn said nothing more.

Before getting into his car, Flynn checked under the hood and chassis. He offered Bench a ride to Deseret Book. First, though, they drove by the blackened wreck of the blue sports car on Second North.

Bench felt trapped in a nightmare. Christensen was dead, Hofmann could be dead by morning, and now the police were trying to finger Mark. The information he had given them would probably help them do it, too, Bench thought, and he had no reason to believe the police were right. In fact, it was ridiculous to think that easy-going Mark Hofmann would hurt anybody. He had never shown the least hint of violence or meanness in all the years Bench had known him.

Bench wanted to get home to his family, near Hofmann's home in Millcreek, the quiet neighborhood between Salt Lake City and Holladay. Bench had to sort out his thoughts and desperately needed more information, some kind of guidance. His whole world was turning sinister and strange.

Quitting time did not come for investigators Wednesday night. About 8:00 p.m. Don Bell got a call from Shannon Flynn. He did not know how Flynn reached him, but he recognized Flynn's name from his interview at the bank. In fact, Bell had listed Flynn's name next to Hofmann's in his suspect column, since they were evidently doing business together.

"I'm going to purchase Mark Hofmann's home," Flynn

told him, "and I just wanted you guys to know that I had a safe delivered there. It's unlocked and in the garage. I thought you might be searching the house and I don't want you to ruin it."

Bell pulled the receiver away from his head and looked at it. A search of Hofmann's house *was* planned—in fact, it had probably started, but how did Flynn know?

"How well do you know Hofmann?"

"Not that well. I've sold some documents with him. Most recently I sold some old Mormon money and a Jim Bridger note to Deseret Book for $20,000. Mark was having financial problems so I signed the check over to him to put on a bank loan."

Bell took notes; this fit with the Tanner interview.

"You'll probably find out," Flynn continued, "that I conned Deseret Book into thinking I was the seller of that material. Mark didn't want them to know it was his stuff."

Bell's amazement at the case grew again. "Did that concern you? He's selling the stuff and doesn't want them to know it's his?"

"No, it's done all the time in the document trade."

"I see," Bell said and arranged to meet Flynn in his office for an interview at 10:30 the next morning.

The next search warrant was served in the glare of television lights outside a red brick split-level house marked by a sign, "Haus Hofmann," on the lamp post. Immediately, investigators spread through the house as D'Elia paced across the porch in the chilly evening air between media cameras and the warm living room. A burglar alarm had sounded as the officers opened the door with a key they had gotten from Hofmann's family. Television cameras out front recorded one officer ripping out wires.

David Biggs strolled through the house as the officers searched. He looked at the calendar on the kitchen wall. "Temple night" was noted in each month, including October, in a small, feminine hand. Biggs considered himself a moderate Mormon. Church members who planned on attending the temple each month were, in his book, pretty dedicated people.

The rooms downstairs, which Hofmann obviously used for

his document business, were chaotic with piles of documents, books, and miscellany. No one knew what the papers meant. But within fifteen minutes, a sergeant upstairs called for the deputy in charge of the search. Inside the back corner of a closet, they had found a letterman's jacket turned inside out, wadded into a ball. Officers turned the jacket right side out. It was green with gray sleeves and the letter had been removed.

They took the jacket to D'Elia and told him where they had found it. He looked it over and nodded. This was important, they knew, as they spread the jacket out and photographed it.

D'Elia, leaning against the open door, his back blocking the cameras, drew a long breath. "My God, you aren't that smart," he murmured. "We thought you were smarter than that."

That night, as print and media journalists worked frantically, Chief Willoughby announced on live television that Mark W. Hofmann was the "prime suspect" in the Salt Lake City bombings. Since Hofmann was in the hospital, the city was safe, the chief said. Federal charges would be filed in the morning. The frequent press conferences held by Willoughby, county sheriff Pete Hayward, and federal agents purportedly informed and reassured the public. But they also exacerbated inter-agency competition and fueled an increasingly skeptical media.

As Biggs drove D'Elia home, the two had talked through the case's puzzles. Why would Hofmann try to bomb Gary Sheets? Who was the third bomb for? Pinnock? One of the attorneys in the McCune Mansion? Could they tie Hofmann to Gary or Kathy Sheets or to CFS? Had Sheets invested in documents with Christensen, just as he had supported the salamander letter project? Had Christensen confided in Sheets and the two of them threatened Hofmann with some kind of exposure?

D'Elia did not mind giving the ring of prediction to his "gut feeling." Referring to suspect, motive, and bomb-building site, he surmised, "Okay, Biggs, Mark Hofmann's the bomber, the salamander letter's a forgery, and it's Emigration Canyon."

3

AN UNPRECEDENTED
INVESTIGATION

By Thursday morning investigators were reasonably sure that, with Mark Hofmann in the hospital, the bombings were over. They did not deny the possibility that he had accomplices, however, and the media was quoting both the chief of police and "sources close to the investigation" that there could be other arrests. Meanwhile, Hofmann's friends and colleagues, even those who knew him only by reputation, doubted that the police knew what they were doing. As bomb threats continued Thursday and throughout the weekend, some Mormon historians and document collectors fled to self-imposed exile. Brent Ashworth moved his family from a motel in St. George (in southern Utah) to a motel on the outskirts of Salt Lake City where he could keep appointments without endangering his family by taking them home.

Thursday morning, essentially in hiding, Brent Metcalfe clung to one pleasant fact. Just before the bombings, he had finally found concrete evidence that the salamander letter was authentic. Given its critics, even after an expensive authentication process, that was a victory Metcalfe treasured, scared as he felt. He didn't know whom to fear. Hofmann? The police? The press? Was he being set up? Was he a target? Repeatedly, he arranged the first three days of the week in his mind, looking for a clue, a solution. He thought back further and added other pieces, but the pieces did not fit and no satisfying picture appeared.

When he had last talked to Steve Christensen, Christensen

had been looking for Hofmann. Metcalfe knew there had been problems with an unnamed deal involving church leaders and a bank loan. "If Mark would just talk with me, we could get this straightened out," Christensen had complained. So during their last conversation, Metcalfe asked if the situation was resolved. "Oh, that's fine," Christensen brushed off the question, "I just need to talk with Mark."

Now Metcalfe did not know what to make of that memory, or of a lot of others. He did think that the police and press ought to know all the facts before condemning Hofmann and his document business. Ironically, Metcalfe also knew that the salamander letter, the most controversial of Hofmann's documents, was genuine, even as the press speculated that the murders were tied to forgery.

Shortly before the bombings, Metcalfe had heard about an Episcopalian prayer book that had belonged to Nathan Harris, brother of Martin Harris, the author of the salamander letter. In the back of the book was a poem, apparently in Martin Harris's hand. Handwriting had been a major authentication issue for the salamander letter because Harris had left behind only a few signatures. Metcalfe had learned that Hofmann had purchased the prayer book from Deseret Book, where it had been stored in a vault for over a decade. If the handwriting in the back of the book matched the salamander letter, Metcalfe believed that would clinch the debate about the letter's validity once and for all. He had badgered Hofmann for photocopies, since Hofmann had sold the book to the LDS church.

Monday evening, the night before the murders, Metcalfe and his wife, Jill, drove to the Hofmann home. When Brent saw the photocopy of the poem, he could hardly contain his delight. Even a cursory comparison with a photograph of the salamander letter seemed convincing. Metcalfe suggested showing the handwriting to Dean Jessee, one of the two Mormon historians from Brigham Young University who had studied the salamander letter. Hofmann, in a hurry to keep an appointment with Shannon Flynn that same evening, had agreed. The Hofmann children were playing around their father's feet, Metcalfe remembered suddenly.

And why not? Mark had been the same as usual, not a madman, no serial bomber, Metcalfe thought. Now he was seriously injured and publicly accused. Metcalfe had talked with him on the phone several times Tuesday. Before and after Hofmann murdered? Ridiculous.

Metcalfe had arranged to meet Jessee Wednesday morning in the parking plaza of the Church Office Building. There, before the third bombing injured Hofmann, Metcalfe showed Jessee the photocopies of the handwriting in the prayer book. Jessee looked at all of them carefully. He pointed to the Nathan Harris hand and then the other, which appeared to be that of Martin Harris. "You can tell these people came from the same family," Jessee said.

When Jessee finally said yes, the salamander letter was written in the same hand as the poem in the prayer book, Metcalfe was elated. Everyone knew that Jessee, a recognized expert on Mormon handwriting, was conservative in his pronouncements. Not only had the paper and ink proven consistent with the early nineteenth-century period, but now the handwriting itself had additional backup. Metcalfe suffered the irony that he could not tell Steve Christensen about this—he had invested so much in that letter. Metcalfe was looking for Hofmann to tell him about the handwriting when he heard about the car bombing.

At that point, Metcalfe had been taken into protective custody. He and Jill had both answered questions, then allowed officers to search their car, their apartment, and the apartment Metcalfe's parents sometimes let him use. Almost as fast as Hofmann had become a victim, Metcalfe became a suspect. And he remained afraid of becoming a victim himself.

Meanwhile, Thursday morning, Detectives Jim Bell and Don Bell returned to LDS Hospital. They knew Hofmann would be groggy and in pain, but questioning him was crucial. The nurse in charge suggested that one of them ask the questions and that he stand near Hofmann's less injured ear. Led to a trauma unit, the detectives introduced themselves. Jim Bell asked Hofmann if he would talk with them again, and, once again, Hofmann agreed. He was more coherent than they had anticipated. Bell then read Hofmann his Miranda rights from a printed card. "Do you understand?"

Hofmann, swathed in bandages, his right arm in a sling, and his right leg in traction, said yes.

"Are you still willing to talk to us?"

"Yes, I am."

As he had the day before, Bell asked him what happened when he had gotten to the car. Again Hofmann replied that he had opened the door and a package had fallen.

"Did you park the car at that location?" Bell asked.

"Yes."

"Where did you go then?"

"I had a meeting in the basement of the Church Office Building, then I came back to my car."

"Did you at any point go to the McCune Mansion on the corner?" Workmen on the mansion roof had reported seeing a young man with a briefcase cross the street toward the building. The media had picked up this story, discovering that Steve Christensen's attorney once had an office there and that Dean Larsen, one of Gary Sheets's business associates, still did.

"No."

"Did you go anywhere else?"

"I went to the trunk before I opened the car door."

"Who do you know who would want to kill you?"

"I don't know anybody who would do this."

Jim Bell took off the kid gloves. "Well," he said, "I'm fairly confident that you're the bomber. We did a search last night and recovered pipe and gloves from your car trunk and a letterman's jacket from your house."

"No," Hofmann said, "I didn't do it." Bell thought Hofmann looked slightly anxious.

"I'm telling you that we did a search and we've got the letterman's jacket you wore when you delivered the bomb to the Judge Building. We've got pipe and rubber gloves from your car. We're confident that you're responsible, and we want to know why you selected these particular people to kill."

Hofmann did not reply but squirmed on the bed. The medical alarms, attached to monitor his vital signs, sounded.

"You'll have to leave," the nurse said. The detectives began to protest that they needed a few more questions answered, then took another look at Hofmann and cleared out.

When defense attorney Ron Yengich heard that the police had come to the hospital to talk with Hofmann on Thursday, he asked the hospital staff to call him if they came back. He did not want his client talking without the benefit of an attorney, especially since the police chief had publicly accused him of murder.

Yengich and co-defender Bradley Rich had first met at the University of Utah law school. Products of the 1960s, both chose careers as criminal defense attorneys, strongly influenced by the Warren Supreme Court and its emphasis on human and personal rights. In the firm of Yengich, Rich, Xaiz, and Metos, Rich and Yengich did not usually work together, for their personal styles differed. Yengich was a colorful "head-banger" whose pithy rhetoric replayed perfectly on the evening news. Rich was articulate and even-tempered, well versed in fraud cases and the myriad details they involved. This case, they soon realized, would threaten to consume them both.

Jim Bell joined Ken Farnsworth and they drove north on Interstate-15 to Centerville where they parked in front of a blue-and-white frame house on Mountain View Road. The front yard was fenced, and small bikes reminded them that Steven Christensen had been a father. For more than six hours, Farnsworth had personally observed both the Christensen and Sheets autopsies. He knew all he needed to about the big, blunt nails that had been dug from Christensen's flesh and the galvanized pipe, blasted into a heavy corkscrew that had gored deep into his chest. But Farnsworth, like Bell, had virtually no sense of Christensen as a person.

Farnsworth, though, was shadowed by a clear memory of Christensen's body at the Judge Building. The early pandemonium had ceased, and he and Bell and a few other officers were methodically gathering evidence. Farnsworth occasionally glanced toward the unidentified body. The hallway seemed eerie. Although he did not—could not—know what that man's death represented, Farnsworth nonetheless sensed a shift in his own life. He had one silent question for an equally silent corpse: What the hell did you do to get yourself blown up?

At the Christensen home, the white front door opened to a hall, with a staircase on the right side. The detectives were shown into a small, formal parlor decorated in blue and white, furnished with a sofa, a painted chest, a piano, and several chairs. Terri Christensen was flanked by her father, Randle Romney, and her father-in-law, Mac Christensen. On the piano was a figurine of a father listening to his young son.

Calmly, Christensen described her husband's schedule in the days before the murders. Steven hadn't left the house until after 7:30 Tuesday morning. He had worked Monday, Columbus Day, but spent that evening and the preceding weekend with his wife and their three boys. Bit by bit, the detectives drew out information from three willing but baffled people who had no idea why Christensen had been murdered or by whom and who knew very little about either the McLellin collection or Christensen's business dealings. No, he had not used drugs. No, he would not fear a grand jury investigation of CFS or criminal prosecution. Their answers were so calm, so articulate, that Farnsworth began to wonder how they could discuss — of all things — the violent, brutal murder of their son and husband without so much as a quaver. Mac Christensen answered his thoughts.

"You must wonder why we're so unemotional and controlled. I assure you that enough tears have been shed in the last couple of days that we wonder if they're not all shed. But we're not callous, uncaring people."

The detectives told the Christensens that they thought Hofmann was responsible for the bombings and promised to keep in touch.

Thursday is traditionally reserved for the weekly Salt Lake Temple meeting of the LDS First Presidency and Council of Twelve Apostles. Underground tunnels lead from the Church Administration and Office buildings directly into the temple. The most solemn and official business of the church is transacted during those private Thursday meetings. In fact, it was during such a meeting, on June 9, 1978, that President Spencer

W. Kimball announced that black men should be allowed to hold the priesthood. One by one, his counselors and the Twelve sustained his statement, changing a century-held doctrine and practice overnight.

Meetings in the temple are seldom disturbed, but this Thursday after the triple bombing, Elder Dallin Oaks was called away. Shannon Flynn, who had accompanied Hofmann to see President Gordon B. Hinckley a week earlier, was at the Church Administration Building, insisting that he see Hinckley. Flynn had seen how accessible Hinckley was to Hofmann, but today, on his own and increasingly frantic, he could not get past the front desk.

Leaving the administration building, Flynn burst into the Search Room in the historical department across the plaza. By now he seemed nearly hysterical. After a few telephone calls, at about 12:15 p.m., Flynn walked back across the plaza and was ushered into Oaks's office, next door to Pinnock's. Oaks had talked with Hofmann alone on Tuesday but had since grown cautious. This time he had two church security officers present and a secretary to record the conversation.

After introductions, Flynn began describing himself and his relationship with Hofmann as well as various document deals. "The police want to talk to me because they found a check which was made out to me from Deseret Book last week, and that check was endorsed over to Mark Hofmann. I had sold some things to Deseret Book for Mark."

Flynn explained that Hofmann and Christensen had come to Flynn's house at around 12:30 p.m. and that both "were quite nervous because the loan at First Interstate Bank had been called due on demand." Hofmann needed Flynn's $20,000 check from Deseret Book to pay towards the loan. Flynn told Oaks that he knew Hinckley had arranged the loan for Hofmann not only because Flynn had been told that, but because he knew Hofmann's financial situation well enough to know that Hofmann could never get an unsecured loan for that amount.

"Do you know anything about why he got that loan?" Oaks probed.

"During the weeks before, he had purchased the McLellin collection. He needed those funds to get that collection. He had tried to get money from other people. One of the partners is someone I know. I went to Arizona with Mark, trying to arrange for money."

"Have you seen the McLellin collection?" Oaks asked. "First hand?"

"No, I just know what he told me. I did see just a part, a papyrus," Flynn said. "He told me President Hinckley had arranged the loan for him at the First Interstate Bank. Plus, he specifically said someone had helped him."

"What was your relationship to him? Are you partners? Or are you loaning him money?"

"Partners. Not in business generally, but in specific deals."

"Are you partners in the McLellin collection?"

"No. He came to me and told me that President Hinckley was nervous to have it." Flynn had been told that a non-Mormon minister and others were about to procure the collection. Hinckley was intent on getting the papers first and having the loan repaid right away, Flynn said, but due to the failure of another deal, Hofmann had not been able to accomplish this.

"Was anyone else's name mentioned in connection with obtaining this loan?" Oaks asked after Flynn explained the details.

"No."

"Where did that $20,000 check go?"

"To First Interstate Bank."

"How can we be of help to you?" Oaks asked.

"I want to find what posture I need to take. The whole room is falling down."

"You are about to talk to the police," Oaks said. "Let me tell you that I know something about this transaction. You will understand when it comes out.

"As soon as I learned that Mark Hofmann had been the object of a bomb," Oaks continued, "I knew that I had some facts that would help the police. Within sixty minutes of the incident, I had talked to two FBI agents. I told them everything I knew about it.

"The church is going to cooperate fully and it has absolutely nothing to hide," he continued. "Sometimes there are some confidential transactions, but this is a murder investigation. Confidentiality is set aside." Oaks then urged Flynn, who had liberally sprinkled his account with Hinckley's name but never mentioned the lower-ranked Hugh Pinnock, to differentiate between what he knew first hand and what Hofmann had only told him.

"Mark Hofmann has told you some things that are not true," he cautioned, quickly adding that he was not criticizing Hofmann or anyone else. He suggested that Flynn say nothing to the press, and the meeting ended approximately twenty minutes after it had begun—about two hours past the time Flynn had agreed to meet with Detective Don Bell.

Soon after 10:30, Bell called the number he had for Flynn and reached his father, who answered his queries abruptly. Bell decided to be equally abrupt. "We had an appointment. If he'd prefer, I can get a warrant. But when I instruct someone to be here regarding a homicide case, I expect him to be here."

At 11:45, Bell was sent to Mormon-owned KSL-TV—the local CBS affiliate—to seize some videotapes. Wednesday night, Hal Passey, the Judge Building jeweler, had been featured on the news viewing a videotape of Hofmann. While he had not made a positive identification, Passey had noted on television a resemblance to the man in the Judge Building. Because of the possibility that he had been influenced by the reporter and the video, Passey would be considered a tainted witness if Hofmann ever went to trial. Bruce Passey, his son, was now the only usable eyewitness to the early morning visitor in the Judge Building. Problematically, Passey had described the jacket as green with tan sleeves, whereas the sleeves were gray. But when police took him back to the dimly lit lobby and showed him the jacket, Passey was sure it was identical to the jacket he had seen on the man carrying the package to Steve Christensen.

Bell waited unsuspectingly in the lobby of the television station. A camera man soon came in and the receptionist's telephone rang. "Okay," she said, into the receiver, "you can bring them in." The photographer switched on his lights and started filming, as the station director handed over the subpoenaed tapes to Bell. As he left, Bell found Channel 4—the ABC affiliate—filming from the sidewalk. Obviously, this was not his day.

No sooner did he get back to the police department than he got a call from someone in LDS church security. "I understand you're looking for Shannon Flynn. He's over here."

"He had an appointment here at 10:30," Bell said, wondering why church security was involved. Flynn's father must have known where to call, he concluded. "We can do this the easy way or the hard way. If it's more important for Shannon Flynn to go to the church than to keep an appointment with police, we'll do it the hard way."

"He's meeting with Elder Oaks," the man at the other end explained.

"So?"

"I thought that would make a difference."

"It makes no difference to me."

"The FBI guys are here, too. I don't see why you're being so hard about this."

"Look, this is really none of your business," Bell began.

"Just a minute. I'm giving you to the FBI." An agent came on the line. "Are you doing our investigation?" Bell asked. "If you are, it sure would be handy to know that down here."

The agent apologized profusely. "Listen, we don't want to be involved. Our boss got a call from Webster [William Webster, FBI director], who got a call from Senator Orrin Hatch [R-Utah], and told us to come over here and give assistance. So we're here."

"I can understand that," Bell said. (He did not know that the FBI had already interviewed both Oaks and Pinnock.) Thanking the agent, Bell decided to call Pinnock.

"Elder Pinnock's in the temple," a secretary told him.

Bell told him who he was and what he wanted.

"He'll be in the temple all day."

Bell sighed. "Could you have him call me when he can?"

In a few minutes, Martell Bird, former FBI agent under J. Edgar Hoover and currently chief of LDS church security, returned Bell's call. He introduced himself. "We understand you want to interview Elder Pinnock."

"No, I want to interview Mr. Pinnock."

"He's quite a busy man."

Don Bell's thinning patience collapsed. He informed Bird

that the city was conducting a homicide investigation, adding, "and the part that really burns me is, what is *your* involvement in this? Twice now you guys have called to tell me about my interviews."

Hot-tempered, Bird quickly became as upset as Bell, and soon they both hung up. In a few minutes, Bell's phone rang again. "This is Hugh Pinnock," the caller said in a measured voice. "If you can come over right now, Detective Bell, I have made time in my calendar."

On the way to 47 East South Temple Bell thought through what he had learned about Pinnock since first hearing his name the night before. Bell had left the Mormon church at age 18, but he had family members and friends who were devout. They told him that Pinnock was well-off financially and on the board of directors of First Interstate Bank. "What is he supposed to do for the church?" he had asked one confidential source.

"He's a troubleshooter."

"What does that mean?"

"You know, if there's a real delicate problem somewhere— maybe an excommunication or something—he's sent out to handle it."

A mutual friend remembered Pinnock from college. "We were all sitting around at a fraternity party telling what we were going to do in life. Pinnock said he would do one of two things, be president of the United States or president of the church."

Bell arrived at the old granite administration building, checked in with security, and was ushered to office 402. He asked Pinnock what he knew about Hofmann, but Pinnock wanted to talk about the tragedy of the bombings and how he had known both victims.

"I knew Mark Hofmann through Steve," he said, eventually coming around to the subject. "At one point I helped him arrange a personal loan he wanted to purchase the McLellin or McCellin—something like that—collection."

Bell looked hard at him. This scarcely sounded like the church leader described during the bank interview as deeply involved in the McLellin transaction. He said nothing.

"I knew so little about the McLellin or McCellin thing that

I had to get up and go see Elder Oaks." Pinnock smiled cordially. "You've heard of Elder Oaks, haven't you?"

"Believe I knew of him on the [Utah] Supreme Court," Bell said.

"I asked Elder Oaks if we were interested in this McLellin or whatever. He said, well, he'd heard something about it, but we were not interested, especially not interested in buying it. If someone wished to donate it, that would be fine.

"I called a friend at the bank," Pinnock continued, "and told him he'd be seeing Steve Christensen and another individual coming over. If everything was in proper order, I said, it would be nice to give this individual a loan. Of course," he added, "those decisions are up to the bank.

"Later on, when Hofmann fell behind on the loan, I felt I should help the bank because of my position." ("Church or bank?" Bell jotted.) "I called Steve and asked if he could get Mark Hofmann to pay. He said he would handle it."

Bell put on his sternest face. "You mean to tell me the church was not involved in this transaction?"

"The church was not involved in this transaction," Pinnock said. Bell noted the answer, then drew an arrow from it to the word "lie."

"I kind of kept up on the loan after that," Pinnock went on. "I thought it might look bad for the church, due to my position, and I wanted to get it cleared up.

"One evening Steve Christensen and Mark Hofmann showed up at my house and we worked out a new deal for repayment. There was a check made out to Shannon Flynn for $20,000. I said, 'Take that check immediately and apply it to the loan.' Hofmann was selling something called the 'Oath of a Freeman' that was holding everything up. He said the Library of Congress was going to buy it for $1 million, but the price had dropped to $350,000. I told him that wasn't a figure to quibble about. It would more than pay off the loan."

Bell wrote furiously, trying to keep up with the words if not the contradictions of Pinnock not knowing Hofmann well or arranging the deal but then offering to restructure the loan completely.

"I suggested that Steve go with Mark when the deal was

finalized. I also suggested that instead of donating the collection we find a buyer."

"You did?"

"Oh, yes," Pinnock expanded. "You know, people love to donate things to the church, but sometimes we have to caution people to be aware of their own financial obligations. I suggested that he sell it to a party who was friendly to the LDS church."

"What do you mean?"

"Oh, a lot of times, people friendly to the church make donations. I helped him find a buyer in Canada who would buy the collection and donate it at a later date. I suggested that Steve authenticate the documents for the Canadian buyer. They were set to close Tuesday morning at Steve's office."

Bell felt his pulse quicken. They were back to a deal at the Judge Building the morning Christensen was killed.

Pinnock would not tell him the name of the buyer but said the attorney's name was David West, Sr. Within minutes Pinnock also mentioned the name David Sorenson, and Bell jotted it down, assuming he now knew the buyer.

"I'm not sure how I heard about the bombings," Pinnock said, "but later that day I saw Mark in the church parking lot."

"Right here in this building?" Bell was surprised. In his mind, Hofmann was a serial bomber squirming in a hospital bed. Yet he and Flynn apparently were familiar with the church's headquarters and its leaders.

"Yes. He said he'd just come from Elder Oaks's office."

Oaks's office? Bell wondered. "Did you inquire why?"

"Oh, no. We talked about Steve's death, and his wife, and how awful it is. Then we discussed what was to be done now that Steve was dead."

Setting up the deal again, Bell figured; but wait a minute — why is Hofmann bypassing Pinnock who arranged the whole deal? "So did Mark Hofmann know Oaks?"

"Well," Pinnock said, "the thing you're going to have to learn is that when people come to this building, they say, 'I want to see the First Presidency,' or 'I want to see Elder Oaks,' but they don't. They see me or someone like me. Then they

leave and tell their friends they saw President Hinckley or whoever. I don't really think he saw Elder Oaks or anybody."

"I see."

"You might want to call Al Rust," Pinnock suggested. "I
believe he had some involvement with these documents."

"I'll do that."

He rose and so did Pinnock. "I wonder if you'd like a copy
of our new hymn book," Pinnock said. As supervisor of the
project, Pinnock was especially proud of the new hymnal. "It's
just been printed."

"No thanks," Bell answered. "I think I'd better get back to
the office."

When he arrived, Bell found Flynn, who had been waiting
for an hour. But before he could see Flynn, he was summoned
to the chief's office.

"What have you gone and done?" Willoughby demanded.

"I just did what normally would be done in any homicide
case—interviewed the people involved."

"I've got a room full of LDS security officers asking me
how come you're giving them problems."

"So do you want me to walk in and apologize, chief?"

"No, you do what you need to do. We'll handle the public
relations."

"Tell the church security people that if they'll stay out of
my way, I'll stay out of theirs," Bell offered.

Don Bell was not the only detective to trip over church
security. Jim Bell had his concerns, as well. A church security
officer had met him on the sidewalk by the Judge Building
Tuesday morning after the bombing, when Bell had gone out
for equipment. "We have thick files on Steven Christensen and
Mark Hofmann if you'd like to see them," the officer had said.
Bell was not familiar with either name, since at that point the
victim had not been officially identified. He asked the agent to
take the files to the SLCPD. Later, when he knew who both
Christensen and Hofmann were, Bell asked for the files but
learned that they had never arrived. When he had checked back
with church security, the entire incident was denied.

Now Don Bell walked down to his office to see Shannon

Flynn, who apologized for missing the morning appointment. "I had to go to the church first."

"Why?"

"To find out what to tell you."

"What if they told you to tell me nothing."

"Then I wouldn't be here talking to you."

"So obviously they didn't tell you that."

"No, they said to come over and tell you the truth. I just didn't know if they wanted me to tell you all the truth."

Bell shook his head and took out his note pad. Flynn explained that he had worked full time for Hofmann for about eighteen months, since April. "He got $185,000 from the church to buy the McLellin collection. Mark told me that President Hinckley called Harvey Tanner at the bank. I drove him to the bank to pick up the check and I saw Tanner's business card attached to it."

"Why buy the McLellin collection?"

"The church wanted it off the streets. Mark and Hinckley had a legal agreement that there would be no copies. Mark had seen the collection and told the church what was in it. Mark said the collection would be very embarrassing to the church. Hinckley talked Mark into giving it free of charge."

"How do you know Mark really knows Hinckley?"

"I've been with Mark when he went to see Hinckley. I waited in the little office outside. I was at Mark's house once when Hinckley called."

Flynn described how the pressure to repay the bank loan was channeled through Steve Christensen. "In July federal bank examiners were in town and found the loan." Bell made a note to check that out. He later found that the unsecured loan had, in fact, caused an internal problem at the bank.

Bell and Flynn talked about the $20,000 check, and then Flynn mentioned that Christensen had been trying to find Hofmann the Friday before. "He said he had the $185,000 check and he couldn't find Mark. I was excited about that because Mark owes me about $30,000. We didn't find him, though, until after bank hours. He was supposed to meet Steve early Tuesday to consummate the $185,000 deal."

There it was again: the McLellin transaction at the place and time of Christensen's death.

Flynn then told Bell he was convinced that Hofmann was a victim, that he would never kill anyone. Almost on his way out the door, he added, "I know Mark dabbled in explosives in the past."

"Wait a minute," Bell said, but Flynn refused to say any more.

While detectives, deputies, and agents interviewed scores of people connected with the case, ATF bomb expert Jerry Taylor visited the Sheets residence. As he had done at the Judge Building and on Second North, he calculated the angle of the blast by the physical evidence. Then he walked a little distance into the trees and returned in a minute with the key component he knew must be hidden there. "Here's part of the mercury switch," Taylor announced.

The deputies and officers who had combed the area Tuesday stared at the small piece of glass and wire prong in Taylor's palm. That switch, when tipped, would connect the circuit to a detonator, exploding the bomb. A mercury switch from the Judge Building had been found in the sweepings saved from the scene. And although none had been found on Second North, this was not surprising considering the fact that fire and water had destroyed and dispersed much of the evidence.

When he left the Sheets home, Taylor headed for the nearest Radio Shack store since the name Radio Shack had been imprinted on the batteries in the bombs. He checked the white, plastic battery packs, the C-cell batteries, and the mercury switches in stock. Sure enough, they matched the bomb parts, so he purchased a package of each. When he took them to the clerk, he was asked for his name and address, which was then noted on the receipt.

Taylor returned to police headquarters and told the detectives, "Here are your bomb parts, here's my receipt. Go find out who bought the parts to the bombs." Immediately police began canvassing Radio Shack stores all over the valley, and eventually spread even farther, sifting through hundreds of thousands of receipts. Almost as soon as they started looking, they found a receipt made out to an M. Hansen at 2056 East 3900 South. Mr. Hansen had purchased a mercury switch and a D-cell battery pack from the Radio Shack at the Cottonwood Mall in south Salt Lake City. The battery pack was the wrong size for the bombs. However, investigation proved that the address M. Hansen gave was both false and near Mark Hofmann's home. That was encouraging, particularly when Jim Bell saw the name M. Hansen during a search of the Hofmann house the following day.

The investigation seemed to know no bounds in terms of interest from various agencies. Late Thursday afternoon law enforcers from the U.S. Attorney's Office, the Salt Lake County Attorney's Office, the Salt Lake City Police Department, the Salt Lake County Sheriff, the FBI, and the Federal Bureau of Alcohol, Tobacco, and Firearms met. Both officers and their chiefs attended. A serial bombing evidently connected in some way to the Mormon church was bizarre, political, and important. Careers and departments could be made or broken on such a case. The ATF and FBI represented federal jurisdiction for crimes involving explosives. The SLCPD and county sheriff respectively owned the turf for the homicides. As Salt Lake County Attorney Ted Cannon called it, this was a meeting of the "bigs"—cordial, serious, and strategic.

Speeches were made about cooperation and trust between agencies. It was clear, however, that every agency wanted the case. Captain Robert Jack, of the county sheriff's department, was named head of an inter-agency task force. The LDS church security's role surfaced, with the news that the ATF and FBI agents from out of town were "checking in with the church first to coordinate." Ted Cannon noted this information curiously, jotting beside it, "Ward?" U.S. attorney Brent Ward, who oversaw those agencies locally, was an active Mormon, as were Utah's two senators who influenced the futures of federal appointees. Did Ward know things they didn't? Cannon wondered. Now Ward was suggesting that D. Michael Quinn, a BYU historian familiar with the recent Mormon document discoveries, be entrusted with the task of identifying the documents found in Hofmann's car. They had been hung to dry on lines in the police shooting range.

D'Elia did not like the idea of Quinn examining the documents—Quinn sounded too close to Hofmann—but he had other beefs, as well. He was angry at the sheriff's department because they had known about Hofmann and his letterman's jacket before the third bombing, but they had failed to pass the information on to the Salt Lake police. He was miffed at the police because he was their prosecutor and had been at the Judge Building, but still when the third bomb came, they did not call him. "We've all got to work together like professionals on this one," he finished up, then looked around, a little chagrined. Geez, am I in a fight with everybody? he wondered.

Now the meeting was moving toward the nitty-gritty. The detectives and investigators reported their findings. After Don Bell summarized his interviews, he added his opinion: "The church is stonewalling us." Immediately he found himself in a vigorous argument with prosecutor Robert Stott, currently trying a death-penalty case in Third District Court, and with U.S. attorney Brent Ward. Both were familiar with the Mormon history community and let it be known that they believed the police had accused the wrong man.

When the meeting ended, arguments about the case were more numerous than answers. Clearly, charges were not about to be filed. Don Bell, Biggs, and D'Elia, along with CAO investigator Sergeant Richard Forbes, trooped downstairs to open Christensen's safe deposit boxes seized from First Interstate Bank. Another box, this one taken from the CFS building, had yielded Christensen's will.

Bell opened the boxes. The first was empty. He opened the second and pulled out a piece of papyrus encased in plexiglass. He held it up.

"Is that a piece of Joseph Smith papyrus?" Forbes ventured.

"What the hell is a piece of Joseph Smith papyrus?" D'Elia asked. He soon gathered that Smith had used Egyptian papyrus to produce The Book of Abraham, a Mormon scripture.

Back at the SLCPD, Bell went to a meeting in the chief's office. Again he reported his findings, and again his description of inconsistencies in interviews involving Mormon church leaders provoked argument. One police major was especially upset. "Why do you keep saying 'they' when you mean the church?" he demanded. " 'They, they, they.' There are five million 'theys.' Are 'they' all lying?"

To Bell, it seemed like a good time to go home.

On his own way home, Ken Farnsworth picked up some homework for the case. Born and raised a Mormon, Farnsworth had served an LDS mission in France, then set about forgetting everything related to Mormonism. He had read only a line or two of newspaper articles on the salamander letter and other document discoveries before snorting and turning the page. Given today's meetings, however, he decided to purchase a copy of the church scriptures, The Book of Mormon, the Doctrine and Covenants, and The Pearl of Great Price (which included The Book of Abraham). Steven Christensen had extensive files on papyri, so Farnsworth figured he could learn that subject indirectly from the scholar whose murder he was determined to solve.

D'Elia was on a similar errand, buying texts on Mormonism. He decided that after eleven years in Utah it was about time. Tonight he was going home with papyrus on his mind.

The exhaustion and frustration of law enforcers at that point were magnified among the families of the murder victims, who still had no idea why their loved ones had been killed. Thursday evening, both the Sheets and Christensen families held viewings at separate mortuaries. For the Sheets, the occasion was something of a reunion, since they had been hiding. They were shocked to discover that their father could not recall having ever met the police's prime suspect.

"I saw his picture in the paper," Sheets told his children, "and just thought, 'My, what a fine-looking young man.' "

So why, they wondered, *why* had their mother been murdered?

Terri Christensen greeted the many visitors from her daze. "No more Valium," she told herself that night, deciding she could handle the funeral the next day better without medication.

Jim Bell's front door looked particularly good to him Thursday night; he had not seen it since Tuesday morning. However, he had been home only a few minutes before a phone call told him, "Mark wants to confess, and you'd better move it because Yengich is on his way."

Bell got back in his car and jammed his foot on the accelerator, driving south from Bountiful to LDS Hospital in Salt Lake's northern avenues at 85 miles per hour. He hurried down the hall and found Ron Yengich, who had obviously just arrived.

"Hi, Jim. I've advised my client not to talk," Yengich said.

Bell stepped closer to the bed. "Mark, you don't have to listen to him. If you want to talk, you can. But you have to tell me what you want to do."

"I don't want to make a statement," Hofmann said.

"I haven't even had a chance to talk with my client," Yengich told Bell, who nodded, as Yengich motioned everyone out.

The room seemed full of security officers, an SLCPD officer, and a nurse. Bell followed the other officers out, and when the door closed behind him, he stood against it and debriefed his officer. He did not want anyone barging in to disturb the meeting inside. No one pushed against the door, trying to leave.

Bell was told that Hofmann had awakened and had motioned to the police officer. Hofmann had said he wanted to make a statement and asked for a tape recorder. The officer had asked hospital security for a tape recorder, and two agents had joined him at Hofmann's bedside. At that point, however, the nurse came back in and intervened. Yengich had been called, and the nurse had kept them from talking to Hofmann until he arrived.

Bell considered arresting the nurse for obstruction of justice but decided against it. He would stay cool, keep his mouth shut, and see what happened.

After five minutes, Bell opened the hospital room door. He saw Yengich turn away from the hospital bed. The nurse, who had stayed in the room, stood between the attorney and the detective. Bell assumed she had overheard the conversation and knew in an instant she could be a witness for the prosecution. Yengich was staring at her and past her at Bell. For a moment Bell thought Yengich was going to vomit.

At 7:30 a.m. Friday, the next morning, Don Bell got a call asking that he go directly to LDS Hospital and assist Jim Bell, who had returned to the hospital. "Is he going to cop?" Don Bell asked, referring to Hofmann. He wouldn't be surprised to hear a confession about now, not after watching the injured man squirm and the alarms go off when they had confronted him yesterday morning.

"Something happened last night. We don't know what's going on." Bell went up to the inner room where Hofmann was and found him alone. Not even a guard stood in the anteroom. "Do you know what's going on?" he asked a nurse.

"We're getting the patient ready for surgery." Hofmann's badly injured knee was scheduled for an operation.

"Hi, Mark," Bell said. Hofmann nodded.

Thoroughly confused, Bell went to the wall telephone and called the station. "Am I supposed to be up here?"

"Yengich is up there and so is Jim Bell. Something happened earlier."

"Okay, I'll find them."

Someone directed him toward a closed door down the hall. He opened it and realized with embarrassment that Yengich was in a conference. Yengich recovered quickly. "Hi, Don."

"Oh, sorry."

Yengich said, "These are Mark's parents, Bill and Lucille Hofmann."

Bell shook their hands. "Ron, could I talk to you a minute?" Yengich escorted him out and shut the door.

Bell got right to the point. "Is he copping?"

"We're wondering."

"Is there a meeting going on?"

"I'm not sure who's still here."

Bell and Yengich were old friends, despite being cop and defense attorney. "Tell you what, Ron, if you'll cop him we'll drop the death penalty."

Yengich grinned back. "If you don't go for the death penalty, I'll cop him."

Don Bell found Jim Bell waiting for him in the lobby. By now Jim was furious with the nurse who had intervened between Hofmann and police and with himself for not having arrested her. "Well, Jim," Don said, "I think they might be willing to cop him." Jim Bell did not think so. "We'll fight for that nurse." They went down to the county attorney's office and found D'Elia ready for battle.

Friday morning when D'Elia came into the office, he found out two things. First, that Yengich had stopped chief of justice Bud Ellett on the courthouse steps and asked whether they would be interested in reducing Hofmann's case from a capital offence, implying there might be a guilty plea in the offing.

"Too soon to talk about that," D'Elia told Ellet, "but this is sure interesting to know." D'Elia figured that something had gone wrong in Yengich's chat with Hofmann the night before — maybe a confession. Next, he discovered that a nurse had stayed in the room while Hofmann had talked with Yengich.

"Yengich just waived his attorney-client privilege," D'Elia said. "I'm going to get that nurse." If they ever talked plea-bargain, they wanted to do so from a position of strength; if they went to trial, the nurse's testimony could be vital.

By 8:30 D'Elia got a subpoena from Biggs, and by 9:00 it had been served. By 10:00 the nurse, Valerie Larson-Lohr, appeared at the county attorney's office, with an attorney, Charles Dahlquist of Kirton, McConkie and Bushnell, counsel for the LDS church and LDS Hospital.

D'Elia's eyebrows went up when he heard the firm's name. "What the . . . ?"

"I think there's an attorney/client privilege involved here," Dahlquist told D'Elia. "I'm instructing my client not to respond."

"You can't do that," D'Elia protested. "You don't have any standing in the case."

D'Elia went across the street to the Metropolitan Hall of Justice, housing Third District Court, and looked for Judge Dean Conder, who had signed the subpoena for the nurse. Now he wanted an order compelling the information. But Conder was out and no other judge would touch the order. When Conder appeared, D'Elia said, "I've got to talk to you about a hearing this afternoon."

By that time Yengich had been alerted by Dahlquist. At the 2:00 p.m. hearing, Yengich was ready. "If I asked the nurse to leave and she would not leave because of her patient's wellbeing, then she would be protected," he argued.

"For right now, Ron," D'Elia said, "I won't ask what she heard." He turned to Conder. "Just give me the nurse and let me talk with her about the conditions in the room." Conder scheduled a hearing for that afternoon. "All right, but you can only discuss conditions, not whatever she overheard."

D'Elia walked out, shaking his head. Yengich clearly wasn't happy about him going after the nurse, and D'Elia felt like a hard guy. Even a defense attorney was a colleague, and he sensed that this issue could mean a malpractice suit against Yengich because he had allowed the nurse to stay in the room. But Yengich's attitude had doubled his suspicions, and he wanted that nurse on the stand. "It's gotta be a confession," he told Farnsworth and Bell, remembering his earlier conversation with Ellett. He sensed their excitement.

Judge Conder excluded the press from the hearing. At 4:15 p.m. D'Elia began deposing Larson-Lohr, whose name Conder kept out of the record. The story emerged in pieces between D'Elia's careful, placating questions and the nurse's sometimes bristling answers.

Larson-Lohr told how she had first cared for Hofmann the night after he was injured on October 16. Following the initial surgery on his leg and other bomb injuries, at about 2:00 a.m., Hofmann had been taken to a special procedures room, secluded from the main traffic of the wing. The room was not an intensive care unit, though it had special equipment. Until that night, it had never been used. Now its isolation and the police guard in the anteroom afforded safety for a bombing target or security for a bombing suspect.

She said that when Hofmann arrived in the room, he was unconscious, still paralyzed from the anesthesia. He had a dressing around his head, with a scalp laceration on the left side. His right knee had an "external fixator device" on it to keep the bones in place. Pillows propped his right arm and shoulder, and a dressing showed blood. His right hand was badly burned and salved with a scarlet dressing.

Half an hour later, Hofmann's eyes fluttered. A little after 3:00, he could follow simple commands with his left hand. By 3:45, he was complaining that he could not breathe through the tube in his throat. Larson-Lohr and a technician removed the tube, as a uniformed officer stood nearby. Then Hofmann asked for his wife.

"I said his wife could not come in; the police would not allow it." Hofmann said he understood.

"Did he ask anything else?"

"No."

"Did he ever explain to you what happened?"

"No."

The nurse and patient conversed the rest of the night about his injuries, his pain, his need to have his right arm and hand repositioned. She detailed the injuries to his right leg—the knee-cap was gone, the tibia (bone below the knee) was fractured and would require further surgery.

At 7:45 a.m., she left the hospital and returned that night at 6:45. This time when the nursing supervisor briefed Larson-Lohr on Hofmann's condition, she mentioned that he had been questioned by police that morning. That contact had elevated his blood pressure, which had stayed high for some time. Also, Hofmann's attorney had asked that he be contacted if any other police officers questioned him.

That evening, the 17th, Larson-Lohr had injected morphine into Hofmann's intravenous feeding tube about 8:30 p.m. The analgesic relieved his pain and promoted sleepiness for about three hours, then slowly began to wear off. Around 11:30, she left the sleeping patient's room to enter information on the main computer. As she called up the program, someone told her that Hofmann's vital signs were signalling a change. She hurried back and saw security officers and uniformed police standing around his bed. She assumed that they had wakened him and that, in his groggy condition, he felt confused and threatened.

"But the question is, do you know whether the officers woke him up?" D'Elia asked.

"No."

"Do you know whether he asked for the officers?"

"No, I don't."

"Let's go back to the point of where you are entering the room again after the computer, and you see a number of individuals, specifically uniformed officers and security guards around Mr. Hofmann. What did you do?"

"I walked up to Mark and asked him if he needed something."

"What did he say, if anything?"

"He said that he would like to make a statement and wanted a tape recorder and asked that whatever was said in the room not be said elsewhere." She continued, "I didn't hear the rest of the conversation to them. I said, are you aware that you could have your lawyer present."

"Is that within the normal course of your duties?"

"Yes, it is."

"To advise somebody that they have the right to remain— excuse me, that they have the right to have the advice of counsel before making any statement?"

Larson-Lohr and D'Elia sparred for a few minutes over legal and medical aspects, then D'Elia asked, "What did you do?"

"I went out and called the nursing supervisor. Then I walked directly back to the room; and there was a lot of commotion and I was trying to get Mark calmed down."

"What was Mark doing or saying that you had to get him calmed down? Or what was it that you discerned from any of the monitoring devices that he had?"

"Both his blood pressure was elevated and his heart rate was elevated and he was shaking real bad. When I went to take his temperature, he couldn't even hold a thermometer hardly in his mouth."

The nurse said she told the security officers to move away from his bed, which they did. The SLCPD officer had already moved back.

"What did you do at that time?"

"I washed—his face was hot. He was sweaty. He was sticky.

His skin was cold and clammy to touch. So he asked me to have a wash cloth for his face and I washed his face and I was talking to him, trying to calm him down."

After she washed Hofmann's face and neck, Larson-Lohr added, she overheard the officer on the telephone. She quoted him as saying that "the nurse called the lawyer. I don't know why she did. And she won't let me near the bed."

"Who won't let him near the bed?"

"The officer said I won't let him near the bed."

"You, in fact, would or would not let him near the bed?"

"I never said anything to the officer."

"How long did you try to calm Mr. Hofmann down?"

"Probably about five or ten minutes. He started settling down, and the officer made it quite clear that he was not happy with me for having called the lawyer and that he wanted to talk to Mark before his lawyer arrived."

She described how she continued to divert her patient, talking to him of other things, and swabbing out his mouth so that he could not talk.

"Did you say anything else to the officer who was on the telephone, besides what you have related so far?"

"He informed me that I was not a lawyer; I was just a nurse, and I made a comment, 'Just a nurse?' That was about all I said to him."

When Yengich arrived, she testified, he had asked her only if she was the nurse caring for Hofmann and had then informed Hofmann that he should not put her in that position again. At first the SLCPD guard inside the room refused to leave until Bell arrived, and then the officers went outside. At that point, Larson-Lohr said, she sat down a little way from the bed.

"Could you, in fact, have left the room?" D'Elia asked.

"I didn't feel comfortable leaving the room at that time."

"You didn't feel comfortable. But the question is, could, in fact, you have left the room and monitored the vital signs in the center of the I.C.U.?"

"To monitor is one thing; to see your patient is one thing. You can't rely on the monitors."

73

"That's right. The question is, again, with respect to monitoring his vital signs for a period of time for only five minutes or so, could you have done that?"

"I could have, but I was more concerned with my patient."

"I realize the qualifications. Now, you stood there, and you watched your patient during the interview with Mr. Yengich; is that right?"

"Yes."

"You were facing him at all times?"

"I was facing him, so I could see him out of the corner of my eye during part of it."

On cross-examination, Larson-Lohr's attorney, Charles Dahlquist, was brief, re-emphasizing the nurse's concern for her patient's condition and her right to follow her best nursing judgment. He asked if she had particular reasons for her concern about the officers around her patient's bed.

"Several different officers made the comment that we can put him back together so they can execute him, and that he got what he deserved and things like that," she said. Ken Farnsworth, listening from the front row, recalled making such a comment the night before when Hofmann was unconscious. Realizing then that Larson-Lohr was offended, he had backtracked. Now she did not point him out.

"And the second reason why you felt it was necessary for you to be in the room?"

"The second reason is that my patient was agitated. His vital signs were outside the normal limits." She added that high blood pressure in someone in his condition could cause problems like a stroke. "Just to see him agitated, I was really concerned about keeping him calm."

In response, D'Elia argued that police officers were expelled from the room during Hofmann's talk with Yengich. Therefore, the nurse had no cause for alarm at that point.

After adjoining the hearing and considering both sets of arguments, Conder ruled in D'Elia's favor. "It appears to me that there is no privileged communication in this case and the witness is ordered to testify regarding any conversation she may have overheard between Mr. Hofmann and attorney Yengich on the morning of October 17, 1985." Conder then ordered that sealed copies of his decision be delivered to the attorneys; at that point he left town.

"By the way, we got the nurse," D'Elia told Yengich when he ran into him in the hallway after picking up the decision. "I know you meant to appeal, so we'll hold off until you file."

Yengich agreed. Meanwhile, D'Elia realized, he would have his hands full holding back the police and deputies. He figured he could afford to play the gentleman on this one. Once the prosecution had the nurse's testimony, he figured the bombings case could fold up fast. And not a minute too soon.

While D'Elia and Farnsworth were in court that Friday battling over the nurse's testimony, Dave Biggs and Jim Bell were back at Hofmann's home. Since the original search warrants for bomb evidence and a letterman's jacket had been served Wednesday, sixty to eighty officers working around the clock had gathered considerable information.

In the probable cause statement drafted to get this warrant, Hofmann's contacts with high Mormon officials were cited. To them he had promised a McLellin collection that had not been delivered. The collection was supposed to be in safe deposit boxes, but it had not been found there. They knew about the bank loan Pinnock had arranged, and they had heard rumors about more Mormon documents. This time they were seeking materials related to any old papers related to Mormon history. They also went a step further and asked to seize any tool or machine that might be used to alter documents.

Moving toward Hofmann's downstairs northeast bedroom, Bell viewed cautiously the hundreds of papers officers brought him. Although they seized eighteen boxes of material, he felt that they were leaving an amazing amount of material behind simply because they did not have probable cause that it related to the bombings. Standing amid the mess in the downstairs rooms, Biggs noticed a deputy's shoe on some material that looked like the packing material surrounding the papyrus he had seen at the CAO. "Would you please move your foot and seize that?" he asked.

The officers carried out boxes of documents, books, blue and green plastic card files, a photocopy of the Book of Mormon manuscript, a soldering gun and chemicals, and a box of Hofmann's LDS mission slides. On top of one box, Bell picked up a manila envelope with the name Mike Hansen printed on it in black, felt-tipped pen. The same name was jotted on the photographic proof of an antique-looking note reading, "Livingston-Kincaid." The police had no idea what that was, but they took it. They also seized a copy of document expert Charles Hamilton's *Great Forgers and Famous Fakes*, wondering if Hofmann might have found it handy.

Bell returned to the station. He looked through the documents in the firing range, then, his hunch growing, headed to the eighth floor to find Farnsworth. Bell knew nothing about Mormonism or document dealing, but he figured that might be as much an advantage as a disadvantage on this case. He thought the whole scenario around Hofmann seemed fishy. "Those documents are all forgeries, and this case revolves around documents," he told Farnsworth. "It's just too good to be true. We'll have to find out about the experts who said this stuff is good."

"Jim," Farnsworth broke in, "I just talked to the experts and all the documents *are* good."

"No, they're no good," Bell insisted. "Everybody's out looking for this stuff, and only Mark finds it."

"Well, we'll keep working on it, but so far it looks like they're good."

The media was still working overtime to inform the public about the mysterious bombings. Thursday, the story of the McLellin collection transaction involving Christensen, West, and later Schmidt surfaced, was plugged into the city edition of the *Deseret News* right at press time. News of coin dealer Al Rust's connection to the McLellin collection broke also, adding confusion and suspicion. The bombings continued to lead the news on television and radio, with teasers tantalizing readers and listeners during the day. Both Salt Lake newspapers gave the story front-page attention, risking bad information and potential legal problems to keep up or pull ahead of their electronic competition.

This new information added to the intrigue of an already

bizarre mystery. Where was the McLellin collection? Was Christensen an agent for the church? Was the church somehow involved in the murders? Or could Hofmann, along with Christensen, have been bombed by anti-Mormons or fanatical Mormons who didn't want the McLellin collection to change hands? And where did Gary or Kathy Sheets come into this? Christensen, Sheets, and Hofmann were all linked to the salamander letter. Were they all linked to the McLellin collection as well?

As police focused on Hofmann as their prime suspect, his reputation nevertheless grew with reports that he was marketing the first document printed in the American colonies, the "Oath of a Free Man," to the Library of Congress. Outside the history community, the public, which had just learned that Hofmann discovered significant Mormon documents, was now being told that he was a major national dealer as well.

On Friday "the story" shifted to the families of the murder victims, as thousands attended funerals. Directions to Christensen's funeral were unnecessary; a stream of parked cars led to the Centerville 13th Ward, where mourners overflowed the chapel, entry, and halls, gathering around the windows and doors outside. Christensen's casket had been opened for the family but was closed before friends, ward and stake members, and business associates paid their respects. After the services the mourners moved to the cemetery, where Terri Christensen had arranged to bury her husband as close as possible to B. H. Roberts, a loyal but contentious Mormon intellectual and general authority during the early twentieth century, a man her husband had greatly admired.

That afternoon, Kathy Sheets's funeral in Holladay was similarly packed with family, ward and stake friends, neighbors, and Gary's business associates. The somber services were brightened—and simultaneously dampened—as a chorus of the Primary children she had taught performed a medley of her favorite songs.

Outside both funerals, police with trained dogs inspected the cars in the parking lots for bombs, and officers filmed the mourners as they left the church and reconvened at the cemeteries.

Friday also brought considerable speculation among reporters and historians about the documents seized from Hofmann's car, for a papyrus fragment had been glimpsed in the television footage. Had Hofmann been delivering the McLellin collection? More than one historian and archivist volunteered to look through the evidence, but investigators were leery. They were quickly learning how interconnected the history community was and did not want to give access and information to prospective defense witnesses. Besides, some Mormon historians were defending Hofmann and his document discoveries in the press, lamenting the fate of possibly valuable documents seized by the police. As had been suggested at Thursday's meeting, the U.S. Attorney's Office contacted BYU historian Michael Quinn. He agreed to examine the documents in evidence but, like many of his colleagues, was concerned for his personal safety.

Friday evening, Quinn began sorting through the charred, wet documents hanging on lines. Most of the papers seemed related to an S. J. R. McMillan, a Minnesota senator in the late nineteenth century. Only one of his letters, signed by an LDS church leader of the period, had anything to do with Mormonism. And none seemed either historically or monetarily valuable except, perhaps, for a few postal marks or autographs. A scorched papyrus in plastic hung beside the papers, and the police seemed surprised that Quinn showed little interest in it. Privately, Quinn totaled the papers' value to no more than a few thousand dollars at best. This certainly did not resemble the famed and costly McLellin collection.

After a couple of hours, an officer approached Quinn. "Hey, isn't this you?"

Quinn looked at the paper in the officer's hand, a letter he had written to Hofmann several months earlier. "Yes, that's me. I'd given Mark some tips on the possible whereabouts of the McLellin collection, and in turn he'd promised me access to the contents of the collection. I just wanted photocopies. But when I heard he was selling it or had it, I thought I'd better remind him of our arrangement."

The officer left, stunned that the man going through their evidence had written to the murder suspect about the McLellin collection—which was what he was expected to find in the evidence.

Saturday morning Quinn was eased out the door of the police station. Quinn soon learned that reporters knew or suspected he had seen the evidence, and he was unimpressed with the efficiency and confidentiality of the investigation. Nevertheless, he sent his report to Ward and later talked with Farnsworth.

On the eighth floor of the SLCPD building, Hofmann's friend and employee, Shannon Flynn, a plump, amiable young man with a self-important manner was being interrogated. Farnsworth and other investigators wanted to know what Flynn knew about Hofmann and explosives.

They talked about gun shows, Flynn's knowledge of guns, and his own gun collection. They now knew that, with Hofmann, Flynn had purchased a copy of *The Anarchist's Cookbook*, a handbook for drug and weapon making, at the Cosmic Aeroplane bookstore in downtown Salt Lake on September 20. But Flynn was not saying so.

The officers edged closer. "Have you ever bought anything having to do with a bomb?"

"No," he replied.

"Has such an item ever been in your hands?"

"No."

They asked the question every way they could find to allow Flynn to say, "Oh, yes, I bought this book." He did not. Finally, Farnsworth pulled a copy of the book out of an envelope and watched Flynn almost fly out of his chair.

"Who the fuck do you think you're dealing with here?" Farnsworth yelled. "Don't you know you've got sixty years of accumulated police experience in this room with you? And look at you lying. Your eyes are twitching, you're jumping around in your chair."

Flynn composed himself as best he could. He told them he had bought two blasting caps for Hofmann in Richfield, a small central Utah town.

"What were those for?" Farnsworth asked.

"I don't know. He didn't say."

"Did you ever ask?"

"No. It was just a casual, passing thing."

"Weren't you curious why he wanted blasting caps?"

"No, not particularly."

"Well, why Richfield?"

Flynn explained that they went down to see the person he had bought his condominium from—and for which Hofmann had paid the $7,000 downpayment, he added. He described an Uzi machine gun he and Hofmann had purchased. Flynn portrayed the machine gun as a toy. He said he had taken his troop of Explorer boy scouts on an outing to shoot the Uzi. Clearly the gun had been altered to make it fully automatic. An ATF agent motioned Farnsworth into the hall.

"Listen, he's just incriminated himself on that machine gun. I've got to give him a Miranda right now, or the rest of the interview's not going to be any good."

They went back and the agent read Flynn his rights. They continued asking about blasting caps and other materials. Flynn gave them permission to search his home. However, in a major case, both Farnsworth and Bell favored getting a warrant to prevent legal mix-ups later on. This time it would have to be a federal warrant.

They handcuffed Flynn who now seemed fearful for the first time. Again they asked him if he had helped Hofmann make the pipe bombs or deliver them.

Again Flynn held his ground. No, he had not.

Early the next morning the media filmed Flynn's arraignment in federal court for illegal possession of a machine gun and followed investigators to his house and storage shed. "We found an Uzi machine gun, other illegal—other suspected illegal firearms," an ATF agent told reporters, "and evidence related to the current bombing investigation." They removed from Flynn's home smokeless gunpowder of the same type used in the bombs, his copy of *The Anarchist's Cookbook*, and an unopened kit for making false moustaches. In Flynn's shed, the suspected bomb-making site, they found nothing relevant to the bombings.

Saturday, Gerry D'Elia took the day off. It was his birthday and his parents were visiting from New York. He refused to go to Richfield to check out blasting caps. "Send a cop," he told Ellett, "or let David go."

Later that afternoon, sipping a drink in front of his television, D'Elia heard the investigators' statements regarding Flynn and the bombings-related charges they expected. D'Elia laughed. "Well, maybe the feds will file charges," he told his parents, "but nobody's cleared nothin' with me."

By Sunday, nobody in law enforcement was laughing. Flynn was free on bond. He and his attorney, Jim Barber, responded to reporters' questions with Flynn looking more like a helpful, confused citizen than a serial bomber. "I've been a little pawn in a very big game," Flynn told reporters. "It's been a great tragedy to me and my family as far as what supposed connection there has been, which, I believe, has been conclusively proven there IS no connection. It has effectively destroyed my livelihood now."

Flynn's connection with Hofmann, his experience with munitions, and even the false moustache kit intrigued the investigators but proved nothing. The news media, which had again followed law enforcement out on a shaky limb, began to lace their reports with doubts about the investigation. Police felt a backlash when people they questioned indicated that the police were making unjustified and premature accusations.

D'Elia foresaw these and other complications as he listened to the news with frustration. "Will you guys please keep quiet?" he pleaded with the investigators on the television screen. "Because everything's going to come back to nip us on the ass."

In the increasingly frustrated, confusing atmosphere developing between overworked investigators in competing agencies and tired reporters scrambling for scoops, the murder mystery twisted, thickened, and turned ugly. Like the police and the press, the public was stymied. Hundreds of unreported rumors filtered through newspaper offices, investigators' meetings, and public and private conversations. Word spread that CFS had been threatened by Iranian investors; that LDS church security agents had guarded and threatened Hofmann in the hospital; that a fourth bomb had been meant for Hugh Pinnock but that the story was being hushed up; that Gary Sheets had over-insured both Christensen and his wife shortly before the bombings; that Hofmann still had the McLellin collection and would soon make it public; that documents had been forged by a ring of alienated homosexual Mormons intent on discrediting the church. For months these and other rumors were checked by reporters and investigators and found groundless. But periodically a rumor would surface at a party or on a radio talk show and flourish for a while before expiring.

Behind the scenes, the investigation continued around the clock. The task force had disintegrated and agency heads were wrestling for control and prestige, often by using a very willing press. In the process, two men—Hofmann and Flynn—had been accused directly in the media, but no homicide charges had been filed. If Hofmann had neared a confession, he had changed his mind, and it would take a court ruling to find out what he had said.

"LDS Official Secured Hofmann Loan," trumpeted the *Salt Lake Tribune* on Monday morning, October 21. The headline did not surprise investigators, but it intensified public interest and beckoned to a watching national press. In the wake of this public disclosure, the dust rose faster than from the bombs themselves. Somehow the Mormon church *was* involved in the bombings. Reporters from across the United States descended on Salt Lake City, only to pick up telephones to call local reporters. They needed a fix on the players and questions before coming up with answers. For instance: What's this about a salamander?

4

MATTERS OF CONTROL

News that a practicing Mormon — a bishop, for instance — is involved in a major crime usually hits Utahns hard. Salt Lake's triple bombing entered a new realm of the sensational with reports that a general authority had been financially involved with an accused bomber, one murder victim, and a collection of controversial Mormon documents. Additional stories that both Mark Hofmann and Shannon Flynn had met with general authorities shortly after the bombings further complicated the scenario.

In an attempt to combat rumors of church involvement, Hugh Pinnock issued a statement through the LDS public communications department. "On the last Friday in June of this year," he began, "a friend of mine, Steven F. Christensen, called, mentioning he had something important to talk to me about. He came to my office. With him was Mark W. Hofmann. I had neither met nor talked with Mr. Hofmann before that afternoon."

Pinnock described their conversation about the McLellin collection, which Hofmann proposed to buy. After learning that Hofmann expected to receive "a substantial payment from the Library of Congress on the sale of a paper he had found, titled, 'The Oath of a Free Man,' which was reportedly the first printed document in America, I called two banks." The first was Zion's First National Bank — once owned by the church. Finding the person he wished to contact was out, Pinnock had next called First Interstate — where he served as a director — which gave

Hofmann a signature loan. "The next I heard about the 30-day loan was when it was past due. . . . I called Steven Christensen and he began working with Mr. Hofmann in order to get the bank loan paid. I have never seen the McLellin Collection. Until last week I assumed there was a collection and that it was valuable."

The church also announced that it was sending the 1830 salamander letter to the FBI for analysis. While President Gordon B. Hinckley had, upon releasing the letter in May, cautioned members that its authenticity could not be guaranteed, the church, led by its historians, had since backed the document. The letter's defenders fully expected the FBI report to coincide with the authentication performed earlier.

While the media explored the possibilities raised by these developments, the investigation continued. Jim Bell, coordinating reports and assignments, had learned from the sheriff's department that a thirteen-year-old boy living next to the Sheets family had seen a van late the night before the bombings. Hofmann owned a two-tone Toyota van. If his van had been used to deliver one or more bombs, or if the bombs had been constructed in the van, evidence might still be found there. Investigators decided to find and seize the van.

Early Tuesday morning, October 22, before dawn, Ken Farnsworth drove to John Stone Drive in Sandy, Utah, where Hofmann's parents lived. Mark and Doralee's light copper-colored van was parked in the driveway.

"Hot damn!" Farnsworth whispered, "we found the van and won't have to hunt it down." He called Bell and an ATF agent. "Bring the warrant and meet me in Sandy." Farnsworth parked his car a little distance from the still-dark home. Now he need only wait.

The police had gathered by the time Doralee Hofmann, nicely dressed, and her oldest child left her in-laws' home about 8:00 a.m. The officers approached her with their warrant.

Farnsworth said good morning. "We've got a search warrant, Mrs. Hofmann. We're going to have to take the van."

She stared at him, nonplussed. "Well, I've got to go see

Mark in the hospital and I have to take my son to Cardon School."

"Transportation won't be a problem," Farnsworth said, offering to drive them himself. "We know this is inconvenient, and we'll do what we can to help you. But we've got to take the van."

By that time, Bill Hofmann had joined them. "Let's step inside the house," he suggested. Farnsworth explained to him that they were going to do a material search of the van. He could see that both Mark's father and wife were frustrated and bewildered.

"Wait just a minute," Dori Hofmann said. "I've got to take something from the van."

"No, you can't take anything out."

"But this didn't come with the van. I just put it in there myself."

She opened the van door and an envelope fell out. Farnsworth picked it up.

"What's in here?"

He drew out an old piece of paper and a small store receipt. It had begun to drizzle, and Farnsworth had heard plenty about protecting old documents. He was concerned about the old-looking paper but soon realized that Dori Hofmann was more interested in the receipt, printed at the top with the name Argosy Bookstore.

"Where did you get this?"

"It was in my house."

"If it was in the house we would have wanted to seize it during one of those searches."

"Well, it was just lying there."

"It was in the van this morning, and so we've got to take it."

"Okay, but don't lose it. That's an extremely important piece of paper."

"I promise you we won't lose it," Farnsworth said. He looked again. The items listed included the "Oath of a Freeman" for $25.

Farnsworth dropped off a pensive Michael Hofmann at the private Cardon School on 2700 South, then headed toward town with Doralee. At about 900 South, he decided to try to approach Dori about her husband's involvement with the bombings.

"I know if you've been reading the newspaper and watching TV you've got to be baffled by all this," he began. "I'm a primary investigator in the case, and I just want you to know that Mark is the bomber. This is a very serious situation for you, and you ought to know this could be a death penalty case."

The suspect's wife recoiled in the seat, closing off her ears with her forearms. "Don't say that. I don't want to hear any more."

Farnsworth stopped. Almost immediately he regretted his words. He stopped at the hospital entrance and watched her make her way inside. The next time he saw Dori Hofmann, when he served another search warrant, he apologized, but she shook it off. "No problem. Just a bad day."

As headlines multiplied in the national press and the local media kept teams of reporters and editors working full time on the bombings story, the Mormon church called a press conference. That, in itself, was history-making. Except to announce plans for new temples, church leaders and reporters seldom sit down in the same room.

Early on Wednesday, October 23, reporters filed into the first floor auditorium of the Church Office Building. Television cameras lined up and directed their glassy gaze at the stage. Three church officials, President Gordon B. Hinckley, Elder Dallin Oaks, and Elder Hugh Pinnock, took their places behind a table.

Hinckley's presence was particularly significant. With a long record of church service, he had become a general authority in 1958, an apostle three years later, and had served almost continuously as a member of the First Presidency since 1981. He had encouraged church leaders to use modern technology, particularly the public media, in the church's interests, and had been highly visible in dedicating eighteen new Mormon temples worldwide since 1980.

Public communications director Richard Lindsay opened the press conference by welcoming those present and explaining that Hinckley and Oaks would each read a statement. Following that, they would answer questions.

"May I say at the outset," Hinckley began, "that our deepest sympathies are with the families and associates of those who have been victims of the bombings in our community. That such tragedies could occur here is beyond our comprehension." He then discussed the church's mandate to preserve its history and his own role as advisor to the church's historical department.

"I first met Mark W. Hofmann in April of 1980 when he was brought to my office by officers of our Historical Department. I was advised that he was then a student at Utah State University in Logan, Utah, and that in the pursuit of a hobby in collecting early Mormon documents he had secured an old Bible with the signature of Samuel Smith (brother of the prophet) in it." Hinckley reminded the press that within the Bible's pages, Hofmann had found the Anthon transcript — a paper, gold and brittle with age, with characters apparently copied by Joseph Smith from the gold plates. "The discovery and acquisition were released to the press and widely publicized," Hinckley continued. "There was nothing secretive about it."

He cited other purchases from Hofmann, moving into early 1985 and the salamander letter. "I received in behalf of the church from Mr. Steven Christensen, the Martin Harris/W. W. Phelps letter, which he presented to the church as a donation. This document, which the press has been wont to call the salamander letter, we made public and it has been written and spoken of extensively. . . . While I had received a letter earlier indicating Mr. Christensen's desire to donate the document to the church after research on it had been completed, I have no recollection, nor any record of his ever having been in my office until the day he presented it to the church."

As he discussed the church's acquisition of the salamander letter, Hinckley introduced and dismissed Steven Christensen, adding only, "Nor has he been in my office since then." After mentioning the hundreds, even thousands, of visitors he receives yearly, Hinckley moved to the McLellin transaction.

"Mr. Hofmann came to see me this past June and indicated that he had access to what he called the McLellin collection. I had never heard of the McLellin collection and asked what it contained. He indicated that it contained various letters, some affidavits and related items. He said he wanted to donate the collection to the church. There was no discussion of our purchasing it.

"Mr. Alvin Rust had delivered to my office, a letter, the day before Mr. Hofmann came, in which he indicated that he had put up money to make it possible for Mr. Hofmann to buy the collection. When Mr. Hofmann mentioned the collection to me, I told him that I had received a letter from Alvin Rust and wanted to know whether he had paid Mr. Rust for the money extended him. He indicated that he would do so and I told him that when he had settled his account with Mr. Rust, then we could discuss the matter of his making a contribution of the so-called McLellin collection to the church."

Noting that he did not know Rust or Shannon Flynn, Hinckley continued. "Not long after that I left for Europe to take care of church business. More recently, Mr. Hofmann called and asked my secretary if he could see me. This time the topic was the so-called Kinderhook Plates [which had been forged in the nineteenth century in an attempt to discredit Joseph Smith]. I saw no reason why we should have them and said so. That is the last time I saw Mark W. Hofmann."

As Lindsay had said before him, Hinckley mentioned that they would soon have to leave to dedicate the new genealogical library, then passed the microphone to Oaks. Pinnock, whose statement had already been released, sat silent, looking unhappy and uncomfortable.

One reporter nudged another, "Did you hear about Pinnock's new church assignment? Mission president in Antarctica."

Oaks began by explaining his position as Pinnock's ecclesiastical superior and the fact that their offices are adjacent. He then related how Hofmann had come to see Pinnock the afternoon of the bombings. Since Pinnock was out, Oaks had met with him. Oaks added that after hearing the next day that Hofmann had been injured by a bomb, he had met with law enforcement officials "and told them all of the above and everything else I had been told or knew about Hofmann, Steven Christensen, and the McLellin Collection." Oaks described his meeting with Shannon Flynn in some detail, adding that he had turned over a transcript to police and to Flynn's attorney.

"To the best of my recollection," Oaks finished, "I have met Steven Christensen only once. He was standing in Elder Pinnock's office sometime last summer when I stepped in to deliver a message to Elder Pinnock. I shook hands with Christensen on that occasion. We had no other conversation other than an informal greeting."

The reporters' questions that followed ranged from the subject of the church's procedures in buying and preserving documents to subjects more closely related to the McLellin transaction. In answer to one question, Hinckley explained that he had not responded personally to Rust's letter because Hofmann had assured him that the matter was resolved.

Another reporter asked if Christensen had told any of the three church officials that something had gone awry in the McLellin transaction — that there was anything wrong with the deal or the documents.

Hinckley answered first. "I had never heard anything, no."

"Nor had I," Pinnock said. "That was . . . " He paused and tried again. "Mr. Christensen and I talked several times about that and there was no suspicion ever communicated that there was not a McLellin collection."

"Nor had I," Oaks added. "I had no communications with Steve Christensen and I had never heard that."

"Next question please," Lindsay said.

After some discussion of why the officials had believed the McLellin collection to be valuable, Pinnock was questioned as to the appropriateness of his conduct in arranging the bank loan.

"When they came in that Friday afternoon," he explained, "and when at that time I called two banks, I had not thought it improper. I was calling on what I thought was a legitimate transaction. I will say that there come into our offices many people asking questions, but we would certainly not use our office for a favor for someone that was inappropriate."

"Would you do it again?"

"No."

As the reporters continued to ask questions, Oaks took charge, requiring that they rephrase their questions more to his liking. Little new information was gained before Lindsay announced that the brethren had sixteen minutes to walk across the plaza to the genealogical library for the dedication. The press conference was over.

The reporters left with mixed feelings. The unprecedented opportunity to question Mormon leaders gave them another lead story, yet, somehow, the church leaders had made the press's questions—from document acquisition to unsecured bank loans—sound outrageous and their own actions justified if inscrutable. Not much light had been shed on a bewildering double murder. Nevertheless, the conference was carried live on local stations, and the *Deseret News* ran two extra pages in its city edition to print an unofficial transcript. The *Tribune* printed a complete transcript of the news conference a few days later.

County Attorney Ted Cannon and others in his office were amused by the press's polite deference to church leaders. Elected officials should have it so good, they mused. Cannon particularly liked the way "Judge Oaks" refused to entertain reporters' questions until they restated them to his liking.

Most disturbed by the press conference were some of Steven Christensen's close friends and family members. Hinckley's and Oaks's statements indicated that both had far more contact with Hofmann—an accused murderer—than with Christensen, his alleged victim. Those near to Christensen that autumn knew that he had rearranged his last months and weeks around the McLellin deal when calls and meetings with church leaders had been frequent. Good Mormons all, Christensen's mourners tried to believe that the church leaders' statements held literally to the truth. Perhaps Christensen had only been in Hinckley's *office* once. Perhaps he had only met Oaks once, last summer when Oaks brought Pinnock a message. (He had not said what message or from whom.) Yet the overall impression, they felt, misled the public about Christensen's activity and intent in the months before he died. If there was some reason for this disassociation, why didn't an explanation — even a private one — come with it?

Police Chief Bud Willoughby sent a letter to his staff the same morning. First, he commended the SLCPD for a job well done on the bombings case, then requested that everyone avoid talking to reporters. "I am confident that we will bring this particular case to a successful conclusion in the very near future," he added.

Willoughby had felt since Friday that they were ready to arrest and charge Hofmann, but the CAO wasn't satisfied with the motive. Willoughby and Sheriff Pete Hayward had ceased their public statements but knew that the longer the case went without charges being filed, the more extreme and unjustified the early accusations against Hofmann would appear.

Throughout, Willoughby had been busy handling jurisdictional problems and shielding his overworked officers. When Senator Orrin Hatch had called him soon after the bombings, offering the FBI's assistance, Willoughby had said, "Hold on. We can handle this." The FBI had been involved by Tuesday, anyway, and once church officials spoke with FBI agents they were reluctant to repeat the process with city police. Plus Willoughby's officers and LDS church security agents had tripped over each other a few times.

By the second week of the bombings, the inter-agency task force was a joke, Hayward was disgusted that charges hadn't been filed yet and would soon reassign his detectives to other, more promising cases, but ATF, FBI, SLCPD, and CAO investigators were still hard at it.

On Wednesday, October 23, Farnsworth and Bell were dispatched to LDS Hospital to get photographs of the suspect's injuries. They were led to the trauma room where Hofmann was still guarded constantly by police. After small delays, which seemed designed to stall them until one of Hofmann's attorneys could get there, they were allowed inside the room. Brad Rich soon arrived.

The detectives found Hofmann alert despite his serious

injuries. His right hand was still so badly burned that it was impossible to roll the fingers in ink, so the photographer took close-ups of his finger pads. Farnsworth looked at the singed hand with part of one finger missing. "Maybe there is a God," he told himself. "He got the hand that wired those bombs."

They photographed the mean-looking traction that entered Hofmann's right knee, otherwise covered with mesh bandage. The detectives knew he had a skull fracture on the left side of his head, lacerations, and burns and shrapnel wounds, including one large piece lodged under a shoulder blade. Rich and the police helped Hofmann shift position so the photographs could be taken, chatting meanwhile. As Hofmann moved, Farnsworth noticed that his genitals were a dark purple color. If he'd been half-kneeling on the car seat when the bomb exploded—as witnesses had indicated—that would make sense, he thought. The force of the blast would have partially passed under him, causing a painful burn.

"Mark, were your testicles injured?" he asked.

"Yes, they used to be black," Hofmann said in his soft, clipped voice. Farnsworth took that as a non sequitur and did not ask any more questions.

When the photographs were finished, the detectives left. "Let's get the hell out," Farnsworth muttered to Bell as soon as they cleared the door. "I'm beginning to see why people think that Mark couldn't possibly have murdered. I'm beginning to think it myself, and I know he did!"

Super cops, investigators for the Salt Lake County Attorney's Office have been called with both respect and derision. (CAO investigators work in conjunction with police, helping CAO prosecutors fill in the missing pieces.) Dick Forbes had been on the Hofmann case since October 17, the day after Hofmann was injured. On Tuesday, the 22nd, he got a call from Jim Barber, Shannon Flynn's attorney. "Shannon wants to talk," Barber said affably. "Why don't you come on over."

On the way, Forbes thought through what they knew about Flynn. He had bought blasting caps for Hofmann and with Hofmann had purchased a copy of *The Anarchist's Cookbook* and an Uzi machine gun, which they had made fully automatic. Forbes started the interview by asking about munitions.

Flynn described how he and Hofmann had discussed making fertilizer bombs, using bottled fertilizer and blasting caps. But he seemed to know nothing specific about the pipe bombs that had killed two people and injured Hofmann.

Most interesting was Flynn's description of the Monday night before the bombings. He and Hofmann had gone to see a history buff that evening, he said, and had talked with him until 11:00 or 11:30. Afterward, Hofmann had dropped Flynn at his condominium. "He said he was going to go get a Coke because he was going to be up for a long time." At that point, however, Flynn had left Hofmann and had no further information.

They next talked about Hofmann's debts. Flynn said Hofmann owed him money, as well as to Lyn Jacobs, and Brent Metcalfe, all of whom had worked for or with Hofmann. He also owed money to Curt Bench and Wade Lillywhite at Deseret Book, to Al Rust, and to several collectors. He said that a financial consultant named Tom Wilding was owed about $300,000, which Wilding had raised from investors. Flynn then went into detail about a series of deals and investments. Forbes took careful notes, hoping that at some point all this would make sense.

Stories were beginning to appear in the media about investors in a variety of Mormon and Americana documents. "The Haunted Man," a manuscript by Charles Dickens, apparently involved several investors who were unaware of one another. The stories suggested that Hofmann was double-dealing.

When the federal agencies learned of Forbes's interview with Flynn, they suggested jailing Forbes for interfering with their own investigation, and certain officers in the SLCPD said they would loan the feds their handcuffs. They too had been planning their next move regarding Flynn and the homicide investigation. Once again, County Attorney Ted Cannon got busy putting out interagency brush fires. A whole procession of officers, representing various agencies, filled Flynn's living room soon after that.

On Friday, October 25, Hugh Pinnock repaid the $185,000
First Interstate bank loan he'd helped to arrange for Hofmann
from his own funds, saying he felt a moral obligation to do so.
Resolving the debt did not necessarily resolve curiosity surrounding the debt, however. The notion of a church leader repaying a
bank loan owed by a murder suspect seemed odd to some, sinister to others.

As days passed with still no charges filed, news reporters
kept a spotlight on Hofmann and his documents. On Sunday,
October 27, KUTV's political editorialist, Rod Decker, hosted
a discussion of the salamander letter by former Church Historian
Leonard Arrington and Utah State University special collections director A. J. (Jeff) Simmonds.

Arrington, like most historians, did not believe that the
bombings had cast any doubt on the documents Hofmann had
discovered. Several LDS historians at BYU had invested time
and scholarship in Hofmann's finds, now being woven into the
unfinished tapestry of Mormon history.

Arrington's friendly opponent, however, was not Mormon
and had voiced doubts about the salamander letter's authenticity even before the bombings. Simmonds, once Arrington's
student, considered himself a friend and previous mentor of
Mark Hofmann. During the late 1970s, Hofmann had attended
Utah State University (USU) in Logan, ninety miles north of
Salt Lake City. To Simmonds, Hofmann had shown his first
major discovery, the Anthon Transcript, even before it was taken
to Arrington and church leaders in Salt Lake City.

Simmonds, like most in the history community, had a "box
story" from the aftermath of the bombings. The day after
Hofmann had been injured, Simmonds had returned to his office
to find a box on his desk. When he opened it, a buzzer sent
him flying across the room. Recovering, he found that the package also contained a bottle of gin—a gift gleefully mentioned
in the student newspaper the next day.

A certain amount of paranoia was probably excusable, however, and Simmonds was afraid to drive his car, with its USU
faculty sticker, to the KUTV studios in Salt Lake City. He borrowed a car and asked a cousin, a former deputy sheriff, to
accompany him. His cousin rode with a loaded revolver drawn

and pointed at the car ceiling. When they arrived at the local NBC affiliate, people inside the lobby separated, staring at Simmonds and his armed bodyguard.

Under the heat of television lights, Decker questioned Arrington and Simmonds. Arrington listed all the reasons the letter was deemed authentic—paper and ink tests, handwriting comparison, and other checking. The salamander letter fit, Arrington explained, within a historical context that included other references to folk magic. However, Simmonds maintained that the letter was too pat—a forgery, probably done in the nineteenth century by an anti-Mormon.

Decker found it ironic that a prominent Mormon historian would defend a letter that seemed to attack the origins of the LDS church and that a non-Mormon historian suspected it. However, Arrington insisted that he saw no threat to church tradition. The salamander letter represented its author's—Martin Harris—account of the discovery of the gold plates, not Joseph Smith's. Yet Simmonds, who had no stake at all in Joseph Smith's mission, thought the letter sounded too close to anti-Mormon propaganda to ring true.

The salamander letter, it seemed, was also something of a chameleon that could change color across the historical spectrum in surprising ways.

As October waned, Gerry D'Elia's study of Mormon papyrus only turned his focus back toward the homicides. In terms of physical evidence, the CAO had several fragments, including the piece of scorched papyrus pulled from the sports car's trunk and the papyrus fragment framed in plexiglass that Christensen had locked in his safe deposit box. Farnsworth had told D'Elia that both were fragments torn from two large papyri east coast document dealer Kenneth Rendell had consigned to Hofmann in September.

Rendell, who had authenticated the salamander letter, was unhappy with the case unfolding in Utah. Reporters' and Farnsworth's questions about the broken-up papyrus were frustrating. Rendell had called the CAO and threatened that if they charged Hofmann he would guarantee a defense fund and place himself at the head of a delegation of expert defense witnesses when the case came to court. Despite those threats, the papyri fragments remained important and elusive clues.

Delving into the history behind the evidence, D'Elia had learned that Joseph Smith in the 1830s had purchased a mummy and some papyri rolls, later "translating" The Book of Abraham from one of them. An illustration from the papyrus, called Facsimile 2, appears in Mormon scripture, but some scholars recently demonstrated that the illustration bears little or no relationship to Smith's text.

Christensen had written in his personal journal and elsewhere that Facsimile 2 was in the McLellin collection. But, as D'Elia told investigators, "This isn't Facsimile 2. Facsimile 2 is round. I can draw it for you. Steve would have known that this is not Facsimile 2." Yet the indisputable fact was that Christensen—midway through the McLellin deal—had locked it up.

D'Elia soon learned that Christensen, for whom he was gaining real respect, had also noted in his journal that the real Facsimile 2 might not match the illustration in Mormon scripture, making it particularly controversial in terms of Joseph Smith and his claims to prophecy. Perhaps Steve hadn't been entirely surprised by a fragment so dissimilar to scripture—and perhaps he had felt it necessary to keep the historical discrepancy quiet, D'Elia decided.

D'Elia could understand such a position, but his own query into theology and history led him to dismiss Mormonism as a religion. By now he thought he understood enough to pass judgment. Son of a bitch, he said to himself, Joseph Smith put it over on everybody with this papyrus and now Hofmann's doing it again.

"Hey, Stott!" D'Elia, scripture in hand, heralded the prosecutor at the office, knowing that Bob Stott was an active Mormon and well versed in LDS history. "You know what's really dumb? On this papyrus, there originally would have been a penis and this guy would have been stroking it, causing an ejaculation and bringing this guy back to life."

Stott was not amused. He explained that Joseph Smith had used his papyrus as a catalyst for revelation and had not meant to render a literal translation of Egyptian death ritual.

"Yeah, that's cool. I understand," D'Elia said. He walked away smiling.

D'Elia did not know that Stott and the Hofmann case were moving toward a merger. Stott's current case, which was being tried in the Third District Court, would soon end in a death-penalty conviction, and Stott had been in on some of the early strategy meetings on the bombings. Unlike Biggs and D'Elia, Stott knew of Hofmann and his document discoveries long before the double murders. Stott had roomed during law school with a future Mormon historian, had attended Mormon History Association meetings on occasion, and had read about Hofmann's discoveries in Mormon magazines and journals. He had difficulty picturing Hofmann as a serial bomber and considered the police case circumstantial. Stott didn't like a circumstantial case without an obvious, provable motive.

Ted Cannon viewed Stott as one of his most experienced and cautious prosecutors. Utahns were accustomed to seeing Stott's impassive face — except his flexing jaw muscle — wavy light hair, and guarded blue eyes on the evening news. Cannon wanted the Hofmann case tried and knew Stott tended to plea bargain any charge that promised less than a sure victory. Nevertheless, at this point, Cannon felt he needed Stott's cool head and high public profile.

Cannon also wanted Mike George, the investigator working with Stott on his current murder case. George was, Cannon believed, the best investigator in Utah. George had cracked the stalemated Bradshaw murder, sending New York heiress Frances Schreuder to prison on the testimony of her son, Mark, who had shot his grandfather on his mother's instructions. George had befriended the young man until he learned the truth about the murders. During court recesses, Cannon lobbied Stott and George to free themselves for the bombings case. However, Cannon did not say anything about Stott to D'Elia and Biggs — he did not want to hamper their hardworking enthusiasm. Still, he was not about to trust a screamer like this case to their inexperience, and he knew only too well his own tendency to "charge up the hill."

Near the end of October, Stott agreed to enter the case but on one condition. He wanted total control regarding major decisions. If it was to be his case, it would be his case entirely, and neither Cannon nor anyone else could tell him whether to take a guilty plea or go to trial. Cannon agreed, figuring that as county attorney he could keep the case on track.

On October 28, Stott joined the daily bombing meeting in the "war room." When the attorneys and investigators returned to their offices, D'Elia confronted Stott. "What are you doing up there, Stott?"

Stott looked apologetic. "Hey, Ted came to me and told me he wants me to get a feel for this case. Maybe advise you. Not do anything, just maybe advise."

Biggs and D'Elia looked at each other and headed for Biggs's car. There wasn't much they could say about this development — any case could be juggled or reassigned, and Stott was a senior prosecutor. All they could think about was how hard they had worked. "You think maybe we're not really trusted?" D'Elia muttered.

Meanwhile, Cannon was considering cooperating with U.S. Attorney Brent Ward in having the nurse in Hofmann's hospital room deposed by a federal grand jury in order to gain her testimony. That would mean dividing the case between federal and state courts in order to share the information. A case had been tried in both courts (by Stott for the state) during the 1970s after a racist drifter had gunned down two black joggers in Salt Lake City. Cannon had not been happy about that situation, but with the bombings case, he had to consider all options. They needed to know what the nurse had heard. Maybe the police were confident about Hofmann's guilt, but no one else was.

About two weeks after the incident with the nurse, Cannon visited the offices of Kirton, McConkie, and Bushnell. On one side of the firm, Cannon knew, LDS church business was transacted. Wilford Kirton, senior partner, was out of town, so Cannon went to see Oscar McConkie, whom he knew through neighborhood and church connections. "What's with Charlie Dahlquist?" he asked in his best old-boy manner, explaining why they needed to question the nurse and that Dahlquist had advised her not to talk.

McConkie soothed Cannon's feelings without promising anything except to talk with Dahlquist. When he did, Dahlquist was furious that Cannon would go over his head to McConkie. Nevertheless, Cannon perservered.

Every day saw another "skull session" to discuss the investigation, which by now had been parcelled out systematically. Two CAO investigators were looking carefully into CFS, while Biggs and Forbes were picking up the suspected frauds that Farnsworth had found. Mike George was cataloging police reports and trying to put together a computer program for the case. D'Elia was working with the police, developing the murder case and sharing their frustration that no charges were imminent.

By the time Hofmann was released from LDS Hospital on Halloween, October 31, the CAO was still disinclined to charge him with the double homicide they believed he had committed. The police had sufficient "probable cause" evidence to arrest and jail him, but prosecutors saw too many problems to risk charging Hofmann prematurely, then losing him at the preliminary hearing.

Hofmann's homecoming prompted a flurry of media stories. Kenneth Rendell appeared on television news, confirming that the papyrus he had sold to Hofmann had nothing to do with Mormon documents.

One of Hofmann's neighbors, beside her front door, told reporters, "I feel like Mark has been crucified, that he's a victim. That's all. I can't say enough good for the family and for Mark."

Eastern document expert Charles Hamilton confirmed that he had authenticated one of the Hofmann documents—the Joseph Smith to Josiah Stowell money-digging letter which Hofmann had sold to the Mormon church—but refused to say if he had changed his mind.

"All of the facts that I know about," defense attorney Brad Rich told the media, "are certainly consistent with him not being guilty, as well—either being set up or being a potential victim." Some people began to wonder whether Hofmann might sue the police, the media, or both.

To keep Hofmann in town, U.S. Attorney Brent Ward filed a machine gun charge similar to the one leveled against Shannon Flynn against him as soon as he was released from the hospital. D'Elia and Biggs were grateful to Ward for that, although Ward told the press that this charge had nothing to do with the bombings.

Hofmann's attorneys pounced on that admission early. "The fact that they have not filed today anything related to the bombings, means they have a weak case on that," defense attorney Rich gloated in the press.

"It's one major investigation," Ron Yengich added sarcastically. "They don't have sufficient cause to charge my client with what they keep saying that he is, i.e., the prime suspect in the bombings, so they've got to show the public that they're doing something."

Farnsworth accompanied Hofmann from the hospital on the 31st, noting how the suspect's eyes darted continually, taking in everyone's reaction, watching, measuring, though Hofmann said little. The Hofmann family asked for police protection, and an officer stayed in the home the first day before Yengich persuaded the family that police were not necessary.

The afternoon after Hofmann came home, Brent and Jill Metcalfe visited. Both were appalled by the extent of Hofmann's injuries. Staring at his friend, Metcalfe painfully remembered the doubts he had expressed to friends, reporters, and even police. At that moment he was convinced Mark had not done anything so terrible as to kill Steve Christensen and Kathy Sheets. Jill Metcalfe simply sat down on the bed and wept.

November 1 saw Mark Hofmann's first public appearance since the October bombings as he arrived at federal court for arraignment on the machine gun charges. The press arrived early at federal court, located above the U.S. Post Office on Main Street and 400 South, about a block from the Judge Building. Nervously, they waited outside the courtroom for a look at Mark Hofmann, whose status as a bomb victim had kept them working nonstop for two weeks.

"Did you go to the vigil at Hofmann's house last night?" one reporter asked another, referring to the gang of media that had staked out the house in hopes of glimpsing the suspect or getting a statement.

"No. Did you?"

"Yeah, but nothing happened."

"What did you do, trick or treat?"

"Yeah. The Hofmanns were passing out brown-wrapped packages."

Eventually, security guards multiplied and defense attorneys Yengich and Rich appeared. An officer told the press to stand back.

A door opened and Hofmann, pale in a dark blue sweater, appeared in a wheelchair. Reporters saw his right profile as he passed without glancing at them. A red and blue quilt covered his lap and injured right hand. No one spoke. Reporters stared at the smallish, bespectacled young man who had survived a bomb blast only to be accused of building a bomb. So this was Mark Hofmann. A mad bomber?

Reporters followed Hofmann into the courtroom, squeezing along benches. U.S. District Magistrate Ronald Boyce took the bench as all but Hofmann rose. Boyce began to advise the defendant of the charges, but Yengich interrupted. "Excuse me, Your Honor, but my client has great difficulty hearing."

At Boyce's suggestion, Yengich pushed Hofmann close to the bench. Within minutes it was all over. Hofmann had pleaded not guilty to owning an illegal firearm. The judge set a $50,000 bond, requiring a $5,000 deposit, and confined Hofmann to Salt Lake County and a daily call to pre-trial services. The press was escorted out, and soon Hofmann was wheeled by. This time, reporters saw his left profile. Again, Hofmann had no comment.

Photographers, grouped outside the building, filmed furiously as Hofmann's father and attorneys helped him into his car. Their persistent lenses captured Hofmann's wounded right hand and the bloody scrapes that showed around the bandages. They caught his grimace as the wheelchair bumped down a curb. The cheery quilt, which had seemed incongruous in the somber courtroom, showed up well on color television. The media and newspaper coverage pictured Hofmann without his glasses that day. The man in the Judge Building had not worn glasses.

Hofmann, who had worn glasses inside the courtroom, had removed them to go outside.

In Provo, 45 miles south of Salt Lake City, Brent and Charlene Ashworth were trying to return to normal living. Brent was no more or less nervous with Hofmann now out of the hospital because he figured the police had gotten the wrong man. Still, the panic had calmed, and they could not stay in motels forever. Finally they returned home, edgy and tired. Charlene's parents called from Phoenix, and encouraged Charlene and Brent to meet them in LaJolla, California, for a relaxing weekend. Twice Brent had talked Charlene out of the idea because he worried about leaving the children with relatives after so much insecurity, but in the end he was persuaded that his sense of disaster was excessive.

The Ashworths enjoyed the weekend in southern California. Sunday night, November 3, they stopped at a drive-in for hamburgers. As they waited for their order, Charlene's mother came running into the restaurant. She had received a call from Provo, she gasped. Their seven-year-old son, Samuel, had been in a serious accident.

Brent threw a $10 bill on the counter, and they ran out, driving to the nearest telephone. He called the Provo hospital and talked with a surgeon. Sammy, he learned, had been knocked from his bicycle by a car and had sustained a critical head injury. The car had been driven by three teenagers who had been drinking.

All the way home, Ashworth castigated himself for leaving their children home with relatives. All their routines had been altered by the bombings. One small thing that loomed immensely now—he and Charlene had never let their children ride their bikes on Sunday.

Now their lives, still chaotic, centered around a hospital room where Samuel remained comatose. They brought their other children to see their brother and gratefully accepted help from people in their Mormon ward. Sammy's hospital room was crowded with messages and tokens of sympathy. Among them was a message from President Gordon B. Hinckley, whom

Ashworth had met on numerous occasions, often when he brought interesting documents to the church.

Despite his experiences with Mormon leaders and his own position as a bishop, Ashworth, confronted with his son's injury and his own sense of guilt, felt spiritually incapacitated. It would be weeks before he could lay his hands on his son's head and give him a priesthood blessing. Like his wife, he could only stand by the bed and talk to his son, lost in a tangle of tubes and bandages. On November 5, he saw on the television in the hospital room that Spencer W. Kimball, the church's venerable president and the man he revered as prophet, was dead.

On November 3, the day Samuel Ashworth would be injured, at about 9:00 a.m., officers swung into the quiet Salt Lake neighborhood off the Interstate-80 exit at 2300 East. Their other searches of the Hofmann home had been done in Mark Hofmann's absence; now he was home. They called Hofmann's attorneys but reached neither.

They drove down Gregson Street, turned onto Marie Avenue, and parked the car. Farnsworth picked up the search warrant and walked past the Haus Hofmann sign in the front yard. The van, which had been returned after analysis, stood in the driveway.

This time they were looking primarily for drill bits and machine gun shells. They knew there were shells downstairs in one of Hofmann's rooms. Tests would show whether they were fired before or after the machine gun was altered to make it fully automatic. They also knew that he had the old parts from the gun and the manual—evidence that he, not only Shannon Flynn, had been involved in altering the machine gun.

Dori Hofmann came to the door. "We've got another search warrant," Farnsworth told her. "We don't want to cause your kids any problem, so we'll wait outside while you call a neighbor to come and get the kids."

"Okay. I have to call Mark's dad."

"That's fine. We called the attorneys, but they weren't in. You can call Mark's dad if you want."

While they waited outside, the Hofmann's ward bishop and one of his two counselors came by. They stopped at the police car and asked what was happening.

"We've got to do another search," Farnsworth said. "We're waiting for the little kids to leave."

The bishop and counselor nodded, went up to the Hofmanns' door, and were let in. After a bit, Bill Hofmann arrived and brusquely walked up to the house. The three Hofmann children left with a neighbor. The police got out of the car and approached the house.

Farnsworth said hello to Bill Hofmann. "We have to search the house again," Farnsworth said. "Upstairs, downstairs, and the garage. Now I don't personally believe that there's anything we need in the kitchen or the bedrooms, but we're going to do our job and search all of it."

Bill Hofmann, always courteous before, was obviously upset. "Oh, you're just harassing them."

"No, we're not harassing anybody. Why don't you come and sit down and let me tell you a few things."

Farnsworth could see Mark Hofmann in the bedroom at the end of the hall as he and Bill Hofmann sat down on the living room couch.

"Don't believe everything you hear in the news media," he began. "There isn't any question that Mark is responsible for these bombings and killed those people. He blew himself up and he's responsible for his own injuries. I know this is hard on you. He's your son, and I can understand you being defensive about him. But the fact is that if he hadn't been injured, he would be in jail now. Even now, we would have arrested him as soon as he came out of the hospital. But the attorneys won't back it up, and they'd just let him out again, so there's no point."

Bill Hofmann listened carefully.

"So what it amounts to is you have a grace period here. One of the real ironies is that if he went to jail, you wouldn't see him another day on the outside. So every day he's here, even though he's injured, is a free day you have with him.

"Now I know this is Sunday morning and you don't like us doing the search, but we have new information and we've got to search again."

Bill Hofmann looked at Farnsworth with cold, blue eyes. "And you've called the press," he said.

"No, we didn't call the press," Farnsworth replied. "You have a neighbor out there who has a problem, and I think he called the press. We're out searching Shannon's house right now, and nobody called the press at Shannon's house."

Farnsworth did not really expect to make better inroads with Bill Hofmann than he had with Dori; he just thought someone ought to tell him the truth. Farnsworth might have saved his breath, however, for later that week Bill Hofmann would appear on television to defend his son and comment that he believed the police would actually manufacture evidence against Mark if they had to to make a case.

As the third search of Hofmann's home ended Ron Yengich appeared. "What's going on?"

Farnsworth handed him a copy of the warrant. Yengich, warrant in hand, approached the media, busily filming from the sidewalk. "They have searched this house three times now," he proclaimed. "Can't they get it right the first time? This police force ought to be reported to the Committee on Un-American Activities for Sunday searches like this."

Investigators removed black magic markers, wires, solder, pipe, masking tapes, motor oil, and drill bits from the home. The most significant result of the Sunday search was a bag of used brass shells fired from the machine gun after it had been altered to be fully automatic and a Radio Shack catalogue with D-cell battery packs circled. M. Hansen, police knew, had purchased such a pack along with a mercury switch. If Mr. Hansen had made the bombs, however, he had revised his method to C-cell batteries and, for that purchase, no receipt had been found.

One block from Haus Hofmann, as investigators searched, members of the Garden Heights South Ward were joining in a special fast for the Hofmann family, "that the truth may be known soon."

The bombings investigation was tense behind the front lines. As Bob Stott began to speak up in the daily team meetings, D'Elia and Biggs became increasingly uneasy. They could feel the decision-making power shift. On November 4, D'Elia challenged Stott again. "What are you doing here, Stott?" Stott left the room and returned with Ted Cannon.

"I understand there's some confusion about who's in charge here," Cannon said. "Well, Stott's lead prosecutor after me, Biggs is C and D'Elia's D."

He and Stott left together, giving Biggs and D'Elia time to recover. Biggs and D'Elia had already been over some bumps regarding the role of lead prosecutor. D'Elia had assumed the role from the beginning, but Bud Ellett, justice division administrator, had talked with Biggs about taking over the lead spot. Biggs had agreed but never had brought it up with D'Elia. He knew D'Elia (who had invited Biggs to assist) would be furious, and they still had a lot of work to do before either would be delivering opening or closing statements in court.

D'Elia, however, had sensed the shift in authority and challenged both Biggs and Ellett on it. Biggs had told D'Elia he had been asked to lead the case, but Ellett had denied it. Now, with Stott's assignment to the case, the jockeying between D'Elia and Biggs had become moot, just as Ellett said he knew it would.

On Tuesday, November 5, Hofmann and Flynn pleaded not guilty to grand jury indictments of illegal possession of a machine gun. The same day D'Elia and Farnsworth took the murder investigation east. They went to New York to investigate Hofmann's contacts there and to check some of the claims about his Americana documents, particularly the "Oath of a Freeman." By then they knew there was a second copy of the "Oath of a Freeman" in existence. Shannon Flynn had told them he had been assigned by Hofmann to market it with Sotheby's auction house in Brazil. Flynn and his wife had even visited Brazil, where Flynn once served a Mormon mission.

Investigators had been hearing about the "Oath of a Freeman" ever since the bombings. Hofmann's discovery of the first printed document in America greatly enhanced his reputation as a solid and significant document dealer. They decided to visit Justin Schiller and Raymond Wapner, the New York book dealers who were marketing the Oath for Hofmann to the Library of Congress for a reported $1 million or more. Hofmann, with the same luck he had shown with his Mormon memorabilia, had found the broadside of the Oath in New York City's Argosy Bookstore and had purchased it for $25, as shown by the receipt taken from his van.

Schiller and Wapner, they found, were convinced that Hofmann was innocent, the victim of conspiring authorities in Utah. The book dealers clearly regarded Hofmann as a pleasant bumpkin who'd made a marvelous find. "Mark Hofmann, a bomber?" they snickered. They were outraged that the publicity about the Utah murders and Hofmann was threatening the Oath's sale.

"Other than the Oath that Hofmann brought into you," D'Elia asked, thinking of the "second Oath" Flynn had mentioned, "have you ever seen a similar document?"

No, they said, they hadn't. But they denied it with such emphasis that D'Elia could not help wondering if, in fact, they knew of the second copy. But where was it? If they knew, Schiller and Wapner were not about to say.

D'Elia and Farnsworth also went to the Argosy Bookstore and found the clerk who had sold Hofmann the item. She recalled writing the title on the sales slip, particularly because Hofmann had come into the shop a second time and told her of his find. He had spent some time sorting through the same area in hopes of finding other rare documents, she said.

When they showed her a photocopy of the Oath, though, she looked perplexed. She remembered a shorter text, but with the same title.

D'Elia and Farnsworth then flew to Boston to talk with Kenneth Rendell, an antiquities dealer with an international trade. He had sent Hofmann two papyri in September, he said. He identified photographs of the various fragments as having been broken from his original. Breaking up a papyrus makes no sense, Rendell told them, since its value decreases dramatically.

When D'Elia and Farnsworth returned to Salt Lake City, Cannon looked down the table at the CAO members of the bombings team and said, "Look, we've got to get this case away from all these agencies," he said. "Somebody has to take charge, and it's going to be us."

He summed up the status of the various agencies. The sheriff's office had virtually dropped out after charges were not filed following the first two weeks of investigation. When Hofmann went home from the hospital, the deputies on the case had moved on, too. Most of the police officers had been reassigned, though Bell had access to them when he needed manpower, and the CAO could and did assign Farnsworth and Bell investigative tasks. The ATF agents were no longer camped in Salt Lake City but were still coordinating services and offering their technical help. That left Brent Ward, the FBI, and the grand jury, which had also indicted Hofmann and Flynn in connection with the machine gun but was disinclined to go beyond that. "I'll warn Brent that he'll have a dog fight on his hands if he tries to stay on this case," Cannon said. Besides, the team agreed, Ward would get the CFS investigation as soon as the investigators working on it wrapped things up. The feds had better fraud laws anyway.

Meanwhile, city officers were still creeping along their tedious course. They had eliminated every pickup that could have conceivably been following Mark Hofmann the day he was injured. The number of Radio Shack receipts they had sorted was approaching the 500,000 mark. Bell had 5,420 items from Hofmann's house or car to identify and catalogue. And officers were still tracking down every mercury switch sold recently and checking out people named Mike Hansen.

At the Utah Attorney General's Office, Special Agent George Throckmorton shook his head as he set down the newspaper. A questioned document examiner, Throckmorton usually dealt with forged credit cards, wills, and tax statements, not nineteenth-century documents. Still, he knew that the authentication of the salamander letter, as described in the press, simply could not have been done.

Although he had no official capacity in the bombings case, as November passed, he began checking claims made in the press about the authenticity of the documents Hofmann had discovered. The more he checked, the more his suspicions grew.

Throckmorton knew Dean Jessee, the BYU historian who was considered a leading expert on the handwriting of early Mormon leaders. He and Jessee had talked, months before, about an upcoming conference. At the time, Jessee had mentioned that he wanted more training, although he'd studied handwriting comparison on his own and had a lot of experience with Mormon documents.

"But how do you detect simulations?" Throckmorton had asked. "How do you know that these documents you examine aren't forged?"

Surprised, Jessee had answered with what seemed to Throckmorton a non sequitur: "Why would anybody want to forge a church document?"

That was all, but the conversation haunted him as he read the newspapers and followed media reports. Then Jessee called, and they met at the Salt Lake City Public Library. Jessee was preparing a paper on the salamander letter, and the news reports on the bombings were making him uneasy. At the library, Jessee showed Throckmorton a letter from eastern dealer Kenneth Rendell, stating that the salamander letter appeared authentic. He showed him statements from Al Lyter, an ink expert, and William Krueger, a paper expert.

Throckmorton asked for copies of all the documents that Jessee knew came through Hofmann; he picked them up at Jessee's home a few days later, along with photocopies of Joseph Smith's known handwriting. Throckmorton then called Lyter and Krueger and discussed their findings. As they had stated in the report, the ink on the paper was iron gallotannate ink, consistent with inks used in the nineteenth century. The paper was also consistent. But those consistencies did not make the letter authentic, for such paper was still available and the ink could easily be made. Throckmorton called around and checked Rendell's credentials, which consisted mainly of his experience in the international rare book and document trade. He was not a trained forensic document examiner.

Finally, on Sunday evening, November 17, in front of the television, Throckmorton remembered the Mormon documents in his briefcase and decided to take a look. He scanned them carefully, one at a time, then went through them again. He decided something was definitely wrong.

One letter—the Joseph Smith to Jonathan Dunham letter, which Hofmann had sold to Brent Ashworth—particularly disturbed him. Jessee had given Throckmorton copies of two other letters Joseph Smith had written from Carthage Jail in Illinois. These were owned by the Reorganized Church of Jesus Christ of Latter Day Saints in Independence, Missouri. The Dunham letter was written in Carthage Jail the same day as the other two, just before Smith was murdered, but the handwriting looked different and it had been written with a completely different writing instrument. Throckmorton began to wonder how Joseph Smith, in jail, could have changed his handwriting, his writing instrument, and his paper within a few hours.

Next he compared all the letters discovered by Hofmann. Martin Harris's handwriting in the salamander letter, Joseph Smith's handwriting in the Dunham letter and in the money-digging letter to Josiah Stowell, and the handwriting in a letter from Lucy Mack Smith, Smith's mother, all looked similar. Yet according to Jessee, the letters purportedly had three authors, spanning nineteen years and several states.

Throckmorton knew that handwriting similarities could result from either social class characteristics unique to a particular system of writing or individual characteristics unique to one person. Perhaps the similarities in writing were class characteristics, held by a great number of people during the nineteenth century. Nevertheless, Throckmorton had his doubts. He called Jessee. "I think you've got yourself a three dollar bill," he said.

For CAO investigator Mike George, the Hofmann case had so far meant sixteen to twenty hours per day organizing police reports into a computer program. Gradually, as he sorted police memos into computer files, he concluded that there was no provable reason for Hofmann to commit murder. The reports of double-dealing and unpaid investors suggested frauds, serious ones, interrupted by the bombings. But had the Oath sold, Hofmann could have "bought back" the frauds.

George agreed with Stott's emphasis on motive. That piece

of papyrus looked like fraud, all right, but Hofmann had too much going for him in this community and too little at stake, ultimately, to kill. They had to prove not only that he made and set the bombs, but why, or they would never get a capital murder conviction.

They had other problems: one witness had been tainted, the ink on the Christensen package did not match the pen in the trunk, and the handwriting expert who had examined it had said her tests were inconclusive but she personally did not think Hofmann wrote it.

Unlike the SLCPD detectives and the ATF investigators, George had not seen the victims, talked with their families, or gathered evidence. For him the case was a matter of analysis. There had to be a powerful motive for this young man with such a remarkable career to commit a double bombing and then to go looking for a third victim. He had no record of violence, no criminal record at all. Typically, bombers aren't successful businessmen with young families.

Also, George had read all the historians' and authenticators' statements that the Hofmann documents were genuine. He had gotten a tape of a KUED-TV program. On it, Brent Metcalfe had explained the similarity of the handwriting in the Nathan Harris prayer book to that of the salamander letter. George watched it repeatedly. He knew that the paper and ink on the Anthon Transcript had been checked, as well as practically everything on the salamander letter.

Eventually, the case's contradictions formed a neat equation in George's mind. If the documents are genuine, he decided, Hofmann didn't commit the murders — cops, letterman's jacket, and van notwithstanding; if the documents are fake, he's our man.

In the process of studying the documents, George had learned a new word, "provenance," meaning the history or genealogy of a document. The Anthon Transcript had no meaningful provenance — it was simply found in a Bible which had been purchased from a Mr. Ansel White. The provenance for the salamander letter was confusing; perhaps he should begin by investigating that, George decided.

When on November 20 Throckmorton called George from

the Attorney General's office, he sounded frustrated. By then he had talked with various reporters, law enforcers, archivists, and historians about the Hofmann documents and the experts who had authenticated them. "Mike, nobody's listening," Throckmorton said. "Those Hofmann documents really need another look."

George explained his intention to investigate provenance since the documents had been authenticated.

"Well, let me explain what authentication means," Throckmorton said. He noted how an expert never wants to get cornered on a document and always needs to give the owner something of what he wants. "You can say that iron gallotann-ate ink is consistent with ink used in the nineteenth century, but it could also have been made yesterday in the bathroom sink. You can say that paper is consistent with nineteenth-century paper; but if you avoid whiteners or other recent additions to the stock, you can buy rag paper today that's just the same. Besides, it might not be that hard to get old paper. You could steal it from books published at the right time, or whatever."

George was definitely interested. "But these documents look old."

"Well, if you were forging them, that's what you'd have to figure out. How to make them look old. How to get the paper foxed—you know, gold with age—and the ink that reddish tint you see on old letters. That would be the hard part, but not impossible."

George invited Throckmorton to come down the following day. In the meantime, he refrained from doing somersaults and settled for running down the hall to Cannon's office. He looked around the circle at Stott, D'Elia, and Biggs.

"I just talked to Throckmorton, and he says our docu-ments might not be authentic."

He watched Cannon's face light up and then put in his bid. "I want to work on the documents."

"Go for it," Cannon beamed.

George picked up a little reading material—Mormon scrip-ture, Dean Jessee's *The Personal Writings of Joseph Smith*, and Fawn Brodie's controversial 1944 biography of Joseph Smith, *No Man Knows My History*. He read with fascination, beginning to see where and how the documents fit into Mormon history, into Mormon politics, into the Mormon market. At last he was free of computer programs, memos, and flow charts. He was a cop on the street again, working one hell of a case.

The next day Throckmorton met with the prosecutors and investigators and repeated what he had told George. Almost immediately he was "borrowed" from the attorney general's office to work on the Hofmann case.

"Would you like to see the originals of the documents?" Stott asked.

"Yes, I would. But first let's call in Bill Flynn from Phoenix. I'm a Mormon, and you're going to need an expert from outside Utah on this case." Flynn, a forensic document examiner for Arizona, was considered among the best in the field, Throckmorton explained.

During this time, the Utah Supreme Court was finally hearing arguments on whether the hearing on the nurse's information should be open to the press. On November 27, the court ruled that the press could attend but postponed this hearing until December 2. While the "battle of the nurse" pended, on November 25, Dean Jessee came to the CAO to answer the team's questions about Mormon documents. He named nine documents that had come from Hofmann and explained their significance.

The CAO needed the hopeful twist. Their adversaries, Yengich and Rich, had arranged for their client to take a polygraph test, assuring him that if the test results were not good, no one need ever know. However, Hofmann had seemed entirely unconcerned, had taken it without apparent worry, and had passed with an unusually high score. Although the test was not admissable in court, Yengich and Rich had released the results to the press, hoping to reclaim the presumption of innocence needed if their client were ever charged.

The media was definitely beginning to turn in Hofmann's favor, as friends and scholars continued to discuss his career and good name and as prosecutors and police fell into an unhappy silence. The media reported that "a nationally recognized expert in polygraph examinations" had written to Yengich that the polygraph test results indicated that his client "was telling the truth." The test had also been verified by a "world-renowned polygraph expert" and psychologist at the University of Utah.

Polygraph tests also cleared Shannon Flynn of any bombings involvement and showed that Dori Hofmann was telling the truth when she said that her husband was at home until after 8:00 a.m. the morning the bombings occured. Some members of the Hofmann family, encouraged by the polygraph results, even wanted the nurse to tell what she had overheard Hofmann tell Yengich and felt that Yengich's resistance in court falsely implied that Hofmann had, indeed, confessed to murder.

Given the defense's new energy and the weeks that had passed since the bombings, the prosecution was tense. D'Elia admitted that "the Supremes" (his term for the Utah Supreme Court) were not as receptive to his arguments regarding the nurse's testimony as he had hoped. If they lost that testimony now, not only did they lose the incriminating statement they hoped she had overheard, but the defense would win a double victory in the arena of public opinion.

Cannon, who had maintained contact with Dahlquist, suggested that Larson-Lohr and her husband might want some protection from the press and from various investigative agencies, who could close in quickly once the court decision came down. A few days later, the CAO sent investigators in a motor home to protect the nurse's home in Salt Lake County. With time, as Cannon had hoped, one of the investigators succeeded in learning from a person close to Larson-Lohr two apparent facts the prosecutors felt were essential—that Hofmann's remarks had been indirectly incriminating and that the third bomb had not been intended for suicide.

While these machinations continued backstage, the *Salt Lake Tribune* pulled a journalistic coup. On Thanksgiving morning, when the two Salt Lake newspapers publish only one edition, the *Tribune* broke the story that their reporter Dawn Tracy had found the McLellin collection in Texas. Details were scarce, but clearly Tracy had used the leads historians had known about for decades. She had located the son of one of McLellin's friends who had in his possession three small journals written by

McLellin. The journals proved to be interesting but not earthshaking. Whatever else McLellin had collected had evidently disappeared years ago. More importantly, the son had never heard of Mark Hofmann.

On November 29, the day after Thanksgiving, the entire bombings team sat down in the war room to assess their case. They rehearsed the old and new evidence. They had the Judge Building witnesses, the M. Hansen receipt and Mike Hansen papers from Hofmann's house, the witness who saw the van at the Sheets house, Hofmann's letterman's jacket, the piece of Rendell's papyrus and evident fraud, plus apparent double dealing with other investors over American documents. They had also found in Hofmann's Toyota van one grain of smokeless gunpowder like that used in the bombs.

More recently, a search of Emigration Canyon leads had produced a bus driver who thought he had seen Hofmann there the afternoon of October 15. A search of the shed beside a house the Hofmanns had considered buying had produced some interesting evidence. A drill that could have been used to drill an end cap to wire the pipe bombs had been left on the counter, and the light had been left on while the owner was away. The owner's son could not remember exactly when he had made that discovery, but it had been around the time of the bombings. Tests showed that a drill bit recovered from Hofmann's home matched the hole in the end pipe recovered from Hofmann's knee. Maybe Hofmann made the third bomb while he was supposedly "driving around" in the canyon the day he was injured.

Police had driven up and down Emigration Canyon and had tried to make phone calls from mobile telephones like Hofmann's to see if his calls on Tuesday could have been made from the canyon. That seemed unlikely, they concluded, and virtually impossible for the bus driver to have seen Hofmann, who had been talking with Dallin Oaks at the Church Office Building very near that time.

Despite those intriguing but inconclusive leads, the case made sense to the detectives interviewing the witnesses. Curt Bench, the Deseret Book manager, had told them that Hofmann and Christensen had been under extreme pressure because of the unpaid bank loan and that Hofmann had been desperate for money. Kate Reid, Hofmann's former fiancee, had described Hofmann's ambitions while in college to find documents that would disprove traditional Mormon history. This did not prove forgery, of course, but it would certainly tarnish Hofmann's public halo. The detectives had not learned yet of Throckmorton's suspicions, but they knew that prosecutors were waiting for a ruling on the nurse's testimony or for the chance to depose her through the federal grand jury.

Still, the detectives became increasingly frustrated with their inability to convince Stott and Biggs to press charges. Hofmann, whom they believed had blown two people apart, was home with his family, telling friends what to say to police and reporters, and selling his documents in the East. The police chief wanted charges filed and the families of the victims were confused and distraught.

Stott felt differently. "We may not have a chargeable homicide," he said, putting the bleakest opinion before the bombings team.

Farnsworth had heard enough. "Okay, let's have it out," he barked. "Who in this room thinks Mark Hofmann is guilty. Raise your hand."

Hands went up, some reluctantly. Stott determinedly kept both hands on the table and stared back icily at the furious detectives. "That's not a relevant question," he said with his best courtroom calm. "Yes, you have enough evidence to arrest him, but we don't have enough evidence to try a capital case. Hofmann's got an alibi, he's passed a polygraph, he's a bomb victim himself. I have to go beyond my belief. I have to have a likelihood of conviction. He's our best suspect and he probably did it, but at this point, I don't think we'd even get him bound over for trial."

Nobody left the room happy. "I know what we have to do to get ready for court," Bell lamented to Farnsworth as they strode across 400 South and back to the station. "But I don't know what it's going to take to get a complaint."

5

THE MICROSCOPE
DETECTIVES

December began brightly for defense attorneys Ron Yengich and Brad Rich. Six weeks ago their newest, and most notorious, client had lain in a hospital bed in critical condition. Now he was not only recovering from his physical injuries but beginning to rebound from the harm to his public image. When the Utah Supreme Court decided to protect the conversation Valerie Larson-Lohr had overheard, the victory of Hofmann's successful polygraph was all the sweeter.

Yengich and Rich knew that as defense attorneys their task was often misunderstood by the public. Constitutionally, every person charged with a crime is presumed innocent and is entitled to the best possible defense. However, if a client confesses guilt but wants to plead not guilty, the conscientious defense attorney is faced with a dilemma. As an officer of the court, he or she should not allow a client to commit perjury. Yet taking the stand is often the client's best, most convincing defense. Thus, "Did you do it?" is not necessarily a helpful question.

As usual, Yengich and Rich stuck to specifics in their conversations with Hofmann, who was eager to help. This time they had an intelligent client caught in what seemed a true murder mystery, possibly involving the Mafia, the Mormon church, fanatical Mormons, bad investments, or some combination of all four. Furthermore, their client had passed a polygraph; he was white, a Mormon with high connections, a husband and father, with no previous criminal record. He had a strong, law-

117

abiding family that was convinced of his innocence. He was thus a dream client and his trial—if it came—could make for a dream case: high profile with a likelihood of success.

In the weeks following Hofmann's release from the hospital, Yengich repeatedly proclaimed his client's innocence. Rich was only slightly more cautious, figuring that if Hofmann was involved at all it was peripherally. Hofmann certainly did not seem like a violent person. The bombings were potentially capital offenses, yet the attorneys knew that Hofmann was not the sort of client who, in Utah, got the death penalty. Rich was both offended and relieved by what he perceived as a cultural reality. In any case, the evidence against Hofmann seemed circumstantial, the motive vague, the aggravating circumstances unprovable. All three would have to be much stronger to bring down verdicts of first-degree murder.

The defense had another advantage. From the beginning, Yengich and Rich had been able to track the prosecution in the daily newspapers as leaks, infighting, and disagreements among agencies provided interesting copy for stories. If this much was getting picked up by the media, the real divisions must be fierce, they concluded. Rich even began to wonder if the case against Hofmann might simply dissipate, vanishing on dissident winds.

Though not giving up, the prosecutors were far from happy. They hinted to increasingly skeptical reporters that the defense would not have fought to keep the nurse quiet had she not heard something significant. But both sides were also saying informally that the "battle of the nurse" had been a personal contest to embarrass Yengich. That trivialized the issue, but it was better than admitting that either Hofmann had confessed (which the defense disavowed) or that the prosecution had sustained a serious loss (which the prosecution denied).

"What'd you do? Attach the wires to the third finger of his right hand?" Gerry D'Elia taunted Yengich and Rich, when he went to pick up the polygraph results. The defense attorneys could afford to laugh at the reference to Hofmann's blown off fingertip. They were obviously jubilant.

D'Elia and the police were not only frustrated at the defense and the press but at Ted Cannon and Bob Stott for refusing to file charges. There had been a time when the defense had seemed ready to collapse with a guilty plea based on what the nurse had overheard, a time when they had been convinced that Hofmann was on the verge of confession. Now it was the defense's turn to flex muscle.

Publicly, of course, the CAO put the best possible face on the situation. Yes, Cannon said, they still considered Hofmann the prime suspect in the bombings. Yes, the investigation was continuing; the loss of the nurse's testimony had only a negligible effect on their case. Meanwhile, the case continued to demand fourteen-to-eighteen-hour days.

George Throckmorton worked feverishly to discover whether forgery was a glue that could hold the case together. First, he needed the documents that Hofmann had sold to the LDS church and to other collectors. He could begin with photographs, then move to the originals, he told Dean Jessee.

Jessee shook his head. The investigation was unpopular among historians. "Leonard won't let you have them," he guessed.

Throckmorton telephoned Leonard Arrington, now head of the church history institute at BYU. He knew Arrington had been widely quoted in the press stating that at least five of the Mormon documents Hofmann had discovered were definitely authentic. Neither Throckmorton's professional interest in documents nor his membership in the LDS church had acquainted him with the new Mormon history attributed to Arrington and his staff. Now Throckmorton introduced himself and told Arrington he needed photographs of the Hofmann documents. Arrington said he could offer no help, except to suggest that Throckmorton pursue some other line of inquiry. "You're on the wrong track," he advised, as they ended the conversation.

Throckmorton next tried to get the photographs from employees in the church's archives at the Church Office Building. For a time, prosecutors and investigators had taken their questions directly to the archives staff, but a memo had instructed employees that any contact with investigators or the press should be cleared through church attorneys. Legally, the prosecutors could not fault the procedure, but, practically, the added red tape slowed the investigation.

A number of meetings took place in December between church and CAO representatives to discuss the examination of certain documents in the church's possession. Church attorney Wilford Kirton was leery of allowing investigators access to the papers. "We cannot divulge the content of these documents," he insisted during one meeting. "It's my responsibility to protect these documents and President Hinckley."

Explanations that the documents in question had already been published did not seem to convince Kirton. Finally, Ted Cannon, who had spoken with church attorneys frequently, called Kirton and told him in no uncertain terms that, one way or another, the investigators had to examine church documents. Meanwhile, when state attorney general David Wilkinson heard Throckmorton complain about the church's lack of cooperation, he said he might be able to help. Later Wilkinson told Throckmorton that if he had any problems to let him know— he had a friend in Dallin Oaks.

"Slap them with a subpoena," D'Elia suggested repeatedly when the bombings team met. But Cannon and Stott opposed the idea.

Finally, all parties agreed to meet on December 5, including Apostle Oaks, church attorney Kirton, Throckmorton, George, Stott, and archives administrators Earl Olsen and Glenn Rowe. Stott explained that they needed the originals of the documents Dean Jessee said came from Hofmann. Some of these documents had been published in Jessee's 1984 book, *The Personal Writings of Joseph Smith*.

After some discussion, Oaks agreed. "We need to cooperate," he said. "We need to be entirely open in this matter, because the church has nothing to hide. We need a subpoena for these documents. Then history will show that the church cooperated."

Throckmorton bit his tongue as Stott smoothly said he would be happy to supply the church with a subpoena. Oaks and Kirton presented a paper for Throckmorton to sign, stating that his notes, test results, and photographs would be returned to the church. Afterwards, however, Throckmorton told Stott he would not agree to sign anything like that and the subject was dropped. Oaks, his legal experience showing, valued docu mentation. He requested a letter from the CAO stating that the church had cooperated fully with the investigation.

While church and CAO attorneys were meeting, Curt Bench and Wade Lillywhite from Deseret Book went to visit their friend, Mark Hofmann, at home. Hofmann looked bad, particularly his injured hand and knee. Dori Hofmann was glad for the visitors and the opportunity to express her anger at the police. "They say the most horrible things about Mark!"

"Well, they're just doing their job," her husband put in mildly.

"That's fine for you to say," she exclaimed. "You don't have to deal with them. I'm the one who has to answer the door and the telephone and write checks at the store. You don't know what it's like!"

As the four chatted, Lillywhite looked around him. Mark's parents were in another room, watching the children, and Dori seemed both insecure and persecuted. Lillywhite, who coveted the Hofmanns' inscribed copy of Jack London's *Call of the Wild*, asked how the valuable children's book collection Mark had helped Dori assemble was doing.

"Mark assured me that all the children's collection is okay," Dori Hofmann answered pleasantly. "Isn't that right, Mark?" He smiled and nodded.

"This is all so ironic," Bench put in. "Do you remember that I'm the one who told you about Steve, Mark?"

He did. "I think it was a few minutes after nine o'clock when Mark called home and told me to get myself and the kids out of here," Dori recalled.

"I guess you know this business about us being witnesses isn't any of our doing," Lillywhite said.

"Oh, yeah, I understand that," Mark Hofmann answered. Somehow, despite Hofmann's bandages and wheelchair, despite all that had happened, the old friends talked and joked as usual, reassured that Mark was the same pleasant, laid-back person they had known; there was nothing sinister about him now or before the bombings.

The more Bench thought about the visit as he went about the day's business, the more questions the police had raised returned. That afternoon he found himself driving back to Haus Hofmann on Marie Avenue.

"Mark, what's this about you carrying a package to your car?" he asked.

"I wasn't," Hofmann said. "After I opened the car door, I saw something falling and I instinctively grabbed for it."

"When he first came to," Dori put in, "he thought he'd been hit by a car."

"I see. Also, I was just wondering about that nurse," Bench added. "You know, she was supposed to have overheard a confession."

"The word confession was never used. The police had been rather abusive, and I wanted to make a statement just to clarify my activities up to the time of the bombings." He looked Bench in the eye. "I couldn't confess to anything because I didn't do anything."

Bench nodded.

"My attorneys won that nurse thing before the state Supreme Court," Hofmann added. "I won't have to pay any fees on that one."

"Right. This conversation really helps. Just one more thing. What about the letter jacket?"

"Oh, I figured that out. See, I went to see Steve on October 10 and we were both in the elevator together. I was wearing my letter jacket, and Steve made some comment about it. The people in the elevator kind of chuckled. I think the witness must have been one of them, and he has that day confused with the day of the bombings."

"I guess that could happen."

"Sure. My attorney told me there are four stores in town where you can buy jackets just like that."

"So what do you think is at the bottom of all this?"

"I don't know. It's so bizarre and incredible, I just can't believe it. I go from theory to theory."

"Did you know about those McLellin papers down in Texas?"

"Sure, I knew. But Don Schmidt asked me not to go after them because he was going to get them for the church."

"What's happened with the 'Oath of a Freeman'?"

"Well, the Library of Congress did about $30,000 worth of tests on it through the FBI. They think it's authentic, but there was some confusion that made them miss a deadline. It still could sell."

"I guess that would be pretty handy at this point." Bench looked at his friend and sighed. Christensen was buried and here was Hofmann, terribly injured and enduring suspicion and libel.

"You know," Hofmann added, "I think Shannon and I will probably write a book. Eventually the truth on all this is going to be known."

Bench left feeling much better. He was under pressure from both the police and his superiors at Deseret Book to keep quiet about what he knew; he had been told he would likely testify someday. But he did not mind telling friends the answers to some of the questions that had been tugging at everyone. Bench knew that word would spread and that people would be reassured about Mark. He figured that if he had to cooperate with the police against his friend's interests, he owed him at least that much.

The following day, December 6, Throckmorton went to the Church Administration Building to get an 1825 treasure-digging letter Joseph Smith had written to Josiah Stowell which had been housed in the First Presidency's vault. Although the text of the letter had been released the previous May, it was still considered sensitive. After some discussion, Francis Gibbons, secretary to the First Presidency, arranged to have the document retrieved. On his way back, Throckmorton went to see his former stake president, Richard Lindsay, now in charge of church public communications.

Throckmorton told Lindsay that he was working on the investigation and that the implications for the church could be far-reaching. "I'd really like a blessing from one of the church leaders, one who's not involved in any of this."

Lindsay told him they routinely discouraged church members from asking for blessings, since church leaders were busy men, but he had to admit that this was an unusual situation. "I'll let you know," he said.

Throckmorton was accompanied to the state crime lab, where the documents would be photographed, by an amiable church archivist who chatted and ate his lunch, a briefcase full of valuable documents at his feet. When they got out of the car, the archivist slipped on the snowy curb, and the briefcase fell and opened. Documents worth tens of thousands of dollars fluttered to the ground around them.

After all he had gone through to get hold of the documents, Throckmorton could not keep quiet. "Hey, they sent you along to protect these things," he chided, as they snatched up the yellowed papers. "You're throwing them all over the snow."

By December, the investigators needed detailed information from the church leaders who had been involved in the McLellin transaction. They knew more than they had in October and were prepared to probe more deeply, so they planned their strategy carefully.

First, Jim Bell and Ken Farnsworth dropped by Hugh Pinnock's office to tell him an interview was imminent. Even their introductions were calculated. Bell announced that he was originally from Canada by way of Detroit. He was not and never had been Mormon. Farnsworth said that he had been raised a Mormon in Salt Lake City and had served a mission in France, though he was no longer involved in church activity. As they expected, Pinnock turned in his chair and spoke directly with Farnsworth. Bell observed closely.

Farnsworth began by explaining that they considered Pinnock an important witness. Pinnock knew whatever Christensen had known about the McLellin deal — and whatever Christensen had known, they needed to get into court. What Hofmann had told Christensen that Christensen related to Pinnock could be ruled out as hearsay, Farnsworth explained; so they needed to hear what Hofmann had told Pinnock directly. Hard as it might be for Pinnock to believe, Farnsworth added, they were convinced that Hofmann had killed Christensen and Kathy Sheets. "It's absolutely imperative that we know everything that was happening between you and Steve and between

124

Steve and Mark. We need to know about Hinckley and Oaks and the bank and the telephone calls—all of it. Also, you'd best be prepared to explain this in court."

As Farnsworth talked, Pinnock gradually drained a pitcher of ice water, brushed lint from his trousers, shifted about in his chair, and paced around the desk. Bell could not remember ever seeing a more nervous potential witness.

On the way out of the building, Bell told Farnsworth he would not be coming back. "You get the church guys," he said. "I'll deal with the chief's office."

Farnsworth agreed. "It's a good thing we met with Pinnock on his own turf—his desk, his office. Think how nervous he'd have been anywhere else." Not that any alternative had been discussed.

On December 6, Farnsworth, Mike George, and an FBI agent met with Pinnock in his office, along with church attorney Oscar McConkie. Pinnock read relevant references from his daytimer and personal journal, as the investigators took careful notes. His first reference to Hofmann was on June 28 when Hofmann and Christensen had told him about a McLellin collection in Texas and Pinnock had arranged the First Interstate Bank loan. He had met with them from 11:25 a.m. to 12:45 p.m., Pinnock said, then he went to Oaks's office, and afterwards began calling banks.

On July 12, Pinnock informed the officers, Hofmann had brought in a photocopy of a land deed from the McLellin collection. Pinnock showed them a photocopy. Two of the many names at the bottom were significant in Mormon history, he said—Sidney Rigdon and Solomon Spaulding. The investigators considered this information important, for they now had another piece of the elusive McLellin collection.

Then, in early October, Pinnock explained, the bank loan was overdue and Harvey Tanner of First Interstate had called. Christensen and Hofmann had come to Pinnock's home, and the deal had been restructured after Hofmann admitted he could not afford to donate the collection. Pinnock had suggested arranging for a buyer who would make the donation. Hofmann had been concerned about his reputation. "What will President Hinckley think of me?" he had asked.

The next day, October 4, Pinnock related that he had met with Oaks. Pinnock had noted beside that appointment Oaks's desire that the McLellin deal close right away. Pinnock listed his contacts with Christensen, Sorenson, West, and Hofmann, all encoded with Pinnock's system of initials. When he came to Friday, October 11, Pinnock added that he had seen Hofmann in the lobby early that morning, waiting to see Hinckley.

"Did they meet?" the investigators asked.

"I don't know."

On October 14, the day before the bombings, Pinnock had been in touch with those involved in the deal. Pinnock said he had heard of Christensen's death on his way to speak at a funeral and of Sheets's death afterward. He, Oaks, and Hinckley had discussed the bombings, he said, and the McLellin deal had been rescheduled for Wednesday. Then when Hofmann was injured, everything changed.

"All we know is what we read in the papers," Pinnock quoted aloud from his journal, obviously reliving the aftermath of the bombings. The strain in his voice grew as he related his fears for his own family. His voice broke and tears came. Behind the mild, urbane surface, Farnsworth saw what must have been a desperate man.

Following the interview, the investigators asked for copies of the relevant journal entries, shook Pinnock's hand, and agreed to stay in touch. They left feeling encouraged. Some questions remained—what Christensen had believed about the papyrus fragment he had locked up, for instance—but most of the interview fit with the evidence. The records from Hofmann's car telephone, for example, showed numerous calls to church head-quarters, at first to the general switchboard. Hofmann had called Pinnock's office several times around July 12 and October 3, important days in Pinnock's diary. Closer to the bombings, Hofmann's calls were placed to Hinckley's private number, each lasting a few minutes. Now, according to Pinnock, they knew that Hofmann had been looking for Hinckley the Friday before the bombings—the day the McLellin deal failed to close. The investigators sat down and drew up a list of questions for Hinckley.

First, they needed Hinckley to provide the kind of background he had at the press conference, but in more depth. How had Hinckley met Hofmann? Had Hofmann dealt with general authorities other than Hinckley, Oaks, and Pinnock? What kinds of moneys had been exchanged for the various documents Hofmann had trafficked? They had questions about the Kinderhook Plates and more about the McLellin collection. They needed to know when Hinckley found out about the McLellin papers, how often he had discussed the collection with Hofmann, and where those conversations took place. They needed the letter Alvin Rust had written to Hinckley and information about Rust's part in the McLellin deal. They would ask whether Hofmann had ever shown Hinckley a papyrus, representing it as Facsimile 2.

Finally, they needed to know more about Hinckley's relationship with Christensen. Had they met regarding the McLellin collection? Was there a document-acquisition plan, as they had been told, setting Christensen up as a collector for the church? Had Hofmann previously occupied that position officially or unofficially? This question was particularly important, because the investigators suspected that Hofmann had discovered he was about to be replaced as the "church's man" in the document business. Perhaps the nails in the Christensen bomb had been meant for revenge.

On December 9, three days after their interview with Pinnock, investigators returned to the Church Administration Building to interview Hinckley, who was represented by Kirton. Hinckley took the initiative by mentioning that at the press conference he had been unable to recall the second document he had purchased from Mark Hofmann, other than the Josiah Stowell letter. He had checked, he said, and found he had authorized the purchase of a letter from David Whitmer, one of three witnesses to the gold plates of the Book of Mormon.

Hinckley retraced the information he had given at the press conference regarding his position as advisor to the history department and later as second counselor in the First Presidency. Hinckley said he had met with Hofmann two or three times in 1985 about the McLellin collection. In between those visits, Hinckley had received a letter from Rust regarding the collection and had told Hofmann to resolve his arrangement with Rust.

On October 10, Hofmann had inquired whether the church would like to purchase the Kinderhook plates, Hinckley said, but he had declined purchase.

"What was in the McLellin collection?"

"He said there was Facsimile 2, journals and affidavits. Mark said he wanted to donate it to the church."

"Do you know if Facsimile 2 has been acquired by anyone?"

"Not by anyone I know of."

"Can you describe to us your contacts with Steven Christensen?"

"The only time Christensen was in my office was on April 12, 1985, when he donated the Martin Harris letter."

Despite the note of finality in Hinckley's voice, the investigators continued to press for more information about Christensen. Had he been given any calling, formal or informal, to procure documents for the church? Hinckley said he had no such understanding and referred the investigators to Don Schmidt, the archivist who had retired the autumn before Christensen had donated the salamander letter. Hofmann had never had such a calling, Hinckley said.

The investigators wanted to know how close the relationship had been between Hinckley and Hofmann. Had either called the other one at home?

"I can't personally recall Mark Hofmann calling me at home. My secretary may have his numbers, but I do not."

They asked about the papyrus piece Christensen had locked up. Hinckley said he had never seen it, and his only reference to Facsimile 2 was that Hofmann had mentioned it in June.

"When did you find out about the $185,000 First Interstate bank loan?"

"I don't remember."

"Elder Pinnock showed us a photocopy of a document signed by Solomon Spaulding. When did you see that?"

"I'm not aware of that."

"Elder Pinnock never showed you that?"

"Not that I recall."

The questions came back to Christensen, but Hinckley

repeated the statement about Christensen being in his office only once. They tried another tack. "When did you hear that the McLellin collection was controversial?"

"I'm not aware that it was controversial. I don't remember hearing that. Mark Hofmann said he wanted to donate it to the church."

"Do you have journals or a daytimer that might refresh your memory on some of these points that are so important to the investigation?"

"No, I don't have anything that would help you. I don't keep a daytimer." The investigators, aware of Pinnock's meticulous journal, Christensen's sporadic one, and the fact that Curt Bench and many Mormons considered journal-keeping a religious duty, received this information skeptically.

Within the historical department it was known that Hinckley often sent drafts of entries from his journal to church employees and others present at meetings he attended in order to check for accuracy and completeness. Hinckley subsequently explained in a written statement, "When the inquiry concerning Mark Hoffman [sic] was in progress I was interviewed by a number of investigators and I recall that one asked whether I kept a detailed journal. I responded that I was an erratic and inconsistent journal keeper and that my secretary reminds me quite frequently of blanks in that record; further, that I do not ordinarily make detailed records of visits or conversations. I do not keep a 'Daytimer.' "

The journal question was only one dead end in the interview. Afterwards, Mike George left Hinckley's office unexpectedly angry. When he interviewed a bandit he expected lies, not when he interviewed a respected citizen and church leader. He soon realized, however, that his anger was simple—his fellow investigators, born and raised Mormons, were furious.

The investigators rechecked Hofmann's mobile telephone records. Hinckley had indeed received a call from Hofmann in the early afternoon on October 10, the day he inquired about the Kinderhook Plates. Hinckley said that had represented his last contact with Hofmann. However, the telephone record showed that the next morning Hofmann had called Hinckley's office from his mobile telephone at 7:30, fifteen minutes before he called Christensen at work. On October 14, the day before the bombings, Hofmann had called Hinckley's office both in the morning and the afternoon, each call lasting two to three minutes. It was unknown, however, if Hofmann spoke directly with Hinckley.

Later that month George interviewed several of Christensen's business associates he happened to catch at the CFS building. As he questioned, he heard Hinckley's name mentioned frequently. One man said that Christensen had been pulled from a meeting by a call from Hinckley. A week later, another call to an associate's office had come from Hinckley's secretary before Christensen arrived. When Christensen came in, he returned the call, then left immediately. That incident had occurred within a week of the bombings. George needed to know what was distracting Christensen from an already hectic business schedule. Hofmann, Hinckley, and Christensen. George had had his chance with Gordon Hinckley. Hofmann, as the suspect, was categorically unreliable. What he wouldn't give for five minutes with Steve Christensen right now.

Throckmorton, at work on the documents, knew only fragments of the whole investigation. He worked in a relative vacuum as he prepared for William Flynn's upcoming visit.

On December 10, Throckmorton called Richard Lindsay at the Church Office Building to check on his earlier request to see a church leader uninvolved with the case. "George, you need to go to your bishop for the blessing," Lindsay said. "Don't even come over here any more. We don't want to look like we're influencing you in the slightest. The church has to stay completely away from this case."

"All right. I wasn't thinking about it like that," Throckmorton said. He understood Lindsay's point of view, but the reaction increased his sense of isolation and personal risk. The conservators, archivists, and historians he had talked with recently had not hidden their incredulity when he announced that the tests done previously on the Hofmann documents had been insufficient to determine authenticity.

The ink, paper, and handwriting had already been evaluated and tested, they countered. The content of the documents fit into the historical context of early Mormonism. Furthermore, some of the documents had been purchased and publicized by the Mormon church, which certainly had at its command the resources to establish authenticity. Not only manuscript experts but Mormons on every level seemed convinced the documents were genuine—from the LDS history division to members of Throckmorton's own ward, who had mentioned after worship services that he was following the wrong lead. And now church leaders wanted him to stay at arm's length.

Throckmorton knew that this case would probably be more important and challenging than any in his career, including his detection of forgery in the famous "Mormon will" of billionaire Howard Hughes. However, he also felt the growing stress of shuttling weekly between the state attorney general's office and the CAO, as well as being publicly called a crackpot. He decided to take Lindsay's advice and call his bishop.

In the East, Hofmann's documents were defended by collectors, investors, and book dealers. The "Oath of a Freeman," in particular, was growing in stature as its investor-agents, Justin Schiller and Ray Wapner, cited tests and experts. In the press, Library of Congress officials announced that negotiations had ended. They refused to specify reasons but insisted that authenticity was not a question. On December 10, the original of a famous Daniel Boone letter, which Hofmann had discovered, sold at a Sotheby's auction for around $40,000. The letter was significant because its text confirmed the story of Daniel Boone crossing the Cumberland Gap, fighting Indians, and exploring the frontier. The text was known, but Hofmann had found the original. With no charges forthcoming in Utah, eastern dealers and collectors openly backed the soft-spoken Hofmann, who was obviously the target of some church/state conspiracy in the wilds of Utah.

On December 11 the SLCPD brought Alcohol, Tobacco, and Firearms agent Jerry Taylor back to Utah to explain the evidence against Hofmann his colleagues had gathered. Taylor laid out everything from technical evidence collected at the scenes to an ATF profile of a bomber—someone in control of his emotions but who hated deeply. Most of the investigators felt the evidence pointed undeniably to Hofmann. Only Stott was unimpressed. When he rose to leave before the presentation ended to keep a lunch appointment, Ken Farnsworth challenged him. Farnsworth told Stott they had brought Taylor back solely to convince Stott they were ready to go after Hofmann. But Stott did not believe that Taylor's testimony could convincingly link the bombs and carry the case—at least, not yet.

The team that headed south to Provo carefully tailored this initial interview to fit Brent Ashworth. David Biggs, Ashworth's first cousin, eased the introductions by chatting about family members. Throckmorton got busy photographing the documents Ashworth had purchased from Hofmann, including a letter written by Lucy Mack Smith (Joseph Smith's mother), the Nauvoo letter from Joseph Smith to Jonathan Dunham (which had first piqued Throckmorton's suspicions), and a letter written in blue pencil to a Walter Conrad signed by Martin Harris. Mike George began asking the questions. They soon found that Ashworth was a walking chronology of information on Hofmann, for the two had dealt closely for several years. Ashworth had utter faith in his Hofmann documents, but he was not so positive about the man who had sold them to him.

Ashworth told them he thought they suspected the wrong guy. "Mark Hofmann's a liar and a cheat, but he's not a murderer."

Why a liar and a cheat? Ashworth began telling them about his document deals with Hofmann. As their conversation neared the time of the bombings, the investigators became even more intent. In fact, Hofmann, they learned, had visited Ashworth the Sunday before the bombings, the first casual visit to his home without something to sell. Hofmann had given Ashworth a check for a document he had on consignment.

Ashworth had mentioned problems with Hofmann's checks, so the investigators asked, "Did this one clear?"

"No, it bounced."

Ashworth mentioned that he and Hofmann usually did business in Salt Lake on Wednesdays. "When he visited you on Sunday, did you talk about coming to Salt Lake on Wednesday?"

"I think we did. At that point, I was still planning to come to Salt Lake on Wednesday, but since I was there on Monday and Tuesday, I didn't go."

"Would Mark recognize your car?"

"Oh, yes. We often did business in my car, sometimes in his."

"Did he know where you parked?"

"Yes. There's a spot near the doors in Crossroads Mall's parking plaza that I can usually get. We meet at our spot by the elevators in the mall, but that's not very private."

Hiding his excitement, George drew a number 3 in the margin and added a question mark.

As the team prepared to leave, Ashworth surprised Throckmorton by letting him take the originals of his Hofmann documents. Throckmorton thanked him, but when he told Ashworth that the Dunham letter was a forgery, Ashworth protested, "That's impossible. Dean Jessee authenticated it. I always went to Dean before I bought anything from Mark."

Throckmorton tucked the letters in his briefcase as Ashworth admonished to handle the documents with great care.

Before returning to Salt Lake City, Biggs, George, and Throckmorton went to lunch, as elated as they were hungry. Excitedly they discussed how they had all watched the case come together in Ashworth's study, his expensively framed documents beaming from the walls. They did not think he realized it yet, but each felt sure that Ashworth represented the mysterious third target of the bomb that had injured Hofmann. They were not sure why, yet it seemed clear that Hofmann had expected to find Ashworth in Crossroads Mall that Wednesday. Also, Ashworth had bought documents that they suspected were forgeries. Hofmann knew Ashworth mistrusted him, but not as a bomber. He would not have suspected Hofmann of wishing him harm.

Brent and Charlene Ashworth also went to lunch that day. Brent thought he might be a suspect in the case, for the investigators had asked him many questions about where he parked and when he and Hofmann met.

"Brent," Charlene said, "did it ever occur to you that they might think Mark was after you?"

He had not, but the thought turned in his mind.

Later the three prosecutors paid Ashworth a visit and showed him a receipt that had been recovered from the Hofmann bomb scene. The scrap of paper from Waldenbooks in Crossroads Mall placed Hofmann near his and Ashworth's favorite meeting place on the day they usually met only minutes before Hofmann returned to his car and was injured by a bomb. Ashworth stared at the receipt—*had* the third bomb been for him?

D'Elia, Stott, Farnsworth, and Bell were not convinced that Ashworth was the third target. But all of them saw Ashworth's value to the case. They asked him to go through the evidence removed from Hofmann's home and car, a jigsaw puzzle turned upside down into thirty boxes. If Ashworth could not put the puzzle together, at least he might recognize a few of the separate pieces. Since he was an attorney who had once been a prosecutor, he also understood the problems of pre-trial publicity and evidence leaks.

During lunch one day as Ashworth sifted though the evidence and listened to Farnsworth ruminate about all the reluctant informants in the case, he said, "Ken, give me your opinion of me."

Farnsworth grinned, looked him over. "I think you're honest."

"That's nice to hear."

"I see you as a bragger-collector. You want to own the best and most important things in Mormon history. But that's okay if that's your interest. Hell, why not?"

"Well, you're right," Ashworth conceded. "That's all true."

As he picked through the boxes of papers seized from Hofmann's home, Ashworth gradually became convinced that Hofmann was involved in intentional fraud. One day, for example, Ashworth came across an unsigned note that said "Livingston-Kincaid." He recognized it because he had purchased a note like it, except that his had been signed with Jim

Bridger's "X" and then co-signed. This note had "Mike Hansen" printed at the bottom. Ashworth recalled that Hofmann had once shown him a sketch of the note, drawn in ink and pencil.

Some days Ashworth could still convince himself that, despite any dishonesty, Mark was simply not a mad bomber. Still, Ashworth knew from the police that an M. Hansen had bought bomb parts. Gradually, he decided that Mike Hansen was a part of Mark Hofmann he hoped never to meet.

Thus when Dori Hofmann called Charlene Ashworth in December to express their sympathy concerning Sammy's accident, both Brent and Charlene were uneasy. On the telephone, Charlene thanked her for calling, adding, "You've had a terrible tragedy in your family, too."

"Well, it would be a lot worse if I didn't know that Mark is innocent," Dori said. She went on to defend her husband, explaining that she knew he was at home at the time of the bombings. "He's just like Joseph Smith, being prosecuted for righteousness' sake." Charlene noted that Dori had substituted the word prosecuted for the usual "persecuted" applied to Joseph Smith, but let the slip pass. In fact, Charlene said little, for she knew that Brent had serious doubts now about the authenticity of his Hofmann documents. But when Dori added, "Mark is just such an honest person," Charlene withdrew completely from the conversation. She had seen their family life repeatedly upset over the years because of her husband's deals with Hofmann. She had tried without success to keep Brent from buying documents from Mark, but she could not tell that to Dori.

Other friends of the Hofmanns' also struggled with mixed feelings. One morning Hofmann came into the Deseret Book store in the ZCMI mall. He was in a wheelchair with his wife pushing him, and Shannon Flynn in tow.

"You look better, Mark," Curt Bench said.

Hofmann gave him some money on a private investment apart from Hofmann's dealings with Deseret Book. "Thanks for taking care of this, Mark. I know things are rough financially."

"I take care of my friends first," he told Bench.

Bench later noted that comment in his journal, adding, "I have to agree. He does take care of his friends first."

Wade Lillywhite was also glad to see the Hofmanns, and he promised to bring by his wife, Kimberly, and their baby, whom the Hofmanns had not seen.

"Mark's either innocent or he believes he is," Lillywhite told Kim on the way to Haus Hofmann. "I want you to see for yourself." Again, Lillywhite left the Hofmanns feeling satisfied and awaited his wife's confirmation. But no sooner had the door shut behind her than Kimberly Lillywhite looked up at her husband. "He's guilty as sin."

"What are you talking about?"

"I just felt darkness and evil in there. It was overwhelming." Lillywhite didn't know whether to feel amused or alarmed. Aside from the ramifications of the murders, Hofmann had brought hundreds of items to Deseret Book, selling them below value, much to the benefit of the rare books department. Lillywhite and Bench had run the department with the highest profits in Deseret Book's system of twelve stores and had won the praise of their superiors, largely due to Hofmann's documents.

Whatever documents were in question, thought Bill Flynn flying into Salt Lake City, he ought to be able to help Throckmorton wrap up the Hofmann case and be home again in a couple of days. Flynn was on the executive committee of the Southwestern Association of Forensic Document Examiners and had known Throckmorton for several years. He knew nothing about Mormonism and only a little about the bombings.

Throckmorton had prepared for the examination in a small office behind the archives search room on the second floor of the Church Office Building. Church officials had installed a lock on the room but still required that the LDS-owned documents be returned to the safe each night. Irked by this mistrust, Throckmorton in turn refused to have church employees present during the tests, and each evening he put the other documents inside his locked briefcase and handcuffed the briefcase to an overhead sprinkling pipe.

On December 17, the two forensic examiners went down into the hall behind the search room and unlocked the door. In this Mormon stronghold, Flynn felt like an outsider. For the next two hours Throckmorton explained his suspicions, as Flynn quietly concluded that Throckmorton's position in the case juxtaposed two of the most important things in his life — his profession and his religion. Professionally, Flynn could already see, this case had enormous implications, even though Throckmorton's information was fragmented. Flynn told Throckmorton he was glad to be aboard. "I'll pay my own way back to Salt Lake the next time if I have to," he said.

They went to the video spectral compactor and began the first test under infrared light, to check for alterations or abnormalities. They had the documents Dean Jessee had identified as coming from Hofmann in one pile and a control group with known provenances in another. The infrared did not show any erasures or alterations in the handwriting. Flynn moved on to ultraviolet light, and Throckmorton began arranging handwriting samples.

Flynn had expected the forger to show his hand rather early with either anomalies or anachronisms. An anomaly, such as an artificial whitener on the paper, would show that the document was forged because no such whiteners were used in the nineteenth century. An anachronism, such as the use of a word before it was coined, would likewise reveal forgery. But the Hofmann documents showed no such signs, nor any visible alterations.

Flynn decided he had been overconfident. This forger, if there were a forger, was going to provide an intellectual challenge — to say the least.

"George," Flynn said, "what do you think about this?"

Throckmorton took a look. Flynn had the Joseph Smith letter to Maria and Sarah Lawrence, two sisters he was supposed to have married polygamously. Under ultraviolet light, the ink appeared to be running in one direction, rather than haloing out evenly as it aged. Flynn moved on to the Thomas Bullock handwriting on the Joseph Smith III blessing and saw a similar phenomenon.

RLDS Church Historian Richard Howard had brought three documents to Salt Lake City from Independence, Missouri, and was spending the day in the search room while Throckmorton and Flynn examined them. One, the Joseph Smith III blessing, was extremely important to the RLDS church because in it RLDS tradition was confirmed as Joseph Smith promised his son succession to the church presidency. Howard had received the blessing for the RLDS church in a trade from the LDS church after both had become involved in a messy transaction with Hofmann in 1981.

Mike George came to Howard at the end of the day and told him the Joseph Smith III blessing would have to stay in Salt Lake City for the time being. George gave Howard the two Carthage Jail letters he had also brought — which seemed to have nothing to do with Hofmann.

As Flynn and Throckmorton continued the examination, not only did the ink on the Hofmann documents appear to have run in one direction, but there appeared to be more bleed-through onto the other side of the paper than was usual. Neither was known to indicate forgery — still, they were intriguing.

Throckmorton placed the Joseph Smith III blessing under the microscope to take a closer look at the tiny script. As the ink was magnified sixty times, he noticed that it was cracked, like alligator skin.

"What about this cracking?" he asked Flynn, who came over.

"I don't know." Flynn reached for another document and put it under the microscope. The cracking was emphatic on some documents when magnified, much less on others. Usually, such cracking appeared only under much greater magnification.

The hour was growing late when the first break in the examination came. Just before closing, Throckmorton suggested a game of serious intent. "You hand me a document and I'll tell you which ones are from Mark."

"You're on." Flynn handed him one.

"This is from Mark."

"Right." He gave him another.

"This isn't."

"Right."

They continued with Throckmorton "guessing" right each time until he pronounced one document from Hofmann and

Flynn said no. Throckmorton noted which paper it was. Then it happened again. He made note of that, too. The rest he guessed correctly. Before leaving, Throckmorton asked Glenn Rowe, the church archivist, to check the origin of the two documents that he had guessed wrong.

"I'm going to go look up ink cracking," Throckmorton said as he dropped Flynn at his motel that night. Throckmorton did and found only that cracking was a characteristic of old ink. The next morning, back at the Church Office Building, he told Flynn, "The cracked ink may not be important."

Still, both men were encouraged that they could recognize Hofmann documents without looking at the identifying tags. Glenn Rowe knocked at the door, and Throckmorton stepped outside. "I'm sorry, we made a mistake," Rowe told him. "Those two documents you asked about did come through Mark Hofmann. Somehow we lost the provenance in the filing system. I hope it didn't cause you any trouble."

"No trouble," Throckmorton said, "thanks." Heartened, Throckmorton and Flynn kept working. By the end of the second day they were confident that the pronounced pattern of ink cracking on the questioned documents and the uni-directional running of the ink were unique to Hofmann documents. That knowledge would not do them any good in court, however, until they knew what had caused the phenomena and what they meant. Still, it was a beginning.

That afternoon Throckmorton and Flynn had visitors: Gerry D'Elia, Mike George, and Dick Forbes. As he entered the room, D'Elia threw open his trenchcoat, revealing a green letterman's jacket without the letter. Startled, Throckmorton whistled, "Is that *it*?" then explained the joke to a bemused Flynn."

Excitedly, Throckmorton and Flynn reviewed their observations. D'Elia could see they were onto a convincing motive for murder. Ever since Bob Stott had come on the case, D'Elia had taken an increasingly aggressive stance to balance Stott's conservatism.

"You've got it," he told Throckmorton and Flynn. "That's enough for me to file charges." By the preliminary hearing, D'Elia figured, the experts would be ready.

As 5:00 p.m. approached, Throckmorton and Flynn gathered up their equipment and notes, then returned the documents and cleared out of the office. The following morning they met with Ted Cannon and the bombings team at the county attorney's office and told them what they had found.

"Documents—true or false?" Cannon had asked in his daytimer. False, the forensic analysts were telling him now, but only in private. Their own reputations were riding on their testimonies, and the double-murder motive might depend on their suspicions.

"If you'll work on the cracking, I'll find out what can make ink run like that—deacidification or whatever," Throckmorton said as he drove Flynn to the Salt Lake International Airport.

Virtually unobserved by the bombings team at the CAO and the SLCPD, Christmas had come to Salt Lake City. The city glittered, particularly Temple Square, with thousands of tiny lights hung on trees. Off-beat downtown stores such as Cosmic Aeroplane were selling glossy red gift paper adorned with stylized white salamanders—amusing, except for the bombings.

The Sheetses, like the Christensens, were in mourning, but grief over Kathy's death was not their only torment. Sheets's company, CFS, was in its last death throes, and its failure would ruin the financial base of three Sheets families—Gary Sheets, with Gretchen and Jim still at home; Roger and Heidi Jones; and Joe and Katie Robertson. Sheets was no longer bishop. He had resisted giving up the position, but after KSL-TV ran an investigative story on CFS, a story Sheets believed misrepresented several facts, he decided that his calling might embarrass the Mormon church and asked to be released. Meanwhile, an FBI investigation of CFS was continuing, and lawsuits and prosecution loomed ominously. Following the public release of Hofmann's polygraph test results, rumors about Sheets had mushroomed and CFS investors were hit with serious losses.

Only gradually did Sheets begin to absorb the extent of his losses personally and professionally. As realization enveloped him, so did a growing depression. One day as Katie Robertson cleaned the family home, she heard a door shut. Her father was home. Red eyes hinted that he had been crying.

She knew that he had needed an exorbitant amount of sleep lately, and she sighed, thinking that he was probably heading for the bedroom. Her mother had always kept the shades up, never satisfied with the amount of light that filtered into the room from outside. Her father, though, kept the shades down and on especially bad days did not bother to make the bed.

"You okay?" she asked, as Gary avoided her gaze and poked his head and shoulders into the refrigerator.

"Sure. Fine."

Robertson, a woman more petite than her mother had been and growing even thinner, put down her cleaning cloth and walked over to him.

"Dad, I don't care if you cry. It's okay to cry."

He turned, almost falling into her arms, and wept for a long time.

The Sheets, like the other survivors, found the public interest in the bombings a problem. Everyone, it seemed, had their own opinion which they did not mind voicing. Yet few seemed able to comprehend the grim everyday heartbreak the families woke to each morning. One day a sheriff's deputy returned to Katie Robertson her mother's watch and wedding ring. The family had searched the walkway and creek after the bombings and questioned the woman who found their mother regarding the position of her hand and arm, but the jewelry seemed to have disappeared entirely. Later they heard that the watch and ring had been recovered during the autopsy. The vacuum following the blast had sucked them into the gaping wound in Kathy Sheets's torso.

Katie Robertson opened the sack and took out the jewelry. In places, it was still crusted with her mother's blood. Her sister, Heidi Jones, took the watch and put it away, just as it was. Robertson decided to take the ring to a jeweler's and have it cleaned. When she handed it over the counter the jeweler looked at it and cooed, "Have you been doing some antiquing, dear?" She could find no adequate reply.

Brent and Charlene Ashworth divided the holiday season

between their home, ward, and Sammy's hospital room. Slowly he was emerging from his coma, and though he was paralyzed and blind, his main body functions like breathing and digestion appeared to be intact. They were hoping to bring him home after the first of the year, but they knew that their son was forever changed.

One afternoon, while presiding over a sacrament meeting, Ashworth thought through his troubles and found himself overwhelmed. He had bought such wonderful documents from Hofmann, taken them to the church, spoken about them to thousands of church members, appeared with them in church publications, borne testimony to the events they witnessed — and now, he knew from his contacts with investigators, they might be forgeries. He had brought Hofmann into his home, let Hofmann upset his family.

Worst of all was seeing Samuel in a hospital bed and feeling that his own hobby had indirectly caused his son's accident. If he had not been involved with Hofmann, Ashworth reasoned, he and Charlene would not have gone to California and Sammy would not have been riding his bike on Sunday.

Ashworth left the meeting, went to his office, shut the door, and called David Biggs. "David," he said, "here's one bishop in Utah who wishes he could trade places with Steve Christensen."

Mark and Doralee Hofmann's extended families rallied to their support. The year's final months had been horrifying and traumatic, but they were grateful for Mark's life and convinced that he would be vindicated of the charges against him. Mark was well enough to attend the usual family Christmas parties. Bill and Lucille Hofmann had raised Mark and his sisters, Heidi and Jody, in the house Mark and Dori were buying on Marie Avenue. The neighborhood was close-knit and mostly Mormon. Many people remembered Mark as a child and repaid years of the Hofmanns' kindnesses by supporting the family in their current trouble.

The evening of the Garden Heights South Ward Christmas party, several of Hofmann's friends went to the Hofmann home to help wheel Mark out to his van. In a few minutes, the

Hofmann family entered the church cultural hall, crowded with ward members of all ages. Dinner was followed by a program, and people visited with one another before, during, and after the planned events. Throughout, Hofmann sat near the back of the hall in his wheelchair, his baby daughter on his lap, answering greetings and comments cordially. Mark was not much on small talk, ward members knew, but anyone could see the poor guy was not a bomber.

Terri Christensen took her boys and went to her parents' Montana ranch for the holidays. The months since the bombings had been terrible, particularly the weekends when she was used to having Steve at home. Monday became her favorite day of the week; Friday the most dreaded, for then the empty weekend stretched ahead of her.

Terri, like Steve, was the oldest of eight children. Her sisters rotated spending days and evenings with her to help with the children and lend emotional support. It helped, but not enough. She spent many days alone at home weeping while her boys went to school and preschool. The best times were when the detectives visited to discuss the case, linking her to Steve. She was learning about areas of Steve's life he had never shared. Another bright spot was Don Tanner, one of Steve's best friends and a former missionary companion, who lived in their ward and arranged to be their monthly "home teacher." "I'd like to tell the boys stories about their dad so they won't forget him," he told her. She agreed, listening to stories about her husband's pranks, good deeds, problems, and triumphs.

Once she caught Tanner alone and asked, "Did Steve talk to you a lot about his feelings and what was going on inside him?"

"No, not much." She nodded, relieved, then confessed her worry that he had been sharing his intimate feelings elsewhere. With her, Steve had usually given the impression that everything was under control. She struggled to understand the pressure he had felt.

At night when the boys were in bed, she could retreat to her own bed with her books on death and grieving. She knew she had a process to go through and was determined to grieve now and get it done. Curled in bed with a book propped before her, she was haunted by the thought of how proud Steve would be of her now that she was doing so much reading. He was the one who always had a book in hand, at his desk in the family room, in the car as they vacationed with friends, once even when they went to the symphony. (She had let him know the last was unacceptable, and he never did it again.)

Despite the self-help books and the kindnesses of family members and friends, she spent those early months despairing. As the child within her grew, she dreaded the birth. "Steve's the only one who can help me now," she told herself often, "and Steve's not here."

After Christmas when they returned to Salt Lake City, Terri looked forward to January 9, 1986, with a double sense of dread. That day, which would have been Steve's thirty-second birthday, was the day she had chosen to give birth. She'd had all her children by Caesarean section, and she wanted this last child of Steve's to be born on his birthday.

When the day came, her mother stayed with her during surgery, and she was more comfortable than usual and delighted by the sight of her son. She and Steve had selected the name Jacob to go with Joshua, Justin, and Jeremy, but she broke tradition and named the baby Steven.

Visitors commented that the infant looked like his father. His eyes were dark like Terri's, but, like Steve's, they were almost too large for the sockets and oddly wise. "He looks just like his dad," Steve's friends teased in Terri's hospital room. "He even has bags under his eyes."

The immediacy of her baby's needs focused Terri's attention firmly on the present. As she recovered and began caring for her baby, she found herself happy, even interested at times. She noticed for the first time how much help and support others were giving her, and she was grateful. Steve was gone, she was still alive. Now she realized how much she wanted to live.

6

THIS CASE IS MADE
IN THE SHADE

The Salt Lake City bombings investigation entered 1986 under increasing pressure from law enforcement and the media for charges against Hofmann — or someone. The murders that had seemed so near resolution within hours or days of the homicides now appeared to be in a state of confused irresolution. Although law enforcement officers tried to maintain a calm public posture, behind the scenes, the pace was relentless.

Bill Flynn, in Phoenix, polled forensic document examiners throughout the United States by telephone and letter. They sent him photocopies of tests and articles, but none had seen anything related specifically to cracked ink or uni-directional running under ultraviolet light. Between experiments, Flynn read, questioned, and compared notes with George Throckmorton. Flynn knew the Salt Lake authorities wanted Hofmann charged soon and that the case could be in court within ten days after that unless Hofmann was not released on bail. If he was, they would have a little more time.

Early in January, Throckmorton sorted through the Hofmann evidence spread out in the police firing range. The room was also full of file cabinets and boxes from Christensen's office. At the end of the range in the dirt where spent bullet shells normally fell were the contents of Hofmann's blasted car.

Ken Farnsworth stayed with Throckmorton as he sorted through the evidence. The CAO was unhappy with

Throckmorton because of an article that had appeared in the December issue of *Utah Holiday* magazine. The article highlighted Throckmorton's suspicions of the Hofmann documents, including his controversial opinion that the documents had never been authenticated by an expert with appropriate credentials. Throckmorton had not talked to reporters since coming on the case, but that was not redemption at the CAO for past indiscretions.

Down in the shooting range, Throckmorton had a gripe of his own. The wet documents from the trunk and back seat of Hofmann's car had been laid out on the dirt to dry. "Geez, Kenny," he objected, "I can't tell what was burned and what's just dirty."

He spent a few hours sifting through the papers on the ground, then began on the boxes. There were hundreds of documents from the trunk bearing the name McMillan. Disguised by fire and water damage, was this supposed to have been a fake McLellin collection?

Throckmorton observed some signed Butch Cassidy photographs and saw photocopies of minutes of meetings of the Council of the Twelve Apostles from the early 1960s. He also found a photocopy of a letter from former church president David O. McKay stating that church members could drink decaffeinated coffee without violating the church's health code, the Word of Wisdom. (Later, Throckmorton was amused to find a photocopy of the letter mounted above the coffeepot in Dick Forbes's office.) Throckmorton was also interested in the hundreds of typewritten letters bearing the letterhead of former Mormon president Heber J. Grant, each addressed to a different correspondent.

Throckmorton rotated between the attorney general's office, the SLCPD, the CAO, and an office he had opened at the state crime lab. His research slowly eliminated deacidification or other standard treatments as a cause for the ink peculiarities on the Hofmann documents, but the news from Phoenix was not good. Flynn had not been able to find any discussion at all of cracked ink, nor had he been able to reproduce the phenomenon.

One day church archivist Glenn Rowe drove to the state crime lab to hand Throckmorton two letters. The newer letter, typed on First Presidency letterhead, indicated that church leaders had searched their vaults, including the First Presidency's, and had found only one other letter which had come from Hofmann and which they were now attaching. "This is all we have," they essentially informed Throckmorton.

The document was an 1865 letter from Thomas Bullock, an early church historian, to Brigham Young. Throckmorton knew Bullock's name. He had been the scribe for the Joseph Smith III blessing, which Richard Howard had brought to Salt Lake City from the RLDS church. The Bullock letter informed Young that Bullock was refusing to send Young the blessing. Because the letter had been kept in the First Presidency's vault, Throckmorton knew it was controversial. Anxious to see how this additional Bullock item looked under a microscope, he took the letter into the lab and found what he expected: the secret Bullock letter looked like all the other Hofmann documents.

Flynn returned to Utah on Thursday, January 9, bringing with him homemade inks. He and Throckmorton worked at the state crime lab for the next two days trying to discover the forger's recipe. By now, Flynn could not help but be impressed with Hofmann's skill. On Monday, when Flynn and Throckmorton reported to the CAO they still had not solved the puzzle of the ink. They could get their own old ink formula to crack slightly—but not enough or in the right pattern to call the Hofmann documents forgeries in court.

After Flynn returned to Phoenix, Throckmorton went back to the SLCPD evidence room. He thumbed through Charles Hamilton's *Great Forgers and Famous Fakes*, which had been taken from Hofmann's basement, and found a formula for iron gall ink, common in the nineteenth century. A hunch growing, he took the book and got on the telephone to Flynn.

Flynn, also, had rummaged through the evidence one day in December. Talking with Throckmorton now, disparate items began to make sense. He had seen sodium hydroxide among the evidence but had not known its purpose. He remembered reading that ammonia could artificially age ink by dramatically speeding its oxidation. Perhaps sodium hydroxide produced a similar effect. He had also seen Hofmann's copy of Hamilton's book but had not tested any of the old ink formulas it contained.

"This book was in Hofmann's possession," Throckmorton suggested with a cop's logic, "not in a library somewhere. This ink formula has to be it."

"I'll give it a try," Flynn responded. "I'll be in touch."

David Biggs began the new year by contracting a virulent case of flu and missing several days of work. About 10:30 the night of January 13, Ted Cannon called. "I've got to have you here tomorrow," Cannon insisted.

Biggs knew the pressures regarding the Hofmann case, but he had more immediate concerns. "Ted, I really can't get too far away from the porcelain facility. I'm sick."

"I don't care if we have to bring in a bed for you. I've got to have you here."

"Okay, Ted. See you tomorrow."

Cannon and the attorneys met in the fifth floor war room the next morning. Charts marking Hofmann's movements, financial dealings, and documents ringed the walls. With weary determination, they all sat down at the long table and began discussing the case. As usual, Cannon wrote lists and acted as moderator. Stott and D'Elia evaluated the case, countering strengths and weaknesses. Biggs pushed two chairs together, lay down, and listened. At lunch, they broke.

Bob Stott followed Biggs back to his office and shut the door. "You know why you're here, don't you?"

"No, I don't know why Ted dragged me out of my sickbed to be here."

"Ted wants charges filed. Gerry will go for it."

Biggs said nothing. He and D'Elia had been a team from the start.

"I don't think the case is ready," Stott added. "I want you to side with me."

Biggs sighed. He was always the swing vote between D'Elia and Stott. "Well, I don't know what else the investigators are going to get," he reasoned.

"Why don't we send Forbes and George back east to secure document witnesses? Flynn and Throckmorton are still tentative on the ink, at least until they can reproduce the cracking. We've got to bring around Charles Hamilton and Kenneth Rendell. You know the press will go to them as the great experts. We can't afford to have them against us." A pause. "I want you to side with me," Stott said again.

"Why should I do that?"

"Because we need more. You know that Ted won't let D'Elia issue the case alone."

Biggs nodded. "I'll think about it."

That afternoon Cannon brought up the subject of filing charges. Stott immediately suggested they send Forbes and George back to talk with Rendell and Hamilton, as well as break down the provenance on certain documents. D'Elia, who had been pushing since early December to file charges, brought the discussion back to Cannon's question. He figured they could file charges and then bring in the evidence Stott wanted. "Ted, if you want the case issued, I'll issue it," D'Elia said. The power struggle lay exposed. Stott had been Cannon's choice, but Stott would not file and Cannon was ready. D'Elia had been on the case from the first and was willing to file but did not have Stott's reputation and experience.

Flat on his improvised couch, Biggs made his decision. He sided with Stott but made it sound like a compromise not a vote. They would send the investigators back east and wrap things up as soon as possible — then, as Cannon put it, "get the damn show on the road."

Cannon, gathering his papers to leave, assumed his most jovial manner in referring to the vote that had not happened. "Biggs, I don't know why the hell I asked you to come in here," he said. "You've crossed me once now. Don't ever cross me again."

D'Elia could read that comment easily. He caught Cannon alone. D'Elia understood the police department's outrage with the delay and knew that it bothered Cannon. "Ted," he said, "let me take the case. I can take the pressure. I feel confident with the case."

He could see Cannon considering his words. "Ted, I've got three balls. One was shot off in Vietnam, but I've still got an extra one."

Cannon cracked up. "Yeah, that's right, D'Elia. You're a fighter. Okay, Stott's got one week, and then if he doesn't file, you will."

D'Elia, who had never been to Vietnam, went to see Stott. "Okay, Bob, what do you want?" He sat down, and they planned the trip back East.

The next day, January 15, before the investigators left, Flynn called Throckmorton. "That's the formula, George," he announced. "I'm getting results!"

Flynn had a difficult time translating old terminology like "Roman vitrol" into iron sulfate and finding additives like gum arabic to give the acidic, homemade product some viscosity. He had followed the formula in Hamilton's book, then added gum arabic as suggested in an old book on ink, and applied chemicals to age the ink. When he placed the ink sample under a microscope he saw what he had seen in the Church Office Building: ink that cracked like alligator skin.

Triumphantly, Throckmorton held an open house at the state crime lab for a very select group—the bombings team. The prosecutors, investigators, and detectives listened closely as he explained the anomalies they had found on the Hofmann documents and how their reproduction of those anomalies indicated forgery. He had some litmus paper out to test whether documents had been deacidified and explained that he had determined that deacidification played no part in the ink anomalies.

Throckmorton got home in time to hear the evening news that night, which included a story that he had developed "a litmus test for forgery." Obviously some erroneous information had reached the media. Historians and archivists who knew that deacidification was used routinely to keep aging ink from eating through paper found the report patently absurd.

After the demonstration at the crime lab, Farnsworth left with an idea. Police had taken from Hofmann's home some very nice, full leather-bound first editions of Dean Jessee's book, *The Personal Writings of Joseph Smith*. Farnsworth had been careful to see that they not get damaged. Guessing that Jessee's book had to have reproductions of at least several Hofmann originals—maybe more—Farnsworth decided he would like a copy for his own library.

He called Curt Bench at Deseret Book and asked if he could find one of the first leather-bound edition.

"That's a $110 book."

"Well, I know, but I want it. Get the lowest serial number you can."

"Gee, I don't know if we even have one on the shelf," Bench said. "I'll see what I can do."

Farnsworth swung by the ZCMI Mall and headed for the downstairs rare books department at Deseret Book. This department had really grown during the last few years. He wondered how many Hofmanns had been sold.

He found Bench. "Here's your copy."

Farnsworth took a look at the volume; the serial number read 31. "This is amazing. How come you could get this?"

"That was Steve Christensen's copy."

"What? You're kidding."

Bench shrugged. "He couldn't afford to have more than one copy any more, so late last summer he turned this one in."

Farnsworth paid for the book and walked away, still shaking his head. Now he had an expensive rare book, eventually a collector's item, containing forgeries by the man he was determined to put in prison; and the book had been owned by the man whose murder he had sworn to solve.

When he told Terri Christensen about the purchase, her surprise held a different irony. "My husband gave up a *book*? That's news to me!"

D'Elia arranged to meet Dick Forbes and Mike George in New York on Monday, January 27, to help them "talk to those New York boys." The two investigators, who took an early flight east, had time to play tourist at the sites of Mormonism's birth. They rented a car and drove to the Hill Cumorah, where the Angel Moroni repeatedly led Joseph Smith to the gold plates. After a trip to the visitors' center, run by the LDS church, they drove to the top of the hill.

Before they left, Forbes got out of the car to take a photograph. He climbed a little knoll, clicked the camera, then jogged back to the car. Jumping over a bit of snow in the parking lot, he came down hard on the ice and heard three cracks in his ankle as he landed. Sprawled on the frigid pavement, he waited painfully for George to get out of the car and help.

George felt that this mishap called for a religious interpretation. "You notice," he said, hoisting Forbes into the car, "that these salamanders don't go after Catholic boys."

George drove to a hospital in Newark, New York, and helped Forbes into the emergency room. A television set was tuned to the launch of the Challenger. As the doors shut behind them, the spaceship exploded before their eyes.

While Forbes waited to get his ankle x-rayed and set, George picked up D'Elia, then returned to get Forbes. By the time they got him out of the hospital, the day was gone, and on the way to their hotel they lost his prescription for pain pills. About 1:00 a.m., they settled into a Syracuse hotel for the night.

The next day, D'Elia and George went to New York City to see antiquities expert Charles Hamilton in his 59th Street apartment. They knew that Hamilton had authenticated the letter from Joseph Smith to Josiah Stowell; Hofmann had given Hinckley a letter to that effect. As they expected, Hamilton was charismatic but defensive about his friend, Mark Hofmann.

The Utahns did not make any accusations. Instead, George handed Hamilton the Josiah Stowell letter and asked if he had seen it before.

"Yes, I've seen this before. I authenticated it."

"How much did Mark Hofmann pay you for it?" D'Elia asked.

"He didn't pay me anything for it."

"Don't you know he's telling people he bought it from you?"

"No, he didn't buy it from me."

"He told President Hinckley of the Mormon church that he got it from you."

"Well, that's a big lie," said Hamilton.

"Would you fold that letter for us?" George asked.

Hamilton did, along the folds. The letter sat puffily before them rather than flat and creased like a cover letter that has been sent through the mails.

"Ah, what a stupid son of a bitch," Hamilton said.

George and D'Elia exchanged glances.

"Who?" D'Elia ventured.

"Me, that's who!" Hamilton roared. "This doesn't even fold right."

One by one, D'Elia and George handed Hamilton the other Hofmann documents. By the time they left, Hamilton had reached the hoped-for conclusion. Hofmann was no longer the "sweetest guy, who sat right there with his wife," as Hamilton had described him. He was a rotten sneak who sold fakes.

On Wednesday, despite his broken ankle, Forbes and D'Elia went to Boston to see Kenneth Rendell, the international dealer who had declared the salamander letter authentic and had consigned two papyri to Hofmann. They had not forgotten Rendell's threat to lead a parade of expert witnesses in Hofmann's defense.

D'Elia and Forbes chatted politely, then handed Rendell the Hofmann documents one by one, omitting the salamander letter. Rendell looked through them suspiciously. In a few minutes, he took them into the next room to view them under ultra-violet light. He did not like the bluish cast in the paper. They let him see the salamander letter again. He knew it came from the same source — Hofmann — and that made him uncomfortable, but he still saw no sign of forgery. However, the other documents looked definitely suspicious, he said.

If Forbes had not injured his ankle, he and George would have flown directly to California to find Frances Magee, a previous owner of the Nathan Harris prayer book. But Forbes decided to get his fractured ankle, sore underarms and wrists back home — where further x-rays revealed his ankle required resetting.

George flew alone to Lynville, California, and found the apartment complex where Magee lived. She had owned the Episcopalian *Book of Common Prayer* that Deseret Book had sold to Hofmann. In the back of the book was a handwritten poem that matched the handwriting in the salamander letter, thereby bolstering its apparent authenticity.

George approached Magee as he had Hamilton, letting her draw her own conclusions and, to a degree, solve a portion of the case rather than handing it to her already solved. He preferred that a potential witness or suspect feel a step ahead of him rather than a step behind. He chatted with Magee and her husband about the salamander letter and the case. The Magees were not Mormon, but her first husband had been Mormon and a descendant of Martin Harris, the author of the salamander letter. Her mother-in-law had frequently discussed Mormonism and the family's history with her.

George showed her the prayer book, and she leafed through it. They discussed the signatures in the front of the book, and she explained who the names represented. When she came to the back she pointed to the poem — just as George had hoped — and said, "This wasn't in here."

"How do you know?"

"Poems are a hobby of mine. If this had been here, I'd have written it down and put it in an envelope that I keep in my kitchen."

"How often did you read this book?"

"Oh, I used to read it all the time. I really loved this little book."

"Have you ever heard of the lost 116 pages of the Book of Mormon manuscript?"

"Oh, I know about those! My mother-in-law was a granddaughter of Martin Harris. You see, Martin brought home the manuscript that Joseph had let him take, and Grandma Lucy Harris was so mad at him for helping Joseph and giving him money and everything that she took the manuscript and threw it in the fireplace!"

George listened carefully. He knew that the 116 lost pages of the Book of Mormon, if found, would probably have commanded more than $1 million. "Some people are saying that the suspect was going to find the 116 pages."

"Well, no. That's impossible because Lucy burned them up."

"We don't have much writing from Martin Harris. Do you

see what the value of the 116 pages might be, especially if Martin Harris's handwriting begins to appear."

Magee's eyes sparkled as she began to put that aspect of the case together—the salamander letter, the prayer book with matching handwriting, and the 116 pages, which, long ago, Grandma Lucy Harris reportedly had burned. She agreed to come to Salt Lake City to testify about the prayer book.

As the investigators' successes on the coasts were reported to the team in Salt Lake City, efforts to tie down loose ends intensified.

"There's something I'm looking for," Ken Farnsworth told defense attorney Jim Barber one day over the telephone. Barber's clients Shannon Flynn and Lyn Jacobs had been subpoenaed to testify against their friend and former employer, Mark Hofmann.

"What's that, Kenny?"

Farnsworth described a photocopy of an early nineteenth-century land deed he had that Hugh Pinnock had given him—part of the reputed McLellin collection. The deed was signed at the bottom by Sidney Rigdon, one of Joseph Smith's early followers, and Solomon Spaulding, the author of a manuscript some Mormon critics regarded as a source for the Book of Mormon. If Rigdon and Spaulding had known each other, perhaps Rigdon had acquired Spaulding's unpublished manuscript and made it available to Joseph Smith, who may have drawn material from it to produce the Book of Mormon. The land deed presented ostensible proof that the two knew each other—something Mormons and anti-Mormons had argued about for years.

A little later Barber called him. "Lyn says to look for your land deed at Cosmic Aeroplane book store."

Farnsworth was surprised. He had interviewed Jacobs, who had made his disdain for Farnsworth obvious. At that time, Jacobs had said that he expected Hofmann would repay all his debts and that the McLellin collection would appear, complete with affidavits, journals, Facsimile 2, correspondence, and possibly, Jacobs added, a copy of the Book of Commandments. That interview had yielded little that was useful, but lately George had been working on Jacobs, trying to turn him around.

Farnsworth called Steve Barnett, the rare books man at

Cosmic Aeroplane, and arranged to meet him at the store. Barnett pulled the land deed out of a drawer. He had bought it from Hofmann on September 20, he said, for $400. The two talked a little longer before Farnsworth, satisfied, asked if he could take the document with him. Barnett's testimony ought to be very useful in court, he thought driving back to the station. Hofmann had sold a piece of the supposed $185,000 McLellin collection for a pittance, right under Christensen's and Pinnock's noses. His estimation of Jacobs rose a notch, too.

Once the investigators returned, there was no question that Hofmann would be charged with homicide and forgery. Forbes and Biggs had developed the fraud cases involving the papyri fragments, which Hofmann had offered to various investors. Hofmann had other investments still outstanding, including a Charles Dickens handwritten manuscript, "The Haunted Man," and the "Oath of a Freeman." Some were prosecutable, some were not worth the bother. But prosecutors intended to prove that the papyri had been misrepresented, that the Oath had been forged, and that the Dickens manuscript had never been Hofmann's to sell.

Altogether, the alleged crimes were now spread over a six-year period and involved a variety of victims. Each case, however, had to present a "single criminal episode," meaning that each allegation must be connected to the others. Gradually, the twenty-seven felony charges materializing against Hofmann were grouped into four "informations" or cases.

The attorneys debated how to file the homicide charges. The Sheets homicide had always created a legal difficulty, for there was no motive for Hofmann to kill Gary Sheets, let alone Kathy, except as a diversion to the Christensen murder. The only evidence linking Hofmann to Kathy Sheets were the sightings of both a van and a sports car like his near the Sheetses' residence around the time of her murder and Jerry Taylor's testimony that the bombs had been constructed and delivered by one person. The third bomb was another problem, but they could at least prove Hofmann had a bomb in his car and had lied about the explosion that had injured him. Basically, however, the three bombs depended on the motive for Hofmann to murder Christensen.

Bob Stott liked an ironclad case when he went to court, and even then he prepared for every possible eventuality. He hated losing on any point. "Let's charge the Sheets homicide as a second degree," he suggested to Cannon, Biggs, and D'Elia. "That way we don't risk it pulling down the Christensen homicide."

D'Elia and Biggs recognized the validity of his concern but argued the other side. They believed the Christensen evidence strong enough to carry the other charges. Cannon agreed, partly because the argument fit his own fundamental standard of prosecution—charge crimes where they fit the penal code, try them at that level, and go for the penalty designated for the crime by law.

By the end of January, reporters were buzzing around the county attorney's office, worrying about their deadlines and preparing their stories. They knew charges were imminent.

Farnsworth had a vacation coming but did not want to be gone when they arrested Hofmann. He left his travel schedule with the CAO and SLCPD but checked in with Jim Bell on Sunday night, February 2, just in case.

"It's weird over there," Bell told him, referring to the CAO. "It's weirder than it's ever been. I hate to have you come back early, but I'm 95 percent sure they're going to charge him."

Farnsworth returned early. On Tuesday morning, February 4, the detectives went over to the CAO to find that the State of Utah had filed four felony cases against Mark W. Hofmann. Hofmann had met Yengich that morning and was being booked into jail. They went over to the jail and found him. It was the first time Bell had seen Hofmann, now on crutches, on his feet. "He's a dead ringer for the composite drawing," he told Farnsworth.

The homicide case listed two counts of first-degree murder for the deaths of Steven F. Christensen and Kathleen W. Sheets on October 15, 1985. Each murder charge listed four aggravating circumstances, justifying the capital charge: more than one person had been killed during the criminal episode; the perpetrator had endangered others beside the victim and perpetrator;

the homicide had been committed for pecuniary or other personal gain; and the homicide was committed by means of a bomb. Two second-degree counts of delivering a bomb, and a third-degree count of constructing or possessing a bomb on October 16 followed. Included in the murder case were one count of theft-by-deception—a second-degree felony—in connection with Alvin Rust's investment in the McLellin collection on April 23, 1985, and also four counts of communication fraud. Communication fraud was a new state statute, modeled after federal law, regarding schemes to defraud whether or not money changed hands. The communication frauds involved the bank loan from First Interstate Bank and the proposed sale of the papyri fragments found in Christensen's safe deposit box and in Hofmann's trunk. The murder charges included a recommendation that Hofmann be held without bond.

Another case included eleven counts of theft by deception, second-degree felonies. Here the alleged victims were collector Brent Ashworth, Steven Christensen and Gary Sheets, the Church of Jesus Christ of Latter-day Saints, and Gordon B. Hinckley. The case did not mention forgery, but the conclusion was not difficult to reach, since the dates of the crimes began in April 1980, when the Anthon transcript came to the church, and coincided with the purchase of other major documents, including the January 1983 sale to Hinckley of the Josiah Stowell letter.

The remaining two cases consisted of theft by deception charges and alleged communication frauds, naming Ashworth, Rust, and Deseret Book as victims, as well as Thomas Wilding and Wilford Cardon, investors in Hofmann's Americana documents. (A fifth case involving several printed documents was filed a few weeks later, bringing the total to five cases of thirty-two felony charges against Hofmann.)

The magnitude of the cases kept the press and others scrambling to sort and interpret the charges. Church attorneys soon complained to Ted Cannon that President Hinckley did not appreciate being named as a victim in one of the charges, since he had been acting as an agent for the church. Cannon promised to talk to prosecutors about dropping Hinckley's name from the case. The "probable cause" statement, explaining the reasons for the allegations, was sealed, an action that would be challenged in court the following day by the Society for Professional Journalists, representing the news media. At issue was the public's right to know the crimes Hofmann was charged with in open court versus the defendant's right to an unbiased jury if and when the case went to trial.

Hofmann was arraigned in Fifth Circuit Court that afternoon, Judge Paul Grant presiding. Security officers lined the walls of the packed courtroom as Hofmann, wearing a torn white tee-shirt and blue slacks, swung on crutches through a side door. He kept his eyes on his attorneys, flanking the podium, or on the judge.

Tall, athletic, and devoutly Mormon, Grant easily recognized the appreciative audience in his courtroom. "Are there any normal people here?" he quipped from the bench. "Or just journalists and lawyers?"

Determinedly casual, the defense attorneys raised the subject of a bond hearing, which would determine whether or not Hofmann would remain in jail until the preliminary hearing—mandatory within ten days if the defendant is imprisoned. The defense waived a reading of the charges, and the judge set a bond hearing for 3:00 p.m. the following afternoon. A hearing on releasing the probable cause statement would immediately precede the bond hearing. Within minutes, Hofmann was swinging back out the door to return to jail.

Outside the courtroom, Yengich and Rich met with reporters. "The first thing is to get Mark out of jail," Rich told them.

A reporter asked Yengich about their intended defense. "The defense will be that he's not guilty and we've said that pretty firmly throughout the whole proceedings," Yengich answered. "We don't have to prove nothin'."

If the shotgun approach to filing charges seemed overwhelming to reporters, Yengich saw it as a way of finally dealing with the allegations against his client. "Now we have a framework," he told reporters. "It's the first time that we can match it up with what the facts are. He is not guilty and we will put on evidence. I can assure you, that if we get to that point, evidence will be adduced on Mark's behalf."

"Not guilty of murder?" one reporter pressed. "Or not guilty of theft by deception, forgery, and fraud?"

Yengich looked into television cameras intently. "Not guilty."

The following day an attorney for the Society of Professional Journalists argued for the release of the probable cause statement and Dave Biggs objected. Grant ruled in favor of the press, maintaining that the statement represented only the bare facts in the case and would constitute no great prejudice to the defendant.

With that, the hearing to determine whether or not Hofmann could be released from jail on bond before his preliminary hearing began.

Gerry D'Elia called Ken Farnsworth to the stand to summarize the homicide evidence against Hofmann. Farnsworth began with the Judge Building, describing how Hal and Bruce Passey had ridden up the elevator with a man carrying a package addressed to Steven Christensen on October 15. Such a package was soon seen by Janet McDermott, who had bent to pick it up but then had changed her mind. He then described the scene at Naniloa Drive and mentioned the young boy living next door to the Sheets, who had seen a strange van the night before the bombings. He explained that detectives had later shown the boy photographs of various vans.

"Did he identify a van?" D'Elia asked.

"He named the make and model of each van pictured," Farnsworth said. "When he came to number six, Hofmann's van, he said, 'That is the kind of van I've been telling you about.' "

Either the same or a similar van was sighted later that morning, Farnsworth testified, when another neighbor and her son dropped off the morning newspaper at about 6:00 a.m. She had seen an unfamiliar van enter the Sheetses' driveway and, as she drove back down Naniloa Drive, pull out again. She, too, had identified a vehicle similar to Hofmann's van. A third neighbor had seen a blue sports car like Hofmann's in the area the evening before the bombings.

D'Elia asked Farnsworth about the evidence sent to the ATF lab. Tests showed, Farnsworth testified, that the bombs were in boxes measuring about twelve by twelve by six inches, that they were of similar design and had been built and delivered by the same person. The Christensen bomb, however, had been packed with blunt nails.

At this point, the hearing was recessed until 11:15 the following morning. As reporters filed out of court, they were handed copies of the probable cause statement. Evidently Judge Grant had made up his mind even before the arguments. Grant motioned one veteran reporter to the bench. "The church is involved in this," he said, nodding toward the statement, "so take it easy on the church."

The next morning, the bond hearing continued. Reporters and Hofmann's family and friends gathered outside the courtroom. As Bill Hofmann paced, Dori Hofmann, fine-boned and demure, waited in a tight knot of friends and family. Shannon Flynn rocked on his heels nearby in a three-piece gray suit. Finally, the crowd followed the Hofmanns to the fourth floor courtroom. Again, the press made it a packed house. Yengich, sporting a new haircut, and Rich joined Hofmann at the defense table. D'Elia, Stott, and Biggs sat opposite them. At a nod from Grant, D'Elia quickly finished his questioning of Farnsworth.

Yengich began his cross-examination with the Passeys' identification of Hofmann. The composite drawing Bruce Passey had assisted with, Yengich emphasized, had included a moustache but no eyeglasses.

"Did you interview the Passeys again October 17?" Yengich asked Farnsworth.

"Yes."

"And you showed them a photo array?"

"Yes." Yengich zeroed in. Hadn't these witnesses been shown photographs of Hofmann by the media before they saw the photo lineup?

"Hal Passey had."

"And what was that?"

"A videotape of Mark Hofmann discussing the Anthon Transcript."

"Did Hofmann have a moustache in the video?"

"No, I don't believe so."

Perhaps the photo array had been tainted by the video-tape, Yengich suggested.

He then turned to the topic of the witnesses near the Sheets residence and asked whether a telephone antenna on the back of the van had been noted. No, Farnsworth said. How about a license plate number?

"No."

"Did anyone mention the state on the license plate?"

"No."

Yengich then asked if an expert had examined the hand-writing on the packages.

Yes, Farnsworth said.

"And didn't that expert conclude that it was not Mark Hofmann's?"

"The tests were inconclusive since the sample was not large enough." Yengich asked about differences in the bombs. The first had cement nails, and the others did not, Farnsworth agreed.

"Were there sufficient fragments of the bombs to recover latent prints?"

"Yes, there were."

"Were there any latent prints?"

"No, there were not."

Finally, Yengich brought up the financial problems of CFS and gave the judge a list of CFS investors.

"Hadn't Christensen been with Sheets four or five years as vice president of J. Gary Sheets Associates?"

"Yes, he had."

"And weren't there allegations that investors had connec-tions with people in Nevada who might have been related to financial dealings?"

"There were some Nevada investors."

"Mark Hofmann hadn't invested with CFS, had he?" Yengich asked.

"I have no knowledge of that," Farnsworth said.

Yengich pressed on. "Because of the financial problems at CFS, hadn't there been some acrimony between Sheets and Christensen?"

Yes, Farnsworth said, he had been told there was.

"And wasn't it suggested to you that you investigate CFS and these investors?"

Yengich showed Farnsworth the list of CFS investors. Farnsworth said that most had been interviewed.

"Did you pursue any further investigation of these people?"

"No, that didn't seem to be indicated."

A murmur went through the crowded courtroom.

Next Yengich brought up the probable cause statement filed with the charges. The defendant reportedly had told Jim Bell that when he got into the car a package fell to the floor. He went to grab for it and then there was an explosion. However, witnesses said Hofmann was in the driver's seat doing something before the explosion, Yengich reviewed. He then argued that one witness had seen Hofmann only after he was blown out of the car, according to police reports. What about that inconsistency?

Farnsworth said that the witness had later changed her mind and now recalled that Hofmann had been "humped over" in the driver's seat.

"That interview was not provided to defense counsel," Yengich protested.

On redirect examination, D'Elia allowed Farnsworth to elaborate. The witness, Farnsworth said, had seen a man walking west and enter a vehicle. The man appeared to be kneeling on the seat moving items in a frantic manner on the passenger side. When the vehicle blew up, the witness saw Hofmann blown out of his car. Another witness saw a man moving packages, then looked away until after the explosion.

D'Elia allowed Farnsworth to reinforce his testimony regarding CFS and the inconclusive report on the handwriting, then summed up. He told Grant that the evidence encapsulated weeks of investigation and hundreds of witnesses and was an indication of what the state would present at the preliminary hearing. He concluded, "We have met our burden of proof, Your Honor. We ask that the defendant be held without bond, as the court sees fit."

Yengich summed up next for the defense. "All persons shall be bailable, Your Honor," he said, "as a constitutional right, unless there is strong evidence that cannot be based on hearsay." He reminded the judge that his client was presumed innocent and that no reasonable hypothesis suggested otherwise. "Thus the prosecution has not met its burden in presenting a clear and convincing case. This is a circumstantial case at best," he said. "It is not convincing, nor is the evidence strong.

"A motive has not been given," he further argued. "Though it's not required at this hearing, it still is needed with circumstantial evidence."

When Yengich finished, D'Elia, bearing the burden of proof, had the last word. "If we start on motive, Your Honor, we'll be here for three weeks," he began. Rebutting Yengich's points, he returned to the eyewitness identifications. He handed the composite sketch to the judge. "If you take off the glasses," he said, "and the moustache, the double chin is there, the mouth and nose are about the same, the piece of hair falling down with a kind of cowlick—that's not a bad likeness."

Every eye turned toward Hofmann. A lock of hair fell across his forehead. He did not touch it. His eyeglasses were on. Then all eyes turned toward the judge. Was this a case of mistaken identity after all? Was a hapless citizen being mistaken for a murderer?

"Inasmuch as this is one of the more important decisions for me personally," Grant announced, "I'll not give a decision now but mull this over and contact counsel later today." Court adjourned.

Paul Grant would later say he had not been eager to take the Hofmann case in the first place. He was an experienced judge, who thought notoriety more likely to cost him his reputation than make it. Because he was Mormon, he had asked Yengich in a conference before the hearing if he preferred a judge who was non-Mormon or at least inactive. "No," Yengich said, "we'll trust your impartiality."

Now he had to decide whether or not to release a young man with no criminal record, a supportive family, and an injured leg, who was accused of two vicious murders. If Hofmann were free, he could help with his own defense and facilitate the preliminary hearing. Releasing him would give the prosecution more time to prepare their case than if he were locked up. There had been a pretty good shooting match at the bond hearing, Grant decided. He would give Hofmann and his family the benefit of the doubt. But once he set a preliminary hearing date, Grant wanted no postponements.

Later that day Grant released Hofmann on $500,000 bail, of which only 10 percent was required for bond, as negotiated through Pre-Trial Services. Three of Hofmann's aunts offered their property to make bond and insure their nephew's appearance at the preliminary hearing scheduled for April 14, more than two months away.

In the meantime Bob Stott and the CAO investigators tried to secure the cooperation of all conceivable witnesses before the case went to the preliminary hearing, let alone to trial. They did not expect the defense to introduce witnesses at the preliminary hearing, which would only determine if the evidence justified a trial. But Stott, particularly, wanted the CAO's case built like a bastion.

About two weeks after charges were filed, A. J. Simmonds opened his office door at Utah State University special collections to Mike George and Dick Forbes. The three men sat down, and lighting the first of many cigarettes during the interview, Simmonds began answering their questions.

They took notes furiously as Simmonds described Hofmann bringing in the Bible with the Anthon Transcript glued inside it, Simmonds's own excitement, and his efforts to remove and open the document. He told them he still thought the transcript was genuine. "The one damn thing that really tipped me on the Anthon was that in the word 'caractors,' it was misspelled the same way on the Whitmer transcript. But on the Anthon, someone had inserted an H very lightly after the C in very pale ink above. It was very interesting. You'd miss it if you didn't look for it."

He mentioned the peculiar adhesive, so old it was brittle. "Do you have any samples of it?"

"I might still have a few flakes around somewhere. I'd have to look."

After about forty-five minutes, Forbes heaved his heavy leg cast up on to the desk, leaned back, and said, "Now what do you know about the letter to the Lawrence sisters?"

Simmonds was stunned that the investigators knew about the letter linking Joseph Smith directly to the early practice of polygamy. Simmonds described how Hofmann had brought it in and how he had doubted its authenticity. Grudgingly, Simmonds complimented the investigators on their expertise.

"We've had a real crash course," George told him.

They discussed other documents, including a fragment of the original handwritten Book of Mormon manuscript, for which Simmonds had traded Hofmann a first edition Hawaiian translation of the Book of Mormon. Hofmann had said the Book of Mormon was for Lyn Jacobs. Simmonds showed them the fragment, encased in plastic.

The investigators told him that just before the bombings Lyn Jacobs had put up his entire collection of first editions as collateral on one of Hofmann's deals and had subsequently lost it to foreclosure. "So your Hawaiian is gone," Forbes summed up.

They asked if Simmonds had ever seen a Livingston- Kincaid note. Simmonds did not think so but checked a couple of sources. He handed the investigators a Deseret Currency Ledger Book in which the serial numbers on early Mormon money had been registered. "Mark photocopied a portion of that. You probably found the photocopies in his basement."

The investigators looked through it curiously. "Look at that," one said to the other, pointing at a type of printing. Simmonds felt nervous and offered to let them take the journal back to Salt Lake City.

Forbes wrote out a receipt. "I think you should know," Forbes said, "that we've checked over 600 documents, not eleven. We laid them out, one after another, and we could see the progression in the forgeries. This is the finest forgery operation we've ever seen, but the Hofmann documents are all forgeries."

Simmonds nodded toward the encased fragment of the Book of Mormon. "And what do I have here? A Mark Hofmann original?"

"I would suspect," George said.

Simmonds did not want to believe it. "I don't know," he mused, "when I first knew Mark in 1979 or 1980 when he was in this office, he was just a kid. Sort of a slob."

"He's still a slob," George said, thinking of the basement room. As they stood to leave, George asked, "Well, Mr. Simmonds, what have we overlooked?"

"Well, to begin with, the defense will call every Mormon historian and they all have their reputations on the line. Leonard Arrington is going to outweigh any three chemists."

"Thank you for your time, Mr. Simmonds," Forbes said.

"Thank you, I think, but you two certainly don't bring a hell of a lot of good news."

"We're not in the good news business," George replied.

"One bit of good news. You were right about the Lawrence Sisters letter," Forbes said.

"It was forged?"

"One of the first."

"Who got stuck with it?"

"The church got it. And you were right about the salamander letter. Two out of three ain't bad."

On President's Day, Detective Jim Bell insisted on organizing the evidence for the preliminary hearing. He and Farnsworth began spreading out items to mark and catalogue on the SLCPD gym floor next to the evidence room. Certain pieces were sure to be used as exhibits, but others might be wanted or needed and they had to be able to put their hands on them quickly.

As they sorted through paper after paper, item after item, Farnsworth picked up a scrap they had puzzled over before. It had come from Hofmann's home and had a list of company names and telephone numbers. One detective had tried to track down the numbers, but they were not local and no prefix was listed.

The name Mike Hansen was on the list, too, and one company, Cocks-Clark Engraving Co., had appeared on another piece of paper. "We've gotta figure this baby out," Farnsworth told Bell. He began reading down the list. "Where is there an Arapahoe Drive and a 25th Street?"

"Sounds like Denver," Bell said.

Farnsworth looked at him. "How do you know that?"

"Oh, I spent some time there. Denver has streets with those names." Farnsworth went to the telephone book, found the Denver prefix, and began calling. Maybe Cocks-Clark Engraving wouldn't be open on a holiday, but luckily someone answered the phone.

"Hi, this is Mike Hansen," Farnsworth said. "I'm having some trouble with my income tax and you people did some work for me. I can't remember exactly when it was, but I think it was in the last year or two. It might have been the 'Oath of a Freeman,' but I'm not sure. It could be something else. How much trouble would it be for you to check through your records and let me know?"

"Oh, that's fine. Where can I reach you, Mr. Hansen?"

"Uh . . . well, I'll tell you what. I'll call you back tomorrow."

The next day Farnsworth eagerly telephoned "Denise" at Cocks-Clark. "Oh yes, Mr. Hansen. I found your order. It was for Deseret Currency." What the hell is Deseret Currency? Farnsworth wondered, as he thanked her and made arrangements for her to send copies of the papers to the police post office box. Farnsworth knew that in Utah there was Deseret Book, Deseret Industries, the *Deseret News*—Deseret everything having to do with the Mormon church. He figured Deseret Currency was bound to be important.

Farnsworth and Bell headed across the street to tell the attorneys and investigators. When they finished, Mike George leaned back in his chair, hands behind his head, and gave Farnsworth a long look. "I think Mark's met his match," he said. "I don't know who's more devious, Mark Hofmann or Ken Farnsworth."

Farnsworth took the comment as high praise. Hot damn, this was going to be fun after all. He and Bell continued checking the other numbers on the Denver list. Some turned out to be taxi companies. The address that "Mike Hansen" had given when he had ordered the Deseret Currency plates was Dori Hofmann's brother's address—with one digit changed. When the paperwork came on Monday, there was a bonus. Mr. Hansen had had two separate plates engraved to print Deseret Currency. The police soon learned that Deseret Currency was money made in pioneer Utah. Hansen had ordered both small and large denominations.

On a hunch, they called Biggs and with another detective went to the Salt Lake Stamp Company. They went through the records and found an order for a personal address stamp for a Mr. Austin Lewis. It had been ordered by Mike Hansen in December 1984. They figured it, too, would fit in somewhere.

"How many companies do engravings like this?" they asked the manager.

"Only two do novelties, DeBouzek and Utah Engraving."

Police had shown mug shots at those shops, but Hofmann and Shannon Flynn had been recognized from media coverage, not because they were remembered as customers. "So they're not going to remember Mark's face," Farnsworth theorized. "We've got to talk to the guy who does the engraving. I'll bet he'd remember his work just because it's something other than invitations."

Thursday Biggs and Farnsworth went to Debouzek Engraving and talked with the owner and the engraver.

"Would you recognize your own work?" Farnsworth asked the engraver.

"Yes."

He handed him a copy of a small document western explorer Jim Bridger was supposed to have signed with an X, plus a copy of the "Oath of a Freeman." The engraver looked at them for a moment, pointed to the Oath, looked back at the officers, and said, "I made that." He brought out the negatives for the Oath and presented them to his excited visitors.

"I've got another one," he added, bringing out the negative for a poem with the same title but a shorter text. He looked up the receipts for both. One was ordered by Mike Hansen, the other by Mike Harris using Mark Hofmann's telephone number. Before the group left, they also had negatives for the table of contents to an early LDS hymnal, edited by Emma Smith, and a negative for an engraving plate with Jack London's signature. "This one's a winner," Farnsworth said, waving the London signature. He expected they could match it to an inscription in Hofmann's first edition copy of *Call of the Wild*. From various file cards and practice sheets in evidence, Farnsworth suspected that Hofmann had been raising the value of rare books by adding the signatures of authors and other important historical figures. "This case is made in the shade," he exclaimed.

Next they went to Utah Engraving, looking for the Jim Bridger manuscript negatives. They knew from Shannon Flynn that the notes appeared in December 1984 or January 1985. The company had boxes filed by every six months. They took one, about five feet long, from October 1984 to April 1985, and full of negatives. Bell, who had joined them, began going through receipts, while Biggs and Farnsworth sorted through the negatives. In only the second pile he picked up, Farnsworth found the Jim Bridger negative. He took it back to show his captain, who looked at Farnsworth and drawled, "You know, they aren't going to believe you anymore than they believe Mark Hofmann. They'll think this is a setup, you found so many of them."

Farnsworth walked back to his office, happy. Now they had a blank Bridger note, a photocopy with Mike Hansen written on it in ball point pen, and the negative from which the printing plate had been made. They had negatives for two variations of the "Oath of a Freeman," one that matched photographs of the Oath in the East and also matched an edited proof taken from Hofmann's home. Next the investigators went to Denver and Kansas City and got the negatives for the Deseret Currency and a pamphlet called the *Latter-day Saints Emigrants' Guide*. In Kansas City, Hansen had paid for the work with cash and with Hofmann's personal check. Farnsworth declared this the best week in the whole investigation.

The FBI tests on the salamander letter had been inexplicably slow, but finally the letter was returned with a report indicating no signs of forgery. Essentially the FBI relied on the same ink, paper, and handwriting tests (using the same samples) that Steve Christensen's paid experts had used a year earlier, except that this time the Nathan Harris prayer book was available for handwriting comparison. As before, ink, paper, and handwriting checked out.

On February 15 Throckmorton took the salamander letter to the state crime lab. "It's a forgery," he told Ted Cannon later, "just like the others."

But Throckmorton had been exploring forensic territory and knew that no other expert could verify his claims, except Bill Flynn. Al Lyter, who had verified the consistency of the ink on the salamander letter, came out to review their procedures. He found nothing wrong with them yet was not certain of their conclusions.

"I'd have to spend a lot more time looking at old documents to be sure that the cracking and running is so unusual."

The CAO balked at paying Lyter to spend days at the Library of Congress going through documents, and Lyter was not interested in volunteer work. Stott did not like leaving Lyter unconvinced, since Lyter might become a defense witness, but they seemed to have reached an impasse.

"Well, I won't disprove you," Lyter told Throckmorton finally over the telephone.

"Okay, Al. Thanks."

They would all have to be satisfied with that. Meanwhile, Stott assigned himself and Mike George the task of bringing around the Mormon historians who had previously worked with some of the Hofmann documents. Stott knew that street-smart cops and academics represented two different kinds of intelligence, each of which tended to disrespect the other. Stott felt he could bridge the abyss. Both he and George had studied Mormon history. He knew how important the Mormon documents were to the church, its members, and its historians, and he was both fascinated and appalled by the documents he believed were Hofmann forgeries. Also, he looked forward to talking with the historians for personal reasons, since he had admired them at a distance. Now that the eastern experts were coming around, it was time to give the historians enough information to let them draw the right conclusions.

Stott and George went south to Brigham Young University where they spent hours in separate interviews with several of the faculty, none of whom seemed to think the prosecutors had a case. George concluded that the only difference between LDS historians and Mormon religion teachers was that the historians still sounded like defense witnesses while the religion instructors pointed out anachronisms and other problems in the Hofmann documents. One BYU religion professor, Richard Anderson, was particularly helpful and agreed to prepare as an expert witness for trial.

Stott had previously read D. Michael Quinn's articles and respected his research. Several years before, Quinn had given Hofmann some Texas leads on the McLellin collection but knew nothing of the deal. He had written articles on the process of presidential succession in the LDS church, had delivered papers on the salamander letter, and was currently researching Mormon origins. Quinn had been upset when after sorting through evidence shortly after the bombings reporters had called to ask what he found. Willoughby had promised confidentiality and Quinn considered his experience evidence of an investigation out of control.

Stott was convinced that Quinn's 1976 article on the succession crisis that followed Joseph Smith's death in 1844 (published in *Brigham Young University Studies*) had been the genesis of Hofmann's Joseph Smith III blessing. But Quinn saw the blessing's discovery as a coincidence that both verified his research and fit into a much larger context. He explained that the blessing had a provenance and had been authenticated, concluding that Stott "was as opaque as a painted wall." Stott, meanwhile, was rapidly losing his admiration for Quinn.

George decided to try his hand at changing Quinn's mind. "You're aware of the importance of the prayer book in authenticating the salamander letter," he began. Quinn nodded. "What if we can show that the writing in the back was never there before Mark Hofmann had the book?"

Quinn was interested, so George told him about Frances Magee in California. She had owned the book for years and said no handwriting had been in the back.

Quinn thought it over, then shook his head. "Well, that wouldn't convince me," he said. "People's memories get very sloppy."

Stott and George began to realize that Quinn, suspicious of the police already, would not be dissuaded by anything they could tell him.

This case, Stott concluded privately, was going to be impossibly esoteric to present to a jury. At least at the preliminary hearing he need worry only about a judge.

Throckmorton's assignment was to turn around Dean Jessee. Throckmorton welcomed the opportunity to talk with Jessee, whom he had not seen since becoming part of the investigative team. "I apologize for not getting back to you sooner," he told Jessee, who welcomed him cordially.

He sat down with Jessee for about three hours, went over the Hofmann documents, and pointed out the various inconsistencies that led him to conclude they were forgeries. Convinced his case was persuasive, Throckmorton prepared to leave. Jessee shook his hand on the way out and said, "Well, I'm really looking forward to this case coming to court, so I can find out which of Hofmann's documents are forgeries."

Throckmorton went out the door stunned. Hofmann's documents, he realized, had been so bolstered by the scholarship and reputation of experts that if they went down at all, it would be one at a time. To Throckmorton, anyone suspected of forgery was completely discredited. Yet Jessee had mentioned a rumor that Hofmann had recently found some new Nauvoo letters — letters that Jessee was hoping to see. Nauvoo letters, Thockmorton mused. What next?

Even A. J. Simmonds in Logan had not yet been "turned around." Simmonds answered a call from Ron Yengich with less anxiety than he had felt talking with Forbes and George. The investigators had shaken him, he admitted, but gradually he had reconstituted his belief in Hofmann and his documents — at least some of them. He still believed the salamander letter to be a nineteenth-century forgery. When Yengich asked, "Would you consent to take the stand for the defense?" Simmonds answered, "Yes, I would be pleased."

"I've been meaning to come up and see you," Yengich said, "but we're very busy."

"I know you are. Would it ease your schedule if I drove to Salt Lake to see you?" Yengich thanked him.

Moments later, Simmonds's wife came to his office. "Jeff," she said, "the county attorney's office just called to say that you're on their witness list."

When Simmonds and his young son walked into Yengich's office a few days later, Yengich explained that he would have to leave for a court appointment in about forty-five minutes. Setting up a tape recorder, Yengich began, "Mr. Simmonds, are you making this statement of your own free will?"

"I am," Simmonds said, feeling the formality of a court suddenly descend on the room, though his son continued to color in his coloring book.

Yengich led Simmonds through the chronology of events involving Hofmann, then suggested, "Okay, tell me about Mark."

Simmonds said the detectives had asked when Hofmann had read Fawn Brodie's controversial biography of Joseph Smith, *No Man Knows My History*. He had thought Hofmann hadn't read Brodie until after he had brought in the Anthon transcript, but upon checking his document purchases, Simmonds discovered that Hofmann had read the biography before that. "I got out Brodie to identify the characters on the Anthon, but I think the police are looking at Brodie as some sort of handbook for Mark's forgeries."

"What do you think about the Anthon now?"

"I still think it's a genuine document."

"What else did the detectives ask?"

"They were interested in the question of provenance of the documents. They wanted to know if that was crucial in manuscript collecting. I told them it's important, but it's not like real estate, after all. I buy a lot of things from Sam Weller, for instance, but Sam rarely tells me where he gets things."

"But you trust Sam, don't you?"

"Yes, and I don't think there's anything particularly suspicious about a dealer's unwillingness to reveal the source of the material he's selling. You see," he added, warming to the subject, "a university has all the advantages. If we can't purchase a document, we can provide a tax write-off. As a last resort, we could confer the American equivalent of knighthood — we could grant an honorary degree."

Yengich laughed and took a note. "I'll have to remember that. Anything else that interested the detectives?"

"They wanted to know about manuscript collecting in Utah." Simmonds stressed the newness of the business, and continued, "They asked me whether anyone besides Mark had turned up important materials." Simmonds obligingly listed several Mormon collections and diaries at various Utah universities.

"Let's talk about the salamander letter," Yengich said. "Did you think it was a nineteenth-century or a modern forgery."

"Initially I didn't know. Finally I came down on the opinion that it is a nineteenth-century forgery." He began to explain but sensed that Yengich seemed familiar with the reasons he had given on television programs.

Yengich, gazing out the south window of his office into a rain-washed alley, asked, "Do you think Mark is a bomber?"

"No."

"Do you think Mark is a forger?"

A pause. "No."

Yengich turned and looked at Simmonds.

"I rule that out for a purely technical reason, in addition to any other reason," Simmonds explained. "Mark uses a ball point pen or a felt-tip. He doesn't write with a fountain pen. There is a whole other technology involved with a fountain pen. It's not easy to transfer between those writing technologies. At least I don't think it is."

Yengich took notes.

"Also," Simmonds added, "getting back to the bombings. I've seen Mark really take the heat, especially with the Joseph Smith III blessing when he was being attacked by both the Utah church and the Reorganized church."

Yengich nodded.

It was almost 2:00 when the interview ended. Simmonds stood and his son packed his crayons and coloring book. Yengich extended his hand. "I'd like to come to Logan and have a longer talk."

"That would be fine."

Simmonds led John out to the hall and knelt to zip his son's coat before braving the rain again. He heard Yengich telling the receptionist, "We need to get a transcript of this as soon as possible."

They stopped at Sam Weller's bookstore on their way back to the car, and Simmonds described the interview. When he finished, Weller asked, "Do you want to hear the latest?"

"Naturally."

"Now they're looking at forged books."

Driving back to Logan through the downpour, Simmonds could only conclude that if this crazy case went to trial, he'd likely testify for his old friend, Mark Hofmann—and against him.

Shortly afterwards, Stott and Biggs accompanied Ken Farnsworth back to 47 East South Temple for more interviews with church leaders. The issue of access to the questioned documents in the church's possession had been settled, though occasionally church attorneys got wind of the CAO whisking documents out of state for testing and asked about their safety.

With the death of Spencer W. Kimball, a new president had recently been appointed. Hinckley, now first counselor, was joined by a younger apostle as second counselor, thereby relieving Hinckley of much of the burden he had previously shouldered. As before, the investigative team first interviewed Hugh Pinnock.

Pinnock surprised Farnsworth by bringing up the papyrus fragment Christensen had locked up in his safe deposit box the week before he was killed. "You know that papyrus," he said. "That's Facsimile 2."

"Well, Steve didn't think that was Facsimile 2, did he?" Farnsworth blurted. He immediately saw by the look on Pinnock's face that he had spoken amiss. Sure, Farnsworth told himself as the prosecutors began asking questions, Facsimile 2 was supposed to be in the McLellin collection and Mark would always get the benefit of the doubt—if Mark said it was Facsimile 2, it was Facsimile 2. The fact that it did not resemble the sketch in the scriptures would be all the more reason for Christensen and Pinnock to keep it out of circulation.

Gradually, as the interview continued, the attorneys realized that Pinnock's potential testimony was, in some ways, not going to help their case. Their murder case involved a situation in which one man was pressuring another to consummate a deal, but Pinnock portrayed himself as benevolent and helpful to Hofmann and Christensen—and only from a distance.

Biggs thought he could make headway if Pinnock understood more about the case. He told Pinnock the $185,000 loan he had helped arrange had gone to Alvin Rust as payment on an old debt.

"Now Mr. Pinnock," he said, inviting his confidence, "I'm not accusing you. We know that the church is a victim in this case, and we regard it as such. It just seems natural to me that since you had arranged a substantial loan for Mr. Hofmann, that loan wouldn't have been made without your support, would it?"

"No," Pinnock said, rather grudgingly.

"Then the loan director calls and tells you that nothing's been paid on that loan, and would you please check with Mr. Hofmann," Biggs reviewed. "You couldn't get hold of Mark, but you got hold of Steve and asked him to get hold of Mark. Now, Mr. Pinnock, at that point you probably weren't too upset, but weren't you concerned?"

Pinnock thought. "No, not concerned. Just relaying information."

"Then when Hofmann bounced a check for $188,000 and the bank calls you . . . Didn't the bank call you?"

A pause. "They may have. I don't know."

"Didn't Harvey Tanner call you and say, 'Hugh, if Mark doesn't pay, we're looking to you to pay.' Now *I'd* start getting upset."

"No," Pinnock said genially, "we were concerned for Mark about his problems and we wished to be helpful to him in resolving them."

"You never indicated to Steve Christensen that you were concerned or upset?"

"No."

Stott and Biggs began to relate the warnings of criminal and civil action that Christensen had passed on to Hofmann and the concerns he had mentioned to his friends. Pinnock seemed unaware, amazed. "Steven said that?" he asked. "I don't understand why he would have said that."

When they pressed Pinnock on Christensen's confidences to several friends that the church would extend him a line of credit to assist in document deals in the future, Pinnock withdrew further. They perservered, and Pinnock became absolute. "I adamantly deny that Steven Christensen had any official position as document agent for the church or held any financial position."

"Why would Steven have told his friends this?"

Pinnock admitted, as he had to Farnsworth in an earlier conversation, that the subject may have been discussed informally, but that was all.

By the time the interview ended, Biggs was restless with frustration. He wanted to grab Pinnock by the lapels and say, "It's okay to be human. Anyone would be upset in that situation."

When they learned that Dallin Oaks was out of town, the prosecutors made an appointment to interview Hinckley, again represented by Kirton. Hinckley would be a material witness, since he had purchased several documents from Hofmann for the church. And he would, by virtue of his church position, carry incalculable weight as a witness. They needed to hear a preview of his testimony by reviewing with him his history with Hofmann and with Christensen.

But Hinckley seemed barely able to remember Hofmann. He traced the purchase of various documents succinctly until they came to the salamander letter.

"Do you remember your conversation with Lyn Jacobs, who brought in the letter?"

"Just that it was brief and I didn't like him."

Hinckley recalled Christensen's donation of the salamander letter in April 1985, the one time Christensen came to his office. He remembered the substance of the letter he had received from Alvin Rust in June regarding the McLellin collection. As the questions neared the time of the bombings, Hinckley recalled no contact with either Hofmann or Christensen, except that he had refused to buy the Kinderhook plates from Hofmann in October.

"You must understand," Kirton interjected, "that these events occurred near the time of General Conference. With President Kimball ailing, President Hinckley was the *de facto* leader of the church. It's surprising to me that he can remember anything at all around that time, let alone someone who was as infrequent and nondescript a visitor as Mark Hofmann."

Faced with having Hinckley appear twice on the witness stand, Kirton offered some counsel to Stott and Biggs as the interview ended. He described Hinckley as a "big gun," whose testimony need not be "fired" at the preliminary hearing. Wouldn't the prosecutors be smart, Kirton suggested, to delay Hinckley's testimony until trial? Hinckley added that he was not eager to testify anyway.

Stott politely thanked them for their comments, then added, "I'm in charge of the case. I know how to prosecute it, and I have to have President Hinckley at the preliminary hearing unless the defense agrees to a written summary of President Hinckley's testimony. If we feel as prosecutors that it's necessary for President Hinckley or Elder Pinnock or anyone else to testify, they will testify."

They shook hands, said good-bye, and left. On the way out, Biggs slapped Stott on the back. "You just lost your bishopric," he kidded, referring to Stott's future in church leadership, "but I'm proud of you."

The issue was not so easily settled, however. It was clear that church leaders would not testify that they were pressuring Christensen to help Hofmann come through with the McLellin collection. Other witnesses, including Curt Bench, could give some idea of the pressure Christensen had been under, but Bench was never on the inside. They could call Christensen's business associates, who would tell of telephone calls and meetings with church leaders, but they would be discrediting their own star witnesses.

"If we're going to make this case fly," Biggs told Stott privately, "we've got to put the church leaders on the stand. We've got to get someone to explain to them that it's okay to have been upset with Hofmann on that document deal. We need them to say that much. It's very simple: Mark didn't have the McLellin collection, they were applying pressure, Christensen

179

was in the middle and got killed. The Sheets bomb was a diversion. The forgery is really an undercurrent."

Stott disagreed. "I don't think they're covering up intentionally or unintentionally, Dave. They're busy people trying to recall minor events, at least minor at the time."

"Come on, Bob. You've already given up your bishopric. Pinnock won't admit the pressure, Hinckley can't remember, and we can't find Oaks to save our lives."

"Okay, maybe subconsciously they don't want to remember."

"But how are we going to get them to admit what was going on? Will you talk to Kirton-McConkie and ask them to explain how important this is?"

Stott agreed but added, "We can get around it at the preliminary hearing."

"Yeah, we can. But when we go to trial and everything has to fit, we're going to have a problem."

Stott had to agree that Hinckley would not be a good witness. A loss of memory wouldn't look good for a church leader, Stott felt, and certainly wouldn't help their case.

Mulling over the situation, Biggs had an idea. Before the trial, it might be possible to get the three church leaders alone. He would present the case to them, explain what they believed happened in October 1985 and why, and show them how crucial their forthright participation was. He would go back to the beginning and weave the case together strand by strand. *Then* they would understand.

SECTION
TWO

7

ONE FOLD

As young girls in the late 1930s, Kathy and Joan Webb played together for hours, sharing a small plastic doll. A slit and a sash from a scrap of fabric, and the doll had an extensive wardrobe.

"Little darlings" in a family of ten children, Kathy and Joan were the youngest, twenty-one months apart. They and their older sister were born to their father's second marriage and did not, like their siblings, live through the trauma of a mother's death. Their father, Nathaniel Hodges Webb, was a schoolteacher, then principal in Salt Lake City. He and his first wife, Hazel Peterson, were raising seven children — from three to thirteen years old — when Hazel died. Two years later, Nathaniel married Virginia Wyss, a twenty-eight-year-old woman who had never been married.

Nathaniel was a loving but impractical man, who was deeply in debt at the time of his second marriage. Virginia, a new stepmother as well as wife, put the family on a strict budget and garnished the older children's earnings. Their older siblings enjoyed giving them books and toys, and their mother, who seemed to understand children instinctively, had relaxed her earlier strictness. By the time Kathy and Joan were aware of family fortunes, times were easier.

Kathy, the youngest, was born in Salt Lake City on July 31, 1935. Kindred spirits who shared a world of fantasy, she and Joan created their own dialect, spoken by the "Hoogabooga" family they believed lived where an airplane signal light shone on the hill opposite their home on 1300 East. Together they attended elementary, junior high, and high school. Their father grew increasingly infirm during those years, and when Kathy was sixteen he died.

Joan, quieter than her sister, watched Kathy's popularity blossom in high school and at the University of Utah. They remained friends, despite Kathy's dates every weekend and Joan's free calendar. At the University of Utah, three young men seemed especially interested in Kathy. Dick Anderson, Kathy's high school sweetheart, began dating sexy, sophisticated girls in college, and Joan did not think Kathy fit the category. Joan preferred Clark Cedarloff, who was popular but not quite the ladies' man. Anderson and Cedarloff were on LDS missions when a third suitor, James Gary Sheets, asked Kathy to marry him. Sheets, a young man from Richfield, Utah, had virtually raised himself after the death of his parents. He had already returned from a mission and was ambitious, full of ideas on how to make money. Joan met Gary for the first time when he breezed into their house to pick up Kathy, saying, "Hi, I'm Gary Sheets. Can I use your telephone?"

Gary was too brash for Joan's tastes, but she could see why Kathy was impressed. He was attractive and dynamic. Despite their romance, Kathy refused to give Gary an answer until after Dick returned home from his mission; then she made up her mind to marry Gary. She knew if she married Gary her children would have advantages she had not enjoyed.

Gary and Kathy Sheets married in 1958. Gary sold insurance, and for a time, Kathy taught school. They had little money, like most young couples, and socialized with other salesmen and their wives.

Already Kathy could see that some salesmen's wives were at a disadvantage with their outgoing, professional husbands. She gradually learned to say, "All right, Gary, if you want $50 for shirts, I want $50, too. I want it right here in my hand for whatever I want to spend it on, and I want it now."

Joan married Lloyd Gorton, as low-key as Gary Sheets was aggressive, and the sisters stayed close, although Kathy lived east of Salt Lake City in Holladay and Joan west in Taylorsville.

Gorton tended her sister's children for a year or two while Sheets taught. Sheets's first daughter, Heidi, was dubbed "H" by Gorton. Katherine, called Katie, entered the Sheets family three years later. The Gortons had two young daughters also, and the sisters combined activities frequently. Gretchen and then James Gary Jr. joined the Sheets family. The only boy, Jimmy was immediately nicknamed, "Dream Prince."

As a mother Sheets became famous at her children's elementary school for her practical jokes, especially on April Fools Day. One year she rounded up the neighborhood preschoolers and brought them to Gretchen's classroom, explaining to the surprised teachers that Gretchen could care for the children on the playground. Another time she sent a box with Katie, accompanied by a letter describing an illness, which had just been diagnosed. The letter instructed her teacher to give Katie three green pills at noon, one yellow pill at 1:30, three blue ones at 2:30, and so on. When the teacher opened the pill box, she found only a note—"April Fools." A third year, a large cake appeared in the teacher's lounge. Lettering on the cake read, "Happy April Fools from Mrs. Sheets. Eat, if you dare." Had anyone dared, they would have found the cake delicious.

After a few years, the teachers began taking particular note of the "Sheets kids" in their classes. Although the elementary school celebrated its 25th anniversary after Jimmy Sheets had begun junior high, Kathy was invited to attend the celebration. With due ceremony, school officials presented her a dozen long-stem roses, minus the roses.

With the success of J. Gary Sheets Associates (JGSA) and the launching of CFS Financial Corp., the Sheets became affluent. Gary and Kathy designed and built a house with a private driveway that branched from Naniloa Drive at about 4600 South. The wooded setting sacrificed practicality for beauty, with a steep driveway that dove toward the Sheetses' triple garage and was impossible to negotiate in deep snow. They learned to park before storms in the parking lot of their local Mormon ward meetinghouse at the top of their driveway, then hike in and out. Despite the uncurtained glass and high ceilings, Kathy had only one complaint about the house: she could never let in enough sun.

Kathy expressed herself throughout her home, designing a massive front door flanked by stained glass windows that featured tulips with the letter S curved into the foliage. The dining room, parlor, and forest green master bedroom were decorated formally. At the center of the house was the pantry, a counter with stools opposite cooking appliances, and a heavy picnic table with benches — all adjoining a family room with a huge overstuffed sofa. The only piece of furniture of any significant value was a tall, painted oriental desk. Kathy kidded admiring visitors with the deadpan report that she had decorated it at her ward Relief Society.

Throughout, her signs spoke: "Silence: The Master is Watching TV Sports"; "BE ALERT. The World Needs More Lerts"; "Keep Your Temper. You'll Need it Later"; "Lord, Help Me To Endure My Blessings"; "When God Created Man, She was Only Kidding"; and "The Likelihood of Someone Watching You is in Direct Proportion to the Stupidity of What You are Doing." Her home represented both process and product, as functional as it was welcoming. When a tap leaked or the dishwasher broke down, she fixed it.

Year by year, souvenirs, drawings, photographs, and signs accumulated. In response to the sometimes self-congratulatory Christmas letters she received from certain friends, Kathy designed a Christmas letter using satiric sketches of her family but adding her own captions: Gretchen hanging little Jimmy by his ankles; "scholar Katie" reading *Mad Magazine*; Heidi balancing in her mother's high heels; Gary on the telephone (of course) with Jimmy beside him; and Kathy, a "famous noncook," scorching something on the stove.

In the late 1970s and early 1980s, as Gary's business success became apparent, Joan watched her sister for changes. But Kathy seemed the same person she had been when she and Gary struggled to support their young daughters. One day she sprinkled pennies in front of the house before kindergarten let out, just for the fun of watching the children pick them up.

During those years, it was easy for the Sheets to grow casual about money. Although Gary ran his company at an arm's length, he had a hard time accepting the fact that Kathy kept her checking account the same way.

"I can't believe how you can go through money," he would chide. "I thought I married a girl from a poor family who knew how to conserve and economize."

She would grin at him. "That's right, Gary. You taught me everything I know."

Other evenings he would come home and she would say, "I'm so angry at the bank." Her aversion to dealing with money was a family joke—her bank statements were neatly filed by date but never opened.

"Well, how come?"

"They say I'm overdrawn and I know I'm not."

"Let me see your checkbook."

"No."

"Come on, Kathy, let me see your check book."

Just as he had corrected math papers for her during their courtship, he would have her check register straightened out in a few minutes. "I'll have to bail you out again."

During those years of affluence both Gary and Kathy were notoriously generous. Gary loaned young Mormons money for their missions and never noticed whether or not the loans were repaid. Kathy promised Joan that when she received her degree in psychology from the University of Utah, she would treat her to an all-expenses-paid trip.

As their children began leaving home, the Sheets remodeled to create dressing rooms and a small study for Kathy next to the master bedroom. The study and bedroom were Kathy's haven. If her children heard the theme from a favorite television drama or from an old movie from beneath the closed door, they knew that whatever they wanted could wait. In 1983, Kathy added a huge gold hourglass to the momentos in the study. On one end was engraved, "Kathy and Gary, June 30, 1958; Even better now than it was then. Let's turn it over and go 25 again."

On walks with her friends, Kathy discussed her role as housewife and mother at a time when many women were seeking careers. She was happy with her choice, her involvement with her high-achieving children, and her busy schedule. Tuesday, for example, was "Grandma day," when Kathy collected her mother from a nearby nursing home and brought her home to spend the day. They would have lunch on the deck overlooking the swimming pool and enjoy the sun on the creek, the birds in the trees. When that became impossible, Kathy visited her mother every Tuesday in the nursing home.

Christmas was Kathy's favorite time of year. She watched anxiously as Katie Robertson teetered between a ladder and the stairs to drape lights over a twenty-foot tree in the foyer. Then Joan Gorton prepared the food for a joint family party held at the Sheetses' home, which Kathy decorated throughout. One year, the sisters stole some needed item from every family member, gift-wrapped it, and gave it back to them at the party. Another year, they drew names and exchanged designer tee-shirts. Kathy's read, "Pierced Ears Are Urp-Gag," for pierced ears were her pet peeve and urp-gag her choicest epithet.

People were at the center of Kathy Sheets's life, her family, friends, and ward members, and also an enduring fascination with human behavior. She loved to relate how when Gretchen was about four years old and on her way to a movie with her sisters, Kathy had told her about a little girl named Audrey, who went out to the lobby alone to get a drink and then could not find her mother and sisters again in the dark theater. When she finished, Gretchen responded with a story about a little girl named Audrey, who counted the rows of seats as she walked out to the lobby, and then counted them again when she reentered the dark theater, walking directly to her family. "Right then I realized that raising the third one was not going to be like raising the first two," she would summarize.

Feelings were important to Kathy, and when conflicts came, she wanted to deal with them, in detail and at once. Gary did not like the emotional atmosphere of such situations.

"Just drop it, Kathy," he would insist, heading for his dressing room. "Just let it go."

"Gary, you come back here and talk this out!"

Gary and Kathy Sheets were two very different people, who had, nevertheless, built a successful marriage and home and were well through the challenges of raising four children. They had chosen separate spheres of responsibility—Kathy at home, Gary in business and community affairs. If Gary was seldom home, Kathy learned to compensate by traveling with friends, taking a class, or starting a project. One year she happily shepherded her family through Europe and the Middle East after Gary decided business would not allow him to vacation.

When the family occasionally discussed either Gary or Kathy dying prematurely, it was always in a humorous vein. "Well, just don't marry anyone cute," Kathy would pout. "And don't sleep with her first."

Not only did Sheets take advantage of her sister's psychology studies through frequent conversations, but her other confidante, Betty Lynn Davis, was a social worker and marriage counselor. The two spent hours on the telephone, and after a long conversation, Sheets would say, "You're my therapist."

"Kathy, you're mine," Davis would reply. She could see how easily Sheets drained her energy when someone else needed help. "Kathy, you've got to take care of yourself first," she would admonish, only to hear, "No, I've got to do this."

Not until CFS received a negative financial report in June did Kathy Sheets realize that her world was endangered. Even then, the full impact did not register immediately. She and Joan Gorton celebrated Gorton's new psychology degree by vacationing in British Columbia, as promised. At the end of the trip, Kathy told her sister that Gary's company was in trouble.

After their return, the summer turned grim as the company floundered. The sudden death of a young father in her ward prompted Kathy to spend uncounted hours with the widow, a pregnant mother of five, until her baby was born. Joe and Katie Robertson's infant, Molly, contracted pneumonia soon after birth and needed weeks of special treatment. Each day Kathy brought a gift to her granddaughter at the hospital.

By autumn 1985 tension in the Sheetses' home had increased. Heidi had worked for her father for five years and understood more about the company than Kathy did. Kathy often called and asked her daughter to explain Gary's terse reports of events in the office. Despite the increasingly alarming news, Kathy tried to be optimistic when she spoke to others, "Gary's a great salesman and a good businessman," she told Joan. "He won't be down for long."

Kathy Sheets carried with her that fall a sense of impending doom. Her fears crystallized in August when Steven

Christensen had left the company, for Steve had been Gary's "organizer," his detail man, even calling Kathy to give her flight times and weather reports before business trips. She knew her husband depended on Steve, young as he was, to lend expertise to a company that only knew how to sell at full throttle.

In 1974, when Gary and Kathy Sheets were designing their dream house, Steven F. Christensen, twenty, was serving a two-year Mormon mission in Australia. One day as he and his companion Don Tanner passed a tailor's shop, the door was open, and steam billowed out. "That's where I was when I was fourteen years old," Christensen commented, "working in the tailor department of my dad's store."

The oldest of eight children born to Fred (Mac) C. and Joan Christensen, Steve was a precocious child, burdened by a sense of responsibility. Too young to remember the incident, he had pulled his younger brother from a full ditch. His earliest memory, he later wrote in his journal, was of playing with the little girl across the street when he was five. He refused to let his brother join the fun, he remembered with remorse. As he grew, he loved chemistry sets and books, and every Christmas Eve read a new book late into the night. In high school, he was an honor student, an avid debater, and served on various student activity committees.

Steve's parents were social, giving people. Mac, a chronic workaholic in retail clothing, was a hard taskmaster who liked rows of shirts to line up like soldiers. An intensely personable man, he greeted familiar customers with a hug or slap on the shoulder, declaring he had just what they needed at a special price. On television, his gesticulating "Have I got a deal for you!" commercials made his Mr. Mac retail clothing stores a Salt Lake City sales institution.

Privately, Mac could not resist a good cause. When the Teton Dam in Idaho washed out, he sent a truckload of Levi jeans to the area. When an automobile accident killed the husband of a young friend and injured their daughter, he provided the young widow with an apartment and appliances and bought her daughter a new wardrobe. Joan Christensen's life revolved around her friends and her LDS ward; she passed on to Steve her love of books.

In Australia, Mormon missionaries Christensen and Tanner told each other about their backgrounds. Tanner confessed to a wild youth. Christensen's idea of rebellion had been borrowing a Volkswagen for a date instead of using his father's Lincoln Continental, or paying for dinner with rolls of quarters. Tanner liked Christensen enormously. Christensen was not dull or rigid but curiously adult, as if he had been born in a suit with a briefcase under his arm.

Tanner was a new missionary in Australia when he met Christensen for the first time. They were struck by a physical resemblance to each other, and both had the impression they had met before. They could never discover how they might have met, for Steve had been raised in Bountiful, north of Salt Lake City, and Don in Payson, southwest of Provo.

There were twelve Italian-speaking missionaries in Australia when Tanner arrived at this mission-within-a-mission in Brunswick, a Melbourne suburb populated by Italians, Lebanese, and Greeks. Christensen and his new companion lived in a bungalow that barely contained their two bunks and tiny kitchen.

When Christensen received a letter appointing him leader over a district of missionaries, he went out in an alley behind the bungalow and yelled, "Oh, shit!" Tanner was delighted— both at the unmissionary-like response and because as district leader, Christensen could arrange their schedules so that the two of them could work together.

Christensen was a natural leader, Tanner thought, and under his direction district meetings changed. Now each had an agenda and reading material, complete with scripture references, quotes from church leaders, and anecdotes. After meetings, the missionaries would break into groups and go out proselyting.

As they walked from house to house, they talked. Christensen told Tanner about "Wolfy," a young missionary who had arrived in Australia with hair below his ears, wearing a long trenchcoat and hiking boots. He had met the mission president at the airport, saying, "Hi, Pres. I'm Elder Wolf, but you can call me Wolfy." Wolfy had been a dedicated missionary who made many converts to the church, although his methods were unconventional. It was obvious Christensen had liked him.

One of the church's chapels in Melbourne was the target of periodic vandalism by local children armed with rocks and spray paint. Christensen's response was to organize a neighborhood youth soccer league. They began registering children from eight to thirteen and invited the children's parents to church for an organizational meeting. They held soccer matches every Saturday for months. After the first game, a ward member treated the children to punch and cookies, and then the missionaries took them on a tour of the chapel, explaining the purpose for each room. After that, the vandalism stopped.

Tanner surmised that missionary work was only the outer manifestation of Christensen's inner quest. Christensen was continually buying religious books, reading, then sending the books home or giving them away. He stayed up nights, drinking RC Cola to keep awake while he studied, until he decided the practice cheated his missionary duties. After that, he compiled a list of questions to research once he got home. By the time he left he had more than 500.

Christensen sometimes tried out his question on his mission president. Once Tanner overheard a conversation between the two while driving in the mission car. Christensen posed his questions, then after some discussion, his mission president turned around in the front seat. "Steve," he said, "I not only don't know the answers; I've never thought of those questions."

In February 1975, Christensen was released from his mission and returned to Utah, to the University of Utah, and to his books. Before long, however, he discovered a major distraction — an attractive, blond, high school senior named Terri Romney.

As a junior high school student in Bountiful, Terri had known Steve slightly. She had moved to Utah with her family from Los Angeles when she was eleven and, like Steve, was the oldest in a family of eight children.

By the time Terri began high school, Steve was on a mission and Terri was waiting for another missionary. She was not engaged but did not feel free, either, and life was getting dull. When Steve returned home, Terri's father asked him to speak at a fireside at their home. Terri flirted a little. A few days later Steve called her father. "Would you mind if I asked your daughter out?" After the third or fourth date, Terri would recall, Steve was ready to get engaged, but she had other plans that included the missionary she had been corresponding with and attending BYU in the fall.

In July Don Tanner returned home from Australia and found Christensen at the airport with four concert tickets in hand. Tanner quickly gathered that Christensen had been squiring around his girlfriend and *her* friend and that he was now supposed to complete the foursome. Like most returned missionaries, Tanner's clothes were worn and outdated. Christensen threw open the doors to his closet and said, "Okay, take what you want. Whatever you need in there is yours."

Embarrassed, Tanner froze, but Christensen simply went through his clothes and pulled out ten or fifteen shirts, a couple of sport coats, and some trousers. The concert date with Steve Christensen, Terri Romney, Don Tanner, and Kris Bell was a success, and the two couples began double-dating frequently. Christensen was attending business classes at the University of Utah, while Romney and Bell were enrolled at BYU. Tanner decided to live at home in Payson and commute to the Y.

Romney enjoyed college. A piano student for ten years, she majored in music. She found, however, that she missed Christensen more than she had anticipated and looked forward to seeing him on weekends. On weekdays, Christensen divided his time between his father's store and his classes at the U. His idea of fun was to curl up with a good book, not Romney's idea of a good time. As their relationship deepened, she worried about those differences.

By January, Romney and Christensen were unofficially engaged. Romney, who would be in town over the holidays, assumed she would be spending Saturday with Christensen, but he casually mentioned he planned to spend Saturday working on his files. For him, this was a chance to do something he had been hoping to do for a long time. For Romney, it was an insulting rebuff.

In May, Tanner and Bell got engaged and by August were married. They moved to Logan, Utah, and spent four years at Utah State University. Meanwhile, Christensen and Romney made marriage plans for the coming September in the Salt Lake Temple. Christensen was twenty-two and Romney nineteen.

"Nine months and one week later," they would tell friends, they became parents with the birth of Joshua Steven. Justin followed eighteen months later, about the time they purchased a home in Centerville, Utah. Both were busy, Terri caring for the babies and arranging their house, Steve working full time, majoring in finance and considering law school. Christensen was becoming dissatisfied selling suits for his father and saw in one of his customers, Gary Sheets, a major opportunity.

Christensen gave Sheets a document that organized his professional and personal life and showed him how to improve his efficiency. Sheets hired him at a salary of around $30,000 and a 10 percent interest in J. Gary Sheets Associates that would increase in time. Christensen left school, for a high salary no longer depended upon a college degree. Before long, Christensen recommended Don Tanner for a job with a company tangential to CFS.

At JGSA, Christensen was responsible for syndicating the projects that CFS salesmen contracted. If, for example, a CFS client wanted to invest in an apartment complex, JGSA would design the contract, charging fees and part of the profit. Steve rose fast in the company through a combination of personal study, a fine-honed sense of organization, and a demanding pace that required self-imposed, self-enforced deadlines. He seemed older than his mid-twenties and more schooled than he was. Sheets gave him a free hand.

Steve and Terri Christensen became an integral part of their Mormon ward and community in Centerville. Jared, their third son, arrived in 1982, the year Christensen became ward bishop, one of the youngest in the church. Despite the honor, the Christensens had mixed feelings about the call, for it involved a great deal of time and responsibility. Terri Christensen was not entirely happy about her own part as "first lady" or "mother" of the ward. She knew that a bishop's wife must be everybody's friend, from the newest arrival to the most difficult ward member. Initially, she doubted her ability to begin conversations and greet newcomers and did not consider herself the paragon of perfection that people seemed to expect from the bishop's family. However, she, like her husband, had been raised to accept church callings, and she quickly found herself more capable than she had supposed.

Soon after Christensen became bishop, the Tanners bought a home in the ward. Don Tanner noticed that Christensen set his own style as bishop right away, just as he had in Australia. He shortened or eliminated leadership meetings and paid attention to both the clock and the spirit during worship services. He was direct about delegating responsibility and asking for his congregation's support. "You know, I didn't ask to be bishop," he confided more than once over the pulpit, "but I need to do this job, and I need your help."

Christensen believed that everyone in the church should be a volunteer; none should become expert enough in a position to be considered a professional. Aware of people complaining about church responsibilities they did not particularly like, Steve one evening asked ward members to remain after services. He then informed them that he had felt inspired in calling only about 20 percent of them to their current positions, and he invited them to request a change if they felt a change was warranted. Some did.

When he realized that he was counseling an increasing number of women in his ward who felt undervalued and overwhelmed by their demanding roles as wives, mothers, and sometimes income-bringers, he visited the Relief Society and told the women to relax. They were only human, he said, and should not let themselves be depressed by comparing themselves to an unrealistic image.

Christensen particularly resisted regional meetings designed to instruct bishops and other ward officers. He considered himself competent and did not like spending time in meetings he considered superfluous. "Bishop, are you committed to this program?" his superiors would ask, only to hear, "No, I'm not going to do it that way. This is how I handle that."

He brought the Tanners and others their yearly temple recommends, required to enter Mormon temples, without first conducting the required personal worthiness interviews. He refused to excommunicate ward members who transgressed church teachings but was willing to spend hours counseling with them. Mormons are prohibited from drinking alcohol, coffee, or tea, and from smoking and using recreational drugs. But Christensen tended to look the other way if a coffee-drinking member needed a recommend to see a son or daughter marry in the temple. When a couple in his ward received clearance from the church's social services agency to adopt a baby, he dashed barefoot through the snow to give them the news. Like his father, Steve confronted people's personal disasters immediately, even if it meant using his own funds.

In 1983 when heavy spring flooding in northern Utah threatened many neighborhoods, the LDS church organized a veritable army of sandbaggers through priesthood ranks. Christensen bought a jeep to haul the sandbags and virtually camped beside the dikes, telling others he had made a deal with the Lord to care for his family while he kept an eye on the flood.

As a bishop, Christensen seemed eager for congregational closeness, for a kind of democracy that complemented his efficiency with a maverick image. He preferred to visit people at home rather than to call them into his office at the meetinghouse, and many visited his office at CFS. He let his congregation know that he was not perfect. He drank caffeinated soft drinks, swore on occasion, and attended R-rated movies. He let his humanity be known, just as he accepted the individual eccentricities of his flock—except gossip about other ward members.

When people asked questions about Mormon history or doctrine, Christensen tried to present all sides of the issue without imposing an answer. "I tell my ward members they don't have to come to church if they're living the gospel," he would say, fully aware of the ironies for attendance-oriented Mormons. Heaven, he liked to say, was not going to be divided between good Mormons and good people.

His own religious questions continued to entice him. Once a week he would stay up all night reading his mushrooming library. He invited speakers to early morning seminars he organized for friends and interested employees. He frequently underwrote Mormon theological conferences and scholarly publications and traded photocopies of speeches, letters, articles, and other information with friends. He classified himself as a believer and found Christianity and the Mormon church necessary and socially beneficial in his life. He also saw the new Mormon history as an indispensible part of the ongoing search for truth.

At twenty-six, Christensen was surprised and honored by a request to serve on a central church committee to study and define doctrinal issues for church lesson manuals. At the same time, he was authoring a column called "Sunday School Supplement" for the independent LDS *Sunstone* magazine. Designed for teachers in church classes, the column drew the ire of Elder Hugh Pinnock (a *Sunstone* reader himself), who objected that official Sunday school manuals were sufficient for teachers. Pinnock did not know that Steve Christensen was the author, but when Christensen heard of the protest, he changed the column's title and continued to write it. Meanwhile, he and Pinnock became friends.

Terri found it difficult to interest Steve in activities she and others found relaxing. Christensen was absorbed by business and his own interests. His desk sat in the family room, both an advantage and disadvantage. While he worked, he was part of his family, for Terri was nearby watching television, and their boys played around them. But still, he was working. When company came, Steve sometimes loved to play the host; at other times he simply withdrew and let the party surge around him.

Terri and Steve learned to enjoy shopping together. Some Saturdays, Steve would take the boys shopping to give Terri "a day off." They otherwise had to schedule their social life, trying to go out once a week, often to movies. There, in the dark theater, Steve could relax, often roaring at comic scenes until Terri was embarrassed. At home, he would watch videos with the boys, and together wrestle and laugh.

Though Steve controlled their income, Terri managed their home and spoke her mind. Steve had told her he liked to see her independence. "Sometimes I wish you *were* a little mouse," he would tease when she stood up to him. Yet she also knew that when he did not want to deal with her opinions or worries, he simply did not tell her what concerned him. Until she realized that CFS was in serious trouble, she had not worried about money. Steve had always provided well, and she had always assumed he had everything "handled."

Unlike his boss, Gary Sheets, Christensen tried to be home between 5:00 and 10:00 p.m. to see Terri and his sons, even if it meant working all night at his desk at home or returning to work early the next morning. He wanted his family to have more of him than he had had of his father. That was not easily arranged, however, particularly as business pressures began mounting in 1984 and 1985. A pending bankruptcy, a new company, and the expectation of a new baby preoccupied both Terri and Steve. But Christensen's abiding passion for Mormon history distracted him from even these challenges in mid-1985 as he attempted to arrange the purchase of the McLellin collection from Mormon document dealer Mark Hofmann.

About a month before Steven Christensen celebrated his first birthday, Mark William Hofmann was born on Pearl Harbor Day, December 7, 1954. His parents, William and Lucille Hofmann, led lives much like those of Mac and Joan Christensen and of Gary and Kathy Sheets. Following World War II, they had all married and raised active Mormon families. They encouraged their children to fill church missions and to attend college and looked forward to the promise of grandchildren and comfortable lives centered around home, church, and community.

William Hofmann married Lucille Sears in December 1947. Bill, or Willy, as the family called him, was nineteen, his bride eighteen. Both, born near the end of large families, were familiar with economic hardship. Bill was the eighth of twelve children, Lue the youngest of nine. By the time the newlyweds celebrated their first wedding anniversary, Bill was leaving to serve an LDS mission in the Netherlands, after which he joined the military. Lucille stayed in Salt Lake City for three years while her husband preached Mormonism, then joined him in Germany where Heidi was born in July 1953. Bill and Lue's sacrifice of their first few years of married life to the church became a symbol of religious devotion in both the Hofmann and Sears families.

Mark William arrived seventeen months after Heidi, by then

the family had resettled in Salt Lake City. Initially, Bill found work as a mortician with Evans and Early Mortuary. Providing for his growing family, Bill changed jobs several times, becoming a sales representative for copying and printing manufacturers. After a few years in Buena Park, California, the Hofmanns moved their family to a new subdivision in the Millcreek neighborhood of Salt Lake City. They purchased their red brick split-level home on Marie Avenue, a quiet street winding into a cul-de-sac. The avenue had far more children than traffic.

An elementary school was close by, a Mormon wardhouse was a block to the north, and a grocery store sat only a few blocks to the south. The neighborhood was close-knit, mostly Mormon. The Hofmanns soon became known as friendly, helpful, yet very private people.

Both Bill and Lucille held a variety of church positions. Their children, Heidi, Mark, and Jody, attended meetings regularly and were obviously familiar with the scriptures and Mormon doctrine and quick to answer questions in class. Mark knew his way through the Bible and The Book of Mormon at an early age. By the time he was sixteen, he had already memorized the sacramental prayers, and there was never any question he would serve a full-time, two-year mission when he turned nineteen. In virtually every way young Mark seemed to be a model Mormon boy.

Proudly watching their son progress in the church, outgrowing his childish pranks, Bill and Lucille Hofmann would occasionally confide to close friends and family members that their hopes for Mark as a future church leader—perhaps even general authority—were high indeed. "Mark and I were in Sunday School class together for years," one member of his ward later remembered. "It was a big class and there were some little hellions. Mark was the kid who never sassed the teacher, never was rowdy. He never sat on the back row and threw spit wads in church."

8

THE BOY WHO NEVER THREW
SPITWADS IN CHURCH

"**W**illy's son Mark was born today," Mark's grandfather, Karl Edward Hofmann, noted in his journal on December 7, 1954. An only son, Mark was born between cousins Tom Eatchell and Michael Woolley. Mark's mother and aunts had been taught that boys were special and that men were in charge, traditions of both Mormon and German culture. Mark also embodied the dreams of two upwardly mobile families. His father, William Hofmann, was a first-generation American who emigrated with his family from Switzerland. His mother, Lucille Sears, was the youngest child of a polygamous Utah family which, in her generation, became mainstream American. In this sense, Lucille was also first generation. The culture of her youth differed from that to which she was becoming acclimated.

Mark's grandfather was depicted as a man of extraordinary faith in Spencer J. Palmer's *The Expanding Church*: "Brother Hoffmann [sic] was an architect and wanted to go to America. To this end, he had saved 13,000 German marks (about $3,000). However, [the president] of the Swiss-German Mission called him on a mission. Without questioning authority, he went on the mission in 1914 and was assigned to serve in his native Germany.

"During World War I, Brother Hoffmann served in the German army medical corps. After six weeks' service, a shell exploded in front of him and a comrade as they were bringing the wounded back from one of the trenches. The explosion killed his companion, and Brother Hoffmann's leg was so severely wounded that it had to be amputated. The army doctors tried to console him by telling him how well he could get along with a crutch. 'I don't want one,' he said. 'I am an architect, and what I want is an artificial limb that will permit me to earn my living.' "

While still in the hospital, Hofmann was called as a mission leader in Germany. "So Brother Hoffmann directed the affairs of the mission in Germany from his bedside in the hospital during World War I. He gathered the patients together around his bed and taught them the gospel. All told, he bore his testimony to about two hundred people."

Hofmann was homeless, crippled, and, like other architects, unemployable. "Mornings and evenings he poured out his soul to the Lord in fervent prayer. He cried, 'Father, I sacrificed to you everything I had: my savings, my leg, and my time. Today I have no work. Now it is up to you to help me.' " In response, he soon found work and prospered. Required to work on Sunday, he changed jobs and prospered even more. He credited his success to his payment of a 10 percent tithe to the church.

This story did not mention that in January 1918 Hofmann married Margrete Seline Katharina Albisser, also a Mormon missionary. A son was born in October, and Margrete was released as a missionary shortly before a daughter was born a year later. The family moved to Zurich, where Margrete had servants to help with the housework and the children. Soon after William's birth in 1928, the couple decided to emigrate to Salt Lake City.

At first, they stayed with relatives and friends, then purchased a two-story house near the city center and bought furniture on credit. Edward found a job with the LDS church as the editor of the *Beobachter*, the church's German weekly newspaper. Wages were low during the 1930s, however, and members of the Hofmanns' home ward helped meet the needs of the growing family, now numbering fourteen. Later, Hofmann performed occasional interior architectural work for the church. He read and collected books and eventually passed his library on to his oldest son.

During hard times, Margrete sent her older children to the Growers Market to buy vegetables wholesale and peddle them. She kept her own cow and garden and saved virtually everything. Despite the pinched pennies, the lack of luxuries and household help, Margrete ensured that holidays saw the dining room table loaded with homemade clothes and gifts.

Once the language barrier was breached, the Hofmann family was admitted to the Salt Lake Temple in June 1929. Mormon doctrine takes literally Matthew 18:18, "Whatsoever ye shall bind on earth shall be bound in heaven." The Hofmann family was "sealed" to one another for "time and all eternity."

"Right is right and wrong is wrong, no matter what the subject," Edward taught his children. Every morning the family knelt in a circle to pray, until, as the children got older, their schedules made morning prayer impractical. Even then, every evening the chairs around the dinner table were reversed until the family knelt for prayer. And each Sunday, the family convened for scripture reading and discussion, again formalized by prayers.

Edward was firm in his opinions. Offended in later years by the church's decision to build a gym instead of a meetinghouse in central Salt Lake City, he refused thereafter to sustain the leader he held responsible. "All in favor," a local church officer would intone routinely, as a wave of uplifted hands washed through the Assembly Hall on Temple Square. "Any opposed." Hofmann's hand would rise, every time, alone.

His determination was reflected in his son, Bill, who graduated from high school with an award for perfect attendance since kindergarten. Even injuries suffered in a car accident his senior year—when he had a record to protect—did not keep him away.

Most of the Hofmann children married young. Bill, the only son to serve a mission, was followed later by his sister, Gloria. Soon grandchildren rushed into the house on Colfax Avenue, raiding Grandma's pantry, avoiding Grandpa's cane, and climbing on his knee for the Hershey bars he kept in a desk drawer. For years, the home provided a family hub. Bill and Lue Hofmann dropped off Heidi and Mark late one Christmas day and went to the hospital for Jody's birth. About two years later, when Mark was five years old, his grandfather died.

Expectations for the Hofmann family's second generation in America were high, and much of the family talk centered on their accomplishments and ambitions. Cleanliness and hard work were two hallmark virtues impressed upon the children. "Willy knows how to work and he knows how to clean," Mark's cousin, Tom, remembered hearing from his grandmother, who turned the house inside out to clean each year. "That's why he is successful."

Among the second and third generations of Utah Hofmanns, Mark Hofmann and Mike Woolley were regarded as the family's "little geniuses." Both were curious, loved to experiment, and enjoyed playing alone. Born just a month apart, they understood each other. Mark, especially, had a passion for fire and explosives. Their attempt to make nitroglycerine, for example, in the furnace room of Mike's home during a family party was not something they boasted of to their parents. When the intended mixture would not ignite, they decided to distill it. In the process, they noticed a strange vapor rising from the substance. Impulsively, Mark struck a match and held it toward the flask. Fire jumped to the table, and the cousins scrambled to put it out. Outside the room, the family party continued undisturbed.

The two cousins grew up together, for even when Mark's family lived in California, the bonds in both extended families kept Mark and his sisters, Heidi and Jody, close to their cousins. During summer vacations and holidays, they played together and always looked forward to the next visit.

Whether in Utah or California, Bill and Lucille Hofmann's home was inviting, frugal, and orderly. Bill had mechanical skills, which he passed on to Mark. When they visited relatives, Bill routinely made small repairs.

As a child, Mark became proficient at magic tricks. He loved tricking people and practiced his illusions diligently, performing them for his sisters, friends, and parents. He liked coins, too, and made a clock with cut-up coins for numbers. He always seemed to have some "trick" up his sleeve and was punished more often than either sister. Born in the middle between Heidi and Jody, Mark seemed to resent his sisters' ability to please their parents. Still, his parents appreciated his cleverness; perhaps Mark would become a scientist, they would add after praising Heidi's musical talent.

By the time the Hofmanns moved back to Salt Lake City, buying a home near 2300 East, Mark had become particularly proficient at card tricks. Like many other orthodox Mormons, the Hofmanns frowned on the use of playing cards. But not Mike's parents. His mother attended church regularly, but Mike preferred to stay home with his father. Mike knew that Mark went to church every Sunday, but that did not disturb their friendship—they did not talk religion anyway.

Mark and Mike liked to play cards with Mike's paternal grandmother, and Mark was always showing off his newest tricks. One night the three played for hours. Mark won hand after hand. Mike knew he was cheating but could not discover how. In desperation, he decided to try a few tricks of his own. Mark soon discovered his cousin's clumsy attempts at cheating and scolded him roundly.

Mark's descriptions of his methods were intriguing, though Mike was not sure he believed them. Once Mark said he won a hand by watching the cards reflected in his thumbnail. Mike looked at his own thumbnail, then decided the explanation was implausible.

Although Mark was only a month older than Mike, he was stronger and more aggressive. He liked to demonstrate his physical prowess and his ability to ignore stress or pain. One day when Mike accompanied Mark to his swimming lesson, Mark pointed out a platform, two by eight feet, resting dangerously about ten inches above the pool bottom.

"Watch me," Mark said, diving in. As Mike watched, Mark swam to the bottom of the pool, passed under the platform, and came up on the other side. Mike refused to imitate the feat.

Mark had no pets, whereas the Woolley home had become overpopulated with cats and kittens. Mark liked to catch a cat and drop it over the balcony twenty feet or so above the ground. The cats survived, but Mike could see that the fall was painful.

Mark was pleasant and respectful to Mike's parents, always remembering to say, "Thanks, Aunt Ruth," and, "I sure appreciate you letting me come." One day, Mike's father helped the boys make gunpowder, and they practiced firing a miniature cannon. Mike kept all his experiments and tools in the furnace room, laid out on a table. The room, with ample space and a concrete floor, seemed the safest place for the boys to play. Mark often brought ingredients from home for their experiments. Once he let Mike know that the alcohol and glycerine they were using had been stolen from a drug store.

Soon after the boys entered junior high school, Mark spent a weekend with Mike and another cousin, Chris Hofmann. After playing in the furnace room, Mark announced that he had concocted 150 different substances that would burn. Given the limited materials on hand, Mike doubted that he could come up with so many and suspected that Mark was adding alcohol to some containers.

That Saturday Mike's mother was trying to catch up on housekeeping and asked Mike to help clean the kitchen. Mike did, leaving Mark and Chris downstairs. Soon he heard someone yelling frantically, "Put it out! Put it out!" He raced down the stairs but found the furnace room empty. He went to the adjoining bathroom and found Mark, his shirt on fire. Chris was batting at the flames with a towel. Mike snatched the towel and smothered the flames. Mike's mother grabbed Mark and put him in a cold shower. She then helped him into the car and drove to the doctor to have a burn on his neck treated.

The burn scarred badly, and eventually Mark entered a hospital for skin grafts. As he convalesced, he began a coin collection. His mother brought him rolls of coins to sort through. Before long, he produced an unusual number of valuable coins. Mike soon learned that he was not the only one to wonder how Mark came up with so many fine coins from a few random rolls.

That same year, Mark tried a coin trick that backfired. He sold a classmate a double-headed buffalo nickel for $10. The coin was in a plastic case. When his friend got home, he opened the plastic case and found an ordinary nickel, with the image of a buffalo embedded in one side of the case. He returned the nickel to Mark and got his money back.

About this time, Mark and other members of his ward

toured the Wilford Wood museum, a private collection of early Mormon memorabilia and artifacts north of Salt Lake City. Mark became interested in Mormon history, historical documents, and artifacts.

Bill and Lue Hofmann purchased a cabin near Bear Lake, bought a motorboat, and enjoyed entertaining family, neighbors, and church groups. On such occasions, Bill spent the day making sure everyone received a spin in the boat. Mark became an excellent water skier, sometimes placing the tow rope in his teeth and letting go with both hands.

In 1970 both Mark and Mike registered at Olympus High School on 2300 East. Mark's sister Heidi was an honor student at Skyline High School, but during Mark's sophomore year the school boundaries had changed. Heidi decided to stay at Skyline, but other students in the neighborhood went to Olympus. Friends remember Mark as "a skinny little kid with a calculator on his belt who hung around the seminary building."

Before long, Mark and Mike began to move in different directions. To his parents' disappointment, Mark's grades were poor, his absences from Mormon seminary classes frequent, and he seemed unmotivated to improve. When they both took chemistry, Mike concluded that Mark had no head for it. Gradually, Mike moved toward a more intellectually minded crowd and let Mark go his own way.

During his junior year, Mark became friends with Jeff Salt, who was a year ahead of Mark in school but only six months older. In high school, Jeff, like Mark, was uninspired by most of his classes. Captain of the track team, Jeff interested Mark in running, and Mark made the team. Mark did not appear to enjoy running, though he performed credibly, and never fit in with the rest of the team. He seemed always on the edge of the group, watching and calculating. Both Jeff and Mark earned letters and wore Olympus's green letterman's jacket with gray sleeves. The boys frequently wore the jackets when they went to the University of Utah library, where they researched science and math topics with an intensity that would have surprised their high school teachers.

About this time Mike Woolley got Mark to join a soccer team. One evening as Mike drove home half a dozen teammates in the car his father had bought him, Mark, in an obnoxious mood, kept flipping Mike's head with his fingers. By the time Mike stopped at Mark's house, he was furious, and during the scuffle, he punched Mark in the jaw. Mark, angrier than before, closed the car door on Mike's head.

When Jeff Salt visited Mark at home, they frequently played pool or ping pong in the game room downstairs. Mark was very competitive and only enjoyed the games he won, moving on to another when Jeff became skilled enough to beat him. By nature a collector, Mark never seemed to throw anything away, while Jeff kept few possessions. As the two researched, Mark gravitated toward anthropology and biology, while Jeff leaned toward math and physics.

One Sunday at Mark's house, Jeff casually remarked that the ward home teachers would be making their monthly visit to Jeff's home later in the day. Bill Hofmann, overhearing, told Jeff that he should go home so that he would be present for the visit. Jeff protested that they were not coming until later — and he did not think it crucial that he be present — but Bill insisted that the boys stop their game so Jeff could go home.

Through such incidents and subsequent conversations with Mark, Jeff became aware of a conflict between Mark and his parents, particularly between Mark and his father. Bill Hofmann's absolute faith in Mormonism left no room in his world for contradicting theories or ambiguous facts. His son, on the other hand, was intrigued by information that was not taught at church. Mark's parents encouraged his learning, hoping that their son's scientific bent might result in a medical career, but any topic that seemed to threaten Mormonism was unacceptable for discussion.

"I brought up evolution at the dinner table last night," Mark would smirk, walking to school with Jeff. As Mark described such conversations, they followed a pattern. He would introduce a subject that was bound to prove difficult. His father would expound what he believed was the church's point of view, then Mark would lay out his evidence. As his mother withdrew, Heidi would support her father's position, though Jody would be interested in what Mark had to say. His father would become upset, and Mark would sit back, amused at what he considered his father's naivete.

Yet Jeff sensed conflict beneath Mark's confidence. Mark, it seemed, could not be himself in his own home. On the other hand, Jeff could also empathize with Mark's parents. The church taught that families would have eternal life together as long as all the members remained faithful. Any dissonance Mark might produce threatened his family's eternal happiness, something Jeff understood through his own experience with parents. However, Mark did not accept this, and when his parents' beliefs differed from his own, he simply invalidated them.

Like poking his tongue into a sore tooth, Mark mulled over a family secret, one he was not supposed to discuss with anyone. His mother's parents, he explained to Jeff, had married polygamously some time after the "second manifesto," a 1904 church pronouncement forbidding the practice of plural marriage. His mother, born in 1929, was the youngest child of that marriage and had grown up keeping her parents' marriage a secret.

Many Mormons — including some general authorities — viewed the first manifesto, issued in 1890, as little more than an expedient compromise with the federal government, which was imprisoning church leaders and impounding church property in efforts to stamp out the practice. The second manifesto, however, was more of an imperative, and the few church authorities who continued to perform new plural marriages did so in the face of church discipline. In the case of his mother's family, Mark confided, her parents' marriage was legally and publicly unrecognized, although the family insisted that the marriage had been sanctioned by the church. The church would not comment officially and had asked the Sears family to keep the entire matter confidential.

Athelia Call, Lucille Hofmann's mother, had been raised in one of the church's stalwart polygamous families. Her grandfather, Anson Call, and her father, Anson Call, Jr., were prominent patriarchs. Athelia, born in Lincoln, Wyoming, was the second daughter of nine children and had been raised in Mexico, in a colony settled by polygamists who had fled the U.S. government's raids.

In February 1906, William Gailey Sears, age thirty-three, and his wife, Agnes McMurrin Sears, visited the Calls in Mexico. Like the Calls, Sears had been raised in polygamy, and he and his wife were childless. Eighteen-year-old Athelia Call, a Cinco de Mayo princess, married William and returned with them to Arizona, where William owned a store. Athelia bore him eleven children, nine girls and two boys. The family prospered in Arizona, but as the children grew older, the parents wanted to return to Utah. Sears never found a good-paying job, and in Utah, they were poor.

Throughout, the two wives stayed close friends. Athelia named her first daughter after her husband's first wife and, after giving birth to a number of children, tearfully gave one of them to Agnes to raise.

By the 1930s, polygamous families had become second-class citizens in Salt Lake City. The church had entered the twentieth century with gusto, leaving relics like polygamy behind and excommunicating new polygamists. When William Sears was called on a mission to Hawaii, only Agnes, or "Aunt Aggie," as Athelia's children called her, accompanied him. Athelia, meanwhile, scraping to support her children, only told them that her marriage had been church sanctioned, not who performed it, when, and where. Her silence was enforced by the excommunication of one of her sisters, who chose to talk. When William Sears died in 1943, his obituary listed two widows. In 1949 Athelia remarried and moved to Ogden, Utah.

Although Athelia Call never renounced polygamy, Mark's generation found the family secret troubling. One of Mark's first cousins summarized the family's dilemma this way: Grandpa could have been a shyster who lied to Grandma about the marriage being proper; Grandpa could have been duped into thinking his second marriage was sanctioned; or they could have actually been sealed by somebody having the authority to marry them polygamously after the second manifesto, in which case the church had lied in saying that no more marriages were being authorized or performed. Those were uncomfortable alternatives for a believing young Mormon.

Mark's mother had grown up accepting this secret and lived with it all her life. She would not debate it now. Mark felt tender toward his mother and did not like that acquiescence. He wanted to know the truth. Who had married Grandpa and Grandma Sears and under what conditions? That answer lay in the Mormon past, and someday, Mark determined, he would dig it up.

In 1971, Heidi Hofmann graduated with honors from Skyline High School. The next year Jeff Salt graduated from Olympus. And in 1973, Mark also graduated from Olympus, but in the bottom third of his class with a C average. His letter in track was his only distinction, and he wore his letterman's jacket often.

When he turned nineteen in December, Hofmann wrote his first and only letter to Jeff Salt, on a Mormon mission in Florida.

Now he, too, was looking forward to a mission. His cousin, Tom Eatchell, was serving in the Pennsylvania-Harrisburg mission under mission president Hugh Pinnock. Pinnock was a favorite in the Hofmann family; one of Eatchell's aunts had worked for him in his insurance firm. Mike Woolley decided not to go on a mission, but Mark was called to the England-Southwest mission. A few months later, Heidi left for a German mission.

When he left for England, Mark Hofmann was a slight, dark-haired young man with light eyes, lush brows and lashes, and an engaging smile. He began his mission in Portsmouth with senior companion Gordon P. Liddle. Hofmann followed the mission discipline, rising at 6:00 or 6:30 a.m. to study. Liddle was impressed with how well this "greenie" knew the scriptures. He noted with approval that if they overslept or otherwise failed to conform to mission rules, Hofmann expressed discomfort. Liddle remained Hofmann's senior companion for six months.

A year later Hofmann became a senior companion in Bristol. His junior companion, Steve Palmer, remembered how the two would spend Fridays together. Friday was "preparation day," when missionaries did their laundry, shopping, letter-writing, and filled out weekly mission reports. Like other missionary companions, Hofmann and Palmer were required to stay together. With their weekly chores out of the way, they would sometimes join other missionaries for a game of basketball. But while Palmer enjoyed the game, Hofmann would sit by the wall and read. Afterward, he and Palmer would go to bookstores or antique shops, where Hofmann would hunt for first editions of the English Book of Mormon. Palmer knew that Hofmann had already found a Cambridge Bible and a third edition of The Book of Mormon. Hofmann bought old things—a sword, Palmer thought he remembered later, and especially old books—a great many books. Surprisingly, most of the books were anti-Mormon. They also visited the library frequently, where Hofmann would study Freemasonry and its possible connections to the Mormon temple ceremonies, though he resolved once in his journal to give it up. He also read Fawn Brodie's biography of Joseph Smith, *No Man Knows My History*, which, Palmer knew, most Mormons thought was scandalous.

Hofmann padded the mission reports, which recorded the hours they spent proselyting and teaching the gospel. Palmer knew this was a common practice among missionaries and was so offended by the unrealistic demands that encouraged falsification that he wrote a letter of protest to the mission president, but nothing changed. Hofmann and he also wrote to their parents once a week. Palmer noticed that Hofmann's handwriting was terrible.

Even though Hofmann was senior companion, he waited for Palmer to take the lead when they taught the missionary lessons. When he did teach, Hofmann generally gave the lessons by rote. Most missionaries eventually substituted their own words.

By August Hofmann was in Bath, senior companion to Ardell Jenks, who had only been a missionary for three months. Jenks admired Hofmann, who never got angry, even when they were chased by irritated housewives waving brooms. Hofmann would give his spare change to panhandlers and once helped some church members rent an apartment. The only time Jenks could remember Hofmann showing any strong emotion was when he bore his personal testimony to the truthfulness of Mormonism. Then he wept.

Jenks also was awed by Hofmann's determination to commit to memory the Bible and the other three volumes of Mormon scripture, beginning with the shortest, The Pearl of Great Price. Hofmann memorized by repeating the verses aloud, each morning, and could quote long sections.

As Hofmann had done with Palmer, the two haunted old bookstores and libraries. Jenks observed that Hofmann would buy any book with the word "Mormon" in it. He read much of what he bought, then shipped it home. He also checked out many books from the Bath library.

Jenks was also surprised to find Hofmann studying *No Man Knows My History*. However, Brodie had been quoted to them by some Jehovah's Witnesses whom Hofmann and another missionary had agreed to debate. Hofmann told Jenks he had written to the mission president and gained permission to read Brodie in order to prepare for the debate. He also made a point of putting a copy of BYU religion professor Hugh Nibley's response to Brodie's biography (called "No Ma'am, That's Not History") inside the book when he returned it to the library. When the debate with the Jehovah's Witnesses came, Hofmann and his partner impressed many of the onlookers, including Jenks. Hofmann liked to say the LDS church could win any religious debate by default.

Hofmann was especially fascinated by six nineteenth-century vintage metal plates and a scroll at the Bath library, donated in 1975 by F. Phyllis Parrot. Parrot's father, William Saunders Parrot, had, in the nineteenth century, posed as a Mormon, created the plates as a hoax, and taken the plates to Salt Lake City in an attempt to expose Mormonism as a fraud. Parrot had also written two anti-Mormon pamphlets, one of which the Bath library had. Hofmann wanted to see the plates up close, but the librarian refused.

When a new librarian was hired, Hofmann tried again and had better luck. He took his new companion, Joseph Judd, to the library to see the brass plates. Judd noted that together with the plates was a pair of glasses set in brass, the equivalent, the missionaries supposed, of the ancient biblical seer stones, the Urim and Thummim, through which Joseph Smith said he had translated The Book of Mormon. For a half an hour or so, Hofmann used a small silver camera to photograph the plates. Judd and another pair of missionaries were nearby, but no library personnel were around.

One day when they went to the library, Hofmann stole an anti-Mormon book. Judd did not notice it until Hofmann called it to his attention, saying, "Isn't it better that I steal this and keep it from being read, than that someone lose their testimony of the gospel over it?"

"No," Judd answered.

Hofmann considered him seriously. "You've got to stay away from this anti-Mormon stuff," he cautioned.

As Hofmann's collection of old books and other items grew and were sent home, he would write to his father, telling him how much the books would be worth in the states.

The missionaries lived in an old building—older than America, they liked to say. The landlady was American, married to a retired English bobby. Electricity for the apartment was paid for by putting money in a box near the landlady's suite. If the renters didn't donate enough money and the electricity went out, Hofmann would read his books by candlelight. He was tight with his money, virtually all of which went for books.

Like Jenks before him, Judd was impressed with Hofmann's ability to keep his cool. One day some children sitting on a fence spat on them. Judd was shaken and angry. "Come on, let's beat them up."

Hofmann calmed him down. "That wouldn't get us anywhere."

The week before Hofmann was transferred again to another city the two missionaries met a family whom Judd would later baptize. Judd credited Hofmann with getting his mission off to a good start.

Hofmann served briefly with a missionary who was sent home for sexual misconduct with a young convert. His last companion was Grant Bierer. Bierer thought Hofmann an odd young man, bookish, quiet, and with strange ideas.

Bierer hailed from the southern United States, and Hofmann liked to speak in favor of blacks, inter-racial dating and marriage, and the prospect of the Mormon church granting the priesthood to black men. Bierer was surprised and offended by his attitude. They spent only a couple of weeks together before Hofmann was honorably released.

Hofmann's parents met him in England, then picked up Heidi in Germany and toured Europe before returning to a double "homecoming" meeting in their Salt Lake City ward.

Shortly before Hofmann left England, an odd event occurred in the London mission — one paralleling the story of William Parrott's brass plates that Hofmann had found so intriguing. A man named Bert Fuchs, living north of London, told some Mormon missionaries that he possessed artifacts belonging to the church. Investigation by the mission president showed that Fuchs had a set of brass plates, both small and large, bound by rings, much as Joseph Smith had described the gold plates. On January 14, 1976, church president Spencer W. Kimball and other officials learned of the discovery.

Fuchs told church leaders that his grandfather had brought the plates from South America (which some Mormons believe to be the site of Book of Mormon events) and told him to give the artifacts to the church whose missionaries would later knock on his door and say certain words. Fuchs also had some parchments, reportedly from Hawaii (which has no ancient written language), which might suggest to Mormons that the Hawaiians, too, were ancient record-keepers and "children of The Book of Mormon."

Fuchs, evidently unemployed, apparently had read the Book of Mormon and appeared knowledgeable about boats and ships. Eventually showing the artifacts to church officials, including Mark E. Peterson, a member of the Council of Twelve Apostles, Fuchs and his family lived for a time at the London mission home, were baptized into the church, then came to the United States. They met with Kimball and other general authorities and were sealed in the temple.

Meanwhile, Paul Cheesman, a BYU religion professor interested in Book of Mormon artifacts, went to England to collect the relics for investigation. He brought to Salt Lake City the brass plates (weighing about 150 pounds), a sword, and a pair of odd spectacles. He spent the better part of a year examining the artifacts, which closely followed Joseph Smith's description of Book of Mormon relics. Although the existence of the Fuchs artifacts was never publicized, rumors about them spread among family members and friends of those involved.

After a time, church officials concluded that Fuchs's stories were vague and that he seemed motivated by material gain. After the plates were found to have been modern creations and the jewels in the sword hilt glass, Fuchs was excommunicated.

In many ways, the Fuchs artifacts foreshadowed things to come. Fuchs met with the head of the church and other high officials. A loyal and discreet church member was sent to bring the artifacts to Salt Lake City where he could examine them, relieving top church leaders of direct involvement. LDS historians and archivists, intently researching in their "Camelot," were never shown the curious relics. By keeping the entire project quiet, church leaders were able to rely on the discretion of a trustworthy middleman outside the hierarchy to protect them from exposure, fraud, or misjudgment.

9

A COLLEGE EDUCATION

Early in 1976 newly returned Mormon missionaries Mark Hofmann and Jeff Salt decided to get serious about their future. Their high school indifference to grades now seemed childish. They would go to college and become scholars.

They chose Utah State University in Logan, 90 miles north of Salt Lake City, the northernmost city along the Wasatch Front. Logan was at once Mormon, rural, and academic; and USU — a public school, not Mormon-owned like BYU — was far enough away to give Hofmann and Salt independence, yet close enough to eat homecooked meals and bring home laundry on weekends. A bus ran between Logan and Salt Lake City, but more often either Hofmann's or Salt's father would give them a ride.

The pair rented a small apartment in Logan and settled in. As they competed for test scores in the classes they shared, Salt concluded that Hofmann did not have to study nearly as hard as he did to make high marks. That first quarter Hofmann passed remedial algebra and earned A's in basic economics and biology.

As he and Hofmann prepared simple dinners, Salt found himself drawn into numerous conversations on Mormon history. Hofmann was well-versed on Brodie's *No Man Knows My History*, which Salt guessed he had read on his mission. Salt felt he could hold his own in these discussions but was less intrigued by the Mormon past. Hofmann seemed particularly fascinated by Joseph Smith, whom he viewed much as Brodie had: a remarkably charismatic fraud. Hofmann talked at length about the way in which Smith was able to "create history." He was intrigued by Smith's ability to get people to follow and trust him, inspiring them to join the church, even though it meant relocation and hardship. Hofmann discussed Smith more as a hero than as a prophet and church founder. Salt knew a lot of people who idolized Joseph Smith, but Hofmann seemed to admire him as a deceiver, the ultimate con artist.

The two returned home that summer. In the fall, only Hofmann returned, driving an old, gray car, alternating too-short pants with paisley shorts, and wearing unbecoming glasses. No one could accuse Hofmann of being preoccupied with appearance. When the handle on his briefcase broke, he wired the case shut. He wore his tennis shoes to shreds, and his high school jeans and shirts saw him through college.

Hofmann roomed in an old house south of campus with several other young men. There were two beds to a room, and Hofmann shared his room with Larry Rock, a senior. Hofmann kept mainly to himself, occasionally going to a movie or a game with other students. Rock was surprised by the bank of old books Hofmann kept under his bed. Rock could see that they were mainly anti-Mormon and could tell from conversations that Hofmann was familiar with their content. He also knew that Hofmann was a returned Mormon missionary.

"Do you believe the church is true?" Rock asked him one day.

"Yes, I'm not bothered by this stuff," Hofmann said.

Rock noted, however, that Hofmann never said evening prayers or read the scriptures, as most returned missionaries did if they remained active in the church. Instead, Hofmann studied for exams or read his anti-Mormon books. He had no magazine subscriptions and hung nothing on the walls. The room was little more than a place to eat, sleep, and clean. That quarter Hofmann pulled A's in psychology and biology and B's in chemistry and plane trigonometry.

During the fall quarter, Hofmann accepted an assignment in his Logan ward as home teacher, visiting church members on a monthly basis. One coed he visited was Kate Reid, a senior and sorority girl majoring in music. She was pretty and popular, as outgoing as Hofmann was withdrawn. After a couple of home teaching visits, the two began to date, casually at first.

Reid's sorority sisters and friends were surprised by her interest in Hofmann. Reid found Hofmann good-looking, bright, eager, and creative. Everything seemed easy for him. He had almost total recall of what he read and planned to go to medical school and become a research physician.

Hofmann had registered in liberal studies, but after going with Reid, he changed his major to pre-dental (with the same basic courses as pre-medical). Hofmann and Reid began seeing each other often. They went to movies on Saturday nights and to church on Sunday. One winter day as they talked in Hofmann's room, Reid told him of a disturbing dream she had had several years earlier. He listened attentively, then went and found his missionary journal. He showed her a passage that described a similar event. He figured out the difference in time zones and told her he must have written in his journal on the same day she had had her dream. She stared at him, feeling that perhaps their relationship was fated.

Reid believed that she was Hofmann's first girlfriend. She'd had far more experience dating, but by Valentine's Day, she also knew that she was falling in love. The two spent more and more time together. Hofmann had registered for winter quarter to repeat the chemistry and plane trigonometry classes in which he only earned Bs. He raised the chemistry grade to an A and got As in psychology and biology. His grade in plane trigonometry remained a B—his first ever, he told Reid.

Reid was flattered that he had sacrificed his grade point average to spend time with her. "We're both perfectionists," she consoled him.

On April 15, 1977, Hofmann and Reid became engaged and set their marriage date for September 7. Both wanted children—Kate suggested two, Mark four. Hofmann presented Reid with a beautiful diamond ring from Schubach's jewelry store in Salt Lake City. He told her the ring was valued at $10,000. Larry Rock was amazed at the large diamond—the largest he had ever seen—for Hofmann never seemed to have any money.

"I sold some of the best coins in my collection," Hofmann

explained, but later Reid was told Hofmann also had time payments to make. Selling coins seemed to provide Hofmann's main source of income at college, for he only worked during summers. He was not, he told Salt, a 9-to-5 person. That kind of schedule was too confining.

That spring Hofmann and Reid's relationship deepened as they made plans for the future. Reid would graduate in June and was willing to support Hofmann's education. She thought a career in medical research would be ideal for him, and she knew his parents supported the idea. Everyone seemed taken with the couple. Lucille Hofmann made them divinity Easter eggs decorated with their names, and Reid was honored by a sorority "rose-passing" ceremony to celebrate her engagement. The couple was photographed for a newspaper announcement in Reid's hometown.

Hofmann taught an Elders' quorum in a ward other than Reid's, giving lessons mechanically from the manual. He told Reid that he had served as a ward clerk and had worked in the temple. If Hofmann did not go home on weekends, they often attended church in Logan, where he kept an arm around her or held her hand during meetings.

Reid was an amateur singer and pianist who often performed at church meetings. Hofmann went with her and watched, but she soon realized that he did not approve. He suggested she decline invitations to perform, for if they went to church, he wanted her on the bench beside him. "Don't be so out front," he would chide. He told her he had chosen her for her looks with the intention of working on her personality.

Hofmann loved her in white, particularly in long, modest dresses. He referred to girls who wore halters and shorts as "sluts." Reid thought his tastes puritanical. Still, he had endearing qualities, such as picking up a fussy baby at church and having it fall asleep in his arms.

In June, Reid graduated, moved to an apartment in Salt Lake City, and took a full-time job. Hofmann moved back with his parents for the summer and began working as a delivery driver. Reid's paychecks allowed her to improve Hofmann's appearance. She bought him Italian jeans and suits. She could not talk him out of his high school letterman's jacket, which he protested was warm and serviceable, but she did convince him to remove the letter. That summer Hofmann lost his glasses while water skiing. Reid was delighted to help him select blue-tinted contact lenses. She was more satisfied with him now, but he was not yet satisfied with her.

Reid's apartment was near the Hofmann home, and she soon came to know her fiance's family well. They were likable, salt-of-the-earth people who seemed to love and respect each other and had a strong sense of privacy.

Mark's older sister, Heidi, had married a schoolteacher and had a son. His younger sister, Jody, a talented seamstress, attended BYU. Gradually, Reid realized the height of the Hofmanns' expectations for their only son. His sisters were encouraged to continue their education, but there was no question that they would fill traditional roles as mothers and housewives. Their brother was not only expected to become a doctor but quite possibly a church leader; maybe, his mother confided once, even the prophet.

Uncomfortably, Reid began to feel that she did not fit the family expectations for Mark's wife. She liked working and intended to pursue a career. Mark did not understand that. "If you want a job," he said, "you can be a Relief Society president like my mom."

"I'm going to earn $20,000 a year!" Reid retorted.

Reid had grown up in a family where religious differences were not merely tolerated but rather accepted. One of her parents was Mormon, the other Protestant, and the family attended both churches. To her, Hofmann's family seemed "very, very churchy." Because Mark had confided in her the family secret about his grandparents' polygamy, Reid listened with sharpened insight when Lue Hofmann once described how she had begun first grade at five years old and had felt herself trying to keep up with the world ever since. Reid privately wondered how much insecurity Lue's family life had added to her childhood, but she couldn't ask. Not only must she now protect the secret, but she also realized that accepting church practices came first in the Hofmann household. Any comment that implied criticism would be considered bad taste, at the very least.

By this time, Reid was so deeply involved with Hofmann

that she was willing to work out these differences with his family. However, she sensed that Jeff Salt, the other person close to Mark, did not approve of their union. She thought he was jealous of the time Mark devoted to her.

For his part, Salt thought Reid attractive but too assertive and liberal to fit the Hofmann family. In fact, Salt thought Hofmann and Reid direct opposites, except that both were strong-willed. He also knew how magnetically they attracted one another.

There were signs that summer that the relationship was growing strained. Hofmann complained that his coworkers were teasing him about giving up his freedom. And Reid mentioned that a former boy friend called or dropped by occasionally, something Hofmann found outrageous. On one occasion, he convinced Salt to help him stake out Reid's apartment. They traced her visitor's license plate to prove his identity. Then Hofmann accused Reid of being unfaithful to their engagement. She insisted that he was nothing more than an old friend and was insulted at their spying.

One night the couple tried to talk through their problems. The next morning they were still talking. Distraught, they drove to Logan to counsel with the bishop of their student ward. "Tell Mark's parents why you love their son and that you hope they will approve of your marriage," the bishop suggested to Reid. "Let them know you're not trying to take him away from them."

Exhausted but more peaceful, the pair drove back. When they reached the Hofmann house, Lue met them and confessed that she had been crying "all up and down the raspberry patch." She feared that they had eloped and that she and Bill had driven them to it. They sat down and talked until everyone's feelings were soothed.

While both Mark and Jeff thought Kate too outspoken and independent to fit Hofmann family expectations, she, in turn, was irritated by Mark's preoccupation with Mormon history. Reid came to despise the big green book he pored over, Jerald and Sandra Tanner's infamous *Mormonism: Shadow or Reality*, a systematic attack on the Mormon church. "How can they disprove the church if they're so sloppy in their research?" Hofmann would criticize the Tanners.

One Sunday he took Reid to the Tanners' bookstore in their two-story, victorian home on West Temple Street near 1300 South. The family was eating dinner, but Sandra Tanner wiped her hands on her apron and came out to talk with Hofmann. Reid resented Hofmann bringing her there, feeling he wanted her proselyted, and refused to listen. She stared instead at the rose bush blossoming in the front yard and listened to the traffic.

When they left, Hofmann was unhappy. "Kate, the Tanners are just ordinary, nice people. You're acting like they're witches."

That August, Reid photocopied Hofmann's patriarchal blessing, given to most Mormon youths as a guide and prediction for the future. The blessing was long but seemed standard, full of the usual promises if he led a good life. She remembered later that it talked about him doing genealogy. She was surprised that Hofmann could tell she had copied the blessing simply by a scratch reproduced from the glass on the copier she used at her office. It marred the copy slightly, something she had never noticed.

The end of August, with the wedding only days away, Hofmann and Reid drove up Millcreek Canyon and prayed to know whether they should marry. In the cool quiet of the canyon, Reid felt an overwhelming negative impression. She interpreted the feeling as the most definite "no" she had ever received to any prayer and then remembered a phrase from her own patriarchal blessing: "Do not be hasty in marriage." She called her parents and sadly returned her shower gifts. Still, she believed they could work out their problems, given a little more time.

The next morning Hofmann told his mother that he had been fasting and praying in the temple and that he did not feel ready for marriage. She immediately ordered printed cards informing the guests that the wedding had been postponed.

The day after their intended wedding date, Reid discovered the iceberg glinting beneath the surface of her relationship with Hofmann. That evening Mark told Kate what for him was an awful truth: he did not believe in Mormonism and doubted the existence of God. He was tired of lying, he said, tired of pretending. If she loved him, really loved him, she would understand.

She did understand; in a way, having it out was a relief. She also knew from hundreds of talks and lessons at church that it was often the woman's role to help a man gain and keep his faith. Just as important, this confession bound him to her in a way he could not be bound to his parents, for his family believed that despite Mark's inquiring mind, he was a faithful church member.

"Let's move somewhere else," she urged. "Let's leave Utah." But for all Mark's stewing and ambivalence, he would not. He wanted to stay near his family and near the resources for his studies of Mormon history. She found that hard to understand.

She recalled several tense conversations between Mark and his parents, usually as they helped Lue in the kitchen. Mark seemed particularly anxious to reach his mother about church history. She would listen — or half-listen, as Kate did — then tell him that such stories did not disturb her testimony of the church. Like her, he had to believe, that was all; he was too analytical, he should have more faith.

Kate, herself a believing if less conservative Mormon than the Hofmanns, understood their feelings and shared many of them. But she was in love with their son. Now that the two of them were levelling about the church, she told him he should be open with his parents. "You can't hide your real feelings about something like that," she reasoned.

He had to, he said — for his parents but not for her. He wanted someone who understood him — who was on his side. If she really loved him, he explained, she could join him. Like him, she could disbelieve but keep up appearances.

Now they knew where they stood, but their private agendas still differed: he wanted her to reflect his own contradictions between appearance and reality — she wanted to mend his faith and make him whole.

That fall Hofmann and Salt did not return to USU but enrolled at the University of Utah in Salt Lake City. Hofmann continued to drop by Reid's apartment after she came home from work. Hofmann was playful and seemed to take a fiendish delight in teasing her cat, Julie, chasing her through the apartment. Once, to Reid's horror, Hofmann told her he had put Julie inside the toilet, closed the lid, and flushed. At the end of the term, Hofmann transferred his credits to USU — an A in calculus and a B in physics.

Winter quarter, Hofmann and Salt continued to attend classes at the U of U, but this time Hofmann did not transfer any credits to USU. Even Salt did not realize that Hofmann's education had shifted from the classroom to the special collections area of the library's archives, where he researched Mormon history and early Mormon money. And when he filled out call slips for Mormon books or manuscripts, he sometimes signed them "M. Hansen" or "Mike Hansen." In the spring, he and Salt returned to USU and roomed together.

USU special collections director A. J. (Jeff) Simmonds could never recall exactly when Mark Hofmann became something of a permanent fixture in his card catalog room. The esoteric materials he requested alerted Simmonds to the dark-haired student who frequently sat at the table nearest the card catalog. Simmonds, a sensitive man sheltered by an acerbic and articulate tongue, noticed the young man reading every page of each volume of *The Times and Seasons*, an 1840s Mormon periodical printed in Nauvoo, Illinois.

Simmonds found something endearing about an undergraduate who researched that exhaustively. Simmonds introduced himself, and they chatted. He offered to help Hofmann locate materials that had not yet been catalogued. More than once, Simmonds pulled a ballpoint pen from Hofmann's note-taking fingers and replaced it with a number 2 pencil — standard procedure to prevent ink notations from marring delicate manuscripts.

Soon the two began moving into Simmonds's adjoining office to carry on their discussions. Simmonds would switch out the overhead light so that the smoke from his cigarettes would not be seen through the window. Hofmann never seemed to mind the cigarette smoke or the coffee that Simmonds drank from a pink mug with USU embossed in gold. Still, since Simmonds, a non-Mormon, could see the outline of Hofmann's temple garments beneath his shirts, he stayed clear of contemporary doctrine and politics.

Simmonds had been on campus since 1961 when he entered as a freshman. Since July 1966, when the card catalog consisted of four drawers, he had been building an extensive Mormon history collection within the archives. He felt that his recently published book, *The Gentile Comes to Cache Valley*, had estranged him from Mormon faculty members and historians. However, he found in Hofmann an avid researcher and an appreciative audience for his tales and historical tidbits.

Simmonds projected the image of a knowledgeable, cynical maverick. His office and the adjacent processing room were plastered with posters, humorous photographs of Simmonds, and cartoons on Mormonism, local, and national politics. In this environment, the two talked Mormon history for hours, Simmonds behind a cluttered desk, Hofmann opposite him in a yellow chair with wooden arms.

In November, a television miniseries aired based on *The Word*, a recent novel by Irving Wallace. Both Simmonds and Hofmann had seen the movie, and, since it centered on the forgery of religious documents, the subject came up. Simmonds loaned Hofmann the book. When he brought it back, they discussed the plot, in which a man, disgruntled with religion, created a fraudulent but convincing new gospel of the New Testament. The forgery was painstakingly prepared, then planted in an archeological dig. Its discovery aroused such excitement that the detection of the forgery ultimately led to murder.

"You know," Simmonds joked, "when I reach the point that I'm ready to retire, I'm going to forge the ultimate Nauvoo diary and sell it to Brigham Young University."

Hofmann laughed. Such a diary would be both controversial and incredibly valuable, especially if it contained explicit references to the early practice of polygamy.

Hofmann asked Simmonds about post-Manifesto polygamy. In response, Simmonds opened the library's collections to him, including diaries and other material on the subject. As he watched Hofmann pore over the collection for hours, he privately labeled him a liberal, temple-going Mormon.

Salt, however, observed that Hofmann had changed during the past two years. He was more reticent, fiercely absorbed now in research on Mormon subjects. He brought piles of photocopies back to the apartment, but he shared little of his thinking. Salt thought his interest, particularly in post-Manifesto polygamy, had become obsessive. He overheard Hofmann confront his mother over the telephone, trying to convince her to reveal the facts of her parents' marriage. Hofmann returned to Logan from weekends at home with tales of arguments with his parents about Mormon issues. He photocopied material for them to read until he finally realized it would not change their minds any more than their convictions changed his.

Salt realized that Hofmann's growing command of Mormon minutiae had not increased his capacity to acknowledge other viewpoints, particularly if they appeared less informed. Kate Reid, who often drove to Logan to bring Hofmann home for weekends, occasionally joined Salt and Hofmann in three-cornered conversations, which Mark liked to steer toward church history.

"You know," Salt once told Hofmann, "Kate would listen better if you weren't so fanatical, waving your arms and yelling."

Reid also saw dramatic changes in Hofmann. She noticed that if she or Salt lost their tempers, Hofmann would retreat behind what she began to call his "mask of smugness." Also, her casual conversations with Salt pointed up inconsistencies in Hofmann's statements to her—inconsistencies that began to look like lies. Unexplained absences, departures, and arrivals seemed secretive. Hofmann could be remarkably unreliable, leaving town, not showing up for appointments, or neglecting to return her calls. Still, he was keeping his grades high at USU, with A's in analytic geometry and calculus, and a one-hour independent study course, during which he read and discussed the new Mormon history.

Shortly after the term ended in June, Hofmann asked Reid what she thought about the most recent event in Mormon history, the long-awaited revelation that black men should be allowed to hold the priesthood.

"Well, if that's what God wants," Reid said with a shrug.

"My parents wondered what you thought. That's the right answer." He seemed amused by the furor among conservative

Mormons following the revelation. Reid did not want to discuss it.

In June 1978, a young man brought to the Tanners' bookstore a five-by-seven-inch letter, beginning "Dear Brother." In the upper left-hand corner was stamped in capital letters, "SALT LAKE TEMPLE," and on the other corner, in partly erased pencil, "Destroy this copy."

Sandra Tanner did not recognize the young man, who said he was from a prominent Mormon family. The document, he said, constituted the ceremony for a second anointing ceremony in the temple, which must be performed by the prophet. The document had belonged to his grandfather and had been found among his papers. Tanner, who often talked with people without asking for their names, especially if they seemed to be Mormon, had learned not to press for information. If she did, the visitor often would not return.

This customer was there neither to buy nor sell. He offered to let her photocopy the document, then took the original with him. Unsure of its origins, the Tanners decided not to publish the blessing in one of their newsletters. They did, however, distribute it to interested people. Slowly, copies of the Tanners' photocopy circled among members of the Mormon history underground.

The summer of 1978 was similar to the previous summer for Reid and Hofmann, except that they were not engaged. Both worked and spent much of their spare time at family activities scheduled by Mark's mother. Reid was impatient with the family's demands on their time. However, she could never get Mark to side with her against his mother on any decision.

By then, Reid's parents were also beginning to question their relationship. "Have you noticed how he encourages you to overeat?" they would ask. "Why does he encourage you to be less attractive, less yourself?" Or even, "Why does he get so much pressure from his family to achieve?"

That fall when Hofmann and Salt returned to Logan, a new romantic development began, circling slowly like a Shakespearean comedy. Doralee Olds, a home economics major from Salt Lake City, and her roommate began seeing Hofmann and Salt. Dori, as her friends called her, was attracted to Salt. Salt liked Olds, but only as a friend — he was more interested in her roommate. Hofmann, meanwhile, had disparaging things to say about Olds. However, by winter quarter, Hofmann was dating Dori Olds, with no explanation for his apparent change of feeling.

One day in February when Reid drove to Logan to give Hofmann a ride home for the weekend, he asked her if a friend of his, Dori Olds, who lived near their neighborhood, could ride with them. Reid complied. She didn't feel threatened by Olds, who seemed quiet and plain and rather awed by the fact that Reid and Hofmann had been engaged.

However, Reid's relationship with Hofmann was deteriorating. One weekend Reid arrived at the Logan apartment to find only Salt at home. He told her Hofmann was in Salt Lake. Reid was distraught at his answer — so much so that Salt was afraid to let her drive back alone. Distressing incidents were becoming all too regular. In fact, twice during their arguments Hofmann hit her and pushed her into a wall. She was more frightened and insulted than hurt, but the second time, Reid loaded up the few belongings he had left in her apartment, took them to his parents' home, and gave them to his mother. But even that had not entirely severed their relationship.

Salt knew how difficult Hofmann could be. He was a demanding friend who ran on his own sense of time and rarely felt a need to compromise. Salt felt Hofmann needed friends and he tried to make room for Hofmann's ego. But occasionally he cut him short. Once in a supermarket when Hofmann exchanged labels on two slabs of cheese so he could buy expensive cheese cheaply, Salt told him to stop. "If you're going to get picked up for shoplifting, do it on your own time," he said.

Now Salt, who had long ago dismissed Reid as a serious romantic interest for Hofmann, watched Hofmann's courtship with Olds approvingly. Olds struck him as intelligent but naive, more Hofmann's type. She was unassuming, obviously in love, and willing to work to put Hofmann through medical school. A graduate of Highland High School in Salt Lake City, Olds had worked as a clerk for the Salt Lake Board of Education, where she was considered cheerful and competent. She was a few years younger than Mark, the middle child of five. Her father's poor health had prevented his working during her childhood and adolescent years, so her mother had worked full-time at a bookbindery. Understandably, money in the Olds home had been tight.

Until early 1979, Hofmann had taken pride in his grades. Spring quarter, he registered for eighteen hours of difficult classes, though he was spending a lot of time with Olds. On April 29, six weeks into the term, he withdrew from all his subjects too late to receive much of a tuition refund. The same day, he wrote a lengthy letter home expressing his feelings toward the Mormon church.

"Dear Mom," he began, "During our Easter feast you gave it as your opinion that certain materials in the Church archives should not be made public because there exists [sic] certain faith-demoting facts that should not be known. While you may take comfort in knowing that this has been the traditional attitude of the leadership of the Church; you have expressed anxiety because I do not share this belief. Since I can get Honors credit for just about anything I write, I thought you might appreciate a letter from me clarifying my ideas in this regard."

Hofmann was not taking an honors class that quarter, though he had taken two previously, in which he had read and discussed Mormon history with the instructor. Instead he was writing a seven-page, single-spaced paper to justify to his mother his differences with the church on the issue of openness and honesty. His theme was that the church should be honest about its history and that individual Mormons should honestly acknowledge their doubts. As an example of institutional hypocrisy, he described a visit with Church Historian Leonard Arrington. "Now that Dr. Arrington is director of the division of history for the Church," he wrote, "one might expect that the Church's attitude toward suppression of records might have changed. This is not the case. I took a copy of [an] article by Dr. Arrington [which called for increased access to LDS church archives] with me to the Church Historical Library when I requested a volume from the Manuscript History of the Church which had not been used since B. H. Robert's [sic] death. His response was 'my hands are tied.' "

Arrington, a symbol of openness and scholarly research, did not actually control access to the archives, although he occasionally smoothed the way for a visiting colleague; nor did his office diary mention a visit during that period by Hofmann or any other young man requesting access by showing him a copy of an article he had written. Furthermore, the manuscript history of the church had been microfilmed a decade before Hofmann's visit and was readily accessible. The story only lent credence to Hofmann's scornful conclusion, "Even Dr. Arrington did not have access to it. One wonders how a new history can be written with such limited access to important primary material."

Hofmann then tied his theme of institutional deception to individual honesty: "Personal doubts and uncertainties are seen as temptations rather than as challenges to be explored and worked through. The individual's conscience and the weight of authority or public opinion are thus pitted against each other so that the individual either denies them to himself at the expense of personal honesty or hides them from others and lives in two worlds."

"Hopefully, our concept of the Prophet and the Church will stand up under examination," he wrote, "but if it does not, would it not be better to change our concept so that it becomes consistant [sic] with the facts rather than just ignoring them?

"The truth is the most important thing," he concluded. "Our idea of reality should be consistant [sic] with it." He ended, "With Love," and signed, "Mark."

On paper, Hofmann's plea for honesty was eloquent, though not, in itself, factual. In a highly rational format, he was confronting his mother on a deeply emotional subject. He spoke of a dilemma — a person who lived in two worlds because doing otherwise was neither possible nor acceptable. He proved his point by not mailing the letter. He kept it.

By this time Hofmann and Olds were making plans to be wed in the Salt Lake Temple. Mark, a returned Mormon missionary and pre-medical student, and Dori, a home economics major who was willing to work, seemed a typical couple. They would marry for time and eternity, have children, hold church positions, attend meetings, pay tithing, and thus assure a supportive ward and a secure future within their extended families.

Yet, secretly, Hofmann was still seeing Reid. As usual, Reid expected Hofmann to take her to the fireworks display on July 24th, Pioneer Day. When he announced he had other plans, their fight was particularly bitter. A few days later, Reid heard from friends that they had seen Hofmann in a car with Doralee Olds "practically sitting in his lap."

That Sunday, early in August, Hofmann and Reid sat down in her apartment and had a long talk. Hofmann told her he was going to marry Olds. Despite their problems, Reid was shocked. She literally could not believe it.

Hofmann explained that he had traded in the engagement ring Reid had returned to him for a smaller one for Dori. "I wanted it enough smaller so that people wouldn't think it was the same ring." He said he was tired of watching other men pursue Kate, that he wanted a wife he did not have to worry about. "I hope the kids will look like me," he added callously.

"But why marry her? What's she giving you that I'm not?"

"She was raised in a poor family and she'll never expect more of me financially than I can give her," he explained. "She doesn't care if I don't become a doctor. She'll want a quieter life than you ever would."

"Mark, you can't give up your plans for medical school. I can't believe you'd drop out now."

"No, I want to do the church stuff full time. I'm spending a lot of time doing research, and I think I can have a career in coins and documents."

"I think that's dumb. You don't even believe in the church."

"I have to remain a member in good standing so people will trust me and I can have access to what I need. But I can make good money at this, and eventually the documents I find are going to show people that they believe in a fairytale."

Reid was quiet. Too many times Hofmann had stormed out when she had refused to discuss the church, or had yelled at her if she had not agreed with him. Finally she ventured, "How does Dori feel about you and the church?"

"Oh, she knows I don't believe, but she doesn't care. She

won't give me the hassle you do, and she'll be grateful for whatever money I can make."

For the next few weeks, Reid tried to convince herself that the marriage would never happen. Hofmann dropped by again a time or two, fueling her hopes by telling her how attractive she was, how he missed her. But then he stopped coming.

Mark Hofmann and Doralee Olds were married in the Salt Lake Temple on September 14, 1979, and honored that evening at a reception in the Crystal Heights Ward meetinghouse on Stratford Avenue near the Olds home. Both bride and groom wore white, except for a pink rose pinned to Hofmann's lapel. Jeff Salt, dressed in a powder blue tuxedo, was best man.

That fall, all three returned to Logan. The Hofmanns lived in an apartment northeast of the Logan Temple and frequently invited Salt over for Sunday dinner and board games. Salt had the impression the invitations came more from Dori than from Mark. Now most of his information about Mark's activities came from Dori as well. Talkative Dori Hofmann was as much an open book as her husband was becoming a closed one.

By autumn quarter 1979 Jeff Simmonds was beginning to wonder if he could turn around in the USU special collections library without seeing Mark Hofmann in the green letterman's jacket Mark wore like a badge of honor. All the staff knew Hofmann, but if Simmonds was around, it was Simmonds Mark wanted to see.

Simmonds knew Hofmann had a coin collection. Several times Hofmann had tried to sell him Mormon pioneer currency. But Simmonds was not interested in coins, not even in Hofmann's Nauvoo coin that pictured Joseph Smith as a U.S. presidential candidate.

Then one day in October 1979 Hofmann brought Simmonds a five-by-seven-inch sheet of paper, enclosed in a plastic folder, along with two pages photocopied from Fawn Brodie's *No Man Knows My History*. Obviously Hofmann had done his research on this document, which read "ca. 1912" on the back. In the top right hand corner was the almost-erased instruction, "Destroy this copy," and in the left hand corner was a stamp, "SALT LAKE TEMPLE."

That was enough to arouse Simmonds's curiosity. He read through the text, a temple ritual written in letter form. Hofmann explained that it was a second anointing blessing. Simmonds knew that the rite was secret and could be performed only by the president of the church. Hofmann showed Simmonds the Brodie material. Simmonds checked the footnote Hofmann indicated. It stated that the second anointing blessing given to the saints in Nauvoo had never been described in print.

Excited, Simmonds paid $60 for the document.

"You have to promise not to ever tell where that sealing letter came from," Hofmann said. "Don't tell anyone it came from me."

Simmonds was sympathetic, for he knew Hofmann was an active Mormon. "I'll have to tell my staff."

Hofmann agreed. In fact, he agreed to let Simmonds send a copy to a friend, Michael Marquardt, in Salt Lake City, whose extensive files on the church were legendary. "Just don't mention my name," he warned.

"I'd like to send one to Jerald and Sandra Tanner, too."

"Oh, don't bother. They have one," Hofmann said.

Simmonds made the photocopy, then locked the original in the safe. He was jubilant about the purchase for a while, but gradually his elation faded. Buying up controversial Mormon documents wasn't going to do him any good in terms of professional politics. There was not a damn thing he could do with that particular piece of paper, he decided, except maybe some day give it to the church. Suddenly he wondered why Hofmann had not taken it there in the first place.

A short time later, Hofmann brought in another handwritten document. This was a letter from Joseph Smith to two young sisters, Maria and Sarah Lawrence. The text was intimate, heavily implicating the prophet in polygamy with the teenage sisters, for whom he was legal guardian at the time.

"Where did you get this, Mark?"

"I got it from a collector. I'm asking $125 for it."

Simmonds looked it over. "I think this is a forgery, Mark."

Hofmann did not agree. "I think it's probably real. It's obviously written by a scribe."

"Mark, read the text. It's too pat, too convenient. It cov-

233

ers the multiple wives, the move to California that was once intended." Simmonds turned it over, held it against the light. He did not like the looks of the paper, either. The back looked like a page from *The Congressional Globe*. "Besides, I don't believe that Joseph Smith was in Nauvoo on that date. Tell you what — it was probably forged in Utah about the time the RLDS sent missionaries out — forged by some overzealous person who wanted to prove that Smith was involved in polygamy."

Hofmann shrugged and took the paper back. "Well, you might be right."

Though no one realized it then, Hofmann's college education was nearly over. In early spring 1980, Hofmann succeeded in answering the most pressing questions on his private research agenda — who had married his grandparents, where, and when. He told Kate Reid that former church president David O. McKay had performed the marriage, but that was not true. Although Simmonds had opened the files to him, which had contained the information he had been seeking, he had never confided the family secret to Simmonds. Jubilantly, he now told Salt the facts, vindication of his search.

He also documented his discovery privately, dating it March 1, 1980. "Today I just found out the story of Grandpa's and Grandma's wedding," he wrote in the awkward hand printing he had begun to use on his mission. Joseph Summerhays, a stake president, had married William Gailey Sears to Athelia Call in Juarez, Mexico, on February 21, 1906. Those simple facts comprised the secret.

"The Church should avoid any discrepancy between the appearance and the reality," Mark Hofmann had written to his mother nearly one year earlier in the letter he hadn't mailed. "Not only does Church suppression provide an example of dishonesty, but when individuals discover omitted facts they may feel like they have uncovered some deep, dark secret that provides evidence for abandoning faith."

"I need to keep up appearances," he had told Kate Reid when describing his plan to marry Doralee Olds and pursue a career in Mormon documents.

Appearance was one thing. Reality he wanted to know for himself.

10

THE TREASURE IN A BIBLE

Dori Hofmann told friends she did not mind leaving school to support her husband's studies. She believed Mark would make a fine doctor, and she wanted a home full of children. Meanwhile, she kept their apartment clean and enjoyed cooking and entertaining friends like Jeff Salt.

Her marriage was seven months old when, on April 16, 1980, she came home from work to find her husband looking through the pages of a seventeenth-century Cambridge Bible. She sat down on the couch beside him and soon noticed that two pages were stuck together. As she watched Mark try to separate them, she observed that an old folded paper (or papers) lay between the pages. Somehow it had become glued to the Bible near the seam.

Finally, Mark succeeded in getting the paper out of the Bible, but the glue along its edges held it closed. By peeking inside they could see writing and a signature that seemed to read "Joseph Smith, Jr." They were both excited, but rather than damage the fragile paper, Mark said he would take it to school with him in the morning to see if Jeff Simmonds could help him open it.

When Simmonds looked at the Bible the next day, he saw that the book had been rebound to include a handwritten copy of the "Book of Amos," signed by one Samuel Smith. It was a common name but especially interesting since it had also been the name of Joseph Smith's brother, grandfather, and a great-grandfather. Simmonds soon fixed his attention on the pitch-like glue that sealed the folded paper shut. The signature on one side excited him. What was more, the markings on the other side, he would write later, "were clearly recognizable as the hieroglyphics Joseph Smith said he copied from the Golden Plates" of the Book of Mormon.

Even as he chiseled at the glue and pried, Simmonds realized he might be holding in his hands the missing evidence of a significant and long-debated story. While Joseph Smith was in the process of dictating his translation of the Book of Mormon, Martin Harris, a prosperous farmer-turned-scribe, had carried a copy of the hieroglyphics, in Smith's own hand, to Charles Anthon, a Greek and Latin professor at Columbia College, for verification. After discussing the characters with Anthon, Harris had returned to Palmyra, New York, satisfied that Smith's translation was authentic. He later sold his farm to pay for the publication of the Book of Mormon.

Later, Anthon heard of his part in this story and swore out an affidavit in 1834 disavowing that he had authenticated the translation. He wrote that the paper he had seen "consisted of all kinds of crooked characters disposed in columns . . . Greek and Hebrew letters, crosses and flourishes, Roman letters inverted or placed sideways, were arranged in perpendicular columns, and the whole ended in a rude delineation of a circle divided into various compartments."

Meanwhile, Martin Harris had given another early associate and friend of the Smith family, David Whitmer, his own version of the transcript. On Whitmer's copy the characters were arranged in parallel lines left to right, and no circle was present.

Simmonds could see that the paper Hofmann had found contained columns of hieroglyphs and a circle of sorts, matching Anthon's description. By then, Simmonds's heart was beating so fast that he could not struggle with the glued edges any longer.

"May I have your permission to slit this so we can open it out?" he asked Hofmann, who nodded yes. Simmonds took a scalpel and cut the glued ends open. Carefully, they folded the stiff, yellowed pieces outward.

There was a faded but legible inscription on the reverse side of one of the sheets. Together Hofmann and Simmonds read, "These Caractors were dilligently coppied by my own hand from the plates of gold and given to Martin Harris who took them to New York but the learned could not translate it because the Lord would not open it to them in fulfilment of the prophecy of Isaih [sic] written in the 29th chapter and 11th verse." The inscription was signed "Joseph Smith, Jr."

Staring at the inscription, Simmonds recognized that the word "caractors" was misspelled in the same way as on the Whitmer document. But between the "c" and the "a" on the new discovery, Simmonds saw that an "h" had been penned very lightly. Simmonds knew that Joseph Smith had eventually learned how to spell the word correctly. That faint letter "h" trumpeted authenticity in his mind.

"I think we're dealing with a single sheet," Simmonds said. They photocopied the end pieces and juxtaposed them, then went to work on the glue with solvent, spatulas, and scalpel. Finally, they pieced the page together.

Simmonds ran for his copy of Fawn Brodie's *No Man Knows My History*, which contained a copy of the Whitmer manuscript. They compared the characters and found that they matched, except that on the manuscript before them the characters were beautifully drawn, while on the other they seemed sloppy and hurried. Hofmann looked as surprised as Simmonds had ever seen him. "Do you think this could be it?" he asked excitedly.

The pair collapsed into chairs in Simmonds's office with the manuscript between them. As they discussed the find, another student came into the office with a paper for Simmonds to sign. To him, Simmonds and Hofmann looked gleeful. Excitedly they informed him that on the desk in the smokey office lay a paper that Mormon leaders in downtown Salt Lake City did not even know existed. They told him of the discovery and showed him the document. He lifted it and read the inscription. Forgetting Simmonds's and Hofmann's presence, he studied the characters, copied directly from the gold plates by a man he revered as a prophet. The paper in his hands seemed charged, a sensation he interpreted as a spiritual witness of the truthfulness of Joseph Smith's calling.

After the student left, Hofmann picked up the transcript and the Bible and hurried over to the LDS Institute of Religion on the USU campus to show his find to an instructor, Danel Bachman. Bachman studied the transcript for a few minutes, then reached for the telephone. He called Dean Jessee, a historian in the LDS history division in Salt Lake City.

Jessee was compiling a book on Joseph Smith's holographs. His search had taken him across the United States, and in the process of sorting through nineteenth-century letters, diaries, revelations, and court documents, he had become familiar with the handwriting of a number of other early Mormons. Less than a decade earlier, Jessee had come to public attention by using handwriting comparisons to expose an attempt to prove that Solomon Spaulding, an early nineteenth-century cleric, had written some of the manuscript pages of the Book of Mormon. Since then, Jessee's reputation as a handwriting expert had grown. Like many authenticators in the Americana field, his expertise was based on experience and observation rather than formal training.

Bachman introduced Hofmann to Jessee on Friday, April 18, but it was not their first contact. Jessee had seen Hofmann researching in the church archives. One day, Hofmann had shown him a letter purportedly from Joseph Smith to two sisters, Maria and Sarah Lawrence.

"It's not contemporary writing of Joseph Smith," Jessee had told him. The cursive script had capital letters that looked "doodled," and the paper did not look old. Of course, Jessee allowed, the letter might be a later copy of an original letter.

However, the manuscript Bachman and Hofmann brought to him on April 18 was different. The paper was brittle and gold with age. Jessee was familiar with Charles Anthon's published description of the transcript and realized at once that the figures on the document matched. As might be expected, the rusty old ink had burned through the fragile paper from both directions. Carefully, Jessee examined the faded notation signed Joseph Smith. It did resemble the prophet's writing in his early life, and certain misspellings were consistent with other Smith writings. A laconic man, Jessee nonetheless could not hide his enthusiasm. He would need a few days to make a definite decision, he said, but the handwriting appeared authentic. Unfortunately, neither Church Archivist Don Schmidt nor Church Historian Leonard Arrington were in town—ironically, Arrington had gone to USU. Hofmann and Bachman returned to Logan ecstatic.

Arrington heard about the discovery that day, for after the USU conference Arrington was attending, his former student, Jeff Simmonds, pulled him aside. Simmonds took him to his office, showed him a photocopy of the find, and told him that Mark Hofmann was bringing the document to the church.

On Monday, April 21, Bachman and Hofmann returned to the Church Office Building to find that Jessee was convinced the handwriting was Joseph Smith's. The three of them showed the transcript to Arrington. They discussed the Bible in which it had been found for some time. Hofmann explained that he dealt in coins, currency, and old books, and had heard of a sale in the midwest involving documents belonging to Joseph Smith's sister, Katharine. Among the items was the Cambridge Bible, which had been purchased by a friend whom Hofmann refused to name. Hofmann said he procured the Bible for a few dollars and later found the transcript.

Arrington called G. Homer Durham, official advisor to the history division, and soon Durham went for his superiors, Elders Gordon B. Hinckley and Boyd K. Packer, both members of the Council of Twelve Apostles. After some discussion, they decided to show the transcript to the First Presidency that afternoon.

Privately, Durham told Arrington he was leaving to attend a Rotary luncheon and asked him to take Bachman and Hofmann to lunch and stay with them. Arrington, too, was a Rotarian, but he followed instructions.

Church president Spencer W. Kimball had been in frail health since a blood clot pressing on his brain had required surgery in 1979. That morning he had an appointment with an optometrist and during the afternoon was scheduled to meet with the president of U.S. Steel. The latter appointment was cancelled in order to view the Anthon transcript.

Hofmann, Bachman, Jessee, and Arrington convened in the Church Administration Building, along with two church secretaries and a photographer. Soon they were joined by Hinckley and Packer, then by Kimball and his two counselors, N. Eldon Tanner and Marion G. Romney. After introductions and handshakes, the church leaders examined the document and the Bible, with its Smith family signatures.

"Don't you think it would be a good idea to leave this with the church archives people and let them test the ink and paper to see if it's authentic?" Hinckley asked.

"Well, how long do you think that would take?" Hofmann wondered.

"How about a year or two?" Kimball suggested. Hofmann agreed. Hinckley also suggested that Hofmann leave the Smith family Bible with the church to provide a context for the discovery.

After some discussion, photographs were taken. Hofmann appeared awed by all the attention.

The Anthon transcript was received by the church with considerable joy. The year 1980 was important historically, for it marked the church's sesquicentennial anniversary. Arrington had announced plans in 1973 to publish a sixteen-volume history of the church to herald that landmark. However, earlier projects by history division employees had met with disapproval from some church officials, and by 1980 the sixteen-volume project had been scrapped.

The sesquicentennial year had dawned amid other problems, as well. On December 5, 1979, the church had excommunicated feminist Sonia Johnson, who opposed the church's efforts to defeat the Equal Rights Amendment. The story of her excommunication had led the national news as the year closed. Features and investigative stories thereafter focused on the church's treatment of women and its anti-ERA activities in several states.

When Hofmann brought church leaders the Anthon transcript only two weeks after April's General Conference, it provided a welcome diversion. Fortuitously, the find preceded the annual meeting of the Mormon History Association (MHA), scheduled in New York in early May. The church was not inclined to encourage such meetings, but this year church public relations advertised the meeting, stressing the discovery of a new document that verified Joseph Smith's account of copying characters from the gold plates. Though the characters matched Anthon's belittling description, more importantly to Mormons, the transcript strongly implied the physical presence of the gold plates and Smith's truthfulness in describing his translation process.

An MHA session on the Anthon transcript was hurriedly put together, featuring Arrington and several other historians commenting on the document as Bachman showed slides. Even before this, the church held its own press conference during which Dean Jessee explained the factors that pointed toward authenticity and Hofmann displayed his discovery. With the Anthon transcript, church leaders and historians found a happy meeting ground.

First historians and then the editor of the church's official *Ensign* magazine asked Hofmann for a provenance of the Anthon transcript. Finding it in a Bible was one thing, but they wanted to know where the Bible had been during the last century. Hofmann explained that the collector he had purchased the Bible from did not want his name known. He confided to some that the deal had not been consummated, but then he finally revealed that he had bought the Bible from a Mr. Ansel White in Salt Lake City. He also provided a notarized affidavit describing his discovery and asked Jeff Salt to sign an affidavit also. The document was examined at BYU under infra-red light, and no erasures, alterations, or other anomalies were detected.

With all the publicity over the Anthon transcript, Hofmann suddenly found himself very busy. For the second year in a row, he dropped his spring classes at USU. He had earned B's and C's during winter quarter. Now he told Salt he was leaving school, even though he was prepared to take the premedical exam that is required of college juniors intending to apply to medical school.

Salt objected strenuously. "There's a big risk in leaving school, Mark." He did not think the document business could compete favorably with a college degree and a medical profession.

Mark and Dori Hofmann discussed their future, and Mark

convinced Dori that he could make as much money or more dealing documents as he could as a doctor.

Meanwhile, Simmonds saw Hofmann far less frequently after he found the Anthon transcript. He was surprised when Hofmann came to his office one day looking pale and shaken. Hofmann was not thinking about the Anthon transcript but about the second anointing blessing he had sold to Simmonds for $60 the past fall.

"You told," Hofmann accused.

"Mark, I didn't," Simmonds protested. "I haven't told a soul. Well, except my staff. I told you I'd have to tell my staff."

"Word's gotten out," Hofmann said, very tight-lipped. "I'll buy it back from you."

Simmonds felt lousy. "Mark, I've had that special archival class hanging around here. There are some real super-Mormons in there. Do you mean they found out?"

"They're the ones," Hofmann said and named two students. "They just confronted me over at the institute and said they knew I'd sold you that document. If the church leaders find out, do you know what that could mean?"

"Not really," Simmonds said, shaken, "but I assume it wouldn't help your dealings with the church on the Anthon transcript."

"It's more than that. I could be excommunicated and then have to go through a special temple ceremony to have my rights and blessings restored before the church would even look at me again."

"Well, Mark, I don't know what to say except that I'm sorry," Simmonds said. He did not see Hofmann again for quite a while but read about him and the Anthon transcript in the newspapers and in church publications. Simmonds kept the second anointing blessing tucked secretly away in his safe.

In May, Mormon-owned KSL-TV traveled to Logan to film a documentary on the Anthon transcript. A reporter interviewed Hofmann in Danel Bachman's office at the LDS institute. Hofmann and Bachman were obviously good friends. Bachman seemed as happy as a child over the extraordinary find, but, perplexingly, Hofmann showed little emotion. The history and meaning of the transcript, plus an interview with Church

Archivist Donald Schmidt, came together well on film. But the reporter needed to capture visually the excitement of the discovery itself. Insistently she questioned Hofmann, trying to prod him into showing some enthusiasm.

The thirty seconds that aired captured all the emotion available. In that span, Hofmann, a young man with longish brown hair, wearing a brightly printed blue polyester shirt, spoke directly into the camera. "It appears to be the earliest Mormon document," he said, "and the earliest Joseph Smith holograph." His eyes shifted and he half smiled, then looked back as he continued, "Also, I think it's exciting just to think that apparently this piece of paper was copied by Joseph Smith's own hand—the characters were—just right from the gold plates that were right there." A smile reached his eyes as he finished, then faded into a distant gaze.

As Hofmann's fame spread, scholars and would-be scholars contacted him to research the document. One researcher called the day after the church press conference. H. Michael Marquardt, a former Mormon and friend of Jerald and Sandra Tanner, wanted photographs and more information. Hofmann obliged. From the first, Hofmann made no secret of his growing relationship with church leaders and his familiarity with church archives. Marquardt saw those as obvious advantages. Hofmann soon discovered that Marquardt's mind contained almost as much data as his files when it came to Mormon history, and he tapped that resource often. He also weighed the fact that Marquardt and the Tanners were anathema to church officials. "In public we don't know each other," he admonished Marquardt.

That spring and summer a number of articles appeared in magazines and journals discussing the Anthon transcript. The Tanners even prepared a booklet on the topic. After the latter appeared, Hofmann went to their bookstore. As he introduced himself, they thought they were meeting him for the first time. He asked about copyright laws and their reprinting of the transcript. Jerald Tanner insisted they were within their rights, and Hofmann did not press the issue. In fact, he ordered five copies of the booklet. Meanwhile, at least one non-Mormon scholar deciphered the first four lines of the transcript, reporting that the document was composed of approximately five ancient Arabian scripts.

In July, the LDS *Ensign* magazine published an article by Bachman, complete with photographs of the Anthon transcript and a sidebar by Hofmann describing his discovery. "Of course my wife and I felt that such an important document should be in the keeping of the Church," Hofmann wrote. "We're happy that it will be available for scholarly study and delighted to have had a part in shedding more light on the Church's past."

By then, the Hofmanns were no longer students in Logan but suburbanites in Sandy, south of Salt Lake City, and expecting their first child. Hofmann was active in various collectors groups, had published an article on medallions, attended lectures on coins and currency, and was developing an increasing variety of contacts. The pressure for a more complete provenance for the Anthon transcript continued, however, and that summer Hofmann traveled with his parents to Illinois to trace the sale of the Bible. His parents had a different reason for the trip. Lucille Hofmann was a stake Relief Society president and wanted to attend a special ceremony honoring the role of women in the church scheduled to take place in Nauvoo.

While in the midwest, Hofmann located a woman named Dorothy Dean who sold antiques. At Hofmann's request, she allowed him to examine her sale records. One amount received did not list the name of a purchase beside it. Hofmann discussed with Dean the possibility that it might represent the sale of the Bible to Mr. White. After he returned home, he typed up an affidavit stating that the sale occurred, then sent it to Dean to sign. He presented the signed affidavits to the church as a provenance, and, on October 13, the Anthon transaction was consummated. In exchange for giving the document to the LDS church, Hofmann received Mormon coins, currency, and a first edition of the Book of Mormon, worth a total of $20,000.

That fall, Kate Reid happened to run into one of Hofmann's aunts. They chatted for a few minutes. Perhaps to soothe Reid's feelings, his aunt told her about an incident that had happened at a family party at the Hofmann's Bear Lake cabin.

Everyone had been dancing, she said, cousin with cousin, husband with wife, and Dori had wanted Mark to dance with her, but he would not. After Dori dozed off, Mark woke her roughly and said, "If you want to dance, dance now." The aunt shook her head. "He wouldn't have treated you that way," she told Reid.

Afterwards, Reid could not put the incident out of her mind. Finally, she called Hofmann's house. She told him what she had heard. "You chose Dori, Mark, and you'd better treat her right. I just called to tell you that if I *ever* hear of you hitting her, I'll tell your parents."

Once that was done, the conversation continued. Reid had heard that Bill Hofmann had been diagnosed with Hodgkin's disease and expressed her sympathy. She thought Mark was frightened, because he could barely discuss the subject, answering her questions about the prognosis and treatment in monosyllables.

More cheerfully, he reported the success of the Anthon transcript, how the telephone was ringing all the time now with people interested in his discovery. Reid concentrated on the familiar sound of his voice. Then his tone changed, and she knew that Dori had walked through the room.

"I miss you," he said after a minute.

"I miss you, too." Reid still nurtured hopes that one day Mark would come back to her.

"This isn't good," Hofmann said. "My feelings about you are too strong to have you in my life at all." Finally, they said good-bye.

In early November, Hofmann checked on his order with the Tanners for the five copies of their Anthon booklet he had requested. They sent him a letter explaining that the order had been lost but that they were backordering the booklets. In January 1981 he stopped by their bookstore. His package was in the mail. He stayed to talk with Sandra Tanner, and the conversation turned to Joseph Smith and treasure digging.

Hofmann pulled from his pocket a triangular metal medallion and showed it to Tanner. On one side were small characters exactly like some of those on the Anthon transcript.

"That's interesting," Tanner said.

"Yes, it's called an abracadabra talisman," Hofmann told her. "Would you like a copy of this?"

"Sure." She made a rubbing of the medallion and stapled it to his order form. After he left, the order and the rubbing were filed away. When Jerald Tanner later began researching treasure digging and magic among early Mormons, the rubbing remained in the file, forgotten.

The discovery of the Anthon transcript opened the scholarly community to Hofmann. One new contact, Buddy Youngreen, a Provo collector of Joseph Smith family memorabilia, talked with Hofmann early in 1981 about a long-debated blessing Joseph Smith, Sr., the prophet's father, had supposedly given to his grandson, Joseph Smith III.

"Do you think the prophet, himself, gave his son a blessing promising him succession to the church presidency?" Hofmann asked.

Yes, Youngreen answered, he and most historians he knew thought so. Youngreen told Hofmann when the blessing was probably given and the evidence to suggest that such an event occurred.

In February, Hofmann called Michael Marquardt. During their conversation, Hofmann mentioned a blessing by Joseph Smith, Sr., to his grandson, which, Hofmann said, he had seen in the First Presidency's vault. Marquardt was interested and asked if Hofmann had a photocopy.

"I couldn't photocopy it." Next Hofmann asked if Joseph Smith would have been in Nauvoo on a specific date in early 1844. Marquardt checked an article in the *Saints Herald*, published in Missouri by the Reorganized Church of Jesus Christ of Latter Day Saints, and said yes.

At the time of his death, Joseph Smith had left the question of succession open, leading various groups and individuals to claim the mantle of leadership. Whereas succession from father to son was the practice of the RLDS church, succession from presiding apostle to presiding apostle was the LDS tradition. A blessing from Smith to his son would lend considerable credence to the RLDS tradition.

Nevertheless, Mormon author Linda King Newell, who by 1981 had spent five years studying the life of Joseph Smith's wife, Emma, believed such a blessing had been given. Emma Smith had stayed in the midwest, after her husband's murder, rather than follow the majority of church members to the Rocky Mountains. The resulting enmity between Emma Smith and Brigham Young had tarbrushed her reputation among LDS Mormons for more than a century.

Newell and her co-author Valeen Tippetts Avery had just finished writing a chapter on the probability that Joseph Smith had blessed his son as successor, when they heard that the original blessing had been discovered. The discoverer, they learned, was Mark Hofmann, the same lucky young man who had found the Anthon transcript.

When Newell saw the blessing, her initial reaction was that the date was wrong. From other nineteenth-century sources, she believed Smith had given the blessing during the spring of 1844. Gradually she adjusted her thinking; perhaps spring-like weather or a January thaw had influenced the reminiscent accounts. People's memories were not always reliable. In any case, since the blessing was extant, Newell and Avery's chapter was now no longer needed in the biography.

The document, dated January 14, 1844, began, "Blessed of the Lord is my son Joseph, who is called the third . . . " Farther down, the key sentence read, "For he shall be my successor to the Presidency of the High Priesthood; a Seer, and a Revelator, and a Prophet, unto the Church; which appointment belongeth to him by blessing, and also by right."

Such a document did not fit comfortably with LDS tradition, nor did the Joseph Smith III blessing have the intriguing discovery story that accompanied the Anthon transcript. Hofmann had borrowed $10,000 from Salt Lake City coin dealer Alvin Rust to buy a Thomas Bullock collection, which had contained the blessing. Bullock, Hofmann explained to Rust, had been a church clerk and, therefore, scribe for the blessing.

Looking for a buyer, Hofmann showed LDS church archivist Don Schmidt a photocopy of the blessing on February 16. Schmidt immediately recognized the importance and potential controversy but kept a poker face. "I'd have to see the original."

"I could probably get a Book of Commandments from the RLDS," Hofmann said.

Schmidt thought this ambitious. "Where did you get this, Mark?"

"It came in a collection I purchased from the Bullock family in Coalville, from Allen Bullock to be specific."

With no commitment from Schmidt, Hofmann next showed the original of the blessing to University of Utah special collections director Everett Cooley. Cooley, too, was interested, but the university's collection was not for trade.

On February 24, Hofmann called an RLDS historian and told her about the blessing. The next day RLDS church historian Richard Howard called Hofmann back. He was very interested in the blessing and arranged to fly to Salt Lake City and meet Hofmann on March 2 at the Church Office Building. Hofmann promised that he would not sell the blessing before March 8, by which time Howard thought he could make arrangements for its purchase if it was authentic.

The following day, February 26, Dori Hofmann gave birth to a son. Mark's cousin Mike Woolley was surprised to hear that they were naming the baby Michael after him. The excitement surrounding the baby's birth made Hofmann difficult to reach, and LDS archivist Donald Schmidt urgently needed to talk with him. The church wanted the blessing, so Schmidt drove to Hofmann's Sandy home on Saturday, February 28. He asked about the status of the blessing. "Are the RLDS interested in this document?"

"Yes, they are."

Schmidt avoided competing for documents. "You finish your negotiations with them one way or the other," he said. "Then let me know." However, Schmidt extracted Hofmann's promise that he would speak with Elder G. Homer Durham before meeting with Richard Howard.

At 8:00 a.m. on Monday morning, Hofmann met with Schmidt and Durham. The message was clear: the church wanted the blessing if Hofmann could free himself from his dealings with the RLDS. Hofmann thought he could.

However, at 9:00 a.m., Hofmann walked across the lobby, met Howard, and reconfirmed his commitment to the RLDS offer. "I need to have the March 8 date extended," Howard told him. He asked to have until March 17 to complete preliminary tests on the document before the purchase. Hofmann said fine and offered to bring the blessing to the midwest for testing.

That afternoon Hofmann met with Durham and Schmidt again. Despite the promise he had made to Howard only hours earlier, he sold the blessing to the LDS church for $20,000 in trade, again accepting various forms of early Mormon coins and currency. These included printed White Notes, the first currency used in the Utah territory, which were distinguished by an embossed seal of the Twelve Apostles. In turn, Hofmann provided the church with an affidavit giving the blessing's provenance.

Hofmann did not tell Howard about the sale. Since Howard had left Independence before Hofmann's letter guaranteeing the March 8 date had arrived, Hofmann rationalized that technically he was not committed to the RLDS.

Yet while Howard was still in town, Hofmann met with him, Buddy Youngreen, and historian D. Michael Quinn to discuss the blessing. Like Newell, Youngreen thought the January 17, 1844, date was wrong—Joseph had blessed his son in the spring, he said. Quinn had something else on his mind. A dispute between Thomas Bullock and Brigham Young over historic documents seemed to have lost Bullock his job as church clerk, Quinn related. Perhaps it was natural that the blessing had been found among Bullock's papers, since there was reason to believe Bullock might have kept such a blessing from Young.

On March 4, back in Independence, Missouri, Howard began calling experts to authenticate the blessing. He expected to hear from Hofmann within a day or two. Meanwhile, he met with RLDS church leaders on March 6 to discuss the purchase. The discovery of such a blessing was exciting, since many church members would view it as solid documentation of their religious heritage. When Howard returned to his office he found a note that a reporter had called from the *Sunstone Review*, an independent Mormon publication in Salt Lake City. He returned the call.

Howard was shocked to hear that the LDS church had purchased the blessing. Numbly, he hung up and called Hofmann, who confirmed the sale. Howard then called his old friend Don Schmidt to ask for a certified copy of the document and permission to publish it. Schmidt was away, so Howard left a message.

Monday morning, back at work, Schmidt called Howard and asked him to put his request in writing so he could forward it on to his superiors. Howard agreed, but his numbness and surprise were galvanizing into anger. He wrote not only to Schmidt, but to Hofmann. His letter to Hofmann indicated that copies would go to Schmidt and the RLDS attorney, implying, as Howard would later recount, the possibility of legal action.

While Howard's letter was still in the mail Hofmann called on friends he knew would pass the news on to others. He dropped by Michael Marquardt's home at 8:20 a.m. on Thursday. He had been keeping Marquardt posted on the blessing transaction. "I think they already had a copy of the blessing in the vault," Hofmann confided. "When I showed it to Francis Gibbons, the secretary to the First Presidency, he thought it looked familiar." Hofmann dropped other tidbits. "I have another letter written by Thomas Bullock," he said. Marquardt, as usual, kept notes.

Friday, March 13, Schmidt received his letter from Howard. He was appalled. He'd had no idea that Howard felt violated by the transaction. Immediately, he called Howard and offered to return the Joseph Smith III blessing to Hofmann so that Howard could purchase it.

"I don't want anything to do with Hofmann," Howard fumed. "If anything, I'd rather deal with you and the church directly."

Hofmann received his letter from Howard the same day and quickly met with Schmidt and Durham. Within the next few days, a trade was arranged. On March 18, Howard flew to Salt Lake City and exchanged an RLDS church copy of the Book of Commandments, a rare volume of early Mormon scripture, for the blessing. The trade was publicized, and word spread that Mark Hofmann, the premed student who had found the Anthon transcript, had uncovered a blessing from Joseph Smith to his son, promising him succession. The LDS church pronounced the blessing an "interesting historical footnote," while the RLDS church cautiously noted the vindication of its history. Their lost grail had been found.

The bad feelings over the transaction were quickly smoothed over. Howard and the RLDS church had the blessing, which, the LDS church publicly admitted, meant much to them. Hofmann had $20,000 in trade. Al Rust was repaid at a profit. And Hofmann had somehow managed to retain his good name with the Mormon church, though Richard Howard would never deal with him again.

Hofmann confided to friends that LDS officials had strong-armed the deal, forcing him to be evasive with Howard. His story about the church already possessing a copy of the blessing demonstrated not only that church leaders were duplicitous but that Hofmann had access to a vault that was inaccessible to others.

The Thomas Bullock collection, from which the blessing came, proved even more lucrative for Hofmann than the $20,000 the blessing had brought in trade. In marketing the Bullock collection piecemeal, Hofmann showed Al Rust four *handwritten* White Notes—currency that had preceded the printed variety by weeks. These rare handwritten notes had been issued, but none were known to be extant. Like the printed notes, which Hofmann had received from the LDS church in trade, they bore the imprint of the seal of the Twelve Apostles, a stamp that had been lost for generations.

Rust took one look at the White Notes and swallowed hard. "You'd better take those to the church," he said.

Hofmann did, selling four notes to Schmidt for $20,000 in trade—the third transaction of that size within six months. He then sold four to Rust for $12,000. He also sold both men gold dust folders and other items from the Bullock collection.

During the first few months of 1981, Mark Hofmann had made $52,000 in cash and trade on Mormon documents alone. Though he appeared to shun publicity, his reputation flourished. Rumors stemming from Howard's accusations of double dealing also grew. In May, Hofmann spoke on the Joseph Smith III transaction at Mormon History Association meetings in Ogden, Utah. Howard sat in the back of the hall, arms folded across his chest, periodically muttering, "Bullshit!" under his breath during Hofmann's version of events.

But the blessing itself, unlike the transaction, proved good. Howard had it authenticated by James Dibowski, Albert Somerford, and Walter McCrone. Experts deemed the paper and ink consistent with nineteenth-century products. Howard also relied on the LDS church's strong assurance that the blessing was authentic, although they had not performed scientific tests. Eventually the blessing was included in the RLDS Doctrine and Covenants in a section titled "Historical Documents."

Salt Lake City church leaders and certain historical department employees did have a powerful reason to believe in both the blessing's authenticity and Hofmann's integrity. Amid the furor, Hofmann had brought in another document, also part of the Bullock collection. Hofmann gave the letter to Gordon B. Hinckley free of charge — not as a document dealer but as a faithful Mormon.

"Private," the letter read at the top in Bullock's distinctive script. Dated January 27, 1865, the letter was written from Salt Lake City. "Dear Pres. Brigham Young," it began. "My rheumuatism being very much improved today, i sit down to write you a letter hoping that we may be reconciled. I have attempted to speak with you privately, but on account that you are too busy to chat with me, since my dismissal from the Historian's Office, I resort to paper and ink.

"I have only the kindest regards for you," Bullock wrote, noting his seventeen years of "faithful employment." "I have never said that you are not the right man to head the church, and if a man says otherwise, he is a *liar*; I believe that you have never pretended to something that did not belong to you. Mr. [Young Joseph] Smith has forfeited any claim which he ever had to successorship, but I *do not believe* that this gives you license to destroy every remnant of the blessing which he received from his Father, those promises *must* be fulfilled by some future generation.

"I will not, nay I cannot, surrender that blessing, knowing what its certain fate will be if returned, even at the peril of my own livelihood and standing." After a few conciliatory sentiments the letter ended with another request to talk privately.

When Hofmann gave Hinckley this letter, he knew that the church would not release the letter's content. It clearly implied that Brigham Young would have destroyed a historical document challenging his standing as prophet and the LDS tradition of succession. Hofmann also realized that the letter tended to strongly verify the Joseph Smith III blessing.

You had better have this, Hofmann told Hinckley. The Thomas Bullock letter, reaching a church leader more than a century after it had been written, was immediately dispatched to the First Presidency's vault.

11

A BOOM IN
MORMON DOCUMENTS

Mark Hofmann's discovery of
the Anthon transcript and the Joseph Smith III blessing stunned
and delighted the Mormon intellectual community—a group
some members liked to call the "unsponsored sector." Here
Mormon historians, artists, writers, and other scholars responded
to the church's trends toward uniformity and bureaucracy with
their own brand of independence and diversity. Rumblings of
official church disapproval—evident in occasional firings, trans-
fers, or official censorship—merely heightened a sense of group
cohesion and contagious paranoia.

Against such a backdrop, Hofmann's own touch of paranoia did not seem particularly unusual. He told Jerald Tanner
in 1980 and Michael Marquardt in 1981 that he did not like
talking on the telephone because he believed the church was
tapping it. Another time he attributed the tap to the Internal
Revenue Service. Friends noticed that Hofmann's telephone was
sometimes out of service, but they attributed this to his lack of
regular income. Despite his lucrative trades with the church,
Hofmann drove a pickup truck that frequently broke down.
The Hofmanns' lifestyle seemed simple—even spartan, although
Hofmann splurged on video equipment early in his new career
and enjoyed playing tapes of his church press conferences for
friends.

The Hofmanns fit easily into their Sandy neighborhood of
middle-class, young families purchasing split-level homes. Their
baby was one year old, and Dori was expecting a second child.

Both Mark and Dori held leadership positions in their LDS ward, with Dori in the Relief Society presidency and Mark in the Elders' quorum presidency. Mark's vocation stirred some neighborhood interest, but he was so quiet, even secretive, neighbors decided he did not want to draw attention to the undoubtedly expensive documents he stored at home. Dori's pride in her husband's success was evident.

Hofmann's career was based on more than just two discoveries. In 1981, he purchased a large collection of letters, including a number from and to Joseph Smith, from Steve Gardiner in Utah County. He borrowed $22,500 from his father and on May 18, 1981, paid Gardiner $20,000. In November, he borrowed an additional $25,000 from Al Rust which he also paid to Gardiner. The documents added to the collection of Mormon money Hofmann had received in trade from the LDS church for his major discoveries. Rust was especially interested in the currency. The letters sold for a few hundred to a few thousand dollars each.

About this time, Hofmann met Lyn Jacobs, who worked in the church's genealogy department, at Deseret Book. They found that their interests coincided. Jacobs was particularly attracted to early foreign language editions of Mormon scripture, which he collected and traded. Known for his quick mind, his facility with ancient and romance languages, and his access to the church library's closed stacks, Jacobs did a brisk business trading rare books for duplicate copies of other books with Church Archivist Donald Schmidt. Hofmann soon found it convenient to have Jacobs deal with Schmidt in his behalf.

Hofmann and Jacobs became friends with Brent Metcalfe, a returned missionary working for LDS church security. Unlike Jacobs, Metcalfe had not been to college, but his passion for Mormon history drew him to the historical department's search room in his free time. The library on the first floor and the search room on the second became favorite meeting places. Although Hofmann did not work for the church, he used its library and archives for his own research and talked history and documents with church employees. Jacobs and Metcalfe, whose fathers worked for the church, liked to swap stories with Hofmann.

Hofmann also kept in touch with Marquardt, who gave Hofmann a photocopy of the printer's manuscript to the Book of Mormon — before it had been arranged into chapters and verses. Hofmann then hired Jeff Salt to list every word in the manuscript on a separate index card. Hofmann said he was interested in the book's authorship, grammar, and syntax, and wanted to analyze the book in a way similar to the "word study" that had been done at BYU. The work was tedious, but Hofmann paid well and the job was a boon while Salt continued his schooling.

As Hofmann's reputation spread, his contacts among dealers and historians grew. One day that spring Hofmann brought hair samples from Joseph Smith and other early Mormons into the rare books department of Cosmic Aeroplane in downtown Salt Lake City. Steve Barnett, the manager, sold the collection to Buddy Youngreen and later mentioned the transaction to Brent Ashworth, then living in Payson, Utah. Ashworth had heard of Hofmann's connection to the Anthon transcript and the Joseph Smith III blessing. He decided to get in on the action.

A vice-president and corporate attorney with Nature's Sunshine, a vitamin and health supplement firm, Ashworth was also a city councilman and LDS bishop. He had traded and purchased Americana manuscripts for years with some expertise and even more passion. After getting Hofmann's number from Barnett at Cosmic Aeroplane, Ashworth called Hofmann and introduced himself.

"Yes, I know who you are," said Hofmann. "I've been meaning to contact you."

"I wondered if you have any letters of Joseph Smith?"

"As a matter of fact, I do have one I bought in Texas. It's a letter from Joseph to his wife Emma."

"Really!" Ashworth was impressed. "I'd like to see it." He arranged to go to Hofmann's house in Sandy.

Ashworth met Dori and their young son, Michael, then sat down. Hofmann brought out a short letter.

"How much are you asking for this?"

"$6,000."

Ashworth suggested a trade. After some discussion, he wrote a $4,000 check and traded Hofmann $2,000 worth of his own documents.

Later, Ashworth took the letter to Dean Jessee for authentication. Jessee made comparisons and said the handwriting appeared to be Smith's. Soon Ashworth and Hofmann were doing business often. Some of the items Ashworth traded to Hofmann appeared in Hofmann's catalog of Mormon manuscripts which he issued in 1981, and Ashworth recognized others from Gardiner's collection. Ashworth was also soon buying from Hofmann documents he had initially sold to Gardiner.

"Welcome to my first list of Mormon Manuscripts," Hofmann's first retail catalog began. "I have actively bought and sold Mormon Autograph material for several years, but in the past have dealt with a very limited group of individuals and institutions. Hopefully, this list will change all that! I am best known for the discovery of the 'New Anthon Transcript' last year and the 'Joseph Smith III blessing' a few months ago, but I have literally hundreds of Mormon Autograph items in stock. For this reason I earnestly solicit your Want List. The following pages contain some of the highlights of my inventory, however, most of my Mormon material is priced between $5-$50 so let me hear from you." "All items," Hofmann wrote, "are unconditionally guaranteed." He offered a two-week return privilege, free sixty-day layaway for items $300 and more, and reserved the right to change prices without notice. His list included thirty-five items, described in detail. The most expensive, listed at $9,000, was a small collection of papers relating to the December 1843 trial of Mormon folk hero Orrin Porter Rockwell, Joseph Smith's bodyguard.

Early the next year, on a Saturday morning, March 6, 1982, Ashworth got a call from Hofmann. "I have an important letter to show you," Hofmann said.

"Okay, Mark. Come on down."

About an hour later, Mark and Dori Hofmann appeared at the Ashworths' front door. Dori went off to talk with Charlene Ashworth, and Mark and Brent sat down to business. Hofmann took out a letter written in blue pencil and signed by Martin Harris, a friend, scribe, and sponsor for Joseph Smith even before the Mormon church was organized. Ashworth looked it over.

"You'll see that it's written in a different hand than the signature," Hofmann said diffidently.

Ashworth knew that samples of Harris's handwriting were virtually non-existent. "Any idea whose handwriting this might be?"

"We think it's in the handwriting of his son, then signed by Martin Harris."

Ashworth read through the letter. In it, Harris vowed that he had seen the angel who delivered gold plates to Joseph Smith and that he had seen the plates. The letter verified Harris's testimony as one of the three witnesses to the authenticity of The Book of Mormon.

"This is wonderful, Mark. I'm very impressed." He read it again and knew he had to have it. He immediately offered Mark the three best items in his collection — letters written by Abraham Lincoln, George Washington, and Robert E. Lee. "I'd say those are worth about $27,000."

The deal was made. Before long, as their transactions multiplied, Ashworth and Hofmann developed a pattern. Ashworth frequently went to Salt Lake City on Wednesdays to meet with his firm's securities attorney in the Crossroads Towers. He would stop by Hofmann's house in Sandy on the way to the city. If they had business to do, Hofmann would often come downtown in the afternoon, and they would meet in a foyer near the elevators in the Crossroads Mall.

Ashworth, who enjoyed his reputation as a wheeler-dealer in memorabilia, wondered why the obviously talented Hofmann seemed modest, almost sheepish. After a few missed appointments and bounced checks, which Hofmann always made good, Ashworth concluded that Hofmann was not much of a businessman and a little unreliable. Nevertheless, his documents were wonderful.

One spring morning, as they both sat at the Hofmanns' kitchen table eating slices of Dori's pie, Mark said he had found a large collection of postmarks — stampless "cover letters" that folded into an envelope. Among them was a letter signed "Lucy

Smith." "I don't know whether it might be Joseph's mother or sister."

"Well, what about the content?"

"It looks like it has Mormon content."

Virtually every Wednesday after that Ashworth asked about the letter. Their conversations went much the same way: "Mark does it look like you can get the Lucy letter?"

"Well, I don't know. I might." And later: "It looks like I will."

"I want that letter, Mark," Ashworth insisted. "Will you sell it to me?"

"Sure, Brent, you're my best customer."

Meanwhile, Hofmann went to coin dealer Al Rust and convinced him to advance him $15,000 to purchase the letter. He would pay Rust back at a profit, he said, just as he had with the Joseph Smith III blessing.

Around this time, Ashworth lost his bid for mayor of Payson and took the loss hard. He and Charlene decided to move their family to Provo, purchasing from his father the home Brent and his siblings were raised in. When Hofmann finally acquired the Lucy Mack Smith letter—which evidently *was* written by the prophet's mother—he brought a typescript to Provo and showed it to Ashworth in his new study, lined with impressive manuscripts and photographs like a small, historical museum.

Ashworth carefully read the typescript of the three-page letter. His elation at finally seeing the content soon became astonishment. Written by Joseph Smith's mother while her son was translating the gold plates of the Book of Mormon, the letter shed considerable light on the translation.

"Dear Sister," the letter began, "It is my pleasure to inform you of a great work which the Lord has wrought in our family, for he has made his paths known to Joseph in dreams and it pleased God to show him where he could dig to obtain an ancient record engraven upon plates made of pure gold and this he is able to translate."

Lucy Smith went on to describe the contents of the translation, some of which were not included in the published version of The Book of Mormon and evidently represented material from the lost 116 pages of original Book of Mormon manuscript.

"Mark, this is the greatest thing I've ever seen," Ashworth said, feeling even that was an understatement. He read through the pages again. "This is really marvelous."

"Well, I don't have it yet." Hofmann said he was waiting for the letter to arrive from back east, but the two began negotiating. On July 29th, when Hofmann finally brought the letter in, he seemed tentative. "Maybe it really should go to the church."

Ashworth jumped up. He began pulling framed documents off the study walls, including an original copy of the 13th Amendment to the Constitution. "Here, why don't you take this?" He then added a Benjamin Franklin item, a rare 1857 John Brown letter, an 1820 Andrew Jackson letter, a book that had belonged to Solomon Mack, Lucy's Smith's father, and a history inscribed by Lorenzo Snow, fifth president of the LDS church. When he calmed down and they ran a tally, they figured the Lucy Mack Smith letter had sold for about $33,000 in trade.

The two agreed not to reveal that Hofmann had sold the letter to Ashworth. Hofmann thought it might hurt his business with other collectors, including the LDS church. Ashworth did not want to mention Hofmann anyway. The letter was his. He planned to take it to the church and let them release its contents.

Dean Jessee examined the letter and compared it to another Lucy Smith letter, which the church owned. He became convinced that the handwriting was the same, and was particularly impressed by the fluent style and language.

When Ashworth told Hofmann he had arranged to meet with President Spencer Kimball on August 23 and then attend a press conference, he was surprised at Hofmann's response.

"I really got taken with the Anthon transcript," Hofmann complained.

"You really feel that way, Mark?"

"Oh, yeah. You wait. When you take that letter in, they're really going to corner you."

"What do you mean?"

"When I had the Anthon and the Joseph Smith III bless-ing, they reminded me of my temple covenant to consecrate everything to the church. They said I ought to turn the docu-ments over to them."

"Well, it's not my intent to give this to the church," Ashworth said. "Maybe someday, but not now."

"Wait and see. You're really going to feel the pressure."

The day before the press conference, Hofmann told Michael Marquardt about the Lucy Smith letter. In the text of the let-ter, he said, Lucy mentioned selling their farm for what looked like too high a price. But research was proving the letter right.

"I'd like to see it," Marquardt said.

"I can get you a photocopy. Brent Ashworth has the original." When their conversation ended, Marquardt called several friends and told them about the interesting letter.

That evening, Ashworth got a call from the director of LDS public communications. Ashworth expected him to sound as excited as he felt, but instead he was upset. Word had leaked about the Lucy Smith letter. "Who have you been talking to?" he wanted to know.

"Nobody," Ashworth said. Actually, Ashworth had con-fided in a close friend and in his father but had asked both of them to keep it quiet. "Listen, why are you so worried about the letter, anyway? It's the best thing that ever happened to the church."

"We don't want to lose control of the story. I think it's gone out over the wires."

Concerned, Ashworth called Hofmann and told him about the call. "Is this coming from you, Mark?"

"No, I haven't told anyone, but the church historical depart-ment leaks like a sieve."

After they hung up, Ashworth's telephone rang again. He found his friend Steve Barnett on the line. "Hey Brent, guess what? Some letter of Joseph's mother has been found." Shak-ing his head in amusement and disbelief, Ashworth tried to sound noncommittal.

Meanwhile, Hofmann got back to Marquardt. "Mike," Hofmann said, "the church is furious that word has leaked about the Lucy letter. They're threatening to cancel the press conference."

"Oh, really?"

"I know you've been talking," Hofmann accused, "because I just got a call from Steve Barnett. Now the story's gone out on the AP and UPI wires, and the church is extremely upset."

"Well, how do you know that, Mark?"

"I know. My source is very close to Hinckley. So keep it quiet."

The next day when Brent and Charlene Ashworth took the Lucy Mack Smith letter to the church, they were escorted to President Kimball's office where a photographer took a picture of the Ashworths beside the church president. That photograph and others were used extensively by the church to publicize the letter.

Kimball was slow and quiet. "Are you giving this letter to me?" he rasped genially.

Ashworth hesitated, then said, "I'll see that you get a good copy of it this afternoon."

Later, Francis Gibbons, secretary to the First Presidency, told the Ashworths that after they left the office, Kimball had commented, "You brethren may not be aware of it, but I'm related to the Lucy Mack family." That story capped an already momentous day for the Ashworths.

Hofmann was not present at the press conference or featured in articles published by church magazines, but rumor quickly spread that he had discovered the document. Several times Hofmann tried to talk Ashworth into trading the Lucy Smith letter to the church. "You could get a full Mormon gold set, Brent. It would be worth about $180,000. I could do it for you—take it in and get a full Mormon gold set."

"No, Mark, I don't want the money. I didn't get this for money anyway. I'd rather display it. Maybe someday I'll have my own little shop."

Soon Ashworth found himself speaking to various groups about the Lucy Smith letter and his other documents. He felt that the Lucy Smith letter proved Joseph Smith's prophetic mission and wanted to feel it in his hands when he bore testimony of Joseph Smith and the church. Ashworth's opinion of the letter echoed in a later article published by the church in which it was termed "the single most important document external to The Book of Mormon."

As October General Conference approached, Ashworth learned that church officials were amending the title of The Book of Mormon to include the subtitle, "Another Testament of Jesus Christ." He decided to take his testimonial note signed by Martin Harris to church leaders, who were glad to see it and publicized it with a second press conference.

Two weeks after conference, Hofmann sold the church the Harris note's fraternal twin—a testimonial from David Whitmer, another witness to The Book of Mormon translation. This note, Hofmann said, had been found in the same envelope as the Harris note, and both were written to a man named Walter Conrad, who had asked for their opinion of Joseph Smith years after the prophet's death. The sale of the Whitmer letter gained Hofmann $10,000. Gordon Hinckley had authorized $15,000 for the purchase, but Hofmann reduced the price in a show of good will.

Privately, Hofmann told Ashworth that Hinckley had called him after seeing Ashworth's Harris note and asked why Hofmann had not brought it to the church originally. At that point, Hofmann had offered the similar Whitmer note at a good price, and everyone was satisfied.

As Ashworth and Hofmann continued to meet, their discussions broadened. Often they talked about forgeries in the national market and how to avoid being cheated. Also, Hofmann was interested in outlaws of the Old West. When he learned that Ashworth had been a prosecutor in Carbon County, Utah, before moving to Payson, he grilled Ashworth about his major cases, including several murders. The pair also liked discussing their relationships with Spencer Kimball and Gordon Hinckley. Ashworth felt that his meetings with these men were spiritual highlights, and he shared some of his experiences with Hofmann, who, he felt, could understand. Sometimes Hofmann changed the subject, but other times he topped Ashworth's stories. "President Kimball has made me some very special promises," he said during one discussion.

Hofmann, Ashworth, and Church Archivist Don Schmidt formed three points of a sometimes tense triangle, since Hofmann was likely to take his best Mormon items to the church or to Ashworth. Schmidt had decided that building a personal collection would be a conflict of interest, so he built up the church's collection as if it were his own. Schmidt saw Ashworth as a Mormon who put his own desires ahead of the church's mandate to collect its history. On the other hand, Ashworth saw Schmidt as a competitor, for he felt that he was fulfilling a mission to buy faith-promoting documents and publicize them.

On one occasion, while Ashworth was preparing to publish in *Brigham Young University Studies* a John Taylor journal dating from the 1840s he had recently purchased, he omitted one page of the original in a photocopy he sent to Church Archives. Schmidt noticed the omission and sent him a letter asking if it was intentional and if he could have a copy of the missing page. Ashworth could not resist twitting him. He wrote back, "Well, the page you mentioned is blank, but the next one is pretty interesting." He sent no copy.

Later, Ashworth learned that an LDS ward in Spanish Fork had kept all its old records, including ledgers and minute books dating back to the 1850s. He called Schmidt who he thought would want the materials. When their resulting meeting ended, Schmidt walked over, put his arm around Ashworth's shoulder, and commented to those nearby, "You know, the only problem with Brent is that he's so darn selfish."

Perhaps he meant the comment as a joke, given Ashworth's help with the minute books, but Ashworth was stung and retorted, "Well, at least I make my documents public!"

As these and other nineteenth-century Mormon documents came to light, they not only reached the public but were sifted into the careful scholarship of historians researching and writing Mormon history. Linda Newell and Valeen Avery were completing their Emma Smith biography, *Mormon Enigma*, which dealt with Joseph Smith and polygamy, a complex and delicate subject. Newell had begun tracing sources that indicated Smith may have been in the process of abandoning polygamy shortly before he was killed. However, she had heard of a letter from

Smith to Maria and Sarah Lawrence. Newell went to the LDS history division to see the letter. Access to primary sources was tightening, but she was given permission to see it.

The letter, dated June 23, 1844, was written four days before Smith's death and resembled another letter he had written about one of his other plural wives. Newell thought the handwriting odd but was told that this was a copy of the original and had been found in the Thomas Bullock collection.

The letter was obviously intimate. "Keep all things treasured up in your breasts, burn this letter as you read it. I close in hast [sic]. Do not dispair. Pray for me as I bleed my heart for you."

Newell could only conclude that Smith was a polygamist up to his death. "The letter documents the fact that Joseph intended to go to Washington and, if he did not have success there, would consider going to Texas or California," Newell and Avery wrote, adding wryly that "The letter also illustrates that he had a propensity to take his problems with him. He wanted Emma to inform him that evening if she decided to go to Cincinnati, because he did not want her and the Lawrence sisters in the same town."

The boom in Mormon documents from 1981 to 1985 included not only the sale of important letters but also of several pieces of the original manuscript of the Book of Mormon. On October 21, 1982, Hofmann sold Ashworth a half-page fragment from the "Book of Mosiah" for $5,000. To meet that price Ashworth traded his Wild Bill Hickok letter, Hickok's last letter, written from Deadwood, South Dakota, in July 1876. Later, Ashworth bought a second fragment, this one a full page from the "Book of Helaman" for $25,000. Both delicate fragments were subsequently featured in an article in the church's *Ensign* magazine, complete with color photographs.

Hofmann also sold Ashworth some fragments so tiny and smudged they could not be read, but he gave Ashworth an infrared lamp to read them by. Ashworth never tried the lamp. Instead, he gave it to Charlene, and every Halloween thereafter the Ashworth house wore a spooky red glow.

The Mormon market was becoming so lucrative and brisk that Ashworth proposed a partnership with Hofmann. Such an arrangement would give Ashworth an exclusive line on Hofmann's discoveries. They discussed the possibility of Hofmann moving to Rochester, New York, to look for the lost 116 pages of the Book of Mormon. Meanwhile, Ashworth would handle the Utah market and the legal work. The subject came up one day while the pair were sitting in the living room of Mark's house in Sandy.

"We're not going to move," Hofmann said. "We've got family here."

"Well, we can still be partners."

"No, there's really not enough money in this for the two of us."

Randy Wilson, a Salt Lake collector interested in Western Americana, met Hofmann through mutual acquaintances. Wilson watched Hofmann's dealings bemusedly. One thing he could never understand was why, when Hofmann had so many fine items he could market himself, he sold them wholesale to Deseret Book. One time he asked Hofmann, who explained that he liked to give Curt Bench a break once in a while.

Wilson's deals with Hofmann were less frequent. "I got the first edition Book of Mormon you asked me for," Hofmann told Wilson one day, "but there's another item I could get for you instead."

"Oh, what's that?"

"*The LDS Emigrants' Guide*, used by the Mormon pioneers." Wilson was interested.

"But it'll be two or three weeks before I can get it," Hofmann told him.

One night he called Wilson about 10:00 p.m. "I've got your *Emigrants' Guide*. I'm bringing it out."

Wilson admired the little volume though he thought the margins too small. Soon thereafter Don Schmidt asked Wilson if he had seen the volume. "Yes, I've got one," Wilson said.

"Did you talk to Peter Crawley about it?" Crawley, a math professor at BYU, also dealt in rare Mormon printed material.

"No."

"Well, I've got one, too, and Deseret Book sold one. When I showed Peter mine, he said it was bogus."

Wilson called Crawley, then Curt Bench. Examination showed that they all had the same thing—a volume in which the page count did not match that in genuine copies. Crawley knew that a pirated edition of the book had appeared in California ten years earlier. Maybe Hofmann had acquired some of those.

They called Hofmann. "I'll have to get back to my man in Chicago," he said, "and tell him to give me my money back."

Meanwhile, Hofmann wrote a check to Wilson, but the check bounced. Wilson called Hofmann again.

"It's feast or famine around here all the time," Hofmann complained. "Don't worry about it, Randy. I'll get the money to you." Eventually, Hofmann did, about six weeks later. You just had to expect that about Mark, Wilson concluded; he might have checks bouncing all over town, but eventually he'd make good.

During the latter half of 1982, Mormon documents became the topic of articles in the national press. The *New York Times* ran a story on the Lucy Mack Smith letter, saying it backed Joseph Smith's account of church origins. A photograph of Ashworth and his Lucy Smith letter characterized the year 1982 in the church's almanac, as well.

In September, separate interviews with Hofmann appeared in *The Sunstone Review* in Salt Lake City and in the BYU student *7th East Press* in Provo. Hofmann cagily mentioned some finds, refused to confirm others, and speculated about documents that might be discovered in the future.

Peggy Fletcher, president of the Sunstone Foundation, interviewed Hofmann and concluded that he lacked social skills. Writing for the *7th East Press*, Jeffrey Keller was also unimpressed. Both found Hofmann mercenary. Keller's article was even titled, "Making a Buck Off Mormon History."

"Hofmann has since enjoyed privileged access to otherwise restricted Church archive material, including the First Presidency's vault," Keller reported. "One reason for this privileged access, Hofmann thinks, is the fact that 'I am not a historian. I'm not going to write an expose of Mormonism.' "

"My basic business technique," Hofmann explained to Fletcher, "is to turn over material as fast as I can. If you buy things at a good price, there's a tremendous amount of money to be made. I try to sink as much of it as I can back into the search. My strategy isn't necessarily to get top dollar for every item but just to sell it so I have more money to keep looking. The real reward in the whole business is being able to see things that no one else knows about. It gives me a kick to know that this is original stuff, that no one else on earth has pieced this together or knows what this says. So there's the pleasure. It's like being a detective."

"Do you consider yourself an active Latter-day Saint?" Fletcher asked.

"Yes. I'm an eighth-generation Mormon, and my mother is a stake Relief Society president right now." Hofmann avoided mention of his own church activity.

"Do you look for specific documents to substantiate the Mormon historical claims?"

"You can't really do that; you have to take what you can find. I don't think documents really change anyone's mind anyway. For example, the Anthon transcript. The anti-Mormons used it for their purposes and the Mormons used it for theirs. The same thing with the Lucy letter. I think most people are a little like that. You have your beliefs and you don't usually let things change them too much."

As her final question, Fletcher wondered, "If you found a document that was potentially embarrassing to the Church, would you consider hiding or destroying it?"

"Oh, no. That gets into a matter of ethics. It's not my role to burn a document just because I don't like what it says. (Not to mention that it's not a very profitable thing to do in the business world.) The closest I've ever come was with the Joseph Smith III blessing which shook up a few people in the Church. It surprised me that the Church didn't buy it up quick and stash it away somewhere, but I guess the Historical Department is trying to be more objective and get away from that sort of thing."

And as for his future, Hofmann told Keller optimistically, "I doubt that business will dry up in my lifetime."

12

THE BIRTH OF
THE SALAMANDER LETTER

The boom in Mormon documents continued into 1983, though Camelot was gone, replaced by a grim professionalism. A change was coming, too, in the new Mormon history, for the faith-promoting finds that blossomed in 1982 now seemed in short supply. Information swapping in the "Mormon underground," however, became even brisker as photocopies of purported document texts circulated.

The letter Mark Hofmann took on January 11, 1983, to Gordon B. Hinckley, by now second counselor in the LDS first presidency, was of major significance. Dated in 1825, when Joseph Smith was only nineteen years of age, the Joseph Smith to Josiah Stowell letter replaced the Anthon transcript as the earliest Smith holograph. More importantly, the letter described an occult means of finding buried treasure and portrayed Smith as a treasure digger, an image the church had tried to deny ever since the young preacher proclaimed himself a prophet and his parlor-full of followers became a church.

Stowell, a farmer in Pennsylvania, had hired Smith and his father to hunt treasure for him—an enterprise not uncommon to rural New Yorkers. The region was rich with tales of Indian mounds, buried Spanish gold, and village seers.

In the letter Hofmann brought to Hinckley, Joseph Smith had written with little punctuation, misspellings, and sporadic capitalization: " . . . since you cannot asertain any particulars you should not dig more untill you first discover if any valuables remain you know the treasure must be guarded by some clever spirit and if such is discovered so also is the treasure so do this take a hasel stick one yard long being new cut and cleave it Just in the middle and lay it asunder on the mine so that both inner parts of the stick may look one right against the other one inch distant and if there is a treasure after a while you shall see them draw and Join together again of themselves. . . . "

Hofmann had already had the letter authenticated by Charles Hamilton Galleries of New York before meeting with Hinckley. Hamilton, the author of several books on autographs and forgery detection, was considered a leading expert in authentication.

Hinckley read the letter, then wrote Hofmann a check for $15,000, making the Stowell letter Hofmann's first major cash transaction with the Mormon church. Hinckley gave the Stowell letter to secretary Francis Gibbons to put into the First Presidency's vault. Access to the vault came only through Gibbons and was rarely granted.

A few days later, Hofmann visited Brent Ashworth and told him about the letter and its sale. "President Hinckley said that letter will never see the light of day," Hofmann confided. "I promised President Hinckley that there aren't any copies, but, actually, I could let you see one."

"No, that's all right, Mark," Ashworth replied.

Hofmann also told Michael Marquardt about the letter and described its contents. Marquardt wanted to see the signature, but Hofmann said no, the sale had not yet closed.

In March, Hofmann sold to the church, again through Hinckley, a second important document: the original contract that Joseph Smith and Martin Harris had signed with printer E. B. Grandin in 1829 to publish The Book of Mormon. This time Hinckley authorized a $25,000 check. The church, Hofmann was told, was delighted to own the contract.

Some time later, a church employee noticed eleven faint rows of uninked type impressed into the reverse side of the contract, indicating that the contract had been laid on the type in Grandin's office, lightly imprinting an advertisement for the shop. He reported to others in the history division that this was proof the document had come from Grandin's shop.

The E. B. Grandin Book of Mormon contract was made available to the history division for study and publication, as were the testimonial notes from Martin Harris and David Whitmer and the Anthon transcript. Like most of the other documents, the Grandin contract was prominently featured in the church's *Ensign* magazine and other journals. But the Joseph Smith to Josiah Stowell letter, like the Thomas Bullock to Brigham Young letter, was kept under lock and key. However, word of the Stowell letter surfaced, and soon scholars were petitioning for access to the letter on their own.

Fragments of the original manuscript to The Book of Mormon also continued to circulate. In spring 1983, Hofmann offered his former USU mentor, Jeff Simmonds, a faded fragment with torn edges about five inches long and about two inches high. The paper was covered with handwriting on both sides that had faded to a light gold color.

"What do you want for it?" Simmonds asked.

"Your Hawaiian first edition of The Book of Mormon. I have a friend, Lyn Jacobs, who collects foreign editions."

"Well, Mark, if this is going to Jacobs, why isn't he up here making the deal?"

Hofmann said he and Jacobs would work out the transaction between themselves. Simmonds gathered that Jacobs was too shy to deal with him directly. He asked Hofmann to leave the fragment with him.

"That's fine. I'm going back to New York to look for the lost 116 pages of The Book of Mormon manuscript. I've got some good leads."

"Really! That would be quite a find." Simmonds wondered what the dollar value would be for lost pages of Mormon scripture. Astronomical, he assumed.

While Hofmann was gone, Simmonds researched the fragment. Then he insured the document, made an appointment to see Dean Jessee to examine the handwriting, alerted sheriffs all along his route to Salt Lake City, and took the fragment to the LDS historical department. Jessee looked it over carefully, then commented that he had seen it before.

Simmonds did not press Jessee but silently concluded that Jessee was telling him he had seen it among the LDS church's fragments. Perhaps Hofmann had received it in trade. When Hofmann returned, Simmonds closed the deal.

On one of his trips to USU that spring, Hofmann became interested in a register book for Deseret Currency, Mormon money used in early pioneer Utah. The register noted the bills issued by serial number. For a time, Hofmann sat patiently copying notes, then asked Simmonds if he could photocopy some of it. Simmonds agreed.

When Simmonds returned after an errand, he found that Hofmann had photocopied until he had run out of coins.

"I'm glad you only copied half," Simmonds said edgily. "We have a policy here about not photocopying *all* of anything."

"I hope you're not angry."

"No. I'm not delighted, Mark, but I'm not angry."

Some time afterwards—neither Simmonds nor his staff could later remember exactly when—both Hofmann and Lyn Jacobs called to see if Jacobs could photocopy the rest of the book. Jacobs drove to USU, but the staff could not find the register.

Meanwhile, Brent Metcalfe was running afoul of his superiors in church security because of his interest in church history and his ties to independent Mormon publications. After a reprimand, he agreed to restrict his research and writing. But his probation ultimately ended in his dismissal. Church security accused him of copying sensitive material; Metcalfe insisted he had followed their instructions to the letter. He and his wife, Jill, were both disillusioned and bitter about what seemed to them an arbitrary and politically-motivated dismissal. A disappointing experience in the temple afterward further shattered their religious expectations.

That spring Metcalfe had become interested in Joseph Smith's involvement with money digging and folk magic. Soon he was discussing magical symbols like toads and peepstones with Hofmann, Marquardt, and others. He even outlined an article he hoped one day to write on New England folk magic and the Book of Mormon. Despite Metcalfe's love of research, the paper was never written. But Hofmann was interested and showed Metcalfe a metal talisman, or magical amulet, inscribed with characters like those on the Anthon transcript. Metcalfe was impressed, realizing that the Anthon document might tie Joseph Smith directly to the occult.

Metcalfe hunted employment for the next several months before Steve Christensen heard about his dismissal and called him in for an interview. Christensen hired Metcalfe as an assistant at J. Gary Sheets Associates to help Christensen organize his own books into a lending library and hired Jill Metcalfe to type notes for Andrew Ehat, a graduate student whose research in Mormon history Christensen was supporting. Ehat, in turn, prepared an index of his own extensive files for Christensen's use.

Late in the fall of 1983, word began to circulate, slowly at first, that a letter had been found somehow linking Joseph Smith with a magical white salamander. Hofmann approached Boston antique document and book dealer Kenneth Rendell at the Boston Book Fair and asked if he would authenticate such a letter. "Where does it come from?" Rendell asked.

"Lyn Jacobs. You know him."

Rendell knew that Jacobs dealt in rare books but he was not interested in authenticating a letter that would arouse as much controversy as Hofmann predicted this one would.

A little before Thanksgiving, Hofmann told Ashworth that Jacobs had found an important Martin Harris document. Weeks later, when Jacobs came home for Christmas from Harvard, where he was a master's candidate in New Testament studies, Hofmann mentioned he was in town.

"What about the Martin Harris document?" Ashworth wanted to know.

"Oh, well, it was probably just a document signed Martin Harris or 'M. H.,' but it's not really Martin Harris." As Hofmann told it, Jacobs had thought the document was a genuine Martin Harris, but when Hofmann had picked him up at the airport, he had convinced Jacobs otherwise.

Yet on November 29, Michael Marquardt got an intriguing call from Hofmann. "I found a letter written by Martin Harris," Hofmann said.

"Really. Where did you find it?"

"It's in private hands. It has a Palmyra postmark on it."

"What's the content like?"

"Here, I've got a copy. I'll read it to you."

Marquardt took notes frantically as Hofmann read through the astonishing letter.

"I hear Joseph found a gold bible," Hofmann read, "& he says it is true I found it 4 years ago with my stone but only just got it because of the enchantment." The letter continued, "the old spirit come to me 3 times in the same dream & says dig up the gold but when I take it up the next morning the spirit transfigured himself from a white salamander in the bottom of the hole & struck me 3 times & held the treasure & would not let me have it because I lay it down to cover over the hole when the spirit says do not lay it down Joseph says when can I have it the spirit says one year from to day if you obay me look to the stone after a few days he looks the spirit says bring your brother Alvin Joseph says he is dead shall I bring what remains but the spirit is gone Joseph goes to get the gold bible but the spirit says you did not bring your brother you can not have it look to the stone Joseph looks but can not see who to bring the spirit says I tricked you again look to the stone. . . . "

The story of Joseph Smith finding the gold plates was present but embedded in a context that suggested ceremonial magic and ghoulism, a strange contrast to the traditional story of the Angel Moroni.

After some discussion, Hofmann hung up, but Marquardt stayed on the telephone, calling friends. About a week later Hofmann called back, and Marquardt got him to read the letter again. Again, Marquardt took notes. Then they discussed authenticity.

"How can you authenticate the handwriting?"

"There isn't really a sample to compare it with," Hofmann said. "The letter does have correct postage, though. I checked that."

On December 11, Marquardt went to the Hofmanns' house, now in Millcreek, east of Salt Lake City, for Mark and Dori were purchasing Mark's childhood home from his parents. Marquardt stayed about five hours, joining Mark, Dori, Michael, and their most recent addition, Karen, for dinner.

After dinner, Hofmann and Marquardt went on talking. Hofmann said he was taking a cashier's check for $18,000 to

Boston to purchase the letter. He wanted to make sure that somehow the contents of the letter would be made public. "How do we get it out?" Both agreed that it should not be dismissed as anti-Mormon propaganda.

Marquardt took notes as they listed "positive" elements that could be emphasized in publicizing the letter. For one thing, it was important to describe Martin Harris. After all, he had been a responsible citizen of Palmyra, New York, and had financed the publication of The Book of Mormon.

"Grandin contract," Marquardt noted, remembering a recent article in the *Ensign*.

"There's Harris's trip to Charles Anthon with the characters from the Book of Mormon," Hofmann added.

"Anthon transcript," Marquardt jotted beside the notation.

"Also there's the note Harris dictated to Walter Conrad. I sold that to Brent Ashworth. It might balance out the salamander letter in some Mormons' minds."

The salamander letter was so controversial it would have to be supported by respectable Mormon historians, they thought. "I've got an 1828 dictionary," Hofmann contributed. "Why don't we look up 'salamander' and see what it meant then?"

They found that a salamander could be a mystical creature, capable of living in fire. Someone living in the 1820s could equate a glorious angelic messenger with a salamander that changed into a spirit.

Hofmann ran downstairs and returned with a triangular metal amulet. He showed Marquardt that some of the engraved characters were identical to those on the Anthon transcript. This, too, might link Joseph Smith with magic at the time he was translating The Book of Mormon. As they returned to the subject of the salamander letter, they agreed that Hofmann should get an interview with the *New York Times* and have the letter reviewed in *Newsweek*. Exhausted, Marquardt finally gathered his notes of the five-hour discussion together and went home.

Two days later, he heard from Hofmann again. "Word about the Harris letter has leaked. It's gotten back to the person who has the letter — and I just got a call from the owner."

"Where was the leak?" Marquardt asked, wincing.

"The leak was in Idaho. I figure you must have told somebody." He had. Hofmann had never said the letter was confidential, and Marquardt knew that a friend in Idaho had called three eastern dealers to learn more about the letter. Word had obviously gotten back to Hofmann, so Marquardt assumed that one of the dealers was the owner. He passed that word on. Marquardt's friends, Jerald and Sandra Tanner, were interested in the letter but could not afford Hofmann's high asking price. If they could not buy the letter, they at least wanted a certified copy of the original.

Shortly before Christmas, Lyn Jacobs, home from Harvard on vacation, took the original of the letter to Donald Schmidt at church archives. Schmidt got a brief look at the letter before Jacobs pulled it back. "I expect six figures for this one," Jacobs said. "I want one of the early pioneer $10 gold coins the church has."

"You can forget that," Schmidt responded. "Where are you going to sell that letter if the church doesn't buy it?"

Jacobs shrugged, then made an appointment to see Gordon Hinckley. He took the letter with him, but the interview was brief and unsuccessful. Jacobs was put off by the fact that Hinckley asked more questions about him than about the letter. Jacobs later met with Hofmann and told him that he had been unable to interest the church in purchasing the letter. Undaunted, Hofmann telephoned Ashworth and said he and Jacob were offering the Martin Harris letter for sale. "I thought you said it wasn't anything."

"Oh, I was just pulling your leg. Really, it's the most fantastic letter. Lyn wants $50,000 for it. We're offering it to you first."

"Whose letter is it, yours or Lyn's?"

"Lyn would get $40,000 and I'd get $10,000, because I had the necessary contacts. Lyn did a great job finding this letter."

Hofmann and Ashworth got together. "Here's the typescript," Hofmann said.

Ashworth read the long letter. He had just finished reading E. D. Howe's *Mormonism Unvailed* [sic], published in 1834, the first major anti-Mormon publication. Howe's influential book contained several affidavits from Joseph Smith's neighbors regarding his involvement in magic and treasure seeking. To Ashworth, the Harris letter seemed *too* familiar, too pat. He handed it back. "Mark, this thing's got to be a fake. Besides, this really ought to go to the church. You shouldn't put any collector in the position of owning a letter like this."

Hofmann went back to Schmidt and told him he thought he could get the letter for the church, if Gordon Hinckley were interested. Hofmann knew that the letter's price and its controversial contents required higher approval. Schmidt had heard that Hofmann was somehow involved with the letter and had gathered that Ashworth and perhaps other collectors had seen it. He read the letter through. "Well, if there's a reasonable price I'm interested in it."

"Okay, let's talk about it." But that afternoon Hofmann dropped by again and said that the letter had been sold. The church was interested to know where the letter was going. Hofmann obliged.

During the first days of January, Brent Metcalfe had brought a note to his employer, Steven Christensen, informing him that Hofmann had found a document linking the coming forth of The Book of Mormon and money digging and that Hofmann was on his way over.

"Tell me as soon as he gets here," Christensen replied.

Hofmann arrived and showed Christensen a copy of the letter. Christensen was very interested but questioned the letter's authenticity. Metcalfe, who had only heard about the letter, was overwhelmed. True, he had read similar information in other sources. But in the letter, the experience with the salamander was so poignantly stated. As a result of his research, Metcalfe had already concluded that Harris had a supernatural world view, linking religion and the occult. For Harris, there would not have been much difference between an angel of God and a talking white salamander.

Hofmann consulted with Jacobs, and the two agreed on an asking price of $40,000 to be paid in several installments. On January 6, business-like as always, Christensen presented Hofmann and Jacobs with a contract in which the document passed from Jacobs to Hofmann and then to Christensen. The contract included a non-disclosure agreement and, at Hofmann's insistence, an authentication clause. Christensen suggested they rely on Dean Jessee for authentication, but Hofmann wanted more extensive tests, and Christensen agreed to split the cost. Hofmann suggested Kenneth Rendell.

Now that Christensen owned the controversial early Mormon letter, his excitement was high. He wanted Mormon historians to study and authenticate the letter and was anxious to enlist Ronald Walker, a member of BYU's Joseph Fielding Smith Institute for Church History (named for a prolific but dogmatic former Church Historian and church president), and other experts.

Soon after the contract was signed, G. Homer Durham, the general authority who had replaced Leonard Arrington as Church Historian, inquired about the letter. On January 9, Christensen responded, describing his purchase and plans. "I'm sure you agree that it needs some commentary," Christensen wrote wryly, adding that the letter seemed to be the only extant sample of Martin Harris's handwriting. Some day, he added, he would donate the letter to the church. He closed respectfully, "I hope this meets with your approval."

On January 13 Christensen received Durham's reply. "We appreciate you buying the letter," Durham wrote, adding that he was also pleased Christensen intended to donate the letter.

Christensen's salamander letter project began taking shape. He spoke with Walker about helping to research the newly discovered document, then invited Jessee to join their ranks. Durham's letter, a copy of the salamander letter, and a cover letter from Metcalfe, who had been assigned to the project, were forwarded to Walker's and Jessee's supervisor, Leonard Arrington.

Walker, who had not read the letter for himself, visited Arrington at home the morning of January 18, 1984. "As I entered his living room," Walker later wrote, "Leonard showed me rather matter-of-factly a copy of a recently found document, which I found unsettling. 'At face value,' I wrote that evening in my journal, 'it is explosive. . . . It confirms several other documents that have been recently found, indicating the 'treasure-hunting' activity of Joseph Smith prior to the organization of the Church. These 'finds,' I wrote, 'will require a re-examination and rewriting of our origins.' "

Walker was appalled by the letter's contents. However, Arrington did not find the letter necessarily troubling. "This is Martin Harris's account, not Joseph Smith's," Arrington said. "Anyway, he's quoting Joseph Smith, Sr., not Joseph Smith, Jr."

Arrington had seen depictions of salamanders in European art galleries and knew that Napoleon's soldiers had been called salamanders because they could supposedly withstand fire. Undisturbed, Arrington encouraged Walker and Jessee, in separate meetings, to work on the project if they wanted to.

Walker thought that their initial study—one that would give the letter a context in early New England folk magic—would be a hasty, dirty job but one that had to be done responsibly. As more information on Mormon origins accumulated, however, the study Walker envisioned became a major project that would require more time. He and Jessee saw Hofmann as a victim of his own luck, for Hofmann reflected their own discomfort with the letter.

Christensen formalized each person's projected participation in a letter. He would pay Walker and Jessee each $6,000 for their time and make a generous donation to the Joseph Fielding Smith Institute. "I am in a position to support . . . this venture," he wrote, adding with characteristic irony, "and I will be greatly rewarded for whatever quiet involvement comes my way."

No sooner had Christensen finalized his research project than Hofmann was back with another proposal. If Christensen would immediately pay him the $5,000 payment on the salamander letter, due on July 24, Hofmann would sell him literary and legal rights to the transcript of an 1825 money-digging agreement he had just found. The contract involved Joseph Smith, Sr., Joseph Smith, Jr., and Josiah Stowell. Hofmann had thus far been unable to procure the original, he said, but was still trying. Christensen agreed, writing to his attorney, Alan Smith, that he was hoping to buy the original on February 6 for $15,000.

The transcript of the money-digging agreement paralleled

the 1825 Joseph Smith to Josiah Stowell letter, still unknown to Christensen and the public. One version of the agreement had been published in the *Salt Lake Tribune* in 1880, but the whereabouts of the original was unknown. The agreement lent credence to the salamander letter and to the rumors of the Stowell letter, Christensen explained to Alan Smith.

Smith and Christensen talked about the salamander letter often. Smith, who was not only Christensen's attorney but a friend and fellow history buff, had benefitted from Christensen's vast private files. The two cultivated a religious faith that remained open to discovery. Smith concluded that Christensen could believe that Joseph Smith had produced The Book of Mormon through whatever means the evidence supported. Whether Smith used seer stones, witchhazel wands, or the Urim and Thummim, whether Smith spoke with angels, salamanders, or old spirits, Christensen was prepared to back responsible research, regardless of its conclusions.

While Christensen coped with the challenges of his new letter, Hofmann was occupied with other customers. Ashworth, who had turned down the salamander letter, had his heart set on another document more to his liking. Some months back, he had visited the RLDS archives in Independence, Missouri. There he had seen two letters Joseph Smith had written from Carthage Jail on the day of his death. Smith had surrendered to a Missouri posse, knowing that his life was in peril. He spent his last few days jailed with his brother Hyrum. Days later, both brothers were killed.

Smith's assassination made him a martyr to his people, and he remained so to modern Mormons. Reading these letters, Ashworth was deeply moved. When he returned home, he had asked Hofmann about the possibility of finding another Carthage Jail document.

Repeatedly, Hofmann had assured Ashworth that he would give Ashworth first right of refusal on any item coming from Carthage Jail. Finally Hofmann told him he had actually located a little-known plea for help written by Joseph Smith to General Jonathan Dunham of the Nauvoo Legion, the Mormon city's militia.

"Remember, Mark, when you get that letter, it's mine," Ashworth had said. Hofmann agreed.

Yet at about 9:00 p.m., on January 27, 1984, Ashworth answered a telephone call from his mother-in-law in Tempe, Arizona.

"Brent?" she began. "I thought I'd better tell you. I just read in our local LDS newspaper that Mark Hofmann sold a Carthage Jail letter to Dick Marks." Ashworth knew Marks, a collector in Phoenix.

"What? That can't be. Are you sure?"

"There's an interview with Marks about the letter."

Ashworth was too upset to talk further. Late as it was he hung up and drove to Salt Lake City. He pulled in the driveway beside the wrought-iron sign reading, "Haus Hofmann," then pounded on the front door until Mark appeared, wrapped in a bathrobe.

"What is it, Brent?"

"Mark, I've just heard about the sale of the Jonathan Dunham letter to Dick Marks! What's going on?"

They stepped inside, closing the cold January night behind them.

"Is it true?" Ashworth asked, taking a deep breath.

"Yes, it is." The Dunham letter, in fact, had sold late in 1983.

"But you promised that letter to me. You remember our agreement that I would have first right of refusal on that letter?"

Hofmann shrugged. "I had to put the deal together in a hurry." He fell silent.

Flabbergasted, Ashworth got up to leave. "You're a liar."

"Brent, come back and get it off your chest. Don't leave mad."

"Mark, I just got it off my chest, and I feel worse now than when I first came. I'm really disgusted with you. You're dishonest, and that's all there is to it."

Driving west along Interstate-80 to Interstate 1-15, then south to Provo, Ashworth felt no better. Their conversation replayed itself in his head. At one point, he had exclaimed, "Mark, it's not just the money. It's our friendship that's at stake here."

Hofmann had not said much. Well, Ashworth thought, what can you expect from a guy who keeps saying he's not in this for the historians or for the church but for the money. Obviously he wasn't in it for friendship, either, Ashworth decided. Still, Hofmann's documents were remarkable. He had better keep their business relationship intact, Ashworth concluded, even though their friendship would never be the same.

By February 1984 when Dean Jessee's *The Personal Writings of Joseph Smith* appeared, many members of the Mormon historical community knew that at least one Joseph Smith document—a letter to Josiah Stowell—was missing. Unfortunately, nothing could be done about it since no historian had seen the original and church officials would not confirm its existence. Everyone knew that the church restricted certain materials from public use and kept others totally unavailable; but now the whispers were growing that the church had something to hide.

Brent Ashworth was not the only Mormon history buff to buy Jessee's book the moment it came off the press, but soon he was the angriest. Not only was the Joseph Smith to Jonathan Dunham letter included, but Ashworth also found a photograph of a brief revelation Joseph Smith had sent to his brother Hyrum, dated May 25, 1838, that hinted at treasure digging. Called the Far West letter, Hofmann had promised Ashworth first right of refusal on that letter, too. Within the hour, Ashworth was at the Hofmanns' front door. Dori answered.

"Is Mark here?"

"He's not home."

"I'm really mad, Dori. You see this book? Dean's book is out. This letter, right here, was promised to me, but it went to the church."

"Well, I don't know anything about it."

"I'm really ticked off. Where's Mark?"

"I don't know, and I don't really know when he'll be home."

Ashworth left, his anger settling into discouragement. He got on the freeway, followed the 600 South loop downtown, parked, walked to church headquarters, and went to Don Schmidt's office.

"Don, I was promised a letter that you've ended up with—this 'treasure letter,' the Far West letter from Joseph Smith."

Schmidt looked at the photograph. "Yes, I have that."

"And you got it from Mark Hofmann?"

"That's right."

"That liar!" Ashworth burst out. "He promised me that letter!"

Schmidt was unruffled, as usual. "Come on, Brent, settle down. Sit down a minute."

"Look, Don, if you don't believe me, okay. I know we're competitors of sorts. But as a member of the church, I'm warning you. In confidence, I ask you to be careful, Don. That's all. Just be careful."

Ashworth left, but the incident followed him. By the following week he had calmed down and was ready for business as usual when he and Hofmann met at their spot in Crossroads Mall. Almost immediately, however, Hofmann confronted Ashworth, angrily quoting back to him his words to Schmidt, including calling him a liar.

"Well, it wasn't quite that way, Mark."

"No? Let's go over to Don's office and tell him that. I want you to take it back."

Ashworth, surprised that Schmidt had told Hofmann about his warning, decided he had better talk his way out of this one to stay on Hofmann's good side. "No, I'm not going over there. Don's no friend of mine, anyway, you know that. You know I was upset about those letters, but I didn't accuse you like that."

Hofmann dropped it, but the cloud between them lingered.

Those involved with Steve Christensen's research project were trying to keep the salamander letter and the related study quiet. Hofmann had warned Michael Marquardt that the letter's buyer did not want publicity.

Ron Walker and Dean Jessee had been pressing for the letter's provenance. Christensen had promised them he would camp on Hofmann's doorstep until he got it. Finally, they were told the letter had come through an autograph collector in the East named Elwyn Doubleday, who, in turn, had sold it to another collector named William Thoman, Jr., who sold it to

Lyn Jacobs. Jessee talked with Doubleday, who said he was 99 percent certain the letter had come through him. Jessee's next task was to locate all signatures or other handwriting samples left by Martin Harris.

On February 7, Christensen wrote to his attorney Alan Smith. He wanted to know how he could best control releasing the salamander letter and the money-digging agreement transcript. Hofmann had not offered the original of the money-digging agreement for sale after all, he told Smith, but had instead brought him a notarized statement attesting to the document's authenticity. Christensen's concern about information leaks was justified when Richard Ostling, a *Time* magazine reporter based in Los Angeles, called for a story. In addition, Peggy Fletcher wanted Christensen to write an article describing the letter for an upcoming issue of the *Sunstone Review*.

In late February, Christensen was apparently scheduled to meet with President Gordon B. Hinckley to discuss the letter. On February 24, he jotted a note to himself: "President Gordon B. Hinckley - 1:30 p.m. 1. don't cave in. 2. will not embarrass the church." But in another note, Christensen implied that the scheduled meeting did not take place. Hinckley subsequently acknowledged meeting twice with Christensen—at a United Way luncheon in October 1984 and when Christensen donated the letter to the church in April 1985. Christensen "may have telephoned me on one or two occasions to confirm that he was having research done on the letter," Hinckley remembered, "and that when this was completed he would give it to the church."

Despite the confidentiality of Christensen's research project—or perhaps because of it—word of the unusual letter spread quickly among historians—with sometimes convoluted interpretations. Michael Quinn was told by a BYU colleague, "There's a new document in which the messenger who came to Joseph Smith appeared as a worm."

"I don't believe it!" Quinn exclaimed and telephoned Leonard Arrington. Arrington, aggravated by the description, told Quinn he knew the letter's content and that its buyer had engaged researchers to study it. Quinn made calls until he learned that Ron Walker was one of the researchers. He called Walker, who was reticent. Quinn persisted, telling Walker he had heard that Smith's messenger had the form of a worm.

"It's not a worm," Walker said. "It's a salamander."

"That helps a lot! What does it mean?"

"We've been working on it a long time. We can't release the letter before we find a way to prepare the public for it. The salamander is just one issue it raises."

"Well, can you read it to me or let me have a copy?"

"No, I'd need Steve Christensen's release."

Quinn knew Christensen. He had sponsored several of Quinn's speeches at the annual Sunstone Symposium, had invited him to participate in a short-lived foundation to study Mormon history, and had even given him gift certificates for clothes. Quinn telephoned, but Christensen was not giving out copies either; in fact, Christensen seemed cold on the telephone. Before long, transcripts of the letter began to circulate, but Quinn refused to read them. He would wait for the letter to be officially released.

For a time, Christensen managed to maintain some control of the salamander letter. On March 7, he issued a press release titled, "Letter from Martin Harris to William W. Phelps." Christensen did not release the text of the letter but described the research project he had organized and announced that authentication procedures were planned.

Meanwhile, Christensen's friend and administrative assistant, Randy Rigby, had become worried about the project. He felt that Metcalfe told him about the salamander letter with glee and an expectation that Rigby's faith would be shaken.

"It doesn't bother me, Brent," Rigby said. "In fact, in some ways, it just reinforces my testimony of the church."

Rigby observed the project's progress, assuming that Metcalfe's association with Christensen, Walker, and Jessee would help him handle the conflicts he found in church history. Rigby concluded it wasn't working and confronted Metcalfe. "What do you think about the church now, Brent?" he asked one day.

Metcalfe explained that he thought The Book of Mormon emerged from the mind of Joseph Smith. "I believe it's spiritually beneficial but not historically correct."

"How are you doing, now that your feelings about the church have changed?"

"I'm doing okay. I really love my family. They mean a lot to me. You know, when you lose something in your life, you turn to your family and other things that are meaningful."

Rigby was bothered by Metcalfe's response. When he could, he caught Christensen alone and leveled with him.

"Look, Steve, I don't know what's going on with your project or how much it means to you. But I personally feel that Brent's lost his testimony of the church working on that letter. To tell you the truth, I'm very worried about him."

"I'll talk with him," Christensen said.

He and Metcalfe had several conversations about the salamander letter. "You know, Brent," Christensen said, "even if I knew that the money digging explanation for Joseph Smith were true and that the church's traditional account was not, I would still remain a member. I need religion in my life and I need it for my family. There are so many good things the church does for people."

But Metcalfe, still smarting from being fired by men he thought should be inspired to act differently, could not agree. He saw the church's revelatory claims closely bound to the church's requirements for individuals. When one couldn't take the church's claims literally, he concluded, then neither need one take literally the church's commands.

As research on the letter progressed, Christensen wrote to Gordon B. Hinckley, inquiring about the rumored 1825 Joseph Smith to Josiah Stowell letter. He also asked about an early history of the church purportedly written by Oliver Cowdery, Smith's scribe during the translation of The Book of Mormon and first official church historian. Jerald and Sandra Tanner had suggested some months earlier that the church might be suppressing a Cowdery history that was said to contain references to the occult.

If the letter was answered, it took the form of a telephone call from Hinckley to Christensen inquiring about the project generally. The specific inquiries were not mentioned, and Christensen and Brent Metcalfe both were left to wonder if

Hinckley's silence was his way of confirming the church had the 1825 letter and the Cowdery history.

By now, Metcalfe's curiosity was piqued. Hofmann had been rumored for years to have full run of Church Archives, including the First Presidency's vault. "Have you ever seen the Oliver Cowdery history in the First Presidency's vault?" he asked Hofmann. "It would be the church's earliest history and could shed some light on the salamander letter."

"Nope."

But earlier Hofmann had asked Michael Marquardt, "If ever I'm in the First Presidency's vault, what documents should I look for?"

Marquardt had considered, then checked with the Tanners, who suggested the Cowdery history. Marquardt put the Cowdery history at the top of his wish list. He gave the list to Hofmann but heard nothing back.

Because of the salamander letter's potentially controversial impact, Ron Walker and Dean Jessee were still pressing for provenance and authentication before publishing anything. However, Walker was finding considerable circumstantial support in other historical sources for the letter's occult imagery, and Jessee had, with Hofmann's help, located several Harris signatures and a few additional words in Harris's hand. All the handwriting samples appeared to be consistent with that on the letter. With that much support, Walker and Jessee discussed with Christensen the possibility of finding an eastern publisher for a book-length analysis of Mormon origins. Christensen agreed that the project was far-reaching and should receive wide exposure.

In August, the *Salt Lake Tribune* picked up an article by *L.A. Times* religion writer John Dart, headlined, "Joseph Smith: His Image is Threatened, Letter Attacks Origin of Book of Mormon." Beside the article ran a sidebar, "LDS Spokesman Says Letter Is Not Threat." As the salamander letter incited a war of words between the press and the Mormon church, at risk were the church's image and the faith of its members.

But in the periodic newsletter Jerald and Sandra Tanner issued from their bookstore, Jerald Tanner expressed doubts about the letter's authenticity. Tanner claimed that the letter's close parallels in content to E. D. Howe's *Mormonism Unvailed* were suspicious.

Hofmann found Tanner's challenge to the letter a serious one, and on August 23 he visited with Sandra Tanner. "You, of all people, should not be attacking this letter," he insisted.

Later that month, John Dart, conscious of his large Mormon audience in California, wrote another *L.A. Times* article, titled, "Mormons Ponder 1830 Letter Altering Idealized Image of Joseph Smith." In it, he included Tanner's criticisms.

While published articles speculated about the letter's effect on Mormon history, several dozen people in the Mormon history community received a typescript of the Joseph Smith to Josiah Stowell letter, mailed anonymously from New York. The typescript offered proof that such a letter existed and lent contextual support to the salamander letter's authenticity.

Meanwhile, the press battle continued. "Historians Testing Authenticity of Martin Harris Letter," announced the *Salt Lake Tribune*, "Tests May Not Be Known Until 1985." A week later, the *LDS Church News*, a weekly supplement to the *Deseret News*, ran an article entitled, "Harris letter could be further witness." If authentic, the article explained, the letter was not a threat to the church. But, the article concluded, the letter might not be authentic, anyway.

Early in October, in this embattled atmosphere, Christensen asked Brent Metcalfe to represent him at a convocation at the LDS Institute of Religion adjacent to the University of Utah in Salt Lake City. Following his generally well-received talk on the salamander letter and its historical context, Metcalfe began answering many questions that lasted well beyond the allotted time. As the discussion became heated, a religion teacher brought the topic to a matter of personal testimony, not scholarship.

Gary Sheets had paid scant attention to Christensen's salamander letter project, until an apostle remarked in General Conference in early October that no one should write or sponsor a book that would lead some into disbelief. JGSA was paying Metcalfe, and Sheets gathered that Metcalfe had "lost his testimony" while researching the letter. Christensen and Sheets had discussed publishing a book on Mormon origins with an eastern publisher, and Sheets thought some money might be made. Now, however, Sheets decided that since he and Christensen were both bishops, they should not be involved in something so controversial. He raised the subject with Christensen.

Christensen agreed to end JGSA's support of the project, partly for his own reasons. Walker and Jessee were not going to mesh with Metcalfe as co-authors of any book, he had already concluded. Also, he was beginning to have second thoughts about owning a document that was so volatile. He informed Metcalfe, Walker, and Jessee they were welcome to continue researching and publishing on their own but his direct involvement would discontinue. He left the clear impression with Walker that if a book manuscript was ever finished, he would be interested in sponsoring its publication.

On October 16, Christensen attended a United Way fundraising luncheon and sat beside Gordon B. Hinckley. "I was introduced to" Christensen at this time, Hinckley later wrote. "There was no discussion of historical documents, our only conversation concerning the business at hand, the United Way." Christensen had been deliberately seated beside Hinckley by a friend making the luncheon arrangements. Afterward he told friends that the luncheon, as hoped, gave the two men an opportunity to discuss the salamander letter at length. When he returned to his office, Christensen wrote Hinckley a long letter documenting the end of the letter project. Christensen outlined the project's inception and personnel, including "a young man by the name of Brent Metcalfe" to work on the letter, "while still in the full employ of Gary Sheets and myself.

"I was also successful and fortunate in obtaining the research skills and services of Dean Jessee and Ron Walker to work on the project," Christensen wrote. "Since that time I have been careful to see that I personally covered their expenses and remunerated them for their time." He described his intended financial donation to the Joseph Fielding Smith Institute for Church History at BYU and his wish to provide "appropriate research" to "accompany a document of such varied contents."

Christensen then complimented Hinckley on his recent General Conference speech, leading him to the conflict the salamander letter posed to church tradition. His next few sentences, as he wrote, revealed his own ambivalence. "Most likely we will always be learning new things historically from our past; however, I believe that the Church has more pressing work to accomplish than to be consumed by questions and contradictions from the past. While it is better that we lead forth in historical inquiry rather than leaving the task to our enemies, those so engaged must have sufficient faith that the day will come when all is revealed and the pieces will all fit together."

Christensen raised the possibility of donating the letter to the church or selling it back to Hofmann for more than $50,000. "What I would appreciate knowing," he concluded, "is whether or not the Church feels strongly about owning the letter. If it would be more of a thorn than a rose, I would gladly let Mr. Hofmann sell it to Yale or some other institution which would pay his 'highway robbery' prices. If the Church would like it, it is yours for the asking—just tell me when." Christensen added a personal note about his experiences as a bishop, then closed the three-page single-spaced letter, "Very Truly Yours."

One day, as he visited with Hofmann at his Millcreek home, Ashworth glanced at the bookshelf by the door and noticed a book on LDS mission presidents. "I wish I'd realized you have that book," Ashworth told him. "I could have used that. I just gave a whole collection of letters by a mission president in the South Seas to the church."

Hofmann's ears pricked up. "What mission president?"

"His name was William Gailey Sears. I've had a whole bundle of his family correspondence with and between his wives. Since I've been getting documents from you, I've been disseminating a lot of my other stuff."

Suddenly Ashworth noticed that Hofmann appeared upset. "That's my grandfather," Hofmann said. "I didn't know you had his letters!"

"Well, I don't have them now. Sorry, but I didn't know there was any connection, so I donated them all to the church."

Frustrations went both ways that autumn. "Mark, your name is mud around here," Ashworth told him during one of their regular meetings at Crossroads Mall. "You two guys"—he included Lyn Jacobs—"are really screwing the church. You're getting a horrible reputation."

Hofmann shrugged. Ashworth tried to hold him personally accountable for the rumors and transcripts circulating through the history community. "You promised me that the salamander letter wouldn't go anywhere. Also that the Josiah Stowell letter wouldn't go anywhere."

"Well, this whole salamander letter problem is really Lyn's fault. Lyn sold it to Steve Christensen as a tax investment. Christensen had always intended to hold it for a year, then donate it to the church."

"Well, what about the 1825 Stowell letter?" Ashworth pressed. "You had the only copy of that." He did not add that Hofmann had offered to show him that copy immediately after promising Hinckley there was none.

"No, that leak wasn't me. Charles Hamilton, who authenticated it, blabbed it all over."

"Anyway," Ashworth continued, "you're getting a bad reputation around Utah County and around the church, too."

"President Hinckley knows the truth."

"Well, have you seen him recently?"

"Yeah. I was up there just the other day."

There was not much Ashworth could say to that. Hofmann always had the inside track, it seemed. "Well, Mark, what would you do if you were me? I'm out there telling people about the Lucy Smith letter and the Martin Harris testimonial letter, and they bring up the salamander letter. What would you do in my place?"

Hofmann looked at him coolly. "I'd just say it was a forgery."

By early 1985, Boston rare documents dealer Kenneth Rendell, whom Christensen had engaged to aid in authenticating the salamander letter, had sent the letter to William Krueger, a paper specialist in Wisconsin, and to Al Lyter, an ink expert in North Carolina. Rendell then personally examined the postmark, the handwriting, and the physical appearance of the paper and on February 13 wrote to Christensen that there was nothing to indicate that the salamander letter was anything but authentic. Christensen, Walker, Jessee, and Metcalfe all felt secure with the analysis.

By that time, Christensen had been promoted to vice-president over syndication at CFS and was trying to cope with the company's mounting financial problems. Hofmann's offer to buy the salamander letter back from him at a profit was tempting. But, as Christensen explained to a new friend, businessman and sometime collector Franklin Johnson, the letter threatened the balance he had managed to achieve between the institutional church and his own independence. He did not want to appear to church leaders as an "enemy of the church," as critics and whistle-blowers were generally labeled.

On February 26, Christensen again wrote to Gordon Hinckley asking if the church would like him to donate the letter. He noted that the proceeds from a sale would be useful but added that he was not interested in selling the letter to the church. If the church wanted the letter, he would donate it as promised and trust in the Lord to help him financially. Hinckley responded with a telephone call. Yes, the church wanted the letter. Accordingly, on April 12, 1985, Christensen brought the salamander letter to Hinckley as a gift to the church. Ten days later he received a thank-you letter from the First Presidency.

That same month, Brent Ashworth went to see Gordon Hinckley. He felt comfortable dropping by without an appointment. Once when Hinckley had entered his office with two apostles and saw Ashworth waiting, Hinckley had excused himself and talked with Ashworth for a few minutes.

These days Hinckley's greeting was often, "Well, Brent, what's new on the lost 116 pages?" a half-humorous prod. Hinckley could also be depended upon to mention the church's enemies and the threat to the membership he felt they posed.

This particular meeting stayed with Ashworth because it was unusually tense. The Josiah Stowell letter was by now an open secret in the historical community. Recently, a church spokesman had been quoted in the *Salt Lake Tribune* denying that the church had such a letter. But scholars were preparing papers on the treasure-seeking letters, including the Stowell letter, for May's Mormon History Association meeting. Also,

Ashworth had known personally for two years that Hinckley had bought the letter from Hofmann.

Preceding his visit, Ashworth had written Hinckley that he had just spoken to his 10,000th church member about his documents. Now Hinckley brought up Ashworth's addresses to church gatherings and made a suggestion. "Tell people we've got nothing to hide."

The Stowell letter jumped into Ashworth's mind. He did not know what to say. After an awkward pause, the expression on Hinckley's face changed, as if he wondered—or knew—why Ashworth was silent.

On May 3, as the Mormon History Association was meeting in Kansas City, Hinckley called the church's public communications department and told them the church had the 1825 Stowell letter. He recommended they announce that they had made a mistake. The text of the Stowell letter was released along with a carefully worded statement that did not acknowledge authenticity. Both the local and national press gave the two spectacular letters extensive coverage.

The same day a high-level church official called Ashworth. "The Brethren want to know about the story that the 116 pages are coming forth."

"Really? What's going around?"

"Rumor has it that the lost pages have material on money digging in them. Do you know anything about that?"

"I don't," Ashworth said, "but I'll check around. I'll get right back to you."

Ashworth phoned Hofmann, "Do you know anything about a copy of the 116 pages that talks about money-digging?"

"Oh, it's an old fake," Hofmann said. "It's on thirty-one leaves, sixteen and a half pages. It folds like an insurance policy."

Ashworth was stunned by the specifics. "You're kidding. What else?"

"Well, it says the 'Book of Lehi' on the outside, and it's tied with a pink ribbon. It would cost about $5,000. I wrote down excerpts from it for Don Schmidt in 1982."

Later Ashworth called Schmidt. "Don," he said, "I'm working for another department, but it's the same church. I need to know about this 116 pages business." He related Hofmann's information and asked about the excerpts.

"Oh, I don't think I've got a copy of that," Schmidt said.

Ashworth thanked him and called Hofmann back.

"Well, maybe I can find a copy of my notes."

Ashworth contacted the man at church headquarters, who was newly alarmed. "The Tanners say they're going to publish it," he reported.

Ashworth called Hofmann again. "What's this about the Tanners? Do they have a copy of the fake, or what?"

"No, don't worry, they don't have a copy of anything. I'm going to fly to Bakersfield and get it. In fact, I've got the tickets."

"Okay. Listen, you mentioned $5,000 for the original of the fake. If you get it, I'll pay you $10,000 for it."

But Hofmann did not go to Bakersfield. The next week he again told Ashworth he had bought tickets, but for the second time did not go. Finally, Ashworth said, "Mark, what are you going to do about this?"

"I don't really want to go down there, Brent. It doesn't interest me that much."

Ashworth thought of all his calls to the church hierarchy and bit back his exasperation. "Well, I'd like to at least get the sheet you promised me with your notes." Eventually Hofmann gave Ashworth a photocopy of a single page that read "Book of Lehi" at the top.

"You can have this, but it's fake," Hofmann said. "Every time it says, 'My father has written about this on the plates,' it's underlined. That made me suspicious."

After Hofmann left, Ashworth stared at the page. He could tell that one page had been trimmed and another pasted on before the photocopying had been done. Nevertheless, he called his friend at church headquarters and told him to quit worrying about the lost 116 pages.

Almost immediately, church leaders had something new to worry about—accusations in the press that they were suppressing an early Mormon history written by Oliver Cowdery.

Press reports of a suppressed early Mormon history had their genesis in a hamburger restaurant not far from Hofmann's home, where Hofmann and Metcalfe were eating lunch. They talked casually at first, then Hofmann began relating an experience he had had that Metcalfe suddenly realized was important.

Hofmann said he had been at a meeting with Gordon Hinckley and secretary Francis Gibbons. "Hinckley was asking about the salamander project," Hofmann said, "and so I asked, 'Well, what other documents does the church have that contradict the traditional story of the Book of Mormon?' "

Gibbons left the room, Hofmann continued, and returned with a book he opened on the desk. "President Hinckley looked at it and I looked at it," Hofmann said. "I thought then that Hinckley might not even know what that volume was, but I recognized Oliver Cowdery's handwriting. I read a part about Alvin going to the hill, and I saw a reference about the salamander."

As Metcalfe listened, spellbound, Hofmann detailed the differences between the account in the Cowdery history and the content in the salamander letter. Metcalfe had him confirm the similarities: yes, Alvin Smith, Joseph's older brother, was in the history. Yes, there was a talking salamander, but not a white salamander.

"What about flames?" Metcalfe asked. "Did it mention flames?"

"No, there's nothing like that in the part I heard. This passage came about a quarter of the way into the book."

"Wow," Metcalfe breathed. "If the story of the plates is a quarter of the way in, think what must come before that."

Before leaving the restaurant, Hofmann swore Metcalfe to secrecy. "If anyone hears about this, Hinckley and Gibbons will know immediately that it was me who leaked it. You can't tell anybody."

Metcalfe endured the secret for a while, but by summer, he convinced Hofmann to let him leak the story to the press. Metcalfe met with *Salt Lake Tribune* reporter Dawn Tracy and told her the story, which she reported without knowing Metcalfe's source. Metcalfe also arranged for Hofmann to meet with *L.A. Times* religion writer John Dart on the condition that Hofmann remain anonymous. As Hofmann recounted the story to Dart,

Metcalfe listened closely. He found no discrepancies in Hofmann's retelling.

"Mormon Origins Challenged Anew Over Purported History," Dart's resulting article announced. "Church Alleged to Possess 150-Year-Old Evidence." Dart explained the significance of the Cowdery history and the emergence of the salamander and Stowell letters. "The source interviewed by the Times," Dart wrote, "described the Cowdery history as a book bound partly in leather, with marbled cardboard covers measuring about 8 inches by 10 inches in width and height and between half an inch and three-quarters of an inch thick. The pages are lined, he said.

"The source said he decided to be interviewed about the history because the Cowdery documents provide corroboration for the salamander references in the Harris letter, which some Mormons are claiming is a forgery.

" 'I don't remember the exact wording, but it said that Alvin [Joseph Smith's older brother] located the buried gold plates with his seer stone,' he said. 'I remember clearly that it was not a private venture. Alvin had other people with him, including Joseph.' "

Church leaders found such stories difficult to handle. They did not know the source or even if they had in their possession a Cowdery history. A different Cowdery manuscript existed, but no history matching the description in the reports and rumors could be found. Still the secrecy that had already developed around documents and the church's mistrust of historians fueled suspicions that the volume did exist — perhaps in a secret vault. The church's inability to deny categorically that it possessed such a history seemed to some a verification.

As intriguing as the Cowdery history was, Brent Metcalfe was even more excited by Hofmann's apparent discovery of some of the missing 116 pages of the Book of Mormon manuscript. Metcalfe knew about the Bakersfield forgery, but Hofmann had also indicated the possible existence of a second manuscript, one that could be real.

One evening over the telephone, Hofmann quoted part of the Bakersfield manuscript that read, "I writeth the manuscript with my own hand."

"What do you think, Brent?" Hofmann asked. "Don't you think we would expect it to read, 'I wrote it with mine own hand'?"

Metcalfe agreed that the second version would sound more natural. The first section of The Book of Mormon contained an account written by Nephi, a young man who traveled with his family from the Old World to the New and kept a history on plates of gold. In the newest manuscript he had found, Hofmann said, there were prophesies by Nephi's father, Lehi, made in Jerusalem before the family emigrated. Lehi was evidently a miner by profession and had a "cornucopia mine" producing gold, silver, and precious stones.

Metcalfe almost dropped the telephone. He had studied The Book of Mormon extensively and had been fascinated by its mention of Lehi's family abandoning gold, silver, and precious stones in the Old World, only to discover treasure in the new land.

"There's a strong parallel," he told Hofmann, "between Lehi and Jacob in the Old Testament with Joseph Smith, Sr., and between Nephi and Joseph the son of Jacob and Joseph Smith, Jr."

"I see what you mean," Hofmann said, sounding impressed.

"The thing is," Metcalfe said, warming to his argument, "since Joseph Smith, Sr., was a money digger, Lehi as a miner is exactly what you would expect. Fawn Brodie, in *No Man Knows My History*, showed that Nephi was the fruition of Joseph Smith's desires. For instance, Nephi found gold and silver and Joseph had been a money digger. Nephi was the third son but was strong and became a leader in his family. Joseph had a lame leg and was the third son. And then Lehi's family left Jerusalem and came to the valley of Lemuel. Joseph Smith's family lived on Lemuel Durfey's property in New York before they acquired their own farm."

"Well, it makes sense that Lehi and his family would return to Jerusalem to get their gold, silver, and precious things and get the plates of Laban," Hofmann said, "especially if Lehi was a miner."

"That's right."

Metcalfe, watching history unfold before him, was beside himself. Each discovery seemed more momentous: the salamander letter, the Stowell letter, the Oliver Cowdery history. Wait until the lost 116 pages sewed together the truths about the real Joseph Smith.

On May 27, 1985, Christensen, in a letter to President Hinckley, rather disparaged the gift he was making to the church of the transcript of the money-digging agreement Hofmann had sold him for $5,000. If released, it would support the other money-digging documents, something he knew would not please church leaders. Still, he informed Hinckley, he and Hofmann were trying to acquire the original contract.

The following day, Hinckley answered by return mail, thanking Christensen for the text of the money-digging agreement, adding that "the enemies of the church are having a great time. Their efforts will fade as the church moves forward," he promised.

The next month Hinckley responded to questions by a group of Mormons touring the Mesa, Arizona, Temple near Phoenix. "You don't worry about salamanders," he admonished. "They don't trouble me. I have those letters—one I purchased, the other was a gift. I knew the uproar those letters would cause. So why release them? Why not? Let the storm blow over so we can get on with the work. Let's get it behind us.

"I'm not concerned about Martin Harris's description to W. W. Phelps," he continued. "What concerns me is what happened to Martin Harris and W. W. Phelps. I know that the man [Martin Harris] went on to testify of Jesus Christ and later came across the plains, hat in hand, so to speak, to rejoin with the Saints. That says more to me than all the letters in the world. Fifty years after the date of that letter Martin Harris bore a strong testimony of the Prophet Joseph Smith."

1.

2.

1. Fire fighters prepare to leave the Judge Building on 300 South and State Street in Salt Lake City after a bomb on the sixth floor killed Steve Christensen, October 15, 1985. (Photo by Ravell Call, courtesy *Deseret News*)

2. Gary Sheets embraces his daughter Katie and her husband, Joe Robertson, near his Holladay home after learning that his wife, Kathy, had been killed in a second bombing. (Photo by Lynn Johnson, courtesy *Salt Lake Tribune*)

3.

4.

3. Terri Christensen greets mourners at the cemetery following a funeral service for her husband, Steve. (Photo by Tom Smart, courtesy *Deseret News*)
4. A police officer inspects the sports car belonging to the third bomb victim, Mark W. Hofmann, on 200 North Main Street in Salt Lake City. (Photo by Tom Smart, courtesy *Deseret News*)

5.

6.

7.

5. Gordon B. Hinckley, second counselor in the First Presidency of the Mormon church, reads a statement at a press conference on October 23, 1985. To his right is Dallin H. Oaks, of the Council of Twelve Apostles; to his left, Hugh W. Pinnock, of the First Quorum of Seventy. (Photo by Tom Smart, courtesy *Deseret News*)

6. Curt Bench relaxes in his successful rare book department at Deseret Book in 1985. (Photo by Howard C. Moore, courtesy Curt Bench)

7. Detective Ken Farnsworth, assigned to the Christensen and Sheets homicides, testifies at a bond hearing after months of investigation. (Photo by O. Wallace Kasteler, courtesy *Deseret News*)

8. Detective Jim Bell, who coordinated the homicide investigation, identifies fragments from the bomb that killed Steve Christensen. (Photo by Tom Smart, courtesy *Deseret News*)

9. Sergeant Michael George, investigator for the Salt Lake County Attorney's Office, organized a computer program for the Hofmann case, then investigated document forgery. (Courtesy Michael George)

10. George J. Throckmorton's suspicions regarding the Hofmann documents helped to crack the stalemated bombings case. (Courtesy George and Caroline Throckmorton)

11.

12.

11. Salt Lake County investigator Sergeant Richard Forbes investigated Hofmann's frauds. (Photo by Tom Smart, courtesy *Deseret News*)

12. The prosecution team meets in County Attorney Ted Cannon's office. Left to right, prosecutor Gerry D'Elia, Ted Cannon, prosecutor Robert Stott, chief of justice Bud Ellett, and prosecutor David Biggs. (Photo by Ravell Call, courtesy *Deseret News*)

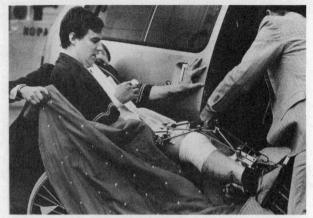

13.

14.

13. An injured Mark Hofmann is helped into his van on November 1, 1985, after being arraigned on illegal possession of a firearm. He has removed the eyeglasses he wore during the arraignment. (Photo by Tom Smart, courtesy *Deseret News*)
14. Steve Christensen in his office at CFS Financial Corp., after purchasing the 1830 salamander letter in 1984. (Photo by Ravell Call)

15.

15. The children of Steven and Terri Christensen in December 1986. Left to right, Jared, 5; Justin, 8; Steven, 1; and Josh, 9. (Courtesy Terri Lauder)

16.

16. Kathy Sheets, stooping, is surrounded by her family a year before the bombings. To her right are Joe and Katie Robertson; to her left, grandson Danny, held by his father, Roger Jones; Gary and Gretchen Sheets and Heidi Sheets Jones are behind her; with Jimmy in the tree. (Courtesy Katie Robertson and the Sheets family)

17.

18.

17. Twelve-year-old Mark Hofmann, center in a plaid shirt, and his Boy Scout troop enjoy a hike. Jeff Salt is at the far left.
18. Elder Mark Hofmann prepares to leave the Salt Lake International Airport on January 24, 1974, for an LDS mission to England.

19.

20.

19. Jeff Salt and Mark Hofmann stand outside the Logan, Utah, apartment they rented in May 1976 while attending Utah State University.

20. A. J. (Jeff) Simmonds checks a reference in his office in the USU Special Collections section of the library in the late 1970s. (Courtesy A. J. Simmonds)

21.

22.

21. Mark Hofmann, left, shows the newly discovered Anthon transcript and Samuel Smith Bible to the LDS First Presidency: N. Eldon Tanner, first counselor; President Spencer W. Kimball; and Marion G. Romney, second counselor. Apostles Gordon B. Hinckley and Boyd K. Packer (rear), advisors to the church's history department, look on. (1980 LDS press photograph)
22. Collector Brent Ashworth shows the Lucy Mack Smith letter to President Spencer W. Kimball. (1982 LDS press photograph, courtesy Brent Ashworth)

23.

Canandaqua June 18th 1825

Dear Sir

My Father has shown me your letter informing him and me of your success in beating the mine as you suppose but we are of the oppinion that since you cannot ascertain any particulars you should not dig more untill you first discover if any valluables remain you know the treasure must be guarded by some clever spirit and if such is discovered so also is the treasure so do this take a hazel stick one yard long being new but and cleave it just in the middle and lay it asunder on the mine so that both inner parten of the stick may look one right against the other one inch distant and if there is treasure after a while you shall see them draw and join together again of themselves let me know how it is Since you were here I have almost decided to accept your offer and if you can make it convenient to come this way I shall be ready to accompany you if nothing happens more than I know of I am very respectfully

Joseph Smith Jr

24.

23. Lyn Jacobs describes his document dealings with Mark Hofmann to reporters at *Sunstone* magazine soon after the bombings. (Courtesy *Sunstone*)

24. The Joseph Smith to Josiah Stowell letter on money digging was sold to a top Mormon official in early 1983 and housed in a secret vault.

25.

26.

25. The Ashworth family in 1983: Charlene, with David; Brent, with Emily; Samuel, to the right; Amy and John, to the rear; Matthew, to the left; and Adam, in front. (Courtesy Brent and Charlene Ashworth)

26. Mark and Doralee Hofmann approach Fifth Circuit Court the morning of April 14, 1986, for the preliminary hearing that will decide whether 32 felony counts against Hofmann will be bound over to Third District Court. (Photo by Jack Monson, courtesy *Deseret News*)

27.

28.

29.

27. Left to right, Mac Christensen, Ken Farnsworth, Terri Christensen, Ted Cannon, and Dick Forbes listen to testimony as the preliminary hearing opens. (Photo by Tom Smart, courtesy *Deseret News*)
28. Bill Hofmann talks with his son, Mark, during a recess. (Photo by Ravell Call, courtesy *Deseret News*)
29. Shannon Flynn testified as a prosecution witness during the preliminary hearing but, like many of Hofmann's friends, believed that Hofmann was innocent. (Photo by Ravell Call, courtesy *Deseret News*)

30.

31.

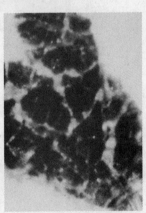

32.

30. Experts from the Bureau of Alcohol, Tobacco, and Firearms built these two bomb facsimiles. The top reconstruction has nails taped to the pipe, representing the weapon that killed Steve Christensen. (Photo by Paul G. Barker, courtesy *Deseret News*)

31. Bill Flynn joined ranks with George Throckmorton to pronounce Mark Hofmann a forger. (Courtesy William J. Flynn)

32. Magnified sixty times, the ink on the Hofmann documents appeared cracked, producing a peculiar "alligatoring" effect. Throckmorton and Flynn linked this phenomenon to the artificially aging of homemade ink. (Courtesy George J. Throckmorton)

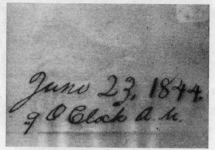

33.

34.

35.

33. The date of the Joseph Smith to Jonathan Dunham letter as it appears under ultraviolet light. Note the clip mark, where the wet document was hung up to dry, and the downward running of the ink.

34. The Deseret Currency Association note on top is genuine, the other is forged.

35. A microscopic flaw in the emulsion of the capital letter "M" in the text of the "Oath of a Freeman" helped to match a printing negative to the first and second Oaths. (Photos 33, 34, and 35 courtesy George J. Throckmorton)

36.

37.

36. Bill and Mark Hofmann walk with defense attorneys Ron Yengich and Brad Rich to Third District Court to enter Mark Hofmann's guilty pleas on January 23, 1987. (Photo by Steve Fidel, courtesy *Deseret News*)

37. Mark Hofmann talks to reporters outside the courthouse before pleading guilty to murder and forgery. (Photo by Jack Monson, courtesy *Deseret News*)

38.

39.

38. Flanked by his attorneys, Mark Hofmann tells Judge Kenneth Rigtrup (out of camera range to the left) that he killed Steve Christensen and Kathleen Sheets. Present are, back row, left to right, Sandra Rigby, Mark D. Lauder, Kris Tanner, Terri Christensen, Joan and Mac Christensen, Stan Christensen, Scott Christensen; second row, Randy Rigby, Stuart Christensen, Gretchen Sheets, Heidi Jones, Gary Sheets; front row, Katie and Joe Robertson, Roger Jones, and Don Tanner. (Photo by Don Grayston, courtesy *Deseret News*)

39. Mark Hofmann responds to a question from a member of the Board of Pardons, as Brad Rich listens, on January 29, 1988. (Photo by Tim Kelly, pool photograph courtesy *Salt Lake Tribune*)

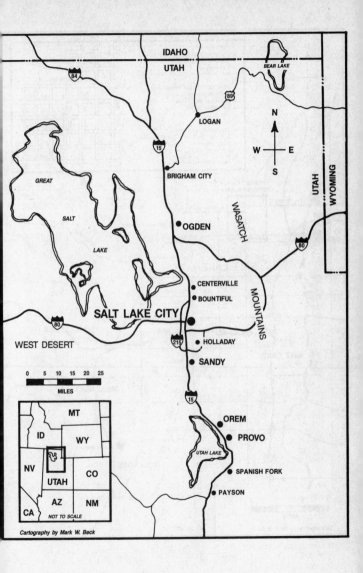

UTAH'S WASATCH FRONT

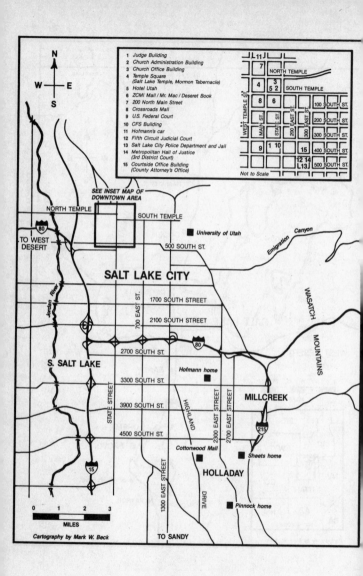

SALT LAKE METROPOLITAN AREA
OCTOBER 1985

13

THE "OATH OF A FREEMAN"
—A POT OF GOLD

During the first half of 1985, Mark Hofmann was less preoccupied with the salamander and Stowell letters than were historians, the press, and the Mormon church. Hofmann told Lyn Jacobs, Shannon Flynn, and Brent Metcalfe, who circled him in separate orbits, that he was moving into Americana documents full time. Sometimes he said he would leave Mormon documents and pass on anything he found to Jacobs, or to Flynn. Both Jacobs and Flynn had claimed to be Hofmann's heir apparent, and part of the intrigue during visits to Hofmann was finding out who knew what about which document.

Hofmann's associates were vastly dissimilar, with Jacobs, Metcalfe, and Flynn relating much more closely to Hofmann than to one another. Jacobs, intellectual and flamboyant, could hardly talk classical music with Flynn, who liked heavy metal music and was interested in munitions and the Vietnam War. For his part, Metcalfe seemed to enjoy little else as much as Mormon history, theology, and church politics, the group's common interests, though Hofmann's, Flynn's, and Metcalfe's wives tended to find such topics wearisome.

Metcalfe was endlessly amazed by Hofmann's ability to uncover missing bits of Mormon history. And in mid-1985, Hofmann arranged to have Metcalfe work for him full time doing genealogical research. In March 1985, Flynn left his employment as a photographic supplies clerk to work for Hofmann full time. Not only did Flynn help with document deals, but, armed with a butterfly knife and occasionally carrying a gun, he also served as Hofmann's bodyguard and sometime chauffeur, stimulated by the secrecy and money surrounding Hofmann. Jacobs, commuting between Harvard and Salt Lake City, had gleaned some rare books for his own collection through his dealings with Hofmann. The salamander letter had brought him notoriety, and Hofmann paid well for the errands and favors he occasionally asked.

The shift toward Americana investments had a significant impact on Hofmann's lifestyle. Not only could he afford to hire Flynn full time, and later Metcalfe, but he also purchased a blue Toyota MR2 sports car, then a Toyota van. A mobile telephone allowed him to do business on the road. In March 1985, this change was symbolized by a sales slip for an extraordinary new discovery. Purchased for a mere $25, this document promised a virtual fortune which Hofmann began to depend upon and spend against as he made other deals and commitments to clients and creditors. The sales slip, from Argosy Books in New York, listed, along with other items, the "Oath of a Freeman," which, Hofmann told friends, was the first document printed in colonial America and was worth more than $1 million.

Just as he had taken his first major Mormon discovery, the Anthon transcript, to a friendly expert, Hofmann took the "Oath of a Freeman" to two friendly experts in New York, Justin Schiller and Ray Wapner of Schiller-Wapner Galleries, Ltd. From Schiller and Wapner, Mark and Dori Hofmann had purchased many rare first edition children's books, often paying top price, though Hofmann friends lamented that he could find the same books at lower prices elsewhere.

As the book dealers would later write, Hofmann showed them the broadside, printed in 1638, and naively asked if they thought he could get $10,000 for it. Their enthusiasm, after examining the document, was overwhelming, and they assured him that he could do much better than that. After some discussion they agreed to represent Hofmann in offering the Oath to the Library of Congress for $1 million, later raised to $1.5 million. Hofmann agreed to give the book dealers a cut in the document, printed by Stephen Daye, known for his famous

Bay Psalm Hymn Book. What was incredible to them was that Hofmann, an affable hick from Utah with a nose for Mormon documents, had stumbled across the document in a stack of unimportant items in a book store. Not until he brought it to them, had its true significance been understood. Like Simmonds and others before them, Schiller and Wapner shared in the excitement of an amazing discovery, later describing the experience for reporters and the *Maine Antique Digest.* Throughout spring and summer of 1985, as they negotiated with the Library of Congress, various tests showed the broadside to be authentic.

The impending sale of the Oath cast a glow over Hofmann's dealings in Utah. He occasionally confided his discovery of the Oath to friends and clients, showing the receipt as provenance. Two of those with whom he shared the news were Curt Bench and Wade Lillywhite at Deseret Book, where Hofmann's business had steadily increased.

Lillywhite, a tall, blond Californian, had brought his rare books and expertise to Deseret Book in Salt Lake City in March 1984 to join Bench's profitable department. Confidently, Bench and Lillywhite set ambitious goals for the next ten years. Their success had already been quick and phenomenal. Store officials and members of Deseret Books's board of directors were full of praise and encouragement. Privately, Bench and Lillywhite began calling Hofmann their "bread and butter."

Hofmann brought them Americana, including signatures of Daniel Boone, Abraham Lincoln, George Washington, Martha Washington, and the song "America" in the hand of lyricist Samuel Francis Smith. Mormon items included a ticket issued for the *Maid of Iowa,* a steamship owned by Joseph Smith, other Joseph Smith items, Brigham Young autographs, and documents signed with an X by Orrin Porter Rockwell, Joseph Smith's bodyguard.

"Greetings," Hofmann would say with his characteristic tight smile, as he entered their downstairs corner. He would toss a document on the counter top and ask, "How's it going? Would you guys be interested in this?"

They would haggle over price, deciding retail value, then

Hofmann would ask, "Can I get a check today?" Or simply, "I need $4,000 today."

Hofmann usually appeared unannounced, and after doing business he often stayed to chat. "Lyn's over at the church committing highway robbery," he would confide, referring to Jacobs's success in trading books. Hofmann consistently came up with enticing tidbits about Mormon leaders and knew the latest rumors about controversial documents. Always, he would swear Bench and Lillywhite to secrecy before sharing his information — but within a week, they would both hear the same rumor from two or three other persons.

Bench and Lillywhite occasionally socialized with the Hofmanns, though the invitations were impromptu and seemed to involve an agenda neither understood — maybe Hofmann was just cultivating business, though the sporadic parties sometimes revealed another side of Hofmann.

On New Year's Eve 1984, Brent and Jill Metcalfe accompanied Mark and Dori Hofmann, along with Dori's sister and brother-in-law, to their ward party. They had a good time, though Dori wanted to dance and Mark did not. He compensated by grabbing four party-favor horns, sticking them all in his mouth and blowing with the music. The Metcalfes were delighted to see him loosen up and enjoy himself.

Another January evening, Wade and Kimberly Lillywhite left a party at the Hofmanns' early, but Randy and Connie Wilson and Shannon and Robyn Flynn followed the Hofmanns through the snow to the hot tub in their back yard. As they hurried along, Wilson, a handgun buff, asked Hofmann about a 30.06 rifle he had helped him sight. "Do you ever shoot that now?"

"No, I've got a new toy," Hofmann said, soon chest deep in the warm water.

"What's that?"

"It's an Uzi machine gun."

"Is it a semi- or a fully-automatic one?"

"It's fully automatic."

"I've got one too," Shannon Flynn put in.

"Do you have a class B license for it?" Wilson asked Hofmann.

"No."

"Well, you ought to get one or get rid of the darn thing. It's a felony if you don't have a license."

The conversation turned to other topics. Periodically, Hofmann and Flynn, clad only in their swimming suits, would leap from the hot tub to roll in the snow, then sprint back.

Curt and Pat Bench heard about the Uzi at another party.

Once, Hofmann casually mentioned that he and Shannon carried a handgun in New York when they visited burlesque theaters and Harlem night spots.

"What did you say?" Dori asked, quickly looking up.

"I said that Shannon carries a gun in New York."

"Oh." She turned away.

Everyone who dealt with Hofmann knew he kept odd hours, made sudden, unscheduled trips out of state, and was practically inaccessible by telephone. Visits by repairmen seemed ineffectual in keeping the Hofmann line open, and Mark hinted darkly that it was bugged. Often the Hofmanns simply kept the telephone unplugged on the kitchen counter, plugging it in only to make calls. For that reason, friends and business contacts tended to drop by the Hofmann home.

The Hofmanns seemed to welcome the visits, Dori conversing animatedly and Mark interjecting juicy comments that were often church-related. The three Hofmann children, born in as many years, climbed on Mark's lap as he talked. However, when the newest baby, Johanna, cried or when Michael and Karen acted "too hyper," or when dinnertime came, visitors could see clearly that Dori was responsible for domestic matters. She kept the house clean, sewed, canned fruit, and paid close attention to the children. Her family visited frequently, and she was active in her ward and friendly with women in the Relief Society and in the children's Primary. Mark's family, who dropped by less frequently, and his business friends completed the Hofmann social circle.

Sometimes Dori complained to her guests about Mark's unreliable schedule and frequent trips. The family's income fluctuated considerably. While the hot tub, video recorder, van, and Mark's sports car were luxuries, the Hofmanns sometimes depended for their meals on the emergency food storage in the basement, which the Mormon church recommends for all members. Dori occasionally lamented that Mark would not even give her a few dollars for groceries, feeling entirely dependent on Mark and anxious about money.

Dori's criticisms, voiced before company, led some to believe that the soft-spoken Mark was henpecked. However, her protests made little impact on his coming and going, and more than one visitor winced at how curtly Mark set Dori straight when she tried to assert herself. If he told her to take care of the baby or leave the room while he talked business, she complied, no questions asked. On more than one occasion, Jill Metcalfe felt like slapping Mark, though she usually liked him very much. Wade Lillywhite silently decided that Dori was more slave than wife.

Even the parties seemed to be for Dori's benefit. She would call the Benches or Lillywhites or Wilsons to say, "Please come over Friday. Mark's been gone for a week and I'm going crazy looking at three kids and four walls." When Lyn Jacobs was not at Harvard, he dropped by frequently, often bringing a girlfriend. Flynn and Metcalfe came by also, sometimes bringing their wives. If women were present, the men moved to the kitchen or bedroom to talk business.

The Hofmanns were casual; neither cared much about appearance. Jacobs, who paid close attention to his wardrobe, and in 1985 sported a rhinestone salamander on his lapel, despaired of Mark's plebeian tastes. Hofmann's "business suits" tended to include thong sandals or, more often, jeans, though he wore a suit and white shirt for major transactions; this Jacobs christened his "going to see President Hinckley suit." When the Hofmanns went out to dinner with friends, both Mark and Dori dressed simply and Dori often brought the baby along.

Mark Hofmann enjoyed relating how once, when he and Dori were in the hot tub with Shannon and Robyn Flynn, Robyn had put her hand on Mark's leg, thinking it was Shannon's. Hofmann kept still as she moved her hand farther up his thigh. Finally he said something. They had all laughed at her embarrassment. Hofmann still laughed whenever he told the story.

One night, when the Benches visited, Curt noticed wine bottles in the wastebasket. Bench was obviously curious. Dori said, "Oh, if you're wondering about those, they're left from when Brent and Jill came over. They brought their own bottles."

Bench later mentioned the bottles to Metcalfe, who smiled. Everyone had been drinking that evening but Dori, he said, who had excused herself with the mention of an alcoholic relative. Jill Metcalfe knew that Dori did not like Mark to drink, especially in public. In Utah, he was usually circumspect, but Dori knew that on New York business trips liquor became a major form of entertainment. Bench never saw him drink. In fact, when the Benches had dinner with the Hofmanns at a Chinese restaurant during a New York book fair, their attempts to order a virgin daquiri from the Chinese-speaking waiter proved as entertaining as memorable.

By spring 1985, the "Oath of a Freeman" promised a bright future for Hofmann in the Americana market, for he had been successful with other Americana. In 1984, Hofmann and Flynn had sold Arizona oil executive Wilford Cardon, Flynn's former LDS mission president, a Betsy Ross letter for $12,000. Jim Bridger notes, signed with Bridger's "X," had sold for around $5,000 each. Hofmann had also begun pooling other investors, thereby allowing him to purchase and resell documents, including a forty-nine piece "national collection," for which he received $45,000 from Al Rust.

A new investor, Gene Taylor, seemed as willing to advance Hofmann up-front money as Al Rust had been for years. Taylor, a shirt tail Hofmann relative, first became interested in Mormon documents when Hofmann started to receive media attention. A successful businessman with an office south of Salt Lake City, Taylor had mentioned to Hofmann the year before that he would like to own a first edition of The Book of Mormon. A few weeks later, Hofmann called to say he had just found a copy in good condition. When Taylor saw it, he found that it had been inscribed by his wife's great-great-grandfather. He took out his checkbook.

When Taylor's wife later heard from Hofmann that he had some letters written by one of her husband's ancestors, she purchased them as a Christmas present for him. Afterwards she told Hofmann she thought they had been the best present she had ever given him and asked Hofmann to notify her if he came across similar documents.

Late in January 1985 Hofmann went to Taylor's office with a proposal. He told him about a rare letter written in 1775 by Daniel Boone, which, when printed in 1830, made Boone famous. The letter described Boone's journey over the Cumberland Gap into Kentucky, creating a prototype of the eastern American frontier experience. The whereabouts of the original letter had been unknown for years, Hofmann said. Now he had a chance to purchase not only that letter, but an entire Boone collection, which he had discovered by tracing descendants of one of Boone's friends. Surveys and notes were included in the collection of fourteen items, Hofmann said.

"I think I can buy the collection for $70,000 and sell it for between $150,000 to $200,000," Hofmann explained.

Taylor was as thrilled about the collection as he was about the investment itself. They drew up an agreement, with Taylor investing $50,000 and Hofmann $20,000. Ultimately the imbalance favored Hofmann as discoverer, for when the collection sold, the original investments would be repaid, then the profit divided 50/50. Both signed the agreement, and Taylor presented Hofmann with a cashier's check for $50,000.

"I'll go back to North Carolina this weekend and call when I get the collection," Hofmann said.

Later, however, Taylor happened to speak with a brother in Boston, who mentioned that Hofmann had come by at the time Taylor had thought Hofmann was in North Carolina. Surprised, Taylor called Dori. She said Mark was gone and seemed blank about North Carolina.

Taylor's concerns were allayed, however, when Hofmann called. "I got the collection, and I saved $10,000 on the purchase," he reported. "I got it for $60,000, and I also sold a couple of items in New York." The two met on February 6. Hofmann wrote out a personal check for $11,071.43, returning the unused portion of Taylor's investment and paying his share of the profit in the sale of a Daniel Boone survey to Charles Hamilton in New York.

The immediate profit paled beside the rest of the Boone collection. Hofmann showed Taylor the famous Cumberland

Gap letter, in which Boone described his exploits. "Dear Conrad," Taylor read, then his eyes swept over a text that evoked visions of Indian skirmishes and tussles with bears and wildcats. When he looked up again, Hofmann told him, "I have three surveys I think I can sell to Hamilton."

"Fine, Mark. You're the expert."

In his enthusiasm, Taylor went to the University of Utah library and began researching Boone to learn more about the man whose papers he had purchased, most of which he had not yet seen. On February 25, when Hofmann paid Taylor another $12,500 for the sale of the other surveys, Taylor asked, "Where's my collection, Mark? I want to see my collection."

"Well, I've sold the important items, but I can get you photocopies." Meanwhile, Hofmann had a new deal to propose to his more-than-satisfied customer. He described to Taylor two pages of the original Book of Mormon manuscript, housed at the University of Chicago Library. He anticipated a purchase price of $50,000 and suggested they invest equally. After some discussion, Taylor agreed, and gave Hofmann a cashier's check for $25,000.

Before long, Taylor got a call from Hofmann. "I sold the Book of Mormon pages to a California dentist for $90,000," Hofmann said. "That's $45,000 for each of us." Once again they divided the profit, which amounted to $20,000 each.

On March 11, Hofmann dropped by Taylor's office. During their conversation, he mentioned a collection of rare books that he said Justin Schiller had. The collection was the most valuable deal yet, and, once again, Taylor was interested. He agreed to reinvest his recently received $45,000, then added $5,000 in $100 bills and a cashier's check for $74,000 for a total of $124,000, or half the asking price. Hofmann said he would buy the books and then sell them to a Mr. Fleming for $450,000.

Taylor's confidence in Hofmann was bolstered not only by his profits but because Hofmann showed him a photocopy of the "Oath of a Freeman," which he said he had found. "This may be the first printed document in America," Hofmann said, obviously pleased. He explained that Schiller would market it in return for an interest in the sale. "The Library of Congress is considering it, and my identity hasn't been divulged," Hofmann offered. "We want to handle this through a Swiss bank account, so that I won't have to pay taxes on it."

"Mark, you can't do that," Taylor objected. "If you make a profit, you have to pay taxes on it."

Hofmann thought there must be a way around the IRS.

"Look, I've got a friend who is a tax attorney in Los Angeles," Taylor volunteered. "I'll talk to him. We may be able to figure out a way to postpone the taxes or average them or even get a note and pay it off over twenty years and pay the taxes on it as you go."

"When you find out what I can do, maybe you could come talk with Schiller about it."

"Sure, Mark. I'll see what I can do."

About a week later, Hofmann returned $5,000 to Taylor, saying that, once again, he had been able to save $10,000 on the purchase of the books. He had sold the books to a collector named Fleming, he said, but had not yet been paid.

"Did you get a contract?" Taylor asked.

"No."

"Did you get the money?"

"Not yet. But I trust him."

Taylor was pressed with other business and did not have time to argue. Nearly a month later, Hofmann sent him a personal check for $2,375, half the profit for a Book of Mormon he had acquired by trading off an early edition of Shakespeare's plays.

Still, by April 15, when Taylor was scheduled to leave the country on vacation, he had not been paid for the rare book collection transaction. He could not get Hofmann on the telephone, so he drove to Haus Hofmann. It was worth the drive to hear Hofmann say he had just received a check from Fleming for $360,000. He wrote a personal check to Taylor for $180,000.

The next day, Taylor deposited the check, paid a few debts, and went to Mexico. When he came home, he learned that the $180,000 check had bounced.

He tried to call Hofmann but could not reach him. Finally, he tracked him down through in-laws. Hofmann was attending the Mormon History Association meetings in Kansas City, Missouri, where the salamander and Stowell letters were the subject of several papers. Taylor told Hofmann that his personal check for $180,000 had bounced.

"Yeah, I know. I'm really sorry, Gene."

"What I can't understand, Mark, is that when I tried to collect on it, someone at your bank said that I was supposed to hold the check, that it wasn't supposed to have been deposited. Since they said it shouldn't have been deposited in the first place, they told me not to redeposit it. Now what's the story?"

Hofmann apologized for the confusion and said he would get in touch with Fleming again.

The next weekend Taylor returned from Boston about 9:30 p.m. to find the transaction still unresolved. He drove directly to Hofmann's house and rang the doorbell. "Did you get the money, Mark?"

"No, I didn't."

"Well, we're going to go to New York together and see this Mr. Fleming."

"Fleming said he was going to wire $100,000, and that much has come in." Nevertheless, Taylor insisted they go to New York on May 9. But that morning, Hofmann called to say he was sick and could not go. Taylor heard later from Dori that Mark had been meeting with church leaders about the salamander letter but would meet him on Temple Square. Taylor found Hofmann, who gave him a cashier's check for $100,000 and a personal check for $65,000.

"I can make that personal check good in a couple of days," Hofmann said. "I should be getting another $70,000 right away, then we'll go back to New York and collect the rest."

"That's fine, Mark."

The trip was postponed again, however, Hofmann explaining that he was now busy meeting with church leaders about the Stowell letter. The next thing Taylor knew Hofmann's $65,000 personal check had bounced and Hofmann did not seem to be anywhere. In fact, Haus Hofmann seemed vacant.

Finally Taylor located Hofmann at his sister's house in Bakersfield, California. Hofmann returned Taylor's call from Disneyland. "This check should have cleared," Hofmann said, the background noise of the park behind him. "Fleming wired the money."

Taylor then called Hofmann's branch of Rocky Mountain State Bank and asked about a wire from Fleming in New York. There had been no such wire. Exasperated, Taylor resigned himself to waiting until the Hofmanns returned home from vacation.

In a few days, Hofmann called Taylor, full of apology. "I'll get a cashier's check." They arranged several meetings before finally making connections, then Hofmann gave Taylor a personal check for $30,000. "I'll make it good, Gene."

Taylor looked at it. "I don't want your personal checks." He handed it back, adding the returned check to it. "From now on, I just want cashier's checks."

With the rare books deal still unresolved, Taylor loaned Hofmann an additional $15,000 on June 10 to invest in a rare manuscript by Charles Dickens, entitled, "The Haunted Man." Meanwhile, Taylor was eager to auction his Boone letter at Sotheby's in New York, and Hofmann seemed equally anxious to have Taylor explain to Schiller his tax ideas regarding the "Oath of a Freeman" sale. Taylor arranged to go with Hofmann to New York for the Sotheby's auction on June 13. The morning before, he dropped by the Hofmanns' home.

"You'd better call Sotheby's," he told Hofmann. "I need to know the time of the auction."

Hofmann placed the call. After he hung up, he said, "Gene, the auction isn't tomorrow. It's been delayed until the 25th."

Taylor was disappointed. He and his family were leaving on vacation to England on June 20th. "Well, I'll go back and meet this Mr. Fleming anyway. At least let's get the books back if he won't pay in full."

They flew to New York and met with Schiller and Wapner. Taylor admired their first editions of children's books, and they discussed the Oath. Hofmann told Taylor he had arranged for them to see Fleming in the afternoon.

First, though, Hofmann was eager to show Taylor where he had found the Oath. He took him to Argosy Books and pointed out the clerk he had bought it from. Over lunch, he, Taylor and Schiller discussed the Dickens manuscript in which they were all investing. Schiller and Hofmann left lunch early to attend a meeting about the transaction.

Taylor wandered around New York for a while. He dropped by Sotheby's and discovered that no rare document auction had been scheduled for June. The next one was not until October 31st for documents like the Boone letter. He asked to speak with someone in charge and learned that Hofmann had not consigned the Boone document or any other document for auction.

"We'd be interested in that letter if you'd like to consign it," the director told him.

Taylor walked back to Schiller and Wapner's, mulling over this information. Hofmann was not there, but Schiller was. "Mark will be back about 3:00," Schiller said.

Taylor frowned but hid the depth of his frustration. "We were going to see Mr. Fleming about that book deal."

Schiller looked startled. "Oh, I don't know how you'd get in to see Mr. Fleming. He's impossible to see."

After a few questions, Taylor concluded that the appointment with Fleming, like the auction at Sotheby's, was fiction. He waited impatiently for Hofmann, before flying on to Florida. The moment Hofmann appeared, Taylor confronted him.

"I want the Boone letter to sell, Mark. I expect you to make good on that deal." He told him what he had learned at Sotheby's.

"I gave that letter to Lyn Jacobs, a partner of mine, to consign at Sotheby's. I thought he'd done it."

Taylor walked Hofmann out to the sidewalk and yelled, calling him dishonest. Hofmann listened, "humble as a puppy dog." Finally, utterly discouraged, Taylor left to catch his flight to Florida. As soon as he reached home, he would have to pack his family off to England. After returning, in mid-July, Taylor received a cashier's check from Hofmann for $40,000, a payment on the rare books investment. By then, however, Taylor had already made up his mind against future investments with Hofmann and was determined to sell the Boone letter to settle his account.

In June, anticipating that the Oath would soon sell, the

Hofmanns began shopping for a new home. Hofmann called a realtor and boyhood friend, who accompanied them to various luxury homes. Hofmann particularly liked a house in Emigration Canyon, east of Salt Lake City. The 3.5-acre lot included a satellite dish, a guest house, a pump house, and an underground garage. On the other hand, it was relatively isolated from family and friends, as well as from their children's private school. The Hofmanns also looked at houses in Olympus Cove and Indian Hills, elite neighborhoods in Salt Lake City, but Hofmann always returned to the Emigration Canyon house, which Dori liked less than he.

As summer passed, anticipation over the Oath's imminent sale grew. Brent Metcalfe was visiting the Hofmanns one evening when Shannon Flynn came in, home from a trip back east for Hofmann. He showed some reports to Hofmann, who was visibly moved.

"I can't tell you what this is about now, Brent," Hofmann said, beaming, "but sometime I will." As Metcalfe later discovered, the Oath had passed all of its authentication tests.

Meanwhile, Brent Ashworth heard that Wade Lillywhite had purchased an original, signed copy of the Lincoln-Douglas debates for around $17,000. The grapevine next reported that the Lincoln-Douglas document's authenticity had been questioned, so Hofmann had taken it back. Thus, when Ashworth heard that Steve Barnett at Cosmic Aeroplane was considering the same item at a reduced price of $9,500, he called Barnett. "Why don't you send me a copy of the inscription," Ashworth suggested.

When the inscription arrived, Ashworth looked at it closely, then called Barnett. "Steve, this isn't Lincoln's handwriting. It's close, but it's not Lincoln."

"Mark told me that Charles Hamilton had authenticated the inscription," Barnett replied.

Ashworth looked at it again and shook his head. "Well, this is a fake. Did you get it from Hofmann?"

"Yeah."

"I've got a Lincoln in my collection."

"Would you send me a copy of that?"

Ashworth did. Barnett agreed that the signatures looked

different and returned the document to Hofmann. The next time Ashworth visited Hofmann, Hofmann met him angrily at the door.

"How dare you tell Barnett that my Lincoln was no good!"

"Well, it was obvious, Mark. It was not the same signature. It's not a Lincoln."

"It's not obvious at all. Charles Hamilton authenticated it."

"Then talk to Hamilton. As far as I can tell, you somehow got hold of a fake. That's all there is to it."

Their debate rekindled an old conflict: the note Joseph Smith had written in Carthage Jail which Hofmann had sold to another collector. Ashworth had never given up trying to get that letter.

"What do you think Dick Marks would take for it?" he asked Hofmann virtually every time the two of them talked. Finally Hofmann said he thought Marks might be amenable to a sale.

Early in July, while Ashworth was at the Crossroads Office Tower in Salt Lake City, he got a call from Hofmann. "Brent, the Joseph Smith letter is available."

Ashworth flushed with excitement. "That's wonderful, Mark. How much?"

"Sixty thousand dollars."

Ashworth's joy quickly turned to outrage. The letter had been virtually stolen from him, he felt, and the price had since tripled. "The price is too high, Mark. I won't pay it." Ashworth had gone through the disposable income he had made in the stock market, had floated loans, and even sold some company stock to buy Hofmann's documents. Charlene Ashworth did not want her husband dealing with Hofmann at all, not only because it was expensive but because there were too many frustrations, each of which Brent took hard.

"Okay," Hofmann said.

Ashworth hung up but could not ignore his disappointment and anxiety. Despite feeling that Hofmann had added insult to injury, Ashworth had to admit he still wanted the letter. The following Wednesday morning, when he went by Hofmann's home, he said as much.

"Deseret Book owns it. They bought it from Marks, and they want $60,000 cash."

"Does it all have to be cash?"

"Yes, it does."

"Well, that rules me out." At least I gave it a try, Ashworth comforted himself, walking out to his car. Early on Saturday afternoon, Hofmann called. "I'd like to come down to Provo and talk with you, Brent."

"That's fine. Why don't we meet at the BYU library?" Ashworth did not want Charlene to know he was dealing with Hofmann again. But as he headed out of the house, she caught him and asked where he was going. He confessed.

"Why are you wasting your time on Mark?"

"I'm trying to get him to come through on that Dunham letter. Dick Marks has sold it to Deseret Book."

"If you're going to see Mark, why don't you take those fake photos you bought from him."

"Good idea." Ashworth met Hofmann at the library, but it was crowded, so they decided to go to Ashworth's father's office in Provo. As they walked down the steps, Ashworth handed Hofmann two of four old West photographs he had bought from him. "Mark, I'm returning these. They're fakes." He showed him that they were mounted on paper not available when Matt Warner and Butch Cassidy were alive.

"Yeah, I see what you mean," Hofmann said, telling Ashworth where he had gotten them. "You have to be careful of that guy," Hofmann warned. Then Hofmann once again offered Ashworth the Dunham letter. "I'm authorized to sell it for Deseret Book. They've relented so that there can be a part-trade part-cash deal."

"So how much do you want in cash?"

"I need $30,000 in cash, $30,000 in trade."

"I just don't have the cash right now, Mark. I did have a line of credit approved for $17,000 at First Interstate Bank. I'd be happy to use that. I could come up with $2,000 more, so that would be $19,000 in cash."

"Well, how about the trade items?"

Ashworth offered him several letters Hofmann had asked to buy back before—letters by Joseph Smith and one by Brigham

Young. Hofmann agreed—$19,000 cash and the three letters. The next week they met in the Crossroads Mall and closed the deal.

Ashworth told no one about his purchase of the Dunham letter and was startled to hear the rumor that he had bought the letter for $100,000. He drove to Hofmann's house. After Hofmann finished his shower, he came into the living room, wrapping a robe around him. "What's up, Brent?"

"How come word is out about the Dunham letter?" Ashworth inquired.

"I haven't told anyone. It must have come from Curt Bench."

Ashworth drove to the ZCMl Mall and confronted Bench.

"Brent," Bench said, "we haven't even told the executives here at Deseret Book about that letter yet. If word's out, it must have come from Mark. It didn't come from us." Ashworth knew an impasse when he reached one. The grapevine always seemed to know more—accurately or not—than the people who comprised it.

During the summer of 1985, as Hofmann awaited the Oath's sale, his financial situation became increasingly complicated. The Dunham letter deal, for example, was far more convoluted and unusual than Ashworth realized. Since Deseret Book had paid $90,000 to acquire the letter, they had sold it to Hofmann for $110,000. Thus Hofmann lost more than $50,000 to get the Dunham letter to Ashworth, still owing Deseret Book $110,000 plus more than $6,000 sales tax, since Hofmann had never bothered to get a tax number and had to pay sales tax. He also owed Gene Taylor and other Americana investors, and he and Dori were still house-shopping. Of course, once the Oath sold, he could repay everyone and everything. Meanwhile, on July 26, he took out a second mortgage on his house for around $26,000. He had not made a house payment to his parents since March.

Then, on July 30, Hofmann gave Bench some disappointing news: the Library of Congress had declined purchase of the Oath. Library officials were asking for further testing and had been annoyed by a price increase from $1 million to $1.5 million.

315

However, Schiller was now offering the Oath to the American Antiquarian Society and Hofmann expected the Oath ultimately to bring him a fortune.

On August 8, Mark and Dori Hofmann made an offer on a plush house on Cottonwood Lane in Holladay, the neighborhood south of Millcreek, and paid $5,000 in earnest money. Dori, in particular, loved the house, with its tennis courts, large kitchen, and built-in aquarium. It was near their present ward and the house where they were now living. It was reasonably close to Cardon School and Dori's parents' home near Sugarhouse.

They scheduled the closing on the house for October 15, but meanwhile their debts continued to mount. The utility companies and mobile telephone service were pressing for payment. Around August 22, the Internal Revenue Service returned to Hofmann a bounced check for more than $8,000. His payroll checks to Metcalfe and Flynn were bouncing and even his $48 registration check to the annual Sunstone Symposium was returned for lack of funds. He postponed the closing on their new house, which would have required a $50,000 downpayment. A fortune gleamed in the distance, but debts, bills, and non-payment threats towered nearby.

Deseret Book was more than anxious about Hofmann's unpaid balance for the purchase of the Jonathan Dunham letter. Even the chairman of Deseret's board of directors was getting nervous. After considerable discussion between July and September, Hofmann drove a few blocks east on September 12 to Bench's home and handed him a $100,000 cashier's check. Bench was glad to see the check but reminded Hofmann he still owed $10,000, plus the $6,000 sales tax. Friday morning, September 13, with a sigh of relief, Bench deposited the cashier's check in Deseret Book's rare books account at First Interstate Bank.

Later that morning, Bench and Lillywhite were surprised to see Hofmann come into the store looking pale and on the edge of tears. He was accompanied by a dark-haired, dark-complected man who was not introduced. Bench assumed he was an attorney. While the man waited nearby, Hofmann told Bench he desperately needed money. Since the $100,000 check had been deposited, Bench agreed to talk with his superiors about advancing him a loan.

Later that afternoon, Hofmann returned, still accompanied by the stranger. Bench took them upstairs to meet with his boss and discuss a loan of $100,000. Hofmann told Bench privately he would do anything to get the money. He offered a collection of rare books as collateral, which he offered to buy back for $150,000 within six months. Mystified, Bench said he would call Hofmann and let him know about the loan.

Saturday morning Hofmann called Bench and told him he would not need the loan after all. "Okay," Bench said, wondering how Hofmann's debts had been so quickly resolved.

The question was soon compounded by a second call at 11:30 a.m. This one was from Steve Christensen, Bench's book-buying friend. "Curt, I've got to ask you what's going on," Christensen said at once. "I understand that a $100,000 check from Mark Hofmann to Deseret Book just went through First Interstate Bank."

Bench thought the call was unusual. How could Steve know about all this? Nevertheless, without asking the questions crowding into his mind, Bench told Christensen his information was right and explained about the Jonathan Dunham letter.

"Curt, a certain general authority, who is a director of a local bank, asked me to find out about Mark's recent transactions, including the $100,000 check for Deseret Book," Christensen related. "You see, Mark borrowed about $185,000 from this bank on this general authority's recommendation."

"Really?" Another debt, Bench thought, dismayed.

"Yes. He said the money was to acquire the McLellin collection, which would be considered collateral for the loan and later be given to the church."

"I know. Mark talked to me about the McLellin collection."

"The note is overdue," Christensen said. "Mark hasn't been in touch, and he doesn't seem to be reachable."

"Oh, I know. He's impossible to reach."

"This general authority and I are trying to keep criminal action from being taken against Mark," Christensen explained. "But we also want to protect the church from the scandal and embarrassment that could result from the fallout of this situation."

After a moment's thought, Bench decided to tell Christensen about Hofmann's efforts the previous day to raise money. Christensen listened intently.

"I appreciate you telling me this, Curt. The situation I'm describing is really important. A problem like this could destroy Mark's reputation and credibility and could hurt his chances of dealing with President Hinckley in the future."

"It sounds serious. Will you let me know what happens?"

Bench stared at the telephone for a minute. The McLellin collection—he thought Mark said he had sold that to the church. Obviously, Hofmann's finances were even worse than Bench had surmised. More than that, something here simply was not making sense. Who was monitoring the checks at First Interstate Bank and telling the general authority—who told Christensen—what was going through Deseret Book's rare books account? And what did Steve have to do with the McLellin collection?

14

THE MCLELLIN COLLECTION
AT ALL COSTS

Steve Christensen's unexpected
call to Curt Bench on Saturday, September 14, indicated that
Christensen had become a link between powerful men and Mark
Hofmann. Christensen did not need to identify Hugh Pinnock
specifically as the one who had arranged a loan for Hofmann—
the mere mention of a general authority-bank director apprised
Bench of the seriousness of the situation. If the church—as
well as Hofmann's relationship with President Hinckley—was
threatened by scandal, Bench sensed a double emergency.

Since late June, the McLellin transaction had been an incredible adventure for Christensen. But by September, the adventure was turning into a nightmare, and the personal stakes were
rising.

Pressures on Christensen had been gradually mounting. In
January 1985 he had been promoted to vice-president of
syndication at CFS. Already critical of some CFS policies,
Christensen launched his own investigation into various company
deals. Two months later, he began confronting CFS president
Gary Sheets and other officers with disturbing facts. For example, hundreds of thousands of dollars had been invested in an
ethanol manufacturing plant in New Mexico. Accordingly, Sheets
had planned to take a hefty tax deduction in 1985. But,
Christensen discovered, nothing of the plant existed but a
concrete foundation. Sheets was shocked. Where had the money
gone? No one knew, except that it had been paid to the devel-
opers.

The regional collapse during the early 1980s of the office building construction boom hit CFS especially hard. The company had invested heavily in such over-built areas of the country as Houston based on the expectation that the national market was at rock bottom and would soon revive, returning a high profit. It did not.

CFS had also become heavily indebted following the construction of its own office building at 300 South State Street in 1982. Company officers had purchased the site expecting to reduce renovation costs by using tax credits available for the restoration of historic buildings. However, the write-off was unavailable, and the cost of correcting serious structural problems exceeded the original estimate by several million dollars. In addition, the idea of selling condominium office space in the building did not catch on. In 1984, CFS tried to refinance the project debt, only to find that the building's value was less than its debt—providing no owner equity. Pension fund debts were added to the company's deficit, ruining CFS's credit rating and preventing it from issuing further limited partnerships, which had constituted its prime source of income.

Despite the remodeling costs, no expense had been spared in decorating the fifth floor, which CFS occupied. Christensen's small but expensively decorated office was next to Sheets's especially lavish one. Sheets, who usually won the company's annual racquetball tournament, had a court installed on the fifth floor. Christensen steered clear of racquetball but installed oak bookshelves to house his rapidly expanding library. Books were delivered almost daily, stacking up in cardboard containers.

Between late 1984 and early 1985, a "working fund" was established at JGSA, directing several investments into the company itself. Sheets, known to loan, spend, or give away money as quickly as he made it, used some of this money to resolve debts.

In addition, CFS had also invested in "diversified products," highly speculative and unfamiliar markets ranging from water slides to jojoba beans. Some of these investments involved bank financing, guaranteed personally by CFS officers and by Christensen, who was in charge of preparing the contracts. In 1984, after federal laws had placed greater liability on investment attorneys and accountants, the Los Angeles law firm that had prepared CFS's investment proposals discontinued those services. CFS retained a New York firm but shifted most of the responsibility of preparing investment proposals to Christensen and his staff.

Christensen had always worked hard and risen fast; now as a new vice-president, he managed to be remarkably intimidating with lawyers and businessmen despite his lack of a college degree in either field. He had never emulated Sheets's back-slapping, cheek-kissing friendliness around the office, nor Sheets's interest in office sports. Sheets gave away forty season tickets to the Utah Jazz basketball games to clients, but only once did Randy Rigby and Joe Robertson convince Christensen even to participate in the company golf tournament. Christensen enjoyed himself but commented, "Would you believe my grandfather can do this eight hours a day?"

The Christensens' condominium in Park City was used by Terri and the boys, since Steve couldn't get away from work. On business trips, he entertained himself by visiting local bookstores, the appropriate page from a telephone directory in hand. He attended only part of a CFS conference in Las Vegas, but on the one night he was in town insisted on attending one live show after another, playing as hard as he worked.

Rigby and Robertson were amused by Christensen's resistance to the diets his wife frequently prescribed. They'd watch as he'd order two double cheeseburgers, two orders of fries, then—as a nod to his waistline and energy level—a Tab.

"Don't you think you'd better go easy on the hamburgers?" Robertson would venture.

"No, I've got to get it now. When I get home, Terri's just going to give me that nutri-drink stuff."

Terri Christensen knew little about her husband's business dealings, but the long nights Steve spent at his desk in the family room, bent over CFS contracts gave her the message: "CFS is broken. Steve, you fix it." More nights than usual, she left her husband at his desk when she climbed the stairs to their bedroom. When she and the children woke, he was usually gone. Robertson or Rigby would find Christensen at his desk in the CFS building early in the morning. The pyramid of Tab cans stacked beside him bore silent witness to the hours he had already worked.

As Christensen peeled back the expensive veneer at CFS to reveal the problems underneath, he decided that the company had about two months to set itself straight. Secretly, his fear grew that the company might be beyond salvaging. He had personally arranged more than one hundred syndications and would become legally and personally responsible to those investors.

Christensen had always intended to be well-off financially. He had dropped out of college and left his father's retail store to enter the corporate fast lane at a salary of around $30,000. He eventually made more than $300,000 per year, much of which he reinvested in the company. He loved luxury and had purchased three BMWs in a row, moving up the line each time, selling the earlier models to Rigby and Robertson. He helped to underwrite the cost of the annual Sunstone Theological Symposium and donated to other publications and organizations related to Mormon studies.

Gradually, Christensen became convinced that business failure was a genuine threat, but he vacillated for a time between hope and despair. On May 1, 1985, Christensen compiled a personal financial statement. He had $5,000 in the bank and more than $200,000 in notes with JGSA plus more than $58,000 in CFS stock. He placed other investments and holdings at a retail value of more than $300,000 and estimated his personal library to be worth $275,000 retail. The latter proved to be greatly overestimated. His debts were few, except that he was a general partner in numerous CFS transactions. If the company failed, he would be ruined. Yet in May he bought a computer system that further indebted himself and his associates, implying he saw a future for CFS.

That hope evaporated completely in June when CFS received a financial statement from accountants that placed the company firmly in the red. Sheets called a meeting of officers. Sheets owned 42 percent of the company, Christensen about 15 percent. "Maybe you guys had better all leave CFS," Sheets said gloomily. "I'm the guy they're going to hang."

The others insisted they would stay, but a few weeks later

company president Stan Benfell resigned after rumors circulated that CFS was being investigated by the state securities commission. The rumors were false, but Benfell's resignation fueled other rumors. Word of CFS's problems was spreading fast, endangering contracts and hampering future sales. With Benfell gone, Sheets began paying attention to administration, which he had previously avoided in favor of setting an example as the company's lead salesman. He found they had spent $300,000 in 1984 on travel alone and knew they could at least reduce that cost. He began looking for other ways to trim, people to lay off, measures that would allow CFS to survive as a no-frills operation.

Beyond CFS's problems, it was Christensen's avocation—his love of Mormon history—that brought him the greatest pressures. Like Christensen, Paul Toscano, one of the bankruptcy attorneys Christensen had hired to advise CFS, studied Mormon theology and history. In May 1985, with the salamander and Stowell letters newly public, he told Christensen that a set of metal plates, some large and small, all thin and finely inscribed with hieroglyphics, had been found in England and given to the church in the mid-1970s.

Christensen shook his head and laughed. "Wow," he said. "How good is your source?"

"Very good. He saw them himself and described them to me."

"So the church has the gold plates."

"Well, the story's weird, but that's what it suggests." Toscano, who'd kept the story quiet for years, added his own assumption, that the church had not publicized the find because scholars might raise questions about the plates' workmanship or language. Christensen found the story credible enough to tell several friends and a study group that he believed the church possessed the gold plates.

The following month, on June 28, Christensen scheduled an appointment with Hofmann to discuss the McLellin collection. Hofmann said he had located the collection in Texas and had already discussed the matter with President Hinckley. The collection's price was $195,000, he said, and thus far he had paid $10,000 in earnest money. However, his option to buy would expire on June 30, and there were others who were interested in the papers for their possible value in re-evaluating Mormon origins. Christensen was the fourth person from whom he was seeking financial support, Hofmann said.

Christensen asked what the collection contained. Hofmann described documents, in three boxes the size of orange cartons, including the original Facsimile 2 papyrus from The Pearl of Great Price. Christensen knew how controversial such a papyrus could be, especially if it had been altered prior to its publication in the early 1840s in a Mormon periodical.

Hofmann said that McLellin had kept an affidavit from Joseph Smith's wife, Emma, indicating that Joseph's first spiritual experience was not his first vision of God the Father and Jesus Christ but centered on The Book of Mormon. Again, Christensen recognized the threat to Mormon tradition, writing in his journal, "The Emma Smith affadavit could be particularly damaging since scores of individuals would like to disprove the occurence of a First Vision. A more recent attack on the first vision experience are those who try to claim that it was really Joseph's brother Alvin who had the experience and that Joseph merely stepped into his place upon Alvin's death (see the Salt Lake Tribune article dealing with Brent Metcalfe and the Oliver Cowdery History.)"

As Hofmann talked, Christensen considered the potential impact of these papers, including thirty years of journals by an articulate enemy of Joseph Smith, on the historical underpinnings of Mormon doctrine. Scholars might be able to explain the omission of Smith's first vision, but the affidavit would focus even more public attention on Smith's experience with the gold plates and possibly money digging.

What was more, Hofmann said, the McLellin collection also contained the only known copy of a revelation in which Smith at one time considered selling the copyright of The Book of Mormon to raise money—a book Smith claimed to have translated "by the gift and power of God."

For years, Christensen had advocated an open approach to Mormon history but faced with such a threat to the faith of thousands of church members, he decided to intervene, despite his own financial problems.

"After a thirty minute review of the facts and potential options," Christensen wrote, "I suggested to Mark that we contact Elder Hugh Pinnock, not necessarily because he was a General Authority, but more particularly because he was a man of financial expertise with a wide circle of friends & contacts. I called Elder Pinnock over the telephone and I was fortunate enough to get through to him. I briefly reviewed the facts with him. After a short discussion he indicated that he could arrange for the funds within one hour and that Mark and I should come over to his office as soon as possible."

By the time they reached Pinnock's office, Hofmann had explained to Christensen that his Americana discovery, the "Oath of a Freeman," was expected to sell to the Library of Congress for $1.5 million. At present, he could not afford to buy the McLellin collection, Hofmann said, but once the Oath sold, he could purchase it and donate it to the church. "That way," he explained, "I can say that I never sold the McLellin collection to the church, and the brethren can say they never purchased it."

Wryly, Christensen noted in his journal, "With any luck no one will ever ask Mark if he donated the material," then added his own rationalization. "Though this form of dialogue walks the fine line of 'honest intent' behind the pure reading of the question and reciprocal answer, it perhaps saves the Church for the time being from having to offer an explanation on why they won't release the material and/or be under a public relations move to counter the contents of the collection." Ironically, Christensen, who only a year earlier had written to Gordon B. Hinckley, asking about the Josiah Stowell letter, the rumored Oliver Cowdery journal, and any other items relevant to the salamander letter, was now trying to help church leaders dodge similar future inquiries.

Inside office 402 at the Church Administration Building, Christensen and Hofmann talked with Pinnock about the McLellin collection for more than an hour. Then Pinnock excused himself and went to speak with his advisor, Dallin Oaks, who had been an apostle only three months. Oaks said the McLellin collection might have some value, but he did not want the church directly connected with the purchase of any documents that might raise the issue of deliberate suppression. What about a bank loan? Pinnock asked. Could he assist in that? Oaks consented.

Approval given, Pinnock called Zions First National Bank, which despite the church's divestment of ownership in the early 1960s, retained close ties. But bank officers were attending meetings of the Utah Bankers Association. Pinnock then called First Interstate Bank and spoke with Robert Ward, a vice-president. Christensen and Hofmann went to the bank, where Hofmann provided minimal information and promised to provide the bank with a copy of his contract with the Library of Congress. Shortly thereafter, Shannon Flynn drove Hofmann back to First Interstate to pick up a check for $185,000.

Christensen was clearly surprised at the speed and ease of the transaction. "It was remarkable to both Mark and myself that Elder Pinnock was willing to assist with only a brief explanation," he recorded in his journal. "It was as though he sensed completely the potential damage which this material would cause the Church." In fact, Christensen noted, before they left Pinnock's office, Hofmann was given four telephone numbers at which he could reach Pinnock over the weekend and the assurance that Pinnock would have $185,000 in cash in case a cashier's check was not considered legal tender on a Sunday. Pinnock also offered a prop-jet and/or an armored car to transport the collection to Salt Lake City, "however, Mark dissuaded him," Christensen wrote. Hofmann said he would send the material home, fully insured, via registered mail. Meanwhile, he would keep Pinnock and Christensen informed. Once in Salt Lake City, the collection would be kept in safe deposit boxes until Hofmann received payment for the "Oath of a Freeman" and could donate the collection to the church.

Obviously elated but unable to share the day's incredible events with anyone, Christensen continued writing in his journal under the heading, "miscellaneous items." First, he wrote that Pinnock told Hofmann that he would like to talk with him sometime about "retaining his services to track down two items"—the lost 116 pages of the Book of Mormon and another item Pinnock would not identify specifically. "Mark and I believe," Christensen speculated, "that he was referring to the Gold Plates from which we have the Book of Mormon. I personally believe that the Church already has them in its possession (unknown to perhaps the majority of the Twelve and other General Authorities)."

Pinnock later wrote in a memo that Christensen had guessed wrong. "When I talked with Steve Christensen and Mark Hofmann in my office on Friday June 28, 1985, I mentioned a lady in Pennsylvania, who claimed to have the missing 116 pages. I also mentioned another item of interest, but we did not discuss it further at that time. I had heard there had been a 'Urim and Thummim' located somewhere in the Northeast. It was the item to which I was referring. If I remember correctly, I cleared that item later with Steve, explaining to him about the alleged 'seer stone.' "

The church's rumored suppression of history surfaced again in the press the very weekend Hofmann was to procure the McLellin collection in Texas. In the *Los Angeles Times* an article by religion writer John Dart announced, "Mormons forbid Female Biographers of Smith's Wife to Address Church." The article reported a ban forbidding authors Linda King Newell and Valeen Tippetts Avery to speak in church meetings about their new book, *Mormon Enigma: Emma Hale Smith*. Despite the book's favorable reviews, some top LDS leaders were unhappy with its contents. Newell and her husband subsequently met with Apostle Oaks, but the ban was not lifted for another ten months.

Fortunately, for the moment, a far more sensitive subject — the McLellin collection — remained out of the public eye. The following Tuesday, July 2, Christensen wrote to Pinnock, "Thank you for your sufficient and gracious counsel" regarding the bank loan. Christensen said he was sure Pinnock's actions had spared the church unnecessary turmoil.

This feeling of accomplishment was jarred the following Saturday, however, when Dawn Tracy reported in the *Salt Lake Tribune*, "Ancient Mormon Manuscript Found, Sold in Texas," with a photograph of Facsimile 2 from The Pearl of Great

Price. This time Tracy's source was not Brent Metcalfe but Mark Hofmann himself.

"Mr. Hoffman [sic] said terms of the sale agreement stipulate he is not to divulge the name of the buyer nor the amount of the sale. He said the collection may be made public when the documents are authenticated," Tracy wrote. "Church spokesman Jerry Cahill stated the church does not own or possess the collection. Mr. Hoffman said he did not sell the collection to the Mormon church." The remainder of the article speculated on the importance of Facsimile 2 and the debate already concerning the papyrus.

Christensen clipped the article, typing at the top: "This is the collection referenced in my Journal Notes of June 28, 1985. Needless to say, there are errors in the article."

Brent Ashworth had no sooner read about the sale than he got a call from Tracy. "Were you surprised to see that?" she asked.

"I was very surprised," he answered, "because Mark had just told me he didn't have the collection—and then here's the article the next day."

"You can probably tell by the article that I talked to Mark."

"Well, he told me yesterday he didn't have the collection and he hadn't seen it." Ashworth remembered an early Mormon hymnal he had bought from Hofmann, which Hofmann said had come from the McLellin collection. Ashworth had wanted an affidavit from Hofmann to that effect but had not received it yet.

Also pending was an offer Hofmann had made to Ashworth in June to buy back the Lucy Mack Smith letter for $250,000. Hofmann said he had a California buyer for it. Periodically, Hofmann renewed the offer. "Brent, I've firmed it up with my man who wants to offer you a quarter of a million dollars for the Lucy Mack Smith letter. He'll pay you 10 percent down, sending you a $25,000 check, and the rest within ten days."

"Okay, Mark, fine. Have him send the check and a signed letter saying he'll pay the rest of it in that short period of time and I'll heavily consider it."

Ten or fifteen minutes later, Hofmann called back. "Brent, I've just spoken with my man again, and he wants eight items from your collection. He'll offer you around $450,000 for the eight items. He'll send you $50,000 now and the rest within a few days."

"Fine, Mark. Write it up, send me the check and letter."

Ashworth ran the items suggested through his mind. Most had come from Hofmann himself and were easily the best items in Ashworth's own collection. The offer did not arrive in the mail. Thereafter, when Ashworth and Hofmann met on Wednesday, either at Hofmann's house or in the Crossroads Mall, Hofmann would say his man needed a little more time to put the deal together.

On July 9, Hofmann stopped by Deseret Book and told Curt Bench about the McLellin collection and its contents. As usual, Bench recorded the incident in his journal, adding, "Mark said he has agreed to try to find things for the Church and prevent them from falling into anti-Mormon hands."

Christensen recorded in his journal Hofmann's characterization of two men — Wesley Walters, a Presbyterian minister, and George Smith, a California businessman, who were both active in the Mormon intellectual community — as "anti-Mormons" wanting to purchase the McLellin collection. Hofmann and Christensen cited this as evidence that Hofmann had to move quickly to secure the papers.

What Christensen did not say was that he had recently discussed with Smith the possibility of Smith's underwriting some of the research projects Christensen had either inaugurated or envisioned. For their part, neither Walters nor Smith knew anything but rumors about the McLellin collection.

On July 10, Hofmann informed Pinnock that the McLellin collection had been purchased in Texas and secured in safe deposit boxes in Salt Lake City.

Sometime near that date Christensen and Hofmann were seen rushing out of Christensen's office in a panic. By then, Joe Robertson was working almost constantly with Christensen, trying to resolve CFS problems. When Christensen appeared and breathlessly asked, "Joe, may I borrow your car? My jeep's in the shop, and I have to meet with President Hinckley," Robertson, unquestioningly, handed over the keys. Hours later, about 3:30 p.m., Christensen returned with the same man and introduced him as Mark Hofmann. "This is Joe," he added, "the guy whose car we borrowed." They exchanged nods, and Christensen returned the car keys.

On July 12, in fact, Hofmann gave Hugh Pinnock a photocopy of the land deed bearing the names of Sidney Rigdon, a minister who converted to Mormonism and became Joseph Smith's counselor, and Solomon Spaulding, whose early nineteenth-century unpublished fable, *Manuscript Story*, had been asserted by some critics as the basis for The Book of Mormon. Mormon researchers and leaders had maintained that Spaulding and Rigdon were not acquainted. The land deed silently proved that they were.

While the McLellin deal pended, an anonymous phone call to LDS public communications inquired one day about a bank loan to Hofmann to buy the McLellin collection. Press leaks were obviously a major threat.

Randy Rigby dropped by Christensen's office one day to find a pair of binoculars propped up in the north window, directed toward the church office buildings.

"What's this, Steve?" he asked, knowing his friend was no sportsman.

Christensen smiled. "Well, when the brethren are looking in on me, I want them to know I'm looking back at them."

During an occasional lull in the McLellin transaction, Christensen's attention would be diverted by the portending disintegration of CFS and personal bankruptcy. For a year or so, Christensen and business associate Franklin Johnson had discussed Mormon history. Now they began talking professional ruin and personal survival, a subject Johnson understood from his own experience. "Go down to nothing," he advised. "If people can see you don't have anything, they won't go after you."

Christensen followed Johnson's advice, divesting himself of research commitments, selling his BMW, cancelling subscriptions. He put up for sale two wooded lots where he had once hoped to build a new home with a two-story library. He even stopped ordering books—except for books on bankruptcy, which he read assiduously, soon beginning to sound like a bankruptcy attorney. Most painful was exploring options for selling his library at the best possible price and the last possible moment.

Johnson, a generation older than Christensen and most of his friends, thought Christensen cynical, that success had come a little too easily for him. Failure was a shock. Christensen felt guilty for his part in drawing investors to CFS deals that had proven unsound. Most difficult, Johnson thought, was the loss of a large amount of money Steve had invested for his father.

Johnson had known Mac Christensen for years and was surprised at how often Steve, who seldom mentioned personal relationships, talked about his father. Johnson knew that Steve's love for his mother, Joan, was deep and simple, but as a super-achieving oldest son, he and his father had a complicated relationship. Steve had inherited his father's workaholism and compassion. Yet Christensen disparaged the super-salesman image wherever he found it, despite his own persuasive abilities. Mac Christensen had a mercurial disposition; his oldest son had learned to keep a smooth surface. He had left his father's business to achieve success on his own. All that was gone now, and with it his father's money. Johnson knew how Christensen was dreading telling his father what had happened.

Once the conversation took place, however, Steve reported that it went better than expected. His relief was visible. As the summer passed, additional talks between son and father began to resolve old conflicts. Although Steve had always seemed precocious, that summer Johnson watched Christensen struggle toward a costly new maturity.

"How can one be a Christian and drive a BMW?" Christensen wanted to know during one of their talks. "How can one be a Christian and live in a materialistic, fast-lane society?" they expanded the question. Yet material means also allowed one to do good. How to balance the material with the spiritual?

By August, Sheets and Christensen had reached a clear impasse over the future of CFS. Sheets knew how much impact Christensen had on morale, and Christensen had made some very negative statements about the company's chance of survival. "Now, Steve," Sheets said when the showdown came, "I need your support in this. You can't keep saying that we're going to fail."

"Gary, I can't honestly say anything else."

"Can't you say that we've got a chance?"

"No."

Christensen had set up a "phoenix committee" to develop a plan for the inevitable bankruptcy. The term had implied hope, but the dark humor at some meetings suggested less euphonious titles. The plan involved Sheets stepping aside while a core of officers sold CFS assets and resolved what debt they could. They presented the plan to Sheets in the board room, but Sheets shook his head. "No, I can't give up."

As one member of the phoenix committee would say later, it wasn't really Gary Sheets's fault. CFS was his baby and they were telling him the baby was ugly.

However, Sheets pressed Christensen for support. "Steve, can't you say we're going to fight this thing together and give it our best?"

"No. I can say we're going to go down the toilet together and then we'll rebuild." He explained their plan again.

"Well, I just can't accept that," Sheets replied. "If that's the way you feel, you're going to have to leave."

Afterwards, Rigby caught Christensen privately. "Steve, what are you going to do?"

"I wish I knew."

"You know, I think there's plenty of business out there," Rigby said, "but people are getting killed by our high overhead and syndication fees. If we kept things simpler, I bet we could make a go of it."

"I feel the same way," Christensen admitted.

The two decided to become partners and extended the opportunity to Joe Robertson.

On August 4, Steve Christensen resigned from CFS.

"I'll tell you what I'm going to do," he told Joe Robertson. "When I go before the judge in bankruptcy court I'm going to plead insanity. I'll wear a Hari Krishna costume and dance around. Then when it's over, I'll whip off the costume and head off to Tahiti in my Bermuda shorts."

More seriously, Christensen contacted an attorney to ask

about potential criminal liability for the investments he had arranged. He brought with him documentation of CFS finances and, on an attorney's advice, began resolving his own involvement in the hope it would lessen his personal liability. He also spoke with a friend and attorney, Alan Smith, about different forms of bankruptcy and which were best. His personal indebtedness was light, but his CFS debts were enormous. During their conversations, Christensen learned that he had given the church the salamander letter during a period of time legally defined as "fraudulent conveyance," when any valuable item may be reclaimed by creditors. "It's an innocent fraud," Smith told him, "but you'll have to get the letter back and make it available as an asset to your creditors."

Christensen told him how embarrassing that would be. "Let me consider the alternatives on the bankruptcy," Christensen concluded. "I'll get back to you."

On August 12, Christensen borrowed approximately $14,000 on his signature. He and Rigby rented an office in the Judge Building, put in a telephone and an answering machine, and ordered letterheads for Rigby-Christensen, Inc. They had an office waiting for Robertson, whenever he could leave CFS. On August 16 Christensen wrote Gary Sheets a memo discussing his future business plans and asking for certain pieces of office furniture to take with him, which would reduce the $20,000 he said JGSA owed him. In a separate letter, he thanked Sheets for an on-the-job education.

Packing his things in his plush CFS office, Christensen gloomily gave a friend an expensive umbrella he had bought in New York City. "You'd might as well have this," he said. "It will just be lost to the bankruptcy court."

His friend thanked him, thinking how quiet and withdrawn Christensen had seemed all summer. He was also losing weight.

On August 18, three days before the Sunstone Theological Symposium convened for its annual meetings, Elder Dallin Oaks made headlines when he publicly decried Mormon scholars who criticize LDS leadership. Church leaders were entitled to the respect and support of their members, he said, regardless of whether their counsel and opinions were right or wrong.

For the second year in a row, speakers at the opening plenary session of the Sunstone symposium discussed the salamander letter. Other sessions on the money-digging letters and the probability that the church possessed the Oliver Cowdery history caused some conference goers to dub the 1985 meeting, "The Salamander Symposium."

On Thursday evening, Steve Christensen appeared on a panel to discuss "Pillars of My Faith." The Hotel Utah ballroom was packed. Everyone knew that Christensen—a Mormon bishop—had purchased the salamander letter, had it authenticated, and then donated it to the church. While people were interested in the personal details Christensen might divulge about the salamander letter, no one knew about the McLellin deal.

Christensen had a prepared paper on Mormon intellectualism, but the session's other speakers focussed on family reminiscences. "I didn't really have anything prepared to tell you about my family," Christensen began. "They won't let me talk about them. We've spent a lot of money in our family trying to cover up our family genealogy rather than do it."

Amid the laughter, Christensen picked up his talk, then looked away from it. "My wife is in Montana with my children up on her father's ranch. She thought that would be a great excuse not to have to attend tonight. But I did read to her and to my oldest son the remarks that I had prepared originally. After I concluded, I was expecting the praise that is due the provider and patriarch of the home." Christensen's voice was by now clearly ironic. "The only comment I received was from my eight-year-old son. He said, 'Well, Dad, I think it would be better if you'd cross out every other word.'"

Gradually Christensen moved to the subject of his experiences as a bishop. He told his audience that the business of releasing and sustaining ward members for various volunteer church callings had changed since he had been called as bishop. "We gave them a third option. We said, 'All in favor,' and of course the hands went up. 'All opposed.' And the third was, 'All who don't give a damn.'"

Christensen was clearly pleased by the enthusiastic response that filled the ballroom. "You laugh," he said, "but it's true.

I'll tell you some bishop jokes. It's a lot better than what I had prepared."

He launched into another story, paused, then said, "If I stutter, it's because I haven't had a caffeine drink for about four hours." He described how a survey of his ward had showed that although 93 percent of all men claimed they visited their assigned families at least once a month, only 28 percent actually did so. "I went back and changed all the quarterly reports for a year and caught pure hell. Ruined the stake averages." He described a stake meeting during which a visiting general authority asked the bishops to set home teaching goals for the next six months. "Hundred percent, one said," Christensen went on. "One crazy fellow said 110. That hit me. I said, 'Well, I can't commit to any percentage. One of two things would happen. I'd have to go out and do it myself, and, frankly, I don't do my own home teaching. To get the brethren to do it, the only way they're going to get anywhere near 100 percent is to lie and I don't think that's anything a bishop should induce on a ward. And he [the general authority] and I had a private chat for two hours."

Christensen tried again to begin his prepared talk. "Let me share with you, if I might — just a couple more bishop stories. This would be great for Johnny Carson where they don't appreciate Mormon culture. Since I've been bishop, we've had a major flood in our ward, had a windstorm, a major fire — burned down a million-dollar greenhouse. The members all want me to get released before we have the earthquake.

"I prepared this talk — the other talk — some time ago. I set it aside. A couple of weeks ago I started looking for it, couldn't find the talk anywhere. I looked and looked, asked my associates, my friends if they had the talk. Did I let them read it? What happened to it? I still couldn't find the talk. Finally, after some diligent searching, I was successful in purchasing the talk off the Mormon underground." That comment and another — "If you can't smile about your religion, you must work in the Church Office Building" — brought down the house.

Finally, he introduced the topic of Mormon intellectualism. "I don't have any college degrees. I was too interested in studying the church to ever manage to graduate from college.

And it has, by and large, been the intellectual stimulation in studying the gospel, the doctrinal development, and church history that has kept my mind alive." He then added a scripture he thought should be written: "Blessed are they that believe; and blessed are they that know why they believe."

Listing his own beliefs, he came quickly to Joseph Smith. "I have a great love and appreciation for Joseph Smith and the phenomenal task that was placed on a very young man with a set of circumstances and environment very much different from ours today. But, by and large, my understanding of church history and the development of doctrine is like unto a garden, which is neither fully planted nor weeded."

The day after delivering his talk, Christensen walked into Franklin Johnson's office and dropped a cassette on his desk. "Here's my Sunstone talk," he said. "I got on a roll and couldn't stop. It'll probably get me excommunicated." He grinned.

The next two months grew serious. August 15, the day Hofmann was to consummate the sale of the "Oath of a Freeman," came and went, and Hofmann had not paid anything toward the outstanding bank loan nor had he donated the collection to the church. Franklin Johnson, Hugh Pinnock's brother-in-law, learned of the McLellin deal from Pinnock when he called to ask Johnson what he knew about Hofmann. "It looks like I'm in trouble," Pinnock said. "Mark hasn't paid the loan and he seems to have disappeared."

Johnson didn't know Hofmann at all, so he called Christensen. "Mark's kind of a flaky guy," Christensen said. "I'll call Hugh and tell him Mark's okay."

On August 26, Christensen wrote to Hofmann that he had been notified by the bank that there had been neither payment nor word from him. He reminded Hofmann of his promise to donate the collection after payment on the Oath. "Please contact Harvey Tanner at this number," he concluded, adding, "Please do me the courtesy of updating me."

By September 1, Hofmann's primary Americana investor, Gene Taylor, knew that things were not going well for Hofmann, for he had shown Taylor a copy of the First Interstate contract. Taylor, who dealt in six figure numbers regularly, was astounded to see that Hofmann had secured a signature loan for $185,000. Now Hofmann was desperate to repay the bank. On September 3, when the loan came due, Hofmann went to First Interstate and wrote a personal check for the principal plus interest. On September 10, the check bounced.

All week Christensen and Pinnock remained in touch, for the whereabouts of the McLellin collection was a major concern. Christensen confided to Franklin Johnson that Hofmann had said other collectors had offered the Texas sellers more than twice the $195,000 asking price. Knowing now that Hofmann was strapped for money, Christensen worried that he would sell the collection elsewhere to pay off the bank loan and keep a profit, and those fears were shared by the church leaders involved. When Hofmann's check bounced, their concerns accelerated. Since the loan had been judged adverse by normal banking standards, its unpaid status created special problems. Meanwhile, the fact that a Mormon general authority had arranged a loan for Hofmann to buy controversial documents and give them to the church was not something anyone involved in the deal wanted to read on the front page of the *Salt Lake Tribune.*

Despite his financial difficulties, Hofmann found time to take his wife to an outdoor concert in Park City. In the crowd, Hofmann spotted his former fiancee, Kate Reid, and pointed her out to Dori.

Reid had come to the concert with nine or ten friends. As the years passed, Reid had tried to recover from her engagement to Hofmann by excluding him from her life as effectively as his marriage had excluded her from his. She had found that difficult to do. When Jeff Salt had stopped to see her on his way home from the bus stop, she had imagined that he would report to Mark. She had moved to another apartment and changed jobs. She had even changed religions, for she wanted solace, not conflict, and she heard Mark's voice echo during Mormon sermons.

Before the concert started, as Reid and her friends were looking for a place to sit, she turned and saw Hofmann staring at her. She looked away. Once she and her friends were seated, she saw the Hofmanns again, some rows ahead, looking back at her. Mark was still wearing that letterman's jacket, she noted, and Dori seemed to have gained some weight. Reid said a few words to her friends, and they all got up and moved.

The next morning, Hofmann called her at work.

"How did you reach me?" she asked.

He said he had traced her through a former employer. Her heart began to pound. She had left instructions not to give out her new company name.

"I saw you at the concert, and I just wanted to know how you are, if you're married."

She wouldn't say much. "How are you?"

"I'm fine. We're doing all right, and we have three kids. How's Julie?"

He had remembered her cat. They laughed. "She's fine."

"We have a Michael," Hofmann said, "but no Julie." They had talked about both names for their children.

"We're buying a big new home out in Holladay, and we'll be moving in a few weeks. Would it be all right if I call again just to talk?"

Reid felt her resolve weakening. "Well, all right."

The next morning he called shortly after 11:00 from a car telephone. There was static on the line. "I hope enough water has gone under the bridge that we can talk about what caused our breakup."

"Mark, it's been too long. Why we broke up doesn't matter any more."

He persisted, but she did not want to hear. "Mark, do you have something specific you want to ask me?"

"No."

"Do you have something specific you want to tell me?"

"Not exactly."

"Well, I really can't hear you well, and I think . . . "

Suddenly he was shouting, screaming into the telephone. "You won't listen! You never would listen to me!" His rage roared through the receiver, and she hung up. Shaken, she realized that she still made Hofmann as angry as she had in the past.

Reid switched jobs again, asked her employer not to give

out her number, and decided that if Hofmann ever called her again, she would contact his parents. She knew they would be unhappy to hear that their son was calling her at all. Telling his parents had always been her most effective threat.

Despite Reid's efforts at letting go, two months later when she heard from a friend that Hofmann was the victim of a bombing, she screamed, grabbed her purse, left work, and was on the sidewalk before she remembered that she was not the person who needed to rush to the hospital to be at his side.

On September 11, Curt Bench had called Hofmann to tell him that an interesting book had been found in the Deseret Book vault: an Episcopalian *Book of Common Prayer* bearing the name "Nathan Harris" in the front along with the notation, "Kirtland, Ohio," where the first Mormon temple had been built. He thought Hofmann might want to market it.

Hofmann came to the store and bought the book for $50. A few days later he returned. "You know that handwriting in the back of the book," he said to Bench. "I found out it belonged to Martin Harris. Nathan Harris was Martin Harris's brother."

Bench was impressed.

"I'll pay you $1,000," Hofmann continued. "I sold it to the church for $2,000."

"Okay," Bench said, "I appreciate you coming back."

This incident was nearly lost in Bench's memory after the strange events of Friday, September 13, when Hofmann had come into Deseret Book shadowed by an obviously unhappy man who waited while Hofmann begged Bench for a loan. Christensen's equally unusual call to Bench regarding an unpaid bank loan had followed the next morning.

On Sunday, September 15, Hofmann went to Gene Taylor to ask for help. He was in a real jam, he told Taylor. The Library of Congress was not going to buy the "Oath of a Freeman," after all, unless he lowered the price. Also, Hofmann told him, he had written a check for a bank loan, but the check had bounced.

"Well, Mark, you've got to learn about bad checks," Taylor said. "You can't give people bad checks. You wait until you make the check good before you give out the check. You need to go to the bank and tell them how you're going to work out this problem."

He had Hofmann list his debts and assets. Hofmann still owed Taylor $68,000, and his other debts were numerous. However, he listed the Boone letter, the Oath, the Dickens manuscript, and various rare books as assets.

"Go home and make a more complete list," Taylor suggested, "and then take it to the bank. You can work this out with them."

To Taylor it seemed ironic that the Hofmanns insisted on showing the Taylors the home they planned to buy. Taylor knew how worried Mark was about the Oath, the bank loan, and his other debts, yet Dori was clearly excited about their new half million dollar home.

The next day Hofmann went to First Interstate Bank to discuss the bounced check. He needed a little more time, he told Harvey Tanner. He had a limited partnership that was going to help out.

Tanner was not satisfied. He called Pinnock again. "Hold his feet to the fire," Pinnock said, assuring him the loan would be paid.

Although Curt Bench knew Hofmann was under financial pressure, he too was being pressured about the $16,000 Hofmann still owed Deseret Book. Bench tried to get a commitment from Hofmann, but with little effect.

Then, on September 19, 1985, Hofmann offered Bench a fragment of Egyptian papyrus. "It's from the McLellin collection," he said, "and this has to be kept very confidential." The asking price was $40,000. Bench declined. "I thought the church had the McLellin collection," he told Hofmann.

"Well, this piece is being marketed separately."

The following day, Mormon Egyptologist Ed Ashment met Hofmann and Brent Metcalfe at the LDS historical department library. Metcalfe showed him the papyrus fragment and asked if he could tie it to other Joseph Smith papyri. Ashment said he couldn't on the spur of the moment but offered to check some references. Then Ashment, tired of chasing rumors about papyri, pulled out a Polaroid camera and snapped a photograph of the papyrus. Neither Hofmann nor Metcalfe would tell Ashment where the fragment had come from. When Hofmann, through Metcalfe, then offered to sell the fragment to George Smith for $30,000, Smith declined. In early July, Smith had acceded to Hofmann's repeated requests to invest in the Charles Dickens "Haunted Man" manuscript, hoping to gain access to any papyri Hofmann had to help with a research project he had assumed from Christensen earlier that year.

Sunday evening, Hofmann offered the papyrus to Brent Ashworth. Since purchasing the Dunham letter in July, Ashworth regarded Hofmann quite warmly. Dori went into the kitchen to tell Charlene about their new home, as the men retired to the den to talk business.

"We are going to need a little more time to complete the deal for the $450,000," Hofmann said at once.

"You know I never got the $50,000 or the promised agreement letter to pay the balance."

"I know. But hang on. They're coming."

Dori entered the room for a moment and was on her way out when Ashworth said, "Mark, I've heard about the Freeman's Oath and the big bucks you're trying to get on that."

Dori paused, turned to Mark and said, "Mark, are you surprised that Brent knows about that?"

He hesitated, then said, "Not really. Word is getting around." Now Charlene was also at the door. "Dear, did you know that Mark and Dori were going to be moving soon?"

"No, I didn't. Why didn't you tell me about it, Mark?"

Mark looked at Dori as if she should not have discussed the new house. When the men were alone again, Hofmann brought up the McLellin collection. He said he had sold the huge collection a couple of months earlier but had reserved a piece of papyrus for himself. "I'll sell it to you if you're interested."

"Well, of course I'd be interested in a piece of Joseph Smith papyrus, but I don't have any money." Hofmann waited out the pause. "How much do you want for it?" Ashworth asked.

"Well, it's $30,000, and I need cash."

"I'd love to see it, Mark, but I can't buy it. I don't have $30,000 in cash. I haven't paid any money back on that huge executive line of credit. So I don't have a dime after our transaction for the Dunham letter in July. But I'd sure like to see it before you sell it."

"Okay, I'll bring it by."

Monday, about 5:00 p.m., Hofmann and Shannon Flynn visited Ashworth at his Spanish Fork office. Hofmann, wearing his green letterman's jacket, carried a piece of papyrus framed inside two pieces of plexiglass held by four metal rivets. He handed it to Ashworth, who looked it over. It had five, almost six, human-like figures and looked genuine. "I don't know anything about papyrus, Mark. I've never collected it."

What about a trade? Hofmann asked. Finally, Ashworth offered a George Washington letter (which he estimated to be worth $20,000 cash). Hofmann agreed. Ashworth stipulated that he would have until Friday to verify to his satisfaction that the papyrus was indeed from Joseph Smith. Hofmann mentioned that the McLellin collection had sold to a Salt Lake businessman for $185,000.

"What's in it?"

"Joseph Smith's revelations and letters—actually a good orange crate full of letters and documents—including six little diaries handwritten by McLellin from 1831 to 1836, one for each year."

"Anything interesting or controversial in those diaries?"

"There are a couple of passing mentions of Joseph Smith, but they're really rather pedestrian. You have to understand I could be in deep trouble if word about this little papyrus piece got out. You've got to keep your mouth shut about this offer."

"Well, Mark, I don't know anything about papyrus. I don't collect it. I need to take this to someone like Hugh Nibley at BYU."

"I don't want you to take it to Hugh Nibley."

"Mark, the only dealer I know that even handle this stuff is Rendell."

"No, I don't want you to call Rendell or Nibley. I want you to call Ed Ashment."

"Who's he?"

"He's an Egyptologist, and he can verify that this piece fits in with the eleven pieces that the church purchased from the Metropolitan Museum of Art in 1967."

"Well, fine, would you call him for me?"

Hofmann called, but Ashment wasn't home. "Well, I want to call Ed first, and then I'll get with you."

The next morning Ashworth called Hofmann but couldn't reach him, so he called Ashment and asked about the papyrus.

"No, I haven't been able to tie this piece in at all," Ashment said. "I'm waiting for some more material Mark promised me."

Ashworth dialed Hofmann's number again and got him. "Listen, Mark, Ed hasn't been able to tie this in at all. I just called him."

"Oh, really? Well, I'll check into it."

Despite Hofmann's objection, Ashworth set up an appointment with Hugh Nibley, a professor of ancient scripture at BYU, but first drove to Salt Lake City, papyrus in hand. He showed it to an attorney friend, then took it to church headquarters and showed it to Jay Todd, editor of the church's *Ensign* magazine. Todd had written a book on The Book of Abraham, so Ashworth thought he could help.

"Well, you really need to take this to Hugh Nibley," Todd said.

"I have an appointment with him later today. The thing is, Mark is such a liar that I really need to verify this."

"That's a little harsh, isn't it, Brent?"

"No, that's what he is. I've had a lot of dealings with him."

At 4:00 p.m. Ashworth was back in Provo in Nibley's office. Nibley thought there might be some relationship with Facsimile 2, but he needed more material.

On his way home, Ashworth stopped by his father's house. "Dad, I've got this opportunity to get an original piece of the Joseph Smith papyrus." He explained the trade. "What should I do?"

"Well, you know what you've got with the George Washington letter, and you don't know what you've got with this papyrus."

Ashworth related his conversations with Ashment and Nibley, then waited. "I would just suggest you hang onto the Washington."

"I think you're right, Dad. Thanks."

SALAMANDER

Ashworth returned the fragment to Hofmann, explaining, "I don't know how else to verify this, Mark." Hofmann had little to say, and Ashworth left.

On September 24, Steve Christensen called Curt Bench at home, only the second time in all the years they had known each other. This time the message was more urgent than before, his information even more specific. He told Bench that two church leaders were upset with Hofmann. Matters had been made worse since they had not heard from Hofmann and he had not taken any action regarding the bank loan.

"They're meeting with Hinckley tomorrow," Christensen said, "and if this isn't resolved, the church will never buy anything from Mark again."

As Bench understood it, Hofmann had paid First Interstate Bank with a bad check. Now the church might pay the bank and sue Hofmann, or the bank might sue Hofmann.

"Mark's supposed to keep checking in," Christensen said, "and he doesn't. It looks like Mark's going to jail or going to be sued or lose his credit and credibility with important people and institutions. What's more, this could leak to the newspapers, and that would be embarrassing to everyone concerned."

Bench was impressed by the seriousness of the situation. Even though Hofmann had asked him not to mention his offer of the McLellin papyrus, Bench decided to tell Christensen about this.

Christensen listened closely but did not comment.

"I have a favor to ask," Christensen said instead. "I know you're close to Mark, and I wonder if you'd go over to his house and stress to him how critical this is."

"Okay, Steve, I'll talk to him."

"Let me know what he says. I'll be trying to reach him myself."

Bench got in his car and went to Hofmann's house. Hofmann answered the door, and Bench suggested that they talk out in his car. He reported his conversation with Christensen. Hofmann confirmed the details of the transaction.

"I appreciate you telling me, Curt, even though it's bad. I'll get it all worked out this week," Hofmann said calmly.

"Listen, Mark, you really need to contact the apostle before he talks with President Hinckley. You've got to pay us this week, too. I'm sorry this is all so heavy. You know I want things to turn out well for everyone."

"Well, I know that. Thanks for coming by."

A few days later, Bench was called upon to defend Hofmann before Bench's superiors at Deseret Book.

By the end of the business week, the bank loan was still unpaid and a First Interstate Bank loan officer had written Hofmann threatening legal action. Meanwhile, loan officer Harvey Tanner asked a superior how much heat he could put on Hugh Pinnock. In response, his superior related a conversation he had had with Pinnock regarding Tanner's efforts to collect from Hofmann. "Keep his feet to the fire," Pinnock had said in reference to Tanner. Now Tanner let Pinnock know that if Hofmann did not come through with the money, the bank would be looking to Pinnock as an unofficial guarantor. Pinnock, as usual, phoned Christensen. After the predictable round of conversations, repayment of the bank loan was set for October 3.

One day late in September as Brent and Jill Metcalfe took the 2300 East exit on their way to the Hofmanns, they missed the turnoff to Marie Avenue. "Pull over into the ward parking lot and we'll get turned around," Brent suggested. Jill turned into the driveway of the wardhouse facing 2300 East, not the Hofmanns' home ward. As they circled behind the building through the parking lot, the Metcalfes saw Hofmann's blue Toyota MR2 in the back corner of the lot.

Brent approached the sports car and knocked on the window. Mark was surrounded by paperwork, Metcalfe saw, but he quickly turned the papers over. As Hofmann opened the door, Metcalfe noticed stress lines in his friend's face.

They talked about Hofmann's financial problems, and Metcalfe, who needed his paycheck, said maybe he should quit working for him.

"Believe me," Hofmann said, "the little bit I pay you is the least of my problems. Look at my track record. Just stay with me. You'll get your money."

Saturday, September 28, Hofmann called Brent Ashworth and asked if he had anything he wanted to sell.

"I still have my David W. Patten document."

"How much do you want for it?"

"I want $6,000."

"Well, why don't I place it for you."

"I don't know, Mark."

"Look, I'll just take it for the weekend. I have a possible buyer and I'll return either the document or your money on Monday. How's that?"

"Okay. I'll let you have it until Monday. By the way, Mark, what about that papyrus? Did you sell it?"

"Yes, I sold it with one telephone call to the same businessman who bought the McLellin collection."

Hofmann drove down to Provo to pick up the Patten document but said he could only get $5,000 for it, not $6,000.

"This is ridiculous," Ashworth began. "Well, all right. If you can get me $5,500 by Monday, I guess I can drop $500."

Hofmann agreed, but when Monday came Ashworth heard nothing. When he did reach Hofmann later, Mark agreed to meet him but did not show up with the document or the money.

On October 3, the day set for the bank loan payment, Hofmann dropped by Gene Taylor's office. He came directly to the point. "Gene, I'm in a big financial jam."

"I'm not going to invest any more, Mark."

"Well, I've got this Mormon money I could give you as collateral for a loan. You can call Al Rust and he'll tell you that it's good. Look it up in your Mormon money book."

Taylor asked, "How much do you need?"

"Twenty thousand."

Taylor happened to have $20,000 in his account. He wrote Hofmann a check and took the currency as collateral.

Hofmann and Shannon Flynn then dropped by Deseret Book. Hofmann waited in the car while Flynn took in some early Mormon currency and a Jim Bridger note to offer for sale. "Are these yours or Mark's?" Bench inquired.

"They're mine. I may want to buy them back later."

Flynn left with a check for $20,000. He owed nearly that much to his former mission president, Wilford Cardon, on other document transactions.

On October 3, still no payment had been made to First Interstate Bank. That evening, Christensen got a telephone call about 9:30 at home from Hugh Pinnock — not the first such call but the most emphatic. The message was unmistakable: Find Hofmann. Christensen explained to Terri that the bank loan was still unpaid and that Pinnock could lose his house over it. He had to find Mark immediately, he said grimly. "We're looking at fraud."

Around 10:00 p.m., Christensen called Franklin Johnson to get Pinnock's home number and address. Half an hour later, Christensen and Hofmann arrived at Pinnock's home on Walker Lane in Holladay. After some discussion, Pinnock suggested a buyer who could repay the bank and donate the McLellin collection to the church.

However, Hofmann introduced a new wrinkle. He explained that Al Rust had an interest in the deal. Pinnock and Christensen worked that out, too. Hofmann could sell his share in the Oath to repay Rust; then the buyer's check would go to the bank. Or vice versa. Fine, Hofmann said, but he would need a little time. Rust had the keys to the safe deposit boxes in which the collection lay, and Rust was on vacation.

The transaction was reconstructed; the problem seemed resolved. Pinnock would find the buyer, Christensen would facilitate the deal and act as authenticator, and Hofmann offered to get a $20,000 check from Shannon Flynn to pacify the bank. Christensen and Hofmann left for Flynn's house. At 12:34 a.m., Christensen called Pinnock on Hofmann's mobile telephone and told him they had the check.

Finally, Christensen picked up his car at Hofmann's house and headed north to Centerville and home. About 5:30 a.m. he called a friend.

"I've been up all night putting this document deal back together. I'm not going to be able to make tomorrow's meeting."

"Okay, Steve. I'll catch you later. Sometime I want to hear about all this."

"You wouldn't believe it. It involves Hugh Pinnock. I was out half the night looking for a guy. We're talking about a file cabinet full of documents."

Later that morning, Christensen went with Hofmann to deposit $20,000 at First Interstate Bank. He called Pinnock, who relayed the information to Dallin Oaks. Christensen and Hofmann soon visited with Harvey Tanner. While Christensen and Tanner observed, Hofmann called Justin Schiller in New York, who said he had a buyer for Hofmann's share in the Oath. Schiller then assured Tanner that $150,000 would be sent directly to the bank. Now resolution of the McLellin deal was just a matter of time.

Friday afternoon, October 4, Randy Rigby looked for Christensen around lunch time but could not find him, so he joined the usual lunch group and walked down to Arby's. That afternoon about 2:00 Christensen finally showed up at work.

"You wouldn't believe this day," he said.

"Yeah, I tried to get you to go to lunch, but I couldn't find you."

"Well, I've been up all night on that document deal. I've got to get something to eat."

Christensen looked like he needed to talk as well as eat, and Rigby was intrigued. He remembered Christensen saying back in June something about "saving the church some face" on a document matter.

"I'll go with you," Rigby volunteered. They walked to Lamb's Cafe near the Judge Building.

"Let me put this day in perspective for you," Christensen began. "Just to get in the mood for it this morning, I went to Crossroads Mall and bought a tape of Miami Vice."

Rigby laughed. He knew how much Christensen enjoyed suspense stories. "What's been going on?"

Rigby listened, amazed, as Christensen told him he had spent the previous night talking with Hugh Pinnock and Dallin Oaks.

"Do you remember the document deal that got started in June?"

"Well, yeah, kind of."

"The whole thing has gone haywire. I spent all night putting it back together again for the church."

Rigby whistled. General Conference was imminent and church leaders were notoriously busy during the preceding weeks.

"The church wants me to be an intermediary. I'm telling you, Randy, this collection makes the salamander letter look like a priesthood manual. There's an affidavit from Emma Smith that discounts Joseph Smith's first vision. The way the deal works now is that we've found an investor. The investor will buy the collection, and we'll pay off the bank and then get the collateral—the McLellin collection. Then sometime down the road, the investor will give the collection to the church but will probably never even see it."

Rigby shook his head. Christensen, obviously, *would* see the collection. No wonder he was living and breathing this document deal.

They went into the restaurant and ordered before Christensen continued. "Know what, Randy? Get this. Elder Pinnock said to me that he had just met with President Hinckley and they would like to fund us—Rigby-Christensen—to be the middleman on acquiring documents. They have no trust or confidence in Mark Hofmann anymore. They would set us up with a line of credit."

"Credit to buy documents?"

Christensen nodded. "To start out with, Pinnock has some leads on where the lost 116 pages of the Book of Mormon are. He said he has some solid leads in Pennsylvania where he was mission president."

"Steve, this is totally out of my area. It's your bailiwick, and I really don't know how to handle it."

"Well, we're partners. In this as well as everything else."

"I told you before, Steve, that you're facing bankruptcy and you need the money. I just need enough to get by. Now on this document business, I want you to take whatever comes in on that."

"No, I'm not going to do that. We'll go 50/50 just the way we planned."

Rigby was so impressed by this startling conversation that he noted it in his journal, stressing the absolute trust the church leaders seemed to have in Christensen.

When he got home that night, Christensen told Terri about the opportunity to buy documents for the church. He obviously was excited about it, but Terri was dubious. Steve had so much going on already—the new business, the bankruptcy. He had just been asked to be a counselor to their stake president, a responsibility a tier up from bishop. Terri was pregnant and Steve had been up all night—the McLellin transaction had been nothing but trouble. Why would he want to do this all the time?

That Sunday, as the Christensens sat together in their family room watching General Conference on television, one of the general authorities spoke on service to the church. Terri felt a pang of conscience. Hugh Pinnock, whose calls came to Steve at both home and work, was, after all, a church leader. Steve had told her that during his conversations with Pinnock, Pinnock frequently left the room to check with his superiors, then returned. Hinckley, with whom Steve also communicated, was essentially running the church.

"Steve," she asked suddenly, "this document buying, is it a calling—something you really couldn't turn down? Or is it just something you want to do?"

His answer was evasive. Terri could not tell if he left the question open because he was going to pursue the opportunity but did not want to worry her or if it was a confidential calling he was not supposed to say too much about.

Despite the confidentiality of the McLellin deal, a number of business associates were becoming aware that Christensen was in contact with high church leaders. One man, for instance, working with Christensen on a satellite network deal, met with Christensen and others in the Judge Building one morning only to have the meeting interrupted by a telephone call from President Hinckley. Christensen, a bishop, must have a serious problem in his ward, the businessman concluded. He guessed from the way Christensen gathered up his papers and excused himself that something was urgent.

The morning after General Conference, Monday, October

7, Hofmann called Christensen's office twice. At noon, Christensen went to First Interstate Bank and rented two safe deposit boxes. As a clerk watched, he opened his briefcase and put something heavy-sounding in one. He locked the box and left. That same day he went to see attorney David West in his Main Street office. West was representing Pinnock's friend and Canadian mission president David Sorenson, who had agreed to buy the McLellin collection. During his talk with West, Christensen learned that West fully intended to take possession of the collection once Christensen authenticated it. He would transfer the documents to his own safe deposit boxes and send the keys to Sorenson. Christensen explained his own preparations to keep the collection safe, but West did not consider the matter negotiable. On October 8, Christensen went to West's office and joined Pinnock and Sorenson in a conference call. The following day, Pinnock spoke with Sorensen, Oaks, Christensen, and Hinckley, either by telephone or in person, about the McLellin transaction.

During the intense weeks of overseeing the McLellin deal, Christensen's connection with Mormon leaders solidified. Pinnock contacted two prospective buyers to interest them in Christensen's personal library, which had recently been appraised at $150,000 retail. When Christensen later bumped into his attorney, Alan Smith, who asked if he had decided how to pursue the bankruptcy, Christensen was hopeful. "Alan, a bankruptcy might not be necessary," he said. "I have something cooking that could clear the decks."

Smith gathered that the mixed metaphor referred to some kind of document deal, probably the lost 116 pages. Christensen obviously was feeling better about his financial situation. His sense of urgency regarding the bankruptcy seemed to have evaporated.

On October 9, Hofmann returned to Deseret Book, but Curt Bench honestly did not know if he could pay Hofmann $13,000 for a half-page fragment of the original Book of Mormon manuscript and other items. Once such a check would have presented no problem, but Deseret Book was skittish about

Hofmann now, though he'd paid the sales tax on the Dunham letter at last.

"If this is a problem for you guys," Hofmann said softly, "I can take my business somewhere else."

"Hang on," Bench told him and went to check with the comptroller. The check was approved. But no sooner did Hofmann leave with it than Bench's supervisor came running down the stairs waving Hofmann's $16,000 check, which the bank had returned. Bench got on the telephone and tracked down Hofmann. He passed on the ultimatum: no more bad checks, no more loans, no more unpaid accounts. Hofmann then took the check he had just been given *from* Deseret Book to the bank to cover the check he was just now writing *to* Deseret Book.

On Thursday, October 10, as Pinnock brought Hinckley up to date on the McLellin deal, Christensen met with an independent financial consultant to discuss limited partnerships. No sooner had they begun talking than there was a knock at the door and a dark-haired man about thirty years old came in. Christensen did not introduce either man to the other, but took his new visitor into an inner office and shut the door.

The consultant waited for five or ten minutes. He could hear voices, but no clear words. Then Christensen shouted, "You can't hide that!"

After five minutes or so, both men came out, sober-faced. The visitor left and Christensen sat down and continued the conversation without comment.

An hour and a half later, Hofmann was stopped for speeding on the desert highway west of Salt Lake City. The trooper later remembered that the wheels and sides to Hofmann's sports car were dirty, as though he had been driving through rough country. The trooper thought a male passenger was present but couldn't be sure.

Hofmann returned to Christensen's office that day. Like Gene Taylor, Christensen asked him to list his debts and assets to help him with his financial problems. Christensen also gave Hofmann a statement he had obtained from David West at Hofmann's request guaranteeing the $185,000 purchase price.

Christensen had added his own note at the bottom that he was facilitating the document transaction.

Another document Christensen typed was undated. This, a contract for the McLellin sale, specified that Hofmann would be responsible for the collection's security and contents. At the bottom he noted an omission to the known contents of the collection: "1 page deed conveying 1/2 acre of land for 1 schillings." Christensen did not mention that the deed, which Hofmann had sold to Steve Barnett at the Cosmic Aeroplane bookstore, had been signed by Solomon Spaulding and Sidney Rigdon. By exempting the land deed from the McLellin deal, Christensen showed he knew Hofmann had already sold it. Perhaps he'd learned that unhappy fact when he'd shouted, "You can't hide that!"

Between his visits to Christensen, Hofmann visited Hinckley and offered to sell him the Kinderhook plates, supposedly ancient texts but actually devised in the nineteenth century as a hoax to expose Joseph Smith's ability as a translator. Hinckley turned him down. Outside Hinckley's office, Shannon Flynn waited for Hofmann.

Other unpleasant surprises about the McLellin collection still awaited Christensen. Fifty miles south of Salt Lake City, in Utah County, quite by chance, Andrew Ehat, the researcher Christensen had supported until recently, ran into Brent Ashworth at a bookstore. They introduced themselves and then had a long, interesting talk. Ashworth told Ehat that the McLellin collection was being purchased by a Salt Lake City businessman. He described the collection and said he had obtained his information from the seller, Mark Hofmann.

Almost immediately, Ehat called Christensen to tell him about the collection, not knowing that Christensen was involved in the transaction. Early the next morning, Christensen returned Ehat's call.

"Where did you hear about this?" Christensen asked.

Ehat told him, explaining that Ashworth's information had come from Hofmann.

After the disturbing chat, Christensen spent a tense Friday trying to find Hofmann. He had a small attache case ready with an envelope addressed to West enclosing an undated letter to Sorenson guaranteeing the authenticity of the collection and the value at $185,000. Toward the end of the letter, he wrote, "Since the items from the collection are varied as to their author and nature, I believe it would be most appropriate for me to hereafter always refer to the collection as the Sorenson collection."

A few months earlier, Christensen had indicated in his journal that he thought Hofmann's intention to deny he had "sold" the church the McLellin collection was a bit thin. Now he was going one better, in an attempt to protect the secrecy of an increasingly threatened deal. His words, "hereafter always," hinted at a policy that all concerned might follow—for no one was likely to ask any of them the whereabouts of a Sorenson collection.

A CFS associate who dropped by Christensen's office that afternoon found Christensen weary and discouraged. He still had not found Hofmann. "How's the cat-and-mouse game?" he asked, guessing the reason for Christensen's mood.

"It's more like cloak-and-dagger," Christensen said. They changed the subject to CFS's problems. Christensen seemed downhearted about his own business prospects and embarrassed about the financial impact on his family.

One of the calls Christensen made Friday in his attempt to find Hofmann was to Shannon Flynn. When he told Flynn the document deal could be closed if they could find Hofmann, Flynn was excited. He wanted his $20,000 repaid.

Flynn caught up with Hofmann late that afternoon. "Mark, Steve said you've got to get that deal done today! The guy involved is back in town and it's got to happen."

"Well, it's too late now. The banks will be closing in fifteen minutes. We can take care of it Monday."

Christensen went home Friday, but his efforts to close the McLellin deal did not end. As he telephoned, the paper under his pencil gradually filled with arrows, boxes, amounts of money, and the names and telephone numbers of Hofmann, his friends, Rust, Pinnock, and Oaks. His efforts were fruitless, and Terri finally reached the end of her patience.

"Steve, I'm tired of this document deal. I'm five months pregnant. I need a husband and the boys need a father." A weekend with the Rigbys in Wyoming had been cancelled, and Steve seemed permanently attached to the telephone.

Terri left the house for a while. When she came back the atmosphere had changed. Steve was off the telephone and did not return to his desk the entire weekend. That's a record, Terri thought. Steve took care of the boys Saturday while Terri went shopping and they all spent Sunday together. This is great, Terri told herself. It doesn't matter if we have a little money or a lot of money. Things are just going to get better from here on.

Friday evening Randy and Connie Wilson and the Flynns visited the Hofmanns at Dori's request. The six of them sat down to a card game. Randy noticed that Mark seemed distracted. It was unlike him to lose every hand.

"Hey, did you ever get rid of that machine gun?" Wilson asked.

"Yes, I did."

There was a pause.

"I still have mine," Flynn said.

Hofmann was becoming increasingly impatient. "Let's finish this and get in the hot tub."

The Wilsons exchanged glances. The last time they had joined the Hofmanns in the hot tub, Mark had kept them there talking until nearly 3:00 a.m. Reluctantly, they changed into swimming suits. But forty-five minutes later, Hofmann had had enough. "Okay, that's it," he said. The evening was over.

Earlier that Friday Hofmann had called Ashworth about the David Patten letter. Hofmann had not returned the letter or paid for its sale. Two days later, Sunday, October 13, he showed up at the Ashworth home unannounced. "Brent, I guess you never expected to get your money," he told a surprised Ashworth. He pulled a check for $4,500 out of his pocket.

"Mark, we both know this is the wrong amount."

Hofmann looked blank, then said, "I just happen to have a blank check. Find me a pen." He rewrote the check for $5,500. Ashworth thought he seemed fidgety. As he left, Ashworth asked, "Can I put this check in? Is this one good?"

"Yes, it's fine. Go ahead and put it in."

He did. It bounced.

Monday was Columbus Day and the banks were closed. Hofmann placed two calls to Hinckley from his mobile telephone, each lasting a few minutes.

That evening, after Hofmann gave Brent Metcalfe photocopies of Martin Harris's handwriting from the back of the Nathan Harris prayer book, he got into his Toyota van and drove to Shannon Flynn's condominium. He and Flynn went to see a Mormon history buff. The three talked for several hours, then Hofmann dropped off Flynn at his home about 11:30 p.m. Hofmann said he needed to stop for a large Coke because he would be up late.

Not far from the quiet streets where Hofmann drove his van, Kathy Sheets sat talking on the telephone to a friend. They discussed Kathy's New York trip. Sheets was in a mellow mood. On her desk lay a letter she had begun to her newest grandchild. Relaxed, Sheets talked until after midnight. She could finish the letter tomorrow.

Steven Christensen, too, spent Monday evening with his family. About 6:30 p.m. he called Randy Rigby to set up a meeting the next morning for 8:00 a.m. "It looks like a routine day," Christensen said.

Later, Christensen got the call he had been waiting months for. About 10:00 p.m. he called Franklin Johnson to cancel their early morning meeting. "I'm closing the McLellin deal," Christensen said. "By eleven, I should be free. Everything's come together." They agreed to meet later in the day.

As Johnson hung up, he thought Christensen sounded happier than he had heard him for some time—elated, profoundly relieved. He thought his young friend had a bit of a "Jesus Christ complex," assuming responsibility for impossible situations, then suffering. Christensen had tried to save CFS and failed, but evidently had succeeded in closing a troubled and difficult transaction. Everything's come together, Steve had said.

The McLellin deal, yes, Johnson thought. But in his mind, Steve's voice resonated further. He sounded as if only beginnings lay before him: new business opportunities, new connections with powerful men, a new church position, a new baby.

With the McLellin deal finally resolved, the fears and worries that had plagued him would dissipate. Johnson, who for so long had listened to Christensen wrestle with disparate selves lately saw him reaching a reconciliation. He knew what he heard in Steve's voice: his new life.

THREE

15

MARK HOFMANN
COMES TO COURT

By the time he faced murder, forgery, and fraud charges on April 14, 1986, Mark Hofmann's name had become as familiar to Utahns as the Wasatch Mountains. Hofmann's preliminary hearing began almost five months to the day after pipe bombs killed Steve Christensen and Kathy Sheets. That delay, like everything surrounding Hofmann, promoted increased interest.

In February 1986, Hofmann had been charged with twenty-seven felonies grouped into four cases. Since then, another case with five charges involving printed documents had been filed. Free on bond, Hofmann had had more than two months to assist in his own defense, but during that time the state had bolstered its evidence. Now the preliminary hearing in Fifth Circuit Court before Judge Paul Grant constituted, in essence, a mini-trial to determine whether sufficient evidence existed to bind Hofmann over for trial in the state's Third District Court on one, two, or thirty-two felonies. Most preliminary hearings take a few hours or, at most, a few days. However, evidence must be presented by prosecutors to substantiate each count — from murder to forgery to fraud — and Grant expected a marathon.

The real contest was not expected for months or even years later in Third District Court, across the plaza in the Metropolitan Hall of Justice. Both prosecution and defense had agreed to join the five cases at the preliminary hearing to expedite matters; but afterward the defense would undoubtedly move, probably successfully, to separate them for different trials in the felony court. That way evidence of double-dealing, fraud, or even forgery would not weigh against their client during a murder trial, in which he could receive the death penalty. In district court, the murder case would stand or fall on its own merits.

Grant also expected a media circus, for his court had had numerous calls from across the country as the hearing approached. To accommodate the anticipated overflow of reporters, Grant had provided an intercom in a room adjacent to the courtroom. However, most of the reporters who lined up outside while police prepared metal detecting equipment had been on the story from the beginning.

David Hewitt, a newcomer to the usual "pack," wrote for the *Maine Antique Digest*. Hewitt admitted to other reporters that he had probably placed half the calls to Grant's court himself, so concerned was the *Digest* about the Hofmann case. He was most concerned about the "Oath of a Freeman," which, like rare book dealers Justin Schiller and Ray Wapner, he believed was authentic. If the Oath had been forged—which Hewitt doubted—the implications for other Hofmann documents which had not been scrutinized in such detail were staggering.

As the police tested their equipment, then began searching reporters, the officers of the court arrived. Gerry D'Elia, David Biggs, and Bob Stott came in a group, appearing confident but edgy, followed by investigators Dick Forbes and Mike George. Not only did they bear the burden of proof, but they wanted to turn around a skeptical public and impress the defense, which was rumored to have some surprises of its own. Defense attorneys Ron Yengich and Brad Rich seemed wired, believing that chances for acquittal were excellent. At the preliminary hearing they could preview the prosecution's case without giving away any evidence of their own and, hopefully, knock out the Sheets homicide and most of the fraud charges. They were accompanied by Bill Hofmann, Mark's father.

Dori Hofmann, smiling tensely in a dove gray suit, followed closely beside the defendant. Mark appeared rested and cheerful in a dark blue suit, white shirt, and tie. Gone was the image of a bandaged, bloody victim in a wheelchair at the machine gun arraignment in November or of a prisoner in a torn tee-shirt and slacks at the bond hearing in February. Now Hofmann swung by the line of reporters looking more like a young Mormon bishop with a sprained knee than a murder suspect. He made no comment, but the half-smile that had become familiar to the media played on his lips.

The press was seated behind the defense table to the judge's right. The victims' families and close friends came in a cluster from the CAO, along with a beaming county attorney Ted Cannon. Mac Christensen was immediately recognizable. Beside him on the bench behind the prosecutors sat Terri Christensen; her hair trimmed just below her ears, she was striking in a white knit suit. Behind Mac and Terri filed the three dark-haired Sheets daughters, Heidi Jones, Katie Robertson with husband Joe, and Gretchen Sheets, with Joan and Lloyd Gorton. (As a witness, Gary Sheets was not allowed to attend the hearings.) Randy and Sandra Rigby and a few other close friends squeezed in near Scott Christensen, Steve's brother closest in age. Across the aisle, Gloria Hofmann, whose home had been pledged for her nephew's bond, took her place in the front row beside her brother Bill. Lucille Hofmann, withdrawn and suffering sleep and weight loss since her son's injury, was at home caring for the Hofmann children so that Dori could attend, just as Joan Christensen would tend Terri's new baby most hearing days.

As the one "pool" photographer allowed in the courtroom by Judge Grant checked the lighting, Hofmann rose from the defense table on one foot, picked up his crutches, and started up the aisle. Nearing the back of the aisle, he met Ted Cannon. The two paused. Hofmann was much smaller, but the crutches propped on either side gave him mass. Neither spoke. Seconds passed. Hofmann stood calmly. Cannon turned to one side and edged past him. Hofmann continued down the aisle as if no one had gotten in his way.

Finally, Judge Grant entered. His sunburned face drew an appreciative chuckle from the press. "Took his kids skiing over the weekend," one reporter guessed. Tall, broadshouldered, and athletic, Grant had a reputation as a sportsman. He also turned out to be something of a clotheshorse, alternating rose, blue, and purple robes with his more traditional black robe several times a day.

The proceedings began with introductions and a few matters of routine business. After Yengich asked that the search warrant files be brought to the bench, Stott, lead prosecutor, moved to delay hearing one case because new evidence had been recovered that would take time to analyze.

What Stott did not say was that Tom Wilding, a victim in several of the fraud charges, had brought the prosecutors a second copy of the "Oath of a Freeman" only days before the hearing. George Throckmorton had matched it microscopically to the printing negative police had found. Prosecutors hoped to match the negative to the first Oath, now being sent to California for a cyclotron test. All of this would require time.

Grant did not want to allow a continuance. "We may be here for a month," he said.

"Hopefully not," Stott replied.

"You may proceed," Grant told Stott.

D'Elia leaned toward Stott and Biggs. "Okay boys," he said, his spirits rising, "this is reality counseling." D'Elia stood and called the prosecution's first witness. Everyone else might consider Stott lead prosecutor, but Gerry D'Elia cared only that "his" homicide case had finally come to court.

Jeweler Bruce Passey was sworn in, then took the witness stand. His task was to identify the man who came into the Judge Building the morning of October 15, identify the letterman's jacket, and the package. His father, Hal, had also seen the man and the package, but a local television station had shown him a video of Hofmann before police had presented him with a photo array. There was another problem with Hal Passey; he was color blind.

A small, inconspicuous man, Bruce Passey wore a tan sweater and slacks that matched his moustache and thinning hair. D'Elia questioned Passey meticulously about his arrival at the Judge Building, the minutes he spent waiting alone in the lobby for his father, and the entry of a stranger carrying a package. "Can you describe that person?" D'Elia asked.

"The fellow was approximately five foot eight to five feet nine."

"And how old?"

"Thirty to thirty-five years of age."

"What about the person's race?"

"He was white—Caucasian."

"What about the person's hair?"

"Dark brown. Medium cut."

How was it styled?

"It was over the ears. It was neatly combed."

"The person's weight?"

"One hundred and sixty-five to one hundred eighty pounds."

What about clothing?

"He had a letter jacket on like you'd wear in high school, without the letter on it."

"What color was the jacket?"

"A green, bright green."

Any other color on the jacket?

"Light brown, a lighter color," which appeared on the sleeves.

Passey could only remember that the man was casually dressed, wearing sneakers. He did not have glasses, nor did he appear to have shaved that morning. "From the darkness in the hallway it looked like he could have had a moustache, but I wasn't real sure on that." The lobby, lit by a chandelier, was dim in the early mornings, Passey said.

"How would you describe this person's entry into the building?"

"Very calmly."

"Did you notice this person carrying anything?"

"Yes. A brown box approximately twelve inches by fifteen inches by six to eight inches deep."

And there was writing on the box. "In the upper left-hand corner of the box was printed a name, 'To Steve Christensen.' "

D'Elia showed Passey state exhibit 3A, a cardboard box, and asked if it resembled the box he had seen that morning.

"It was very close to that size."

Passey described the ride to the third floor, where he and

his father got out. The man had pushed five and stayed on, he said. A little after 8:00 a.m., they heard an explosion.

"Would you be able to recognize the jacket if you were shown it?"

"Yes."

D'Elia brought out state exhibit 2, a green letterman's jacket with gray sleeves.

"Are you able to recognize that jacket, Mr. Passey?"

"Yes. That is the color of the jacket on the fellow in the foyer."

"How about the remainder of the jacket—the sleeves are gray on that, are they not?"

"Yes."

"And you originally described the sleeves as being a light tan color, is that correct?"

"Yes."

"How sure are you that this could be the same jacket?"

"I feel sure that it is the jacket."

"Why the difference between the original description of tan instead of gray?"

Passey said the foyer was too dim for him to see the color clearly. D'Elia showed him another exhibit, a photograph of the jacket.

"Do these sleeves look closer in that picture to what you saw that morning, in color?"

"Yes, they do."

"Did you see this jacket at another time?"

"Yes, a detective brought it in and asked if I could identify it two days later. I said yes, this was the same jacket."

Gradually, D'Elia led Passey to the key question. "With respect to the person that you saw in the elevator and in the foyer of the Judge Building on October 15, 1985, are you able to recognize that person again?"

"Yes."

"Do you see him in the courtroom today?"

Passey answered clearly. "Yes. He's sitting next to Mr. Yengich, wearing glasses and a blue suit."

D'Elia asked if he had been shown a photo spread by police. He had.

"How many photographs were there in that photo array?"

"Eight or nine. They were in a stack. I went through them. One photo that I picked gave me a strong feeling in my stomach, it made me feel uneasy. It was almost the last one. I initialed it with the date on the back."

"Did the picture look like the person in the courtroom and on the elevator?"

"Yes, it looked like him."

D'Elia showed Passey the composite sketch the detective and he had helped assemble. "Is there anything on that composite that does not comport with your recollection on the basis of what you saw in the Judge Building?"

Yes, Passey said; the detective had typed in dark brown sleeves for the jacket. "That's wrong."

"Anything else?"

"The moustache is wrong. I said five o'clock shadow. He looked like he could have had a moustache but it was not distinctive. I told [the detective] I was not absolutely sure of the moustache because of the five o'clock shadow"

Next, D'Elia brought out a fragment of cardboard with the word "Steve" on it and asked Passey if he could identify it.

"It does look like the printing on the box."

Next D'Elia produced a photo array. Yengich, however, said he wanted to inspect it first. Accordingly, the judge called a fifteen-minute break. The Hofmanns formed a tight group around Mark and his attorneys, while the Christensens and Sheets chatted with the CAO staff on the other side of the aisle.

After the break, D'Elia handed Passey an envelope and asked him to look at the photographs inside. "How do those compare with the photos a detective showed you?"

"Yes. I recognized one."

D'Elia showed him the photograph he had identified earlier. Passey's initials, the date, and the officer's initials were on the back.

"For the record, Your Honor," D'Elia announced, "this is a driver's license photograph of Mark Hofmann. I have no further questions of this witness."

Yengich rose for cross-examination. His "Good morning, Mr. Passey" bristled.

Yengich established Passey's age, occupation, and that he was a high school graduate. "Before October 15th did you know a man by the name of Mark Hofmann?"

"No sir."

"Had you ever heard of that man?"

"No."

Yengich retraced Passey's testimony, checking the number of times he had spoken with police, when, with whom, and regarding what information. Finally, he came to Passey's identification of Hofmann.

"You're certain that you told [the detective] that the man didn't have a moustache, but he had a five o'clock shadow?"

"Yes."

"You're certain?"

"Yes."

"Did you describe the jacket?"

"Yes, I did."

"What did you say about the jacket?"

"Bright green color with leather sleeves, not fabric. They looked light tan."

"You never told him that it was a dark brown?"

"That's correct."

"Do you see anyone in the courtroom (who is not sunburned)," Yengich added for a chuckle at the judge's expense, "who possibly has the type of five o'clock shadow you saw in this instance?"

Passey looked around. "Not from this distance."

They went back to the brown sleeves, then Yengich asked, "Now the man that you saw was not wearing spectacles?"

"That's correct."

"He didn't appear as though he was having trouble seeing, did he?"

"No."

Yengich continued to peck away at Passey's testimony. "What's the lighting like in the elevator?"

"It's brighter than in the lobby."

"You didn't have any trouble seeing the color of the jacket in the elevator, did you?"

"No, sir."

"But you still said light brown sleeves."

"Light tan."

Yengich moved to the photo array, reading through the names and dates of birth. Most of the photographs were of people older than Hofmann. Then Yengich returned to Passey's ability to tell color. "In the picture, what color would you say the pantlegs were?"

Passey looked for a minute. "Tannish gray slacks."

On re-direct, D'Elia capitalized on Passey's uncertainty regarding neutral shades. He pointed to the beige carpet. "What color is the carpet?"

"Light tan or light brown, very close to that."

"Your sweater is . . . ?"

"Light tan or light brown." Passey added that when he accompanied the officers to the lobby at noon, the sleeves still reminded him of a tan color in that light.

D'Elia next held up the driver's license photograph. "Mr. Passey, what was it that you looked at in that picture to make your identification?"

"The broad bridge of the nose, the cheekbones, the hair appearance."

"And those things were discernible regardless of the glasses or moustache?"

"Yes."

Passey stepped down. His identification of Hofmann had been strong, yet Yengich had raised questions about his suggestibility after-the-fact. What had he really seen? And what had he come to think he had seen as one police officer after another confronted him with evidence? Yengich's questions about the flaws in Passey's identification hinted that at trial he would try to discredit Bruce Passey's testimony.

Next D'Elia called Janet McDermott, a slim, professional woman with brown hair and eyes and expressive hands. Ken Farnsworth, in trying to convince Terri Christensen she should attend the hearing and hear the evidence for herself, had warned her about McDermott's testimony.

"Janet thinks Steve lived for a few minutes after the explosion," he had said. "She thinks he suffered. He didn't. But her testimony is going to have an impact. Just *you* remember, he didn't feel anything. It was too fast."

In response to D'Elia's questions, McDermott described the position of her office, across the hall from Christensen's office. She and Christensen, she said, had been "cordial acquaintances" who chatted occasionally and picked up one another's mail and packages. She detailed her arrival at work the morning of October 15th and the unknown man she had seen in the hall. She estimated his size at 5 feet 10 inches to 6 feet tall, 180 to 200 pounds, with light brown hair.

The courtroom held its breath as McDermott, moving from question to question, described how three times that morning she had decided to lift the package, then changed her mind. As shrapnel burst through her door and shattered glass flew around the room, she had ducked behind her desk.

"Did you hear anything at that time while you were over at the desk?"

"Yes, I did."

"What did you hear?"

She paused, then spoke tightly but distinctly. "A very high-pitched crying." The silence in the courtroom intensified.

"What did it sound like?"

Janet McDermott looked past the judge to the far corner of the courtroom, as far from Mac and Terri Christensen as her eyes could reach. She fought for control.

"A little child . . . dying."

Terri Christensen numbly moved her hands to her wet cheeks. Around her, Steve Christensen's friends and family tried to swallow their tears as McDermott continued.

Convinced a few minutes later she was being trapped by fire, McDermott described how she had grabbed her belongings and crept out of her office.

"What did you see?"

"Steven Christensen, lying on the floor."

"Where was he?"

"He was part way in his office and part way out in the hallway." She described his wounds.

"How long did you look?"

A pause. "I don't know. Probably at least a minute. It felt like a long time."

Not surprisingly, she had no recollection of damage to the hallway.

"Did Mr. Christensen move at all at that time, while you were standing there staring at him?"

"I don't believe he moved."

The noises she had heard earlier, she said, still were coming from Steve but were much deeper than at first. As she stared, she noticed that his office was still dark—he had not even switched on the light.

Judge Grant kept his eyes on the defendant. He noticed Hofmann react similarly to others—with sadness, slowed breathing. Grant later called this "reverence for the magic of life." He thought it universal.

After verbally walking the witness through the event, D'Elia came to the crucial question: "Can you identify the person that you saw that morning in the Judge Building down the hall?"

"Not positively."

"Would you be able to recognize the person by face again?"

"No."

Could she identify the writing on the cardboard fragment? She did so easily.

D'Elia was finished. Judge Grant called a break.

Reporters went out to the restrooms and drinking fountain. Terri Christensen stood beside her seat, opposite the Hofmanns, but Ted Cannon, directly between the two sides, blocked her view of the defendant. After a minute, Bill Hofmann walked over to his son.

Mark Hofmann stood alone beside the defense table, his right foot slightly above the floor. He looked more relaxed than earlier. McDermott's testimony had been powerful, but she had not identified him.

After the recess, Yengich cross-examined carefully. Not only had McDermott been unable to identify Hofmann in court, but she had also been unable to select his photograph from the photo array or to identify the letterman's jacket for police. McDermott evidently estimated height and weight by her husband, who was five eleven and weighed around 200 pounds. She guessed that Yengich (slightly taller than Hofmann) was five ten. The description she gave of the man she saw was both taller and heavier than Hofmann. The man had been casually attired, she thought, probably in a button-down plaid shirt, casual pants, and a jacket that ended at the waist.

"Have you ever been shown state's exhibit 4?"

"No."

Yengich showed her the composite drawing. "That person looks familiar. It's the same facial structure."

"What about the hair?"

"I don't know."

"You don't know." Yengich's voice was gentle. "What about the moustache?"

"I don't know on the moustache."

"You don't know about the moustache," again softly.

"The eyes and the rest of the face, especially the cheeks, look like the individual that I would have seen."

"You said you didn't know whether or not the man was wearing glasses, is that correct?"

"My tendency is he was not wearing glasses."

"This individual looked at you, and your eyes met his eyes, correct?"

"Yes."

"No further questions of this witness, Your Honor."

D'Elia was on his feet, as Yengich turned toward the defense table. "Mr. Yengich, if I promise not to ask your age, could you stipulate on the record what your height is?" Laughter met his irony, but the pause following the question demanded an answer.

"Well, I'm about five eight and a half," Yengich drawled. "Without heels?" a reporter quipped. "Without heels," Yengich said, winning the laugh.

But D'Elia smiled. If McDermott had overestimated Yengich's height, it followed that she had overestimated the size of the man in the hall. On re-direct, D'Elia returned to McDermott's recollection.

"With respect to what Mr. Yengich was just talking to you about on the composite, you said there was something about the eyes on the individual that you saw at the Judge Building that day that you can remember, and the same with the cheeks. Would you describe for us the eyes?"

McDermott explained that he had relatively small eyes, a little closer together than D'Elia's eyes she said, maybe more so than hers.

"What is it about the cheeks that you recollect?"

"Chubby cheeks. Not a definite cheekbone."

D'Elia tried again. "Besides your husband, is there anyone in this courtroom that you see that resembles the qualities of the person that you saw on the 15th in the Judge Building?"

McDermott scanned the faces before her again. "Um," she said finally. "Mr. Hofmann . . . I'd say maybe even the gentleman sitting next to you if you were seated . . . "

"Mr. Stott?" D'Elia blurted, adding through laughter, "for the record."

Quickly D'Elia established that McDermott could not rule out Hofmann as the man in the Judge Building nor could she rule out the jacket. "Could you rule out this box as the size of the box you saw that morning?"

She looked at it dubiously. "It seems awfully large."

When Yengich rose again, his manner was abrupt but he established only that McDermott did not recall seeing a green letterman's jacket—though she did recall a plaid shirt. McDermott stepped down, and the courtroom took a break.

This time, Hofmann remained seated, oblivious to the strain in his wife's and father's faces. Dori slid her fingers between his shoulder and the back of his chair and left them there a minute.

At that point D'Elia called Margene Robbins, secretary to Tom Wilding, a financial consultant who did business with Hofmann. She testified that Hofmann had come into their office at 9:30 a.m., October 15, wearing a green letterman's jacket with no letter. Yengich cross-examined briefly, then Robbins stepped down.

Judge Grant had announced at the outset that he was prepared to continue as late as 7:30 p.m., but by 4:45 p.m. the courtroom audience was already beginning to stir. But then D'Elia called Gary Sheets. As Sheets, dressed in a white shirt and dark blue suit, came into the courtroom, he was met by a low, ugly murmur.

The prosecution had, from the beginning, contended with the community's suspicion of Sheets, partner of one murder victim and husband of the other. The failure of his business and its subsequent bankruptcy had done nothing to improve Sheets's public image, nor had his appearance on television shortly after the bombings or his presence at a Utah Jazz basketball game the next Saturday evening. Sheets simply had not behaved the way people expected a grieving widower to act.

Before the hearing began, Ken Farnsworth heard a rumor he thought he should check out. Several apparently credible women claimed to have seen Gary Sheets come into LDS Hospital to visit Hofmann the very day Sheets had buried his wife. These women had recognized Sheets from television, and his presence in the hospital seemed to them so strange and suspicious that they had remembered the incident.

Farnsworth knew Hofmann had been guarded by police throughout his hospital stay. There had been no report of a visit from Sheets. Still, he called Joe Robertson, Sheets's son-in-law.

"Well," Robertson said thoughtfully, "I don't see how Gary could have been at the hospital. I was with him out at Steve's funeral in the morning, and then we went right from the cemetery to Kathy's funeral in Holladay. I didn't drive with him, but I just don't see how he could have been there." He offered to call Sheets. A few minutes later, Robertson called Farnsworth back.

"The story's absolutely right. He *was* at the hospital. Gary said he stopped by LDS Hospital after Steve's funeral and on his way to Kathy's."

"He did?"

"Yeah. A member of Gary's ward had been diagnosed with terminal cancer and Gary went to visit him. Gary's just the kind of guy who would think of visiting him for a minute, even on the way to his wife's funeral."

Farnsworth had hung up the telephone, pondering the public and private Gary Sheets. He guessed they were ready for the defense on that one.

"Would you describe for us your wife, Kathy?" D'Elia began.

"I think Kathy was one of the most loved persons I've ever seen. Everybody in the neighborhood loved her. She had a great number of friends. She was a great wife, a great companion, a super mother, a great grandmother."

As Sheets's voice trailed, D'Elia asked about her sense of humor or other characteristics. "She had a great sense of humor, a great wit. I used to tell people the best job of selling I ever did was to convince Kathy to marry me. She was just an outstanding person."

"How would you characterize her relationship with you at the time?"

"It was fine, it was great. We had a great marriage. We were both very busy people, she in her life playing tennis and walking, and doing the things she did with the neighbors and friends, and the grandchildren, and me in the business and the other community things I was involved in."

"How many grandchildren did you have?"

"We have three," Sheets answered, slipping into present tense. "Her children and her grandchildren were her life and her love."

D'Elia then led Sheets through his activities the morning of October 15, driving his son Jimmy to volleyball practice then going to work. Sheets marked on a diagram how he drove out of the garage and up the driveway without seeing anything suspicious. He described how he found out about Christensen's death and then heard of a bombing on Naniloa Drive.

D'Elia asked Sheets about Christensen.

"I first met him when he used to wait on me when I went to shop at Mac's. Steve was the most outstanding, brightest, most intelligent young man I'd ever met in my life. I loved him like a son." His voice broke.

"During the mid to late months of summer 1985, Steve Christensen quit your organization. Would that be a fair statement?"

Yes, Sheets answered and described the impasse he and Christensen had reached regarding the future of CFS.

"What was your relationship with Steve once he left the company? Were there any hard feelings?"

"None whatsoever."

Briefly, they discussed Sheets's involvement with the salamander letter. "I was not really interested that much in it. Steve was fascinated by those things. We were talking about writing a book with JGSA as a business endeavor, but we decided against it."

After D'Elia's questions, Yengich asked to cross-examine Sheets in the morning. Grant agreed, banged his gavel, and the first day of the preliminary hearing ended.

As court convened the next morning, KSL-Radio's Melissa Jenkins reviewed Sheets's testimony in her morning broadcast, then added, "Defense attorneys would not comment on whether they will try to discredit Sheets's testimony. Sources have told KSL that the Sheetses were in the middle of a messy and bitter divorce. Two former CFS employees also say Sheets and Christensen parted angrily."

Meanwhile, inside the courtroom, Sheets's family listened to the cross-examination.

"Prior to yesterday's date, have you been in the presence of Mark Hofmann?" Ron Yengich asked.

"I don't know."

"Were you aware of his name before October 15, 1985?"

"No, but let me clarify that. One of my weaknesses is not remembering names."

"We share that weakness," Yengich said. "Do you recollect at any time Steve Christensen talking to you about Mark?"

"No."

Yengich turned to the diagram on the wall and retraced Sheets's testimony as to the morning's logistics. Eventually he came around to CFS's difficulties, which Christensen had uncovered.

"And there were never any arguments, not even as a father and son might have?"

"No. I don't think we had disputes."

"Steve ultimately left your employ." Sheets agreed.

"Did Steve ever tell you he felt personally responsible for CFS business failures?"

"No, not at all."

After a few other business questions, Yengich asked, "Was Steve an active member of the LDS church?"

Sheets capitalized on the titter in the courtroom. "He was a bishop. That's pretty active."

Gradually, Yengich established that Sheets's involvement with Christensen's interest in Mormon history had been peripheral but that research on the salamander letter had been supported by JGSA funds.

"Now there came a time with CFS when you had some people become quite disgruntled with the way things were being handled. Is that a fair statement?"

"I think that's fair."

"And some of these people were investors, correct?"

"I don't know of anyone who was disgruntled that wasn't an investor."

Yengich diverted here to establish that Sheets knew of no reason why anyone would want to harm his wife and that any bomb at their residence was probably intended for him.

"That's the way I feel, yes."

Yengich probed as to what people might have vengeance on their minds, eventually coming to Las Vegas investors.

Immediately, D'Elia objected. "That's outside the scope of direct examination," he told Judge Grant.

Yengich protested that this might be his only chance to raise these questions. Hofmann was charged with killing Sheets's wife, he said, making Sheets an adverse witness since they were attempting to develop alternative theories for the murders. And investigative reports from the county attorney's office placed Sheets's credibility at issue, Yengich added. "He does not appear to be hostile, but certainly is adverse as that phrase is understood in the law and the rules of evidence."

D'Elia disagreed. The defense could call Sheets if they wanted to, he said. "There is not at this time any indication of adversarial nature between Mr. Gary Sheets and Mr. Mark Hofmann. He didn't even know the man."

Grant ruled that Yengich could explore the area, a popular decision in the courtroom because of rumors about Las Vegas investors, the Mafia, and Sheets's previous experience as an insurance writer.

Yengich went into some detail about various investors, then came back to the day of the bombings. He asked whether Christensen had been insured by either JGSA or CFS.

"Just by CFS." He explained that early in 1985 insurance had been purchased for all company officers. Christensen's had not been cancelled since it was paid annually. The $500,000 premium had been paid to the company after his death.

"After you were aware of Steve's death, but before you found out about the bombing at your own house, did you have any personal fear for your own safety?"

"No."

"And you've indicated that your marriage with your wife was a great marriage, is that correct?"

"Yes."

"Did you have insurance on her life?"

"All I had on Kathy was $5,000 with our group medical plan."

Yengich then asked Sheets if he could identify several individuals, evidently involved in some of CFS's Las Vegas deals. Sheets recognized most of the names and identified the investors. Next Yengich said a woman's name. "No," Sheets said, shaking his head. Again the murmur rose in the courtroom. Yengich made no comment and asked no further questions.

On re-direct, D'Elia asked if the insurance premium paid after Christensen's death had gone into the bankruptcy. Sheets said it had.

"Did you receive any part of it?"

"No."

Grant called for a break. Sheets left the stand and greeted Terri Christensen with a bear hug and a kiss, shook hands with Mac Christensen, adding a hug, then moved on to greet Joan Gorton and Sheets's daughters. They were unhappy about the innuendoes involving insurance and Las Vegas investors but were still unaware of the radio report that the Sheetses had been in the middle of a divorce at the time of the bombings.

When court reconvened, D'Elia called thirteen-year-old Aaron Teplick. The curly-haired boy pointed out his house on a diagram and then the Sheets home next door. He explained how he had awakened around midnight the night before the bombings. Feeling ill, he had gone upstairs to the kitchen for aspirin. As he came up the stairs, he saw lights coming down the driveway. A slow-moving vehicle, a gold-colored Toyota WonderWagon, passed his house, turned around, and drove back toward the Sheets's driveway, where it paused for several minutes. He watched the van until it drove out on Naniloa Drive.

The next day at school, he had heard of Mrs. Sheets's death and told his mother and later the police about the van. He had drawn the van for the police, identified Hofmann's van in a photo spread, then picked Hofmann's van out of a car lot full of vans.

Yengich cross-examined carefully, stressing the difference between gold and copper. The van had been the color of the van in the photograph, Teplick said. He could not say it was the same van, but it appeared the same as the van he saw that night. Teplick's testimony was patient and precise, but the questioning was detailed and tedious.

By the time the next witness, deputy sheriff Jerry Thompson, was called to testify, he had vanished. Grant said the court would break for lunch — and that Thompson had better return wearing iron underwear.

When court reconvened, Thompson apologized for his earlier absence. He described in detail the bomb scene at Naniloa Drive and the discovery of Kathy Sheets's body. As D'Elia held up photographs of the scene, the victim's daughters all ducked. Thompson identified the photographs and described the collection of evidence. He identified a piece of Kathy Sheets's jacket and described how galvanized pipe had been blasted throughout the area. As repairs were later made to the garage and house, more fragments had been recovered.

Suddenly, Terri Christensen was helped from the stuffy room. The piece of Kathy's jacket undid her calm. She felt faint and sick and clearly did not want to be in the courtroom when a piece of Steve's suit or bomb fragments were exhibited.

Next Thompson testified to the search of Hofmann's home on October 16. He described how the letterman's jacket in evidence had been found turned inside out in the corner of the closet. Amid whispers from the press, defense counsel exchanged glances. They knew a letterman's jacket had been found in Hofmann's home, of course — but crumpled inside out in the back of a closet? That held implications they had not expected.

When Thompson finished, D'Elia called Bradley Robert Christensen (no relation to Steven), who had seen a young man approach a sports car before the third bombing. Christensen described in minute detail what he had seen before the bomb exploded. After observing a man walking ahead of him enter a blue sports car, Christensen said he paused for traffic, crossed Main Street, then, after a delay of a minute or two, heard a blast, and raced back across the street to help. He identified the injured man as Mark Hofmann.

"When Mr. Hofmann went to the car," D'Elia finished, "did you see any activity before the car door was open?"

"I vaguely remember him quickly going to his trunk, opening it up."

"Were you able to discern whether or not the car door had been unlocked?"

Christensen was not sure, and D'Elia let it drop. Christensen's testimony was significant, for it directly contradicted Hofmann's statement in the hospital.

Yengich knew that Christensen's first statement to police had seemed more consistent with Hofmann's description. On cross-examination, Yengich was obviously ready to explore that contradictory testimony.

"How many statements have you given to the police?"

"I've given two." The first was a hurried statement given to Jim Bell, before Bell headed up to LDS Hospital to interview Hofmann. The second, Christensen said, had been given three weeks later to ATF and the SLCPD and repeated at "the usual witness preparation" the night before with Bell and D'Elia.

Yengich pointed out that some details in his testimony had not been in his accounts to police. Christensen said his first statement represented only a brief summary of what happened.

"Who suggested that he may have gotten into the trunk of the car?"

"It was mentioned, but it had previously been in my memory."

"Who mentioned it first?"

"I'm not sure if it was Detective Bell or Gerry D'Elia," Christensen said, blind to the implications that the police and prosecution had suggested this part of his testimony.

Yengich asked about the bag Christensen said he had seen Hofmann carry. It appeared to be a gym bag, Christensen said, but it did not have handles. It could have been a grocery bag.

Yengich came to the crucial point—the time Christensen said had elapsed from the time the man entered the car until the explosion—reading him his first statement to the police, in which Christensen said the explosion occurred a second or two after Hofmann reached his automobile, not a minute or two. Yengich pointed out that Christensen's earlier statement had been made closer in time to the explosion than his testimony at the hearing. By now Christensen appeared shaken. Court took a recess before D'Elia began re-direct.

"Is this the first time you've testified under oath in any proceeding?"

"Yes."

"Now, Mr. Yengich brought up the fact, in his words, that a statement about Mr. Hofmann going into his trunk was suggested by Mr. Bell or myself."

Christensen said that was something he wanted to explain.

D'Elia asked how the meeting at the CAO the evening before had proceeded.

"You asked me questions."

"Did I or any law enforcement official ever suggest to you the answer to any question during any interview that you ever had?"

"Never once."

"Okay, now what was the question I put to you?"

"You asked me, 'Could he have opened his trunk?' I paused for a long period of time and said, 'I think you struck a raw nerve.' I mumbled to myself for maybe five minutes."

"And did Detective Bell or I say anything to you?"

"No one said anything. Then I said it's 55 percent that he got into his trunk and 45 percent that he didn't."

D'Elia asked him to explain why the time span between seeing Hofmann approach his car and the explosion was now one to two minutes, where in his previous statement it was much shorter.

Christensen said that immediately after the bombing, his interview had been brief, he had been upset, and he had been cut off frequently in the middle of statements.

"Has this information ever been gone over in detail until you talked to the county attorney's office?"

"Not really."

"Is there anything today that you've said that is a change in your testimony?"

"No, there's no change."

Yengich was not finished. He read Christensen his report verbatim, emphasizing, "And you say one to two seconds. Now was [one of the agents] pressuring you in that statement too?"

"I don't really remember him asking me that. I recall saying two or three seconds. He didn't give me time to think."

Yengich pressed the point further until D'Elia objected and Grant said, "That's enough."

"So you're saying now," Yengich summed up angrily, "that the October 23rd interview would be incorrect. It's incorrect then and remains incorrect today, and that's because you were pressured into saying it."

There was a pause. Finally, Christensen said, "Yes, it would have been."

As Yengich sat down, D'Elia stood and handed Christensen the transcript of his interview and let him read it. D'Elia then read aloud a rambling sequence about the bag Hofmann carried and Christensen running to the car. The part in question read, "uh . . . uh . . . one or two seconds . . . "

"Was this one to two seconds comment interjected into another thought?"

"Definitely. It was done several times. I was thinking about something else."

Christensen was excused. If he had crossed Main Street before hearing the explosion and running to Hofmann's aid, the time span would, of course, have been more than a second or two. Nevertheless, the discrepancies in his statements would give Yengich fodder for trial later.

After the clash Christensen's testimony had provided, D'Elia's next witness, a clerk from Radio Shack, ended the day anti-climactically. She identified a receipt she had written to a Mike Hansen for the sale of a C-cell battery holder, a package of photo lamps, and a mercury switch on October 7, 1985. (This receipt, twice overlooked, had been found during the third search of that store's files after charges were filed.)

Brad Rich cross-examined, asking the number of customers she served and whether she remembered Mike Hansen. She did not. As court was dismissed, everyone rose exhausted. Leaving the room, reporters discussed Christensen's testimony. Nobody said much about Mike Hansen.

On Wednesday, April 16, Officer James Bryant testified about Hofmann's arrival at LDS Hospital. Bryant's brief testimony set the stage for Jim Bell, the next witness. In what came as a disconcerting surprise to the prosecution, Bryant indirectly implied that police knew Hofmann was a suspect almost immediately but did not read him his Miranda rights. Evidently, Bryant had been informed by the police dispatcher, as Bell had not, that Hofmann might be a suspect. But since Bell was on his way, Bryant did not read Hofmann his rights or interrogate him at length.

Bell, who had not heard that Hofmann was a suspect until after speaking with him, reviewed his interview with Hofmann at the hospital, then identified several twisted pieces of pipe that had been recovered from the Christensen bomb. As he testified, Bell watched the suspect. Most of the time, Hofmann shuffled papers or wrote notes, but he always looked up, Bell noticed, when the detective held up bomb parts. When he lifted aloft a foot-long skewer and announced that it had pierced Christensen's chest, Bell was astonished to see Hofmann's eyes glaze over. He had heard from experts that bombers had sexual interest in explosions. Jerry Taylor would testify soon, and Bell resolved to ask him about this.

Bell identified a papyrus fragment encased in plastic, a black felt-tipped marker, two rubber gloves, a pipe elbow, and some documents, all of which had been recovered from Hofmann's car.

He also described the Radio Shack searches, which had quickly turned up a receipt with M. Hansen and a phony address on it. In a later search of the Hofmann house, Bell had seized a manila envelope bearing the name Mike Hansen. Now he identified the envelope.

"Now did you see that Mike Hansen envelope yourself?" D'Elia asked.

"Yes, I did."

"Where was it?"

"It was in a box in the southeast basement bedroom, lying right on top, folded over like this."

This was important, for the defense was expected to move to suppress much of the evidence recovered in the searches on the grounds that police did not at the time know what they were looking for. Since Bell knew the name Mike Hansen or M. Hansen was associated with the purchase of items similar to those used in the bombs, his recognition of the Hansen envelope was key to the prosecution's use of it as evidence.

Ron Yengich did not want to cross-examine Bell until he looked through the evidence the police had seized, later consolidated into one room. After some debate, Grant ruled that Yengich could spend lunch hours and evenings going through the evidence with Bell and Farnsworth, then cross-examine Bell later, out of sequence.

Thereafter Yengich met Bell or Farnsworth daily in the evidence room next to the police gym. As they sorted, he asked the detectives to set aside certain items — a receipt for a ward fast offering, receipts for the rental of children's movies, a greeting card printed "To a wonderful father, husband, friend and lover," and a sheet of paper covered with Hofmann's printing, dated March 1, 1980, which began, "Today I just found out the story of Grandpa's and Grandma's wedding."

As they sorted, a rapport grew between Yengich and

Farnsworth. Glancing at Yengich's notepad one day, Farnsworth saw that Yengich had jotted "Hoffman." Farnsworth pointed out the misspelling.

"Well, for what he's paying me, that's the best he gets," Yengich quipped.

Another time, the two broke loose to shoot a few baskets in the gym. Farnsworth, who had the advantage in height, outshot Yengich easily. Then they agreed to shoot baskets for Hofmann's felony counts. Immediately, Yengich's accuracy improved. He won the murders, and Farnsworth got only the Lucy Mack Smith forgery and a couple of frauds. Farnsworth bounced the ball across the court and wiped his face. "Back to court," Yengich suggested.

"I sure hope that's not an omen," Farnsworth muttered as he locked up the evidence room.

After Grant ruled that Yengich could review the evidence before cross-examining Bell, Jerry A. Taylor, ATF regional director in San Francisco, approached the stand. Taylor, who obviously testified often, answered the questions in a military staccato. He gave an impressive list of qualifications before D'Elia began questioning him about the Judge Building bombing. He described the scene and the analysis of the evidence gathered there.

"Do you have an opinion as to the make up of the Judge Building bomb?"

Taylor replied that the evidence at the scene plus lab reports indicated that the pipe bomb had contained smokeless gunpowder. One cap on the end of the pipe had been drilled to allow the insertion of a model rocket ignitor, which was connected to a mercury switch and batteries. When the mercury switch was tilted to a position that allowed it to contact the C-cell batteries, the circuit was completed. The bomb, he added, had been contained in a 6-by-12-by-12-inch box.

"How do you know the size of the box?"

"I read it on a piece of cardboard recovered at the scene."

Prosecutors smiled at defense attorneys. Bill Hofmann had

earlier left the hearing to copy the evidence list and had returned with a box exactly that size. As soon as prosecutors and police had showed an interest in the box, it had disappeared.

Next Taylor described the collection of evidence on 200 North after the car bombing. He identified several pieces of the bomb, then said that an intense fire had destroyed much of the evidence inside the car—only three fragments of cardboard had been recovered and no mercury switch was found.

They moved to Naniloa Drive, and Taylor identified the mercury switch he had detected in the woods.

"How does the Sheets bomb compare with the Christensen bomb?"

"It is identical in structure."

"How do they compare with the Hofmann bomb?"

"Again it is a pipe bomb the same as the others and identical to the other two devices."

D'Elia asked for differences between the bombs.

"The first bomb had a large quantity of nails confined in the box and taped around the pipe. Nails are common in certain devices if you want to kill an individual rather than just destroy property."

"Do you have an opinion with respect to the authorship of these incendiary devices?"

"Yes. The same person constructed all these pipe bombs."

Did the bombs have safety devices?

"There is no evidence of any type of safety. It was capable of being functioned immediately. This makes an extremely hazardous weapon. The person that makes it would be the person who handles it."

Grim-faced, Mac Christensen leaned forward, elbows on knees, staring at Hofmann as Taylor continued. "The same person who made the devices positioned the devices. When you put an extremely dangerous bomb inside a cardboard box, there's no way that anybody else could get it to its location without causing serious injury bombing themselves."

Taylor explained that the bomb parts were identical to items sold in Radio Shack stores, describing his own purchases there.

After eliciting considerable detail, D'Elia focussed Taylor's attention on the bomb that had injured Hofmann.

Does the evidence indicate where the bomb was in relation to Hofmann?

"His right side. Damage to his right leg, arm and shoulder, and he received some pretty bad burns to his right hand. The approximate distance of the bomb to the hand was very close, the rest of the body within eighteen inches."

Was Hofmann inside or outside the car?

"He was inside the vehicle based on the damage caused to the vehicle and the damage caused to Mr. Hofmann."

After a short break, Taylor set up a chair on the floor in front of the witness stand, sitting in it as if in the driver's seat. He explained that the explosion of a pipe bomb is directional, with the end caps blowing off first as the points of least resistance. The bomb had been on a diagonal when it exploded, between the floorboard on the passenger side and the top rear corner behind the driver's seat. The explosion occurred just below the top of the console between the seats.

"Mr. Taylor, I'm going to give you a hypothetical," D'Elia said. "An individual goes to the driver's side. When the door is opened, a box falls from the seat to the ground with the person outside the car at that time reaching into the car toward the box as it's falling—and then the explosion occurs. How does that hypothetical comport with the evidence, in your opinion?"

"That didn't happen in this case," Taylor said. "The bomb did not explode on the floor but up by the console."

Taylor took the stand again, and D'Elia brought in exhibit 38, a facsimile of the Christensen bomb, complete with nails. The ugly device was wired with a buzzer. As D'Elia approached the defense table, he tipped the bomb and the buzzer sounded. He handed the bomb to Yengich. Taylor kept his eyes on Hofmann, who wiggled excitedly in his seat.

His testimony over, Taylor walked out of the courtroom and found Jim Bell in the hall. "That guy just had an orgasm in court," Taylor told him.

On cross-examination, Yengich was interested in Taylor's experience testifying in Nevada. Yengich was obviously leading up to the Mafia theory for the bombings.

First, he traced Taylor's qualifications, then had Taylor compare the three bombs in detail, emphasizing that they varied slightly in length and diameter. Yengich emphasized that no manufacturer could be identified for the pipe or smokeless gunpowder. Furthermore, no bomb-making site had been found.

"Have you ever testified in any cases where the bomb was reported to have been the result of a Mob or Mafia type incident?"

"That type of device is not used by the Mob or Mafia."

D'Elia was up, even as Yengich turned away. "Why not?"

"The pipe bomb doesn't have near the effectiveness as five or six sticks of dynamite that the Mafia likes to use. When you use five or six sticks of dynamite you don't have to worry about the victim living or a vehicle being damaged. It's blown over a block and a half. It's a sure thing."

When D'Elia and Yengich finished with the details of bomb manufacture, Judge Grant had a simpler question. If you drew an imaginary line down the middle of the car lengthwise, Grant wondered, where was the bomb?

Taylor said the bomb had been in a position parallel to the length of the car, then tilted up and down with one end toward the floorboard and the other toward the upper part of the driver's seat.

Taylor's testimony concluded the bombings evidence *per se*. Beyond the tedium of times, descriptions, and lab reports, the prosecution had portrayed a tragic scenario of two people unsuspectingly picking up deadly packages; of an unaware widower rushing to comfort survivors, unconcerned about his own safety; of a young businesswoman confronting horror outside her office door; of a boy, who had an interest in vehicles, watching out his window as a van prowled the dark street; of investigators piling up evidence; of a returned Mormon missionary kneeling in the street and commanding a dying man to live.

All of this had, of course, been chipped at by the defense. The possibility remained of mistaken identity, of high-pressure investigators manipulating evidence or abusing a suspect's rights.

MARK HOFMANN COMES TO COURT

Mark Hofmann seemed in good spirits as the first phase of the preliminary hearing shifted into the second. But the eyes that watched him from the press section behind the defense table were becoming suspicious. Across the aisle, the Christensen and Sheets families listened and waited for justice.

16

DOUBLE IDENTITY

The testimony of witnesses during the first week of preliminary hearings had been predictable. From here on, however, witnesses entered, testified, and left, sometimes taking only minutes, adding their pieces to the complicated mosaic that prosecutors hoped would make sense when they had finished. For their part, defense attorneys wanted no clear picture to emerge—tantalizing or incriminating bits were not enough. The burden of proof rested with the prosecutors and the clarity of their case.

Dave Biggs called on a number of printers and clerks to identify order forms for negatives of printing plates. Mike Hansen had ordered a Jack London signature; an address stamp for Austin Lewis, a San Francisco socialist acquainted with London; and the table of contents to an early Mormon hymnal, the first line of which began "The Spirit of God." Earlier, in 1982, Hofmann had ordered four rubber stamps resembling early Mormon currency.

Brad Rich countered by asking each witness if he or she could remember Mike Hansen or identify him. None could.

After lunch, Jim Bell took the stand. He told of fingerprinting Hofmann in LDS Hospital, then identified some rub-off letters and pencils taken from Hofmann's house.

Immediately after Bell's testimony, a finger print examiner for the Utah Crime Lab fitted a key piece of evidence into place. He had discovered a left-hand ring fingerprint on the order forms used by Mike Hansen to order the Austin Lewis personal address stamp. The fingerprint, he said, was Mark Hofmann's.

A low whistle rose from the press section. "Bye-bye, Mark," one reporter whispered.

Ron Yengich had only a few questions, then Judge Grant called a recess. The defense was clearly frustrated. They had known prosecutors had evidence relating to a Mike Hansen but had not realized how much. Like the letterman's jacket crumpled in the closet corner, the fingerprint was an unexpected blow. They were working night and day now, just as prosecutors and investigators had earlier, and the stress was accumulating. As their voices sharpened, they joked less with reporters and conferred less frequently with their increasingly subdued client.

Reporters were not bothering to lower their voices during breaks, though they sat directly behind the defense table. One reporter asked another, "Did you hear what Dori asked Mark last night when they got into bed? Mark, who's Mike Hansen?"

When court reconvened, Biggs called Hofmann's friend and former employee, Shannon Flynn. More comfortable in jogging sweats, Flynn appeared in court wearing the gray suit he had worn at the bond hearing. His round face was flushed, and he removed his suit coat before testifying. His deep voice and ponderous manner seemed better suited to a church pulpit, but a tic fluttered periodically near his right eye.

Flynn's position at the hearing was difficult. Like Hofmann, he had been accused and arrested by investigators and had defended himself and Hofmann to police and reporters. Yet Brad Rich had told reporters before the hearing began that if Hofmann was guilty, there were "some empty chairs at the defense table"—implying that Hofmann had accomplices. Hofmann and Flynn had visited gun shows together, had discussed explosives, had co-owned an Uzi machine gun, had been together part of the day when Hofmann received a speeding ticket in the desert, and had spent part of the evening prior to the bombings together. Flynn was obviously vulnerable. His attorney, Jim Barber, sat behind Yengich and Rich, though Dick Forbes waved him over to the prosecution side of the aisle. Clearly, Barber and Flynn were looking out for his interests first. Still, Hofmann seemed to take a close second, for Flynn, questioned by Biggs, sounded more like a defense witness than one for the prosecution.

Flynn filled in details about his role in selling documents for Hofmann to Wilford Cardon, Flynn's former LDS mission president. He also explained how he had signed over a $20,000 check from Deseret Book to Steve Christensen and Mark Hofmann after midnight the night of October 3. Then Biggs moved to the time of the murders.

"On October 14, 1985," Biggs said, "were you with Mr. Hofmann on that evening?"

"For a period of time I was." Flynn described their visit to a Mormon history buff.

"How did you get there?"

"We drove there in a vehicle."

"And whose vehicle was it?"

"Mr. Hofmann's vehicle."

Hiding a smile, Biggs persisted. "And what vehicle of Mr. Hofmann's was it?"

"It was what is commonly known as a Toyota minivan."

While Biggs reached for an exhibit, Flynn mopped perspiration.

"Does this photograph of a van look familiar?"

"It *looks* like the van owned by Mr. Hofmann."

Biggs established Flynn's bias. "You remain today a good friend of Mark Hofmann's, is that correct?"

"I believe so."

"I believe you told me as late as last Tuesday that you thought him to be an honest businessman. Is that correct?"

"That is correct."

"And you still believe that?"

"Yes, I do."

Flynn gazed at the ceiling lights, while Yengich, Rich, and Barber huddled. Biggs returned to the night before the murders when Hofmann and Flynn had sat talking in the van until about 10:30 p.m. "Do you recall that in an interview you stated that just before you left the van Mr. Hofmann said he had to get a Coca-Cola because he had to stay up for a little longer?"

Flynn said he did not remember. Biggs pressed. Didn't Flynn

remember Hofmann's statement or didn't he remember his own statement to police reporting Hofmann's comment?

"At present," Flynn countered, "I remember neither."

Biggs persisted. "Do you recall ever having a conversation with Mr. Hofmann concerning gunpowder?"

"Um . . . I don't remember any specific conversation, though I believe that we certainly could have had such discussions."

Biggs kept pressing. "Do you recall ever telling law enforcement that Mr. Hofmann was asking you about what was a fast-burning black powder?"

"I don't remember. It certainly could have occurred."

"When you took the Bridger notes to Deseret Book," Biggs said, switching subjects, "what did you tell them about those items?"

"I probably told them that they were mine."

"Was that something that was worked out between you and Mr. Hofmann?"

"Yes, it was."

"Was Mark present with you?"

"He was not. I don't know where he was. I believe he was waiting in the car."

Biggs looked amused. "He drove you down there, didn't he?"

"Yes, he did."

During a break, defense attorneys told Flynn, a witness for the prosecution, that he sounded flippant and to cut it out! Flynn protested that he was simply trying to answer questions precisely and literally.

After the break, Biggs tried again to get Flynn to discuss Hofmann's comments to him, as reported to investigators.

"Regarding the Coke incident, could it also have occurred when Mr. Hofmann got to your house initially rather than when he dropped you off?"

"It could have," Flynn countered genially, adding, "I'll have to rely on previous testimony that something like that happened."

Biggs asked about smokeless powder again but could not get Flynn to recall any specific conversation with Hofmann. Biggs sat down.

Rich began cross-examination lightly. "Now you're talking about Coca-Cola, right?"

"That's right."

"And your memory is not distinct as to that conversation."

"That's correct."

"And if it did occur, you're not sure when."

"That's correct."

Mac Christensen, entertained by Flynn's testimony, turned and winked at his son.

"Concerning any conversation about gunpowder, you have no distinct memory. Certainly that would be a general conversation and nothing more."

"That's correct."

"On through to October 15, did you ever hear Mark Hofmann say anything of an antagonistic or unpleasant nature about Mr. Christensen?"

"Never."

"Had you heard him mention Gary Sheets?"

"Never."

"Did he ever mention Kathy Sheets?"

"Never."

"When you went to Deseret Book, did you have the authority to sell those notes?"

Flynn hesitated. "Yes," he said uncertainly.

Biggs had a few questions on redirect.

"Mark Hofmann and Brent Metcalfe, did they know one another?"

"I believe so."

"You've been together with both of them?"

"Yes, I have."

"As a matter of fact, Brent Metcalfe worked for Mr. Hofmann."

"Not that I knew of," Flynn said stiffly.

At this point, Judge Grant, trying to make sense of Flynn's mixed messages, asked a question. "You received six documents and rode with Mark Hofmann to Deseret Book, then returned to Mr. Hofmann's car. Any particular reason why he didn't take the check then? Was it discussed?"

"Yes. I wanted it. I knew we were going to give money to Wilford Cardon and I was desirous of giving him cash."

Grant nodded, and Shannon Flynn stepped down.

Now Bob Stott approached the witness stand, for Donald Schmidt, former LDS Director of Libraries and Archives, was being sworn in. As Schmidt took the stand, Sergeant Michael George, balancing an archival box on his knees, removed one famous historical Mormon document after another. The documents were marked as exhibits and slowly circulated past the judge and the defense table, while onlookers craned for a glimpse.

Stott established that Mormon leaders accepted Hofmann's documents without question after he had provided affidavits regarding the provenance of his first two major acquisitions. Forensic tests had been few, but Mormon historians had checked them for contextual accuracy.

On cross-examination, Brad Rich displayed his own interest in the documents. "I love this stuff," he said to Stott at one point. But Rich wanted more details, including the information that Schmidt checked with superiors, such as President Hinckley, if a document cost more than $1,500 or might be controversial.

Rich continued his cross-examination the next morning, proceeding item by item through the church's list of forty-eight documents acquired from Hofmann. Before he finished, Dori Hofmann turned on the bench, wrinkled her nose, stuck out her tongue, and protested to the reporter behind her that she was bored. By the time Rich reached the salamander letter, even he was wearing thin.

"Yes, I've heard of it," Schmidt twinkled, evoking a chuckle. Since the church had obtained the letter from Christensen after Schmidt's retirement, Rich's questions soon trailed away.

On re-direct, Stott showed Schmidt an 1835 Mormon hymnal, compiled by Emma Smith, wife of Joseph Smith. Schmidt said he had traded it to Lyn Jacobs. At that time it was missing the last page, the table of contents on which the first title was "The Spirit of God."

"And this appears to be the book you sold to Lyn Jacobs — is that still your testimony?" Stott asked.

"Yes, it is."

Stott showed Schmidt that the missing table of contents was now present as the book's last page. "If a book was incomplete and someone printed on an end sheet to the book and sold it without telling them that the last page was the product of a modern printing, would that be proper?"

"Not in my estimation."

"What would it do to the value of the book if the fact were known?"

"It would reduce it considerably."

Stott took his seat. Already in evidence was the negative for a printing plate that prosecutors had called, "The Spirit of God." It had been ordered by Mike Hansen.

His turn now, Rich switched to a subject of particular interest to the defense. "Isn't Dean Jessee the historical department's expert on a variety of Mormon historical issues?"

"I considered Dean Jessee the person to talk to in connection with Joseph Smith and his handwriting."

Rich pressed Schmidt about Jessee's expertise regarding other early Mormon handwriting, particularly Martin Harris's. Schmidt maintained that no good samples of Harris's handwriting existed, nor did he know of any expert on Harris's handwriting.

Does anyone know more than Jessee? Rich persisted.

No, Schmidt said.

Following a break, Biggs called witnesses, who added small pieces to the emerging puzzle. First, a printing order was identified for two different sets of Deseret Currency, ordered in Denver in 1984 by Mike Hansen. The next witness identified a first edition of Jack London's novel *Call of the Wild*, recognizable by the Jack London signature and Austin Lewis personal address stamp in the front. The plates for the London signature and the Lewis personal address stamp had been ordered by Mike Hansen — who had somehow left Mark Hofmann's fingerprint on the Lewis order form.

Next, Wilford Cardon, the suntanned oil executive from Phoenix, described how Hofmann and Flynn had convinced him to invest $12,000 in a letter written by Betsy Ross. Cardon had even fronted Flynn $6,000 for his share of the $18,000 investment. (What Cardon did not know was that Hofmann and Flynn had cashed the $12,000 check the same day Cardon wrote it and took pocketsful of $100 bills with them to New York City.) Flynn had photographed the Betsy Ross letter and sent Cardon a copy. Then, Cardon said, the letter had been traded for Jim Bridger notes. Cardon had also invested $100,000 in the Charles Dickens "Haunted Man" manuscript, sending the money directly to Justin Schiller in New York.

With these successes behind him, Hofmann had approached Cardon in June 1985 and asked him to invest in the McLellin collection, apparently at President Hinckley's request.

"Mr. Hofmann told me it was important that the church not purchase the documents outright, but that they be put in the church's hands for safekeeping," Cardon explained.

Cardon had felt uneasy about the proposition, so Hofmann had called Hinckley's office, only to find that Hinckley, dedicating a temple in East Germany, could not be reached. They left the proposition at a draw—if Hinckley wanted Cardon to proceed, Hofmann said, Hinckley would call. He never did.

Cardon said he had met with Hofmann and Flynn on a business day. He guessed June 30, unaware that this was a Sunday. Investigators had placed the meeting between June 23 and June 26, just before Hofmann approached Christensen.

In September, Hofmann and Flynn had proposed that Cardon invest $250,000 in the "second Oath of a Freeman" to pay Hofmann's personal debts, but the deal had not gone through. Then Flynn's bad check had ended Cardon's involvement.

Biggs asked Cardon if he had questioned Hofmann about the McLellin collection. Cardon said yes. "I said, 'Were you able to complete the McLellin purchase?' He said, 'Yes.' I said, 'Where is it now?' He said, 'It's been deposited with the First Presidency.'"

On re-direct, Biggs asked pointedly, "Were you ever told by either Mr. Hofmann or Mr. Flynn that the Betsy Ross letter is not authentic?"

"No."

"Was there any representation that the Bridger notes are not authentic, that they had been produced very recently?"

"No."

"Would you have been involved in the sale of the Bridger notes had you known that they were not?"

"No."

"Did Mr. Hofmann ever inform you that he received $150,000 from Al Rust in April for that same McLellin collection?"

"No."

After Richard Marks, another Arizona collector, testified briefly, Rich rose and suggested that court recess. Such requests were becoming familiar. Stott said calmly that he had another witness waiting outside. Rich tried again, his frustration showing, but Grant told Stott to go ahead. With an angry shrug, Rich took his seat. Beside him, Hofmann stared straight ahead.

Stott called Glenn Rowe, the soft-spoken director of LDS libraries and archives, who enumerated the church's recent document acquisitions from Hofmann. Rich's cross-examination reiterated Rowe's testimony, after which court was dismissed. The first week of the hearing had ended.

Rich caught the prosecutors outside the courtroom. "Jesus Christ!" he said. "If you guys had this much, why didn't you tell us?"

The prosecutors laughed, as relief washed over them. These days, reporters, tagging their steps as they crossed the street to the county attorney's office, congratulated them on their case. Some even hinted at overkill.

The second week of testimony began with Alvin Rust. As soon as Rust took the stand, and each time Bob Stott stepped away to pick up an exhibit, Rust tried unsuccessfully to catch Hofmann's eye.

Rust first identified the two sets of Spanish Fork notes he had purchased from Hofmann for $2,500 and $1,500. This information dovetailed with earlier testimony about stamps Hofmann had ordered from Salt Lake Stamp Co. in 1982.

When Grant called a break, Heidi Jones, Gloria Hofmann, and Terri Christensen came in. Jones talked briefly with her sister, Katie Robertson, and her aunt, Joan Gorton, then began asking reporters who Melissa Jenkins was. Over the weekend the Sheets family had heard about Jenkins's radio broadcast describing "a messy and bitter divorce." When Jenkins returned to the courtroom, the three women confronted her.

Jenkins said she stood by her sources—a stewardess on the plane Gary and Kathy Sheets had taken home from New York and a police source. "I tried to call you," Jenkins said, nodding to Jones, "and you didn't want to talk. And I tried to call you," she pointed at Gorton, "and you weren't home."

"We were here!" Robertson exclaimed. "We were in this courtroom."

"If you wanted to know the truth about it, you could have talked to us here," Jones added.

People returning to their seats glanced curiously at the intense group by the aisle.

"Kathy would have been crying on my shoulder," Gorton insisted. "I would have been the first person she told. We're her family. We know more than any police source or some stewardess."

Grant banged his gavel, and the women took their seats but their anger was unpacified. Having Kathy's marriage publicly attacked after her murder was intolerable. The police officers guarding the hearing soon heard that Jenkins claimed a police source. They firmly denied the assertion.

Meanwhile, Rust resumed his testimony, describing his purchase of Deseret currency from Hofmann—first small denominations, then large ones. Lyn Jacobs had been involved in the deal, Rust said. Jacobs had asked him not to let Schmidt know that there were two sets, but Rust refused to keep the secret. In fact, he had felt cheated himself, he testified, because he had paid $25,000 for what he believed was the only set extant.

Hofmann listened to the description impassively. Judge Grant, watching from the bench, did not understand how anybody could rob a man like Al Rust. Rust also described the handwritten White Notes Hofmann had sold him and the church.

"Mark Hofmann came into my store and handed me these eight notes. It really shook me up. I said, 'Don't even tell me what you want for them. They're too valuable. The LDS church archives should have first choice.' "

"Did you later see any more of them?"

"He sold four of them to the church and brought the rest

back to me. I said, 'Wait until I sit down and then you whisper the price to me.' " Rust bought the notes for $12,000.

In early 1985, Rust continued, he heard from Hofmann that an important group of Mormon documents, called the McLellin collection, was coming up for sale in New York.

"He wanted to know if I was interested in helping finance it for $180,000. I didn't have that kind of money, but I said if it does come up, come in and we'll talk about it. In April he came in again. My son was there. Mark indicated to me that the McLellin collection was for sale and was going to be sold for $180,000. He described it as twenty times more important than anything we had ever purchased before."

Stott asked if the McLellin collection was supposed to be controversial or anti-Mormon. Rust said no. Hofmann had told him the collection was extensive, containing around twenty important items. Rust agreed to put up $150,000 and Hofmann $30,000.

"Did he ever inform you that there was anyone else involved in this transaction?"

No, Rust said. "I understood that he and I were to purchase the collection. My son, Gaylen, was to travel with him. The twenty items that were of extensive value would be carried back in briefcases, and the rest mailed back to my store to be sold from my store at a future date. I said, 'I don't have this kind of money. I'll have to finance it through my line of credit with the bank.' Mark said there would be no problem getting the original amount of money back within thirty days."

"Was there any discussion of who the items would be sold to?"

"I didn't ever question Mark. I knew he had a lot of contacts. He indicated the church would be interested."

"Would you have entered into this agreement if you hadn't made the special conditions?"

"No."

"Was an important item in your negotiations the fact of the quick turnover of these items?"

Rust chuckled. "Yes, it was. I was paying interest on the money." Rust described how Hofmann had left on Tuesday, April 23, 1985, with a cashier's check for $150,000 in hand. He and Gaylen Rust went to New York, but returned empty handed except for some shipping receipts. After some delay, Hofmann called Rust and said he had sold the McLellin collection to the LDS church for $300,000. The deal was confidential, he told Rust, "Gordon B. Hinckley being the agent he was dealing with." Rust continued, "He stressed emphatically that I couldn't tell a soul and that no one was supposed to know about the transaction."

"Did he explain why it had to be kept secret?"

"He said the church wanted time to examine the collection before they were bombarded by inquiries."

After many evasions and delays, Rust testified, Hofmann gave him a check for $132,100, the amount due following an earlier payment. The check bounced. Rust, fed up at last, had turned it over to a collection agency.

On Friday, September 13, he continued, Hofmann had burst into his booth at a coin show at the Salt Palace. "Mark came running to my table and indicated that it was urgent that he talk to me. He was very distraught. I've never seen him like that. He was desperate. I followed him out and left my son at the table. He said, 'I'm losing everything. I'm losing my home. I'm losing my car.'" Hofmann described his problems with his First Interstate Bank loan, and Rust agreed to help him raise some money, but had no success.

Rust, who admitted he had regarded Hofmann as a son, testified with the sadness of a disappointed father. It was clear that despite Hofmann's debts and apparent duplicity, even despite the evidence the police had shared with him, Rust had not given up on Hofmann. As Rich gathered his papers to cross-examine, Rust tried again to catch Hofmann's eye.

Rich began with Rust and Hofmann's early transactions. "And you did quite well, did you not? You were paid and profited."

"Yes, I generally made money." Rust said their deals were done on a handshake without contracts, and he kept a running total in his books.

Rich then traced Rust's testimony, extracting the further information that Rust had filed suit against Hofmann.

On re-direct, Stott had two remaining questions. When

had the $150,000 cashier's check for the McLellin collection been cashed? The same day it was issued, Rust said, it was cashed in Salt Lake City.

And had Hofmann made a large payment on his account after that time? Stott wondered.

Yes, Rust said. Hofmann had paid $165,000 on his running total on June 28, 1985. However, only $17,000 had applied to the McLellin loan.

For a moment the courtroom sat stunned. June 28, 1985, was the same day Hofmann had received $185,000 from First Interstate Bank. Obviously, that money, intended to buy the McLellin collection in Texas, had not left town.

On cue, Elder Hugh Pinnock entered the courtroom. Pinnock, in a blue suit, white shirt, and blue tie with a red stripe, beamed, then approached the clerk and raised his arm to the square. His smile seemed out of place. Mac and Joan Christensen quietly took their seats behind the prosecutors' table. Terri Christensen, looking drawn and ashen, joined them. Bill Hofmann, across the aisle, seemed depressed. Quickly, the other seats filled. The only general authority to testify, Pinnock would do so before a full house.

Prompted by Stott's questions, Pinnock outlined his meeting with Christensen and Hofmann on June 28 and told how he had obtained permission from Oaks to arrange a bank loan for Hofmann to purchase the McLellin collection in Texas. On July 12, he said, Hofmann had brought him a photocopy of a land deed signed by Solomon Spaulding and Sidney Rigdon. The next development, Pinnock said, was when the loan came due but was not paid. The bank contacted him, and he enlisted Christensen's help.

Pinnock described the October 3 meeting at his home, during which they restructured the McLellin deal, drawing in Pinnock's friend, David Sorenson, as buyer. That arrangement, too, had been approved by Oaks, Pinnock said.

"Did you ever obtain anything besides this one document from the McLellin collection?" Stott asked.

"No."

"Does any authority in the LDS church even possess the McLellin collection?"

"No."

After Pinnock described his own repayment of the bank loan, Grant called a break.

Returning to Pinnock, Stott summarized the McLellin transaction. Sorenson would pay $185,000, Pinnock said, which would pay the bank loan. Hofmann had said there was an "unsigned agreement" that he could sell his interest in the Oath for $150,000 to repay Rust. Rust would relinquish the McLellin collection, and Hofmann would receive the few thousand dollars left over, Pinnock explained.

Stott established that Pinnock had been unaware of other outstanding debts Hofmann had at the time, then sat down.

Rich politely delved for details. Unlike the minutiae of document acquisition, the questioning of a general authority interested the entire courtroom.

After reviewing the primary dates Pinnock had mentioned, Rich asked, "Was it your obligation, the acquisition of historic documents for the church?"

"No, absolutely not."

"Why were they approaching you?"

"Mr. Hofmann was going to donate a substantial collection to the church. I was seeing him as a friend of Mr. Christensen's."

Rich established that Pinnock had met with Christensen nine or ten times, and with Hofmann, alone, five or six times. He then asked about Pinnock's persuasiveness with First Interstate officials regarding the bank loan.

"I repeated that which I had been told. I believed it was secure."

"Did you suggest to them that they get a security interest?"

"No," Pinnock chuckled. "I didn't talk about those sort of details with the bank."

"You had been told President Hinckley had already been approached. Did you ask him?"

"No. He was in Europe."

"Did you have a discussion with President Hinckley about this subject?" Rich asked.

"Yes," Pinnock said, keeping his answers brief and his smile intact. From the audience, his church attorney smiled back.

"At what point was that?"

"The latter part of August when Mr. Hofmann was going to donate that collection."

Rich pressed for further details about Hinckley's awareness and involvement.

"Did he exhibit an awareness of what the collection was?"

"Yes."

"Did he indicate a desire to have the church become the owner of that collection?"

"Yes."

"So you understood you were authorized to negotiate . . . "

No, Pinnock said. "There were no negotiations."

"In the loosest possible sense," Rich tried again, "that is to say you could continue to facilitate the receipt of these documents?"

Pinnock looked uncomfortable. "Well, I guess in the loosest sense that would be correct."

After establishing that Hinckley had approved the transaction, Rich questioned how well informed Hinckley had been as the deal progressed. Pinnock said he had spoken with Hinckley on October 7th or 8th about both the McLellin deal and the investiture of a new president at Westminster College. He said he had discussed it with Hinckley again "on at least one other occasion," and kept Oaks informed. "It was part of the laundry list." However, other general authorities were unaware of the transaction, he said.

Next, Rich established that the information that traveled up from Pinnock to Oaks and Hinckley did not necessarily travel down the same route. Pinnock testified that he had not known about Rust's letter to Hinckley until the church press conference after the bombings, when Hinckley had described the letter to reporters.

"Did you give Mr. Christensen a blessing of some sort?" Rich asked suddenly, after establishing the chain of command. Rumors had indicated that Christensen had, in fact, been "called" as the lowest link of that chain and, perhaps, in regards to other document deals.

"Oh, no. In August or September we talked on a number of occasions. And we're often called to give blessings. During that time we talked about what his occupation would be. He was concerned about his past business difficulties. I would suspect that during that time I gave him a blessing."

"You suspect that?" Had Pinnock turned his no into a yes?

"Yes, that he would work through his business difficulties. I do that often."

On re-direct, Stott emphasized that Pinnock had reported to Oaks and Oaks to Hinckley regarding the McLellin deal, then asked about the security of the McLellin collection. Pinnock said that no photographs were to be taken, nor were any parts to be sold separately.

Not accidentally, Sergeant Richard Forbes replaced Pinnock on the stand and identified the papyrus fragment Christensen had locked up. Prosecutors would establish that the papyrus had been offered for sale. But only note-takers caught the coincidence that on the same day that papyrus was placed in a safe deposit box, October 7, Mike Hansen purchased Radio Shack items like those used in the bombs.

At the end of the day, in the tense and subdued courtroom, Ron Yengich half-pleaded, half-demanded that Judge Grant allow more time between sessions. Across the aisle, prosecutors and investigators were not sympathetic. Grant heard Yengich out, then decided, "We'll see you at 8:30 in the morning."

Leaving the courtroom, Randy Rigby and Joe Robertson took their unanswered questions with them, along with their frustration. Why hadn't Stott asked Pinnock why Steve had believed he had a future procuring documents for the church? What exactly had Pinnock said in the blessing he "suspected" he had given Steve about his future occupation? Had Steve and Hugh Pinnock really believed that the papyrus fragment was Facsimile 2? Why hadn't Stott asked that? And what about Pinnock's calls to the Christensen home? What about all the meetings Steve—who'd always been so businesslike—had cancelled or postponed, saying he had to meet with Hinckley, or with Oaks and Pinnock?

"Why didn't they ask the good stuff?" Robertson asked. Rigby could only shake his head. That, too, was an unanswered question.

The Spaulding/Rigdon land deed was entered into evidence the next morning as Steve Barnett, rare books manager at the Cosmic Aeroplane bookstore, testified. Hofmann had shown the deed to him in September, he said, and Barnett had recognized the significance of Spaulding's and Rigdon's names appearing together. However, Barnett had found that Spaulding had died by the time the deed was signed and had purchased it at a reduced price for the Rigdon signature.

Kenneth Rendell, the Boston art and document dealer who had earlier threatened to lead a delegation of witnesses in Hofmann's behalf, appeared next for the prosecution somewhat chastened, as the hearing shifted from fraud to forgery. Brad Rich protested he had not known Rendell was scheduled for that morning. Grant answered that Rich could retrieve his notes during a break and ordered that the testimony proceed.

Ignoring the frayed tempers at the defense table, Gerry D'Elia began asking about the salamander letter, which, Rendell said, Hofmann had asked him to authenticate in November 1983. Rendell was not interested at the time. However, in April, Rendell was again approached by Hofmann, who said the letter had been sold and would generate a lot of publicity. Rendell agreed to authenticate the letter.

"What were you going to do when you received that letter for the authentication of the document?"

"Basically, I considered about a half a dozen factors: the history of the letter or the provenance — it came from Lyn Jacobs, who found it at a stampless cover dealer. Mark was a person I had known for five years and a person that I had every reason to believe was reputable and honest. I would normally consider making a comparison of the handwriting, and in this case it just wasn't possible. There was no general handwriting known of Martin Harris."

Rendell described the paper and ink tests he subcontracted to other experts, then his own comparison of the signature with other Harris signatures. He examined the letter under ultraviolet light for erasures or anomalies. At that time, he said, he could find no evidence of forgery and knew of no reason to question its authenticity.

D'Elia asked if he had since viewed the salamander letter in company with other documents. Rendell said he had when D'Elia brought a dozen or so documents to his Boston office and again in Salt Lake City.

"During the course of examination, both last night and six weeks ago, what did you look for and what did you observe in the other documents?"

"All of them had strong indications of being forged just on a strictly handwriting basis. They had a drawn appearance. They had slow, hesitating strokes, there was re-writing and so on. All of the standard type of things that I would look for. They fluoresced a very bright blue and you could see that a chemical of some type had been put on the paper. I'd never seen anything like it before. There were marks from clips, so the documents had been dipped or painted. In one case, there was a document which was perfectly genuine. There were three lines on the back which were very questionable, and only those three lines had been covered with the chemical. There was no question in my mind that there was probable reason to believe that these documents were not genuine."

D'Elia asked his current opinion on the salamander letter. Rendell answered that the way the letter was folded had never made sense. "But as one point, it was not all that significant. I think the bottom line is that I found no evidence of forgery and no reason to believe it would be a forgery. I still find no evidence of forgery in terms of handwriting, but the provenance has changed and the circumstances. This letter is associated with a number of pieces that appear to be forgeries." He added that ink problems would tip the scales significantly.

Next, D'Elia wanted to know about the two papyri Rendell had consigned to Mark Hofmann in September. "How does that ethically figure in?" D'Elia asked.

"Ethically, it's not the right thing to do. Commercially, the value of the parts is not worth the total. If you cut it up, you lose a lot of money." The papyri, Rendell continued, had come from an English collection that had nothing to do with Joseph Smith or the McLellin collection.

D'Elia's questions also drew out the information that Rendell had spoken with Hofmann late in September and told him he intended to come to Utah and visit with Brent Ashworth (who had been offered the papyrus fragment) and others, perhaps even Christensen, with whom he had corresponded.

D'Elia brought Rendell back to the salamander letter and gave him another chance to call it a forgery. "Would you say there is a probability or a possibility it is forged?"

"Commercially, I would not buy or sell this letter. There is not sufficient evidence that it's genuine. Still, there's no hard evidence it's not genuine. If there's a relationship, it's in the ink. I'd defer to Al Lyter. He did the ink analysis." Despite the odd folds, Rendell said he could find no evidence of forgery.

Obviously dissatisfied, D'Elia let the matter drop.

On cross-examination, Rich began with Rendell's background, which included studies at Boston University but no degree.

"So you are essentially self-taught."

"There is no formal training in historical documents."

"But the various components are amenable to formal study, are they not? Do you have any background in chemistry?"

"No."

"Inks?"

"No expertise."

Rich went down the list of various types of forensic training, none of which Rendell had. Like Dean Jessee, Rendell's expertise came from familiarity rather than scientific training.

Under Rich's questioning, Rendell described his study of the salamander letter handwriting, which showed no signs of forgery.

"In fact," Rich suggested, "it would be very difficult for someone to draft a document with that kind of perfection."

"I believe it would be very difficult."

Rich moved on to the papyrus. Rendell had some experience with buying and selling papyrus and a passing knowledge of Egyptian history.

"You have some background in Mormon history?"

"Yes, a moderate amount. I've seen perhaps twenty-five Joseph Smith documents, seventy-five Brigham Youngs." He said he collected Mormon documents and knew the church said that the Book of Mormon came from golden plates.

"Have you ever seen Facsimile 1 and 2?"

"No."

"And you don't have any knowledge of any Mormon connection with Egyptian documents?"

"I have a vague knowledge but nothing specific. When all of this came out I was told about the Mormons being in Egypt. I pretend to have no knowledge at all of Mormon history prior to Joseph Smith."

Since the Mormon church was founded in 1830, Rendell's comment about Mormons in Egypt was confusing. "Well, there's very little Mormon history prior to Joseph Smith," Rich quipped. Everyone in the courtroom laughed, as Rendell looked bewildered.

The papyri, Rendell continued, were both drawn by the same craftsman or scribe. He considered them a little gaudy.

"How was the fragment removed?"

"It looks as if it was broken off to get a ragged edge. I don't believe it was with a sharp instrument."

Rich inquired about his contacts with investigators, finding particularly interesting the fact that one long conversation with Farnsworth and D'Elia in Boston had been taped. Evidently the defense had not received a copy. Rendell said D'Elia had shown him a series of documents, including those named in the charges, and he had examined them one by one.

Though Rendell protested he was not an expert witness on the documents, Rich wanted to know what he thought was wrong with them. The Lucy Mack Smith letter had something funny about the paper and ink, he said, but he could find nothing specifically inconsistent. The Anthon transcript was unusual. There was something strange about the paper. He had put it under ultraviolet, and it had fluoresced a bright blue. Also, he saw something unusual about the ink. He said he had told them to take it to Al Lyter.

On the Joseph Smith to Isaac Galland promissory note (not named in the charges), a chemical had been applied to the paper only in the areas written by Joseph Smith. The signature had been added and the date written over another date. On the Spaulding contract, the date had been altered. On the Grandin Book of Mormon contract, Joseph Smith's signature was too shaky. On the Stowell letter, there was a little unusual blotting. The Joseph Smith III blessing "didn't look to me like 1844."

"The Betsy Ross letter?"

"I had just worked with a Betsy Ross document. The hand-writing didn't hit me as being the same at all. Also, I said that the postmark should be pursued because it appears to be a much later postmark."

"Obviously, the salamander letter was keeping very bad company," Rich said, "but had your opinion changed in any fashion?"

"Not at all. I found no relationship in the handwriting or the way it fluoresced."

On re-direct, D'Elia emphasized that neither he nor Forbes had mentioned forgery or provenance. They had simply shown him the documents.

"I was very, very surprised when you showed me that material," Rendell offered.

D'Elia asked if Rendell was in any way employed by the CAO.

"No."

"Are you being paid anything?"

"No."

D'Elia asked him to fold a blank cover letter properly, so it could be sealed and mailed as a nineteenth-century letter. Rendell demonstrated. D'Elia asked whether the process of deacidification could account for the blue fluorescing Rendell saw under ultraviolet light. Rendell said it could not.

Stott then called Curt Bench, manager of the rare books department at Deseret Book. Bench and Hofmann exchanged smiles, but Bench's voice seemed burdened. D'Elia, who nick-named almost everyone, called Bench "the man with a halo." Indeed, Bench struck people on both sides of the aisle as cred-ible.

Bench described selling the Nathan Harris prayer book to

Hofmann, who returned to pay more money because of the Martin Harris handwriting in the back. He told how Hofmann had visited Deseret Book twice on Friday, September 13, desperately seeking a loan. Then Stott asked about the papyrus fragment Hofmann had offered Bench.

"I asked him if it was from the McLellin collection and he said it was," Bench said.

"Did you tell Mr. Steven Christensen about this attempted papyrus transaction?"

"I did." Although Hofmann had made him promise to keep the papyrus quiet, Bench said, he'd decided to tell Christensen about it after learning that Christensen had some serious concerns regarding Hofmann. Later, Hofmann had asked Bench how Christensen had found out he had offered the McLellin papyrus.

The courtroom was utterly silent as Bench continued. On September 24, Christensen had phoned him at home, Bench said soberly, and told him that church leaders wanted Christensen to find Hofmann. Christensen was asking Bench for help.

"Steve told me that various things could occur if Mark didn't make good," Bench explained. "Some of them were: he would certainly lose his credibility and credit with the church and with President Hinckley; that criminal action could be taken and he could conceivably go to jail; he could also be sued by the bank or even by the church if the church was sued. He could lose his membership in the church."

Bench passed all this on to Hofmann, who "was surprisingly calm, but Mark is usually that way."

On cross-examination, Rich wanted to hear more about the Nathan Harris prayer book. "Are you certain about the provenance of the Harris volume?"

"Quite certain."

"It had been in the safe at Deseret Book for at least a dozen years when it resurfaced?"

"Yes."

"Do you know where it had been before that?"

"It had come through the Harris line, that's documented. Deseret Book bought it in 1973. A corporate officer pulled it out and showed it to me." The book itself, Bench said, was not special, but he was interested in the Nathan Harris insignia.

"You discovered that on the front inside."

"Yes, that's correct. I believe that I remember some writing in the back. I can't say what was there."

"Did you point it out to Mark?"

"No, I don't believe that I did."

"At any rate, he agreed to buy the volume for $50."

"That's correct."

"So by September 11th, Mark indicated to you that he had found the handwriting in the back as well and had sold it for around $2,000?"

Bench said they had agreed on $1,000 in trade since the book was worth more than originally thought.

"Would you have been offended if he'd been able to sell it for that much profit?"

"Probably. I wouldn't have approved of that."

"But he did it of his own volition. And this was approximately a lapse of five days or less."

Bench agreed.

"You never told him of your independent discovery of these writings in the rear of the book?" Rich suggested.

Stott objected. "That wasn't his testimony."

"He may answer," Grant said.

"That's correct," Bench let it pass.

Rich moved to Christensen's call to Bench. "And did Mr. Christensen appear to be acting as a friend, or did it appear malicious?"

"I believe he wanted to help Mark. He called me as a friend and someone who could contact him."

"And Mark dealt with you matter-of-factly, not frightened or out of control. He didn't indicate to you any animosity toward Mr. Christensen. In fact, it didn't appear to arouse his ire at all." In fact, Rich continued, by September 24 Christensen was urging Bench to "light a fire under Mark." Was the threat of consequences coming from Christensen or from someone else?

"He said there was a member of the Seventies who was chairman of a bank, and an apostle," Bench said.

On re-direct, Stott established that reputation was vital to a document dealer. Bench then stepped down.

During the break that followed, Rich told Bill Hofmann he felt they had had a good day thus far. Rendell had not called the salamander letter a forgery (though he had trashed the other documents), and Rich felt that Bench had been fair.

Before he testified, Lyn Jacobs, who had been Hofmann's partner in many deals, confronted Mark at home. Jacobs had been confronted repeatedly by the investigators and the barrage of facts and figures had finally had an effect. "If you're guilty, Mark," he said, "there's nothing I can do for you."

Hofmann looked at him blankly. "Lyn, just tell the truth."

"Oh, I will," Jacobs promised.

Jacobs, slender, bearded, and dressed in a black shirt, black tie, black slacks, and a black and gray jacket, was a striking contrast to previous witnesses. As controversy had swirled around Hofmann, much of it had included Jacobs. Outspoken yet elusive, Jacobs had long claimed to be Hofmann's best friend. The proceeds of their various deals had helped to support his graduate studies at Harvard. As police began investigating him, Jacobs, like Shannon Flynn, had hired attorney Jim Barber. Late in the investigation, Jacobs's obvious dislike for the police had given way to a high regard for investigators Mike George and Dick Forbes. They had done their best to turn Jacobs around and felt they had succeeded far better than with Flynn.

In fact, Jacobs had recently given a lengthy interview to *Sunstone* magazine. Again, he had defended Hofmann but changed his own story about finding the salamander letter. Now, Jacobs admitted, Hofmann had actually found the letter.

Stott began by asking Jacobs if he and Hofmann were close friends.

"I would say very close."

"And do you still consider yourself a close friend of Mr. Hofmann's?"

"I certainly do."

Stott moved on to the question of provenance. Jacobs explained that Hofmann had suggested that he hunt down dealers while on the east coast to see what they had but that he had been too busy with his studies to follow through on Hofmann's request. Instead, he sent a list of dealers' names to Hofmann. In November 1983, Hofmann called.

"Mark mentioned that the idea had been successful. He had picked something up from one dealer I had told him about. Then he read to me the Martin Harris letter." Jacobs explained that Hofmann gave him a share in the letter as a reward for sending the tips, so they both owned it jointly.

"Did he explain to you what he paid for it?"

"I think he mentioned $15 or $20." Jacobs said he saw the letter when he came home about December 16th. "I think it was at my house. We got together almost immediately."

Stott asked Jacobs to identify exhibit 116, the salamander letter, then asked how they had offered the letter to the Mormon church.

"Mark asked me to take full responsibility because he did not want the publicity. It was based on his understanding of my partial ownership of it. It was my part to present the letter, and he turned it over to me. He said, 'It's now 100 percent yours, do with it as you wish.' I said, 'Fine, now tell me what you think I should do.' "

Jacobs next told how he had taken the letter to Don Schmidt and to G. Homer Durham. "We all knew it had to be presented to President Hinckley." Jacobs met with Hinckley but only discussed the letter generally.

Hinckley had asked Jacobs what he wanted for the letter.

"One of the gold coins," he answered.

"Do you know the value of that, money-wise?" Stott wondered.

"Oh, $60,000 to over $100,000."

"So you were starting out pretty good," Stott remarked, cracking a rare courtroom smile.

Jacobs basked a moment. "Well, why not? He thought it was a little high, so I asked for a Book of Commandments, worth $30,000-$40,000. He said he wasn't sure he wanted to buy it."

When Hinckley turned down the letter, they offered it to Brent Ashworth, who also declined, and finally to Steve Christensen, who accepted.

"At this time you were still maintaining it was your document."

"Well, it was. He'd given it to me."

At CFS, Jacobs said, they were met by Brent Metcalfe. "I had known Brent for years."

Stott asked if Hofmann and Metcalfe were friends.

"I assume they weren't enemies."

"Do you know whether or not they were friends?" Stott repeated.

"I don't know. Mark has many acquaintances. I wouldn't say they were *dear* friends."

"Did you receive your so-called share of $5,000?"

Yes, Jacobs said, and he had used it to help pay for schooling.

Stott asked whether Jacobs had later told people that he had located the letter?

"Unfortunately, that is correct."

"And you were doing this under Mr. Hofmann's instructions?"

"Not on Mark's instructions, but at his request — not that I fabricate the story, just that I take full responsibility for the document. It was my decision to fabricate the story several months later."

Stott asked about the Emma Smith hymnal Brent Ashworth had bought from Hofmann as part of the McLellin collection, a book Don Schmidt said he had traded to Jacobs.

Jacobs said he had photocopied and inserted the last page to complete the book but removed it after Hofmann said he had found a genuine page.

"Did Mark Hofmann tell you at that time or any other time that it was the result of a modern printing?"

"He certainly did not."

"Did he tell you he had had a plate made?"

"I never heard of such a thing."

As Stott moved on to Deseret currency, Jacobs kept his eyes on Hofmann. "I was never involved with obtaining it. I was sometimes involved in selling it. I took some to the church on Mark's behalf."

"Didn't you have a source back east? A little old woman?"

"That is not correct. Mark had a source."

"You had nothing to do with the acquisition?"

"I did not. I just know what he told me about it."

Stott was hitting Jacobs with the deals that tended to implicate him with Hofmann, but Jacobs was placing responsibility squarely on Hofmann. Yengich and Barber consulted, and Barber warned him not to push Jacobs.

"I suppose you're familiar with a document termed the 'Oath of a Freeman'?" Stott persisted.

Jacobs denied ever having seen the second Oath or receiving any money for it. With that, court ended for the day.

The next day, Wednesday, April 23, court was delayed. Finally, Judge Grant arrived and explained that Hofmann had fallen and hurt the knee he had injured in the bombing. Yengich stressed that there was no indication of deliberate injury, but moved for a recess. Stott did not object, despite the inconvenience of rescheduling witnesses. Grant announced that the hearing would reconvene on Monday, May 5.

Reports on Hofmann's injury varied in tone and content. Some said Hofmann had slipped on the stairs in his home or in his bathroom. One newspaper reported that he had tried to take his first steps unaided by crutches and his leg was not strong enough. No one said so directly, but the raised eyebrows and knowing smiles in the courtroom suggested that maybe Hofmann had found a way to give the defense more time.

17

A QUESTION OF INK

Ironically, Mark Hofmann's injury and the resulting delay in the preliminary hearings gave prosecutors more time to continue their investigation. The "Oath of a Freeman" had figured in the McLellin deal and was the most prominent Americana document in the fraud charges. More than any other document, it promoted Hofmann's national image as a successful document discoverer.

During the preliminary hearing, a reporter had handed Bob Stott a photocopied page from the July 1984 issue of the *Freemen Digest*, published by the ultra-conservative Freemen Institute. In it was a facsimile of the "Oath of a Freeman." This Oath differed only slightly from the document Hofmann said he had found at Argosy Books in New York City in March 1985.

On April 25, 1987, County Attorney Ted Cannon and one of the investigators visited *Freemen Digest* headquarters in Salt Lake City and asked for its publisher. He was not in, but an assistant told them that the *Freemen Digest* was sent monthly to subscribers and that Bill Hofmann was on the mailing list. When they then asked about Mark Hofmann, the assistant became uncooperative. Cannon promised a subpoena (never served), and the two men left.

A printer before going to law school, Cannon next had a printing plate made from a photographic negative of the Oath and brought several hand presses to the office. He invited prosecutors and investigators to a printing demonstration and ran off scores of Oaths for the interested and amused audience.

Another piece of information delighted investigators. As George Throckmorton and Bill Flynn completed their study of the Hofmann documents, they had told Ken Farnsworth and Jim Bell, "If you can find a calligrapher, we've got it all wrapped up."

Initially police had looked hard at Lyn Jacobs as a possible calligrapher. However, they could find no proof of criminal intent on Jacobs's part. Again and again, the evidence led directly to Hofmann. The investigators' discoveries of printing plates ordered by a Mike Hansen who paid with Hofmann's personal check, gave Hofmann's telephone number, *and* wore Hofmann's fingerprint had considerably narrowed their conclusions. Still, the skill evident in the best of the handwritten documents nagged at them.

When a county deputy told Farnsworth about a telephone call from a woman who said she had taught calligraphy to Hofmann, Farnsworth was elated. He returned the call to Darlene Sanchez.

Sanchez had been sure from the first that police had arrested the wrong man and had not contacted authorities until newspaper reports of the preliminary hearing made her increasingly uneasy. She had known Mark and Doralee Hofmann in 1981-82 when they lived across the street from her in Sandy. They were active in her ward, and she had a clear memory of Mark helping a neighbor move during a rainstorm.

During the summer of 1981, Sanchez told Farnsworth, Doralee Hofmann had signed up for a ward Relief Society "mini-class" in calligraphy. Later, Sanchez taught another course in a community school program, and both Hofmanns enrolled. At the first class meeting, Sanchez invited each student to explain why he or she was interested in calligraphy. Doralee, she remembered, said she wanted to improve her poster-making skills. Mark said he worked with manuscripts and thought these skills would prove helpful.

Sanchez taught the "basic italic" handwriting format. She gave the class an assignment and was astonished when Hofmann brought in a number of beautifully written alphabets, some of which she had never seen before.

"Mark, are these rub-on letters or real?" she had asked.

"No, I wrote them," he had answered.

"I couldn't have taught him much," she told Farnsworth. She had, however, taught him to read the slants in handwriting and how to write fluidly, without hesitating. "If you are able to see and understand the slants in handwriting, you can then reproduce it."

Farnsworth recalled Ken Rendell's testimony and decided that Sanchez would be a useful witness when the case came to trial.

Meanwhile, Throckmorton was still examining documents. He had planned to go to the University of California at Davis to visit the cyclotron examiners who were testing the first "Oath of a Freeman." Instead, he spoke at length by telephone with the examiner who had found the paper and ink to be consistent with other seventeenth-century documents. Throckmorton told the examiner about the photographic negative they had seized and the forgery evidence in the case. Although Schiller and Wapner would view the test as further proof of authentication, the cyclotron examiners decided not to comment publicly. Like the FBI exam of the salamander letter, the cyclotron test was more likely to help the defense than the prosecution. Both tests only looked at consistency of the paper and ink, not artificial aging.

On May 2, 1986, three days before the hearing recommenced, Brent and Charlene Ashworth's son Samuel, badly injured on his bicycle soon after the bombings, died suddenly in his sleep. Sammy had come home from the hospital in January, still paralyzed but with the nerves that controlled basic functions intact. He was growing fast, eating well, and responding to simple instructions. The Ashworths counted themselves lucky. Then, without any sign of infection or asphyxiation (two of the Ashworths' main fears), Sammy died, asleep beside his brother.

"We lost him twice," the heartbroken parents told friends. "First we lost our little boy and then we lost the second Sam we also learned to love." Brent Ashworth, convinced he had been the third bomb target, blamed Hofmann and himself for Sammy's death.

On May 5, the "regulars" gathered on the fifth floor of the circuit court like weary runners in a marathon. Journalists, like David Hewitt of the *Maine Antique Digest*, were still in suspense. Others, less interested in documents, waited only for Judge Grant's decision as to which counts would stick. Few doubted that Hofmann would be bound over, but many questioned whether a trial would be held. Rumors of a plea bargain proliferated. Only a few supporters outside Hofmann's family defended his innocence, and they hinted darkly at a police-church conspiracy to convict him.

This time Hofmann entered court in a wheelchair, pale and withdrawn. His father parked the chair beside the defense table since it did not fit behind. After a day or two, Bill Hofmann would rearrange the table and wheelchair to move his son closer to his attorneys.

"Hi, Mark," Ron Yengich said, breezing past the table that Monday morning, "how's the leg?"

"Okay," Hofmann shrugged.

"Good," he returned, preoccupied with other, more pressing concerns.

As the proceedings recommenced, Bob Stott first called Gaylen Rust, Al Rust's son and manager of Rust's Coin Shop, who described his fruitless trip to New York with Mark Hofmann to purchase the McLellin collection. Next, Wade Lillywhite from Deseret Book echoed parts of Curt Bench's earlier testimony regarding Hofmann's distraught frame of mind around September 13.

Lillywhite, however, also described helping Hofmann assemble collateral for a loan—a piece of papyrus, Mormon money, and some items provided by investor Tom Wilding. But the loan was never made.

Little emerged on cross-examination, but on re-direct, Stott established that Lillywhite, like Bench, had told Steve Christensen that Hofmann had shown him a papyrus fragment from the McLellin collection. The day before the bombings,

Lillywhite testified, Hofmann had offered to sell him Facsimile 3.

Next, a stockbroker described meeting with Christensen early on the morning of October 10. He identified Mark Hofmann as the man who had unexpectedly interrupted their meeting. While waiting for Christensen to return, he heard Christensen suddenly shout, "You can't hide that!" Five minutes later, both men returned, and Hofmann left.

Yengich cross-examined for detail. Hofmann did not have a moustache, the broker said, nor had he been wearing glasses.

Dave Biggs recalled one of the printers. Reporters whispered that this would have something to do with the as-yet undiscussed Oath. Their hunches were confirmed as the printer for DeBouzek Engraving identified a photographic negative and a receipt for the "Oath of a Freeman" ordered by a Mike Harris on March 8, 1985. Mike Harris had given Mark Hofmann's unlisted phone number. On March 25, Mike Hansen had ordered another plate of the Oath—this one with a different text and border.

In the tense courtroom, Brad Rich, on cross-examination, asked about the original artwork used to produce the negative. The artwork would have to be of good quality, the printer said. The murmur in the audience indicated that David Hewitt and others still hoped that the first Oath was genuine and had only been used to make the negative for the second Oath.

"Do you remember what Mike Harris or Mike Hansen looked like?" Rich asked.

"No. I don't."

Jim Bell was next called to identify several key pieces of evidence. First, the Argosy Bookstore receipt for the purchase of the "Oath of a Free Man" for $25, dated March 13, 1985, which was found in Hofmann's van. He also identified a Waldenbooks receipt for 50 cents for a purchase made at 2:30 p.m. on October 16, 1985, about ten minutes before Hofmann was injured. The receipt had been found among Hofmann's papers in the street. Biggs asked if Bell had timed the walk from the bookstore in Crossroads Mall to the 200 North bombing site. Bell said he had made the walk in seven to eight minutes.

Bell also identified a copy of Charles Hamilton's *Great Forgeries and Famous Fakes*, which had been removed from Hofmann's house, a 1982 snow tire receipt signed by Mike Hansen, and the Betsy Ross letter, also taken from Hofmann's house. Biggs added for the record that the letter contained anachronisms — the name of the postmaster and date on the letter were both wrong.

The next morning, Biggs called Thomas R. Wilding to the stand. Wilding's name had been mentioned, but his story proved to be the most dramatic during the five-week hearing. An investment advisor for Summit Financial, Wilding had attended Utah State University, where he had met Hofmann soon after the Anthon transcript had been discovered. In fact, Wilding had sold the Hofmanns their maternity insurance.

Their friendship had been renewed early in 1985, Wilding related, when Hofmann convinced him to organize a private group of investors to buy Americana collectibles. On March 21, Wilding and his co-investors gave Hofmann $22,500 to purchase rare books. Hofmann promised them a 50 to 100 percent return within six months. Hofmann reported success, Wilding testified, including a 100 percent profit on the deal.

"Did he give it to you?" Biggs asked.

"No." Instead, Hofmann gave Wilding his investment plus a 50 percent gain, then put the remaining 50 percent into another investment on April 15. Wilding then raised additional funds for the Charles Dickens "The Haunted Man" manuscript and gave them to Hofmann on May 9. This manuscript was to be purchased for $310,000, Hofmann told Wilding, through Justin Schiller. Wilding called Schiller, who assured him the manuscript was genuine. Hofmann, Wilding, Schiller, and Wilding's brother-in-law Sidney Jensen were all investors.

"Did the defendant indicate that he had approached Wilford Cardon about the Haunted Man investment?"

"No. Not while I was there."

"Were you ever told that Cardon was another substantial investor?"

"I was told that Mr. Hofmann would provide the difference."

Most in the room did not know that Hofmann's checks to

repay Gene Taylor had coincided precisely with Wilding's investments. Since Taylor was not scheduled to testify, Biggs introduced a financial chart into evidence to give the judge a glimpse
of the money flow. The Wilding group's $160,000 had quickly
dispersed. Hofmann added to the collateral he had left with
Wilding's group and kept them informed of developments
throughout the summer.

Wilding then testified that on August 1, Hofmann had
approached him about a Brigham Young collection being auctioned in New York for $20,000. Wilding's investors were excited
by Hofmann's successes and raised $22,600 for Hofmann to
bid at the auction. Again Hofmann gave his personal guarantee and collateral, and Wilding kept careful records. In mid-
September, they were told the Dickens manuscript had sold at
a 66 percent profit and that they could expect their money by
October 16.

Early in September, Hofmann told Wilding that the
Brigham Young papers had netted them a profit of 42 percent
and offered them a chance to invest in his best find so far — the
"Oath of a Freeman." One copy had sold to the Library of
Congress for over $1 million, Wilding said Hofmann had told
him. A second copy had to be worth at least $1.5 million.

Biggs ignored the whispers in the audience and asked,
"Where did he get the first Oath?"

"He found it in a bookstore in New York."

"Where was he going to get the second Oath?"

"From a book dealer in Boston by the name of Lyn Jacobs,"
who would let it go for $500,000, Hofmann had said. An audi-
ble groan rose from the audience.

Biggs wondered why, if it was worth over $1 million, would
Jacobs sell it for $500,000?

"Mark said [Jacobs] had owned it for a year and had seen
enough gain that he would let it go."

Wilding and Jensen had wanted to call Schiller. Hofmann
had agreed but seemed concerned that Schiller not know there
was a second Oath.

"What did he say or do?"

"He said to talk to Schiller about the Oath as a document."
They could discuss it in generic terms, Wilding explained, but
should not mention that a second Oath was being sold.

"Did you conform to that request?"

"Yes."

Meanwhile, Wilding said, Hofmann gave them more collateral. They met at Valley Bank, and Wilding gave him a
$173,870 check to invest in the Oath. When they went to First
Interstate Bank to purchase cashier's checks, however, an odd
incident had occurred. Harvey Tanner, a loan officer, took
Hofmann aside. Watching at a distance, Wilding and brother-
in-law Sid Jensen thought Tanner seemed upset. When Tanner
left, they asked Hofmann about it.

"No problem," Hofmann had told them.

"He never told you that he had a $185,000 outstanding
debt to First Interstate Bank?"

"He did not."

Wilding went back to his office but soon got a telephone
call from Hofmann saying that Sid Jensen had seemed nervous. "If he wants, I'll buy out his $20,000 investment,"
Hofmann had told him.

Next, Jensen had burst into Wilding's office, upset and
anxious. He and another co-investor had compared notes and
found inconsistencies in what Hofmann had told them.

"What inconsistencies?" Biggs asked.

First, Wilding related, indignation growing in his voice,
they had learned that Hofmann had a sizeable loan from First
Interstate. Second, Hofmann had said he was going to catch
an airplane that same day, September 12, and had told Jensen
the airline and flight number. They had called the airline and
found no such flight number. They had driven to the airport to
check the flights to New York, then circled the parking lot
looking for Hofmann's car. It was not there. They tried to call
him. They went by his home, but no cars were there.

"What did you do?"

"Lay awake all night," Wilding said, drawing a chuckle in
the courtroom.

Early the next morning, Friday, September 13—the day a
desperate Mark Hofmann would meet with Rust, Bench, and

Lillywhite—Wilding and a co-investor had confronted Hofmann, who had just stepped out of the shower. Hofmann wanted to know what the big deal was.

"We'll tell you what the big deal is. There are a lot of things that don't jive. You're supposed to be in New York."

"I couldn't go. I'm going to go today and take my son."

Unmollified, Wilding said they wanted their money back.

"That's fine," Hofmann said. "I'll meet you at the bank at 10:00."

"I'll wait," Wilding said.

"You don't need to wait."

"Well, I'll wait."

Biggs broke in to show Wilding a cashier's check made out to Lyn Jacobs. Wilding identified it as a check Hofmann had shown them at a distance to demonstrate that he was going to purchase the second Oath from Jacobs. They met at the bank at 10:30 and got $18,000, Wilding said.

"Was there any discussion about the [remaining] $155,000?" Biggs asked, ironically.

"Certainly there was."

The audience stirred uneasily, watching Hofmann, who seemed impassive, as usual.

Hofmann was evasive, Wilding continued, but said they would get their money back. Wilding stayed with him while he went to the coin show to talk with Rust, then to the ZCMI parking plaza. Wilding got out of the car to allow Hofmann to make some calls. Then they went to a business complex south of Salt Lake City, bringing along some of the collateral Hofmann had. They visited Deseret Book twice, and Wilding waited while Hofmann talked to Bench and Lillywhite. Finally, still lacking the $155,000, they returned to Wilding's office about 6:30 p.m. Sid Jensen was waiting for them.

"By then," Biggs summarized, "you had been with Mark Hofmann since 7:30 a.m." When the three of them met at 6:30 p.m., what was discussed?

"The obvious discussion was where's the money?" Hofmann told them he had sent the money east to an associate and the Oath had already been purchased, Wilding said.

"Wait a minute," Biggs protested. "In the morning he told you he was going to New York himself. Right?"

"Right."

"Before he described going back to purchase it from Lyn Jacobs, and now he's telling you . . . "

Rich was on his feet objecting.

Biggs regrouped. "What did he tell you about how the check had gotten back to New York?"

"He said one of his associates had taken it and gone to Boston and that the Oath had been purchased."

"Did he tell you how he'd get your money back?"

"He said he had others who wanted to invest. They would raise the money or he'd do it himself."

The three of them signed an agreement stating that Hofmann would have their money by September 17. "We questioned him and said, 'That's not a very long time. How are you going to raise that kind of money in that short a time?' And he said, 'Don't worry, I'll do it. I don't need any longer time than that.' "

Biggs asked if Wilding and Jensen experienced any frustration during this two-hour conversation.

"Certainly. There was a large amount of money at risk and there were a lot of people involved."

"What was Mr. Hofmann's attitude during the first hour?"

"I would say almost a detached arrogance."

Biggs asked if his attitude made Wilding angry. "It caused me great concern and it caused Mr. Jensen anger."

"Did Mr. Jensen do anything at that meeting because of anger?"

"He slugged Mr. Hofmann," Wilding announced. "Mark said, 'No one's ever struck me before.' " Wilding did not mention that Jensen, who hit Hofmann in the face, had only one arm.

Hofmann agreed to pay the full amount by October 16, to call them each day until Tuesday, and to provide invoices for the "Haunted Man." In return, Wilding and Jensen promised to protect Hofmann's reputation. They knew his parents and his wife's parents. They would keep quiet until Tuesday. Also, they would check the collateral to determine its actual value.

Hofmann called on a regular basis and said he was working on the deal. Finally, he met with Wilding and said he did not have the money. Wilding brought in his attorney on September 17, and Hofmann signed promissory notes. By now, Wilding said, Hofmann owed them $455,155. He agreed to bring them the deed to his house and the titles to his cars but never did.

After additional discussion, Hofmann met them the morning of September 18 and reluctantly gave them the second "Oath of a Freeman," which they locked in a safe deposit box. "I don't want any of the other people involved to know you've got this," he said.

"If you do what you've said, that's fine," Wilding replied.

Biggs showed Wilding exhibit 137, the second "Oath of a Freeman" encased in plastic. Wilding identified it as the document he had placed in his safe deposit box at Valley Bank.

Hofmann made several attempts to pacify the Wilding group. On September 23, Wilding continued, Hofmann visited him at home around midnight. Hofmann said he had just returned from Arizona, seeking an investor for the Oath. He showed Wilding a partnership agreement with a number of items crossed out. On September 30, Wilding had gone with Hofmann to meet with businessmen in South Salt Lake City because he wanted to keep an eye on Hofmann's collateral, now being shown to the businessmen to raise funds.

Then on October 10 (five days before the bombings), Hofmann had told them about an impending document deal, for which Steve Christensen was acting as agent, that would bring Hofmann $185,000.

"What do you have that's so valuable?" Wilding had asked.

Hofmann answered that it was a large collection of postcards, letters, and other items. Wilding and his lawyer doubted that such a collection could be worth so much, but they were glad to hear Hofmann would be getting the money. They made an appointment for the 11th at 8:30 a.m., but Hofmann did not show. Frantically, they tried to reach him on his car telephone.

At 11:30 a.m., Hofmann called. "Do you have any money from the transactions?" they asked. He said no, but he had something else that would suffice over the weekend. He delivered a letter from attorney David West, amended by Steven Christensen, addressed, "To Whom it May Concern," stating that Hofmann would soon be receiving $185,000. "This is to show you everything is in order," Hofmann had reportedly said. He also showed them a large box of papers in his sports car trunk, including ordinary postcards and correspondence of a man named McMillan. Wilding took them home over the weekend but was unimpressed.

"It had been told you the previous day that the entire amount was coming to you," Biggs reviewed.

"That's correct."

"Did he tell you he had promised money to First Interstate Bank and to Alvin Rust?"

"We knew he had the debt at the bank but it was our understanding that he'd told the bank this money was coming to us. I knew he had dealings with Rust, but I didn't know any magnitude of money or anything of that nature."

"When did you first learn that Steven Christensen was involved?"

Wilding said he had known for a week, but his lawyer only heard on the 11th. His lawyer said, "I know Steve Christensen. Why don't we just give him a call and verify this?"

"What was the defendant's response to that?"

"Mark was extremely reluctant. He said, 'If you call, let me talk. You can listen.' "

They asked why. Hofmann said he was concerned that the deal might not go through. "We didn't think it would be necessary. We didn't want to do anything to jeopardize [the deal]. But it was quite apparent in that discussion that shortly we'd call Mr. Christensen if things didn't happen and Mr. Hofmann didn't deliver what he had promised so many times."

Hofmann said they would have their money on Monday, October 14. But Monday was a holiday and the banks were closed. He did not bring in the titles and deed he had promised but did collect the box of postcards and letters he had left over the weekend. He seemed extremely detached, Wilding said.

On October 15, Wilding and his lawyer met with Hofmann at 11:00 a.m. Hofmann dropped by about 9:30 without an appointment, Wilding said, but Wilding had been out.

"What was he wearing?" Biggs asked.

"Tan slacks, a plaid shirt with short sleeves." Wilding did not recall a coat or jacket. The lawyer turned to Wilding and said, "Our problem has taken a bizarre turn this morning. Have you heard the radio?"

Wilding said yes, he had heard about the bombing. The victim was Christensen. Wilding had noticed that Hofmann seemed to be taking the news hard. He was breathing so heavily, Wilding observed, he seemed to be hyperventilating. Hofmann's hair was damp and newly combed, as though he had just showered and shaved.

Biggs asked if they received the titles and deeds.

"No."

Wilding tried to call Hofmann the next morning, but Dori said she did not know where he was.

Biggs now skipped to the week after the bombings. Between October 20 and 27, Wilding and his lawyer had taken Hofmann's collateral to New York to Justin Schiller. They had tried to see Schiller the previous month, but Hofmann had called them in New York and told them Schiller was out of town.

When they met with Schiller and Wapner, Wilding testified, they discussed the rare books Hofmann had given them as collateral, but Schiller and Wapner seemed uninterested. Then Wilding pulled out the second Oath and showed it to them.

And their reaction? Rich objected that this would be hearsay and irrelevant, but Judge Grant ruled that Wilding could describe what he saw and heard.

"They were totally overwhelmed and dumbfounded and astounded. Schiller was sitting back in his chair. They both got up, picked the Oath up, and held it up to the light."

When the court reconvened after lunch, Wilding was not on the stand. Judge Grant explained that Wilding's testimony would be postponed so that an out-of-state witness could testify. A small, gray-haired woman made her way to the stand. Her name was Frances Magee, from Lynville, California.

With Stott asking questions, Magee explained that she owned the *Book of Common Prayer* that had originally belonged to Nathan Harris. Her mother-in-law had given her the book and had told her about the Harris family's connection to Mormonism. Stott had her identify some Harris signature in the front. He then asked her to turn to the back of the book.

"Was the handwriting that appears on those two pages in the back when it was given to you by your mother-in-law?"

"No."

Magee described how, for thirty-seven years, the book had been in the family. She had enjoyed showing it to friends.

"And at any time was that handwriting ever in the book?" Stott asked for emphasis.

"No, I would have remembered it."

In 1973, Magee continued, she had given the book to a dealer in Glendale, along with some old photographs. When she tried contacting him again, he had died. His wife returned duplicates of the photographs, but the originals and the book had gone with the dealer's estate to the Mormon church.

"To Deseret Book?"

Yes.

During cross-examination, Rich asked, "Did you read this book cover to cover?"

"No, I read portions. I'd look through it."

"It was a conversation piece?"

Yes.

"Do you remember looking in the back, specifically?" Rich pressed.

"Yes. Once we saw what was in the front, we wanted to look in the back and see what else was there."

"Was the book in this same condition?"

"No, it's in worse condition now."

Mike George turned to scan the faces of the reporters. Magee's spunky rejoinders were refreshing, but was her testimony compelling enough to convince them that Hofmann had forged Martin Harris's handwriting to bolster the authenticity of the salamander letter?

Now Rich asked summarily, "Could we contact you further if we have any additional questions?"

Magee looked nonplussed. "If there's any purpose for it, sure," she said.

Stott stood and asked if she had ever been paid for the prayer book. The dealer had given her $600 for a Book of Mormon, she said, but had only borrowed the other items. "And you know the rest of the story."

Excused, Magee moved to leave the stand, still clutching the prayer book. "I need this," Stott told her softly, retrieving exhibit 108. "I hope I get it back!" Magee exclaimed, then left.

With Wilding on the stand again, Rich was eager to undermine his credibility. Quickly Rich established that document and book investments were not part of Wilding's regular business.

"You saw this as an opportunity for yourself and your clients to make money. This was a chance to make not just a few bucks, but a lot of dollars."

Wilding stiffened. "That's what was purported to us."

"And you knew there was some degree of risk."

"Certainly."

Rich then retraced the document deals. Eventually half the courtroom was dozing. Grant called for a break. Afterwards, Rich continued through the transactions, growing increasingly indignant at the pressure Wilding had brought to bear on Hofmann.

"You've got to remember we still believed we were dealing with someone who was an expert in his area," Wilding said.

"And you were making real profits," Rich answered.

Biggs rose to object and Rich rephrased the question.

"You understood that the former transactions were doing well and you profited quite handily."

"We obviously believed it or we wouldn't have given him any more money."

"And then you *followed* Mr. Hofmann for the next several weeks," Rich accused.

"That's not a correct statement," Wilding bridled. The situation did make him nervous, he said. "I wanted Mark to keep in touch with me for the next several weeks and we did try to find him that night. You would too, if you . . . "

"I'm not asking you to justify what you did. You desired to get out of it if you could, and you changed it from a joint venture to an indebtedness."

"Mark agreed there was no problem in refunding the money."

"You confronted Mr. Hofmann at his home in the early morning hours of the 13th," Rich countered, "and insisted that you wanted your money back." What provisions did you have for a breach of contract that had failed in much less than twenty-four hours? he asked.

Wilding repeated that they had decided they no longer wanted to invest and that Hofmann had said he would return their money.

Rich moved to the meeting in Wilding's office on September 13, following a day of trying to raise money. "And at the meeting you were angry at Mr. Hofmann."

"It was not strained at first," Wilding said, but then Jensen had become angry.

"Were *you* angry?" Rich asked.

"I was very concerned."

"Did anyone yell at Mr. Hofmann?"

"I wouldn't say it was yelling, no."

"Mr. Jensen was upset," Rich reminded. "What did he say?"

"He felt Mark was taking lightly our concerns. I don't recall that there was yelling . . . maybe a loud discussion."

"And Mr. Jensen made certain accusations."

"No more than what we'd already discussed, that what was purported to have been done with the money hadn't been done. Then he said, 'I don't think you're taking serious what we're talking about,' and he hit him."

"How many times."

"Once."

Rich moved on to the agreement they had signed. He brought out the fact that they had actually received about $40,000 back from Hofmann by October 16, in several payments.

Had they received any money since then?

Wilding said they had sold some of Hofmann's collateral for around $163,000.

Rich next asked about Hofmann's appearance the morning of the bombings. "You know Mark well enough to tell how recently he shaved?"

That was how he had appeared to him, Wilding said.

"Would you be able to tell what time this morning I shaved?"

Wilding waited for the chuckles to die, than answered, "Maybe if I saw you shortly after you did I would."

"Have you ever seen Mark without his glasses?"

"Not that I recall."

"Did you see him in his letter jacket?"

Often.

"Did Mr. Jensen ever use foul language toward Mark Hofmann, particularly on the occasion when he struck him?"

Wilding hesitated, and Rich broke in, "You understand what I mean by foul language?"

"I don't remember. Probably."

"Did he call him names?"

"No, I don't remember that he did."

"Have you ever been in the armed services?"

"No."

"Did you ever hear Jensen make unkind remarks about Mr. Hofmann on other occasions?"

"No, he doesn't use foul language as a practice."

"Only when he's very upset."

"I don't remember his exact words."

Biggs, on re-direct, emphasized the apparent misrepresentations Hofmann had made and that Wilding had then tried to untangle. Then he asked if any of their agreements with Hofmann had carried penalties.

Wilding said that Hofmann had readily agreed to a significant penalty—$2,000 per day—for every day he did not return the money. "You need to remember," Wilding added through the muted whistles that followed, "that he had promised for several months to return the money."

"When did these penalties start to accrue?"

"They were dated October 14, 1985," Wilding said, the day before the bombings.

"So this was $4,000 per day in penalty," Biggs clarified, since the penalty applied to each of two notes.

"To which he readily agreed."

Rich was interested in the penalty agreement. "You had put some pressure on Mr. Hofmann, had you not?"

"What do you mean, pressure?"

"Obviously, on September 13, there *was* some physical contact," Rich reiterated, as well as "some psychological contact. You say you had put significant pressure on Mr. Hofmann to pay you back, had you not?"

"There was significant pressure to perform what he agreed to perform."

The tension in the courtroom was mounting, with sympathies divided for and against Wilding. Rich wanted to know what he would call "significant pressure."

"I would say it would be significant pressure if we had taken him to the police, and maybe that's what should have happened."

"Or broken his leg?" Rich ventured sarcastically, "or run over him with a car, or . . . "

"Or bombed him!" Mac Christensen suddenly shouted from the audience, as Farnsworth clamped a hand on his arm. Rich wheeled, frustrated and angry. But Christensen and Farnsworth stared straight ahead. Rich wrapped up, then tersely asked to approach the bench. The whispered conference between attorneys and judge clarified the source of the outburst, and the hearing continued.

The hour was late when David Biggs called his first cousin, Brent Ashworth, to the stand. Charlene Ashworth slipped into the courtroom. Hofmann looked back over his shoulder from his wheelchair, and she glanced away, feeling his eyes rest on her. She shivered.

Ashworth introduced himself as a corporate vice-president and attorney and, by avocation, a collector of historical documents in American, western, and Mormon history. Biggs's questions were infrequent, Ashworth's answers fluent, packed with information and self-deprecating humor. He described his enthusiastic purchase of the Lucy Mack Smith letter and identified it for the record. He went on to describe other purchases. He described how he had "fallen in love" with the Carthage Jail letters in the RLDS archives and had asked Hofmann to find and sell him a similar item, followed by his discovery that Hofmann had sold a Carthage Jail letter to another collector.

"Was that a surprise to you?" Biggs asked.

"It was an extreme surprise," Ashworth said, his voice picking up volume and speed as he described his angry late-night confrontation with Hofmann. "Our relationship took a real dive," he said.

Ashworth next described purchasing the Emma Smith hymnal for $10,000 on November 30, 1984. Hofmann had told Ashworth "it was one of the most beautiful copies he'd ever seen, better than the two that the church possessed."

Biggs asked him to identify exhibit 87, the hymn book. "Was that last page in there?"

"Yes, the book was complete."

"Any missing pages?"

"No."

"Did he ever tell you he had a plate made and printed up the last page and added it to the book?"

"No."

"If he had, would you have paid $10,000?"

"No." Ashworth then added, "The next Wednesday I went up to Mark's home and said, 'Mark, I'm thrilled to have that book. I've never seen one so nice.' He told me Lyn Jacobs owned it before and that it was originally from the McLellin collection."

Ashworth outlined several other transactions, beginning with the two Jim Bridger notes he had purchased in December 1984, one of which he resold to Deseret Book. He had not purchased ten notes as Shannon Flynn had testified Hofmann told him.

Ashworth described his pursuit of the Jonathan Dunham letter, which he finally purchased for $60,000 in July 1985, and how he and Hofmann had discussed the letter at their "usual spot in the open area by Waldenbooks at Crossroads Mall."

Biggs asked Ashworth his whereabouts on October 16, 1985, the day Hofmann was injured by a bomb. "I didn't go to Salt Lake City on that Wednesday because I was there Monday and

Tuesday." He had tried to reach Hofmann but had failed. He had last seen Hofmann on October 13, the Sunday before the bombings. Hofmann had dropped in unexpectedly and written a check for the wrong amount, then corrected it.

"Did the check clear?"

"No, it did not."

"Have you ever seen Mr. Hofmann without his glasses?" Biggs finished.

"Yes, a number of times. He wears glasses sometimes, sometimes I've seen him without."

As Biggs took his seat, Yengich told the judge that he would waive cross-examination so that the Ashworths could return to Provo and their son's funeral. The hour was late, and the court was grateful. However, Ashworth's testimony was also proving damaging to their client. When Ashworth stepped down from the stand, he and Yengich shook hands warmly. They had attended law school together. On Friday, with the hearing in recess, prosecutors drove to Provo for Samuel Ashworth's funeral.

No one could say the preliminary hearing was going well for Hofmann. Prosecutors asked Judge Grant if Mac Christensen could speak privately with Bill Hofmann. Grant gave Christensen and Hofmann a few minutes alone in his chambers, then opened the door to see how they were doing. He gathered that Christensen had suggested to Hofmann that Mark end the long legal proceeding by simply pleading guilty. Bill Hofmann had then explained that that was not possible. He knew his son was innocent; he had received a spiritual witness. Grant watched as the two men embraced. The priesthood brotherhood, Grant reflected. For him, it was the finest moment of the hearing.

Wednesday morning, May 7, the question of document forgery dominated as William Flynn, forensic document analyst for the Arizona State Crime Lab, took the stand. Quickly Stott established that Flynn had held this position for fourteen years. Before that he had been a document examiner at the Philadelphia Police Department. Flynn said he had examined nineteenth-century documents — all of which were related to the

Hofmann case—four times between December 1985 and April 1986.

Flynn described the equipment he used to examine the documents. The paper appeared to be genuine, he said.

"Let's talk about the ink. Did you find any peculiar or abnormal characteristics associated with the documents?" Stott asked.

Flynn explained the microscopic cracking; the peculiar unidirectional running; the unusual solubility; and the tampering with number and names.

"Was there anything common to these documents in which you saw microscopic cracking and the one-directional running?"

"Yes. They had all occurred on documents that had been dealt by Mark Hofmann."

Judge Grant, watching the defendant, saw a reaction in Hofmann's eyes. They seemed to brighten with concern for the first time, Grant thought, as if Flynn's testimony struck at him in a way all the bombings, printing, and alleged fraud testimony had not. Grant noted that moment.

"Were there any other documents out of the 461 you examined that exhibited these characteristics?" Stott continued.

"No."

Stott asked him to describe his research and experiments. Flynn said that he had not observed that cracking on other documents and had tried to find the cause. He described his search, including his own experiments with iron gall inks, produced at his kitchen sink.

"Were you able to discover how the cracking effect occurred?"

"There were two problems," Flynn explained. "One was whether or not the ink could be artificially aged, and the second whether that procedure would also crack the ink."

Ink aging, Flynn went on, could be simulated by exposing the ink to ammonia of some type, which would oxidize the ink quickly instead of over a period of years. He tried ammonium hydroxide and found that the ink immediately turned a deep rust color but did not crack. Then he added sugar or gum, common to the period to give the ink body and to preserve it. "When I added either the sugars or gum arabic, then artificially aged them with sodium hydroxide, I got exactly the same phenomenon that I described. The ink aged—and cracked."

Stott went into the technicalities a little further, then asked, "Would any normal preservatives (such as having the document deacidified or washed) affect the cracking?"

No, Flynn said. They had found that washing and bleaching would not crack the ink, though it might remove part of the ink surface.

"Did you duplicate this phenomenon?"

"Yes." Flynn described how he made quill pens from turkey feathers—"widepoint and finepoint quills." He showed several to the judge, and Stott numbered them as exhibits. On one sample Flynn had used modern paper with modern ink from an old formula that included sugar. He had simulated Thomas Bullock's handwriting. He had the Joseph Smith III blessing and the Thomas Bullock to Brigham Young letter among his models. On the second sample, he oxidized the ink in an oven, rather than with a chemical. On the third, he tried a gaseous fume rather than a liquid and obtained similar results. As the simulated documents were passed around the courtroom, Hofmann scrutinized them closely.

"Did you ever use the same process with authentic nineteenth-century paper?"

Flynn said he had used cover letters, then casually stated a hard-won conclusion that itself was history-making in forensic science.

"When iron gallotannate ink is utilized on old paper and aged, there would be no way to ascertain that it was not as old as is purported. The paper would have been genuine and the apparent chemical reaction of the inks is identical to a natural aging process."

This explained why experts from Massachusetts to California had been unable to detect Hofmann's forgeries.

Mike George began passing documents to Stott as he asked Flynn to comment on them. The first was the Josiah Stowell letter, sold by Mark Hofmann to President Gordon B. Hinckley in January 1983 and made public over two years later. Flynn described the cracked ink on the document and said the handwriting was too neat for a young Joseph Smith.

"Joseph Smith was not a good writer," he said. "Once I began to cut my own quills, I realized how important it was to keep the quill sharp. Everybody who wrote with a quill carried pen knives, so they could constantly sharpen their pens. Joseph Smith was not adept at maintaining the point of the quill. You can always write worse, but you can never write better than you can write. The letter exhibits handwriting skill higher than Joseph Smith was capable of. Also, all of the smearing of the ink is in one direction."

"Do you have an opinion as to whether the Josiah Stowell letter is an authentic document?" Stott probed.

The courtroom was beginning to fill with whispers.

"I don't believe it is a genuine document of that era."

"Shit!" a Mormon stringer on the back row muttered under her breath.

Stott brought out the E. B. Grandin Book of Mormon contract. Flynn said the ink on the entire document showed extensive cracking. Under ultraviolet, some of the ink ran in one direction. "I don't believe it is a genuine document of that time period."

Successively, Stott presented Flynn with the handwritten white notes and the David Whitmer to Bithell Todd letter. Flynn pronounced them forgeries. Next came the salamander letter. "There is extensive surface cracking in the ink," Flynn said. Also, he added, one edge had been cut on the left side, probably with scissors.

"Did you compare this letter with any other handwriting?"

"Yes." Flynn had compared the salamander letter to the poem in the back of the Nathan Harris prayer book. "I believe the handwriting was done by the same hand." Neither the salamander letter nor the poem was authentic, he said. Several reporters slipped from the hearing to telephone their newspapers or radio or television stations.

Flynn pronounced the Joseph Smith III blessing, the Lucy Mack Smith letter, and the Jonathan Dunham letter forgeries. After a break, he continued with the Anthon transcript. Although it showed no evidence of cracked ink, the ink had burned through the paper because of its acid content. It contained no sugar or gum arabic, accounting for the absence of cracking. It had an unusual staining pattern, as if scorched by an iron. The Bible, too, was problematic, Flynn said. "I do not believe the transcript was folded in the Bible for any length of time."

Flynn discussed the handwritten "Book of Amos," signed by Samuel Smith. The signature covered an erasure, he said, and in the signature, but not the text, the ink cracked, indicating a different, artificially aged ink.

The land deed signed by Solomon Spaulding and Sidney Rigdon was also curious. The signatures had been written in the same hand, he said, and the date had been altered from 1792 to 1822 by writing over the numbers. The Betsy Ross letter, too, he said, showed a date change from 1837 to 1807. The name Ross was written in a different ink than Betsy.

Stott asked Flynn why he chose Thomas Bullock's hand to imitate in preparing his courtroom exhibits. Bullock had an English style of handwriting he found easy to mimic, Flynn said, for the letters were discontinuous rather than connected.

After a break, Brad Rich began an extensive cross-examination. First he questioned Flynn's credentials. Flynn explained that a forensic analyst applies scientific principles to legal questions. He admitted that he dealt with modern documents 99 percent of the time. However, he had extensive experience with signatures, ranging from thousand-page drug ledgers to signatures on a credit card. Rich asked about ink analysis. Flynn said he did ink analysis often, to determine if a document has been altered or to determine the age of a document.

"Were you familiar with any forgeries of antiquities done in iron gall ink?"

"Yes. The Hitler diaries, the Joseph Mengele papers." He added, "One was a questioned letter by Ludwig Von Beethoven. Another involved some old land deeds."

Rich looked surprised. "So it would have been just a handful of times that you've worked with iron gallotannate ink?"

"Yes."

"Had you ever attempted to synthesize ink before?"

"Never."

"How many inks did you prepare?"

"Dozens. I kept varying the constituents."

Rich and Flynn plunged into the technicalities of artificially aging ink, with little new information surfacing.

During the break that followed, Joan Christensen sat still, watching Mark Hofmann—Steve's age—talk with his father.

On the documents with microscopic cracking, Rich began after the break, Flynn had described ultraviolet bleeding. How much did that phenomenon vary from document to document?

"The cracking phenomenon was fairly consistent throughout the documents."

But was the cracking "equal and similar?" Rich wondered. "Yes."

"How does it appear?"

"It appears as plates or flakes. I did not see that phenomenon on the other 461 documents that I had examined of the same period."

"It has never been used as a test for the legitimacy or illegitimacy of documents?" Rich asserted.

"It has not. The research came to a screeching halt in the 1940s."

"Then, I take it, you are the first expert ever to use this particular test in a courtroom to claim a particular document to be a forgery?"

"Yes, I may be the only expert to ever have seen artificially aged gallotannate ink."

Rich asked if he had an opinion as to who authored the documents. Flynn said no—they would require a fair degree of calligraphic skill, but it would not be insurmountable. "My own forgeries show fairly critically that I did a fairly capable job and I'm not a real good writer."

After some rechecking of details by both Rich and Stott, Judge Grant had a question. "You concluded that the Anthon transcript was a forgery? I'd like you to enumerate for me the specifics that led you to that conclusion."

"Had it been genuinely stored in the Bible for a period of time, the text would have acid-burned the pages of the Bible just as it burned through the paper. There was no evidence of that. That was the primary reason, there was no sugar in the ink, so there could be no cracking. Also, it appeared to have been heated on one area on the front and back. Indeed, it did not exhibit the uniform brown of paper when it's aged. And, of course, there were problems with the Bible."

Flynn stepped from the stand disappointed. He had prepared for more. He had memorized the history of papers, inks, and handwriting development. He knew the Hofmann case would be a landmark in his field, and he wanted to be ready for anything. The defense, however, clearly had hired no experts. Flynn's most vivid memory of the hearing was of a tall judge wearing a purple robe and cowboy boots.

Now it was George Throckmorton's turn. He had returned from Florida to meet with Gerry D'Elia the Sunday before he testified. He had examined documents connected to the Hofmann case for the past six months by then. However, he knew his activity in the Mormon church would be construed in court as prejudice. Consequently, prosecutors decided to let D'Elia, a lapsed Catholic, examine Throckmorton to minimize the Mormon issue.

When Throckmorton took the stand Monday morning, D'Elia first reviewed his credentials. Throckmorton was a certified forensic document examiner for the attorney general's office, a special agent in the litigation division, and owned a private business named Independent Forensic Labs. Currently, he was on the executive committee of the Southwest Association of Document Examiners.

"How much of your work consists of printed or stamped material?"

"About 20 percent."

Like Flynn, Throckmorton described the examination of Hofmann documents, including 75 to 100 self-enveloping cover letters.

Were the cover letters in this case cut in any fashion? D'Elia wanted to know.

"Yes." Throckmorton described the microscopic scissor marks or razor marks. As D'Elia presented the exhibits, Throckmorton identified suspicious cuts on the Spaulding/Rigdon land deed, the Betsy Ross letter, the Josiah Stowell letter, and the salamander letter.

Over Rich's objection, Throckmorton said he had not observed such cuts on any other nineteenth-century cover letters.

How were cover letters normally folded and sealed? D'Elia asked.

Rich objected again that Throckmorton had not sufficient experience to make such an observation. Again Grant ruled that Throckmorton could answer.

"They were all folded in such a manner that the writing or content of the letter was not visible from the outside," he said, adding that sealing wax was in the center portion.

"How does exhibit 116 [the salamander letter] compare to other cover letters regarding the folds?"

"It is different in two respects." Throckmorton explained that when he reproduced the folding, it was possible to pinch the edges and read the handwriting inside. Also, when folded, the cut marks matched, indicating that the letter had been folded first and then cut. Also, folding the letter placed the sealing wax in the extreme upper right corner, and the letter had been cut next to the sealing wax, making it possible to pinch the letter open and read the contents.

D'Elia asked if Throckmorton's research had uncovered information describing how to forge a stampless cover letter?

"In *Famous Fakes and Forgeries* [sic] by Charles Hamilton there is a section including pages 147-149, with several pages on methodology—how to get cover letters, how to cut them, how people have gotten caught in their attempts to forge. You get letters for a legitimate purpose, then erase pencil, cut off half, add dates, and so on."

D'Elia brought out a representative sample of a cover letter and had Throckmorton demonstrate the typical folding. As he did, Hofmann and Yengich held a whispered conference.

Next D'Elia brought Throckmorton a negative for a Jim Bridger note and several of the notes themselves. Throckmorton identified each, then described cracking in the handwritten signatures. What was more, he had matched the notes microscopically to the negative, Throckmorton said. Bits of emulsion, called trash marks, indicated that they were products of a plate made from that negative.

D'Elia allowed a few minutes for Throckmorton to review the handwritten documents described by Flynn earlier. "How many items written in iron gallotannate ink did you observe?"

"Six hundred and eighty-eight documents written with iron gall ink. Of those, twenty-one had cracked ink. They all came from Mark Hofmann."

"Other than those twenty-one from Mark Hofmann, were there any other documents with cracking or running?"

"No."

D'Elia asked about deacidification, which can preserve old documents. Throckmorton said he had deacidified the salamander letter, first a corner, then more, and finally the entire document. There had been no change in the ink appearance. He had done the same with the Joseph Smith to Maria and Sarah Lawrence letter with identical results.

They returned to the Bridger notes, which combined printing, from a modern printing plate, with handwritten signatures that showed cracked, running ink, Throckmorton said. He explained that any disclaimer on the printing plate could be easily removed without affecting the significant parts.

After a brief break, Throckmorton pronounced as forgeries two different types of Spanish Fork notes. Printed in four colors, the notes matched rubber stamps and inks from Salt Lake Stamp. The letters on the notes also matched sheets of rub-off letters confiscated in Hofmann's home. Next, D'Elia showed him Deseret currency notes, identifying them by denomination and serial number and negatives recovered from Cocks-Clark Engraving in Denver. Throckmorton said one of Al Rust's notes was genuine and the source of a plate used to print several of the other notes. Two $2 notes appeared genuine, he said, but notes in higher denominations and some of the lower denominations were products of modern printing from negatives in custody.

As news reports of the Hofmann preliminary hearing aired on television and radio, USU special collections director Jeff Simmonds maintained an unstable ambivalence between suspecting Hofmann and discounting the investigation. When the news of Throckmorton's testimony about the Deseret currency went over the wires, Simmonds, at work in Logan, suddenly remembered Hofmann photocopying the Deseret currency ledgerbooks.

"Get Rust's book," he told his assistant, and they thumbed for the appropriate reference. They found an editor's note, saying that heretofore undiscovered sets of Deseret currency had been found just as Rust's book (which Hofmann had helped prepare) went to press. Simmonds sagged against the wall. "Oh, shit," he said.

Meanwhile, D'Elia turned to the Emma Smith hymnal with its suspicious last page. Lyn Jacobs had testified that his photocopy of the page had been replaced by an original page Hofmann had purchased for $1,000 and tipped in to the book.

Throckmorton said that the page in question seemed to be a flyleaf that had been extracted and printed on. D'Elia asked if the printing negative from DeBouzek Engraving had any relationship to the printed table of contents.

"Yes. The negative was used to make a plate that was printed on the flyleaf of the hymn book." The printing inks were black throughout, he said. However, "the printing process is amateurish. It was printed on a different type of press" than the rest of the hymn book.

After echoing Flynn's testimony regarding the Anthon transcript, Throckmorton went on to match the inscriptions in *Call of the Wild* to the Jack London printing negative and the Austin Lewis personal stamp. Next he was shown the second "Oath of a Freeman," which he pronounced microscopically identical to the printing negative.

"In one of the small m's there is a small, hairline crack evident on the negative where the emulsion on the film itself remained intact. The same discrepancy is on the Oath." A printer's note on the bottom of the negative had been removed from the plate before printing, Throckmorton said.

Is it authentic?

"It couldn't possibly be authentic because it was made from the plate from this negative."

Brad Rich did not see the cracked ink phenomenon as fatal to his client's credibility. The test was so new, so untried. He thought a battle of the experts at trial might well be won by the defense. (But the printing negatives presented a whole different challenge.) After lunch, he was more than ready to take on Throckmorton. "Mr. Throckmorton," he began, "are you familiar with a document known as The Book of Mormon?"

"Yes."

"Do you have a particular belief from whence this volume came?"

"I do."

"And can you tell me what that is?"

D'Elia objected, saying that Throckmorton's religious bias, simply stated, was sufficient. Rich countered that the salamander letter was a powerful motivation for bias, although he had no intention of belaboring the point. The judge ruled for the defense.

Again he asked Throckmorton's belief concerning the origin of The Book of Mormon.

"My belief agrees with the conservative point of view of a member of the Mormon faith. And that's that the Book of Mormon was translated from the plates that were given to Joseph Smith."

"Who gave the plates to Joseph Smith?"

"The Angel Moroni."

"And do you believe that a salamander or toad was involved?"

Throckmorton's face twitched as if suppressing a smile. "I don't believe so."

"Had you expressed your opinion on that prior to your involvement with these documents?"

D'Elia objected again, and this time was upheld.

Rich tried again. "Prior to examining the salamander letter, had you heard of that document?"

"Yes." Throckmorton said he had read something in the newspaper when it was first found.

"Did you have an opinion whether that document was legitimate or not?"

"I didn't know what was in it."

"Had you heard of Mark Hofmann prior to the bombings?"

"No, sir."

"Had you heard about the other documents?"

"I had read about the Joseph Smith III blessing and Charles Anthon transcript. I believe that's all."

"Did you view the contents of the Joseph Smith III blessing as inconsistent with your religious beliefs?"

"I don't know what it said."

"If the contents of that document purport to give the reins of the Mormon church to Joseph Smith III rather than to Brigham Young, would that be inconsistent with your religious belief?"

Throckmorton looked at him an instant. "The letter itself wouldn't cause me any concern."

"You wouldn't accept its content as doctrine?"

"No."

Rich turned to Throckmorton's qualifications, establishing that his experience with "documents of antiquity" was limited. He had known that Hofmann was a suspect in the bombings and that his discoveries made up the questioned documents in the case.

As Rich continued, Yengich and Hofmann held the Anthon transcript to the light and whispered animatedly. This went on for several minutes, gradually drawing the attention of everyone in the courtroom, though nothing was said for the record.

Rich reviewed Throckmorton's and Flynn's discovery of the ink anomalies and their implications. Yawns passed like popcorn down the rows as Rich reviewed Throckmorton's findings, document by document. Eventually they reached the printed documents and the process of comparing negative to finished product.

"But you have not seen any plates," Rich asserted.

"I have not."

Wrapping up, Rich asked, "You were quoted in the press saying you have a litmus test for forgery. Is that true?"

"I was quoted in the press as saying a lot of things," Throckmorton smiled. He explained how he tested the paper for acid, then experimented with deacidification.

Judge Grant had a final question regarding the Nathan Harris prayer book—did the poem in the back have cracked ink?

Throckmorton explained that the absorbency of the paper

left little ink on the surface; he could tell only that the ink had an odd color.

Throckmorton was the state's last witness, but Biggs read two stipulations into the record. The first, from Justin Schiller, stated that Schiller and Hofmann did not have any agreement for the purchase or sale of eighteen rare books from Europe as represented to Tom Wilding by Hofmann; second, Schiller, acting as agent for Mark Hofmann, had purchased a Charles Dickens manuscript entitled, "The Haunted Man," with the following funds: $110,000 received direct from Wilford Cardon in Arizona, $20,000 from Mark Hofmann, and $170,000 from Schiller and Wapner. No funds had come from Wilding. Last, Schiller stipulated that from April 1985 through "at least November 1985" Schiller and Hofmann had owned the "Oath of a Freeman" in a 50/50 partnership.

The second stipulation came from Gordon B. Hinckley, stating that in January 1983 he had purchased the Stowell letter with a $15,000 check from church funds. "Mr. Hinckley accepted the letter for the Church and gave it to Mr. Francis M. Gibbons, Secretary to the First Presidency, to keep and house for the Church. Mr. Gibbons has kept the letter in a secure place since then and turned it over to the County Attorney's Office on January 13, 1986." Hinckley stipulated that on March 4, 1983, he authorized a $25,000 check to Hofmann for the church's purchase of the Grandin Book of Mormon contract. The stipulation ended with the statement that Hinckley "has never seen nor possessed nor has any knowledge of the whereabouts of a document or group of documents known as the McLellin Collection."

Next, Yengich rose and explained that Hofmann, on advice of his attorneys, declined to take the stand in his own defense. Closing arguments were set for May 20, more than a week away.

When the hearing reconvened for closing arguments, Stott addressed a full house. Most of his summary was directed to points of law, particularly the communication frauds involving the papyrus fragments, the McLellin loans, and the Americana investments. Each had been charged separately, and though

Stott asked to have two dismissed, he did not want to lose the others.

"It's a new statute patterned after the federal statute," Stott said. The statute required a scheme to defraud, false statements or promises, and communication made to execute or conceal the scheme. However, criminal intent need not be proved nor need money change hands. Each separate communication, Stott maintained, represented a separate crime. Thus there were several charges involving the same document, for different alleged victims, amounts, and propositions.

The theft-by-deception charges, implying forgery, were also defined. "Persons or institutions gave to Mark Hofmann substantial amounts of money for documents that Mark Hofmann represented to be genuine. If the document was not and Mark knew it was not, then he committed the crime as charged."

As to the theft and fraud charges included in the murder case: "Each of the seven counts centers around a scheme involving the McLellin collection. But each victim is different and each of the counts represents separate false communications. In some, money was given and in some money wasn't given. It doesn't matter under the statute."

Stott announced that the McLellin collection was, in fact, non-existent. "No one's ever seen the McLellin collection, not his creditors, Al Rust, Hugh Pinnock and First Interstate Bank, not his business associates, Wade Lillywhite, Curt Bench, Brent Ashworth, his close friends didn't see it, Lyn Jacobs, Flynn, even Wilding never saw it. And you know how important it was for Mark Hofmann to please Mr. Wilding and his friends — but they never saw it."

Stott totalled the monetary charges at nearly $2 million, which included charges in which money was sought but not obtained.

Finally, Stott came to the homicide and bomb charges. Bomb expert Jerry Taylor had testified that all three bombs were closely related, made and delivered by the same person, Stott reminded the judge.

"Who was that person?" Stott asked rhetorically.

At 6:45 a.m., the morning of the murders, Bruce Passey saw the bomber. He identified Mark Hofmann in a photo lineup, then in the courtroom with no hesitation. He also identified his green letterman's jacket and the handwriting on the package. Janet McDermott saw the package and identified the writing. She could not identify the man in the hall but said he had physical characteristics similar to Mark Hofmann.

Joan Christensen placed a hand over her eyes, as Stott continued. Margene Robbins saw Mark Hofmann between 9:00 and 9:30 a.m. wearing his letter jacket. Aaron Teplick saw a car slowly moving down the road by the Sheetses' house the night before and identified Mark Hofmann's van as the car or "exactly similar." Kathy Sheets, Stott claimed, died to divert attention from Hofmann's dealings with Christensen.

Mark Hofmann, on October 16, was injured, Stott continued. Not only did prosecutors know that the same person had made and planted the bombs, but "We also have something interesting. We have the conflicting statements given by Mr. Hofmann. Mark Hofmann told Jim Bell that he opened the door and a package fell to the floorboards." But Jerry Taylor said the bomb exploded by the seat, not on the floor, but near the console. Hofmann was inside the car, not just getting in. And Brad Christensen saw someone inside the car doing something on the seat.

Next Stott reminded the judge of the testimony from Radio Shack employees, of the apparent bomb parts purchased on October 7, of the mercury switches found at the scenes, of the grain of gunpowder in the van.

"Who's Mike Hansen?" Stott asked rhetorically. He is Mark Hofmann. He ordered stamps and engraving plates. He used Mark Hofmann's checks and telephone numbers and left Mark Hofmann's fingerprint on the Austin Lewis order form. "Just as a pattern of using Mike Hansen to commit crimes" and forge documents developed, Stott said, Mike Hansen was used when Hofmann prepared to commit more serious crimes after buying bomb parts.

Stott listed the aggravating circumstances in the murders. First, there was pecuniary gain — killing to gain advantage or to rid oneself of difficulty. "In the second week of October, there was an extreme amount of pressure on Mark Hofmann." Wilding was threatening to take his house and cars, Christensen was threatening civil and criminal consequences. "If anything came out that would cast a doubt on him, his profession would collapse. He'd never be able to pay back all this money. And what if someone started to take a second look at all these other documents?" Wilding's lawyer knew Steve Christensen and had one copy of the Oath. But Christensen did not know about Wilding's investments or the second Oath. Hofmann talked them out of calling Christensen, but it was clear they would call Christensen if matters were not quickly resolved.

The crimes had been premeditated and heinous; the arbitrary placement of the second bomb showed particular callousness. Finally, Hofmann had apparently been seeking a third victim with the third bomb, for the receipt found at the scene showed that he had been at Crossroads Mall where he regularly met Brent Ashworth minutes before the bomb exploded.

"Steve was at the center of all the pressure. [Hofmann] had to get rid of Steve Christensen. It wouldn't solve all his problems, but it would give him some time. As you know, the only thing a con artist ever wants is time—that's a savior to a con artist—if I can just have another day."

The next morning, Ron Yengich rose to counter Stott's arguments. First, the communication frauds should not be charged separately. Second, all charges involving the Anthon transcript, the Joseph Smith III blessing, and the White Notes should be dismissed, because charges were filed more than four years after the alleged thefts had occurred. The statute of limitations had expired.

Regarding the homicides: "Mr. Stott argued for close to two hours and yet he spent less than fifteen minutes on the homicides. He said that we could have quit after the first three days, and I guess many of us wish he would have. But he didn't nor did he have to. They never tied the three bombs together. Mrs. Sheets's death was glossed over, if ever discussed at all by Mr. Stott." Basically, Yengich said, the only thing similar among the three bombs was that they were pipe bombs—the Christensen bomb had nails and the Hofmann bomb was not shown to have had a mercury switch or packaging.

Both Bruce Passey and Janet McDermott were vague, and Aaron Teplick supposedly saw the van late at night, but the van was also seen early in the morning. Shannon Flynn was with Hofmann the night before and noticed nothing unusual.

The seeming contradictions in Hofmann's statements, Yengich continued, could be due to Jim Bell's bias in reporting them. Brad Christensen was "the young man who willed him to live and performed a religious function, but he also changed his testimony considerably to dovetail with the theory of Mr. Taylor, [on whose theory] the prosecution really hangs their hat. Because if Mr. Hofmann opens the door and it falls out, it doesn't fit the state's theory. So he changes his testimony . . . and tells the court something that is consistent with what Mr. Taylor has said have to be the facts for this man to be the bomber."

The bomb parts are all generic. The grain of gunpowder found in Hofmann's van did not necessarily come from the batch that went into the bombs. Mike Hansen was never identified by any witness as Mark Hofmann.

Next Yengich attacked the state's chronology. A van was seen at midnight and again at 6:00 a.m., Hofmann supposedly was seen at the Judge Building at 6:45 and 7:00, Christensen was killed about 8:00, Margene Robbins saw Hofmann between 9:00 and 9:30, the Sheets bomb went off about 9:38, and Wilding saw Hofmann between 10:30 and 11:00 a.m. Yengich suggested that Hofmann could not have been in all those places at all those times.

Finally, he claimed, there was no motive, and Stott's reference to pecuniary gain pointed up this weakness in the state's case since Hofmann had owed neither Christensen nor Sheets. Yengich pictured Hofmann and Christensen not as adversaries, but as allies, saying that Christensen had been essential to Hofmann. "He was helping him with Pinnock. Steve was the one who was in contact with President Hinckley, he was offering his hand to Mark in friendship, not offering a threat as some others did." The evidence proved his client innocent, not guilty.

"What good does it do to kill Steve Christensen? It does none. Mr. Stott says Steve Christensen was the center of all his problems. I say that that's bull. Steve was helping Mark." If Steve was an errand boy for Hinckley, Pinnock, and First Interstate, Yengich asserted, then logically Hofmann would kill Hinckley and Pinnock, not Christensen. "If Mark killed Steve to give him time, that doesn't ring true and it's not a commonsensical application of the evidence, either. Because killing any of the participants in this particular scheme not only would not buy time but would focus a police inquiry on all the participants involved."

Denouncing the case as "made of maybes," Yengich brought up the remaining mysteries — Kathy Sheets's death and the bomb in Hofmann's car. "The one individual who will not benefit or lose by this complicated scheme that has been laid out by the prosecution is Steve Christensen. He doesn't benefit a lick, doesn't lose a lick. And the real thorns in the side of Mr. Hofmann are not harmed, nor is there any indication whatsoever that they were intended to be harmed, not even the budding pugilist Mr. Jensen." Quickly, Yengich asked the judge to dismiss the charges against his client.

Stott ignored Yengich's rhetoric and addressed only the legal issues. He reviewed the requirements for charging communication fraud and emphasized that each charge represented a separate scheme with separate claims, victims, and monetary goals. Second, he stated that the statute of limitations regarding theft-by-deception relates to the point at which a fraud is detected, not the date when the crime is committed.

Arguments finished, Judge Grant complimented the attorneys, then, with a note of surprise, congratulated the press for acting professionally. He said he needed to check a few matters and would render his decision the following day at 1:00 p.m.

At 1:00 p.m. the courtroom was crowded. Succinctly, Grant read his decision. Because of widespread interest, he said, he wanted to emphasize that he was not determining the guilt of the defendant; but that he found probable cause that these crimes were committed and that the defendant committed each of the crimes. With that, Hofmann was bound over to Third District Court on thirty felonies. Nevertheless, he would continue free on bond until and unless he was convicted.

The Sheets family was prepared for the possibility that the second homicide charge would be dismissed, but after a long internal debate, Grant had decided to bind both homicides over for trial. At the beginning of the preliminary hearing, Grant had thought perhaps Hofmann was innocent. But by the end, he thought him clearly guilty, a pathological liar with no conscience and no remorse.

Prosecutors and investigators left the courtroom, beaming. Grim-faced, Yengich and Rich gathered up their papers hurriedly. "We're looking at this as a three act play," Rich told a somber Bill Hofmann. "All this has been is reading through the script. We haven't even gotten started yet."

Hofmann nodded. Pushing his son's wheelchair to the van, Bill gave reporters and onlookers his own verdict — which his son would enter as his own plea the following week in Third District Court. "Not guilty," Bill Hofmann said.

18

THE WHEELS OF
LEGAL STRATEGY

The week after the preliminary
hearing of Mark Hofmann ended, County Attorney Ted Cannon
called the prosecution team together to organize assignments in
preparation for trial. "Get the trial date set this year," he urged
the prosecutors. "I want this case tried while I'm still in office."
Cannon had announced just before the preliminary hearing that
he would not run for re-election.

Elated by the outcome of the preliminary hearing, the prosecutors nevertheless had numerous leads to trace and details to
secure. Several witnesses who could be counted on to provide
dramatic testimony at trial had not even taken the stand. These
included Kate Reid, Hofmann's fiancee; Darlene Sanchez,
Hofmann's calligraphy teacher; and Charles Hamilton, who
would no doubt steal headlines by describing how he had been
duped, then later had come to regard the Stowell letter and
others as forgeries. Hamilton had, in fact, produced a sample
"paragraph" of handwritten lines from six Hofmann documents,
arranged in no particular order, which gave the impression,
even to the untrained eye, that the documents had been written
by a single hand. And of course, Mormon leader Gordon
Hinckley would be the anticipated witness, though prosecutors
foresaw problems.

Cannon was proud of his team and looked forward to
trial. Something of a traditionalist, he liked his cases charged,

tried, and sentenced at the level of the crime. Deep down, Cannon knew that the Hofmann case might come to a plea bargain, but he was loathe to give up the death penalty.

Now Cannon recruited George Throckmorton full time from the state attorney general's office. In June, Throckmorton went to New York City, armed with the second "Oath of a Freeman" and its printing negative. The U.S. Attorney's subpoena for the first Oath had been ignored, and Schiller and Wapner still insisted that the document was authentic and did not belong in Utah.

Once in New York City, Throckmorton met Charles Hamilton, who took him to Argosy Books, where they were received coolly. Throckmorton also met ATF technician Marvin Rennart at the New York Postal Laboratory. Ray Wapner brought the Oath over and handed it to Rennart, then left. Rennart and Throckmorton put it under the microscope. Within the hour, they matched the Oath microscopically to the DeBouzek negative. They also discovered that the seventeenth-century, handwritten inscription on the back was written in ink that had cracked. They returned the Oath to Wapner, but the test results went to Salt Lake City.

Back in Utah, Throckmorton met with Rod McNeil, a research scientist and head of Environmental Technologies in Palmer, Montana. McNeil had developed a new test to track the movement of ions in ink to show how long ink had been in contact with paper. The artificial aging on the Hofmann documents threw off the test by as much as a decade, but McNeil's tests indicated comprehensively that none of the Hofmann documents had been written before 1920. With McNeil's equipment, Throckmorton and Flynn were also able to analyze the chemical composition of the inks on the Hofmann documents, learning that the ingredients were more available and the composition simpler than they had believed.

While Throckmorton and Flynn continued their research, D'Elia decided to approach New York officials about investigating Hofmann for fraud in his proposed sale of the first Oath. If he were successful, D'Elia figured, Hofmann would have a two-front war to fight. The prospect of time in a New York jail might not appeal to a defendant roaming freely while awaiting trial in Utah. An indictment from New York would give Yengich pause also, D'Elia thought, since New York would be unimpressed by the feisty style Yengich used to advantage in polite Utah.

D'Elia felt fine about "his" murder case except when he thought about a jury. The involvement of LDS church leaders presented a terrific complication. This was a case that would be difficult to try outside Utah—but could it be tried inside Utah? The defense would ask prospective jurors something like, "Would you believe President Hinckley no matter what he said?" Anyone who replied yes would be disqualified for bias. So, D'Elia figured, the jury would first have to be "church-qualified"—made up of non-Mormons, ex-Mormons, inactive Mormons—then "death-qualified"—comprised of jurors capable of giving the death penalty if they felt it was warranted.

Then constitutionality could become a question in a state more than 70 percent Mormon. Ordinarily, jurors are not asked their religious preference, but in this case it would be relevant. Yet it would be impossible to move the case out of state. Hofmann's peers were here, and he was entitled to a trial by his peers. Move the case to Provo, home of BYU and center of Mormon orthodoxy, and you might not even find twelve non-Mormons, D'Elia supposed. But move the trial to racially and religiously diverse Price, in central Utah, and you would really be in trouble, trying both to explain the complexities of the case to rural jurors and counteract anti-Mormon feeling. Utahns simply had too many deep-rooted and mixed feelings about the Mormon church for either prosecution or defense to feel confident about a jury.

While defense attorneys did not particularly want Gordon Hinckley testifying against their client, they saw his involvement as more of a problem for the prosecution than for the defense. Hinckley was a material witness and would have to be called, but Rich and Yengich saw that as a personal conflict for Stott, as well as a strategic problem. Yes, Stott would call Hinckley, and yes, Hinckley would testify. Yet given the structure and reverential nature of the Mormon priesthood hierarchy and Hinckley's high profile, the prospect of his taking the witness stand was difficult to visualize.

The defense had taken a beating at the preliminary hearing. They had expected the eyewitnesses from the bombing sites and the expert testimony regarding cracked ink. What they had not expected was a full blown case against Mike Hansen, who had purchased snow tires, batteries and mercury switches, and ordered printing plates using Mark Hofmann's telephone number, checks, and fingerprint. However, their client's family was supportive, and Hofmann had pleaded not guilty. Yengich's and Rich's battle would be one of strategy, not evidence.

Their first post-preliminary hearing victory came when Judge Kenneth Rigtrup was assigned the murder case and immediately granted the defense motion for separate trials for the murder, forgery, and fraud charges—since they were widely diffuse, stretching over six years and involving a variety of allegations and victims. Rigtrup had been assigned by a new computer program. For years, high profile murder cases in the third district had been heard by Judge Jay Banks, nicknamed "the hanging judge," by defense lawyers. Banks, nearing retirement, was the name that prosecutors had hoped for.

Rigtrup, used to civil cases, now had a trial that involved the state's most powerful institution and would draw national media interest. The prosecutors worried that an inexperienced or insecure judge would tend to rule for the defense, since the defense had the right of appeal. Also, Rigtrup was confined to a wheelchair, having contracted polio while in the army, and might sympathize with the defendant's disability, they stewed. Rigtrup set a murder trial date of March 3, 1987, and the judges assigned to hear the other Hofmann cases set trial dates for later that spring and summer.

When Ted Cannon heard the trial date, he looked down the table at Stott skeptically. "As soon as I'm gone, you're going to plead this in," he predicted.

During the summer of 1986 Stott knew better than to discuss plea bargaining in Cannon's office, but he knew that the Hofmann case was headed in that direction. He sensed the impact the preliminary hearing had made on Yengich and Rich. Each passing week increased Stott's conviction that a guilty plea was coming. For one thing, the defense did not request "discovery," or a listing, of the prosecution's latest evidence. At the very least, Yengich and Rich did not seem in any hurry.

Meanwhile, the families of the murder victims were trying to get on with their lives. Terri Christensen had appreciated the preliminary hearing, once the evidence about the bombings was over. For months before, her main ties to Steve had been the detectives' visits or the stories Don Tanner told her sons when he dropped by. Now, virtually every day, she heard someone describe a different facet of Steve or his experiences. She had caught Ken Farnsworth or Jim Bell after court sessions to ask questions, and began filling in pieces herself from scraps of memory. She also began to sense how many people cared about Steve's death and her loss. She was not as alone as she had thought.

The hearing also forced her to confront an anger she had refused to face before. Now she saw Mark Hofmann in the courtroom every day. He never said a word to her, but she watched him examine the photographs and evidence or listen to the testimony against him. His emotions never showed. She found it difficult to contain her rising anger.

By the time the hearing ended, school was nearly over for the summer. Father's Day was a nightmare, but Terri was soon busy with the boys' schedules and her new baby. She had also enrolled in a course on exploring one's feelings and relationships.

The Hofmann family was relieved when the preliminary hearing ended and the daily media coverage of Mark faded. Most family members did not believe he was guilty, and the continual barrage of so-called evidence was painful. Within the Hofmann family, a protective blanket of silence sheltered feelings. From the first, the case had not been freely discussed, nor speculation entertained. Mark could not have done such things; therefore, he had not.

Mark and Dori brought their children to family outings, though Mark had to get permission to attend the Sears reunion in Vernal, Utah. The immediate family saw this as a heartening sign of his devotion to family solidarity. However, the news that Dori was expecting their fourth child in December came as a surprise to most, given the instability of their situation, the seriousness of Mark's injuries, and the fact that they already had three children, the oldest of whom was five. (The defense attorneys, when Hofmann told them a trifle sheepishly that a baby was expected, figured a new infant might soften a jury. Any and all human touches could be favorable.)

Hofmann entered the hospital again and was prepared for knee implant surgery. However, the donor joint was not available, and the operation never took place. Although Hofmann was seen in public on crutches during the summer and fall, his damaged knee was healing and his walking steadily improved.

Bill Hofmann confided to a few family members that there was more information that had not come out in the preliminary hearing. Perhaps, he said, someday he could tell them more. To others, he indicated that all would not be understood until the next life. He let family members know that he relied on the spiritual confirmation of Mark's innocence he had felt when he had questioned his seriously injured son in the hospital.

Not only had Mark said he had had nothing to do with the murders but also that the Mormon church had the McLellin collection. President Hinckley's stipulation had stated that the church did not have the papers. The conflict for the family was obvious. Yet the Hofmanns had known that some of Mark's transactions with the church had, of necessity, been kept secret by church leaders. Bill had defended the church's secrecy to Mark years ago, just as he had counseled his son that trouble-some religious questions did not pertain to his salvation and that he should not challenge those in authority. The Hofmanns were prepared to sacrifice for the church's sake. Although the months since the bombings had been horrifying, Bill Hofmann would neither criticize the church he loved nor give up on his only son. Others in the family found strength in Dori's testimony to her ward the first Sunday in December, "We know that Mark is being prepared for something really special."

Only a few in the extended family knew that Lue Hofmann, withdrawn since the bombings and continuing to lose both weight and sleep, had confided to a loved one her worst fear—that Mark was, in fact, guilty.

In a "small town" like Salt Lake City, interwoven with wards, stakes, and many large families, the Sheetses were frustrated by reports that the Hofmanns' family, friends, and ward still believed in Mark's innocence. They tried to ignore the situation, but living in Holladay, they occasionally passed Mark, Dori, and the children in their van on the freeway or ran into mutual acquaintances.

As Kathy Sheets's birthday approached on July 31, her friends decided they wanted a lasting memorial. By now they knew that the family home would go into the bankruptcy. The grassy corner of the nearby wardhouse lawn overlooked the woods and stream beside their driveway. Gary Sheets asked the bishop, "I wonder if we could get permission to have a memorial bench to Kathy installed there in the corner."

The bishop looked at him keenly. "No," he said, "I can't give you permission."

Sheets was taken aback, then decoded the message, laughed, and slapped the man's shoulder. "I see that you're going by the old rule: It's easier to repent than get permission." The bishop smiled.

So the family and close friends began making plans. On July 31, a group of tearful people gathered at the corner of the ward lot where the memorial bench stood. The preliminary hearing had established in their minds that Kathy Sheets had died an innocent bystander, probably a decoy. The meaningless nature of her death added to their pain.

Cherie Bridge, a next-door neighbor, delivered her reminiscences as listeners wept. "I remember Kathy," she began. "Costume collections and Halloween — best treats in the neighborhood (especially for the little kids who came early); her new red car after driving a frump car for years. . . . Late night talks with her children, formals, parties, campaign posters, ball games never missed — finally weddings and grandchildren. A ring turned backwards to remember something, a big smile and a voice that could always be heard. We miss you, Kathy," she concluded, "we love you, and in the eternal scheme of things, we will see you for lunch tomorrow."

Financial uncertainty plagued not only Gary Sheets but his sons-in-law as well, since both had been connected to CFS.

Lawsuits, bankruptcy, and an FBI investigation were underway, and Gary's time in the family home was limited. When he became engaged to a woman near his own age who had several grown children, the news, embroidered by gossip, buzzed about town.

Sheets's children liked their father's fiancee and did not want him to be lonely, but they had mixed feelings about the marriage. They asked him to wait a year after their mother's death. He set the wedding date for October 17. As the time neared, however, his intentions waned. Gretchen wrote the family from Europe, where she was taking a semester abroad, that the family should fast and pray regarding her father's engagement. Soon afterward, Gary called Heidi Jones and said he would like to drop by.

When he came in, Jones commented, "I already know what you want to talk about. You don't know if you want to get married."

Sheets nodded, and they talked for a long time. "You know, your mom didn't really want me to marry again," he said.

"If you do marry again, you want to be looking into the future, not back into the past," Jones answered, feeling that her mother would not wish him twenty or thirty years of loneliness. She knew that her father had just begun to mourn. The business crisis was no longer the burning issue it had been; the preliminary hearing was over. Grief and loneliness had waited patiently until Sheets was no longer distracted.

Katie Robertson had all the family home movies put on video cassettes, and they got together to watch them. The experience was more wrenching than nostalgic. Kathy was so vivid, so alive and familiar on the screen, that seeing her was more than Gary could bear. He watched and wept.

His daughters had preceded him on the journey of grief, but they were learning that the road was longer than they thought. It bothered them that the house their mother had designed and cared for was slowly running down. The family sense of mimicry sometimes rescued them. "See!" they imitated their mother saying. "I told you that everything would fall apart without me!"

"Right now, Mom's up there taking a crash course in the Book of Mormon," they'd tell each other — and laugh.

In September, Gary Sheets had knee surgery. "You can have ten years of walking or five years of racquetball," the doctor told him.

"I'll take the five years of racquetball."

He began playing again and felt better. Now that he had lost everything, he had time to talk with his grandchildren every day and grow closer to Gretchen and Jim, still at home.

The second his body hit the sidewalk, Brent Metcalfe woke up. Before that, he dreamed he was walking up the incline toward his parents' condominium in downtown Salt Lake City. Behind him was the Church Office Building and the noise of traffic. He had the definite, sinister feeling that someone was following him, but climbing the hill made it difficult to watch. He heard the gunshot the same moment he felt it.

Metcalfe got up, toweled off the cold sweat, and looked out the window of his apartment into the Arizona night. His clock told him he had slept only three hours, about average now that he faced returning to Salt Lake City to discuss Mark Hofmann with the prosecutors. He had left Salt Lake before the preliminary hearing and had tried to start a new life. His marriage had ended, his job was gone, he had become notorious as one of Hofmann's friends and employees. He tried to forget all that — to forget Steve Christensen, Gary and Kathy Sheets, and Hofmann. He found it impossible. Things were coming together now, things he had sorted through for the last year. But seeing them fit made him no less frightened.

For a long time, as the media reported accusations of apparent double dealing, Metcalfe had not been too bothered. He knew that Hofmann liked living on the edge, having half a dozen deals up in the air, then consummating them just in time. He also knew that Hofmann lied. Like Jeff Salt before him, Metcalfe had figured that out but had learned to accept it. He did not take it personally; in fact, he defended Hofmann to himself and others. Maybe he was pressing Mark for information about buyers or leads or documents that Mark simply could not provide. Hofmann's pragmatic philosophy was to do what seemed best at the moment. Hofmann was bright, easy-going, and had leads on more Mormon documents than other people even knew existed.

Now the dark suspicions about Hofmann left Metcalfe weak. He could not imagine Hofmann or anyone committing those crimes, and Hofmann had looked him in the eye and denied that he had anything to do with them.

As news reports outlined details of the preliminary hearing, Metcalfe found himself calling friends in Salt Lake City for information. When he heard about the Mike Hansen alias and Hofmann's fingerprint appearing on a Mike Hansen printing order, he couldn't stand it any longer. He called Hofmann.

Dori answered and told him he could not talk with Mark; his attorneys did not want him to talk with Metcalfe, or Lyn Jacobs, or Shannon Flynn. Metcalfe asked Dori about the evidence and found that she did not believe any of it. "The reporters ask me why I'm not going to court anymore," she said. "It's just so hard to sit there and hear them say all these things about Mark."

As summer turned into autumn, Bob Stott was happy to see there were still no requests for discovery or other motions from Hofmann's attorneys. He had called Ron Yengich during the summer, but Yengich had refused to discuss a plea bargain as long as Ted Cannon was in office. The defense attorneys believed that Cannon's political position was so shaky that he did not have the strength to allow a reasonable plea bargain, that he would have a hard time giving up the death penalty. However, one day when Stott saw Yengich, he decided to broach the obvious. "You know, we're both going to have to do an awful lot of work before March. If we're ever going to reach an accommodation on this case, we'd might as well do it before we go to all that trouble."

Yengich agreed but was in no hurry. His client was free on bond, apparently at no risk to himself or anyone else. Yengich and Cannon had feuded for years, and he had no desire to give Cannon a guilty plea on a case like this.

However, it did not take a crystal ball for Yengich, Stott, or anyone else to see that Cannon's remaining days as county attorney were few. Since the bombings, his political problems had provided an ongoing sideshow to the Hofmann case, though Cannon had done his utmost to protect the bombings team from his controversies.

"I put my foot in my mouth again," he announced more than once, sliding into his seat at a Hofmann "skull session." "You'll be reading about it, but don't let it bother you. I'll take care of it."

Late in December 1985, news had broken that a grand jury, encouraged in part by Sheriff Pete Hayward, would investigate the CAO on allegations that an arson report which implied county liability had been suppressed. In January, Cannon had denounced the grand jury as politically motivated, half-heartedly apologizing a few days later. In March, he had said he would not run for re-election. "That's the day I neutered myself," he later remarked. Once he became a lame duck, loyalties in his office split between two Republican in-house candidates for Cannon's job. One of them won a muddy primary campaign, then lost to defense attorney and former prosecutor David Yocom, a Democrat, in November.

Yocom was no stranger to the CAO. During the 1970s, he had tried high-profile cases, taking Bob Stott and Dick Forbes under his wing. Although Cannon rejected the idea of a plea bargain, Stott and Forbes kept Yocom — still a good friend and Cannon's expected successor — apprised of negotiations as the summer wore on. The Hofmann case contained the kind of mystery that had always intrigued Yocom. Short of a "smoking gun," there was nothing better than a strong, circumstantial case, he believed, and the Mike Hansen evidence was compelling. Of course, at a jury trial there were always risks. Yocom complied with Stott's request that the Hofmann case not become a campaign issue.

However, Cannon was gone before Yocom could be elected. In October, one of the secretaries in the investigations department released a tape recording that toppled Cannon's teetering career. She maintained that the conversation on the tape represented only one such incident in Cannon's continuing sexual harassment. The county commission asked for Cannon's resignation, but Cannon refused. Immediately, the grand jury added sexual harassment to a list of other indictments. Cannon took a paid leave of absence to fight for his professional survival, but ultimately he pleaded guilty to a misdemeanor count of sexual harassment and was found guilty of criminal defamation and official misconduct. He was fined and served nearly a month in jail. Yocom became acting county attorney soon after the election, for Cannon obviously would not be back.

One day, as Cannon's troubles mounted, Stott dropped by Yengich's office, and the two went for a ride so as not to be seen talking together. Stott did not believe in starting high on a plea bargain and getting talked down, so he gave Yengich an option at the outset. Hofmann could plead guilty to one first-degree murder without the death penalty (meaning Hofmann would serve a life sentence), guilty to two forgeries, and clear up the rest. By "clear up" Stott meant that Hofmann should state in open court that the charges that would be dismissed were true. Or, as another option, Stott said, Hofmann could plead guilty to two second-degree murders (meaning a five years-to-life sentence for each), plead guilty to two forgeries, and clear up the rest.

Yengich thought it over. "I'll get back to you," he said.

Up to that point, Mark Hofmann was virtually the only person in the case who had said nothing about Mark Hofmann — at least, not directly. That silence, especially coupled with the magnitude of the charges against him, had engendered a certain mystique. Defense attorneys suspected that there was enough mystery left in the bombings and forgeries cases to win their client a better plea bargain. When they met again, Yengich had a proposition for Stott. "What if we allow you to interview Mark, and then you drop the second murder to manslaughter?"

No deal, Stott told him. Yengich tried again. "What if we allow you to interview Mark, and you give him a break on the sentencing. He'll plead to second degree, but the penalty will be reduced to manslaughter."

Stott thought it over and agreed. Gradually, the deal evolved until Hofmann need only meet with prosecutors to discuss his crimes. This arrangement promised answers, Stott reasoned, that they could never get otherwise. The fact that so many people still thought they had the wrong man galled him—as did the insistence of historians, collectors, and experts that the documents were genuine. Now he and the other investigators would be vindicated by Hofmann himself, and they wouldn't have to drag the families through a messy trial.

Meanwhile, no one had mentioned these negotiations to Gerry D'Elia, who was worrying about the murder trial scheduled to begin in March. The defense motions had not been filed, Stott seemed to have all the time in the world, and an old courtroom enemy of D'Elia's, Dave Yocom, was stepping into Cannon's shoes as acting county attorney. D'Elia wanted the murder case in court soon. He went to see Stott.

"Okay, Bob," he said, "get off my homicides. If you were sincere about Ted making you take the case against your will, Ted's gone. Now's your chance to get off my cases."

Stott looked at him incredulously. "What are you talking about? You know I can't do that. I probably can't even try the forgeries once the murders have been tried and that evidence has been introduced. The only way to get those forgeries resolved is to bring them in as motive for the murders."

D'Elia shrugged; he thought the forgeries far less important than the homicides. One day he walked across the street to talk with Judge Rigtrup, suggesting how difficult it would be to answer defense motions filed in January or even later and still begin trial in March. The judge set a December 5 deadline for all pre-trial motions to be filed. When defense motions came in, right on deadline, they were so perfunctory that Biggs and D'Elia were amused. "I wrote one of these myself while I was at the Legal Defenders," Biggs scoffed. "All they did was change the name."

D'Elia thumbed through the motions on the way out of the office. "Pitch and sink motions," he sneered, giving them a toss.

D'Elia and the new acting county attorney had struck sparks several times. During Yocom's first weeks he pulled D'Elia off a case he wanted plea bargained, but D'Elia came to court anyway and watched from the back of the courtroom. They even argued publicly about the length of D'Elia's hair. Finally, Yocom transferred D'Elia to the CAO's southeast office, a demotion without a salary cut, which effectively removed D'Elia from the Hofmann case. D'Elia protested to the press and prepared to fight the transfer, then changed his mind and resigned. The Christensens, Sheetses, Ashworths, and other victims were dismayed, the detectives upset, and the public nonplussed, but Yocom said the case was still in good hands. Privately, he was confident that Yengich and Hofmann would ultimately come through with a guilty plea.

D'Elia reasoned that the Hofmann case was all that was keeping him at the CAO anyway. He knew he couldn't work for Yocom. Secretly, he suspected that without him there would be "four cold feet going into that courtroom with the bombing evidence." He nursed the fragile hope that if the case went to trial, he would help prosecute it under contract.

Until D'Elia's resignation, Stott had hoped that D'Elia would be put back on the case. Despite his negotiations with Yengich, Stott wanted his bases covered, and D'Elia covered several. He thought that once tempers cooled, something might be worked out regarding D'Elia. Meanwhile, Stott was juggling pressures from Yocom, the press, the rest of the team, and, secretly, Yengich. Unlike D'Elia and Biggs, Stott had not been surprised by the defense motions. Now he told Biggs to answer them for Rigtrup.

"I can't answer these things," Biggs protested. "They don't have any points and authorities [i.e., legal precedents]. Let's go to court and get Rigtrup to order the defense to provide the case law."

"No, no. I'll just call Ron and tell him to do it. Just answer them as if they were complete."

Biggs set to work. He agreed with Stott that the most dangerous motion was one that proposed separating the bombings charges from the McLellin frauds. Evidence of forgery and fraud provided the motive for the bombings. The question was, did Hofmann's loans for the McLellin collection and his offers to sell papyri constitute one criminal episode? The prosecution said yes; the defense no. The judge would decide what forgery evidence was admissible, but keeping the McLellin fraud part of the homicide case was critical.

Biggs wrote a 30-page brief explaining how the alias Mike Hansen linked both bombs and forgeries. He addressed the complex motive for murder — that Hofmann was protecting a nine-year forgery scheme and that Christensen was pressing him and was likely to discover the second Oath. When Biggs finished, Stott told him his brief was too long. Painfully, Biggs cut it to ten pages. As he worked, Biggs's mixed feelings about D'Elia's departure kept him company. Biggs had always occupied the narrow middle ground between Stott's caution and D'Elia's aggressiveness.

Meanwhile, Stott found it difficult to explain the complicated case to Dave Yocom or to defend the high cost of prosecuting Hofmann. Yocom was not as interested in the case as Cannon, nor had he been present through its difficult unfolding. "If I can't understand this," he told Stott after one thirty-minute discussion of the murder case, "how will a jury understand it?"

Yocom's assessment did not help Stott's growing insecurity about the trial, nor did Yocom's mandate to reduce the office budget. Later, Yocom commented that expense had not been a deciding factor in the plea bargain, but the arrangement had been financially advantageous.

As Stott and Yengich worked out the plea bargain behind the scenes, guilty pleas to two second-degree homicides and two second-degree frauds were established, setting Hofmann's prison sentences at five-years-to-life for the Christensen murder and three one-to-fifteen-years sentences for the Sheets murder and the frauds. However, Yengich had other cards to play. He wanted the sentences to run concurrently, not consecutively; this way Hofmann would serve, essentially, only the five-years-to-life sentence. That would be easy to arrange, since, by Utah law, if the judge did not specify consecutive sentences, they automatically ran concurrently. As long as Stott had Hofmann's guilt established on the murders and his confession of forgery, he agreed not to oppose Yengich's motion for concurrent sentences. It was up to Rigtrup, anyway, Stott told himself; and, ultimately, the Board of Pardons would decide how long Hofmann served.

Stott was excited by the plea bargain—as unprecedented as the Hofmann case itself. Not only would he put Hofmann in prison, but he would extract from him the specifics of his crimes for a still-wondering public. Since Hofmann would go to prison for a long time, Stott trusted, and since the clean-cut, Mormon Hofmann would probably not have gotten the death penalty at trial, Stott figured he was gaining a lot and giving up very little.

Though the plea bargain negotiations were still not known around the CAO or the SLCPD, George Throckmorton became aware in early December that the Hofmann team was disintegrating and that he was the next casualty. First, he heard he would be fired as part of a cost-cutting move, for all new employees could be fired without cause during an initial six-month probation. Throckmorton, who had left the state attorney general's office only a few years before retirement, had been assured by Cannon that no matter how the election went, his position at the CAO would be secure. But when Yocom arrived early, all that changed. Yocom honored Throckmorton's original agreement with Cannon, even accepting the vacation time Throckmorton had accumulated, but now he figured that Throckmorton knew the risks of changing jobs and would simply have to live with the consequences.

Throckmorton's shock eased a bit when Stott began working with him to draw up a contract for his services to prepare for the March trial. The 500 hours required would at least provide transitional income, for Throckmorton knew his former position at the state attorney general's office had been filled. Gradually, however, Throckmorton could see that Yocom and Stott really expected a plea bargain sometime before trial. He had no idea when it would be or how much he could earn before then.

A few days before Christmas 1986, Dave Biggs walked by Stott's office and saw Mike George. Biggs sauntered in and Stott said, "Well, Dave, if you were going to offer a plea bargain, what would your best deal be?"

Without hesitation, Biggs said, "One capital homicide without the death penalty and two first-degree frauds."

"Shit, Stott!" George whistled. "You should have sent him to talk with Yengich," and laughed, Stott joining in.

"What's going on?" Biggs asked.

Stott sat up straight in his chair. "Well, we think there's going to be a plea."

"Oh, yeah? When did all this come up?"

"Well, I've been talking to Ron for a month or so."

"You mean I've been busting my ass on these motions and you've been doing a deal?"

"Yeah, that's about it. Yengich wanted it to be secret, to not have anybody else know but the two of us."

"Is the deal done?"

"Yeah, it pretty much is. Two second-degree murders, two second-degree frauds, and an explanation. What do you think of it?"

Biggs kept his cool. "It doesn't matter what I think. It's done."

Biggs left. Throckmorton came in shortly thereafter, and Stott told him he would have to advise Yocom not to sign Throckmorton's contract. They had a plea bargain arranged, he said, and explained it.

"When did this get started?" Mike George asked.

Stott, always vague about time, figured it out. He decided it would have been between the time Cannon left office and the election.

"So Ted was right," George said. "As soon as he left you pleaded Mark in."

Stott still had to sell his plan to the rest of the team. Police routinely interview felons after conviction, but additional information never affects sentencing nor is it made public. Tangles in the investigation could be traced to Hofmann's lies to friends, clients, and the media both before and after the bombings. So an important question became: How could Stott trust Hofmann to tell the truth, unless, perhaps, they questioned him before sentencing? Chief of Police Bud Willoughby, Ken Farnsworth, Jim Bell, and George Throckmorton all supported pre-sentence interviews, and finally Stott agreed. But Yengich would not have it.

Stott capitulated, explaining to his colleagues, "If we talk to him during the thirty days after the guilty plea, we'll get a more complete account. He's going to prison anyway. He's pleading guilty to murder. Why shouldn't he tell the truth?"

Stott met with Terri and Mac Christensen, then with Gary Sheets. He explained the plea bargain agreement and his reasons for seeking it. He told them that the plea bargain would prevent an extended trial and the possibility of complicated legal procedures. He did not think they were giving up anything, since Hofmann was unlikely to get the death penalty, and a five-years-to-life sentence could keep him in prison for twenty to thirty years at the very least. Both the Christensens and Sheets assured Stott that they were satisfied. They did not want the legal hassles and publicity to continue, nor did they hunger for the death penalty.

Yengich, too, talked briefly with Mac Christensen and Gary Sheets, confiding how difficult the plea bargain would be for Hofmann's parents, who did not know yet that Mark was dealing with prosecutors. Dori, who had recently given birth to their fourth child, Julie, was aware of the negotiations.

Meanwhile, prosecutors learned that, as a further complication, Bill Hofmann believed, like some other conservative Mormons, in the doctrine of blood atonement, which early Mormons had adapted from the Old Testament. The teaching holds that the blood of a murderer should be spilled to atone for the crime. Foreseeing trouble, Stott photocopied an article from *Dialogue: A Journal of Mormon Thought* that disavowed that blood atonement was an official church doctrine and gave it to Yengich to pass on to the defendant's father.

Throughout the plea bargain negotiations, Mark Hofmann had cooperated, discussing the intricacies of the plea bargain so dispassionately that Brad Rich sometimes asked himself if Hofmann understood—at gut level—that he was going to prison. Occasionally, Rich wondered if Hofmann could work out a bargain that included the death penalty with the same calm, so divorced were his rational processes from his emotions.

Keeping the negotiations quiet was critical, for if Hofmann changed his mind and word leaked that he had considered a guilty plea, the effect on a prospective jury could be devastating. Reporters were becoming increasingly suspicious. Stott suggested entering the plea on Christmas Eve, but Yengich still had concerns.

For instance, prosecutors had pursued a fraud indictment in New York on the "Oath of a Freeman"; now Stott said he thought he could deflect that. He called the New York authorities and got a verbal commitment that they would not proceed with their inquiry if Hofmann pleaded guilty to a similar offence in Utah. Yengich said that a verbal commitment was not good enough; he wanted a written statement. That took a little time.

Farnsworth listened closely when Stott read the plea bargain agreement to him, then commented, "This doesn't say anything about the police going out to talk to Mark. It says the prosecutors."

"You know that includes you guys. It includes all of us, the whole team. Whoever needs to be there."

"It doesn't say the police. I'd like to see that written in."

"No, I don't want to write in a hundred little details and have to argue with Yengich over all of them."

Farnsworth insisted, but to no avail. Gradually, despite their skepticism, investigators became excited about the prospects of talking with Hofmann. None gave Hofmann high marks for honesty, yet each thought he could check or discern the truthfulness of any of Hofmann's statements.

Fellow Democrat Dave Yocom drew the unpleasant task of telling County Sheriff Pete Hayward about the plea bargain. To no one's surprise, Hayward was not happy. A few reporters were hearing about the plea and, just as fast, being sworn to secrecy. Christmas came, and even reporters took a few days off.

Then on Monday, December 29, KTVX-TV, Channel 4, broke the story, with KSL and KUTV on its heels. The details of the agreement varied from one account to another, but the two second-degree murders and an admission that the salamander letter was forged were on target. Hofmann's family was outraged by the reports, which they believed were totally erroneous. Yengich, who made no secret of his affection for Bill Hofmann, was furious and accused the CAO of leaking the news. Stott vehemently denied that, but, for a week, the plea bargain swayed precariously between two disturbed camps.

Stott had begun collecting questions for Hofmann from various document victims and collectors. He called Brent Ashworth before the plea bargain took place. "Can you tell me all the documents you bought from Hofmann, Brent?"

Ashworth had recently brought suit against Hofmann for selling him twelve forged documents, but Hofmann had defaulted. "I gave you a copy of my lawsuit. Why don't you check that?"

Stott sounded dissatisfied.

"Well, what does it matter now anyway?" Ashworth asked. "He's not going to tell you the truth."

Stott seemed astounded. "What reason would he have to lie?"

"What reason does he have to tell the truth?"

On January 7, 1987, both sides met and signed the plea agreement, with the written understanding that it would not be binding until formally entered in court. Mark Hofmann agreed to plead guilty to two counts of second-degree murder — a first-degree felony — in the "knowing and intentional murders" of Steven F. Christensen and Kathleen W. Sheets, and to a second-degree theft-by-deception count in the sale of the salamander letter to Christensen. His guilty plea to a second-degree fraud in obtaining money from Alvin Rust for the non-existent McLellin collection completed the guilty pleas.

In return, Hofmann was promised the following: that the State of Utah would dismiss the twenty-six remaining felony counts against him; that the U.S. Attorney would dismiss the federal machine gun charges; and that the State of New York would not prosecute him.

Furthermore, if Hofmann would answer questions regarding the murders and the two frauds before he entered his plea in court, prosecutors would not oppose Yengich's motion to reduce the penalty for the Sheets homicide to manslaughter, nor would Stott oppose a motion that Hofmann's sentences run concurrently. In return, "within thirty days" Hofmann would answer "truthfully and completely" all questions asked by prosecutors concerning other charges or related matters. If Hofmann's answers were satisfactory, prosecutors would state this to the Board of Pardons. Otherwise, they could make a negative recommendation.

For the next two days, at Yengich's home, Hofmann talked with prosecutors about the bombings. No court reporter was present since the conversations were informal and preceded the actual conviction. The agreement actually specified only that Hofmann give his attorney this information, who could then relay it to prosecutors. Stott and Biggs were happy to hear from Hofmann directly.

They were surprised at how easily Hofmann opened up. He described youthful exploits making gunpowder and a cannon with his cousin Mike, and other experiments with explosives. His purchases of bomb parts he assigned to October 5. He knew he was going to make two bombs to kill two people, he said, but was not sure who the victims would be. Maybe Tom Wilding or Brent Ashworth with the first bomb and himself with the second, or perhaps Christensen and Wilding, or Wilding and Ashworth (now omitting any mention of suicide). Finally he decided that Steve Christensen would have to be killed so that the McLellin transaction could not take place, he said. He knew that CFS and Gary Sheets were in trouble and chose Sheets as a diversion so the bombings would seem linked to CFS.

He described constructing the bombs the night before the murders, after dropping off Shannon Flynn and visiting with his wife until she went to bed. He had worked during the early morning hours, he said, when he usually did his best forgeries. He decided on his targets and looked up Sheets's address in the telephone directory, underlining it with the same marker he used to address the packages. The investigators, he asserted, had missed that evidence. After drilling the end caps in his garage, he had gathered every trace of filings and scraps and left it in dumpsters, including one near Shannon Flynn's condominium. Then he drove to the Sheets's house and left the bomb.

Aaron Teplick remembered the hands on the clock wrong,

Hofmann said, for he had been driving his van down the driveway at 3:00 a.m., not 11:45 p.m. He said he left the package in front of the garage door nearest the walkway, later adding that he left it in the driveway five feet from the garage. He thought a car would bump and ignite it, or, since the rocket ignitor might be defective, maybe it would not explode at all. It did not matter since it was just a diversion.

He knew, didn't he, prosecutors asked, that the Sheets bomb could cause death or injury? Yes, Hofmann shrugged, he knew.

After placing the Sheets bomb, Hofmann drove home. His daughter cried out when he entered the house, and his wife called to him to attend to the baby. He had, so Dori had the impression he had been home all night.

Between 6:00 and 6:30 a.m. he went to the Judge Building, Hofmann continued, describing an attractive woman on the elevator with him and the Passeys but essentially denying that Janet McDermott had seen him on the sixth floor. He had left clues for police, he said, by wearing his letterman's jacket and dropping rubber gloves and other evidence in trash cans outside. If the police could catch him, they should.

Stott and Biggs recognized Hofmann's posturing as common to criminals who never want to admit they were not smart enough to elude police. Stott told Hofmann the police had searched the trash cans. Hofmann said he had noticed a bag lady and street people outside. They had probably retrieved the items before the police could find them.

However, when Hofmann said the bombs had safety devices, both Stott and Biggs believed him. Neither could imagine anyone walking around with fully armed bombs. Hofmann said he had used an icepick to punch holes in the cardboard boxes, pulled wires through, and taped them. After he placed the bombs, he removed the tape and connected the wires so that as soon as the packages were tilted, the mercury would complete an electrical circuit and ignite the bombs. In fact, Hofmann expanded, he had noticed one of those icepick holes in the cardboard fragments in evidence at the preliminary hearing, hinting that investigators should have found it.

By 7:00 a.m., Hofmann was home again. At about 8:30 a.m., he said he called the Sheetses to warn them, but no one answered. Then he called Christensen to tell him not to pick up the package, but only got the answering machine.

Next Hofmann explained how easy it was to fool people. The polygraph was only one example. Another was Dallin Oaks—he had spoken with both Oaks and Pinnock the afternoon of the murders, and neither had suspected him of being involved with the bombings.

The third bomb, Hofmann continued, was a suicide attempt. He was distraught over the murders and thought his own death would be best for his family.

Stott had long favored a theory that the third bomb was intended to blow up Hofmann's car to disguise the McMillan papers and papyrus fragment as the now-undeliverable McLellin collection. "Isn't that what you were trying to do?" he asked.

Hofmann easily agreed. "That's partly what I was trying to do." First, he said he went into the Deseret Gym to get a drink of water, then returned and touched two wires together, exploding the bomb.

Stott and Biggs both knew his account contradicted eyewitness reports and physical evidence. Hofmann's hands and face had not been blown away, nor had he held the bomb to his chest as had Christensen and Sheets. But they did not argue, and the conversation ended at this point.

"Frankly," Stott said later, "we were not all that concerned about the murder charges or the McLellin collection or the salamander letter. He was pleading guilty to those. We were more concerned about the other charges. We didn't want to leave them hanging. In those initial conversations, we wanted to determine, if we let him plead guilty, would he be open with us? And I found out yes, he talked and talked and talked. It was not all true, but he would talk and he would give a lot of information."

When prosecutors later debriefed to the rest of the team, some investigators did not believe all of Hofmann's description of the murders. His story about the suicide bomb provided the strongest contrast to the evidence. But there were other problems, as well.

Farnsworth and Bell did not believe the bombs had safeties, other than the mercury switches. The cardboard fragments in evidence had no icepick holes in them; nor was such a thing likely since an explosion seeks the path of least resistance and icepick holes in a box containing a bomb would not remain intact. Hofmann had carried the bombs fully armed, they believed, and he had dropped the third one. Now he was verbally correcting that error, just as he was correcting the recollections of Aaron Teplick and Janet McDermott, and chiding police for not finding his "clues."

Had Hofmann placed the second bomb five feet from the garage in the Sheetses' driveway, investigators realized, it would have been hit by one of the four cars that drove out that morning before Kathy Sheets was killed, or it would have been observed by someone in the carpool. More likely, Hofmann left it by the garage as they had surmised — and as he first indicated — so that Sheets had only to walk a few steps before reaching the walkway, where she was killed.

Also, Hofmann had been in his car by 8:30 the morning of the murders and had telephoned Metcalfe, Flynn, and his bank from his mobile telephone. The mobile telephone records showed no calls either to the Sheets home or to Christensen's office.

Despite the discrepancies, Throckmorton was eager to question Hofmann in detail about his forgery techniques, and Bell and Farnsworth wanted straight answers about the murders. These talks were only preliminary, and with the plea bargain imminent, the team's morale remained intact.

But the plea bargain still stalled because of Hofmann's inability to confront his family. Prosecutors offered to have his prison term postponed for thirty days after he entered his plea. This way he could tell his parents after-the-fact. Hofmann declined but suggested that he plead guilty and be taken to prison before his parents found out. That, however, was virtually impossible, given the media interest — and his attorneys felt that he should tell his parents himself.

Meanwhile, both sides met Judge Rigtrup to work out the details. Rigtrup discussed the dismissal of the remaining charges against Hofmann with the judges presiding over those cases. He had been told, and told them, that the victims' families had approved the plea bargain — and that had an effect on the other judges. After discussion, the judges agreed to dismiss the charges. For his own part, Rigtrup had read the preliminary hearing files and felt that most of the evidence had been aired, constituting, in effect, a public trial. His September decision, denying the prosecution motion to join the five cases, had been almost perfunctory. Now the defense motion to break up the homicide case promised to be touchy. Rigtrup viewed the complicated homicide case, much as Grant had, as a professional liability, more likely to affect his career adversely than favorably.

Also, if Rigtrup heard the murder case and if Hofmann was convicted, Rigtrup knew that Yengich could waive a jury hearing of the penalty phase. That would leave the decision between death and life in prison to Rigtrup. Though he could not predict his decision with any certainty, Rigtrup thought it unlikely that he would sentence Hofmann to death. So it all came down to the same thing. If prosecutors would not fight for consecutive sentences, Rigtrup would go along with Yengich's motion for concurrent prison terms. Judges seldom interjected contrary opinions into plea bargain agreements, and, Rigtrup knew, the final say rested with the Board of Pardons anyway.

The "dress rehearsals," as they were irreverently termed, continued, as attorneys met with Rigtrup to plan the hearing. They decided that when Rigtrup pronounced sentence, he would state that Hofmann ought to spend the rest of his life in prison. The press would pick that up, though such a statement did not have the legal clout of consecutive sentences. Finally, all was arranged and everyone satisfied. The deal was made — almost.

On Thursday, January 22, with the plea bargain imminent, the *Salt Lake Tribune* broke the story. Soon the police officers setting up extra chairs in Rigtrup's chambers were told they could take them down. The plea bargain was off again.

That same day, however, prosecutors met with Hofmann at Yengich's house for another interview. Hofmann opened the discussion by saying the salamander letter was a forgery. He described his research at the University of Utah, his reliance on the 1834 anti-Mormon publication, *Mormonism Unvailed* (which contained the reminiscences of Joseph Smith's neighbors regarding magic and money digging), and his discussions about the occult with Brent Metcalfe. He described stealing paper from a book published in 1830 and adapting Martin Harris's handwriting from his signature and other nineteenth-century handwriting samples. Postmark forgeries came up next, then the "Oath of a Freeman." But Hofmann said he became lazy and had printing plates made. "Obviously, I should have made the Oath plates myself," he said, referring to the microscopic flaws forensic experts had traced.

Prosecutors were pleased by the interview, for the Oath was still being marketed in the East. They asked him if his wife knew he had been forging. Hofmann said he once told her he had forged the Anthon transcript, but she became upset and he had eaten his own words. She may have suspected some things were forged, he added enigmatically, but she thought the Oath and the salamander letter were real.

During the conversation, the doorbell rang. Yengich looked out. "It's your father," he told Hofmann.

"Well, get rid of him."

Yengich talked quietly with Bill Hofmann, who had seen the newspaper story. Bill left, but as the prosecutors gathered their notes and told Mark Hofmann good-bye shortly thereafter, they saw the entire Hofmann family coming up the walk — Bill and Lue Hofmann, Dori with the new baby, and Mark's Aunt Gloria. They nodded politely, and the prosecutors left, wishing they could hear the conversation about to ensue.

Once the Hofmanns gathered in Ron Yengich's home, Mark told them he was going to plead guilty — it was best for everyone concerned. The conversation was painful for all present but not because Hofmann directly admitted guilt. His reasons for entering a guilty plea were pragmatic, leaving his wife and father, at least, still convinced of his innocence.

Months later, Brad Rich flinched discussing that occasion. "The plea bargain was definitely the best thing for Mark," he said, "but it cut the rest of us off at the knees." He included himself and Yengich, the polygraph examiners, and the Hofmann family and friends, all of whom had protested Mark's innocence.

The morning of January 23, 1987, fifteen months after the bombings, Mark Hofmann walked briskly, without limping, from his attorneys' office to the Metropolitan Hall of Justice. His attorneys, father, and an entourage of reporters accompanied him. One reporter's question made Hofmann pause: Did he think his forged documents had damaged the LDS church?

"Oh, I don't think they've been hurt unduly," Hofmann said with a slight smile. He was less pat when asked about going to prison. "Obviously, I know it will be hard on my family, and I feel badly about that. But I think we'll get through it."

Leaving the blaze of television lights, Hofmann in his dark blue, pinstripe suit entered the courtroom and took his seat opposite the Sheetses and Christensens, seated above, below, and in the jury box. Judge Kenneth Rigtrup entered in his wheelchair and opened the session.

During the next twenty minutes, a poised, unemotional Mark Hofmann entered his guilty pleas. The faces before and behind him were solemn, sometimes teary, but only a slight huskiness softened his voice as he said yes, he had killed Steven Christensen; yes, he had killed Kathleen Sheets. Yes, he had forged the salamander letter and robbed Al Rust of his McLellin investment. Bill Hofmann, red-faced, his teeth clenched, watched from his seat behind the defense table.

The officers of the court moved smoothly through legalities. Rigtrup praised Stott and the county attorney's office and granted Yengich's motions. The judge concluded by announcing that Hofmann should spend the rest of his life in prison, then asked that the courtroom be cleared for the convenience of the Hofmann family. Hofmann shot a look at Yengich. "That won't be necessary, Your Honor," Yengich said quickly.

The gavel fell, Yengich handed Gary Sheets a letter of apology from Hofmann to the Sheets and Christensen families. "I'm sorry for what happened," Hofmann had written.

Bill Hofmann watched, as if rooted, when Mark walked past him out the side door, where he was handcuffed and shackled. Yengich ducked back into the courtroom to shake Bill's hand. Now reporters were filing into the hall to catch defense attorneys. The Christensens and Sheetses were hugging one another and passing around Hofmann's letter. Mac Christensen looked across the courtroom at Bill Hofmann, still standing near his seat. Christensen made his way through the crowd and enveloped the smaller man in a bear hug.

As the courtroom cleared, Gary Sheets, too, shook Bill Hofmann's hand and embraced him. "I want you to know we don't bear any ill will toward your family. We think you're a fine man."

A pair of grieved but resolute eyes looked back at him. "I wish you knew that Mark is a fine man, too."

As reporters walked over to a press conference at the police station, the earliest reports hit the airwaves saying that Hofmann had pleaded guilty to first-degree murder and had been sentenced to life in prison. Five minutes into the press conference, however, that simplified view was clarified.

Chief Bud Willoughby stood at the door of the conference room greeting reporters with, "Boy, that's a tough judge." Members of the prosecution team, Yocom, Hayward, and Willoughby, took seats at the front of the room. Ken Farnsworth tried to get Throckmorton to join them, but he kept his seat in the audience. Yocom, sworn to office only days earlier, opened the press conference by thanking all who had worked on the case. He then turned the microphone over to Bob Stott to answer questions. In between queries, Stott commented on the benefits of the plea bargain. They had apprehended the person who had committed the crimes, he said, and now the public knew that. Also, Hofmann would spend the rest of his life in prison.

A reporter quickly pointed out that the judge had not pronounced the sentences consecutively. By law, they would run concurrently.

"That really doesn't matter," Stott said. "What matters is the Board of Pardons and if, after questioning Mark, we tell the Board of Pardons that he cooperated."

"What makes you think he'll tell the truth?"

"We've spoken to him face to face," Stott announced. "I can't go into particulars because we agreed to wait until after the debriefing." He added that Hofmann had been open, honest, and candid.

"But if Hofmann's going to spend the rest of his life in prison, why should he talk?"

Stott explained again that Hofmann would talk to get a good report for the Board of Pardons. The argument seemed circular, returning again to how long he would be in prison — if he got a good report. Finally, there was a dissatisfied silence, which Stott was quick to fill with praise for Ted Cannon and others involved in the preliminary hearing. "We didn't use all our evidence, and we've since discovered more, but it's basically, mostly there."

"What about church influence?" a reporter asked. "Did you choose the salamander letter to appease the church?"

Stott said the salamander letter was chosen to represent the forgeries because it was the best known. But by choosing the salamander letter, which Christensen had purchased, and the McLellin fraud, which involved only Rust, Stott had precluded naming the church as a victim. After a pause, he said, "Let me just add something here. For nine years, Mark Hofmann's been putting something across on the scholars and the historians and the forensic experts and the collectors. Dave Yocom talked about George Throckmorton. He and Bill Flynn uncovered the methods and ways Hofmann did this, and their discoveries will be a strength in future law enforcement. We will benefit in the future from what we learned from Mark Hofmann."

For a moment, Throckmorton wondered if he might be asked to stay on at the CAO. Meanwhile, Biggs and Farnsworth each answered a few questions, then Hayward, Willoughby, and Yocom added their own endorsements. The press conference ended, but the coverage had just begun. More than one news story asked whether — with one five-years-to-life sentence versus the dismissal of twenty-six felonies and federal charges, plus immunity in New York — Hofmann had not just made the best deal of his life.

As it turned out, the praise Throckmorton received at the press conference did not translate into dollars. His bill for overtime was turned down by the CAO, which no longer needed his services. On February 5, 1987, he returned to pick up his final

paycheck. Stott had invited him to lunch, but he found that
Stott had left to play racquetball. Only half kidding,
Throckmorton left a note on Stott's desk: "How soon they
forget."

19

ASK ME YOUR QUESTIONS

Admitted to the Utah state prison on January 23, 1987, Mark Hofmann, thirty-two, was placed in the prison hospital on suicide-watch. The Hofmann family viewed this as harassment from the CAO, though prosecutors and investigators denied any involvement in the decision. Hofmann's attorneys eventually concluded that so much rested on prosecutors being able to talk with Hofmann that Bob Stott had left nothing to chance.

Before entering prison, Hofmann underwent a routine psychological evaluation by Dr. Robert Howell, a BYU psychology professor and clinical psychologist at the state mental hospital in Provo. Howell's task was to determine Hofmann's mental state, including anti-social or violent personality traits.

Hofmann was being labeled a sociopath in the media. Prison officials would consider such a finding by Howell important because sociopaths — apparently devoid of conscience — tend to commit future crimes, and Hofmann had already shown a capacity for violence. Thus sociopaths make poor candidates for rehabilitation or early release.

When he talked with Hofmann, Howell looked for telltale signs of sociopathology, quickly ruling out the standard psychoses such as schizophrenia and manic depression — Hofmann did not appear to be mentally ill. Sociopathology, on the other hand, is a personality disorder with no established cure. In order to fit the category of sociopathic personality, Hofmann must have, by age eighteen, displayed three or more of the following characteristics: truancy, running away from home, physical fights involving weapons, cruelty toward animals, cruelty toward people, forced sexual relations, repeated fire setting, perpetual lying, and stealing.

Beyond age fourteen, Hofmann must have shown three or more of the following: an inability to sustain consistent employment; failure to conform to lawful behavior; irritability and aggressiveness; repeated failure in managing finances; failure to plan ahead; no regard for the truth; no regard for personal safety; neglect or abuse of children; squandering household goods needed to support a family; failure to sustain a monogamous relationship for more than one year; or lack of remorse for injury to others.

Hofmann appeared in Howell's office as a family man with a wife and four young children. He had a reputation as a successful businessman. And despite the criminal charges against him, Hofmann was entering prison as a "first offender." Hofmann's only previous encounter with the law had been an arrest for shoplifting a bag of peanuts in Logan. When Hofmann did not appear in court, the matter had been dropped.

But Hofmann's boyhood friends remembered incidents of cruelty toward animals, a tendency to lie, his delight in tricking people, stealing chemicals, his fascination with fire and explosives, and occasional incidents involving physical violence. Later friends knew that Hofmann worked at irregular jobs, stole books, lied, bounced checks, spent money lavishly but other times could not or did not supply money for groceries or utilities, was fascinated by guns and explosives, and could be physically violent.

Hofmann was, in fact, a businessman with a family whose success depended upon fraud. He had solved his conflict with Mormon values by choosing to "live in two worlds," as he had once written to his mother. His successes made possible his fraudulent career; his soft-spoken, apparent normalcy became a passport to crime.

Howell, at the end of his examination, concluded that Hofmann was not a sociopath. In fact, Howell was distressed by media reports that asserted Hofmann suffered from sociopathology or was a cold-blooded killer. Howell completed his report for the prison. Hofmann qualified for housing in minimum security but was placed first in the hospital and then in medium security. Knowing that his records said he was not a sociopath or mentally ill, Hofmann objected. "Treat me like you would anyone else," he insisted. His notoriety, he and his family feared, would guarantee unfair punishment.

Hofmann had promised to be interviewed within thirty days of entering his guilty plea. Nineteen days passed before the CAO succeeded in arranging a meeting with Hofmann and Ron Yengich. On February 11, George Throckmorton, Ken Farnsworth, Mike George, and Dick Forbes accompanied Bob Stott and Dave Biggs to the prison. They arrived before Yengich and found themselves making small talk with Hofmann.

Farnsworth had brought a copy of the *New York Times*, featuring a story in which document expert Charles Hamilton proclaimed Hofmann the "World's Greatest Forger" for having duped him and others. Investigators watched Hofmann scan the article and then ask, "Don't you think he's just saying that, trying not to look so stupid?"

During the discussion that followed, Farnsworth came to a conclusion. Hofmann was trying to ingratiate himself, his eyes flicking from face to face. "I probably shouldn't tell you this," Hofmann began one comment. Farnsworth swallowed a smile. Telling secrets—the technique that had never failed to endear Hofmann to others.

About that time, Yengich entered the board room. He took one look, said, "Well, we're not going to talk with all these people here," and walked out with Hofmann.

"If you let Yengich keep us out," Farnsworth said, turning to Stott, "it'll be a stupid move. If you start out the interviews letting Yengich push you around and get everything he wants, he's going to ask for more and get more. Now I don't care about all those forgeries, but I want to be present when the homicides are discussed. There's a lot I know about the murders we've never even discussed."

Throckmorton agreed. "I don't care about being at all the talks either, Bob, but Bill Flynn and myself are still the only people who know what was done to those documents. You won't even know what questions to ask, let alone what counter-questions."

"Yeah, and you've never *interrogated* anyone," Farnsworth put in. "Police are trained in interrogation, not attorneys, and this is certainly no courtroom!"

Stott heard them out, then replied, "I'll talk to Yengich one more time and see if you can just be present during the questioning."

Farnsworth and Throckmorton nodded, partly appeased. "Okay, Bob. Will you let us know whether we should stick around?" Throckmorton asked as they opened the door.

Yengich went in and spoke with Stott while the others, including Hofmann, waited. Then Yengich stuck his head out. "Mark, Dave, come on in."

Hofmann and Biggs went in the room and the door closed. Farnsworth, Throckmorton, George, and Forbes waited in the hall for ten minutes before they realized they would not be seeing Hofmann again, that day at least. They left the prison by the back door, trying to avoid news cameras, and walked to the parking lot. Jim Bell had been right. He had not even bothered to come.

Stott realized at that first meeting that Yengich would hold strictly to the conditions of the plea bargain—interviews only with prosecutors. He and Biggs already knew that Hofmann had an answer for everything and thought him unlikely to break under Farnsworth or Bell. Still, if they let Hofmann talk about the forgeries, clearing them up as he had promised to do, Stott reasoned, the rapport they establish might encourage Hofmann to talk to the detectives.

Yengich and Brad Rich expected the prosecutors to press Hofmann for more information about the homicides, then go after a complete list of forgeries. They were prepared to resist the latter, since they did not want Hofmann charged in other states. But when they began, Stott said, "Mark, let's start with the Anthon transcript."

"Let me interrupt, Bob," Yengich said, surprised. "I'm sorry. When do you intend to go to today? I had planned until 4:30."

Yengich and Rich figured that a few hours should suffice, but Stott said, "We'll go as long as we can. We'll go to the

Anthon transcript and go on from there in kind of chronological order."

Yengich sank back, and for the next two hours, Stott and Hofmann discussed the Anthon transcript. Hofmann described creating it in his Logan apartment while his wife was at work. He took the ink recipe from a book, *Making Ink*, he had stolen from the USU library. He aged the ink with hydrogen peroxide and a clothes iron, added signatures to the Bible, and tried inserting the manuscript in several places.

Hofmann occasionally digressed to criticize forensic analysts, telling prosecutors their experts were wrong that quills could not be distinguished from steel nibs under the microscope. (William Flynn later commented that Hofmann's ego exceeded his expertise, since hard quills and soft steel nibs can be indistinguishable.)

Stott asked Hofmann to detail his research for the Anthon transcript. "I wasn't trying to reproduce an ancient document," Hofmann answered. "I was trying to reproduce a document written by Joseph Smith." He had depended on Charles Anthon's disparaging description. "You know, it's just various screwball characters is what Anthon was saying, and I think that's what you have."

Stott was just coming to the pitch-like glue that had fascinated Jeff Simmonds at USU when Yengich said, "That seems like it would be a good place for us to stop. . . . Are you satisfied with his answers as far as what you have been through today?"

"We are satisfied in the amount of information he's given us," Stott said.

Yengich persisted—was Stott satisfied that thus far Hofmann had met the conditions of the plea bargain agreement?

"Yes. I think we'll want to come back and ask more questions."

"I'm just saying you're satisfied," Yengich repeated. "Pursuant to the agreement—today?"

"Yes," Biggs said, and the session ended.

A week later, Stott, Biggs, Yengich, and Hofmann met again and continued the discussion of the Anthon transcript.

Hofmann said he had composed the Joseph Smith holograph on the back in less than thirty minutes, using a nineteenth-century dictionary. He had made the glue from a burnt match tip, ground up and added to wheat paste. The substance was not sticky enough, so he added a little Elmer's glue.

"I was in a hurry," he said. "I wanted to get this thing done that day."

"Why?" Biggs asked.

"I don't know. It's just — I'm always rather impatient. That's probably part of my personality. I wanted to get it done before Dori came home from work."

By now, Biggs regarded Hofmann as something of a sociopath. He knew that impulsivity was frequently a symptom.

He "found" the transcript the next day, Hofmann continued. "My wife was home. I wanted her to alibi for me or be a witness to its discovery."

"Is this skill in copying handwriting, is that something you had to work at or is that something that came easy to you?" the prosecutors asked.

"Although I really don't consider myself an artistic person, I think I have the ability to look at handwriting and copy it," Hofmann said. He added that the calligraphy class he took had taught him nothing new.

Yengich said it was almost time to quit, but first they discussed Hofmann's ability to deceive. "I think I have that ability in my personality," Hofmann said. "I obviously do for the number of frauds that have been committed, you know as far as . . . I don't think I give myself away very easily as far as I can look someone in the eye and lie, for example."

Was this something he could do back in 1980? prosecutors asked.

"Not so much but I soon developed it. I thought that I . . . for one thing, I didn't believe, for example, in that someone could be inspired as far as what my feelings or thoughts were. You know, using that in a religious sense. I thought that I could give myself away by acting nervous or a certain expression on my face or some outward sign."

When time was up, Yengich again asked if everyone was satisfied. The prosecutors said yes. When they met ten days later on February 27, this time with Rich representing Hofmann, Hofmann described his feelings in April 1980 when he took the Anthon transcript to President Spencer W. Kimball and other Mormon officials.

"I believed it would pass their inspection as far as being in Joseph Smith's handwriting. And, as far as how I felt, probably a combination of emotions. There was, of course, a little bit of fear involved since, of course, it was a forged document. There was some excitement involved, a feeling of duping them, I guess."

What were his feelings about the Mormon church at that time? they asked. He replied that he had lost faith in the church around age fourteen. "Therefore, I wasn't . . . I had no fear as far as . . . This is something that I guess Ron wants to be here when I start talking about. Well, I will finish what I was saying."

Rich interjected, "We are very close to an area that I know Ron wants to be here, but I think you can finish this."

"I wasn't fearful of the church inspiration detecting the forgery," Hofmann said. "That's all I was going to say."

Hofmann, then, was saying that he had abandoned all belief in Mormonism years before he went through the temple, served on an LDS mission, and married in the temple. Prosecutors were struck by Hofmann's capacity for outwardly filling his family's and culture's expectations while maintaining a separate inner life.

Stott noticed how fluent Hofmann was when asked how he forged or tested bombs, and how inarticulate he became when asked why he forged or how he felt. Biggs thought that Hofmann's belief that he was immune to "church inspiration" curiously unsophisticated and concluded that Hofmann had not outgrown a childish delight in duping authority.

They listened intently as Hofmann continued. "I won't go so far as to say I wanted to change Mormon history. Let me take that back. Maybe I did. I believed that the documents that I created could have been a part of Mormon history. I'm speaking specifically, for example, of the magic-related items— the 1825 Stowell letter, the so-called salamander letter. In effect, I guess, the questions I asked myself in deciding on a forgery— one of the questions was—what could have been? I had a concept of church history and I followed that concept."

An off-the-record discussion ensued. Prosecutors were still curious about Hofmann's feelings toward the church and his dealings with high church leaders. However, Yengich and Rich did not want any of Hofmann's comments regarding Gordon Hinckley or other church officials to adversely affect their client's future.

Finished with the Anthon transcript, Hofmann moved on to the Joseph Smith III blessing before the interview ended at 5:30 p.m. Both Biggs and Rich left pondering Hofmann's described "passion for forging." Evidently, Rich mused later, the process of forging—doing the research, finding paper, making the ink, anticipating the tests—was far more fulfilling than the end results.

Hofmann had provided impromptu handwriting samples for the prosecutors. Rich was less impressed with the Joseph Smith and Thomas Bullock signatures Hofmann dashed off than with the way Hofmann held his creations to the light and commented on them with pride or chagrin.

When Rich and Biggs met with Hofmann on March 12, the interviews quickened. Expeditiously, Biggs led Hofmann through his printed forgeries of White Notes, Spanish Fork Notes, the Emma Smith hymnal, and the "Oath of a Freeman." Not only did Biggs move faster through the material than Stott, but Rich was less likely than Yengich to object. In this relaxed setting, Hofmann enjoyed the conversation, sensing the others' interest. At one point he leaned over to Biggs and said, "You're just dying to hear this, aren't you?"

Five days later, the trio met again, except this time Mike George was included. Hofmann and Rich did not seem to care. George kept quiet and observed, hoping he could return again and not disturb the SLCPD's chances to participate. The interviews were held in the comfortable paneled board room on the second floor of the main prison building.

This time Hofmann detailed his creation of the Oath— studying type, cutting letters with an exacto knife (though he denied cutting them from the library book investigators had found missing identical letters), using red fungi to age the paper, and cutting a quill. "By the time I forged the Oath, I considered myself a pretty good forger. I thought I had a pretty good knowledge of different techniques that would be used in analyzing it."

"Had you ever done that—looked through a microscope under ultraviolet light at printed and written material?" Biggs asked.

"Yes, I have. I've studied that. You will be interested to know that I also, even before the preliminary hearing, spoke to Ron about my fears as far as the cracking was concerned."

"Oh, really? You had seen that cracking before, yourself?"

"Yes, although I didn't know the cause of it until the preliminary hearing as far as the gum arabic. Undoubtedly when somebody reads this transcript, they'll keep gum arabic out of the formula."

"We are doing an invaluable service here, I guess," Biggs quipped. "One last question," he continued, "before we stop for a minute so Mr. Rich can go get a guard. Hypothetically, if the American Antiquarian Society had been able to and did vote to purchase your Oath on October 15, 1985, for about a million dollars, what would that have done to the financial hole that you dug yourself into by that time?"

"It would have relieved me from it. Hence, I guess you want me to say that the bombings would not have taken place."

"I don't want you to say that unless it's true."

"I'll say it since it's true," Hofmann told him, and they took a break.

Like Rich, George was intrigued by Hofmann's pride in his profession. Hofmann told George that forgery had dominated his thinking for years, since he was a teenager. He loved discussing various tests and confided that he thought he had figured out ways to elude even the newest methods of detection. He had suggested that George was good at his job because he devoted his time, energy, and thoughts to it. Well, Hofmann shrugged, it was the same way with him and forgery.

During three April meetings, the prosecutors presented Hofmann with several prominent Mormon forgeries. Hofmann filled in details, confiding that he had filched the paper for the Bullock letter from an executive ledger book in the USU library.

He created the letter to validate the Joseph Smith III blessing, he said, and gave it to the LDS church. Regarding the Stowell letter, Hofmann said he had met with President Hinckley three times and that Hinckley had said only top Mormon leaders would know of its existence.

Forgery technicalities introduced the third meeting, as Hofmann told the prosecutors how he had used ozone to age the Oath. He placed the document in an ozone-filled glass aquarium and passed an electric spark through the document. They then discussed the forging of the Grandin Book of Mormon contract, including the 1830 Grandin advertisement imprinted on the obverse side to give the impression of paper from Grandin's printing shop.

When they reached the Jonathan Dunham letter, Biggs tried to get Hofmann to talk about Brent Ashworth, the only person for whom Hofmann showed visible contempt, but Hofmann would say little and refused to clarify why he took a loss on the Dunham letter when he was desperate for money.

A defense of his business methods—paying back loans with interest for fraudulent transactions—led to Hofmann's own definition of document value. He explained that at age fifteen he had electroplated the mint mark on a coin. "It ended up going to the Treasury Department, where it was pronounced genuine. And my feeling was that if the Treasury Department—or I should say my rationalization was that if the Treasury Department—pronounces it genuine, that it is genuine by definition."

Stott jumped on this. "That's what I wanted to ask you. Is that the same kind of rationalization you used on these documents?"

"Yes. I never would have done them, obviously, if I thought they could be detected. I thought I was clever enough to avoid that, which, obviously, I wasn't."

"If the expert says they're a real document then the people who bought them really aren't hurt?"

"Yes, that's right. And that's also when I lost respect for forensic examination, I guess."

As they moved back to specific documents, Hofmann added, "I hope you are not going to leave me without going into my rationalization because I can do a lot better job as far as how I rationalized myself."

"If you have something more to add, whatever."

"No. We'll talk about it later. A lot of it deals with my rationalization for the homicides, which we'll get into."

"Did we talk about the . . . You have the Whitmer to Conrad?"

They discussed the details of forging for some time before Hofmann brought the conversation from his forgeries back to himself. "It's hard for a lot of people to accept, I'm sure, that my closest friends and even my wife did not know the extent of my fraudulent dealing. But those people do not know my personality. In other words, I have always been fairly introverted. I have never had really close friends that I've shared information with."

Near the end of the interview, they pursued Hofmann's motivation again. "Do you want to go into any more of the rationalization or do you want to wait on that?"

Hofmann balked. "It is something that's hard to just talk about without being questioned on about why I did a certain thing or whatever."

Biggs saw an angle. "Remember, we were talking about that check. You never did really answer that."

"Which check?"

"On the 13th of October of '85, you drove down to Brent Ashworth's home."

"Oh, he was pressing me for payment on a consigned item and I felt by giving him a check, even if he had to hold it for a while, would satisfy him, and anticipated that I would be getting the funds to pay it."

"Didn't you have more pressing worries at that time?" Stott asked. "The question is why did you take the time to go see Brent on this little bitty thing?"

"Some of it may have been just the feeling of having to get away. I did a lot of thinking while I drove."

The day in question had been two days before the bombings. "Now at that time you had bought some bomb parts?"

"Let's see, when did I buy the bomb parts? I don't remember the exact . . . "

Biggs told him.

"Yes, well this gets into rationalization for the bombs. All along, of course, until the evening that I made them, I didn't really think that I would end up using them. At least to take a life."

"Why is that?"

"My rationalization was that I would prepare myself or have that at my disposal, but that things would work out."

Hofmann reiterated his juggling of suicide and possible targets. "Who was going to be taken out with me was up in the air, if anyone was to be."

Stott tried again. "So were you casing Brent's place with the idea of him being a victim?"

No, Hofmann said. He knew Ashworth's home, so there would be no reason to case it. The prosecutors backed off and went after motive for the forgeries again—what about the sentiment, emotion, and belief people had invested in the documents?

"No, that didn't cause concern in my mind as far as my feelings where it's not so much what is genuine and what isn't, as what people believe is genuine.

"My example would be the Mormon church, which may be a bad example since I'm sure you're both believers in it. I don't believe in the religion as far as that Joseph Smith had the first vision or received the plates from the Angel Moroni, or whatever. It doesn't detract from the social good that the Mormon church can do. To me it is unimportant if Joseph Smith had that vision or not as long as people believe it. The important thing is that people believe it."

Hofmann tried to answer the media perceptions of him. He had not forged revisionist documents to obtain "free money," he said, or to rewrite history. His aim was to correct or be consistent with Mormon history, as he perceived it. "It is true that I wrote the documents according to how I felt the actual events took place. In other words, I believe that Joseph Smith was involved with folk magic; but the idea there was more to keep it in harmony with what I thought potentially genuine, discoverable-type documents may say. In other words, to make it fit the history as accurately as possible so that I wouldn't be found out, or whatever."

On that note, the interview ended.

Even after the plea bargain and during the interviews, Ken Farnsworth continued to work on the Hofmann cases. Other law enforcers said he was obsessed, but he did not think so. There were still a lot of loose ends. He had a roomful of evidence to return, for one thing. Doralee Hofmann had been asking for their typewriter. After the red tape was cleared and Yengich did not come for it, Farnsworth loaded it in his car and drove it out to the Hofmann home. Dori had him bring it in the house and put it on the table. She thanked him and he left.

The next thing Farnsworth knew, Biggs got a call from Yengich, essentially telling him to keep his cops away from Yengich's client's wife. The message was clear that Farnsworth was not going to be allowed to talk with Hofmann. Whether Hofmann would talk to detectives was still a hot question, one that prosecutors and police hoped would still work out. Now Farnsworth hoped he had not ruined Bell's chances. He made it a point to tell County Attorney Yocom that it seemed an outrage that Mark Hofmann was controlling them all.

What the CAO and police hated to admit was that since Hofmann had detailed his forgeries during a dozen interviews, they had little leverage to insist that he talk with detectives, something he obviously did not want to do. The hundreds of pages of transcripts the interviews would already comprise might seem sufficient to Hofmann, his attorneys, or even the Board of Pardons when Hofmann met with the board in January to establish his first parole hearing date. Investigators counted on the parole date being set in 2006 — at the earliest — but they also hoped that Hofmann cared enough about a positive recommendation from the prosecutors that he would discuss the homicides honestly. That paradox, intrinsic to the plea bargain, added tension as the interviews continued. "He's got us by the balls," Biggs admitted reluctantly.

On April 30 and May 15, prosecutors met with Hofmann and talked through the document deals of 1985. Brad Rich found it interesting that Hofmann spoke of the salamander letter in terms of paper, ink, and postmark. The evocative language and imagery, Hofmann stressed, were simply common to the period. Rich thought that the letter had such color; the salamander, a stroke of genius, had captured the imagination of a culture. In the subconscious of Hofmann's computer-like mind, below his interest in detail and technology, had Hofmann absorbed the vivid Mormon past? Rich wondered. Or did the salamander represent the indirect emergence of Hofmann's own personality?

Next came the mythical Oliver Cowdery history and the McLellin collection. They discussed Hofmann's meetings with Gordon Hinckley in the spring before Pinnock and Christensen became involved. Hofmann had described the collection as being in danger of falling into the hands of "the enemy."

"What did you tell him about what it contained and what the enemy was doing?" Stott asked.

"Not too much. How can I put this?"

Yengich urged, "Put it honestly."

"Well, of course, I basically told [Hinckley] that I could tell him what my fears were concerning its getting into the enemy's hands, or whatever." As Hofmann tried to explain the interchange, his language became increasingly broken and confused. Haltingly, he described a protective technique he had developed, telling Hinckley only what he thought Hinckley really had to know. In the case of the McLellin collection, Hinckley was not so interested in the church obtaining it, Hofmann said, as insuring that it would not present the church any problems. "He just wanted to make sure it did not fall into the enemy's hands, which was good since I knew I didn't have it. I knew the church couldn't obtain it."

"Wasn't that a problem that Al Rust was saying that, you know, I understand the church has it and, of course the church knew they didn't have it?"

"Yes, no. That didn't raise a problem in my mind, because I knew that Hinckley knew that I was protecting the collection from Rust, and anyone else as far as where it was. He knew I had previously told him that I had the material in a safe deposit box in Salt Lake City."

Hofmann, again disjointedly, added that he had convinced Hinckley that Rust, a disgruntled investor, might reach the point where he would make the collection public. Thus, Hinckley would see Rust as a mutual problem. However, Hofmann had also tried to use Hinckley to set up a second McLellin scam, involving Cardon. "The idea I had when I went to Arizona to talk to Cardon was that he would obtain phone confirmation from President Hinckley that it would be nice of [Cardon] to buy out the other investor named Al Rust or whatever."

Hofmann would raise the McLellin money again so that Rust would be repaid with Cardon's money. Meanwhile, the church would assume that the McLellin collection was safe, and Cardon would be told the church had the collection. Hofmann had been surprised that he could not reach Hinckley in East Germany, he said, since he had communicated with him easily before when he was traveling.

After that fell through, Hofmann had approached Christensen, who, ironically, took Hofmann to Pinnock and thus back to Hinckley. Now that they were nearing the day of the murders, Stott broached the subject of talking with the police. Hofmann agreed that Jim Bell could attend.

Accordingly, Bell, along with Stott and Biggs, drove to the prison on May 27 to debrief Hofmann about the homicides. Immediately, they learned, the long-anticipated interview was in jeopardy. The three waited anxiously outside the interview room as Yengich and Hofmann conferred inside. Hofmann, believing his prison housing too restrictive, was determined to use the leverage he had in discussing the murders to compel law enforcement to change what he believed was their doing.

Yengich said Hofmann would talk again to Stott and Biggs but not to Bell unless they could make a deal. Stott and Biggs decided to back up the police.

"Nowhere does it state that Detective Bell has to be present," Yengich insisted. "And number two, Mr. Hofmann is prepared to proceed today and answer whatever questions Mr. Biggs and Mr. Stott want to ask."

"It was never indicated in the plea agreement," Biggs responded, "who was going to be there and who was not going to be there. There was never anything said by either Mr. Yengich or your client, that Detective Bell or Farnsworth or the investigators not be allowed in the interrogation. That has been the case up until today."

"We disagree on that, Mr. Biggs," Yengich said, "so that is not my understanding. I guess we can get mad at one another and I'll tell him okay we won't go. If you want me to try to work it out, fine. If not . . . "

"I think you need to work it out," Stott put in, "but our position is unless he wants to change, we're through and we'll report to the board what happened."

"He doesn't go to the board for quite a while, so I'll talk to him," Yengich said.

In the meantime, prosecutors and police took pains to keep secret the fact that the interviews had broken down. As long as news did not leak, Hofmann could change his mind and the public would never be the wiser. The issue was sensitive for the CAO because prosecutors, backed by police, had assured the public at the time of the plea bargain that Hofmann, who was open, truthful, and candid, would tell all.

In fact, Dave Yocom, who had never believed the police would be present at the interviews, quietly called Yengich the week after the impasse was reached. Together they arranged an appointment for Yocom to debrief Hofmann personally about the murders. Yocom knew he would take heat from Willoughby, Bell, and Farnsworth, but he figured that his office's responsibility to the public was a greater concern. Had he been calling the shots when the impasse was reached, he would have continued the interviews and told Bell to go back to work. The night before the scheduled interview, however, Yocom got a call from Yengich. "My client's unwilling to be interviewed at this point." Yocom answered that the door would stay open.

Farnsworth, who knew nothing of these developments, was furious when he heard what had happened at the prison. He was still working hard on Hofmann's Americana forgeries, which he believed were extensive. Evidence suggested that Hofmann was interested in American literature, particularly inscribed first edition books, letters, poems, and even songs. For months, Farnsworth had investigated the Daniel Boone collection

Hofmann had sold to Gene Taylor. Hofmann had given Taylor photocopies of the papers, since he said he had sold the key items. Since then, Taylor had auctioned the Cumberland Gap letter at Sotheby's in New York for nearly $40,000. After considerable sleuthing, Farnsworth learned that Hofmann had photocopied a genuine collection in Minnesota, then created the "original" of the known but lost Cumberland Gap letter.

Farnsworth had briefed Sotheby's on the evidence, and eventually they recalled the Boone letter and sent it to Bill Flynn for testing. The story that it was a forgery broke in the *New York Times*. Locally, KSL-TV began investigating Americana hanging in galleries throughout the nation. Flynn examined a dozen prominent documents and pronounced half of them forgeries. Names like Emily Dickinson, Frances Scott Key, and Mark Twain were joining Joseph Smith, Brigham Young, and Martin Harris in Hofmann's gallery of forgeries.

By July nearly six months had passed since the plea bargain — and still no depositions from Hofmann. News leaked that prosecutors and investigators were being courted by various television and movie scouts. Were they controlling Hofmann's interviews for personal profit? news stories asked. Yocom quickly announced that the depositions were being transcribed and soon would be published. A news conference was set for July 31 — what would have been Kathy Sheets's 52nd birthday.

The night before the press conference, KSL and the *Deseret News* released a public opinion poll showing that 69 percent of those questioned disapproved of the plea bargain. Early the next morning, reporters and private citizens lined up to purchase the published interview transcripts for $60. Mid-morning, Yocom opened the heavily guarded press conference at the new County Complex, saying, "We did not expect a universal approval rate." Through the media, he said, their office had attempted to answer the public's questions — and Yocom, Stott, and, to a lesser extent, Biggs had been accessible to the media. Those who had listened, Yocom asserted, had accepted the reasons for the plea bargain. Now, Yocom said, the interviews with Hofmann were invaluable, though they had been prematurely terminated when Hofmann refused to allow a police officer in the interview room.

Inter-agency rifts had not surfaced at the plea bargain press conference, but now the chasms between agencies were obvious. Willoughby, Farnsworth, and Bell publicly boycotted the news conference since they had not been allowed to attend the interviews. The prosecutors were criticized both for allowing the police to be excluded and for not continuing with Hofmann without the police there. Armed with notes written on a legal pad, Stott fielded questions.

Initially, Yocom had gained Sheriff Pete Hayward's support for the plea bargain, but now Hayward gruffly demanded to know why they had not discussed the murders with Hofmann first rather than risk him ending the interviews prematurely. Stott said they had discussed the murders before the plea bargain and had included a summary of their notes in the transcript.

Reporters had been scanning the 451-page transcript since early that morning, and now several wanted to know if Stott believed Hofmann had been truthful about the homicides. At the first press conference, Stott had said Hofmann was open and candid. Now reporters could read for themselves Hofmann's explanation of the third bomb and his descriptions of afterthoughts and warnings. Stott said he would reserve comment for the Board of Pardons meeting in January.

After Stott fielded a few more questions, Yocom announced that he was talking with Yengich personally about finishing the interviews with Hofmann. If he did talk with Hofmann, Yocom promised, the interviews would be published.

Hayward blew up again, insisting that the conditions of the plea bargain were not being honored. Then television columnist Rod Decker made an on-camera speech questioning whether justice had been served. But it was Biggs who stole the show by speaking off-the-cuff and personally about Hofmann.

"Mark looks like all of us, he talks like us, he was raised here," Biggs said. "But after 11:30 at night, he would forge documents and he would build bombs."

Reporters probed for more of his impressions. Biggs described Hofmann as a manipulative sociopath. As an example, he mentioned Hofmann's account of trying to warn his victims.

"He put that bomb in the doorjamb of Steve's office," Biggs reminded his audience. "Steve could not answer the telephone without picking up that bomb."

So Biggs did not think Hofmann was truthful? Biggs side-stepped this question. Hofmann had discussed gunpowder, bomb parts, and tests, he said, and those things had checked out.

The LDS church followed with its own press conference that afternoon. Unlike the unprecedented press conference in October 1985, no general authorities attended. This time public communications director Richard Lindsay read a statement, then fielded questions regarding document acquisitions. He spoke indignantly of the harm the church had suffered as a result of recent media coverage. What damages? one reporter asked. Fewer baptisms?

No, Lindsay responded, baptisms had risen every year. "Last year was an all time high. Two hundred thousand people were converted." Several times he invited reporters to attend a symposium on the Hofmann documents to be held at BYU the following week.

The media blitz lasted until midnight with documentaries, interviews, and editorials. Every angle of the case was reviewed, especially the controversial plea bargain and depositions, though both prosecutors and defense attorneys defended the arrangement. Biggs tried to sound supportive, but he was quietly applying for positions out of state. By fall, Stott would be as alone with the plea bargain as he had been at the start.

Symposium organizers at BYU had expected only a few hundred people to attend, so when nearly 2,000 participants preregistered the sessions were moved to the special events center. The forum, sponsored by several historical and religious departments, gave Mormon historians the painful opportunity to admit they had been deceived. At both morning and afternoon sessions, the church was portrayed as a victim. By its structure and format the symposium put historians on trial.

Almost immediately, the abyss of misunderstanding between investigators and historians widened. Stott, who was still deflecting criticism about the plea bargain, had been asked to discuss the role historians had played in the investigation. His accumulated frustrations with Mormon historians who could not be "turned around" etched his comments like glass. Citing his interviews with Hofmann, he criticized historians for their gullibility and reliance on the "historical method" to compare Hofmann's documents with other manuscripts. Furthermore, he suggested, they had been arrogant in disregarding the opinions of colleagues who taught religion.

"You can read in the transcript—Mark Hofmann, frankly, is laughing at you, that you believed those stories," he told them. "Mark Hofmann recognized those areas in which you would be the least objective. He recognized your interest in folk magic, he recognized that you better accept something in that area than something that wasn't. His deceptions, his creations, then, in part, were fashioned with that in mind, to meet what you wanted."

Several historians explained, excused, or admitted their mistakes but vigorously protested Stott's view of their part in the drama. BYU historian Ron Walker threw away his speech and wrote another during lunch. "I remember sitting in a sacrament meeting several days after Mark Hofmann had confessed and entered his plea bargain," Walker told his audience. "I felt an overwhelming emotional and spiritual relief. . . . That 'white salamander' that had bedeviled me for so long at last was exorcised. I felt spiritual channels, once hindered and partly clogged, renew themselves. Like many in this audience, I owe a personal debt, and I warmly acknowledge it, to police and prosecutors who exposed Hofmann and secured his confession."

Now Walker, like other historians, blamed the press for not better informing them of the evidence and for contributing to the tension by quoting the historians' statements to reporters. "I would like to enter some guilty pleas," Walker continued. "Certainly Mark Hofmann duped me as he did most everyone else. And certainly these past several years have taught me about the fallibility of document authenticators. Next time around I will be on George Throckmorton's doorstep."

Walker denied disparaging religion instructors and objected to Stott's assertion that Mormon historians' interest in folk magic had inspired Hofmann's creations. "To suggest that we would not have greeted a more traditional account of Mormon origins with enthusiasm is an untruth which the slightest and most casual inquiry could have affirmed."

The banquet speaker that evening, Elder Dallin Oaks, whose speech was later published in the church's *Ensign* magazine, mentioned historians only peripherally. Rather, he went after the press for "Mormon-bashing," particularly the *Salt Lake Tribune* and the *L.A. Times*. He also defended the suppression of some documents, explaining that confidentiality and privacy were two extenuating reasons. "Examples would include diaries or minutes that discuss the private affairs of living persons," he said. "In addition, our belief in life after death causes us to extend this principle to respect the privacy of persons who have left mortality but live beyond the veil. Descendants who expect future reunions with these deceased ancestors have a continuing interest in the ancestors' privacy and good name," he said. He emphasized the church's release of many documents, omitting mention of the Stowell and Bullock letters.

In defense of church leaders who had dealt with and been deceived by Hofmann, Oaks explained that, as ministers of Jesus Christ, church officials must extend trust and love to all people. In one of the few comments regarding the bombings, Oaks denied that he, Pinnock, or Hinckley had threatened Hofmann's church membership. He did not mention civil or criminal repercussions, which, Curt Bench had testified, threatened Hofmann.

The symposium seemed to air, more than resolve, the damages Hofmann's forgeries had caused. Stott, who was criticized but never formally thanked for appearing, concluded he had been set up by conference organizers to do a thankless job. Many historians felt he had been loosed upon them by church leaders like a lion upon Christians. Some participants defended the new Mormon history, explaining how well Hofmann's documents fit with other manuscripts of the time. Michael Quinn, who was not invited to speak at the symposium, had recently finished a 335-page book, titled *Early Mormonism and the Magic World View*, from which all references to Hofmann's documents had been removed.

Some, however, less involved in the politics, found the

conference enlightening. Ken Farnsworth, listening from the audience, had a perfect day. For once the cops had done a great job, the historians had been wrong about Hofmann, and the press was blamed both for saying too much and saying too little. Things could not be better, Farnsworth decided.

Another conference on the Hofmann documents, this one in Palm Springs, also brought together people with battered reputations when Throckmorton and Flynn conducted a two-day workshop for the Southwest Association of Forensic Examiners. Sensitivities abounded within the FBI, which had re-authenticated the salamander letter. So Throckmorton invited the agents involved to tell their own story. On the second day, Flynn and Throckmorton supervised sessions on printed documents, making and aging ink, manufacturing quills, simulating handwriting, and embossing letterheads. Interest was high, and, by the end, some ruffled and competitive feelings had been smoothed.

Hofmann's victims had spent the year trying to reconstruct their lives. In February, Terri Christensen married Mark Lauder, twenty-five, a ward member who had known and admired Steve. In fact, as bishop six years earlier, Steve Christensen had sent Lauder on his mission. Terri's sons were happy about the marriage, and Lauder was oriented toward sports and family activities. Soon the boys began calling him "Dad." After a few months, Lauder went to work in Mac Christensen's retail store.

The Sheets family had filed a $375,000 suit against KSL-radio and its parent company, church-owned Bonneville International, for the broadcast regarding "a messy and bitter divorce." Just before the end of the year the Bonneville suit was settled out of court for an undisclosed amount of money. Sheets had also lined up behind Al Rust, Brent Ashworth, and others in suing Hofmann for damages.

During the summer, Sheets had married Diane Harris Jackson, a divorcee with two children who left New Zealand to join him. She quickly befriended the Sheets's children, and the new family celebrated Christmas together. Gretchen was slated to leave on a mission in January, and Heidi Jones and Katie Robertson were each pregnant.

But by Christmas, Gary Sheets knew he was facing a federal indictment for fraud regarding the JGSA "working fund," which, between November 1984 and May 1985, had directed investments into the company itself. Convinced in his heart that he had done no wrong, Sheets hired a criminal attorney and decided to go to trial rather than plead guilty to a felony.

One day in 1987, Brent Ashworth, on impulse, decided to drop by the Church Administration Building to see President Hinckley. He climbed the granite steps, opened the heavy front door, and gave his name to the secretary. Within a minute or two, he was ushered into the office, where Hinckley greeted him warmly. He asked how Charlene was, how their children were, how were they getting through all the trauma they had suffered. Those questions answered, Hinckley asked if Ashworth knew how Mark Hofmann's family was getting along. Ashworth told him the bits he had heard, nothing much.

"Did you ever get anything from Mark that's real?" Hinckley asked.

"No, but I traded him about half my Americana."

Hinckley shook his head. "That poor young man. He threw it all away."

As Ashworth prepared to leave, Hinckley came around the desk and gave him a hug. Ashworth walked into the spring day remembering an incident a few months earlier when he had passed Hinckley on the street and received no response to his greeting. Then he had felt snubbed. Now he decided Charlene was right—Hinckley simply had not seen them.

Gerry D'Elia and George Throckmorton, both casualties of the CAO, were in private practice during 1987. Toward the end of the year, Throckmorton took a position at the San Diego County Crime Lab, commuting to Utah to testify in various cases and visit his family.

D'Elia tackled some high-profile cases outside Salt Lake County but dropped everything early in the summer of 1987 after his stepson was seriously injured in a hit-and-run accident. The D'Elias spent every possible moment helping him recover from a coma, brain damage, and multiple fractures.

By 1987, it was clear that the man who had fueled Deseret Book's rare books department, Mark Hofmann, had essentially ruined it. Curt Bench and Wade Lillywhite had listed the documents known to have come from Hofmann and offered their customers refunds or credit. Relatively few documents came back, however. Either they had been resold or their buyers were keeping them as souvenirs, hidden reminders of bad decisions, or—worse—passing them on with no mention of Hofmann. Steve Barnett had lost his job at Cosmic Aeroplane, and other booksellers had suffered, but no other store had been devastated like Bench's and Lillywhite's department. As their department shrank, Lillywhite's job was soon one of the first casualties. By the year's end, the rare books department and Bench, a Deseret Book manager for years, were gone, too.

Other Hofmann associates were seeking life as usual. Shannon Flynn was working again as a photographic supplies clerk, the federal fire arms charges against him having been dropped because of his cooperation during the Hofmann investigation; Brent Metcalfe had remarried, found a new job, and was again involved in Mormon studies; and Lyn Jacobs had published a bibliography on foreign language editions of Mormon scripture and was pursuing a Ph.D. in New York. Each portrayed himself, now, not as Hofmann's friend but as Hofmann's victim.

Dori Hofmann, living quietly with her children in her Millcreek home, kept the Haus Hofmann sign on the post in front of the house. Supported by her family, her in-laws, and her Mormon ward, Dori visited Mark regularly, often taking their four children with her. She continued to maintain his innocence. Others, too, remained defensive. One particularly supportive ward member explained, "Other than two incidental murders, Mark didn't do anything all that bad."

In December 1987, as once again Salt Lake City prepared to celebrate Christmas, negotiations intensified concerning Mark Hofmann. Two years earlier, forgery detection had been the watchword; a year ago, the plea bargain had been imminent. Now County Attorney Yocom was trying again to interview Hofmann about the homicides. Yocom and Ron Yengich had

discussed the matter since the release of Hofmann's depositions, and Yengich said they would resolve the matter in December. The CAO would soon be compiling a report for Hofmann's
scheduled meeting with the Board of Pardons on January 8,
1988. The board would consider the report and other information in deciding whether to give Hofmann a parole date, set a
rehearing date to discuss parole, or deny parole altogether — in
effect, life in prison.

The conditions for the anticipated interviews had, of course,
changed. Hofmann need not be questioned by the detectives
who had caught him nor by the prosecutors who had sent him
to prison but by their bosses. Yocom, County Sheriff Pete
Hayward, and Salt Lake City Police Chief Bud Willoughby
now intended to represent Salt Lake County law enforcement
during the debriefing. Both Willoughby and Hayward assured
Yocom that they could update themselves on the case, then
brief Yocom; Yocom regarded himself as highly qualified to
question Hofmann, given his own experience as a prosecutor.
No sooner did the trio gear up for the interview, however, than
Yocom received a letter from Yengich delaying the meeting.
Yocom, Yengich, and Stott met soon afterward.

"Ron, if Mark's hearing's scheduled for January 8, we'd
better get this done," Yocom insisted.

"No, it won't be on the 8th. I'm getting the hearing date
continued," Yengich told him. "We'll get it done. We'll do it
over the holidays."

But the talks never materialized. Meanwhile, Stott, who
was mainly satisfied with Hofmann's earlier answers, had little
interest in continuing the process. The police, who were dissatisfied and wanted to interrogate Hofmann, were not even considered, since Hofmann refused to deal with them. The remaining members of the CAO team who had worked the case were
unimpressed with the idea of Yocom, Willoughby, and Hayward
taking on Hofmann. "You don't know the intricacies of the
case. You're going to look like the three stooges going in there,"
Stott protested to Yocom.

Although the January 8 date was continued by the board
to January 29, no interviews took place. The CAO suggested a
three-month delay so that the interviews could be completed,

but the Board of Pardons was frustrated with Yengich. Instead, they told Hofmann that if he wished a continuance he must file notarized papers in a timely fashion. Hofmann failed to do so but at the last minute sent a handwritten request. Paul Sheffield, the executive director of the Board of Pardons, rejected the request.

The inevitable press leak came on January 20, when the *Tribune* broke the story of the failed interviews, the refused continuance, and the expected letter from the CAO accusing Hofmann of defaulting. Immediately, Yengich and Stott jumped back into the public ring, slugging out the controversial plea bargain, which both claimed as a professional coup. In one story, Yengich angrily rebutted Sheffield's refusal of a continuance and called him "a punk." Though Yengich swore he would attend the hearing as Hofmann's friend, Brad Rich stepped into the fray.

In an unprecedented move—as virtually all moves related to Hofmann were—the CAO released its report concerning Hofmann to the press, as well as forwarding it to the Board of Pardons.

In the report, Stott described the charges and Hofmann's crimes. He said that Hofmann had discussed most of his crimes forthrightly, but objected to several statements and omissions. Stott asserted that the third bomb had been intended to blow up Hofmann's car and damage a fake McLellin collection, and he disputed Hofmann's claim that he had attempted suicide. Stott also protested Hofmann's refusal to discuss documents other than those named in the charges and described the impasse they had reached regarding the police. He noted that Hofmann's inarticulate answers regarding feelings, reasoning, and motivation might be intentional or could indicate "his lack of feelings."

"Inasmuch as Hofmann has failed to honor the conditions of paragraph 9, by refusing to respond to questions about ten of the charges and about other related activities," Stott continued, "the prosecution is free, under the terms of the agreement, to make a recommendation to the Board that it feels is necessary and consistent with justice. That recommendation is the same as Judge Rigtrup's: Hofmann should remain incarcerated for the rest of his natural life.

"Two respected citizens of this state were murdered by Hofmann," Stott concluded. "They were not killed in a fit of passion, jealousy, or anger; rather, they were killed pursuant to a deliberate, calculated plan spawned from greed and a desire to protect a false reputation gained through deceit and fraud. . . . For twenty years, deceit, fraud, and treachery have been inextricably etched into Hofmann's personality. A few years of prison will not eradicate these vile and dangerous traits. Only natural life will begin to adequately punish Hofmann and insure that no one will be tricked, harmed, or murdered by him again."

"Let Hofmann Die in Prison, Prosecutors Tell Board," headlines trumpeted. But Yengich had the last word in the media, pleading with the board immediately before the hearing to release Hofmann in seven years—as recommended by board guidelines.

The three-member Board of Pardons uses a matrix to evaluate the reports and recommendations it receives and to balance the subjective, emotional, and sometimes manipulative pleas it hears from inmates or family members. Inmates are rated by their criminal records. The psychological profile that is prepared when an inmate enters prison is very important, as are reports from social workers.

Hofmann, with no prior criminal record, fell into the "excellent" category, meaning his "risk level," or the probability of his commiting future crimes, was minimal. In addition, his psychological report was mainly favorable, he was housed in medium security, his I.Q. was near genius, he was young, clean-cut, and he had a supportive family and neighborhood. On paper, Hofmann had a lot going for him.

Yet the Board of Pardons found in the Hofmann case puzzling contradictions. There was no criminal history, though multiple charges indicated numerous crimes, including two capital homicides. He had been sentenced lightly, yet both the judge and prosecutor had recommended that he spend his life in prison. Board members Victoria Palacios, Gary Webster, and Michael Norman not only reviewed the material submitted to them by the prison, the police, and the prosecutor but also read Hofmann's interviews before assembling their questions.

The afternoon of January 29, 1988, Bill and Dori Hofmann entered the room — now filled with reporters — where Mark had been interviewed by prosecutors. Dori, slender in a white-and-black-striped dress, was shown to a seat in the front. A worn and slightly lame Bill Hofmann, the effects of ill health visible in his deeply grooved face, sat among the reporters. Brad Rich sat one chair away from Dori, saving the center chair for Mark, soon escorted into the room. Hofmann had obviously lost weight in prison. He appeared slim, healthy, and as clean-cut as ever. As he sat down, he and his wife exchanged smiles and reached for one another's hands.

After preliminary remarks, Palacios read background material into the record, then questioned Hofmann about his forgeries, alluding to his deprecating remarks about the experts.

"Uh . . . that wasn't my intention," Hofmann said. His voice was educated and courteous but toneless and unemotional. He explained that he had been portrayed as "sort of a genius forger or something, which I don't think is accurate. I think that almost to make themselves look like the experts they are, they have to try to build me up — my sophistication or knowledge or whatever — since I fooled them."

"You know, Mr. Hofmann, the same thought occurred to me relative to you." Palacios said she found Hofmann arrogant. Would he care to respond?

There was a pause. "I think my techniques were superior to what had been encountered before," Hofmann said. "Not to sound arrogant, but I think they would have more easily detected the forgeries if they had more experience with iron gall ink."

Next Palacios wanted to know if he had a set of beliefs, a philosophy that guided his actions. Hofmann brightened and said he did, though not religious beliefs. "It's hard to say, looking back, if my actions sprang out of them or if I developed them later to justify my actions," he volunteered.

Palacios then asked why he toyed with others' beliefs through creating forged religious documents.

"I've always been fascinated by the idea of why people believe what they do. Toying with them, I guess, would be more experimentation on my part," Hofmann explained.

So, she asked, you forged the salamander letter, then sat back like a scientist to observe?

Hofmann agreed that he enjoyed that observation. "In other words, it wasn't purely monetary."

Palacios switched to a discussion of the bomb Hofmann had left at the Sheetses' home, noting that he had told the prosecutors that its model rocket fuse might be defective, preventing ignition. "If it didn't go off, it would not frustrate your purpose, would it?" she pointed out. Hofmann agreed. "As strange as it sounds, it was almost a game as far as . . . uh . . . I figured it was a 50 percent chance that it would go off and a 50 percent chance it wouldn't."

Palacios wanted to know why, since Hofmann had such a good technical background, he hadn't insured that the bomb was a dud and spared the life of Kathy Sheets.

There was a pause. "It was certainly an option," he agreed, then paused again. Stott had accused him of evading motivational questions. Now he had another chance to explain himself. "As I said, it was a game at that point. Although at the time, I don't think I considered it not exploding. Certainly I could have made it so it wouldn't. In a nutshell, I just didn't consider it." Paradoxically, he added that he hoped no one would die by the bomb but knew anyone could. "At the time I made that bomb my thoughts were that it didn't matter if it was Mr. Sheets, a child, a dog."

As the dispassionate voice stopped, the room was hushed. Dori Hofmann still clutched her husband's hand, but her body leaned toward the far corner of her chair.

As he talked, Hofmann changed his story of placing the second bomb, saying now that he had set it against the garage door when in the deposition he had described leaving it in the driveway. But his listeners, absorbing Hofmann's matter-of-fact description of his earlier indifference to the probability of blowing someone up, let the discrepancy pass.

"It sounds so callous," Palacios told him, "to be putting together these lethal instrumentalities and not have even decided who would receive them."

"It was callous," Hofmann said, and laughed. "Yeah," he added, a slight nodding motion of the head rocked his upper body for a moment.

"Then why kill Mr. Christensen and Mrs. Sheets if you were going to commit suicide?"

"I decided I would commit suicide after they were already dead," Hofmann explained haltingly.

Palacios gave him an opening—was his decision due to feelings he had after he committed the murders?

"Uh . . . it was in response to feelings. It wasn't so much feeling of guilt as feelings of detection." The evening news had reported his letterman's jacket, he said. "I felt like I was had."

"If you're such a smart guy," Palacios asked, "why did you wear that letter jacket?"

"I've toyed with that myself, as far as why" Hofmann answered, pausing. He did not—or could not—answer the question.

Palacios challenged him again. "You seem so good at things technical, how could you botch the suicide?"

Hofmann had a technical explanation—from what he had heard, he surmised that the pipe had blown up in the wrong direction. He had wanted a clean death, he said, not paralysis or other injury, so he had made a bigger bomb for the car.

Palacios wanted to know why he had bothered to fake a McLellin collection—Stott's explanation for the third bomb—if he was going to commit suicide anyway.

Hofmann seemed to draw a blank until he realized that she was referring to the papers of Minnesota senator S.J.R. McMillan. "That collection had been in my car for a few days," he said, "uh . . . but at the time I anticipated it might be a McLellin collection." There was a confused silence.

"Are you saying those papers weren't a fake McLellin collection?"

Hofmann explained that he had given the papers to investor Tom Wilding at one point as collateral, then Wilding had returned the collection. "It was just there, but I think that I left it in there thinking it would be known as the McLellin collection." He went to this trouble as "protection from being

identified with certainty as the forger and murderer that I am."
The entire scheme, he explained, was to protect his family.

There may not be much point in asking, Palacios said wea-
rily, but what were you really going to do with the third bomb?
"Believe it or not, that was a suicide attempt," Hofmann
said. Palacios shrugged and turned away as Hofmann grinned.
Do you feel any remorse? she wanted to know. Neither psychologist nor prosecutors reported seeing any, she said — only
his caseworker and attorneys said they had. Palacios waited.
"Definitely, I feel remorse," Hofmann finally said, noting that
his expression of remorse was public record.

"For yourself and your family, or for your victims?"

"Uh . . . part of my philosophy of life we were talking
about earlier is that my victims are not suffering at this point,"
Hofmann said, his words still rapid and level. "Uh . . . I believe
their families are. In other words, I feel more remorse or sor-
row for what they're going through."

Now Palacios quickly reviewed his history, pausing to clarify a statement in one report that his LDS mission had prepared him for life in prison. Would he care to elaborate?

"I was living what I believed to be a restricted life," he
said. "I wasn't a believer in Mormonism at that time." The
structure of missionary life and the sense of an alien lifestyle
had taught him to cope with a proscribed environment, he said.
She then asked if his marriage was likely to stay intact. Both
smiled as if the question was frivolous. After a pause, Hofmann
said, "I like to think so."

"You say in the deposition that you staged the discovery
of the Anthon transcript in front of your wife. Did you use her
in any other ways in your criminal activity?"

"I don't know if I did in any other direct way . . . uh . . .
uh . . . but certainly through socializing with potential victims,
people I had in mind to defraud or whatever. She was very
supportive, and no one would have guessed I was the kind of
man I was." Hofmann nodded, rocking slightly, again.

"She was useful to you in that way? Didn't you feel any
compunction using your wife in that fashion?"

Hofmann thought about it. "Strange as it sounds, I didn't feel I was using her. I felt like she didn't ask me questions about my business and I didn't volunteer information."

Palacios wanted to know how much Hofmann had earned as an honest document dealer before the forgeries crept in, but Hofmann clarified that he had sold authentic documents only as cover and had forged for a living.

Palacios said she had noticed how his customers innocently placed orders for the documents they wanted him to find. "I can't believe that people didn't catch on," she smiled.

Hofmann grinned back. "I'm sure neither can they. Neither can I."

Palacios's smile faded. She asked what had happened to all the money Hofmann had made.

" 'Easy come, easy go.' " He laughed.

"Did you have a high lifestyle?"

"In ways, I did, yes. I traveled quite a bit and bought lots of things."

Palacios reviewed Hofmann's prison status. He was in good health, housed in medium security, and he spent his time reading, watching television, and taking a college course. He had been fired as "tierman" (tier janitor), though he was not a disciplinary problem; and he had been accepted as a tutor but had not yet taught. He had unusual family and neighborhood support.

As Palacios turned to Gary Webster, Hofmann waited, smiling and nodding, his wife's arm now drawn across his waist, her hand in his. Webster began his questioning by returning to the Sheets bomb and Hofmann's contradiction of hoping no one would get killed but neglecting to take precautions.

Hofmann smiled. "That's right, it's beyond me, too. Don't try to make sense of it because there's none to be made. It was an irrational decision, obviously, to plant the bombs. I don't know what to say. I wasn't thinking straight at the time."

Bill Hofmann flinched and drew his arms closer to his body. Webster looked hard at Mark Hofmann. "Either you did intend or you didn't intend the bomb to explode," he said softly but intently. "You said you hoped no one would die yet allowed that to happen." This seemed out of character with the planner and methodical forger Hofmann had proven himself to be, Webster said.

"Like I said, at that point it was almost a game. Obviously it was a treacherous thing to do." A pause, then Hofmann added, "I feel like I haven't answered that to your satisfaction."

"You may never answer it to my satisfaction."

"Yeah. Probably not to mine, either."

Hofmann explained how he had concluded that life was worthless and that if he did kill someone, no great harm was done—they might die in a car accident or from a heart attack that day anyway.

Bill Hofmann winced again as a slight murmur ran through the audience. Webster continued to press Hofmann about his selection of targets, and Hofmann insisted that it was a last minute decision.

"I went through several possible names. I felt at that time like someone would have to die, that drastic measures were called for, but I didn't know who. I contemplated suicide at first, then taking someone else out as a diversion. But the night before those first two bombs, I chickened out of suicide and that's when I arrived at Steve Christensen. As I explained in my letter, he was the target because he was involved in a couple of fraud schemes."

Webster began to interrupt, but Hofmann had not proved his point. "I even thought of the possibility of killing people who were not involved in any of the fraud schemes at all, just for the idea of people who were associated with me. And I could tell the fraud victims I was too busy with those deaths or whatever to come through on the frauds. The whole idea was to avoid being caught on the frauds."

Clearly, animosity had not been a conscious factor. Steve Christensen and Kathy Sheets had been murdered in very cold blood. Palacios looked pale. Mike Norman then asked Hofmann how he felt about his own family—his wife living alone, his children growing up without a father.

Silence, then, "Uh . . . it's obviously harder on them than it is on me . . . same with any of the victims. I figure I deserve what I get . . . uh . . . obviously they were unwilling associates, or did not participate in the crimes." Hofmann paused, then added, "How I deal with it or whatever is I try not to think about it, as far as thinking of the various victims or whatever."

Now Webster wanted to know if, since Hofmann didn't care who got killed, he had really tried to warn his victims. Hofmann said that he had, calling the Sheets from a 7-Eleven store and Christensen's office from his home. He did so because he felt guilty, he said, and began wondering if, in fact, there was a God and he might be wrong. But he indirectly hinted at another reason to call Christensen: to see if the bomb had exploded. Since the explosion had not damaged Christensen's answering machine Hofmann could not tell.

Norman asked when Hofmann had first begun to think about killing people—a day before the bombings, weeks, or even at any earlier point in his life. There was a long pause, perhaps twenty seconds, before Hofmann said, "That's a good question."

Hofmann pinpointed his decision to kill as the day he purchased the bomb parts in order to "keep his options open" and "get out of a jam." He then described pondering the question of killing people months, if not a couple of years, earlier, "the idea of my own existence, with myself, my own survival, the issue, thinking about under what circumstances I would take a life."

Norman's hands were over his face, fingertips touching his closed eyes. Hofmann added, "At that time, I wouldn't think that saving my reputation would be a sufficient cause for that."

Norman lowered his hands. "Do you see yourself as a violently dangerous person?"

Silence, then Hofmann said, "No," adding quickly, "but I'm sure a lot of people would disagree."

Norman posed another question. "Do you think, given your crimes, you should ever be free again? I'm not asking if you want to be, but, given your crimes, if you should be?"

Hofmann twisted in his chair as his wife waited expectantly. "Obviously, I want to be free," Hofmann said quickly, "uh . . . " During the long pause that followed, Brad Rich watched his client closely. Was Hofmann struggling to answer logically a question that contradicted his desire? Dori Hofmann watched, too, her profile as soft as a child's. At last Hofmann ventured, "I think that someday I should be free," but gave no reasons.

Dori Hofmann had chosen not to address the board, but Rich tried to alter the picture Hofmann had painted of a man who could plan death like a game, forgery as an experiment, and calmly label himself a forger and murderer. Rich insisted that Hofmann's homicides didn't show the same brilliance and forethought that characterized his forgeries.

"I think these homicides occurred in a moment in Mark's life when he was suffering from a level of desperation under pressures that would have driven any kind of varieties of people over the edge. The board hears every day of people who come in and say I did what I did because of drugs or alcohol, or because they never had a chance in life." There is no easy answer, Rich finished. Something more subtle is going on in Mark's life as he was cast adrift from a traditional and moral upbringing.

Although Hofmann had lost his moral bearings, Rich said, he had killed not chiefly for pecuniary reasons but because he feared the damage that would be done to his family if he was exposed. "Given that pressure, he made a terribly disastrous decision. He hasn't defended it. Mark hasn't asked you to let him off or cut his potential time, and I'm not here to ask for that.

"I *am* asking, don't throw Mark Hofmann away, because in a number of ways he's an exceptional individual." He added, "I don't think he should just be put away and never examined again. Because it is my feeling, having talked to him, that there will come a day when Mark Hofmann will regain his footing, and he's made some giant strides already."

Hofmann no longer lived in that amoral frame of mind he had described, Rich said. In fact, Hofmann was now astonished by his crimes and his memory of them was dim and nightmarish, Rich said.

Palacios picked up a letter that Hofmann had handed the board at the beginning of the hearing. The four pages of cramped printing contrasted sharply with the flowing nineteenth-century script that highlighted the best of his forgeries. The letter was clearly a late attempt to finish the business he had begun with the prosecutors. Palacios told him that his issues with the CAO had "limited utility" for her. In other words, she did not care.

Now she read one of the first paragraphs aloud. "As far back as I can remember I have liked to impress people through my deceptions. In fact, some of my earliest memories are of doing magic and card tricks. Fooling people gave me a sense of power and superiority. I believe this is what led to my forging activities."

You like to fool people, she suggested to Hofmann. You seem to be proud of your forging abilities and you seem to enjoy your notoriety. Is that true?

"The reason for the notoriety is nothing to be proud of, but there's nothing I can do about it."

"Are you proud of the skill with which you did the forgeries?" Palacios probed.

Silence. "That's hard to answer." Another pause. "I wouldn't describe as a feeling of pride . . . uh . . . obviously . . . I guess looking back on it . . . " He took a breath. "Yeah, I guess I am! I'm proud of the techniques I developed."

Palmer asked how Hofmann thought he might earn a living outside prison. "Good question," Hofmann said, sounding surprised. "My only experience at earning a living is dealing in collectibles, and obviously no one will trust me to buy collectibles from me again." Perhaps working with computers or teaching, he decided.

Before leaving, Palacios explained to Hofmann that while seven years was the recommended time for someone like him, they were free to come to their own decision. Hofmann smiled confidently, then turned to his wife, kissed her, and left the room with his guard. He did not acknowledge his father. As the room emptied, Rich read his copy of Hofmann's letter that described the progression of his client's fraudulent career.

"At the age of 25 (1979) I sold my coin and Mormon money collection and decided to forge for a living. Money became the object. This was almost my exclusive source of income from

1980 to October 1985. During that time I forged hundreds of items with at least 86 different signatures."

After describing his bomb-making, Hofmann added a tender touch to his portrayal of murderous deliberations.

"Although I have a poor memory of this time, I remember on the night before the first two bombings going into my children's bedrooms and kissing them while they slept while telling myself that my plot was for their best good."

The second part of the hearing was brief after Hofmann and the board members returned. With little preamble, Palacios announced, "Mr. Hofmann, the board has come to a decision. The reason for our decision is manifold. We are impressed that there are a large number of victims. We are impressed that you exhibit a callous disregard for human life and that the killings were done to cover other criminal activities. By a majority vote, the board has decided that you shall serve your natural life in prison, Mr. Hofmann."

Hofmann, looking steadily into Palacios's face, nodded, rocking slightly. His eyes did not shift or waver.

"Is there anything you would like to say, Mr. Hofmann?"

The nodding stopped. "No, thanks," he said softly, rising without a word, look, or kiss this time, and left the room. The haunting half-smile that so readily identified Hofmann was now replaced by a tight line. As the board members followed, Webster and Palacios gave Bill Hofmann a long, sad look but said nothing. The audience sat motionless for a minute longer, then Bill and Dori Hofmann, looking stunned, were ushered into the hall. His hand on Bill's shoulder, Rich saw them down the stairs. Father and wife, both longtime defenders of Hofmann's innocence, got into a small gray car, Bill at the wheel. They fastened their seatbelts, then drove away as reporters gathered around Rich.

Rich was frankly surprised by the board's decision. He had told Hofmann's family to expect a ten-to-fifteen-year rehearing date. Now he voiced his hope that someday another board would reconsider and say, "Boy, Mark Hofmann has come a long way. Let's give him another chance."

Hofmann's hearing, covered by the media, both chilled and heartened readers and viewers as Hofmann's culpability and fate were laid to rest. Among Hofmann's victims and investigators that evening, telephones spread the news with a sense of relief and joy that felt — at last — like justice.

From the beginning, the Salt Lake City bombings and the Hofmann forgeries played tricks with reality, twisted cultural myths, and turned common assumptions inside out. Long after most people were convinced by the preliminary hearing, the guilty plea, or the interview depositions that Hofmann was guilty, confusing questions still remained — especially how and why.

Steve Christensen and Mark Hofmann, born at opposite ends of the same year, had become one another's nemesis by October 1985. Christensen staked his future on closing a deal that Hofmann's future depended upon eluding. Between them was a collection of historical documents, the McLellin collection. Since the papers did not exist, Hofmann could not sell them, but Christensen had to procure them. Both Christensen and Hofmann perceived themselves as double agents, but there was one important difference. Christensen felt loyalties to both church and history, Hofmann claimed loyalties to neither. Both knew that Gordon B. Hinckley was overseeing the transaction. Hinckley had, in fact, been involved before Christensen and Pinnock had even heard of the collection. Pinnock, who reported to Oaks and Hinckley, said he did not hear the details of Hinckley's involvement, such as the letter from Al Rust, until after Christensen was dead.

In the case of the McLellin collection and other documents, Hinckley did not act with the specific approval of church councils, though he did sometimes purchase expensive and significant documents with church funds. This time, Pinnock, with ecclesiastical approval, arranged a bank loan for the purchase. That loan was traceable and controversial, linking the church both to moneyed influence and to controversial historical documents. Unpaid, the loan turned what began as an elusive scam into a high-pressured transaction that culminated in a double murder.

Pinnock later wrote that the loan for the McLellin collection was the only such loan he had ever arranged, though, he said, he had introduced several friends to First Interstate Bank.

other sources deeply involved in Salt Lake City business circles say that a $185,000 loan given on a general authority's say-so is neither unusual nor particularly large. At the October General Conference following the preliminary hearing, Pinnock was sustained to the Presidency of the First Quorum of Seventy, a step up in the hierarchy—a promotion rather than a punishment.

Although the church denied procuring and hiding controversial documents, it nevertheless had done so, on occasion. Nearly a decade after the Fuchs gold plates incident church leaders were drawn to the McLellin collection, also a fake; only this time Steve Christensen volunteered to be the middleman. As such, he became an essential player when Hofmann defaulted on the bank loan. Christensen could track, assist, badger, and coerce Hofmann in ways that Pinnock, Oaks, and Hinckley could not. Even more, Christensen knew that he would have the happy responsibility of "authenticating" the McLellin collection before its sale. His flair for creative financing, his passion for church history, his loyalty to the church, and his susceptibility to suspense stories fueled his enthusiasm. Furthermore, he also believed that his relationship with church leaders promised him relief from financial disaster by their helping to sell his personal library and proposing that he—not Hofmann—procure documents for the church in the future.

Hofmann had evidently expected church leaders to duck and avoid an investigation that might reveal the McLellin deal, even though the decoy bomb convinced detectives that the Christensen and Sheets incidents were CFS-related. But Hofmann miscalculated the reaction of the church leaders. Instead of abandoning the project, the bombings heightened their sense of urgency. The McLellin transaction was still on track, they told him, and Christensen would be replaced.

So, at some risk, Hofmann drove 90 miles to Logan, Utah, the next morning and bought more bomb components. Now he needed a third victim—another decoy. Brent Ashworth, like Christensen and Sheets, was a Mormon bishop who took both himself and his religion seriously. He and Hofmann had knocked heads more than once. More important, he was easily accessible to Hofmann. He probably would not pick up a strange package that day, but he would not need to, since the day was a Wednesday.

By the time Hofmann reached Salt Lake City, David West and Don Schmidt were already waiting for him. But Hofmann walked down to Crossroads Mall where he and Ashworth regularly met and bought a newspaper, tucking the receipt in his pocket. Brad Christensen, who would rescue Hofmann, was in the mall earlier, but had left, stopping to visit his brother before climbing the hill just behind Hofmann.

Had Hofmann actually met Ashworth in the mall and offered him a peek at the McLellin collection, which Ashworth knew he was selling, Ashworth would probably have driven Hofmann back to his car, just as he had done several times before. Had Hofmann unlocked the passenger door and suggested that Ashworth pick up the box on the front seat or grab it from the back seat while he got more materials from the trunk, Ashworth would have suspected nothing. Then, when Ashworth detonated the third pipe bomb in two days, a shaken Hofmann would need only to telephone Pinnock or Oaks or Hinckley and explain that a bomb left in *his* car had killed Brent Ashworth. This time everybody would duck.

There would be no pressure to proceed with the McLellin deal. This time, theoretically, all of Hofmann's objectives would have been achieved. The McLellin deal would stall, perhaps permanently. The first "Oath of a Freeman" would still be for sale in New York. Hofmann would buy time, and time would solve everything.

The flaw in this scenario lies in the pipe elbow, pen, and rubber gloves Hofmann left in his trunk. Possibly he forgot them because he was preoccupied and rattled after two killings. Perhaps he simply did not think he would get caught, and those items bothered him no more than wearing his favorite jacket the morning he set the bombs.

Even as an injured bomb victim in the emergency room, he had established a defense, warning friends to flee and describing a pickup truck he said had followed him. Waking from a morphine-induced sleep, knowing he was a suspect, Hofmann had summoned a police officer and asked for two things—a

tape recorder and confidentiality. He was going to make a statement—tell a secret. Either shortly before or just after Ron
Yengich arrived, Hofmann changed his mind. Secondhand
sources close to the defense contend that Hofmann told Yengich
that Kathy Sheets never should have picked up that package—
an incriminating statement but not a confession.

Kathy Sheets and Steve Christensen died in the violent par-
oxysm of a simple and difficult equation: the McLellin deal
had to close/the McLellin deal could not close. In order to
convict Hofmann of the bombings, the state had to prove both
sides of the equation.

First, they had to establish the enormous pressure and secret
financing that characterized the transaction, yet no one inside
the deal could or would describe that situation—figuratively a
bombshell. Lacking the general authorities' effective testimony
of that pressure, prosecutors relied on Curt Bench, a messenger from one friend to another, to demonstrate a motive for
murder. They bolstered Bench's testimony with accounts from
Ashworth, Rust, Wilding, and Cardon to illustrate Hofmann's
dishonesty and business pressures. By so doing, they made the
McLellin deal one of many financial pressures, with Christensen
in the busy intersection. He seemed to be a random and inter-
changeable target—an impression confirmed by Hofmann's confession.

Second, prosecutors had to prove that the McLellin deal
could not close by demonstrating the extent of Hofmann's fraudulent document dealings, requiring the discovery of telltale
cracked ink and printing negatives, as well as tracking Hofmann's
dealings through a community of collectors and dealers. The
evidence against Hofmann was overwhelming, but the magnitude and complexity threw confusing shadows everywhere.

Because the evidence was compelling, Hofmann pleaded
guilty. Because the case presented difficult legal and political
problems, the county attorney's office accepted his guilty plea.
The specific deal, however, was Stott's, based on his belief that
Hofmann's confession, detailing his forgeries if not his murders, would clarify the mess he had made of Mormon history
and demystify the case once and for all. Promised Hofmann's
answers, Stott did not resist Yengich's efforts to reduce

Hofmann's sentence but deferred to the judge and the Board of Pardons. Judge Rigtrup also deferred—to Stott and to the Board of Pardons. And when everyone was through deferring, the defense quietly claimed a major victory.

That perceived victory spawned its own small mystery as rumors grew that the LDS church had rigged the deal, that Stott had followed church instructions in arranging the plea bargain or conducting the interviews or criticizing Mormon historians. Stott considered such rumors insulting. Had a trial come, he would have called LDS general authority Gordon B. Hinckley to the stand and Hinckley would have testified. Yet few Utahns could picture such an event, and what could not be imagined would not happen.

In fact, the power of the Mormon church was integral enough that no instructions were needed for Stott to act, nor for both the defense team and the CAO to understand the advantages of a plea bargain, nor for two state judges to regard the case as a professional liability. "You're the luckiest man alive," Judge Grant congratulated Judge Rigtrup once the plea bargain was entered. In a final twist, the Board of Pardons, visibly appalled by Hofmann's smiling, abstract explanation of his crimes, vindicated the prosecutors' strategy and expectations by throwing away the prison key.

Two years after the Salt Lake City bombings, in another blue and orange autumn, Jeff Salt, now an instructor at Utah State University where he and Mark Hofmann had studied, wrestled with his memories. The moment he heard that Mark had been injured, Salt suspected that Mark was into something over his head. And when police declared him their prime suspect, Salt, switching between television stations, knew, gut-deep, that Mark was guilty.

But obscuring that were layers of reason, rationalization. He had no proof, and Mark had been his best friend and an usher at his wedding. Salt guarded his words. It took him time to admit, even to himself, that he was not surprised by anything Hofmann had apparently done. Privately, like others close to Hofmann, Salt was questioning his own judgment, his own perceptions, his image of himself for having such a friend.

Salt knew he had come close to working full time for Hofmann, traveling with him to New York on business, where, Hofmann bragged, the living was high and wild. He had watched Hofmann's employees on television with sympathy. He had stayed in school, not interested enough by Mormon history and too put off by a few bounced checks to work for Hofmann. Besides, Hofmann still had a habit of criticizing people within earshot, or putting friends in awkward situations. Salt could handle him one on one, but there were times when he could not stand being with Hofmann in social situations. Also, his wife, Nancy, did not like Mark.

Most days now Salt believed that, had he not thrown out the evidence years ago, he would have turned over to police a notebook for an organic chemistry lab he and Hofmann had taken together. Salt expended great effort on that lab notebook; he wanted an "A" even though it was only a one-hour class. The notebook was returned with a red "C" on the front. He could not understand why, but he let it go.

Years later, still a student, he had glanced through the notebook but kept getting confused. One experiment merged into another. After awhile, he realized that pages had been removed from the bound notebook so deftly that their loss was scarcely discernible. He had stared at the pages. Why would anybody have ripped out individual pages? Then he realized why his professor had given him a "C" instead of the "A" he deserved. Salt knew that if he had given the notebook to the police, Hofmann's fingerprints would have been all over it. But that would not have quenched the issue that burned in him now. What does it say about a relationship, he asked himself, when someone goes to great trouble to screw you up?

Salt remembered that he and Hofmann had taken organic chemistry in the fall of 1979, right after Hofmann married. Hofmann had not gotten his usual "A," but a "B." He and Hofmann had competed for grades—and, thanks to the missing pages, Salt had gotten a "C."

That memory galled Salt, but it was not the worst. The worst he had not told anyone—not the police, not even the psychiatrist he had consulted to try to understand Hofmann's and his friendship.

He recalled clearly that he and Hofmann had been in a study room on the fourth floor of the Marriott Library at the University of Utah. Outside, it was autumn, probably the fall of 1977. He could remember the atmosphere in the room, too. Hofmann was gauging his reaction, as he so often did, even asking if he was willing to help. And Salt was wondering, why is he telling me this? He was used to his friend's odd ideas and schemes, but this time Mark was talking about murder.

Hofmann had an acquaintance, he explained to Salt, a man named Freed who owned the Lagoon amusement park north of Salt Lake City and who collected coins and currency. Freed had in his safe some items Hofmann wanted. Hofmann knew that Salt had been studying pharmacology and wondered if he would help him find a chemical compound that would induce heart failure. If he gave Freed a drug like that, Hofmann explained, he could take what he wanted from the safe.

Businessman David Freed did have a safe in his office, which Hofmann could see into when he visited. Freed kept his best samples of currency in a safe deposit box in a bank downstairs. These, too, Freed would show to the interested student. The security systems were such that robbery was nearly impossible, unless, of course, Freed opened the safe himself.

Ten years later, with Mark in the Utah State Prison for murders so callous that some still doubted he committed them, Salt was dogged by that memory. It had been a *research* question Hofmann had posed to him, entirely devoid of feeling. Could such a compound be found? produced? administered? The subject had come up again on other occasions before Hofmann finally dropped it. Never once had Hofmann wondered aloud how he might feel if Freed collapsed before him or how Freed's family would suffer.

The literal hell of it was that Salt still could not forget all the hours he had spent listening to Hofmann, putting up with his ego, joking with him, studying. Once conversation had flowed between them, and Hofmann had shared his innermost feelings about the church and his parents. Often, Salt, reticent himself, had wanted to call Mark's parents and say, "Please. Just tell him he's right. Say, 'Mark, you're right,' about something, anything." Of course, Salt never had. Now that his perspective had shifted, he wondered how much Mark had goaded his father, how much venom had accompanied his attempts at intellectual honesty. When had the mischief in Hofmann turned to malevolence?

Gradually, Hofmann stopped confiding and turned inward. He dropped off some of Salt's things at Salt's apartment and left them on the porch without even ringing the bell, though Salt was home. The last time they had lunch together, Salt looked up from his meal at Hofmann and wondered if Mark even knew he was there; he was so entirely detached. Salt wanted to visit him in prison, to ask him how? why? Instead he visited Dori and was left with the impression she was not thinking her own thoughts. She told him that Mark had outsmarted everyone — all the people who wanted power over them — the psychologist and prison officials.

Even during those college years with Salt, Hofmann had planned a murder and forged a temple ceremony he would sell for $60 to a non-Mormon. That early, too, Mike Hansen had researched Mormon history and currency. Years later, when Hofmann felt compelled to build a third bomb, he abandoned his usual alias and combined his father's and grandfather's given names — Bill Edwards — to purchase bomb parts in Logan.

Hofmann graduated from high school with a green letterman's jacket, a trademark of adolescent belonging that Jeff Simmonds labeled his "badge of honor." In that jacket, Hofmann delivered bombs he manufactured with the same delicate balance of care and risk that characterized his forgeries. Everything depended upon his cool detachment. Then both bombs and forgeries required someone else to read them, pick them up, take the impact.

He worked alone, below the ground, on projects known only to himself, his identity obscured by many names. Mark Hofmann, Mike Hansen, Mike Harris, Martin Harris. In his most creative and notorious forgery, he created a white salamander, a clever and defiant trickster. It lived in a hole beside a treasure and had the temerity to smite a prophet of God and exclaim, "I tricked you again."

AFTERWORD

December 1989

Although Mark Hofmann's Board of Pardons hearing ended on a note of finality, the effects of his crimes were not easily absolved nor did the bomber-forger disappear into obscurity. Scores of people affected by Hofmann's crime spree spent the remainder of the 1980s trying to recover. Meanwhile, even confined in maximum security, Hofmann and trouble quietly continued their mutual attraction.

Under new prison guidelines, Hofmann resided in the Oquirrh facility as a Level 2 inmate, the second most secure classification, where he kept a low profile. He did not appear to fraternize much with other inmates, preferring to read or sleep in the cell he shared with another prisoner. A Mormon volunteer at the prison began conducting long conversations with Hofmann weekly, although Hofmann refused all interviews and an offer to participate via telephone hook-up in an independent Mormon lecture series.

Captain Thomas Bona, who supervised the area, answered Hofmann's requests for information regarding University of Utah correspondence courses. Hofmann's crisp, deferential manner and interest in scholarship might be viewed as outstanding among prisoners. Yet Bona gradually came to compare Hofmann with another notorious inmate he'd worked with—Dale Pierre Selby, who'd committed the gruesome 1974 Hi-Fi murders. Selby and his sidekick, William Andrews, had robbed an Ogden, Utah, stereo shop and held five people hostage, forcing them to drink caustic drain cleaner. After raping one captive, Selby had shot the hostages execution style, killing three.

Bona's comparison of Hofmann with Selby would not have occurred to most people. Selby, an undereducated black airman and native of the West Indies, had committed viciously aggressive homicides. Hofmann, the white, Mormon family man, was a literate and clever forger whose frauds and murders were consistently passive-aggressive.

However, the pairing in Bona's mind had to do with the men's personalities, for Hofmann and Selby differed from most prisoners in a strikingly similar way. Both murderers were inscrutable, unwilling to reveal their feelings or opinions.

"That type is more dangerous than most inmates," Bona later said, "because you don't know what the hell's going on in their heads." As docile as Hofmann seemed, Bona's trained instinct flashed the same warning it had around Selby: "Watch your back."

(The names Hofmann and Selby would be publicly linked when Selby later vainly appealed to the Board of Pardons to commute his death sentence. Defense attorneys cited Hofmann's plea bargain as evidence of the system's hypocrisy. That protest became an outcry, following Selby's execution, when Andrews pleaded for his life as well. Though he had administered the drain cleaner, Andrews had left the store before Selby shot the hostages and thus had not directly killed anyone. Many members of Utah's black community rose to Andrews's defense since others who had killed, including Hofmann, somehow avoided the death penalty.)

Bona's intuition that Hofmann could not be trusted was soon underscored when rumors surfaced that Hofmann planned vengeance on members of the Board of Pardons. But since board members come to expect threats of reprisal from criminals disappointed that their requests for leniency go unanswered, the rumors were not taken seriously at first.

Still, Hofmann elicited uneasiness—even his hearing had seemed atypical. For instance, his wife, seated beside him as if to speak in his behalf, had remained silent throughout the proceeding, as had his father. Clearest in board member Gary Webster's memory was the way Mrs. Hofmann's hand seemed *appropriated* by her husband, though no squeezes or pats suggested communication. Certainly Hofmann had been his own worst spokesman, dispassionately describing his crimes. Webster recalled how Hofmann had parried his pointed questions so flippantly that Webster tired of the game and withdrew.

Uneasiness about Hofmann flared when a harassing call subsequently came to the home of the board's executive secretary and the police were notified. An alert reporter turned the police report into a newspaper story linking the threats and concern to Hofmann. The story—plus word that prison officials were intercepting letters from Hofmann with coded passages—gave investigator Michael George of the Salt Lake County Attorney's office an opening, and he began interviewing prison personnel and inmates about Hofmann. An interesting and unsettling picture emerged.

George learned that Hofmann had counseled inmates preparing to meet with the board—an irony considering the outcome of Hofmann's own board hearing. "If the board gives me a bad time," he'd reportedly bragged, "I'll kill those sons-of-bitches." Even before his hearing, George heard to his surprise, Hofmann had asked inmates leaving prison to find out the home addresses of board members Victoria Palacios and Gary Webster. (The third board member would excuse himself, a fact Hofmann had apparently known.)

Some of Hofmann's "fan mail," as well as certain inmates, cast Hofmann as a folk hero who had "shown up" the Mormon church, George was told. Yet Hofmann struck social workers as narcissistic, shallow, and controlling. "He's a Jekyll and Hyde personality," one explained, "who's sometimes macho with other inmates and sometimes very reclusive." "Money is Mark Hofmann's god," another said, adding that Hofmann seemed to have virtually no motivation regarding sex and showed no sign of suicidal behavior.

George's interviews with inmates colored in the picture, and darkened the shadows. After the hearing, Hofmann had allegedly offered one inmate $50,000 (supposedly hidden somewhere) to blow up Palacios and Webster or arrange their deaths. A second inmate, who'd had no contact with the first, said Hofmann had offered him $10,000 and suggested Doralee Hofmann's services in picking up materials for the bombs.

"Mark thinks his bombings were funny," one inmate told George. "He likes to describe them to other inmates to see if the crimes turn them on." The inmate said Hofmann had confided that the third bomb, which injured him, went off too soon. It had been intended for a Mormon who owed him $30,000 and wouldn't pay up. Later Mark changed the story back to a suicide bomb.

Indications of other offenses, small and large, peppered

George's interviews. One inmate offered that Hofmann sometimes smoked marijuana; another said Hofmann had described
an undiscovered homicide he'd committed years before the bombings. George investigated the latter allegation (as improbable as
snow on a green tree) but could find no evidence for the version the inmate recounted.

On March 29, 1988, George and prison investigator Craig
Rasmussen interviewed Hofmann in an empty lunchroom at
the prison. George greeted Hofmann, who'd not only lost weight
but had shaved his head. He still wore his wedding ring but
kept his damaged right hand hidden as often as he could.

The investigators confronted Hofmann with the alleged
threats against board members, and he flatly denied them. Bra-
vado, Hofmann protested, was not part of his personality.

George suggested to Hofmann that the board's decision
must have come as a genuine shock to him and his attorneys.
After all, he'd pleaded guilty to two second-degree homicides
and was probably expecting to serve as little as seven years.
Hofmann denied that too, saying he'd expected no better.

When they confronted him with the inmates' independent
accounts of payment for revenge, his story began to shift. Well,
Hofmann said, perhaps such conversations had taken place but
only because *he* was approached by sympathetic felons who'd
suggested vengeance.

Ah, George thought, now there is plotting to kill but it's
someone else's fault.

Furthermore, Hofmann elaborated, he had no need for
revenge. "I have it good here. I'm fed well and I'm a loner anyway. I have time to read and do whatever I want."

Next the investigators showed Hofmann the letters with
coded portions and demanded an explanation. Well, he said,
he wrote to Doralee daily and the coding was a way of privately
preserving his thoughts for future reference once he was out of
prison.

"You're not going to get out of prison, Mark," George
reminded.

"Oh, I'll get out," Hofmann assured him. "It'll be a while,
but I figure I'll be out in time to see my grandchildren grow
up."

Pressed further to decode the passages, Hofmann invoked the prisoners' honor system: he couldn't break the code, as Rasmussen insisted he must, because he'd written information about other inmates in those passages and didn't care to be known as a snitch.

"I want to talk to my lawyer," Hofmann said, effectively stopping the interview.

Rasmussen hotly informed Hofmann that he was leaving to shake down Mark's cell. George, still seated near Hofmann, could detect no fear or anger—except that Hofmann fell silent. For a time, neither spoke. Then George got Hofmann to comment a couple of times in monosyllables, finally broaching a subject he had not intended to explore.

"Mark," George ventured, "would you be willing to talk about some of the documents that never were discussed with the prosecutors?"

Hofmann cheerfully consented.

Lacking his notes on the subject, George began with manuscripts or currency recently called into question by Al Rust, Brent Ashworth, and Lyn Jacobs. Gradually they worked toward Hofmann's grand scheme to produce some of the lost 116 pages of the Book of Mormon manuscript. These priceless papers would have fit Hofmann's theory of early Mormonism and been authenticated by his forged letters. Presumably, Hofmann would have accomplished a historical coup and reaped a fortune.

Hofmann confirmed that his plan had been almost in place. He compared the venture to his painstaking preparations to forge the Oath of a Freeman, including examining the original *Bay Psalm Book* so he could match or reproduce the paper's distinctive "chain lines." Listening closely, George recalled that Hofmann had once offered LDS church archivist Don Schmidt five figures for just one blank page of the original Book of Mormon manuscript. Schmidt, bemused, had turned the offer down.

George noticed something else. As their discussion intensified, Hofmann's countenance altered. Gone was the indifferent felon; present was the creative forger, wholly in his element. He gestured as he talked, leaning forward on his chair. By the time Rasmussen returned, the two were deep in conversation.

Rasmussen was not happy. In one hand he carried a newly found list of alphabetized forgeries, titled in Hofmann's childish printing: "Mormon and Mormon-Related Items That I Forged." Virtually every nineteenth-century Mormon of note seemed to be on the list, which was printed in three columns on lined prison stationery. Names such as George Q. Cannon and Orson Pratt joined those of Joseph Smith and Martin Harris. On the reverse side was another list, about half as long, this one of Americana forgeries, including Miles Standish, Francis Scott Key, Martha and George Washington, and Mark Twain. In addition, Rasmussen and his crew had turned up another letter with coded portions. Again Hofmann refused to decode the letter. There was nothing George could do to coerce him, but Rasmussen threatened to send Hofmann to a federal prison out of state.

"Go ahead," Hofmann replied coolly. "That would probably be the best thing—to get me out of here. I'm trying to get my wife to divorce me so my kids can grow up with a different name."

Listening, George heard behind Hofmann's words the echo of Br'er Rabbit stuck in the tarbaby and pleading for Br'er Bear to do anything but throw him into the briar patch (his home).

Following the interview, Hofmann was placed in isolation while George headed for the Hofmann home, where Doralee surrendered Mark's letters upon request.

"Can you read the code?" George asked.

"No."

"Well, if you can't read it, what's the point in Mark writing to you in code?"

"Mark wants to keep a diary of his innermost thoughts to use for later reference."

So Hofmann's story was consistent. George knew Mark had not been able to call home in the meantime. He asked to photocopy certain letters and promised to return the originals. The letters were sent to an FBI lab, but the code proved difficult to decipher.

Coded portions appeared sporadically throughout the letters, which were printed in Hofmann's distinctive hand on prison stationery. They began "Dear" or "Dearest" and concluded with "I love you a ton" or simply "Love, Mark." To George, the letters seemed youthful, not only due to the printing but because they read like something a precocious adolescent would write home from summer camp.

In his letters, Hofmann reported on everyday incidents — inmates had thrown hot coffee and tea into a supposed snitch's cell; he'd lost control of his diet and was indulging in candy bars and junk food.

He wrote lightly of the case that sent him to prison. "I had my first experience with necromancy," he noted, reporting that an inmate had informed him that "Cathy" (sic) Sheets's spirit did not haunt Mark because she was unsure he was her killer. He also commented on interviews and talks by prosecutor Bob Stott that had appeared in the media.

Hofmann's letters mentioned his parents and children, asking Doralee to videotape them performing songs and poems they'd learned for the holidays. "It's hard to think that some-day they'll be embarrassed about their dad." He praised her visits and the children's.

For months after the coded letters were discovered, the public remained unaware of their existence. Later that summer, the FBI broke the code and found references to Palacios, Webster, and document expert George Throckmorton, thus apparently verifying Hofmann's alleged threats. The county attorney referred the matter to the state attorney general's office. Although no charges were filed, Hofmann was "written up" for misuse of mail privileges and disciplined. Meanwhile, the story leaked to the media.

About this same time, a second story broke that Doralee Hofmann had filed for divorce and was asking that her maiden name be restored to her and her children. Many Utahns were relieved at this indication that she intended to rebuild her life and protect her children from their father's infamy. The fact that the divorce had been initiated in the penitentiary was not reported, nor that whether the children bore their mother's name or their father's, they continued to ride in the copper-colored van which had delivered bombs and that their home was still clearly labeled Haus Hofmann.

Then, in early August, the divorce reports were eclipsed by the news that Mark Hofmann had been found unconscious in his cell, the victim of an apparent drug overdose. Discovered about noon when his cellmate returned from work, Hofmann was rushed to the University of Utah Medical Center in Salt Lake City, where he hovered near death. An injury to his right arm at first raised questions of assault, but doctors concluded that he had lain so long in one position that his blood circulation had been curtailed, damaging muscle and skin tissue.

Hofmann had swallowed a potentially fatal dose of an antidepressant that produces sleepiness as a side effect. The overdose was linked in the media to the pending divorce, though Hofmann's attorney Ron Yengich said his client had not seemed distraught. The drug, in fact, had not been prescribed for Hofmann, and the apparent suicide attempt surprised Captain Bona and other prison personnel. Since Mike George had finessed the coded letters situation neatly, prison officials asked him to interview Mrs. Hofmann about a possible motive.

George found a very shaken wife who could not get information from the hospital or prison regarding her estranged husband. One rumor had it that Mark had been up walking around and laughing the night following the overdose. George made some calls and told Doralee that Mark was still unconscious but was out of danger. George asked whether she had noticed anything unusual in her conversation with Mark the evening before the overdose.

No, she said, there had been nothing at all.

What about the divorce, George asked. Was Mark upset and depressed over that?

"This is a divorce on paper only," she told him firmly. "I love Mark as much as ever. If you get to see Mark, tell him I love him and the kids love him. We need him there. Committing suicide, if that's what he was trying to do, is a chicken way out."

Prison investigators learned that Hofmann had procured the drug from other prisoners, gradually accumulating a cache. Although Mike George considered the possibility the overdose involved an escape attempt or some other ploy, after consulting with prison officials he settled on an aborted suicide. Not that

Hofmann was necessarily depressed, but, with Hofmann, George didn't think despondency was required. If the trouble over the coded letters and threats had impressed Mark that no board would ever parole him, George concluded, he could rationally decide to take an easy step into oblivion.

Following his hospital stay, Hofmann returned to the same cell in the Oquirrh facility with his arm bandaged and his right hand nearly useless, necessitating surgery and months of out-patient therapy. Furthermore, he was watched closely, his privileges were restricted, and his classification was re-evaluated. Early in 1989, Hofmann was moved to the Uintah facility, the most restrictive at the penitentiary. Again, he was classified as a Level 2 inmate but received more latitude this time, due to a federal court decision requiring that inmates be allowed forty hours a week outside their cells for exercise, commissary privileges, and two ninety-minute visiting periods. With time, Hofmann enrolled in University of Utah courses and enthusiastically studied Latin. Persistent rumors that he somehow had access to a computer circulated outside the prison. But as no computer systems or classes are available to inmates in the Oquirrh and Uintah facilities, the rumor was unfounded.

In October 1988, five weeks after Hofmann's overdose and a few days after the third anniversary of the Salt Lake bombings, news headlines announced: "Ex-Investment King Facing 34 Counts In Felony Fraud Case." J. Gary Sheets, former president of the now-bankrupt CFS, was indicted on more felony counts than Hofmann had been but refused to plea bargain. His trial in federal court was scheduled for late February 1989.

Since Kathy Sheets's death, the family had scattered. In the spring of 1988, two grandchildren were born just four days apart. Roger and Heidi Jones named their third child Kathy after her grandmother, while Joe and Katie Robertson introduced Tommy to his older sister, Molly. The Joneses then relocated to Chicago. For six months Gary and Diane Sheets lived in California. However, Gary found selling insurance difficult and expenses high so they left Diane's grown children there and returned to Richfield, Utah, where Gary had been raised. Following his father's trial, Jimmy Sheets left for a Mormon mission to the Philippines shortly before Gretchen returned home from her mission to Finland.

The Sheets trial lasted five weeks and involved scores of witnesses. Kathy's diary became a contested piece of evidence due to an entry she had written in January 1985 expressing grave concern about Gary's business problems. Prosecutors claimed that the entry indicated Sheets had lured investors long after he knew his company was doomed. Sheets's attorneys insisted that not until the June audit did the death knell toll, and even then Sheets had refused to believe it tolled for them.

Expectedly, Steve Christensen emerged as a pivotal and controversial figure in the testimony, for the charges centered on JGSA, the syndication company he ran for CFS. Privately, some former CFS employees believed that Christensen could have deflected a criminal prosecution. Others thought Steve would have been indicted for his involvement and, unlike Gary, could not have claimed ignorance of everyday operations. Still others saw Christensen as the company conscience who finally cried foul and attempted to correct the uncorrectable.

Former CFS employees, whose own losses had been tremendous, were called to testify, including Randy Rigby and Joe Robertson. As the wife of one leading salesman listened to the question of fiscal and ethical responsibility batted between Sheets and Christensen, she was struck by a memory. One Christmas CFS had thrown a lavish employees' party at a downtown hotel. She'd seen Gary Sheets arrive direct from a Utah Jazz basketball game and begin chatting with and hugging employees and their spouses. "Hi, Gary," she'd interjected, "where's Kathy?" Gary had looked startled. "Steve," he'd called, "where's my wife?" Steve, businesslike as always, had known.

Though witnesses included singer Marie Osmond and several of the Osmond Brothers, the trial's star was Gary Sheets himself. On the stand he displayed the anecdotal skill that had made him a superb salesman, successfully convincing the jury he'd not knowingly defrauded anyone. On April 8, 1989, Sheets was acquitted of all counts. Standing among his former employees, friends, and overjoyed family, Sheets was not surprised by the verdict; he and Diane had gained confidence as the trial progressed that he would not go to prison.

With his own legal problems resolved, Sheets filed a $1 million lawsuit against author Robert Lindsey, whose book on the bombings had quoted the diary passage used against Sheets in court. Sheets also filed a separate suit against *The Globe*, a supermarket tabloid; the suit alleged that an article had said he faced charges when, in fact, he had been acquitted. In addition, Sheets filed an intent to sue former Salt Lake County Attorney Ted Cannon and the detectives and prosecutors on the Hofmann case, claiming that they had given a copy of his wife's diary to Lindsey without his permission. At summer's end, fighting exhaustion and depression, Sheets borrowed money and took Diane back to New Zealand for a two-week vacation.

Though her husband's name came up frequently in court, Terri Christensen did not attend the trial. Her curiosity regarding CFS dealings was nil. In fact, she was thoroughly weary of everything having to do with CFS, forgeries, Mark Hofmann, and the bombings and wished never to hear or say another word about them.

Terri's second marriage soon ended in divorce, but the money Steve had left in trust allowed her to remain at home with her children in Centerville, Utah. Determined to survive the bombings on her own terms, Terri resolved her feelings by reminding herself that Steve had died a martyr to the necessary discovery of Hofmann's exploitation of LDS church leaders and his distortion of Mormon history. If Hofmann's malice had been part of a divine plan, why should she waste her energy hating him?

Some of the investigators who dealt with the bombings case moved on, too. Detective Ken Farnsworth asked to be transferred from homicide to patrol for the few years remaining before his retirement; Detective Jim Bell jumped to the Medical Examiner's Office amid controversy regarding serial murders that Bell considered solved; and George Throckmorton returned to Salt Lake City from California to take a job with the Utah Transit Authority. Occasionally, Throckmorton still examined questioned documents. Although the owners of the Oath of a Freeman insisted their Oath was "not one of

Hofmann's forgeries," other collectors began checking printed documents and handwritten manuscripts. For most, however, the expense of forensic analysis precluded testing.

Meanwhile, the Mormon money market realized significant losses as Mike George's conversations with Hofmann invalidated many of the samples in Al Rust's classic book, *Mormon and Utah Coin and Currency*. Exchanging information, collectors realized that during the late 1970s and early 1980s Hofmann had sustained a quiet trade in now-suspicious coins and currency along the Wasatch Front. Virtually unknown among collectors then, Hofmann had already regarded himself a numismatist.

Coin expert and author Harry Campbell remembered a youthful Hofmann for a 1900 Lagoon Amusement Park token he'd told Hofmann appeared to be unique. Hofmann had said he would offer the token to the park's current owner, David Freed. Freed purchased the small coin unaware that Hofmann had earlier discussed killing him for items in his collection. Now Campbell and Freed both assumed the token was counterfeit, and Campbell regarded with considerable misgiving a Joseph Smith token and Brigham Young's Lion House notes that Hofmann had sold to the LDS church. Still another token, which Hofmann had sold to church officials as an 1846 Utah item, Campbell suspected had actually originated in Britain.

Not only did LDS leaders continue to examine the church's holdings, they freed up attorney Richard Turley, newly appointed history department director recruited by Apostle Dallin Oaks, to prepare a book on "the church's intersection" with the Hofmann case. Turley enjoined archivist Glenn Rowe's help with interviews and a secretary's full-time assistance with computer data. Turley resolved to write church history for a general audience and an undetermined publisher, illuminating the role of church leaders, whom, he believed, other authors had inaccurately portrayed. Turley greatly preferred written materials to interviews, and after cross-referencing and analyzing the three published books on the bombings, he requested personal journals and notes from individuals associated with the case, including investigators.

When city detectives resisted turning over their records,

church attorneys used Freedom of Information laws to compel them. The police only released thirty-nine pages of early notes and memos written by several officers regarding their interviews with church leaders or employees. Not surprisingly, Turley found his own interviews with investigators more complete and productive than the relinquished papers. As a church employee, Turley claimed access to church records never made available to journalists or investigators; but he found it difficult to locate and successfully interview sources who had been aware of the pressures surrounding Hofmann's important William E. McLellin transaction.

Unknown to Turley, at work in the Church Administration Building, church leaders in Hofmann's home congregation quietly and belatedly removed Mark Hofmann's name from church roles more than six months after he pleaded guilty to murder.

When Deseret Book Company's rare books department was dismantled in late 1987, Curt Bench opened Benchmark Books, specializing in out-of-print and rare books. Ten months later, Bench's former assistant, Wade Lillywhite, who had moved to California, was charged with defrauding Deseret Book of more than $200,000. Lillywhite admitted issuing checks from Deseret Book to cover personal debts, pocketing profits, inflating prices, and stealing books. A U.S. district chief judge decided against a possible ten-year prison term and ordered Lillywhite to serve ten years probation and make complete financial restitution.

Lyn Jacobs let several years pass before contacting the man he had called his best friend and business partner. Reconstructing his life, Jacobs now found certain memories of Hofmann especially significant. Once Mark had shown off in a Boston restaurant, scribbling famous signatures across the tablecloth with a crayon. The signatures hadn't looked all that authentic, Jacobs comforted himself, yet he recalled how Hofmann's hand whipped along, how his eyes darted from Lyn to Doralee to Shannon Flynn. All Jacobs had thought at the time was "My gosh, he's writing in cursive instead of his silly printing."

Then there was the night not long before the bombings when Hofmann had given Jacobs a promised scrap of papyrus, supposedly from the McLellin collection he was selling to the church. Hofmann had sworn Jacobs to secrecy, confiding that high-ranking Mormon official Gordon B. Hinckley intended to suppress the collection and wouldn't want anything out.

Jacobs had shaken his head. "Well, Mark, really, I just can't believe the kinds of deception people are capable of!"

Mark had agreed. "For instance, Lyn, you have no idea what deceptions *I'm* capable of."

"What do you mean?"

"Oh, I've done something really awful."

"Come on, Mark," Lyn encouraged, "what is it?"

As Jacobs probed, Hofmann denied murder, adultery, and theft, then minimized dishonesty as commonplace.

Forgery, Jacobs would say later, hadn't occurred to him, and Mark had seemed particularly smug when he couldn't guess.

Now, in late spring, 1989, Jacobs again had forgery on his mind. His personal collection of "clip signatures" of LDS church presidents and Relief Society presidents contained five signatures Hofmann had given him. Jacobs assumed they were forgeries but wondered if the others in his collection might have originated with Hofmann, as well. He decided to write to Mark and inquire. In reply, he received a carefully worded letter from attorney Ron Yengich informing him that the items he had questioned were all fakes.

Around the same time Jacobs wrote his letter, Brent Ashworth traced his old route to Haus Hofmann. For more than three years he had struggled to resolve his debts, regain some confidence in his judgment, and forgive himself and Hofmann. Not that he was alone in being duped, though sometimes it seemed that way. One collector had recently informed Ashworth that President Hinckley had been suspicious of Hofmann early on. "That's not the way I remember it!" blurted Ashworth, who'd always played second fiddle to Hofmann, the concert master.

Ashworth decided to try for reconciliation. He considered a meeting with Hofmann but rejected the idea as unprofitable for him and probably unattractive to Hofmann. But Doralee Hofmann—now Doralee Olds, he supposed—had been so involved in his transactions with Mark that Brent tended to blame her too, perhaps unfairly. Also, he was concerned for her and the children, and she was more accessible and certainly less dangerous than Mark. He decided to visit, confess his hard feelings and his forgiveness, and resolve the matter.

Gathering his courage as he parked at the curb on Marie Avenue, Brent forced his legs to walk past the Haus Hofmann sign on the lamp post, past the copper-colored van in the carport, and toward the door. He wasn't the only one feeling strain, he discovered, for Doralee turned white as he approached.

Inside, the house was much as he remembered. The large family portrait taken shortly before the bombings still hung on the wall, but another that included the youngest child and omitted Mark had been added. The blond children had grown, of course. Michael, eight and recently baptized, looked like his father. He was preparing for a camping trip with other boys from his ward, and his mother helped him assemble his gear. Ashworth had never seen the youngest child, Julie, who brought him a book to read to her when her mother left the room for a few minutes.

Chatting with Dori proved difficult. Reaching to establish a rapport, Ashworth related his concern, years back, over Mark's injuries from the third bomb. Matter-of-factly Dori brought up the death of Brent's son and asked how his wife was recovering. Clearly, Dori considered her life devastated and herself greatly misunderstood.

Dori's hostility toward the police was strong, Ashworth soon learned, and she disliked and dismissed everything she had read about the case. Worse than the publicity, she told him, even some members of her own family criticized her for not distancing herself from Mark sooner and more completely.

"Do you still visit Mark?" Ashworth wondered.

No, she said, though she had for months after filing for divorce. Around Christmas Mark had told her it hurt too much to see her. They still corresponded, though, and Mark's parents took the children out to visit him.

She still loves him, Ashworth concluded; she's very much under his spell.

As if answering his thoughts, Dori said emphatically, "I didn't leave him sooner because he's a good father and a good husband."

"Well, I could see that in him," Ashworth offered.

"I'm glad you could see that," she replied eagerly. Even going to church, she added, had its strain especially when church history was discussed in Sunday school class. "It's hard to know what our history really is and not say anything."

When Brent mentioned Mark's suicide attempt, Dori interrupted. "It wasn't a suicide attempt!" Mark had begun using drugs recreationally soon after going to prison, she told him. And, although she had warned him, he persisted and finally overdosed.

"Gee, we really agree on that," Brent said. "I didn't think he'd try to do himself in."

"He still doesn't have full use of his arm," she continued, flexing her own arm to demonstrate the problem. "But then, he can write equally well with either hand." (Driving home later, Ashworth would remember that remark and burst out laughing.)

Now, as lightly as he could, Brent again brought up the third bomb, which he believed had been intended for him. Dori shrugged the possibility off. "Mark denies it. At least that's what he says," she explained elliptically.

Finally Ashworth ran out of conversation and realized he had hoped in vain for any acknowledgement for his suffering. He stood, groping for a gesture that would give the past its due and free him.

"I hear you're struggling financially," he said. "Would you accept a check?"

Still tense, she hesitated then said yes. He wrote a sizeable check and handed it to her. Later he would learn that it went toward the children's tuition at a private school.

Returning to his car, Ashworth felt lighter. The last time he had walked away from Haus Hofmann, he'd left an icily furious Mark Hofmann behind, holding the papyrus fragment that Steve Christensen soon would lock up. Hofmann and Ashworth had struck a $30,000 deal for the fragment. But unable to verify the piece's authenticity, Ashworth had returned it.

That incident had occurred on the evening of September 26, 1985 — the same day Hofmann had paid an early morning visit to President Gordon Hinckley; the same day Steve

Christensen had called Hofmann to insist again that he pay the bank loan or suffer dire consequences; the same day Hofmann had hauled collateral to Deseret Book trying to raise money; the same day a First Interstate Bank official had written to Hofmann demanding immediate repayment—and, this time, no rubber check!

Ashworth's relief at leaving Haus Hofmann only contrasted with the uneasiness that shadowed him inside the house like a low-grade fear. He hadn't yet heard that Mark had confided to a fellow inmate that his third bomb had been meant for a Mormon man who owed him $30,000 and refused to pay up. But the admission wouldn't have surprised him.

Many prisoners become expert at manipulation, a game Mark Hofmann mastered early in life. Just as he'd arranged the presentation at his Board of Pardons hearing in a way that struck board members oddly, so now does Hofmann arrange his family constellation to fit his present needs.

His ex-wife, who still lives behind his name and depends on his parents for financial support, Hofmann keeps conveniently at arm's length with schoolboy letters. At his request, their four children travel regularly to the prison with their intensely religious grandfather who'd insisted on his son's innocence and squirmed as Mark pridefully discussed murder and fraud. Essentially, Bill Hofmann now serves time too, driving four impressionable children to the worst of places to visit a celebrated criminal who'd been as bad as a Mormon boy could be: he had repeatedly duped prophets of the Lord's true church; he had murdered two people then avoided the only penalty his family believed could atone for his sins.

Perhaps the old silence toward family secrets and disturbing subjects rides with them too, week after week. That silence, more than four years after the Salt Lake City bombings, still envelopes the Hofmanns' extended families and settles over the neighborhood and ward. Also hovering about the Mormon history community and LDS church generally, it communicates an unconscious ethic: if discomfiting subjects are not discussed openly, the world remains a nice place. No one need feel awkward; no one need cauterize or bind wounds.

A FORENSIC ANALYSIS
OF TWENTY-ONE
HOFMANN DOCUMENTS

George J. Throckmorton

This section explains the process and techniques used to uncover the fraud perpetrated by Mark W. Hofmann. Also included are descriptions of the major examinations conducted by forensic specialists, the kinds of tests which were developed and used, and the results obtained.

EXAMINING THE DOCUMENTS
First Examination: 17-20 December 1985

William Flynn and George Throckmorton met in the LDS Church Office Building in downtown Salt Lake City, where a temporary laboratory was set up in a room on the second floor with specially installed locks to insure security. The documents were secured in a large vault each night and were brought into the room in a locked briefcase. No one examiner was ever alone with the documents in order to guard against accusations that any of the documents had been altered.

A total of 81 documents — including 12 from Hofmann — were examined (an additional 5 were eventually added to the list of suspected forgeries). However, this initial examination raised more questions than answers. The documents fell into two groups, one of which had passed through Hofmann; however, the exact nature of either group was unclear. Little "hard" evidence indicated forgery, but enough about the documents seemed suspicious to warrant further investigation.

Second Examination: 7-20 January 1986

This time a room was specially secured and equipped at the Utah State Crime Laboratory. The original 81 documents were again examined, plus an additional 288 documents—including 261 known to have come from Hofmann. At this point, samples of ink were prepared using an eighteenth-century recipe, and experiments were conducted using this ink.

On January 17 the Martin Harris to W. W. Phelps letter, or salamander letter, which had been retrieved from the FBI laboratory in Washington, D.C., was brought to the Utah crime laboratory. This letter, subjected to the new tests, also fell into the category of believed forgeries. By the end of this period, a total of 569 documents—including 276 Hofmann documents—had been examined. Of these, 21 were believed to have been forged, all of which came through Hofmann.

Third Examination: 22 January 1986

This examination was also conducted in the Utah State Crime Laboratory and included all previously examined documents. Flynn and Throckmorton were now joined by Al Lyter, an ink expert from the Washington, D.C., area. They discussed the previous examinations, testing procedures, and results and conducted further experiments.

Fourth Examination: 19 April 1986

During this examination, conducted in a laboratory at Throckmorton's home, all previous tests were repeated and verified. Flynn and Throckmorton were joined by a forensic document examiner from the Bureau of Alcohol, Tobacco, and Firearms Lab in Washington, D.C. By the end of the examination period, all three agreed about procedures and results. Still, it was not yet possible to explain and duplicate all of the various phenomena which the Hofmann documents demonstrated. At this point 688 documents, including 302 Hofmann documents, had been examined. Sixty-one of these were believed to have been forged and could be traced directly to Hofmann.

Hereafter experiments were conducted individually by Flynn and Throckmorton to examine newly found Hofmann documents.

THE TESTS

Initially it was hoped a single test could be developed to detect forgery for all of the Hofmann documents. Unfortunately, the diversity of the Hofmann documents precluded this. In the end, a series of tests was developed, based on hundreds of hours of research and experimenting. No one test was ever sufficient to guarantee results. But applied cumulatively, the tests without exception uncovered the Hofmann forgeries among the over 6,000 documents (including 443 from Hofmann) subjected to such testing.

1. Ultra-violet Examination

BLUE-HAZE. Documents treated with certain chemicals exhibit a particular discoloration under ultra-violet light. This discoloration discloses portions of the document treated with chemicals—for example, to remove or otherwise obliterate ink. Such chemically treated areas generally appear fairly bright in color compared to the rest of the paper.

Entire Hofmann documents were found to exhibit a certain discoloration under ultra-violet light. Our questions thus became: Why had these documents been chemically treated and with what chemical(s)? In the end it was determined that hydrogen peroxide and ammonium hydroxide could cause the characteristics exhibited by these Hofmann documents. These two chemicals cause a rapid oxidation of the iron in iron-gall ink and also cause a slight blue-hazing effect on the paper itself. There is no reason why genuine nineteenth-century documents would legitimately be treated with these chemicals. However, such chemicals artificially age the appearance of iron-gall ink. Only those documents which coming from Hofmann among the over 6,000 documents examined exhibited this blue-hazing effect.

UNI-DIRECTIONAL RUNNING. Ink applied to paper will slowly begin to migrate from the original point of contact. In general, ink will radiate outwards in all directions. Iron-gall ink was the preferred ink for many years because it is relatively impervious to moisture and is fairly permanent. Still, such ink, if in contact with moisture for an extended period of time, will bleed.

Many of the Hofmann documents exhibited a unidirectional running of the iron-gall ink when examined under ultraviolet light. This running suggested that some liquid had caused the relatively impervious ink to run profusely and that the documents had been hung up to dry. Gravity would cause the ink to run in one direction rather than to radiate out from a center. The two chemicals which caused the artificial aging were also shown to cause this uni-directional running effect on documents hung up to dry. None of the over 6,000 documents examined exhibited this effect except those from Hofmann.

BLEED-THRU. Paper treated with certain chemicals frequently becomes translucent, a characteristic most noticeable under ultra-violet light. The writing on the reverse side of a paper becomes more noticeable after treatment. The degree of translucency varies from one paper to another.

It was discovered that documents treated with the two chemicals discussed exhibit this bleed-thru phenomenon. The variability from paper to paper remains an acknowledged weakness of this test. Still, the bleed-thru observed on the Hofmann documents differed significantly from that observed on the other 6,000+ documents examined.

2. Microscopic Examination

ALLIGATORING. Iron-gall ink on the Hofmann documents exhibits a particular pattern of cracking, which resembles the plating of an alligator. This "alligatoring effect" is difficult to describe but is recognizably distinct from the normal cracking which occurs over time with iron-gall ink. After learning to differentiate this alligatoring effect from normal cracking, it was discovered that treating iron-gall ink with hydrogen peroxide and ammonium hydroxide causes this distinctive pattern to appear. Further research showed that treating documents with these chemicals causes a rapid rise and decline of the acidity, which in turn causes certain components in the ink to crack. Not all of the Hofmann documents showed this alligatoring.

But of the thousands of examined documents, only those coming from Hofmann exhibited this effect.

SOLUBILITY. Ink on paper tends to harden progressively as time passes. If ink has been placed on paper at two different periods, the ink placed on the paper first will be harder than the ink placed there later. If the ink formula and paper of two documents are identical, then this principle can be used to compare their relative age.

This principle was used to devise a test for the Hofmann documents. It was discovered that a 15 percent solution of ammonium hydroxide in distilled water would eventually cause iron-gall ink to become soluble. When small portions of such a solution were placed on genuine nineteenth-century documents, very little reaction occurred—even after as much as three minutes. Application of this test to more than 200 documents ranging in age from 100 to 200 years old showed this resistance to the solvent. However, when the solvent was placed on the Hofmann documents it caused an almost immediate reaction—always within 15 seconds. Even acknowledging a wide tolerance for error in the test, it was ascertained that the Hofmann documents are significantly newer than their claimed 100 years.

STAIN. When iron-gall ink is placed on a document, it slowly begins to oxidize, or rust. The iron rust is absorbed into the paper and is all that remains visible after a period of time. Rusting of ink varies according to atmospheric conditions, ink, and paper. Still, the basic principle is sound and provided yet another test for the Hofmann documents. Under the microscope, a sharply pointed stylus can be used to pick away some of the hard and crusted surface of the ink and to expose the underlying paper. In a genuine nineteenth-century document, the paper beneath the ink is brown in color because of the oxidation of the iron. However, when this top layer was removed from many of the Hofmann documents, the paper was not stained brown. As with the solubility test, this procedure could not determine how long any particular ink had been on any particular paper, but it could compare genuine documents with those coming from Hofmann. Again, the Hofmann documents were found to differ significantly from documents dating from the early 1800s.

PRINTING FLAWS. During the investigation, several photographic negatives were found which were eventually traced to Mark Hofmann. These negatives matched various documents and nineteenth-century currencies which Hofmann sold. The negatives themselves had been recently made at printing companies throughout the United States. These negatives formed a crucial link in establishing forgery.

In the 1800s plates used to print money, postmarks, and other documents were made from similar negatives — though today this process is rapidly being replaced with other technology. In making plates, the art work or copy is first photographed. Then a zinc plate covered with a light-sensitive coating is exposed to the resulting negative and etched with nitric acid. The resulting printing plate is inked and used to print a reproduction of the original art work. Hofmann's negatives suggested that he might have had plates made for manufacturing fraudulent documents.

Any scratches or imperfections in a negative will be reproduced on a plate and on the printed documents. Obvious imperfections can be removed or covered up on the negative. But inconspicuous dots and scratches are frequently overlooked, and these smaller imperfections can be seen through a microscope. These "trash-marks" can be used to match a particular document with a particular negative or printing plate. This process can be used to identify the origin of fraudulent printed documents, especially when compared to authentic printed documents and currency when available.

3. SAMD

In the early 1980s, Roderick J. McNeil, experimenting with Scanning Auger Electron Microscopy, devised a technique for determining when certain inks were placed on documents. Scanning Auger Microscopy Dating (SAMD) now measures ion diffusion of inks in paper and determines the age of a document with an accuracy of 15± years for inks made with a heavy metal. This technique has gained wide acceptance among archeometric and forensic specialists for documents written within the past 500 years.

However, the technique is extremely costly. Few laboratories in the United States have the necessary equipment, and only McNeil is considered an expert in the technique. The procedure also requires a fair expenditure of time. Because of the controversy surrounding the case, 7 of the documents were subjected to the entire SAMD technique and several others were partially analyzed. The results of the SAMD agreed with the results of the tests described above. The SAMD provided a fairly precise dating of when particular documents were created.

THE DOCUMENTS

1. The Second Anointing Blessing

Dated ca. 1912. Purchased for $60.00. Introduced 1978-79. On plain off-white paper, approximately 5 1/2 inches by 8 3/4 inches. Upper left-hand corner shows a rubber stamped impression approximately 1/2 inch in height and 2 inches long, reading "SALT LAKE TEMPLE." In upper right-hand corner several words are handprinted, then erased, but remain visible: "Destroy this copy."

This document was not considered highly significant to the criminal charges against Hofmann. However, the handwriting on the document was compared with the handwriting in a diary kept by Hofmann several years earlier. Only two pages in Hofmann's diary are in cursive, but these matched the cursive writing on the blessing document.

2. The Joseph Smith to Maria and Sarah Lawrence Letter

Dated 23 June 1844. Gift to LDS church. Introduced 1978-79. Handwritten on plain paper approximately 8 inches by 11 inches, with a small tear in the lower left-hand corner. Top of document not evenly cut, indicating it has been trimmed by someone using scissors or similar device. Written in iron-gall ink.

The handwriting was found to differ significantly from the known writing of Joseph Smith. It was also found to be quite different in form from other known writing of the era, although this finding was not generalized to prove the handwriting "positively" did not come from the period. All tests—blue-haze, uni-directional running, bleed-thru, alligatoring, solubility, and stain—indicated forgery.

3. The Anthon Transcript and Smith Family Bible

Transcript not dated (1828); 1668 Bible. Purchase price estimated at $20,000 in trade. Introduced October 1980. Approximately 7 5/8 inches by 10 7/8 inches, with writing on both sides.

The Bible appeared to be genuine. An 8-page handwritten insert on lined paper of the "Book of Amos" from the Old Testament ends with the name "Samuel Smith." Since Samuel Smith was the great grandfather of Joseph Smith, among other possibilities, this insert could identify the Bible as a Smith family Bible. However, when examined, the inserted pages were found to contain a watermark with the date 1819, eliminating the possibility that the signature could be that of Joseph Smith's great-grandfather. Neither was the handwriting that of Joseph Smith's brother, Samuel Smith. The ink of the signature was found to differ from the ink in the rest of the handwritten insertion and had been artificially aged with chemicals.

Examination also demonstrated that the brownish discoloration originally interpreted as a reaction between the Bible pages and the transcript was added by artificial means. Some letters from the Bible were stuck to the glue on the transcript, but the lack of staining indicated that the transcript had not been glued in the Bible very long.

The Anthon transcript has a brown, faded-out appearance, and the writing is very blurred and washed out. Various filters were used during the examination to make the document easier to read. The brown staining had ridges consistent with scorching done by a hand iron. Ink tests indicated that the document had been written and aged in a manner consistent with other Hofmann documents. The handwriting on the back of the document was not of the quality or consistency of the known handwriting samples of Joseph Smith. The low quantity of metal in the ink made SAMD examination less precise than usual, dating it to 1940 ± 50 years.

4. The Joseph Smith III Blessing

Dated 17 January 1844. Purchase price estimated at $20,000. Introduced March 1981. Approximately 8 inches by 10 inches. Handwritten, with body of text on one side and a brief notation on the other. A small sliver of paper has been cut from the lower left-hand corner of the paper for paper analysis.

The paper seems to be authentic paper from the period. The form of the writing is close to that of Thomas Bullock, although the slant of the writing is more consistent with Bullock's 1857 period than with that of the 1844 period. In addition, the punctuation, spacing, margins, and style of the blessing differ from other blessings written by Bullock. All tests — blue-haze, uni-directional running, bleed-thru, alligatoring, solubility, and stain — indicated forgery, while SAMD dated it to 1962 ± 25 years.

5. Handwritten White Notes

Dated 1849. Estimated purchase price $3,000 to $5,000 each. Introduced March 1981. On white paper, approximately 2 7/8 inches by 2 inches. Three signatures on each note, frequently in different colored inks. Embossed Seal of the Twelve Apostles in the center of each note.

Artificial aging technique is evident on portions of the documents. The signatures are "similar" to genuine signatures, but close examination reveals indications of fraud. The seal was the same as that of the genuine Seal of the Twelve Apostles. Hofmann had obtained a copy of the genuine seal and made a reproduction for embossing the notes. All tests — blue-haze, uni-directional running, alligatoring, solubility, and stain — indicated forgery.

6. The Lucy Mack Smith Letter

Dated 23 January 1829. Purchase price estimated at $30,000 to $33,000. Introduced July 1982. Supposedly a stampless cover letter written on one single piece of paper approximately 15 1/2 inches by 11 1/2 inches. The paper was tattered and worn. It was taped in the middle, as if the single sheet had come apart at the fold because of age and wear. Addressed portion of the letter exhibited bits of sealing wax, a poor quality postmark from Palmyra with the number 24 visible as the date, and a handwritten designation of 78 3/4 written in the upper right-hand corner, as the postage paid.

Examination indicated that the letter was written on two different pieces of paper (not one which had come apart). Both pages had been cut at the same time, using the same instrument, then taped together. The paper had been artificially aged. Irregularities, inconsistencies, and improper pressure indicated that the postmark was not genuine but probably a facsimile of a genuine one. The handwriting differed from that found on a genuine letter written by Lucy Mack Smith. A practitioner of forensic linguistics compared the two letters and stated that "there is a clear descriptive indication that these two letters were authored by different writers." All tests—blue-haze, uni-direction running, bleed-thru, alligatoring, solubility, and stain—indicated forgery, while SAMD dated it to 1962 ± 25 years.

7. Spanish Fork Notes

No date. Purchase price varied from $1,500 to $2,500 per set. Introduced December 1982. Rainbow Set: Each set with denominations of 10 cents, 25 cents, 50 cents, and 1 dollar. Each denomination printed in a different color—red, blue, green, and yellow. On grey-colored card stock, approximately 3 7/8 inches by 2 1/2 inches. Handwritten number and signature in bottom portion of each note. Small Notes: Denominations of 5 cents, 10 cents, and 25 cents; initials at bottom crossed out with two horizontal lines; unevenly cut, approximately 2 inches by 3 3/4 inches. Rainbow Set: The paper contains artificial brighteners which were not added to paper until 1940-50; rubber stamps ordered by Mark Hofmann from Salt Lake Stamp Company in January 1982 produced impressions which matched the denomination figures on the notes.

Small Notes: The paper seemed to be from the inside cover of an old book. Sheets of "rub-off" letters were found in the possession of Mark Hofmann. One sheet contained letters in the same size and style as those found on the notes. Comparison established a correlation between the size, style, and quantity of letters missing from this sheet and the size, style, and quantity of letters found on the notes. Apparently these rub-off letters were used to make art work which was photographed, and the negative used to make a printing plate. After the notes were printed, the initials were added and then crossed out to indicate that the notes had been used as currency. All tests — uni-directional running, alligatoring, solubility, and printing flaws that were consistent with the negative — indicated forgery.

8. The Joseph Smith to Josiah Stowell Letter

Dated 18 June 1825. Purchase price $15,000. Introduced January 1983. Handwritten stampless cover letter with the body of the letter on one side and an address on the other. Sealing wax on address side in two places. Right side of paper unevenly cut, indicating it was trimmed from a larger piece of paper.

In the letter, Joseph Smith's writing seems too neat. It appears that a finger had been drawn across the wet ink on this letter, smearing it with a "flicking" motion. However these smudges are not consistent with those appearing in genuine Smith documents.

All tests — blue-haze, bleed-thru, alligatoring, solubility, and stain — indicated forgery, while SAMD dated it to 1960 ± 25 years.

9. The E. B. Grandin Book of Mormon Contract

Dated 17 August 1829. Purchase price estimated at $25,000. Introduced March 1983. Handwritten on old-looking, faded paper, approximately 8 1/8 inches by 11 1/2 inches. Four signatures at bottom. Small diamond-shaped papers pasted next to three of the signatures, perhaps an early form of notary. Iron-gall ink. Using oblique lighting, a recessed impression naming the E. B. Grandin printing company is visible on the reverse side.

The advertising stamp on the reverse side was one of Hofmann's most subtle and convincing forgery techniques. The paper was artificially aged. All tests—blue haze, uni-directional running, bleed-thru, alligatoring, solubility, and stain—indicated forgery.

10. The Martin Harris to W. W. Phelps (or Salamander) Letter

Dated 23 October 1830. Purchase price $40,000. Introduced January 1984. Folded, handwritten stampless cover letter, approximately 11 3/8 inches by 8 1/2 inches. Small piece of paper had been removed from upper right-hand corner for paper analysis; small circular holes where ink samples had been removed for testing. Postmark faded and difficult to read.

Most stampless cover letters are folded so that the contents are not visible unless sealing wax is broken. This letter was folded so that one end was open, and the contents could be seen by looking in the end. Also the flatness, vagueness, and ink distribution of the postmark differ from genuine postmarks of the period. All authenticated handwriting samples of Martin Harris are signatures. All other Martin Harris handwriting samples originate with Hofmann. The signature on the letter is similar to other Harris signatures, but this was not enough to verify the handwriting. The paper is genuinely old; however, microscopic analysis determined that the lines on the paper were drawn, not printed mechanically. All tests—blue-haze, uni-directional running, bleed-thru, alligatoring, solubility, and stain—indicated forgery, while SAMD dated it to 1950 ± 40 years.

11. Deseret Currency

Dated 1858. Purchase price $1,000 to $12,000 per set. Introduced August 1984. Denominations of $1, $2, $3, $5, $10, $20, $50, and $100, approximately 4 7/8 inches by 2 1/2 inches. Machine printed, in most cases, on thin tissue-type paper. All contain signature in lower left-hand corner, date in lower right-hand corner, and either a handwritten or machine-printed signature of Brigham Young in the lower right-hand corner. Handwritten number in upper left-hand corner. Iron gall ink.

A total of forty different notes were examined; thirty-six

were counterfeit. The printing process on the genuine notes is significantly better than that on the counterfeits. Negatives were found in Denver, Colorado, which had been used to make printing plates for the currency. The printing flaws found on the negatives match those on the counterfeit notes. Evidence indicates that the genuine $1, $2, and $3 notes were photographed to make negatives and plates. Apparently original art work was created for the remaining denominations, and plates were made from this art work. The forgeries were printed on paper which differs from the paper of the genuine notes. The paper used for the forgeries is characteristically used to protect pictures in older books. Two signatures found on the questionable documents were compared with genuine signatures. They were very similar, but close examination indicated they were forgeries.

12. The Betsy Ross Letter

Dated 29 November 1807. Purchase price $18,000. Introduced October 1984. Stampless cover letter, approximately 7 1/4 inches by 9 inches. Dover, N.H., postmark dated Nov. 26. Letter sent free under authorized signature of Wm. B. Smith, Postmaster, Canandaigua, New York. Folded and sealed with sealing wax.

The top and bottom of the letter had been cut unevenly, and there was evidence that it had been cut after it was folded. The date at the top had been altered from 1837 to 1807 by carefully picking off the ink at the top of the "3" formation and connecting the bottom loop with new ink to resemble an "0." Ultra-violet examination confirmed this alteration. Research with the U.S. Postal Department showed that William B. Smith was not postmaster until 1835. Using a scanning electron microscope, it was determined that the ink in the name "Ross" differs from the ink on the remaining portions of the document. Handwriting examination was not conclusive because of the handwriting sample that had been recently added was so small. However, there were indications that the name "Ross" was of different authorship than the rest of the handwriting on the

letter. Thus the examination indicated that the letter was probably genuine to the time period 1837 and signed by someone
named Betsy.

13. The "Oath of a Freeman" I

Not dated (1638). Never purchased but asking price of $1.5
million. Introduced March 1985. Machine printed document,
approximately 4 1/4 inches by 6 1/8 inches. Border of 1/4 inch
surrounds all four corners of the document. Title "The Oath of
a Freeman" and 27 lines of printed words on face of document. Notation "Oathe of a Freeman" in seventeenth-century
script handwritten on back. Iron-gall ink seems to have turned
brown with age. Edges of paper slightly tattered.

Letter "j" in the word "subject" in fifth line of the Oath
drops below the upper portion of the "d" in the word "doe" of
line six. Close examination disclosed other areas of overlap.
This overlapping of letters could not have occured in genuine
printing from the period. A strip frequently called a "lead" or
"slug" was inserted between lines of type as individual letter
characters were handset into a block. This strip prevents overlap. This overlap indicates that a cut-and-paste method was
probably used to forge the Oath. Letters could be cut from
printed material from the 1600-1700 period and used to make
the art work for a photograph. Investigation confirmed that
Hofmann had a plate made from a negative of the Oath in
early 1985. "The Oath of a Freeman II" (described below) was
printed from the same plate. The second copy of the oath was
submitted for SAMD testing. The examination of Oath I was
conducted in the U.S. Postal Laboratory in New York City.
Many tests that would normally have been conducted on this
document were not undertaken because of limited time with the
document resulting from lack of cooperation among parties
involved.

14. The Peter and David Whitmer to Bithel Todd Letter

Dated 12 August 1828. Purchase price $1,500. Introduced
April 1985. Handwritten stampless cover letter, approximately

11 1/4 inches by 8 5/16 inches. Sealing wax. Faint and distorted postmark, with date "20 August" written over in ink.

Postmark is extremely illegible and indications exist that it is not genuine, although this could not be positively verified during examination. Sealing wax is composed of sealing wax mixed with what appeared to be hardened mucilage, which is highly irregular. A second, partially burned stampless cover letter addressed to Bithel Todd (but without letter contents) was found in remains of Hofmann's car after explosion. Handwriting on the address of the first letter and that on address of second come from common source. All tests — blue-haze, unidirectional running, bleed-thru, alligatoring, and solubility — indicated forgery.

15. The Joseph Smith to Jonathan Dunham Letter

Dated 27 June 1844. Purchase price $60,000. Introduced July 1985. Handwritten letter, approximately 6 1/4 inches by 7 3/4 inches.

Two genuine letters written from Carthage Jail on the same day were compared with this letter. The two genuine letters (four pages in all) are similar in that they were written on the same size paper with the same type instrument. The Dunham letter, however, is written on a different size paper with a different writing instrument. Small rips on the left side of the Dunham letter indicate the paper has been torn out of a book. The handwriting in the Dunham letter is significantly different from that in the other letter. All tests — blue-haze, uni-directional running, bleed-thru, alligatoring, solubility, and stain — indicated forgery, while SAMD dated it to 1962 ± 25 years.

16. The Solomon Spalding-Sidney Rigdon Land Deed

Dated 1822. Sold for $400. Introduced July 1985. Handwritten document, approximately 7 7/8 inches by 12 1/8 inches. An uneven piece of paper, approximately 1 1/4 inches by 2 1/2 inches, had been torn out of lower right hand corner. Paper faded, browning white in color; iron gall ink. Unevenly cut on all sides. The spelling, "Solomon Spalding," differed from that prefered by the historical figure: "Spaulding."

Two different inks were found on the document. The top date ("1822"), the lower date ("1822"), and two names ("Sidney Rigdon" and "Solomon Spalding") were written in one ink, the body of the document in another. The minor areas in the separate ink had been artificially aged. Microscopic examination revealed that the lower date, "1822," had been written over an original date, "1792." The document was probably authentic, except that the lower date had been changed and the three additional entries had been added. All tests—blue-haze, uni-directional running, alligatoring, and solubility—indicated forgery.

17. "The Oath of a Freeman" II

No date (1638). Suggested purchase price $185,000 (used as collateral). Introduced September 1985. Machine printed document, approximately 5 3/8 inches by 7 1/8 inches. A 1/4 inch border surrounds all four corners of the document. Black ink. Title "The Oath Of A Freeman" and 27 lines of printed words on face of document.

This second Oath was compared with Oath I and with the negative made in 1985. This examination took place in New York City at the same time Oath I was studied. The printing flaws and errors on Oath II matched those on Oath I. Oath II did not have the iron-gall ink on the back and therefore the ink tests could not be applied. However the SAMD test was conducted on this Oath with acceptable results, dating it to 1920 ± 75 years. Because of the low percentage of metal found in the ink, the results of the SAMD test were not as precise as generally obtained. However, the results showed that the document could not have been printed in 1638.

18. Jim Bridger Notes

Date 1852. Purchase price $5,000 each. Introduced December 1984. Machine printed note, approximately 3 3/8 inches by 7 7/8 inches, with handwritten portions and signatures. The machine-printed format required certain blank spaces to be filled in when the note was negotiated. Writing in the blank spaces and signatures at the bottom added with iron-gall ink. Apparently Jim Bridger could not write, so he affixed an "X," designated as "his mark." This was witnessed by two other signatures.

Tests on the ink of the signatures and printing indicated artificial aging. The negative Hofmann used to make the plates was found and compared with the note. A handwritten "power of attorney" for Jim Bridger dated 1838 was located in the Missouri Historical Society, which has been there since 1906. "James Bridger his mark" is written at the bottom of the document. The handwriting style and format on this document is consistent with the handwriting on the Bridger notes. This document was probably used as the model to simulate the name of Jim Bridger.

19. *Call of the Wild* Book Plate and Signature

Dated 1903. Used as collateral in summer 1985. First page inscribed by Jack London: "To Buck and his human friend Austin Lewis." A rubber stamp impression (address stamp) on the front cover and also on the title page: Austin Lewis, 3108 Harper, Berkeley, Calif.

The handwritten inscription was found to be a machine-printed copy of handwriting rather than an actual signature. The distribution of ink was not consistent with the deposit of ink left by a pen. A negative of the signature and the impression of the rubber stamp of the address matched these additions to the book and linked them to Hofmann.

20. The Joseph Smith to Hyrum Smith (Far West) Letter

Dated May (1838). Purchase price unknown. Date introduced ca. 1982. Handwritten stampless cover letter, approximately 7 inches by 7 5/8 inches. Very smudged appearance, with brown-colored ink. Edges of the paper well worn and torn. Postmark on face of the letter: "Far West" with month "May" visible but day not discernible.

An examination of the postmark under a microscope showed that it was not consistent with other postmarks from the period. The pressure of the postmark is uneven and irregular, indicating that it was either handdrawn on the document or impressed into the paper with a counterfeit stamp. Neither is the handwriting consistent with the known writing of Joseph Smith and appears to be a simulation executed by someone else. The ink on this document was different from that on other Hofmann documents, in that it was a different color under ultra-violet light. It otherwise exhibited the other characteristics found only on Hofmann documents. The irregularities combined with the counterfeit post mark and questions about the handwriting suggested the document was forged.

21. The Isaac Galland Promissory Note

Dated 11 September 1837 and 14 December 1841. Purchase price unknown. Date introduced unknown. Handwritten promissory note, approximately 7 1/2 inches by 4 1/4 inches. Iron-gall ink on front and back. Signature on the front spelled "Galland" and the back "Garland."

The front and the back of the document reacted differently under ultra-violet light. On the front the ink was stable and clear, with no running or bleeding. The ink on the back demonstrated significant fanning and bleeding. A blue-hazing effect was visible around the ink on the back of the document but no where else. The ink on the front was smoothflowing, while the ink on the back showed the characteristic alligatoring found on other Hofmann documents. The solubility test showed the ink on the front stable for over 60 seconds after being treated with an ammonium-hydroxide solution; the ink on the back began to dissolve within 10 seconds—indicating the ink on the front had been on the paper significantly longer than the ink on the back. Apparently the front of the document was genuine. The writing on the back had been added at a much later date, then treated chemically to artificially age the ink. The monetary value of the document increased significantly with the extra writing on the back.

A FORENSIC ANALYSIS

SUMMARY

During the one-and-one-half-year investigation into the Mark W. Hofmann documents, more than 6,000 documents, reportedly dating from between 1792 and 1929, were examined. Of that total, 443 documents came from Hofmann. Of these, 268 (or 60 percent) were found to be authentic—mostly public court records and other historically insignificant items. Another 68 documents (or 15 percent) could not be proven either genuine or forged. However, 107 documents (or 24 percent) were found to be forged.

SUMMARY

During the past six years, the Southern Poison Lab of W. Hoffmann documents more than 1,500 deaths per year dating from between 1972 and 1978, these examined. Of that total, 262 documents cases that Hoffmann. Of these, 296 (or 8 percent) were resolved as accidents simply by the records and other high yearly magnification being. A number of deaths due to 15 fatal and could not be proven either gender were resolved as yet. No individual, not single period were added to this list.

INDEX

ABOUT THE AUTHORS

LINDA SILLITOE has published articles in *The New York Times, The Philadelphia Inquirer, Utah Holiday Magazine, Sunstone* magazine, and *Dialogue: A Journal of Mormon Thought.* She has been nominated twice for Pulitzer prizes by the Salt Lake City *Deseret News* and has received awards from the Utah Chapter of the Society of Professional Journalists, the Associated Press, the American Civil Liberties Union, and the Utah Navajo Development Council. She recently co-produced a documentary called "Native *and* American." She is the author of the novel *Sideways to the Sun* and a short story collection, *Windows On the Sea.* She currently resides in Salt Lake City with her husband and three children.

ALLEN D. ROBERTS has published investigative articles and historical essays in a variety of publications, including *Utah Holiday Magazine* and *Utah Historical Quarterly.* He has served as co-editor and co-publisher of *Sunstone* magazine and as editorial associate of *Dialogue: A Journal of Mormon Thought.* He is a licensed architect with a background in historical restoration. A board member with the Utah Endowment for the Humanities, Roberts also serves as Utah Advisor for the National Trust for Historic Preservation. He is the recipient of a Best Article award from the Mormon History Association. He currently lives in Salt Lake City with his wife and five children.

GEORGE J. THROCKMORTON, a forensic document examiner, serves on the executive board of directors of the Southwest Association of Forensic Document Examiners and is a member of the American Academy of Forensic Sciences. At the time of the Salt Lake City bombings he was working for the Utah attorney general's office. Together with William J. Flynn, of Phoenix, Arizona, he developed new ink and paper tests to expose the Hofmann forgeries. He is married and has four children.